THE BOOK OF
ILLUMINATION
THE COLOR OF
CHANGE Ed.4

Eric E. Mitchell

The Book of Illumination/ The Color of Change© 4th printed edition
Copyright © 2014 by Eric E. Mitchell

The Book of Illumination©
Library of Congress Control Number: 2014952611
ISBN 978-0-9748080-4-8

Printed in the United States of America

Visit

WWW.BOOKOFILLUMINATION.COM

Attention: Schools and Businesses

Aqualeo books are available at quantity discounts with bulk purchase for educational, business, or sales promotional use. For information, please write to:
thebookofillumination@gmail.com

To Herman and Aphrodite…To The Father and his Sun

May we find ourselves again…In the next life to come

Sword of Omens give me sight beyond sight – **Lion O**

¹And I saw in the right hand of him that sat on the throne a book written within and on the backside, sealed with seven seals.

²And I saw a strong angel proclaiming with a loud voice, Who is worthy to open the book, and to loose the seals thereof?

³And no man in heaven, nor in earth, neither under the earth, was able to open the book, neither to look thereon.

⁴And I wept much, because no man was found worthy to open and to read the book, neither to look thereon.

⁵And one of the elders saith unto me, Weep not: behold, the Lion of the tribe of Judah, the Root of David, hath prevailed to open the book, and to loose the seven seals thereof.

Table of Contents for B.O.I

1 **In the beginning was the Word**, and the Word_was with God, **and the Word was God.**

[2] The same was in the beginning with God.

[3] All things were made by him; and without him was not anything made that was made.

[4] In him was life; and the life was the light of men.

[5] And the light shineth in darkness; and the darkness comprehended it not.

[6] There was a man sent from God, whose name was John.

[7] The same came for a witness, to bear witness of the Light that all men through him might believe.

[8] He was not that Light, but was sent to bear witness of that Light.

[9] That was the true Light, which lighteth every man that cometh into the world.

[10] He was in the world, and the world was made by him, and the world knew him not.

[11] He came unto his own, and his own received him not.

[12] But as many as received him, to them gave he power to become the sons of God, even to them that believe on his name:

[13] Which were born, not of blood, nor of the will of the flesh, nor of the will of man, but of God.

[14] **And the Word was made flesh, and dwelt among us,** (and we beheld his glory, the glory as of the only begotten of the Father,) full of grace and truth.

The Book of Illumination

INTRODUCTION

THE COLOR OF CHANGE

The Book of Illumination

INTRODUCTION
THE COLOR OF CHANGE

INTRODUCTION

The UNIVERSE is alive…those who are awakened can see its power. Throughout the annals of history this UNIVERSE has manifested itself in many ways. Nature is the greatest indicator that validates the existence of a higher being. Have you ever peered over the peaks of the mountains in Aspen; or seen a sunset off the coasts of Maui? Humans who have lower consciousness tend to relate more easily when they see the UNIVERSE manifest itself in a corporeal anthropomorphic form. Since this is the way man relates himself to the divine, I've illuminated the names and personalities of a few major stars of today to highlight how their names embody the makeups of their personalities. (*In the beginning The* <u>*word*</u> *was God; made flesh, and dwelt among us.*) **John1:1, 14**

Magic Johnson, Marshall Mathers, Lebron James, and Usain Bolt are all heavy concentrations of manifested "star" matter. The BRAWN reflected within the body structure and name of Le<u>BRON </u>James sticks out like a sore thumb as there isn't an athlete in today's professional basketball arena with his physique and physical stature. Usain <u>BOLT, </u>who is the fastest man in the world, has a name that also is a testament to his physical manifestation. BOLT as in "bolt" of lightning, is the trait that is indicative of his SUPER human speed which won him several gold medals at the Olympics. Remember <u>MAGIC JOHNSON</u>, the man who beat AIDS. This "magic <u>johnson</u>" was so magical it defeated one of the most horrendous and deadly sexually transmitted diseases the world has ever seen. How about Marshall Mathers? who I like to call (MARTIAL MATTERS.) Breaking down his name we can easily see how he rose to fame through <u>battle rap</u> aka (martial matters.) Mastering these "martial matters" (the <u>WAR</u> with his mom, girlfriend, drug addiction, as well as other rappers) has enabled him to remain atop the rap/pop charts. Even when he makes a love song with Rihanna, *Love the Way You Lie,* his delivery is reminiscent of a tyrant at battle.

Many people discredit the power of the occult (numerology, gematria, and astrology) due to the inconsistencies found in horoscopes, tarot card readings, and the fear of the hidden and supernatural. Capitalism has a way of generalizing information for mass consumption and this generalization "waters"

11

things down often stripping the materials information of its power and true intent. Because this has happened, I have used the biggest and brightest "stars" of today's time, to bear witness that the celestial "stars" of the "heavens" have influence over the "gods" or "stars" of today who are watched on our television screens and seen in their iconic personifications.

For example, Andre Young also known as Dr. Dre is highly regarded as the most successful and iconic producer of rap music. He has produced several iconic rap acts which include the likes of Eazy E, 50 Cent, Ice Cube, Eminem, Snoop Dogg, and 2Pac Shakur. While this information doesn't seem "eye" opening maybe this will; Dr. Dre was born an Aquarius. Aquarius is one of three air signs in the zodiac and represents air in its androgynous fixed masculine form. Aquarius stands atop the air sign pyramid with Gemini in the middle and Libra at the base. Dr. Dre has taken 2 different sets of air signs to the zenith of musical stardom.

Snoop Dogg, and Eminem are both Libras; and each within their respective generations under the tutelage of Dr. Dre had the highest/fastest selling albums of all time.o

Ice Cube, 2Pac Shakur, and Kendrick Lamar are all Gemini's whose birthdays roll in sequential consecutive days. Ice Cube's birthday is June 15th, 2pac's is June 16th, and Kendrick Lamar's is June 17th.

This represents three generations of musical genius that has not only dominated rap, but also with it, proves that history really does repeat itself.
Later I'll show in depth just how much numerology, and astrology, have shaped everything we deem to be religious, and of "God." The people who have true understanding of this knowledge are called the 'elect - the illumined ones' hence the term Illuminati - the secret society that promotes the illuminated beings sent from the "heavens" to replenish the earth. Everything you think you know is a noisy black and white interpretation of something that is colorful and high definition. Since I've given you a glimpse that shows the UNIVERSE IS ALIVE... I must now...at this time ask ...are you?

THE COLOR OF CHANGE

<u>Religion</u>**:** a collection of cultural systems, belief systems, and worldviews that establishes **symbols** that relate humanity to spirituality and moral values ₐ

The origins of "God's" word, people, and covenant, in conjunction with past and present race relations in America, have a link to one another through the scriptures provided in the Book of Genesis. These scriptures bear witness that what many people in the world perceive to be the truth, in regards to God and the people for which his covenant was established, may be a version they have created for themselves and not one that is routed in any fact. Because mankind has yet to show that he can submit to a power greater than himself, his constant ignorance has blinded him, causing the world to degenerate into an abyss of opinions, biases, and an overall apostasy from the blueprint given in the religions of the world that magnify how "gods" emanate to the earth.

Genes 3:5 *For God doth know that in the day ye eat thereof, then your eyes shall be opened, and <u>ye shall be as gods</u>, knowing good and evil.*

People who feel they haven't been affected by the current religious system of ideologies and dogmas cannot understand the importance of a book such as this; as in today's society, the truth is not the truth, but rather an illusion of what the people want it to be. This thought takes me directly to the word romantic. When most people think of romance they think of roses, hearts, and expressions of carnal love; however Webster defines romance as such:

<u>Romantic</u>: (1) Imaginary not based on fact (2) Marked by the imaginative or emotional appeal of what is heroic, adventurous, remote, mysterious, or idealized

According to Webster's definition, romance is defined as things that are imaginary, <u>not based in fact</u> that are marked by imaginative emotions of what is heroic, mysterious or idealized. Due to many peoples fixation on the romantic depictions of what they think God/gods, and Jesus are supposed to look like, they are blinded to the fact that the "gods" have been amongst the people on earth from times of antiquity to the present.

Imagine that every seemingly impossible reference in the Bible like "talking snakes" is an allegory that describes a more profound truth; but because people are looking at the literal interpretation, they are blinded to the allegorical significance; this takes me directly to the word Sadducee.

<u>Sadducees</u>: (1) a member of an ancient Jewish sect consisting mainly of Priests and Aristocrats that differed from the Pharisee especially in their literal interpretation of the Bible and their rejection of oral law and tradition

The Sadducees were a band of Priests and Aristocrats that believed in the direct and literal interpretation of the Torah (*1st five books of the Bible*.) If the Torah says a snake talked, they believe a snake "actually" talked. The fact that Jesus had many skirmishes with the Sadducees lays claim that what the Sadducees thought they understood in terms of the literal interpretations of the Torah according to Jesus, were inaccurate as in *"it's sad you see"* the Torah from this perspective.

Anytime I think about the Bible and the stories represented in it, I recollect on how the church, in opposition to science, like the Sadducees, teaches these stories from a literal point of view. Again talking snakes, women being created from ribs, and men walking on water, are all things that give rise to the argument of the atheist; his standpoint being, he doesn't believe that to be God. However if he was to have the back story and or allegory as to what walking on water, or talking snakes signifies, then he as an atheist may be able to see the profound wisdom and accurate prophecy, that *may* reveal a "God" he was previously unable to see. To break it down further I will say the Bible's stories are routed in deep truths; however these truths aren't ones that are easily understood or recognized by the masses. This is due to the varying degrees of people's comprehension. Some people are able to differentiate and comprehend hidden or deeper meanings while others cannot. Those who have higher levels of comprehension are the ones who progress intellectually which gradually "raptures" them into the higher mysteries of life. This is why certain high ranking members of government and the priesthood are given the specific information that is pertinent and not for the public's view. This specific information is considered esoteric.

<u>Esoteric</u>: (1) designed for or understood by the specially initiated alone (2) requiring or exhibiting knowledge that is restricted to a small group (3) difficult to understand

When you take into account that a large portion of biblical knowledge, prophecy, and information perplexes the masses; it is easily seen how those who have a higher mental aptitude, void of the entanglements of romanticism, have become initiated into the higher and greater mysteries involved with life, death, and resurrection. This initiation takes place when one develops the ability to "read" between the lines to discern the subtleties that add color to all things literal and literary. For example, how was the tortoise able to beat the hare? Was it because the hare slept while the tortoise diligently stayed the course; or was it because of the hare's arrogance? The person who says it was because the hare went to sleep isn't wrong in their answer; however the person who understands what caused the hare to go to sleep is able to really comprehend the hidden lesson. This fable illustrates the undertones coded within the Bible's subtext, and this hidden wisdom like that of the parable, is why people remain captivated and influenced by the information in it.

Storytelling, though likely adorned with embellishment, has been the ultimate way mankind has conveyed and preserved the human experience. Stories sustain a record of human accounts while concurrently arousing the reader's imagination. Though man may evolve technologically, enabling him for the moment to better influence the outcome of his present circumstance, he's still reliant on the records left by his predecessors, as history is known to repeat itself. Whether driven by personal ambition or contributing his talents towards forging a better world, the basic character traits that compel him don't change; neither do the conditions that will inevitably confront him. Although phenomenal breakthroughs and discoveries will further occur, the rules that regulate the human character remain consistent. Time and the elements are the intangible forces that govern the physical world we live in, and will always be the deciding factors in situations, despite man's efforts to manipulate them. This is the explanation as to how prophecies are written, which further makes the great cliché "history repeats itself" have such great significance. Everyone isn't able to scientifically understand this phenomenon, and because of this, many have adopted very fundamental instructions regarding their religious beliefs. These beliefs often stem from traditions their parents gave them. But now an assessment of where and who their parents got their traditions and information from has to be made. Why do I say this? True evolution demands adaptation. To teach a person that snakes talk or that women come from the ribs of men seems absurd right; but because it was in the Bible, and "God said" is attached to it, people believe it. If we look deep enough, we will find the answers to these "seemingly" ridiculous stories.
The people who benefit from the way the religions of Abraham are perceived and taught do not wish for change; and from their perspective, this is understood; for what and who really changes? Men will always be men, and women will always be women. Who and how they are depends on where you catch them in their life's journey. Looking at change from this perspective allows the person with an

inquiring mind to see though change *is* needed, at what cost and to what degree should it be mandated? Especially when you take into account that you can lead a horse to water, but you can't make him drink it. Change in the eyes of those atop could very well seem to be a replacement of the same "new regime" previously in power. This is stated because many regimes superficially seem different but they typically often end in the same result. Change from the eyes of those who petitioned for it seems to be liberation and in many cases these people feel justice has finally prevailed. But who is to say the people who have brought about the change are just? Even if the people are just I'm sure someone could rationalize their perceived justice as "*just*" their point of view. Liberating everyone to do what they want naturally is the ultimate form of chaos. When everyone looks at the individuals who are truly free they are able to see the "chaos" in the individuals free self. However people in their free selves perceive what the masses perceive as chaos to be their liberation.

The Wisdom of Solomon as regarded in Ecclesiastes 1:9 states, "*there is nothing new under the sun.*" This perspective shows that knowledge or lack thereof is what has led people to certain behavior types. *For what has been is what will be and what has been done is what will be done.* Though stereotypes are not considered to be politically correct many are routed in truth. These stereotypes are often delivered to the masses with comedy. The genius of comedy is it allows the comic to deliver harsh truths and stereotypes with laughter, sarcasm, and a smile.

In studying the religions of Abraham and then reading the historical information regarding his life and walk with "God" we find out the land he is living in is in Africa (MIDDLE EAST.) When we look at our own American society today we know as a fact the slave trade is how many Africans who are now considered African Americans got to the United States. In some instances although blacks live in and are from Africa, they have been excluded from many of the major depictions of the Bible's characters in movies like *Son of God, Noah, Exodus* *. The black people who have risen above the Christian point of view, namely Black Nationalists, Black Muslims, and Gnostics, argue that retribution is needed for the enslavement and falsification of the race of those written about in the Bible. However, because these groups are perceived as extremists and are a significantly small sect of individuals the retribution they feel they deserve is often overlooked. On the other hand, the masses of black people who assimilated, integrated, and bought into the "American Dream" aren't really concerned with the falsification of the race and origins of the Bible's heroes; because in their churches and faith, they simply make Christ into whatever race or person they want him to be. This is why those who were zealous in advocating that integration was the answer are now in search of a savior who is most like them.

 Many have heralded Barack Obama as being the "messianic" figure the world has so anxiously been waiting to see. President Obama won the Nobel Peace Prize and the Presidency of the United States and trail-blazed the competition upon the slogan, "Yes We Can." The underlying theme of President Obama's campaign was change, though a further analysis of President Obama's platform reveals the brilliant simplicity of the popular slogan that allowed him to effortlessly ascend the Presidential throne. But what was meant by the change the President advocated? Is the fact that America has never seen an African American president reason enough for change? Does the fact that the Bush Administration, as believed by some, was responsible for many unwarranted deaths via the War on Terrorism, corporate fraud as seen in Enron, and the unprecedented, miraculous victory in the 2000 presidential election seem merit enough for change? In all actuality, when one speaks of change, a plethora of possibilities arises. The use of the word "change" in the generic sense as a campaign strategy was ingenious because a candidate with the attributes of Barack Obama forces the change to be implied. Even though it is a direct point of emphasis, his obvious intelligence, eloquent speech, and charisma, allows the change personified to be witnessed physically. President Obama didn't go into detail about the mistakes of the former administration, because the former administrations mistakes were witnessed by everyone on a global scale. What we're witnessing in America is a slow shift within the ideology of the American government. What difference does color really make as long as the best candidate is chosen? Rarely will you find anyone living in America who is a pure blood of anything; this was the targeted goal of the United States, and is why it is regarded as being the great "melting pot" of the world. This "melting pot" created a situation where everything and everybody is blended together; key word being the "United States" as in the *united states* of existence. Because everything and everybody has now merged the only thing that has become relevant is the truth about human existence and the source from which all humans come; that source as attributed by the religions of Abraham as being God. If everybody believes in one God, why is there so much contention and strife? Why are there so many different religions and why is the world at war over them? Though many people admonish the fact that voting for and electing a President who is half black and half white is the only real solution to the lopsided racial diversity of the United States presidential position; some Black Nationalists feel Barack Obama is accepted in White America only because he is half white. In their point of view this is nothing new as mulattos were always kept as mediators and buffers between slave and slave master.

17

Black Nationalist: a member of a group of militant blacks who advocate separatism from whites who promote self-governing black communities

Mulatto: the first-generation offspring of a black person and a white person

The placing of a "colored" man in office, through the point of view of the Black Nationalist, can appear to be a slap in the face because they feel retribution is what is needed, not another representative or figure head for peace and equality. However the point of view of the Black Nationalist from a global perspective isn't clearly understood. The world can only move forward from where it has come in the past. People who have not been the victims of racism and those who have become willing Americanized citizens can only view the change that has come to America as a great sign of progression, and an overall sense of "anyone" can really become "anything." How and why would anyone want to stop that type of message from being heard or seen in the world? Michael Jackson, the King of Pop, sung about it not mattering if you're black or white and transcended all aspects of racial barriers; President Obama has now personified it.

The world of today seems adamant about healing from the hatred of racism, and bigotry. However if this is truly the case, then the origins of God and his religions have to be revealed. President Obama is a very exceptional man, and all things being equal I would say he is unrivaled among those who have run against him as well as many other past presidents. However, the only way that society can begin to rebuild itself and re-structure itself is if it owns up to its past. Even in the Roman Catholic Religion you must confess before your sins are accepted. If the best of individuals black, white, red, or yellow are to run the world and really make it live up to the dream America has for so long sold and profited from; then a disclosure of where America got its religion from has to be revealed to the masses. If it isn't revealed, how can the world truly say that racism is truly over?

Revelation 10:7 *but in the days of the sounding of the seventh angel, when he is about to sound, the mystery of God would be finished, as He declared to His servants the prophets.*
I came to the following assessment from analyzing history and listening to the stories of those who were disenfranchised, discriminated against, and treated as if they were nothing. This aroused a sentiment that things haven't' really changed in America. In a speech from Malcolm X entitled *House Negro Field Negro* he outlined several things that when looked at in today's society, does raise eyebrows. It was no secret that in slavery times the lighter skin Negroes (namely the ones who are mixed with white) were in the house and the darker slaves were in the field. The field Negroes were given scraps, the house Negroes where given choice cuts of meat. The field Negroes slept in outhouses on cots, the

house Negroes slept in a bed in the master's house. The field Negroes worked all day in the field picking cotton, and corn. The house Negroes did house chores like washing dishes, clothes, and raising the slave master's children. When confronted with this truth from the past I was forced to see if this was still true today. Are the lighter skin blacks given more of the power positions than the darker? This question was one that was so pressing that I must ask the readers to ask themselves the same question as well. Pending on what your answer is will in turn determine if you accept this as still being true today.

There is a popular publication that has circulated amongst the black communities. While this publication serves as propaganda exposing the tyranny of White Supremacy, many blacks feel that it is the very system designed within the publication that has kept blacks at the bottom in regards to social and economic progress. This publication is none other than the infamous Willie Lynch letter; here are a few excerpts from that publication.

WILLIE LYNCH

Greetings, I HAVE A FULL PROOF METHOD FOR CONTROLLING YOUR BLACK SLAVES. I guarantee every one of you that, if installed correctly, IT WILL CONTROL THE SLAVES FOR AT LEAST 300 HUNDREDS YEARS. On top of my list is "AGE," but it's there only because it starts with an "a." The second is "COLOR" or shade. Now that you have a list of differences, I shall give you an outline of action, but before that, I shall assure you that DISTRUST IS STRONGER THAN TRUST AND ENVY STRONGER THAN ADULATION, RESPECT OR ADMIRATION. The Black slaves after receiving this indoctrination shall carry on and will become self-refueling and self-generating for HUNDREDS of years, maybe THOUSANDS. Don't forget, you must pitch the OLD black male vs. the YOUNG black male, and the YOUNG black male against the OLD black male. You must use the DARK skin slaves vs. the LIGHT skin slaves, and the LIGHT skin slaves vs. the DARK skin slaves. You must use the FEMALE vs. the MALE, and the MALE vs. the FEMALE. You must also have white servants and overseers [who] distrust all Blacks. But it is NECESSARY THAT YOUR SLAVES TRUST AND DEPEND ON US. THEY MUST LOVE, RESPECT AND TRUST ONLY US. 2

THE BREAKING PROCESS OF THE AFRICAN WOMAN

Take the female and run a series of tests on her to see if she will submit to your desires willingly. Test her in every way, because she is the most important factor for good economics. If she shows any sign of resistance in submitting completely to your will, do not hesitate to use the bullwhip on her to extract that last bit of [b----] out of her. Take care not to kill her, for in doing so, you spoil good economics. When in complete submission, she will train her offsprings in the early years to submit to labor when they become of age. Understanding is the best thing. Therefore, we shall go deeper into this area of the subject matter concerning what we have produced here in this breaking process of the female nigger. We have reversed the relationship; in her natural uncivilized state, she would have a strong dependency on the uncivilized nigger male, and she would have a limited protective tendency toward her independent male offspring and would raise male offsprings to be dependent like her. Nature had provided for this type of balance. We reversed nature by burning and pulling a civilized nigger apart and bullwhipping the other to the point of death, all in her presence. By her being left alone, unprotected, with the MALE IMAGE DESTROYED, the ordeal caused her to move from her psychologically dependent state to a frozen, independent state. In this frozen, psychological state of independence, she will raise her MALE and female offspring in reversed roles. For FEAR of the young male's life, she will psychologically train him to be MENTALLY WEAK and DEPENDENT, but PHYSICALLY STRONG. Because she has become psychologically independent, she will train her FEMALE offsprings to be psychologically independent. What have you got? You've got the nigger WOMAN OUT FRONT AND THE nigger MAN BEHIND AND SCARED. This is a perfect situation of sound sleep and economics.

THE NEGRO MARRIAGE

We breed two nigger males with two nigger females. Then, we take the nigger male away from them and keep them moving and working. Say one nigger female bears a nigger female and the other bears a nigger male; both nigger females—being without influence of the nigger male image, frozen with a independent psychology—will raise their offspring into reverse positions. The one with the female offspring will teach her to be like herself, independent and negotiable (we negotiate with her, through her, by her, negotiates her at will). The one with the nigger male offspring, she being frozen subconscious fear for his life, will raise him to be mentally dependent and weak, but physically strong; in other words, body over mind. Now, in a few years when these two offspring's become fertile for early reproduction, we will mate and breed them and continue the cycle. That is good, sound and long range comprehensive planning.

Because of the vicious tone and cut-throat mentality expressed in the Willie Lynch letter, many Black Nationalists who have read and understand it, see every attempt at integration as a ploy to keep the blacks as the labor force, and the whites as the labor master's. To the nationalists, it is common knowledge that historically African American men have minimal knowledge of their deity and has such become a wanderer in a society as explained by the Willie Lynch letter that has goals to keep them as functioning inferiors. In their opinion, few black men reach the zenith of self-mastery due to the void of an authentic and fundamental self-identity. This lack of self-identity leaves them unable to achieve maximum self-evolution. However for those who haven't the ability to make the connection between what culturally happened to the black male of the past, at first glance, makes the information in the letter seem appalling and the latest attempt at reverse discrimination against those who enslaved blacks. I guess the question to ask today is, "Is this Willie Lynch mentality still relevant?" The Black Nationalist's feel it is, and the information reflected within the Willie Lynch letter, they say, is as clear as day to see.

Now that this great nation we call America has been built, it is going to take an even greater amount of subjects to keep it that way. The only difference between the subjects of today and the subjects of yesterday is color. As we learned from the Willie Lynch letter, blacks were targeted to be the working class slaves in this American society; however now-a-days immigrants as well as all other social outcasts are highly susceptible to becoming those who turn the wheels of the blue collar working class machine.

I know the reader is asking, how does all this relate to the origins of God, the people he claims as his own, and the current make-over of the political face of America? And with that, how did I turn this into a black thing when religion is universal? When you look at everything that has happened in the world and gather up the facts, you'll find the conditioning you were given as children placed you in a paradigm that would limit your scope of vision. Because younger generations were trained to be narrow minded, as they grew older they formulated their own assessments about their preconditioned behavior; and through rebellion expressed their newfound enlightenment. Due to alternative perspectives about race, politics, and religion surfacing on the internet via the *Zeitgeist* campaigns as well as the *Loose Change* documentaries about 911; some Black Nationalists feel the ruling class of this society has chosen a candidate to represent it like Barack Obama. These nationalists stand on the premises that as long as the governing elite can show the American public they've "superficially" changed, people will still believe in the lie they feel the government perpetuates in regards to religion, racism, and what the Black Nationalists perceive as oppressive governmental control. Barack Obama being half African and half American, appeals globally to the citizens of America. Though America's issues are no longer only black and white, the focus was always on black and white because between the two all other colors seemingly emerge. Either you're closer to the black, closer to the white, or you're somewhere in between. When we talk about black vs. white this conversation goes beyond race. This is stated because even within any specific race you have those who are darker and those who are lighter. History has proven those with fairer skin have been treated better than those with dark skin. The castes systems of India with the Dravidian and Aryan culture are a great example of the disproportionate treatment for those people of the same race that have darker skin. The plight of the American Negroes and the civil rights struggle was the most recent example the world has witnessed in regards to this phenomenon, although this is a known reality for all races of color. Even Webster himself has an opinion on the subject.

Fair: pleasing to the eye or mind especially because of fresh, charming, or flawless quality

Dark: (1) arising from or showing evil traits or desires (2) lacking knowledge

Recognizing this point and looking at it from all sides takes the point of emphasis from the Negroes and their struggles against White Supremacy, and turns the point of emphasis to the state of the world in respects to economy, population, natural resources, and social status. Every group of people who have or are experiencing civil injustices that have used the civil rights struggle to further promote their agendas, should take a proper assessment of the history of the ancient as well as present world.

On the surface, whenever you commercialize anything, the great importance's and details usually become obscure as the most useful instructions for all, are ones that are generic. In this case commercializing the movement against civil rights has done this exact thing. Now many social groups who feel they are discriminated against, protest in the same manner they saw the civil right protestors of the early and late 60's. They do this without really knowing what those early protestors were protesting against. These new protestors relate to the civil rights protestors on a superficial basis, like blacks having the right to sit at a table with whites. They can't however understand what is meant by reparations for the inhumane mental reconditioning of an entire race of people like that spoken of in the Willie lynch letter. This is because the more specific you get, the less universally it will be accepted. We've all heard the cliché' "the **devil** is in the details."

When any social group uses the plight of the American Negroes and compares their struggles as being similar, on the surface it appears to be the same; a fight against civil rights and injustices. However if a microscopic lens where placed on the movements and plights simultaneously, two very different ambitions and motivations would clearly be revealed.

Prior to writing this book I went about the states participating in cyphers, lectures, and study groups with Black Nationalists as well as other religious subcultures. Within one of the focus groups I attended, a point made by one of the Black Nationalists was the gay rights struggle is nothing in comparison to the Negroes struggle. While the point expressed wasn't the keynote of the nationalists' speech, it did strike a chord in the minds of his audience. He went on to say the discrimination of blacks, involves a holocaust of 200 million lives, 400 years of slavery, and another 150 years of socio-economic injustices. When he said this I didn't take his statement out of context as an injustice anywhere is an injustice everywhere. However when putting into perspective the magnitude and the scope of the two movements, I could see why he felt one was petty in terms of the other. You can't hide the color of your skin, and what happens if you're a black person who is gay?

Being black/dark in America was something that used to be considered degenerate within itself; again Webster's definition points this out for us. If you were black then you had a problem just because your skin was dark. The question that hasn't been asked is what does being black really mean, and how does the nature of black people affect society as a whole? When we look at the nature of black people, and analyze the character of their genetic makeup, certain things become highlighted when an overall assessment is taken in regards to the race. These assessments though not true for all blacks were taken, caricaturized, and placed on screen in order for blacks as a whole to see themselves as other races see them. These assessments were depicted through the Minstrel shows of the early 1800's.

Minstrel shows depicted black people in the most disparaging ways. They were showcased as buffoonish, superstitious, ignorant, and lazy. Again, the most creative and less destructive way of communicating the truth without offending is through comedy, because comedy allows for the harsh truths to be told with laughter and a smile. The minstrel show began in the early 1830s and lasted up until the 1960's.

Minstrel Show: an American entertainment consisting of comic skits, variety acts, dancing, and music, performed by white people in blackface or, especially after the Civil War, black people in blackface.

Most people who have insight regarding being gay versus being black can empathize with what is meant by saying one is petty in terms of the other. Those who promote gay rights would use this to further advocate that homosexuals, like blacks, were born that way, and therefore could not change who or how they were. When blacks hear this statement they are detested by it because they feel being black is normal and being gay isn't. But what many blacks haven't factored is when they are being compared to gays, it is the nature of their existence that is in question and the marker on their skin is what makes them identifiable. Civilized society considers the "ghetto" behavior demonstrated by

23

some black people as being degenerate. A great example of this is when Kanye West took Taylor Swift's award and said Beyonce Knowles deserved it. This behavior in whole is seen as chaotic, and the uncontrolled emotion reflected in it is what has caused the civil society to treat blacks as animals due to the unpredictability of their actions. When they see blacks they often look towards the nature, and sometimes overlook the individual. Being born gay isn't necessarily the same as being black because being black has to do with a person's color, not their character or sexual orientation. One can't accurately debate this without offending, but if you think about it, freedom does dictate "how" a person is able to live. I'm not one to argue the specifics of the movements nor am I one to take sides. It's easy to dismiss someone else's pain as small, but the fact they feel pain is reason enough to take notice. But any member of any Black Nationalist sect would tell you the difference between being black and being gay is this: You can't hide the color of your skin. Gays were never hung in mass volumes, targeted and taken away from their homeland, castrated, shackled and beaten with whips, tarred and feathered, and denied the right to vote. They were never segregated as a mandate of the state, and raped in mass volumes. They were never sentenced to prison in mass quantities, aren't considered 3/5ths of a person in the constitution, were never enslaved for 400 years, and they never suffered through the decimation of their language, heritage, customs, and knowledge. These statements come across very harsh, and are usually delivered with a sentiment of frustration and bitterness. It wasn't until the speaker acknowledged that gays were taking over the world before I could figure out how the topic had found its way into his lecture. From his point of view the biggest artists, like Lady GaGa as well as the firing of Isaiah Washington for alleged "gay bashing" was a part of a bigger conspiracy by those in positions of power to promote the "gay agenda." The fact that President Obama appointed the first openly Gay Judge, Deborah Batts, to the Supreme Court with plans to legalize gay marriage further fueled the speakers passion.

As the speaker stood at the podium, with veins pulsating in his neck, emphatically and passionately preaching, my mind began to drift off. As I looked back at American history with an open mind, I saw there were many social groups with causes that swayed more on the liberal side. These groups were discriminated against much to the same extent as gays, and the people who were on the opposing spectrum to conservative mainstream America, had to fight for whatever way of life they wanted to live. Larry Flynnt and the porn industry were discriminated against. Movies like *Deep Throat* which we're instrumental in pushing the censorship barriers in relation to pop culture, we're banned by the government from being screened; and actors involved like Harry Reems and Linda Lovelace, we're blackballed and tried in criminal courts. The hippies, who

were the love children, were also discriminated against. The hard rock and rollers were discriminated against as well. Each of these "liberal" social groups was discriminated against by right wing conservative America that was educated in Victorian principals. These principals were principles taught to them by their religious institutions, which ultimately inherited their influences from the Roman Catholic Church. I guess in the nationalists point of view being black was natural and being gay wasn't. I also take it that the speaker felt if a person feels something isn't right, they have the authority to discriminate against it; and with saying this, I think most people subconsciously operate within this frame of mind. Discrimination is most despised when it is unjust against those innocently trying to do and live by what society deems is right and lawful. A person playing devil's advocate would say, "The fact the person who is an exhibitionist was born that way, gives them the right to walk around that way. Walking around with no clothes on and having everyone looking at them is their right." The exhibitionists argument is being naked is the most pure and natural form of existence and is the way all people were born, and "seen" in their "truest" selves. But what happens when people who are easily aroused see these exhibitionists? What if the aroused person was born with a hypersensitivity towards nudity, and when they see a naked person they cannot help but to pounce on them? Though true and perfectly natural, being naked may arouse some people, and offend others. My point here is that everyone was born a certain way with certain things that make them unique, should they have the right to express themselves, of course, but to what extent should this right be enforced? This could be argued as a debate for civil liberties rather than civil rights. Any private sect can rally around their cause and do almost whatever they want within the confines of their own group.

A great example of this is a practice called *metzitzah b'peh* in Jewish circumcisions. Jewish law requires that all baby boys be circumcised on the eighth day of life. Immediately after the boy is circumcised, the man who performs the ritual, known as a *mohel*, takes a mouthful of wine, places his mouth around the base of the boy's penis, and uses suction to clean the wound. Again, the solution to the social climate and social discrimination that gays as well as those with views considered to be liberal face is solved in them rallying together to protect their way of life. Their causes and plights are more for expression and acceptance, as they want to openly express themselves and be viewed in the same likeness as "normal" people. The blacks just wanted to live. When blacks tried to segregate and ask for their own land so they could live the type of lifestyles they wanted, they were never given the chance to go and be away from a society that acted as if it could not stand them because the color of their skin. I was at this point in my mind when my ears heard the speaker's booming voice echoing in them again.

The Black Nationalists rationalize that even though blacks are and have been allowed to participate in certain management activities; racism isn't shown as long as they remain participants. When it comes to ownership and control then you will see racism rearing its ugly face once again. For instance I was asked a simple question by a member of the Hebrew Israelite community. He asked, *"If you have several multi–million-dollar black entertainers how come they still go through other companies for their distribution, manufacturing and promotion. Wouldn't it make sense business wise for them to come together and merge their industries eliminating the middle men? Why are there no black owned football or baseball teams even though minorities dominate the sport?"* When he posed the question in this way it seemed to be a no brainer; he then informed me, *"When you see blacks becoming involved in high corporate management positions this only means that the playing field has become larger. When you have more territory that is occupied by a certain race or creed of people you need leadership that at least superficially resembles the people they govern. Because the people who used to be the majority have become or are becoming the minority they use the elite of the minority to govern the minority."* The Black Nationalists feel that this is what America is dealing with in terms of leadership in political America. But, before I was able to fully ingest his point of view I was then confronted with the question, what is the alternative?

In another lecture while attending a Black Muslim rally one of the speakers made an interesting comparison, he said that, *"The fact that the same minority of private property owners who have ties to Rome and the Vatican are getting richer, show you the extent of the change not only in America but in the World. The people of America have become accustomed to seeing only certain types of people being permitted and allowed to participate in the high echelons of government; so them being able to witness change by way of a half black president is big."* When I asked him to name his sources as to which people have been getting richer he backed down from his point and receded in implicating the Catholic Church by saying, *"they are the number one real estate owners in the world."*

I understand the point of view the nationalists speak from, but there is also a counter argument. Most people cannot think beyond what they can see, nor do they care for things that do not directly affect them. The governing bodies are merely responding to this apathetic mentality, a mentality that serves as the under currents to the masses personalities, and is viewed by those with ambition as nihilistic. Because this is the way in which many people think, they will always be able to be led. The problem with this type of mentality is if the people can see they are being led, they will rebel just because someone else is the leader. When I thought about this I had to acknowledge that fact because no one tells their child to go be a follower. Everyone encourages their child to be a leader, THE LEADER, whether or not they possess the capacity or ability for it. You don't have organizations that have the title "Future Followers of Tomorrow."

Due to the endurance and strength of the masses, they are very capable of sustaining themselves with little. The only thing that will distract people is oppression. Oppression causes us to deal with the day-to-day hustle and bustle of existence whereby our chaos is quarantined to one day of the week; that day usually being Saturday. If people are allowed to freely practice and exercise "every" right they will become lazy. When prompted by the government to become more productive their seemingly docile personalities will turn into full-fledged anarchy; which for the state is detrimental like cancer is to the human body. This anarchy is seemingly dormant and will only remain that way if the people are distracted.

With the election of President Obama black people in America think they have a person that represents them because no person of color in America has ever been able to hold such a high seat in the American Government. These people have only come to this conclusion from the superficial fact that President Obama's skin isn't all white. People recognizing a color change is an indication that there is still a racist sentiment towards people of color in America, by people of color in America. Reason being is President Obama is just as white as he is black; yet black people acknowledge him as being the 1st black president. The only thing most black people know about Barack Obama is that he stands for change, and for them, that is enough. Barack Obama was raised in Indonesia and Hawaii, places far from the American struggles of the Black Negroes in terms of racism; yet they attribute their struggles to his. The struggles they have dealt with may not have been struggles that he's dealt with, but on the plight of change, people want to feel as if they have a voice. President Obama for them *is* that voice. John Calhoun wrote in his Disquisition on government that, "*The difference between the rich and the poor will become more strongly marked and* *the proportion of ignorant and dependent people will increase. Then the tendency to conflict between them will become stronger; and the poor and dependent become more numerous in proportion there will; be in governments of the numerical majority, no want of leaders among the wealthy and ambitious, to excite and direct them in their efforts to obtain the control"*3b.

If what Vice President Calhoun predicted in the quote above is correct, it makes the defeat of President Obama in any election virtually impossible.

Blacks who have been oppressed for so long now see a huge sign of change; and attribute that change to the full-fledged overcoming of racism in America. This point of view exposes the peoples love for a candidate like Barak Obama has more to do with the lopsided racial diversity of the United States Presidential position than Obama himself. That coupled with the aesthetic aspects of the position popularized by JFK, reinforces the love, adulation, and revere the public has for its new hero. When you put these two things together you can understand where all the adoration comes from, even when the people know little about their presidential nominee.

The present leadership in America is a reflection of all that has happened in America. The people are dissatisfied, and because of this dissatisfaction, they have hit the polls and used their right as a citizen of a democratic nation to force trend by nominating a candidate most suited to their liking. Many people reading this book do not have a clue as to what the war of the holy land and its holy people have to do with the current president, the Bible, or this book. Gil Troy of the Jerusalem Post said, *"Barack Obama compares Palestinian suffering to African-Americans' oppression. This comparison also sloppily and demagogically racializes a national conflict, making the multi-hued Israelis the "white guys," meaning the bad guys* 3. For these reasons, we have to examine history and take an in depth look at scriptures, and the meaning of words, in an attempt to decipher a religion that 4/6ths of the world's population have pledged their allegiances to. All the three major religions of the world (Judaism, Christianity, and Islam) stem from Abraham. Abraham's story is found in the Book of the Genesis, so it's only befitting the next place of reference will be the Bibles 1st Book. I have highlighted a few scriptures in the Bible that were re-translated and re-written by the people who have authored it in its present condition. This was done so the masses can get a different perspective to look at the Bible from; as well as introduce the understanding that the Bible is a book of prophecy and allegory.

When you think about the word prophecy which means a prediction of what is about to come, it totally changes the perspective from which the reader sees biblical scriptures. The fact that many prophecies in the Bible have come true seem reason enough to re-examine every book written in it, even those deemed historical. *Biblos* actually means *the little books* 4 and when you look at the Bible, it is a compilation of "little books" that explains stories about a specific nation of people. What is very haunting and liberating is biblical scriptures speak of a time that's present in conjunction with a time that was.

With all of the information that is circulating around the internet namely misinformation; a releasing of the truth is the only thing that will counter balance the speculation and bad information people are receiving. If the truth causes anarchy it must have been necessary for it because the truth is inevitable. No matter which side you are on, the truth or the lie, each present a great argument for whatever point of view they represent. However the truth unlike the lie requires no acceptance because it is. A great example of this is the fact the Sun gives the world light. Just because you may not believe the Sun does this, doesn't make it false.

Matthew 10:26 (26) *Fear them not therefore: for there is nothing covered, that shall not be revealed; and hid, that shall not be known. - Jesus*

I have also placed within this book, literary elements, as well as movies whose themes tell stories behind the superficial display of action, storyline, and drama. The most pivotal and essential of those literary elements is allegory. When the masses gets a hold of this information I hope it presses them to look deeper into the scriptures of the Bible and closer at the history, prophecy, and the great heroes that have walked the earth in our life time; heroes of old that we both revere as gods in the flesh and immortals.

John 10:34 – 36 *(34) Jesus answered them, <u>Is it not written in your law, I said, Ye are gods?</u> (35) If he called them gods, unto whom the word of God came, and the scripture cannot be broken (36) Say ye of him, whom the Father hath sanctified, and sent into the world, Thou blasphemest; because I said, I am the Son of God?*

<u>Allegory:</u> a form of extended metaphor, in which objects, persons, and actions in a narrative are equated with the meanings that lie outside the narrative itself. The underlying meaning within the allegory has a moral, social, religious, or political significance, and its characters are often personifications of abstract ideas

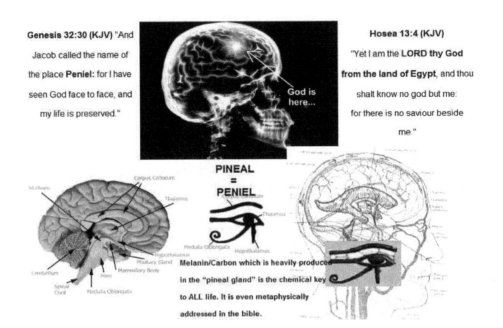

Genesis 32:30 (KJV) "And Jacob called the name of the place **Peniel**: for I have seen God face to face, and my life is preserved."

God is here...

Hosea 13:4 (KJV) "Yet I am the **LORD thy God** from the land of **Egypt**, and thou shalt know no god but me: for there is no saviour beside me."

PINEAL
=
PENIEL

Melanin/Carbon which is heavily produced in the "pineal gland" is the chemical key to ALL life. It is even metaphysically addressed in the bible.

The diagram above epitomizes allegory. It shows how certain words are used in a story to conceal their truest meanings while remaining functioning with practical usage within the story itself. The example above also illustrates just how knowledgeable and creative ancient Egyptians were as the eye of Horus is symbol linked to the pineal gland within our brains.

As indicated in the above diagram, pineal is the place where "God" is seen face to face. This gland also corresponds to the *Egyptian Eye of Horus* which as I will explain later, is the All Seeing Eye that sees the "*walking dead*" as well as everything else "under the Sun." A person having limited knowledge about what is being translated has no choice but to translate with a literal assumption when there is no legend or clues to direct them. This is why romanticism has spread so rapidly and also why Egyptology in the western world has been declared heresy, satanic, as well as the evil "dark" religion. A diagram like the one just seen easily allows the reader to separate the literal from the literary which again is the key to understanding the Bible as well as other esoteric writings. The people who are connected to this gland both physically and metaphysically are the same people for which the **ruler** of the gland, the "Sun God," establishes his covenant with, in the Book of Genesis.

THE GENESIS

In the Book of Genesis, The Ark of the Covenant between God and his chosen people is given to Abraham in the 17th chapter. In this chapter, there is a name change that is established during the covenant between God and Abraham that connotes a significant piece of allegorical information.

GENESIS 17:1-7 and when Abram was ninety years old and nine, the Lord appeared to Abram and said unto him, I am the almighty God; walk before me, and be thou perfect. (2) And I will make my covenant between me and thee, and will multiply thee exceedingly. (3) And Abram fell on his face: and God talked with him saying (4) As for me, behold, my covenant is with thee, and thou shalt be a father of many nations. (5) Neither shall thy name anymore be called Abram, but thy name shall be Abraham for a father of many nations have I made thee. (6) And I will make thee exceedingly fruitful, and I will make nations of thee and Kings shall come out of thee. (7) And I will establish my covenant between me, and the, and thy seed after the in their generations for an everlasting covenant, to be a God unto thee and to thy seed after thee

At face value what does a covenant between God and a chosen people represent? One reading this passage would look at it for its literal significance and say, big deal, God established a covenant with Abraham so what! However if we look at the 15th chapter of Genesis it gives us a very detailed account of what we should expect to happen to the promised seed of Abraham upon whom the LORD's established his covenant with. In the 15th chapter of the Genesis it states that Abram's seed will be enslaved in a foreign land 400 years after which the nation afflicting them would be judged.

Genesis 15:12-14. *"And when the sun was going down a deep sleep fell upon Abram; and lo a horror of great darkness fell upon him. And he said unto Abram, Know of Surety that thy seed shall be enslaved for 400 years; and also that nation, whom they shall serve will I judge: and afterward shall they come out with great substance.*

Prophetic: foretelling events on the basis of observation, experience, or scientific reason

Being that prophetic hints to something that will happen is reason enough to look at the information within these books as speaking to a time that's current as well as a time that was. Though the Genesis is widely regarded as a historical book amongst theologians, the prophecies reflected in it, are undeniable. Again, the Book of Genesis emphatically states within the 15th chapter, Abram's seed will be enslaved in a land that is not their own for 400 years. Upon citing and understanding this scripture we have to factor within our scope of history where a people have been enslaved and afflicted in a foreign land that is not their own for 400 years. The only people in history that have had this happen to them are the American Negroes. Many people who have read the Bible have overlooked this major clue and are unable to recognize its historical significance. However, when the name change from Abram to Abraham is then factored with it, it further corroborates that the enslaved seed of Abraham could very well be the American Negroes. When Abram's name is changed from Abram to Abraham, the latter three letters of his name (Ham) becomes very significant. For those who are reading this book who have no clue who Abraham is, he is regarded as being the father of modern religion. Christianity, Islam, as well as Judaism regard Abraham as being the Patriarch or father of their religions. The name Abram was changed to Abraham to highlight that Abram relates to Ham, who is unanimously believed as being the black son of Noah by scholars and theologians. Ham comes from the word K**hem** which was the original name of Egypt. The name Ham was given to the people who lived there because of their very dark skin. In the Genesis the covenant between Abraham and the LORD is happening in Egypt and the Middle East which is additional evidence that supports the claim to the seed of Abraham being the American Negroes. When we put the 400 year prophecy with the name change we get a clear sight at who the intended people of God's covenant with Abraham are. I can imagine people reading this are saying, *it seems too simple, I know other people have come to this same conclusion*; while others will take this presentation of facts as an error in comprehension. An interesting thought to ponder is maybe the same group of people whose ancestors enslaved the American Negroes, now, after witnessing the plight of these people realize the prophecy regarding Abraham and his chosen seed has to do with the Negroes of America. Perhaps this is why the Black Nationalists feel that Barack Obama was a candidate that was created in an attempt to rectify these heavy revelations.

 Prophetically the Gene/isis or "Gene of Isis" marks the beginning of the new Epoch. An Epoch is a new age when the Sun rises in a new constellation and the energy of that constellation takes effect on the overall consciousness of the people on earth. This gene of Isis is the son of Isis, the "Horus." The Horus, according to Egyptologists, who was originally named Heru, is where the term hero gets its meaning from. The arrival of the Horus also indicates the end of an age is here and the beginning of the Great Age has begun. The age we are leaving in respects to the Sun and the way it rises in different constellations is the Virgo/Piscean Age; the age we are presently coming into is the Age of Aquarius/Leo 6c. **Barack Obama** is the representative of the new Horus who through ritual has been used to usher in the new Epoch; being that he has been elected to the highest office in the land by the (Government of Democracy.) This G.O.D. represents by way of ritual, ancient Egypt, and the new epoch signifies a New World Order, whereby a one world governing system of ideologies and spiritual laws begins to take shape amongst the people of the earth.

PROPHECY

Recognizing the cyclical patterns of the days, weeks, months, and seasons, allows us to step outside of what is going on immediately around us, to take a bird's eye view of the same elliptical patterns that exist historically and prophetically within our immediate society. If we look at enough history and take into account the major events as well as the people involved in them, we are then able to see who is who in respects to all of creation. Compositing the lives of these people while observing planetary orbits and stellar alignments, and keeping in account the law of nature that states *matter is neither created nor destroyed it changes forms*; reshapes how we view these past and current events. This again is achieved by stepping outside of society or as referenced in ancient times as "going into the wilderness." Upon completion of this task is where the clarity and clairvoyance of vision is given that allows these higher cosmic events to be witnessed. The eye opens, consciousness increases, vision becomes **panoram**ic - <u>All</u> Seeing.

Since we have begun to talk about the Genesis and the beginnings from which man attributes his creation, it is also imperative with it, we talk about the people from which God's covenant was drawn. These people are commonly called the Hebrews which derives from the word (Apiru.) In cuneiform tablets found in the tomb of **Akhenaten** is where the legends of the Apiru or Hebrew people were first discovered [5]. Akhenaton was a Pharaoh during the 18th dynasty in Egypt who in the ninth year of his reign, declared there would be only one god, and that he would be the mediator between the people and that "God." During his reign, any inscriptions containing the mentioning of the plurality of gods were removed from all temples.

In the Book of Judges in the Bible, **Ophrah**, is where Gideon a **judge** started the development for <u>judges</u> to become Jewish kings and again the scrolls containing the king making ceremony were found in the tombs of the Egyptian Pharaoh <u>Akhenaten</u>. In the Bible, however, Saul was made king by the wandering (Hebrews) when they started to become <u>urbanized</u> by the reenacting of the king making rituals [6e]. The Apiru's (Hebrews) did this because they wanted to include all people of all levels of society in their monarchy. This, at that time, in the history of the Hebrews, was the ultimate form of democracy because it enabled the lay person who wasn't a blood heir to the throne of the kingdom to become a ruler or king. On the flipside to the customs of passing on a kingdom to the king's son through hierarchal and blood lineages, the Hebrews

33

knew that certain alignments of astral energies created beings who literally were *"sent from heaven"* to the earth to modify its condition. Conflicts often arose between the blood heirs and the person natured "fashioned" to rule when those who were *"sent from heaven"* appeared on earth during the same time a mortal ruler occupied the throne. The relationship between Moses and Ramses depicted this in the Bible as well as King David and Saul. In reference to the king making rituals of ancient Egypt, again, when the Hebrews became urbanized, Saul was advanced to king by the anointing at Ephraim and Gilgal. Being that the ritual of king making took place by the **judges** in **Ephraim** a city likened to (**Ophrah**) 6h we can take this to mean that those who are made kings by this ritual could also be known as sons or a "sun of Ephraim" 6g. Ephraim, one of the twelve tribes of Israel, in ancient Semitic legend was reportedly the son of Joseph and Asenath whose name means "loyal to Anat"6f. In this particular legend, Ephraim was the ARK or sacred carrier of the knowledge of Atlantis, which was the (Polytheistic) civilization that pre-dated the Great Flood; a figurative allegory speaking to the time between the end of the Piscean Age and the beginning of the Age of Aquarius 6f.

Judges 5:12-14 *(12) Awake, awake, Deborah: awake, awake, utter a song<u>: arise, **Barak, and lead thy captivity captive,** thou son of Abinoam. (13)Then he made him that remaineth have dominion over the nobles among the people: the LORD made me have dominion over the mighty (14) <u>Out of Ephraim was there a root of them against Amalek</u>; after thee, Benjamin, among thy people; out of Machir came down governors, and out of Zebulun they that handle the pen of the writer.*

As we see in the Book of Judges, Barak was indeed a **Judge** who is mentioned with the tribe of Ephraim as the one who leads thy captivity captive. When we combine the information from the old world found in the tomb of Akhenaten, a pharaoh with the striking resemblance to President Barack Obama, what we see is essentially the same energy represented in the Bible taking place in our world today in a slightly different form. The humble beginnings of Barak Obama and non-traditional family structure are the attributes that have made him very appealing to the American public. In the eyes of the people he is just like they are; a mortal who through hard work and diligence has become the governor or president of the free world. However when we look at the Kabbalistic pedigree of Barack Obama, an entirely different person is revealed. Barack Obama is both black and white which enables him to relate to both races objectively. He is also a Leo (monarch of the zodiac) born on the fourth day, and the 4th day according to the tarot is the day of the emperor 6. Not only is his outer personality (Leo) "leader" reflected in his overall achievement of becoming the first African/American President of the United States; his inner numeric and tarot reading says the same as the emperor is synonymous to the senate or senator. As many of you may well know, prior to Barack Obama becoming the President of the United States, he was a senator in Illinois. The 4th day is also listed as Aries in Astrology. Aries is linked to the RAM or LAMB of God 6b.

Lion: (2) a person of outstanding interest or importance, celebrity

Lionize: (1) to treat as an object of great interest or importance (2) to worship as celebrity

While Obama is a Leo, the woman he is standing next to, Oprah Winfrey, is an Aquarius (January 29th.) Again at "Oprah" (Ophrah/ Ephraim) the ritual of making a commoner /judge into a king has just taken place before the world. Oprah Winfrey is widely regarded as the most popular and influential woman in America. Upon her endorsement of President Obama he was exposed to one of the largest and most influential social and media platforms on the planet. In latter chapters we will discuss the relationship between the Leo and the Aquarius in how they relate to one another in the form of the "harbinger" known as the "Baptist" (Aquarius) who prepares the way of the Sun – (Leo) the "messiah." – On the next page is an image of Akhenaten's mother, note the resemblance to Michelle Obama. Due to differences in languages and customs between varying antiquious cultures, the words, Mother, Father, Sister and Brother, though close in relation, have alternate meanings. For instance, a mother is also a wife; a wife is also a sister, and a father also a brother. Depending on what aspect of the relationship was translated when the historical records were formulated from the lives of these ancient deities, in turn repositions our viewpoint in regards to their actual relationships between their family members.

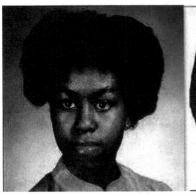

Imagine if it were blasted to the world the same deity who established monotheism had reincarnated to the planet and is now of age and ready to ascend to his earthly throne. How do you think the people would react to this news blast? In a democratic society the people want to elect the person who rules them, and everybody feels their opinion counts as they know best who is supposed to rule. This is why even though an immortal has reincarnated they still must go through the proper channels, schools, and rituals to manifest their old destiny on earth as their new destiny on earth; but one may ask what does this mean? This proves in a 3 dimensional display the great cliché' history repeats itself is true as we have now witnessed the same set of events from ancient times occur while we're living today. Astral or star energies present in people who were literally "written in the book" have appeared before us in broad daylight in similar likenesses as they had when their lives were 1st recorded in ancient scrolls. This at the same time gives the clarity of vision so that all may see and understand the reason why the Sun of Man's cult, which is the cult of resurrection, is the one that billions of people on the earth subscribe to and worship in the form of religion today.

The Government of the United States pays homage to the buildings and customs associated with Ancient Egypt as Washington D.C. (PENTAGON) is a replica of the city of Memphis in Egypt and sits on a pentagram. This is why there are pyramids located on the back of the dollar, and also why through ritual and sacrament the leading presidential figures are initiates into the higher mysteries associated with that of creation and death. Masonry is the system of building ethics these initiates follow, so it is no surprise that in this time during the beginning of the Age of Aquarius a candidate with the attributes of Barack Obama would be used/created by the Government of Democracy (G.O.D) to usher in a new world society. This for the world marks the beginning of a New Age and a New World.

AS ABOVE SO BELOW

Many reading this book have heard the phrase *As above so below*, but have no actual clue as to what this phrase really signifies. As stated previously we have indeed crossed over into a new age and a new world. Known as the Age of Aquarius, or as what pop culture calls today the Age of Knowledge and Information, this new age came about when the sun which was previously in Pisces, crossed over into the constellation Aquarius. This is why we see the ALS Ice bucket Challenge where the most influential people pour out water on their heads in likeness to the depiction of the "Water Bearer" in "heaven" (constellations.) Also synonymous to this age is the merger

between Apple, a company that bears on its logo a bitten apple, and Beats headphones, of which Dr. Dre, an Aquarius, is the co-founder and co-owner. This "apple" again is indicative of the "apple" in the Garden of Eden that allegorically represents the fruit of Knowledge which links knowledge and information with the Genesis and also the Aquarius.

I used the Kabbalah, numerology and astrology to animate the lives of Oprah Winfrey and Barack Obama; had I not, what was previously stated would seem like a far-fetched extrapolation of ideas. However Astrology, the tarot, and the Kabbalah provide a blueprint that illuminates the truest identities of these enormous media icons as well as provides a map to finding other deities who will be animated in latter chapters.

1 Corinthians 15:13-14 (13) *But if there be no resurrection of the dead, then is Christ not risen* (14) *And if Christ be not risen, then is our preaching vain, and your faith is also vain.*

Before progressing to the next chapter which is a thorough examination and breakdown of the numerological as well as gematriacal aspects of Kabbalah, I felt it necessary to acknowledge its most popular icon and advocate. Madonna the most successful female pop-star of all-time has most recently been covered in the media due to her expressed belief in Kabbalah. Not only is she its chief celebrity advocate, but she also was the 1st woman to hint at the notion of a black messiah in her epic video "*Like a Prayer.*" At the time, the superstar leonine heroine lost her Pepsi endorsement and it was one of the most controversial topics of the day. What is equally perplexing about the singer hinting at the notion of a black messiah was Madonna's relationship with Michael Jackson. The two of them were spotted together at the 1991 Academy Awards and though Madonna never acknowledged Michael as such, it isn't farfetched to believe that she felt something "irregular" or "supernatural" about his stardom and persona. Her name says it all as it hints to the Virgin Mary who as we will explain later, after a brief introduction in Kabbalah, has an astrological association tied directly to Michael Jackson.

The Book of Illumination

CHAPTER 1
THE KABBALAH

The Book of Illumination

CHAPTER 1
THE KABBALAH

KABBALAH

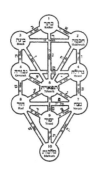

The Kabbalah presents a road map for the spiritual ecstasy of any individual who is "soul searching" to attain harmony with God. According to the Sefer Yetsirah, an ancient collection of writings reportedly written in Palestine between the 3rd and 6th centuries; "God" created the universe by his manipulation of the twenty-two letters of the Hebrew Alphabet and the ten sephirot, which are the nodes on the mystical tree of life. The sephirot are treated in the text as living entities and elements of the divine personality of God that embody the metaphysical values of the numbers one through ten which God emanates his presence down from the spiritual world of heaven into the physical world of matter. This Hebrew alphabet corresponds to the twenty-two paths that connect the sephirot to the Tree of Life. The Zohar, a collection of commentaries about the secrets of the Torah 1st published by Moses De Leon in Spain in the 13th century, promotes the idea that the sephirot views the Tree of Life as a ladder (Jacob's ladder.) This ladder enables the mystic searcher to climb back to the realm of "God" in addition to allowing the divine to express itself within the material world through creation 55.

The Ten Sephirah here are named within this chart. Each Sephirah number is found on the nodes that extend from the branches of the Tree of Life 57.

Sephirah	Hebrew name	English name	Traits
1	Kether	Crown	Highest self,
2	Chockmah	Wisdom	Spiritual purpose
3	Binah	Understanding	Spiritual Awareness
4	Chesed	Mercy	Love, Kindness
5	Geburah	Judgment	Personal power, will
6	Tiphareth	Beauty	Self Identity, ego
7	Netzach	Victory	Emotions, feelings
8	Hod	Splendor	Mind, Intellect thoughts
9	Yesod	Foundation	Sexuality, subconscious
10	Malkuth	World	Physical Body, world

These ten nodes again connect the twenty-two Hebrew letters with the twenty-two paths of the tarot. The tarot is an occult science that merges the destiny of the individual through pictures and hieroglyphs with aspects of their actual and present life. These hieroglyphs are living, and a person who understands them can get a very clear portrait of what a person is going to be like even before they are born.

Hebrew name	Path	#	English	Significance	Tarot Card
Aleph	1-2	1	A	Thinker	Fool
Beth	1-3	2	B, V	Domestic	Magus
Gimel	1-6	3	C, G, J	Travel	High Priestess
Daleth	2-3	4	D	Opportunity	Empress
Heh	2-6	5	E, H	Observer/ control	Emperor
Vau	2-4	6	U, V, W	Choice	Hierophant
Zayin	3-6	7	Z	Aggression/conflict	Lovers
Cheth	3-5	8	Ch	Defensive	Chariot
Teth	4-5	9	T	Revenge	Strength
Yod	4-6	10	I, J, Y	Energy	Hermit
Kaph	4-7	20	K	Wise	Wheel/Fortune
Lamed	5-6	30	L	Driven/ just	Justice
Mem	5-8	40	M	Caring	Hanged man
Nun	6-7	50	N	Introspective	Death
Samech	6-9	60	S	Supportive	Temperance
Ayin	6-8	70	O Oo, Ou	Business mind/ athletic	Devil
Peh	7-8	80	P, F	Talkative/ social	Tower
Tzaddi	7-9	90	X, Tz	Crafty/dodged	Star
Qoph	7-10	100	Q	Thinker (emotional)	Moon
Resh	8-9	200	R	Thinker (rational)	Sun
Shin	8-10	300	Sh	Judgment/drive	Judgment
Tau	9-10	400	T, Th	Honest/altruistic	Universe

Element	Name of Hebrew letter	Personality trait
Fire	Shin	Energetic, inventive, rash
Water	Mem	Emotional, caring, creative
Air	Aleph	Intellectual, logical, organized
Earth	Tau	Physical, practical, homely

Planet	Name of Hebrew Letter	Personality trait
Mercury	Beth	Quick witted, communication
Moon	Gimel	Creativity, the supernatural
Venus	Daleth	Love, Health issues
Jupiter	Kaph	Jovial, good fortune
Mars	Peh	Warlike, physically active
Sun	Resh	Paternal, generous
Saturn	Tau	Melancholy, family-centered

Gematria: is the process of adding the numerical values of a letter in a word, name, or sentence to obtain the complete value of that word or collection of words 55b.

Understanding Gematria allows a person to define names and phrases in their actual meanings in reference to biblical scriptures. This deciphering in turn pulls the reader deeper into what the biblical scriptures are covertly communicating. These processes of Gematria were used to breakdown and translate the Hebrew books into English formats. I placed this pertinent piece of information within this book to show what people think they know about the Bible and what it may mean is pale in comparison to what it is actually saying. Once a person gets to the point where they are literally deciphering the Bible's scriptures they become initiated into the real mysteries that the scriptures entail.

It is premature to explain the tarot before I have talked about Astrology. Astrology acts as a marker that allows a person to readily assess the superficial aspects of their personality as it corresponds to their ultimate destiny. These personality traits are measurements taken from the position of the Sun in relevance to the constellations it revolves through. The Sun then projects the energy of the constellations on the earth and these measurements act as the characteristics that makeup astrological signs. When the Bible says that John and Jesus are preaching that the kingdom of heaven is at hand, they are talking about the end and beginning of astrological ages. These ages are the 12 constellations that the Sun rises in and orbits for a period of 2,160 years.

Aries		♈	Mars	♂
Taurus		♉	Venus	♀
Gemini		♊	Mercury	☿
Cancer		♋	Moon	☽
Leo		♌	Sun	☉
Virgo		♍	Mercury	☿
Libra		♎	Venus	♀
Scorpio		♏	Mars	♂
Sagittarius		♐	Jupiter	♃
Capricorn		♑	Saturn	♄
Aquarius		♒	Saturn	♄
Pisces		♓	Jupiter	♃

In the latter half of this book I will talk more in depth about Astrology and further segue way to show the reader why the Hebrew and Jewish Priests have went to such lengths in covering up this vast system of knowledge. I empathize with them, as this knowledge in the hands of the unscrupulous could be very dangerous; especially during times between ages. In their attempts to disguise this information with romantic mythology, the Romans have been exposed as the culture that has perverted the knowledge of the ancient world causing degeneration to take place in the thought processes of the masses. This degeneration prophetically and directly parallel's the time we are in presently with the same point in the Bible where Jesus begins to preach his message to the world. People forget that the Jesus of Nazareth was a Jew (*by way of the Abrahamic curse/covenant not by religion literally*) (*Jew as in JUDAH*) which means he understood and would have been preaching this method of Kabbalah. By understanding Kabbalah one can easily see how I animated the lives of Barack Obama and Oprah Winfrey by using it.

<u>Worship</u>: reverent honor and homage paid to God or a sacred personage, or to any object regarded as sacred.

Above are the images of the tarot 56. Comprised of the 22 cards of the major arcana (*standard tarot deck*), these images serve as a hieroglyph that examines the inner personalities of people. Tarot cards, and the explanations given through their depictions, explain the inner sol destinies of people much like Astrology. The tarot cards and astrological signs go hand in hand and when used together with the process of Gematria, a person can "literally" discover who they really are. This revelation is one that is so precise and so accurate that at times it is scary. Tarot cards serve as the keys that provide the explanation that tells a person what aspect of the Supreme Being or "god" they are made of. This is the ultimate knowledge of self and also the knowledge that can "rapture" an individual to a higher consciousness whereby they are able to physically witness the pen stroke of God in every person they meet. The tarot cards strength and justice above were switched when Aleister Crowley reinterpreted the tarot decks in his Egyptian Tarot book called *The Book of Thoth*.

Many people do not believe in tarot cards because the Roman Church deemed them as a form of heresy, sorcery, and Satanic Devil Worship. The Papal Bull of 1737 issued by the Mother Church of England outlawed the teaching of Masonry which combines Astrology, and the Kabbalah with the Bibles scriptures, because it (Masonry) was regarded as a science that was too "freethinking"56a. For these reasons books about Astrology and the Kabbalah are found in the metaphysical section of bookstores.

Here in 1st Samuel chapter 17:37 is an indication that those who translated and presented the Bible in its present form are aware of the secret makeup of the god that freemasonry worships, which as I will explain later, takes the form of a Lion and a Bear. The key words that expose this are the numbers 1737 which again was the year the papal bull was issued, and the Book of Samuel which resembles the name of the "fallen "aspect of the angel "Samael" aka [the serpent/LORD (Gabriel)] who cohabitated with Eve. The Philistine in the scripture below is the giant. We'll also discuss this more in depth when we dissect the relationship between the giants that fell to earth, and the way those who were translating this phenomenon have shaped the viewpoints of all who have read the Bible. Recognizing that all of this information was given within one scripture of the Bible adds significance to the hidden "code" and language the Bible was written in.

1 Samuel 17:37 (37) *David said moreover, The LORD that delivered me out of the paw of the lion, and out of the paw of the bear, he will deliver me out of the hand of this Philistine.*

When most people think about tarot cards they think about a reading where a medium or psychic draws cards and reveals their future to them. I do not discredit their abilities however I find those readings to be as accurate as horoscopes. True tarot card readings are about the card that corresponds to the day that any particular person was born on. For instance: if you were born on the fifth day of the month, you would have a personality that is indicative of the Hierophant. This probably means that you have a love for all things mysterious and also have a knack at digging deep to investigate sacred knowledge's for their esoteric meanings. Although this may not be the case for everyone born on this day; all it would take is for someone who is well versed and understands the way tarot works to show the person how their card directly relates to their inner personality. Again, the tarot usually corresponds to the inner personality of the person; which is the side of the person that is seen if the person is known "personally." The astrological sign is the aspect of their personality that is superficial and observed by anyone who comes in contact with them. For example Barack Obama, Shawn "Jay-z" Carter, Beyonce Knowles, Sean "P. Diddy" Combs, Russell Simmons, Nick Saban and Mark Cuban all have the emperor's tarot card. The emperor tarot card represents mastery over the 4 elements and also represents senator and ruling capabilities. All of these individuals have risen to the heights of their professions with uncanny precision and have stayed there exemplifying solidarity and longevity. Below are brief definitions that explain how the 22 cards correspond to a person's inner personality traits.

THE MAGUS: Communication; playful dealings with all possible forms of communication; flexibility, brilliance

THE HIGH PRIESTESS: Access to intuitive powers, healing, independence, inner equilibrium, increased self confidence

THE EMPRESS: Beauty, love; motherliness; femininity; wisdom; connection between spirit and matter; inner and outer wealth

THE EMPEROR: Pioneer, discoverer, leader, initiator; creative wisdom; great leadership qualities; urge for action; adventurousness, new beginnings; fatherhood, authority

THE HEIROPHANT: Spiritual master, teacher, advisor, initiate, inner guide, spiritual father; highest transformation

THE LOVERS: Love, attraction, approaching, connection, union of opposites through Love; becoming conscious through relationships

THE CHARIOT: New beginning, change for the good; introspection, meditation, spiritual growth

JUSTICE: Balance, centering, equilibrium; balancing of opposites, justice

THE HERMIT: Finding one's own light; going inward; completion, harvest; resting in one's own center; wise guide

THE WHEEL OF FORTUNE: New beginning, expansion, creativity, big break-through; self-realization; unexpected fortune

STRENGTH: Passion, multidimensional creativity, talents; strength; integration of animalistic energies; overcoming old fears and conditionings

THE HANGED MAN: Congealed; end of a situation or relationship which is stuck; letting go, giving up; surrendering; learning to see in a new way; the necessity of breaking through old behavior patterns

DEATH: Death and resurrection; transformation; becoming free of old ensnarement's; external changes

TEMPERANCE: Unification of opposites, balance; inner change, transformation, alchemy, a quantum leap; creative power

THE DEVIL: Procreative energy, new vitality; humor; sensuality, sexuality, creative energy; individuality

THE TOWER: Far reaching, inner transformation; healing, the old is destroyed to make room for the new; spiritual renewal; self-knowledge

THE STAR: Inspiration, crystallization, self-recognition, radiating, clear vision, trust in the self; connection to universal intelligence

THE MOON: Final testing; wrong turns, illusion; burning off karma, interaction or struggle with the subconscious, place to new levels of consciousness

THE SUN: Highly creative energy; awareness; fulfilled love relationship; wisdom, spirituality; transformation

JUDGEMENT: Highly discriminating or discerning; open to criticism; critical self-analysis

THE WORLD: Completion, cosmic union; travel liberation form bondage; burning off karma

THE FOOL: Openness, trust ready to take a risk, courage to stand your ground; freedom, independence; creativity; great potential; possibility to take quantum leap; listening to the heart's voice 57

ALL SEEING EYE
Ezekiel's Wheel

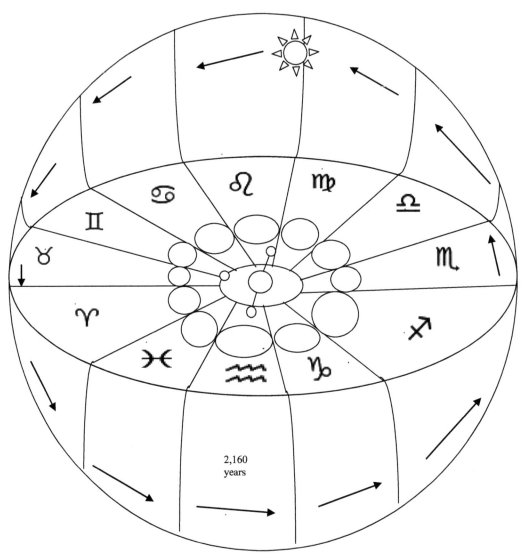

2,160
years

12 ages
2,160 years each
25,920 years total

The Book of Illumination

CHAPTER 2

THE TALENTED TWELVE

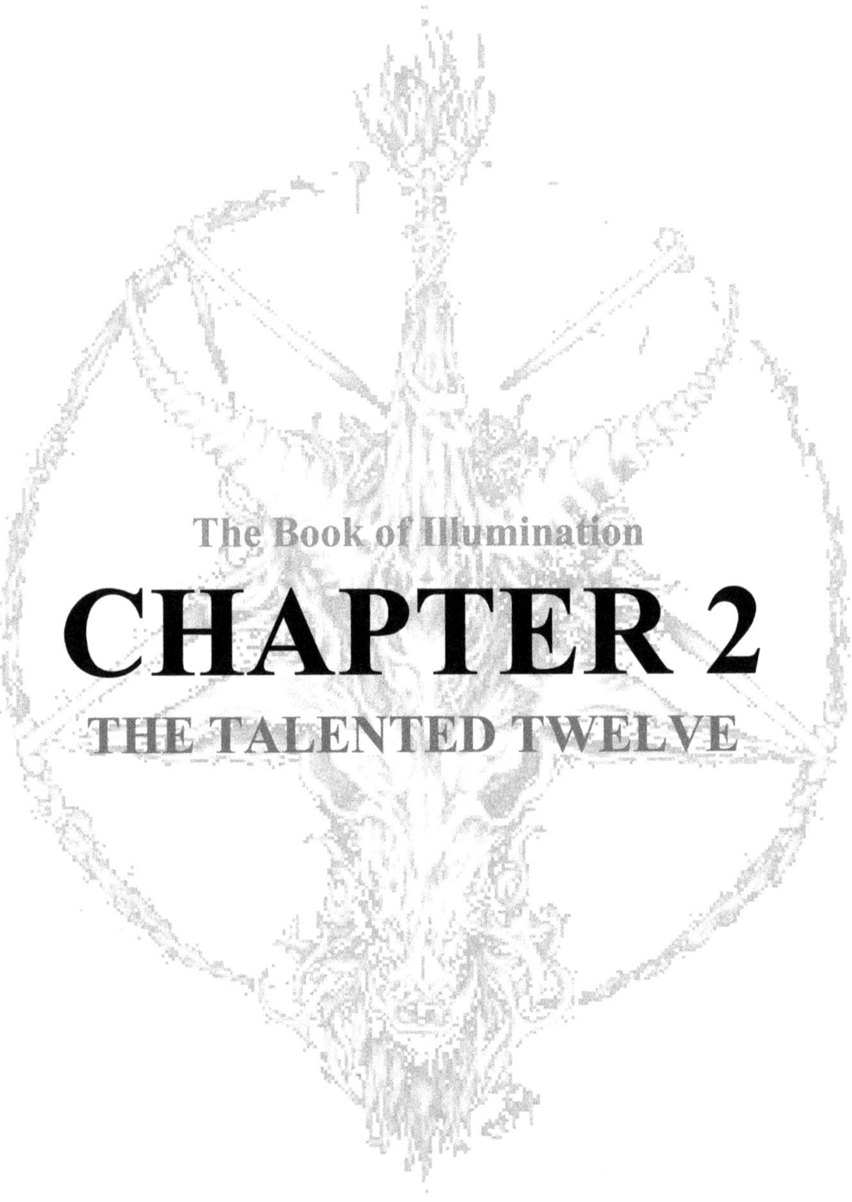

The Book of Illumination

CHAPTER 2

THE TALENTED TWELVE

THE TALENTED TWELVE

In order to fully assess why I said the "gene" of Isis is a representation and sign of the Horus to come, or son of the Virgin Isis; we first must understand what role Astrology plays in the Bible and life of the Sun of Man. You have to place the life of the Sun of Man in its proper context to fully understand the story of Jesus. The myth of Jesus tells more about the human condition than it does about the actual life of Jesus as 18 years of his life are completely missing from the Canon (authorized Bible.) There are so many mysteries involved with the scriptures that if revealed the people would feel alienated by a religion they so eagerly have given their entire lives to. For instance: Jesus and his twelve disciples represent the Sun and the Moon and the other twelve astrological constellations they both revolve through. These constellations all have planets assigned to them and the planets govern the personalities of people on Earth. Cancer (Moon) Leo (Sun) Virgo (Mercury) Libra (Venus) Scorpio (Pluto) Sagittarius (Jupiter) Capricorn (Saturn) Aquarius (Uranus) Pisces (Neptune) Aries (Mars) Taurus (Venus) Gemini (Mercury.)

At this time, it is important to note the correlation between plane and planet. A plane when defined as a noun is: *a level of existence or consciousness.* Plane defined as an adjective means: *completely level or flat.* Planet, a word that has plane at its root, is defined as: *a celestial body moving in an elliptical orbit around a star.* A square, the popular depiction of what most people think a plane looks like, is flat and has 4 right angles at 90 degrees totaling 360 degrees. The shape that most accurately describes a planet's appearance is a circle also 360 degrees. In my astrological model, the star the Sun and Moon revolve around is the Earth itself. The Moon is on the inside of the elliptic 250,000 miles away from the Earth; and the Sun is on the outside ecliptic 93 million miles away from the Earth. Because the Sun is on the outside of the ecliptic, it takes 25,920 years to make a full revolution around the Earth through the constellations whereas the Moon only takes 30 days. The periods between each constellation are what are called the *planets.* Think of them in terms of a pie, or as the diagram displays *planes of existence.* The circle in the middle of the pie has another circle around it, which enables it to make a revolution around the pie (inner circle) alot quicker than the circle surrounding the pie. Again, the circle on the inside of the pie represents the Moon's orbit; and the circle on the outside of the pie represents the Sun's orbit. Beyond the Sun are the constellations. The Sun takes 2,160 years to move through each constellation and 25,920 years to move through them all.

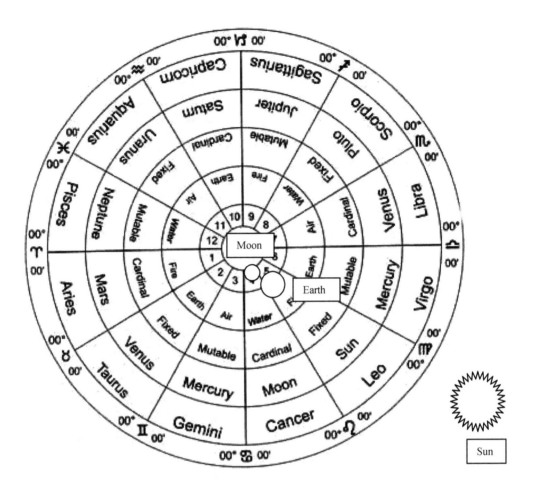

In Latin, one of the old world's primary languages, the days of the week correspond to the planets. Monday = Lunes (Moon day) Tuesday = Martes (Mars) Wednesday = Miercoles (Mercury) Thursday = Jueves (Jupiter) Friday = Viernes (Venus) Saturday = Sabado' (Saturn) Sunday = Domingo (Dios) which means God. Below is a biblical reference that allows the reader to fully see that ancient cultures referenced within the Bible had knowledge of Astrology.

Acts 14:11-12 *(11) And when people saw what Paul had done, they lifted up their voices, saying in the speech of Lycaonia, The gods are come down to us in the likeness of men (12) And they called Barnabas, Jupiter and Paul, Mercurius, because he was the chief speaker.*

The Zodiac is the belt or band of constellations through which the Sun and Moon transit across the sky. Astrologers noted these constellations and attached a particular significance to them. Over time they developed the system of twelve signs of the zodiac *(Aries, Taurus, Gemini, Cancer, Leo, Virgo, Libra, Scorpio, Sagittarius, Capricorn, Aquarius, and Pisces.)* Based on these twelve constellations many ancient cultures considered the Sun, the Moon, and Venus to be particularly important. The **word** Zodiac comes from the Greek word *zodiakos kuklos* which translates to a *"circle of animals."* This is where the circus developed its concept, show, and theme from 58aa. The Zodiac (ideology) however came from Mesopotamia, where the Moon held equal significance to the Sun due to the cultures worship of a feminine "god" over a masculine one. This was primarily because the constellations can be seen at night under the Moon rather than in the day with the Sun.

Many cultures that worship a Moon goddess in place of a Sun god have overlooked the fact that the Moon is a projection of the light from the Sun; which, with the help of "Set," (sunset) allows all the other stars to emerge 58. Another important notation as to why cultures worshipped a Moon goddess over a Sun god has to do with the physical makeup of the two celestial entities. Who can actually say they have looked directly into the Sun with the naked eye and have not been blinded by it? At the same time who has not been awestruck by the presence of a full Moon at night. The beauty and mystery associated with the Moon aesthetically is one of the most breath-taking spectacles in the sky at night. Just as in Egypt where Osiris is obstructed by Set; the setting of the Sun is also another breath taking spectacle in nature, and is why Set is so vital in the life of Osiris (the Sun.) These ciphers as well as many others will be thoroughly explained throughout the following chapters in this book.

58aa The cover of Michael Jackson's *Dangerous* album showcases this circus theme and gives even more insight into the knowledge he possessed both of himself and the world around him. Though the Egyptians worshipped a solar deity, the Sun God Ra, who they believed traveled across the cosmos in a solar boat {Ark} 58ab (indicative of Vishnu/Shiva.) The Babylonians however, were the first culture recorded to have practiced Astrology under Ba'al, the LORD, also indicative of the Hindu God Shiva, who we'll discuss later is mentioned in Old and New Testament Scriptures. The following is a rundown of the 12 astrological signs and their characteristics 58bc.

Aries: the ram is the first astrological sign in the Zodiac originating from the constellation of Aries. In astrology, Aries is considered a masculine, positive (extrovert) sign. It is also considered a cardinal fire sign, and is ruled by the planet Mars. Being the first sign in the Zodiac, Aries is associated with the astrological 1st house. The astrological symbol for Aries is said to represent the head and horns of the ram, and originates from the cluster of stars which constitute the head of the Aries (constellation). Ariens are the warriors of the zodiac. They are usually highly competitive and display a "childlike" innocence and outlook on life. This isn't childlike in the sense of immaturity, rather childlike in the sense of seeking fun displaying innocence within that frame of mind.

Taurus: is the second astrological sign in the Zodiac, originating from the constellation of Taurus. In astrology, Taurus is considered an earth sign and is one of four fixed signs. Like the rest of the earth signs, Taurus is considered a "negative", feminine sign, which in astrology means it is rather introverted. Taurus is ruled by the planet Venus (which also rules Libra). Being the second sign of the zodiac, Taurus has been associated with the astrological second house. The Sun is in Taurus roughly from April 21 to May 20. The astrological symbol for Taurus represents the head and horns of the bull. Taureans are partakers of the material world and represent money, finances, and wealth within the zodiac. They are extreme lovers of music and when they become focused on something they are usually unwavering in any attempt to sway them from their goals.

Gemini: is the third astrological sign in the Zodiac, originating from the constellation of Gemini. In astrology, Gemini is considered a "masculine", positive (extrovert) sign. It is also considered an air sign, and is one of four mutable signs. Gemini has been closely associated with the planet Mercury and is considered to be ruled by it. The Sun is in the sign of Gemini roughly from May 21 to June 21. Being the third sign in the zodiac, Gemini is associated with the astrological 3rd house which is associated with communications, siblings, neighbors, local travel, transport, and education. Gemini's are the communicators of the zodiac, quick witted and also showing a dual nature, Gemini's usually are realists and do not sugarcoat the realities that life entails.

Cancer: is the fourth astrological sign in the Zodiac originating from the constellation of Cancer. In astrology, Cancer is considered a yin sign or alternatively feminine or negative sign, meaning it is more introverted. It is considered a water sign, and is one of four cardinal signs. Cancer is ruled by the Moon. Being the fourth sign in the zodiac, Cancer has been associated with the astrological 4th house. Under the tropical zodiac the Sun is in Cancer roughly from June 22 to July 22. Cancereans are the feelers of the zodiac. They are very sensitive and are considered the "mothers" of the zodiac do to their sensitivity and their sign being ruled by the moon.

Leo: is the fifth astrological sign of the Zodiac, originating from the constellation of Leo. In astrology, Leo is considered to be a "masculine", positive (extrovert) sign. It is also considered a fire sign and is one of four fixed signs. Leo is ruled by the Sun. The Sun is in Leo roughly from July 23 to August

23. Leo's are the monarchs of the zodiac. The usually are very dogmatic and considered bossy because of their position in regards to being ruled by the sun. They are extremely positive individuals and show resilience in the face of any opposition.

Virgo: is the sixth astrological sign in the Zodiac, originating from the constellation of Virgo. In astrology Virgo is considered a "feminine", negative (introvert) sign. It is the only sign represented by a female. It is also considered an earth sign and is one of four mutable signs. Virgo is traditionally ruled by the planet Mercury. Under the tropical zodiac, the Sun is in Virgo roughly from August 24 to September 23. Virgos represent the thinking women and were sought after and coveted for their remarkable mental abilities.

Libra: is the seventh astrological sign in the Zodiac originating from the constellation of Libra. In astrology Libra is considered a "masculine", positive (extrovert) sign. It is also considered an air sign and is one of four cardinal signs. Libra is ruled by the planet Venus (which also rules Taurus). It is governed by the 7th House (House of Love & Relationships). Under the tropical zodiac, the Sun enters Libra around September 24 and exits around October 23. Libra, is also known as The Scales of Balance, and is the only symbol of the zodiac that is represented by an inanimate object, rather than an animal or human. Libra is the sign that brings balance to the zodiac. They are usually very stable individuals who often see perspectives from both sides of any debate. Seeing from both sides causes them not to take stances either way but rather they mediate between both sides to bring about compromise and peace.

Scorpio: is the eighth astrological sign in the Zodiac, originating from the constellation of Scorpius. Scorpio is considered a water sign, and is one of four fixed signs. Like the rest of the water signs, Scorpio is considered a negative, feminine sign. Under the tropical zodiac the Sun enters Scorpio around October 24 and exits around November 21. Scorpio is associated with the astrological house number 8, which is associated with natural Scorpio matters - birth, death, transformation, deeply committed relationships of all kinds, and the occult and psychic matters. Scorpio also has associations with three animal symbols: the scorpion, the snake, and the phoenix (or Eagle). Each sign represents different levels of power related to personal strength, individual power, and even intimidation based on cultural associations with these different animals. All three symbols indicate the fierce determination of the Scorpio to triumph over odds and to be ruthless in pursuing goals. Scorpios are the carnal lovers of the zodiac, often vindictive, and calculating they have been vilified for their personality traits.

Sagittarius: is the ninth astrological sign in the Zodiac, originating from the constellation of Sagittarius. Sagittarius is classed as a positive or masculine, extrovert sign; its element is fire and its quality is mutable. Sagittarius is ruled by the planet Jupiter. Under the tropical zodiac, the sun enters Sagittarius around November 22 and exits around December 21. "Sagittars" are known in mythology as Centaurs and are the discerning gurus of the zodiac. Their wisdom and ability to float between both realms of existence between the animal and human world give them the uncanny ability to be awesome judges of character. They are often talkative and use their communication skills to promote their own particular philosophies of life.

Capricorn: is the tenth astrological sign in the Zodiac originating from the constellation of Capricornus. Capricorn is considered an earth sign and is one of four cardinal signs. Like the rest of the earth signs, Capricorn is considered a "negative" feminine sign and is ruled by the planet Saturn. Being the tenth sign of the zodiac, Capricorn has been associated with the astrological 10th house. Under the tropical zodiac, the Sun is in Capricorn roughly from December 22 to January 19. The astrological symbol for Capricorn is said to represent the horns and tail of the goat-fish or sea-goat. In mythology Capricorn has been associated to the God Pan. Capricorns are the most built and refined physically of all the signs

Aquarius: is the eleventh astrological sign in the Zodiac, originating from the constellation Aquarius. In astrology, Aquarius is considered a "masculine", positive (extrovert) sign. It is also considered an air sign and is one of four fixed signs. Aquarius has been traditionally ruled by the planet Saturn, and, since its discovery, Uranus has been considered a modern ruler of this sign. Being the eleventh sign of the zodiac, Aquarius is associated with the astrological 11th house. Under the tropical zodiac, the Sun is in Aquarius roughly from January 20 to about February 18-19. Aquarians are the thinkers of the zodiac and one of 3 signs that are recognized as a human being. They are often ahead of their time in the way they are able to "see into the future.

Pisces: is the twelfth astrological sign in the Zodiac, which originates from the Pisces constellation. Pisces is represented by a pair of fish that are swimming in opposite directions but remain held together at the mouth by a cord. In astrology, Pisces is considered a water sign, and is one of four mutable signs. Like the rest of the watery signs, Pisces is considered a "negative", feminine sign. Being the twelfth sign, Pisces is associated with the astrological 12th house. Since its discovery Pisces has been traditionally ruled by the planet, Neptune has been considered a modern ruler of this sign. Under the tropical zodiac, the Sun is in Pisces roughly from February 19 to March 20 Pisces are the liberals of the zodiac often led by their emotions and equally intrigued by those who inspire them.

Astrology has had a profound influence over the past few thousand years on western and eastern cultures. In the Middle Ages, those who were educated at the time believed Astrology to be the placement of celestial spheres in the heavens that reflected on the personalities of the people influencing their lives on the earth below. Astrology also had a direct influence on both the language and literature of the ancient world as well. For example: influenza comes from the Medieval Latin *influentia* which means "influence" and was named so because doctors believed epidemics were caused by unfavorable planetary and stellar "influences." The word "disaster" comes from the Italian disastro, derived from the negative prefix *dis-* and from Latin *aster/astro* "star" meaning (ill-starred). The adjectives lunatic/ (Luna/Moon, (mercurial (Mercury), (venereal) (Venus), (martial) (Mars), (jovial) (Jupiter/Jove), and (saturnine) (Saturn) are all old world words used to describe personal qualities said to resemble or be highly influenced by the astrological characteristics of the planets. In literature, many writers, notably Geoffrey Chaucer and William Shakespeare used astrological symbolism to show planetary influences in the description of their characters motivations 60.

Angels and Demons, a movie about the conspiracies of the Illuminati and the Mother Roman Church, acknowledged these two men in their attempt to decode the ancient language biblical scriptures were written in. However the secrets that both Chaucer and Shakespeare knew was that Astrology, which at that time was deemed satanic by the Mother Church, was the key and source for all understanding including the understanding of the LORD and the "heavenly kingdom" he plans to manifest upon his reincarnation to earth.

To fully understand the significance and importance Astrology has over western society; one has to have a fundamental understanding of energies, elements, and mathematics. Every person and everything has an energy associated with it. Depending on where the Sun was located when a person was born will determine what type of personality that person will have; which again are measurements of time as well as the position of the Sun. These positions were organized into elemental forms and further caricaturized into astrological signs. Astrology is formulated upon a science that relies on mathematics as its basis for measurement. Though seemingly speculative and designed from superstition, Astrology provides an all-encompassing curriculum for any individual to

 understand themselves as well as other people. It is the ultimate guide to self-discovery and when a person embarks on the journey to find themselves or God, Astrology is the link that shows them what aspect of "God" (which the ancients saw as the *Celestial Hierarchies* themselves, {*Sun, Moon, stars,*}) is in operation within their soul, or as Astrology reveals…their *SOL*

When speaking in reference to the Sun or the Sun of Man as a consciousness, it can be interpreted in many ways. Because the Sun moves through constellations and astrological signs, a person could factor the consciousness associated to the return of the Sun, as the return of the Sun in a specific constellation or sign. This is where symbols and glyphs assist us in finding out where the Sun was when certain stories and ancient myths were developed. Upon doing this is how we are able to formulate prophecies which are stories developed from the planetary position of the Earth in relation to the Sun at the point the consciousness (deity/constellation) descended to Earth. From this acknowledgement, because we understand Astrology, it makes us able to see the people or person who embodies this specific consciousness at the specified and appointed time as illustrated by the stars in heaven.

We then can test this hypothesis mathematically by comparing and contrasting the contemporary myth (person) with the ancient myth (person) to see if there is a match. If there is a match, those persons/entities/celestial embodiments in human form are then recorded into new myths, which are validated by the previous myths that predated them. These myths (celestial embodiments) as main characters are then organized within Holy books like the Bhaga vita, Torah, Qur'an, and Bible as avatars and sons of God. Their heroics are then rewritten in an allegorized narrative and are presented to the uncivilized people of the society by its clergy men. The lives of these avatars are then deified in the next cycle of history when their accounts are dug up, doctored, and published to the new civilization's people.

The Book of Illumination

CHAPTER 3

THE RESURRECTION

The Book of Illumination

CHAPTER 3
THE RESURRECTION

THE RESURRECTION

This new age of knowledge and information has given rise to an insatiable quest for the truth. Trying to discover what is truth versus what is false forces us to call into question what we believe and why. With the current witch hunt storming the internet involving artists who promote the agendas of the 'Illuminati; it is easily seen that the topic of debate nowadays is religion. Young people want to know if it is real, and if so why are they so confused by it. The 90's generation was the generation that did it all. The words of a famous song sum the generation up best, *"Two thousand zero, zero party over we're out of time/ so tonight I'ma gonna party like its 1999"* [7]. In the pre-Y2k rebellion, the youth tore up everything, and they had no idea they were responsible for destroying all that was once held sacred. However in their destructive rebellion, they found something; it wasn't the truth, but it was something almost as sweet. They found that what their parents told them wasn't true, and it gave them an edge on discovering what was. The youth have already been sedated, suppressed, repressed, and everything else under the sun; so on this time around, on this journey, the only thing that is relative is being enlightened. They can no longer be pacified with fairy tales as their experiences have given them the clarity to see beyond the veil as 'they've done it to death.' Everyone who isn't completely broke by the *"party and bullshit"* mentality is either dead, in jail, or *'tryna make a dollar out of fifteen cents.'* This mentality was fueled by hip-hop, but has bled its way into suburban and corporate America. The people are stressed vexed, over sexed, and all tapped out. The only thing that is sufficient enough to quench their insatiable desire to know *is* to know. With that being said, the only plan towards reconciliation is a plan for salvation. So naturally we turn our scopes to the author of salvation, the most popular figure in the history of the world; and in our quest to know, we have stumbled across some interesting facts. The author we speak of is called Jesus, and our findings make him the direct enemy of the very institution that claims to serve him... the church. This is why naturally the next chapter in this book is about Jesus and the resurrection; the same resurrection that I used to animate the examples of Barack Obama and Oprah Winfrey. Reason being is an in depth exploration of the resurrection has to first be understood before I am able to shed correct light on why the Bible was written, why scribes have edited it, and why certain members of the present mother church have tried to conceal this information.

Think back to any time in your life when you heard a story where the headline or initial sentence that drew your interest was very different from how the story actually happened. Quite often, it's discovered at the end of the story, that the story itself was embellished by the person telling it. The embellished or romanticized aspects of the story are what creates the headlines, and these headlines become the story itself. The details of the story somehow along the way become obscure and forgotten. The same pattern of embellishment used to create headlines is also utilized in the art of storytelling whereby by the embellished accounts overtime grows into full-fledged romanticism. People then preach these romantic or embellished beliefs to their children for the sake of not going into detail due to the under developments of their children's comprehension. Logic tells the parents their children won't understand and when these children grow up, they repeat the same cycles their parents repeated with them. From the passing down of these romantic stories and embellishments traditions are then born.

Romantic: (1) Imaginary not based on fact (2) Marked by the imaginative or emotional appeal of what is heroic, adventurous, remote, mysterious, or idealized

We have to keep in mind in "biblical times" there wasn't any television and stories were often embellished and "spiced up" for entertainment and allegorical purposes.

Many Christians today do not know the origins from which "preaching" started. In the ancient Jewish sects they had Priests who served as the spiritual leaders of their congregations and were the holy men that presided over the synagogues who performed ritualistic and educational functions. According to biblical gospels, the Priests Jesus speaks in reference to were known as Sadducees.

Sadducees: (1) a member of an ancient Jewish sect consisting mainly of Priests and Aristocrats that differed from the Pharisee especially in its literal interpretation of the Bible and its rejection of oral laws and traditions

Pharisee: (1) a member of an ancient Jewish sect that differed from the Sadducees chiefly in its strict observance of the religious practices, liberal interpretation of the Bible, and adherence to oral laws and traditions

John the Baptist, according to the Bible, was preaching the kingdom of heaven is at hand. This was done to fulfill an earlier prophecy that stated Elijah must first come and restore all things before Christ appears back to earth.

Matthew 3:1&2 (3) *In those days came John the Baptist <u>preaching</u> in the wilderness of Judaea (4) and saying repent ye for the kingdom of heaven is at hand.*

Matthew 17:10-13 (10) *And his disciples asked him saying, Why then say the scribes that Elijah must first come (11) Elijah truly shall come forth and restore all things, (12) But I say unto you Elijah is come already and they knew him not but have done unto him whatsoever they listed. Likewise shall the Son of Man suffer of them. (13)Then the disciples understood that he spake unto them of John the Baptist.*

Malachi 4:5 (5) Behold, I will send you Elijah the prophet before the coming of the great and dreadful day of the Lord.

John is in the wilderness preaching "the kingdom of heaven is at hand" because he is the resurrected Elijah.

Matthew 11:13-14 (13) For all the prophets and the law prophesized unto John. (14) And if ye will receive it, this is Elijah, which was for to come.

Matthew 4:16-17 (16) The people which sat in darkness saw a great light and to them which sat in the region and shadow of death is sprung light (17) From that time Jesus began to <u>preach</u>, and to say, **Repent for the kingdom of heaven is at hand**.

Matthew 3:1&2 (3) In those days came John the Baptist <u>preaching</u> in the wilderness of Judaea (4) and saying repent ye for the kingdom of heaven is at hand.

John and Jesus preaching the kingdom of heaven at hand is eerily similar to Michael Jackson in his song *Another Part of Me* where he says "*The planets are lining up, bringing brighter days, their all in line, waiting for you, your just another part of me.*" The alignment that Michael Jackson was speaking about was the coming of the new age and consciousness or basically the kingdom (new constellation) of heaven that is moving in place of the last constellation. This new constellation signifies a change in the evolution of the human psyche and John is preparing the people for the coming of Jesus whose message will change the world; just as Michael Jackson was preparing the world for a new "mulattocized" society (age) which would be ruled temporarily by the mystic "Lamb of God" as referenced in the Book of Revelations 52b. However, in the Bible, the people have forgotten why Elijah is coming, and what his coming symbolizes. They haven't a clue as to who they are looking for or what the coming change really represents. This is why Herod the Tetrarch an aristocrat, mistakes John for Jesus.

Matthew 14:1-2 (1) *At that time Herod the <u>tetrarch</u> heard of the fame of Jesus (2) And said unto his servants, This is John the Baptist; <u>he is risen from the dead</u> and therefore mighty works do shew forth themselves in him.*

<u>Tetrarch</u>: (1) A subordinate prince (2) A governor of the 4th part of providence

<u>Aristocrats</u>: (1) Nobles, those who are believed to be superior of their kind

<u>Aristocracy</u>: (1) a governing body or upper class usually made up of hereditary nobility

The previous scripture indicates that Herod the Tetrarch had anticipated a resurrection of Christ before Christ was even slain on a cross; and gives rise to the theory the aristocrats or rulers of that day had knowledge of the resurrection of people or god incarnates from past lives as written in ancient prophecies. Isn't this the same as today, where people are awaiting the return of the Christ? This means that either the resurrection that Paul and the Christian church preach of is misunderstood, or writers (scribes) have come in later and tried to piece together versions of the original stories with those that are false. I say this because Jesus spoke to the multitude and told them that John was the resurrected Elijah. Why wouldn't Herod the tetrarch say," *This is Elijah: he is risen from the dead and therefore mighty works do shew forth themselves in him.*" The scriptures say that "**John**" is *risen* from the *dead* which indicates a writer has read the scriptures and come along later and placed John's name instead of Elijah's in the texts. Again only Jesus knew at that time Elijah was John. This "slip up" shows the Bible has been tampered with unless of course you believe that "God" makes mistakes. John didn't rise from the dead; Elijah rose from the dead in the person of John the Baptist.

According to biblical scriptures, Elijah is said not to have died but went up to heaven in a whirlwind. It is a very easy notion to assume that the writers (scribes) who edited the gospel of Luke, read the Gospel of Matthew first. This is stated because the 1st Gospel written according to history and scholarship was the Gospel of Matthew. I'm sure if the people would have known that John the Baptist was Elijah this question would have been asked, "*Why if Elijah was a spirit taken up in a whirlwind would he be born to physically by traditional birth.*"

Luke 1:39-41 *(39) And Mary arose in those days, and went into the hill country with haste, into a city of Juda (40) and entered into the house of Zacharias and saluted Elisabeth (41) And it came to pass that, when Elisabeth heard the salutation of Mary, the babe leaped in her womb; and Elisabeth was filled with the Holy Ghost.*

If Elijah went to heaven in a whirlwind why wouldn't he return in a whirlwind? And if Elijah went to heaven the same way Jesus went to heaven after he arose from the cross, wouldn't this mean that the returning Jesus/Savior would also come through the womb of a woman (not the sky) just as Elijah in the person of John the Baptist did. The sign Aquarius as I will explain later is an **air** sign (sky) and is also an allegorical symbol that links the sign known as the "water bearer" (Aquarius) to John the **Baptist.** In this sense, the messiah would come from the sky, but he would also still have to come through the womb of a woman.

The reason why Elijah wouldn't return in a whirlwind is because this is figurative language. A language that is so esoteric, only a few initiates in the world know its true meaning and significance. If we are to ever solve the problems of the world then we have to be realistic about what the Bible is saying and why. Until we fully own up to the fact that man has come along and in "God's" name, done some reconfiguring to the biblical accounts, reconfiguring meaning *changed* the Bibles original texts, society will never fully be over its bigotry, racism, religious misunderstanding, and war. One would ask why man would do such a thing like falsify "God's" word in the Bible; the two words that come to my mind are power and control.

Here in Matthew 14:1-2 it is evident the aristocrats are aware that the resurrection of John (Elijah) and or Jesus will cause them to be overthrown. This is stated because back then in that time, aristocrats were claimed to be divinely appointed representatives sent from the heavens to control the fates, and properties of man. Their rule wasn't questioned because their rule was issued from "God" himself. The hereditary lineage of "God" was through Abraham and the aristocrats of that day claimed their rule was divinely appointed from "God" through him (Abraham). If you look at other scriptures ones that are pointed at Pharisees and Sadducees you get this same conclusion. The Pharisees and Sadducees according to definition are the wealthy aristocrats of the church and state, who are acting as if they are divinely appointed from God. Here you have two figures (Jesus and John) who, according to the scriptures, are appointed from "God" (nature.) When the two (John and Jesus) display their powers, the aristocrats and fake priests are exposed. Besides the scriptures informing us that John and Jesus are from above, we know they are from the heavens "stars" because they have abilities that showcase they are a higher creation than regular layman. This expose' threatens the rule of the governing bodies and in the prophecy the governing bodies of aristocrats have teamed up with the governing body of the church to imprison or kill both John and Jesus. *Imagine the magic and magnetism of Michael Jackson and compare it to the abilities of Ronald Reagan.* Who would be considered the "divinely" appointed avatar, and who would be the aristocrat? In biblical times, the people and even some disciples thought that John the Baptist was the Christ. By entering this evidence we can conclude either the modern day preacher, (studiers under Paul and the NT) don't really understand what the resurrection is really about; or the church through clever minded action or skilled writing has re-written and re-translated facts that if spun in a different way, would reveal a totally new Gospel. Think about it, If Herod the tetrarch is looking for Jesus and the whole story of the Gospel is how Jesus is exposing fake priests and aristocrats and they are seeking him out to kill him, why is it necessary Jesus run. If he is like Jason (hockey mask) or any other mythological persona who is immortal why is it necessary that he hide and do his mission in secret? Why wouldn't he just come down from the cross and say, "ha-ha you can't kill me I am immortal!?" After which they would poke him through his heart with a spear and he would look at them and turn the spear and pull it out and say, "You can't kill me I am immortal." This perverse example shows you the immortality that Jesus speaks of has nothing to do with dying a physical death, resurrecting shortly after, and living eternally. If this were the case, it wouldn't have taken a full 2,160 years for him to resurrect.

Matthew 27:42 *He saved others; himself he cannot save. If he be the king of the King of Israel, let him now come down from the cross, and we will believe him.*

What is interesting about the scripture below is Paul is quoted as saying Jesus is the only one with immortality.

I Timothy 6:15-16 *(15) Which in his time he shall shew, who is the blessed and only Potentate, the King of Kings, and Lord of lords: (16) Who only hath immortality, dwelling in the light which no man can approach unto; whom no man hath seen, nor can see: to whom be honour and power everlasting.*

But according to Jesus, he isn't the only person who is resurrected.

Matthew 11:13-14 (13) *For all the Prophets and the Law prophesied until John.* (14) *And if you are willing to accept it, he is the Elijah who was to come.*

Again, the resurrection spoken of by Jesus about Elijah (John) has nothing to do with him dying a physical death; this resurrection has to do with past lives. What is even more enlightening is that Jesus is the only one capable of knowing who Elijah (John) is. Paul stated in II Timothy that Jesus was the only one with immortality; Matthew 11:13-14 has just disproved that. Jesus also tells his disciples to let the dead bury their dead in Matthew 8:22.

Matthew 8:22 *Follow me and let the dead bury their dead.*

Is this a clue explaining what the resurrection Jesus spoke of is *really* about? Is the Sun of Man the first one aware of his immortality and therefore the light to show the world that people resurrect as well? If so, this would explain the mystery of everlasting life that Jesus promises his disciples.

Matthew 10:8 *Heal the sick, cleanse the lepers, <u>raise the dead</u>, cast out devils, freely ye have received freely give.*

What does this mean? Raising people from the dead using this reference of death has little to do with those who are physically dead; and speaks more to those who are spiritually dead. We know this because Jesus also told his disciples to raise the dead yet only He and Elijah were "physically" able to do it. If this doesn't mean to spiritually raise from the dead then what could it possibly mean? Again, if you think this a false notion ask yourself where Jesus has been for the last 2,000 years and then think about why Christians believe he's coming back.

John 6:38 *for I came down from heaven, not to do mine own will, but the will of him that sent me.*

In fact, Elijah and Jesus are two of three individuals who didn't die in the Bible, but ascended to heaven. The other is Enoch, and his ascension is unclear in the account given by the Book of Genesis

Genesis 5:24 *(24) And Enoch walked with God: and he was not for God took him.*

2 Kings 2:11 *(11) And it came to pass as they still went on and talked that behold, there appeared a chariot of fire, and horses of fire, and parted them both asunder; and Elijah went up by a whirlwind to heaven.*

Acts 23:7 & 8*: <u>For the Sadducees say there is no resurrection</u>; neither angel or spirit but the Pharisees confess both.*

<u>Resurrect</u>: to raise from the dead

According to the scriptures, the (Sadducees) doubt the Jesus they are talking to is the one prophesized about in the Old Testament. The Sadducees do this because they believe there is no resurrection. Here we have a sect of Priests who believes that Christ cannot resurrect; so let's examine this notion critically. Maybe their belief wasn't that Jesus could not be resurrected but that a person who has died can't live again after they have died in the same lifetime. I'm not speaking of those who are revived with special heart pumping techniques or jolts of electricity of modern medicine; I'm talking about those who are truly dead! If this is the case it would explain some of the actions of the Jews. Think about it, if a rogue vagabond were to walk up into a church in America and address the clergy (preachers) with the pure unadulterated message of God, what do you think the preachers would do to him? The preacher and his congregation I doubt seriously would recognize him as being from God. It would be no different than Criss Angel who does all of these unbelievable magic tricks. Though he is very skillful and crafty in his magic, I highly doubt that any one would believe that "The God" was his father. They would probably rebuke him as being Satan like they did in *Matt 12:27* when they said that Jesus cast out devils in the name of *Beelzebub.* After which they would all come down to the altar and pray for his spiritual deliverance.

Matt 12:27 (27) And if I by Beelzebub cast out devils, by whom do your children cast them out?

Beelzebub: The chief Devil; Satan

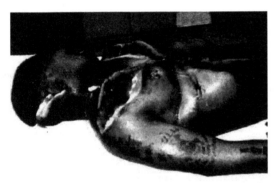 I firmly remember in my lifetime when **Tupac Shakur** died. For year's people thought he was alive after he died and many still think so to this day. Most of the people who thought he was still alive were his biggest fans. You could show them a photo of his autopsy and they still wouldn't believe it. In fact many of his fans would go out into the world and "preach" (profess) him to still be alive. This behavior is paralleled to the disciples of Jesus after his death; because a stranger who never saw Jesus resurrected, wouldn't believe he was alive either.

How do you expect the (Pharisees/Sadducees/Jews) to believe that Jesus was alive if they didn't see him when it defies all logic? Before you cast judgments ask yourself would you? According to scripture, even his own disciples doubted he was real after his resurrection.

Matthew 28:16-17 (16) then the eleven disciples went away into Galilee, into a mountain where Jesus had appointed them. (17) And when they saw him, they worshipped but some doubted.

How can we expect people who never saw Jesus after the resurrection to be believers in it (resurrection) when it says some of his disciples even doubted? The gospels tell us that Mary and his disciples saw Jesus after he died but 1 Corinthians 15:5-8 say that 500 people alongside Cephas and Paul saw him.

1 Corinthians 15:5-8 (5) And that he was seen of Cephas, then of the Twelve (6) And after that he was seen of above five hundred brethren at once; of whom the greater part remain unto present, but some are fallen asleep (7) After that he was seen of James; then of all the apostles (8) And last of all was seen me also, as of one born out of due time.

In conclusion I would have to say that believing in the resurrection in today's times would be very difficult for most people. (The resurrection from past lives actually has factual basis and is accepted in other religions such as Hinduism, Buddhism, and Islam.) I would say most people would react just as the Pharisees did with Jesus when really confronted by a man, who is homeless who says he is the Christ, the one they've been waiting for.

Matthew 8:20 *Jesus replied, "Foxes have holes and birds of the air have nests, <u>but the Son of Man has no place to lay his head.</u>*

Very few, if any in this country accept the belief that a person who has been killed in that same life and body can live again; however resurrection from past lives makes sense. Even the Sun and the Moon follow elliptical orbits. These orbits are those that revolve in circles causing the same things to happen on the planet at the time the planet crosses the same point in its orbit. This is also how we can predict what the weather patterns will be like on our planet during the various seasons. When you look at nature and the seasons we can readily see that everything that happens in that monthly, seasonal cycle repeats itself. In winter its cold and everything is dead, in spring things warm up and life begins to form. In summer it is extremely hot, and life is at its zenith, and in fall, things begin to die. This resurrecting of nature's cycle shows us that there is evidence that makes it possible for belief in life after death. What would also make belief in the resurrection of Jesus hard for people to accept is in the scriptures Jesus is a homeless man who works miracles. Homeless people today are unseen and their contributions go unrecognized. How would one know the person they are talking with is *The Son* of *The God?* This is why so much emphasis is placed on belief alone.

John 6:40 And this is the will of him that sent me, that everyone which seeth the son, and believeth on him, may have everlasting life; and I will raise him on the last day.

John 7:24 (24) Verily, verily I say unto you. He that heareth my word, and believeyh on him that sent me, hath everlasting life, and shall not come into condemnation; but passed from death to life.

John 6: 47 (47) Verily verily I say unto you. He that beleiveth hath everlasting life.

When the Jesus of Nazareth comes back, it will require your belief that a resurrection (from past lives) is possible before you can even begin to fathom the other mysteries and instructions that he is going to give out upon his return. If you can't or don't believe in the resurrection, there is no way you can believe in him. Jesus by nature was fashioned as "God." What I mean by this is that in nature you have all levels of beings like roaches, worms, dogs, cats, birds, and humans. We know that single celled organisms are the lowest on the planc of existence and humans are considered the highest. Humans are considered the highest because of their intelligence levels. This makes them fashioned like "God" or the Creator. In the human realm of existence there are also varying levels of being and consciousness. You have those of low intelligence, and those of high intelligence, those of high skill, and those of low skill, you have those with beauty and those without. Beauty, intelligence, and high intellect are what humans recognize as godly attributes. Jesus is the man fashioned by nature/God who has all of these attributes. Though he has other attributes, these attributes are the ones that are easily recognized with the senses. There are other prerequisites and attributes that are hidden and secret, that if known and understood, people would be able to see what made (Jesus) be referenced as "God" in the flesh or the Son of Man. But these things have been hidden until the end of time before they will be revealed.

Matthew 13:35 (35) That it might be fulfilled which was spoken by the prophet, saying I will open my mouth in parables: I will utter things, which have been kept secret from the foundation of the world.

A lot that goes on in the church today is directly contradictory to the teachings of Jesus, but again, one has to also understand time and place, the setting and the events, as well as the why? Why is Jesus on this mission to be crucified; and why is he telling his disciples they need to go and preach the "kingdom of heaven" is at hand? I used a few examples earlier to highlight the life of Jesus and pull the story into modern times to spawn critical thinking. I want the readers to place themselves in the scriptures. If this is done with accuracy you'll see just how faithless people really are.

A BUM RAP

Remember, according to scriptures, Jesus is a homeless man. Most people consider the homeless to be bums. This makes it extremely difficult for people to be believers in Jesus; especially when he doesn't have any possessions and claims to perform miracles. Again we have to keep in mind, if a homeless man with remarkable powers and intellect were to walk up to you at your job and tell you to follow him, how many people would look at him strange? Who would beckon at his call? Most people when confronted with this situation wouldn't do half as good as the worst disciple of Jesus; yet they conveniently say they would have been loyal to his every word. Naturally because people have oversight and can read the end of the story they can self-arrogate and say, "Oh yeah of course I would have listened to Jesus' every word. What was wrong with the people back then don't they know who he is?" The answer is NO, that's exactly the situation; most of them don't know who he is.

Matt.16:13-14 (13) *Who do men say that I the Son of Man am? (14) and they said, some say that thou art John the Baptist: some Elijah; and others Jeremiah or one of the prophets*

This is why the disciples have to step out on faith in their belief in his words and his actions. A person who is reading the Bible for the first time that stumbles across this passage in the Book of Matthew would be very puzzled as to why two men would abandon their way of life to follow a man who is homeless who they don't even know. So the Gospel of Luke answers these no brainer fundamental questions and fills in the gaps to kill people's speculation about unclear events.

Matthew 2:18-20 (18) *And Jesus walking by the sea of Galilee saw two brethren, Simon called Peter and Andrew his brother, casting nets into the sea: for they were fishers. (19) And he saith unto them, **Follow me, and I will make you fishers of men**. (20) And they straightway left their nets, and followed him.*

Luke 5:3-10 (3) *And he (Jesus) entered into one of the ships, which was Simon's, and prayed him that he would thrust out a little from the land. And he sat down, and taught the people out of the ship (4) Now when he left speaking he said unto to Simon, **Launch out into the deep, and let down your nets for a draught** (5) And Simon said unto him master we have toiled all night, and have taken nothing: nevertheless at thy word I will let down the net. (6) and when they had done this, they inclosed a great multitude of fishes: and their net brake (7) And they beckoned unto their partners, which were in the other ship, that they should come and help them. And they came, and filled both the ships, so that they began to sink (8) When Simon Peter saw it he fell down at Jesus' knees saying, Depart from me; for I am a sinful man, O Lord. (9) For he was astonished, and all that were with him, at the draught of the fishes which they had taken (10) And so was also James, and John, the sons of Zebedee which were partners with Simon. And Jesus said unto Simon, **Fear not; from thence forth thou shalt catch men.***

The Gospel of Luke clears up all speculation and makes it understood why two men would leave their way of life to follow a man who they know absolutely nothing about. They left their respective jobs because Jesus blessed them with so many fish. A man this powerful who is able to provide this abundantly is one any person would follow; which takes no faith at all. Coincidentally, the gospel of Luke was written under the tutelage of Paul who as I will explain later has a questionable ministry. But if you we're reading from the gospel of Matthew alone it would remain a mystery as to how Jesus gained their favor. In St. Matthew 16:6 –Jesus says "*beware of the leaven of the Pharisees and Sadducees."*

Leaven: (1) a substance as yeast or baking powder that causes fermentation and expansion of dough or batter (2) an element that produces an altering or transforming influence.

St. Matthew 16:7 (7) and they (the disciples) reasoned among themselves saying it is because we have taken no bread.

So Jesus replies like this in **St. Matthew 16:11, 12**(11) *How is it that ye do not understand that I spake it not to you concerning bread, that ye should beware of the leaven of the Pharisees and of the Sadducees? (12) Then understood they how that he bade them not to beware of the leaven of bread, but of the doctrine of the Pharisees and the Sadducees.*

Doctrine: a particular principle, position or policy taught or advocated as of a religion or government

According to the definition of leaven, Jesus is referring to the second meaning of the word; warning the disciples not to be influenced by the altering and transforming doctrine of the priests/preachers i.e. the (Pharisees and Sadducees.) On a deeper level, the very fact that Jesus' disciples are mocking him about the leaven of the Pharisees again is an example that shows the mindset that (man) is in. His disciples couldn't fathom that the leaven he is talking to them about is the doctrine/ altering influence of the Pharisees and Sadducees as pertained to their literal interpretations of the scriptures and prophecies. This is also an indication that when deciphering the words of Jesus, people should look beyond the obvious and superficial meaning of what he is saying to the underlying principal and allegorical significance. This illustration is no different than today in how preachers and priests wrongly teach the doctrines of Jesus causing mass confusion and warped religion. The only thought the disciples can muster about the leaven of the Pharisees and Sadducees is their erroneous comparisons to the leaven as being bread. In this passage we can either conclude that the disciples aren't very bright or there is an underlying dissent and doubt that causes them to reveal their confusion and lack of concentration concerning the words that Jesus has spoken. In the passage Jesus asks them, "*How is it that ye do not understand that I spake it not to you concerning bread, that ye should beware of the leaven of the Pharisees and of the Sadducees?*" Jesus posing this as a question in this way shows he is in disbelief of his disciple's ignorance. The reason I don't particularly feel the disciples were of low intelligence is because Jesus in Matt. 13:9-15 talks about giving parables to those with lesser understanding and revealing the mysteries of "God" to his disciples because they are worthy.

St. Matthew 13:9-11, 13, 16, 17 (9) Who hast ears to hear let him hear. (10) and the disciples came and said unto him Why speakest thou unto them in parables? (11) Because it is given unto you to know the mysteries of the kingdom of heaven, but to them it is not given. (13) Therefore I speak to them in parables because they seeing see not; and hearing they hear not, neither do they understand. (16) But blessed are your eyes for they see: and your ears, for they hear.(17) For verily I say unto you that many prophets and righteous men have desired to see things which ye see, and have not seen them; and to hear those things which ye hear, and have not heard them.

David Blane and Criss Angel are extraordinary miracle workers and magicians, however they are not viewed in public opinion or worshipped the same way Jesus is. We live in an elitist society where we worship those who have money. Paris Hilton is most notably famous *just* for having money and she is one of the world's biggest and most recognizable celebrities. To the unknowing person, what would be the criteria that would exalt Jesus above others? Would it be intellect alone, birthright, the performing of miracles, or coming out of the clouds? I would think he would have to satisfy all of these criteria for him even to be considered a candidate who could be the messiah. But even if this were the case only the very elect and well-studied theologians and scholars (Scribes) would know what he was talking about. Could we trust them to make the announcement to the world; especially when we know the scribes who translated this in the Bible were controlled by the Roman Catholic Church? I say this because the way that Jesus is described in the Bible is written figuratively not literally.

Most people still have an infantile understanding of Christ because they are trying to see what separates him from them. For example, Jesus being called the Son of Man; many people have no idea what this means. How would this knowledge affect a society that bases one's status with money and fame? Based on the corruption and falsification of religion in the world today, who would be able to recognize Jesus by way of his message upon his return?

Matt 23:29-30 (29) Woe unto you, scribes and Pharisees hypocrites! Because ye build the tombs of the prophets, and garnish the sepulchers of the righteous (30) and say, If we had been in the days of our fathers, we would not have been partakers with them in the blood of the prophets. (31) Wherefore ye be witnesses unto yourselves, that ye are the children of them which killed the prophets.

Imagine all of the miracles Jesus performed. What do you think it was like being Jesus; having to suffer for ignorant and for lack of a better term, degenerate people. Jesus himself knows the conditions of man because he existed in the flesh as a man. Think about the torment it caused Jesus just in the people's inability to accept truth after witnessing the miracles he performed. According to scripture, Jesus doesn't want to give up his life for a faithless and perverse generation.

Matthew 17:17 *O faithless and perverse generation How long shall I be with you? How long shall I suffer you? - Jesus*

Matthew 26:39 *O my father, if it be possible let this cup pass from me: nevertheless not as I will, but as thou wilt. - Jesus*

Reason being, what would be the point? The people that Jesus encountered then are no closer to salvation than the people of today. When you look at what the church and Paul has produced today it makes you question the validity of the scriptures altogether. *"You will know a tree by the fruit that it bears."* If today you have all the contradictions associated with the Christian Church namely priests who molest boys, homosexuals who are being married, all things which are forbidden in the Bible; it means you need to look to the source to find the culprit

Matthew 7:15-20 (15) *Beware of the false prophets, which come to you in sheep's clothing, but inwardly they are ravening wolves. (16) Ye shall know them by their fruits. Do men gather grapes of thorns or figs of thistles? (17) Even so every good tree bringeth forth good fruit; but a corrupt tree bringeth forth evil fruit. (18) A good tree cannot bring forth evil fruit, neither can a corrupt tree bring forth good fruit. (19) Every tree that bringeth not forth good fruit is hewn down and cast into the fire. (20) wherefore by their fruits ye shall know them.*

The Book of Illumination

CHAPTER 4
THE ANTI-CHRIST

The Book of Illumination

CHAPTER 4
THE ANTI-CHRIST

THE ANTI - CHRIST

 Historically, Peter and Paul are credited with starting the religion of Catholicism. Peter was a direct disciple of Jesus and Paul was a Pharisee who later converted to the Christian faith after wreaking havoc on the followers of Christ. The Catholic Church, also known as the Roman Catholic Church is the world's largest Christian church, and claims over a billion members. This represents approximately half of all Christians and one-sixth of the world's population. The Catholic Church traces its foundation to Jesus and the twelve Disciples. It sees the bishops of the Church as the successors of the disciples and the pope in particular, as the successor of Peter, who is widely regarded as the leader of the Disciples. Catholics cite Jesus' words, in the Gospel according to Matthew to support their view of why the church was built.

Matt.16:18 (18) *And I say unto thee, that thou art Peter upon this rock I will build my church; and the gates of heaven shall not prevail against it.*

Anti: (1) One that is opposed (2) Against

Christ: (1) The ideal truth that comes as a divine manifestation of God to destroy incarnate error

Incarnate: invested with bodily and especially human nature and form

According to the Roman Catholic faith Peter is its leader and the bishops of the church are the representatives of the churches like the disciples are the representatives of Jesus. In the gospels of the NT, Jesus had twelve disciples. After a thorough examination of the life of Jesus we discover that out of the twelve disciples both his most devoted (Peter) and most wicked (Judas) in some way betrayed him. Peter who was supposed to be his most devout disciple denied Jesus before men. In fact it is stated in the scriptures that he said he would die for Jesus.

Matthew 26:35 Peter said unto him (Jesus), though I should die with thee yet will I not deny thee.

But when it came time for Peter to die with Jesus he denied Jesus not once but three times which shows lip profession is in Peter's character.

Matthew 26:69-75 *(69) Now Peter sat without in the palace: and a damsel came unto him saying, Thou also wast with Jesus of Galilee (70) But he denied before them all saying, I know not what thou sayest. (71) And when he was gone out on the porch, another maid saw him, and said unto them that were there, this fellow was also with Jesus of Nazareth. (72) And again he denied with an oath, I do not know the man. (73) And after a while came unto him they that stood by, and said to Peter, Surely thou also art one of them; for thy speech betrayeth thee. (74) Then he (Peter) began to curse and to swear saying, I know not the man and immediately the cock crew. (75) And Peter remembered the word of Jesus, which said unto him. Before the cock crow thou shalt deny me thrice. And he went out and wept bitterly.*

The lip professing of Peter is seen in many instances within the scriptures. Jesus is no stranger to lip profession because he is the victim of it (lip profession) all the time.

Matthew 15:8-9 *(8) This people draweth nigh unto me with their mouth, and honoreth me with their lips; but their heart is far from me. (9) but in vain they do worship me, teaching for doctrines the commandments of men.*

Here is another instance where Peter is in a sense "brown nosing" Jesus. As soon as Peter gains favor with Jesus with this acknowledgement; Jesus says that he is going to build his church upon this rock. Though it isn't specified if Peter is the rock Jesus is talking in reference to, this is what scholars and clergy man of today accept.

Matt.16:13-17 *(13)* **Who do men say that I the Son of Man am?** *(14) and they said, some say that thou art John the Baptist: some Elijah; and others Jeremiah or one of the prophets. (15)* **But whom say ye that I am?** *(16) and Simon Peter answered and said thou art the Christ, the son of the <u>living God</u>. (17) and Jesus answered and said unto him* **Blessed art thou Simon Barjona for flesh and blood hath not revealed this to thee but my father which is in heaven** *(18)* **And I say unto thee, That thou art Peter upon this rock I will build my church; and the gates of heaven shall not prevail against it.**

What is very strange about Peter being the rock that Jesus is to build his church upon is after Jesus has spoken to Peter and the disciples about the church being built upon a rock; Jesus is quoted as calling Peter Satan.

Matthew 16: 21-13 *(21) From that time forth began Jesus to shew unto his disciples, how that he must go unto Jerusalem, and suffer many things of the elders and chief priests and scribes, and be killed and raised again on the third day. (22) The Peter took him, and began to rebuke him saying, Be it far from thee, Lord: this shall not be unto you (23) But he (Jesus) turned and said unto Peter, <u>Get thee behind me Satan: thou art an offence unto me</u>: for thou savourest not the things that be of God, but those that be of men.*

Rebuke: (1) to bluntly check, or reprimand (2) to sharply criticize

Is it any coincidence that the other disciple who was referenced or likened to Satan was Judas Iscariot?!

Luke. 22:3 (3) Then entered Satan into Judas surnamed Iscariot being of the number of twelve.

The difference between Judas and Peter being called Satan is the scriptures say Satan as a different entity entered Judas but Peter was called Satan directly. Jesus looks at Peter and actually calls him Satan; whereas with Judas it states Satan entered Judas before Judas committed the offence of selling Jesus out. Again this latter interpretation is found in Luke a Gospel later written under the guidance of Paul. Luke being a Gentile would not at that time have been allowed to write a gospel according to Jesus' instructions. I only used it here to further showcase my point of how if you are reading from the point of view of Matthew, the church of today has nothing to do with the message of Jesus. However the church of today is very close to the teachings of Paul. So with this, I have cited both scriptures for the reader to understand my most fundamental points, which are: **after reading and seeing that there wouldn't be a church if people where following the instructions of Jesus; scribes and the "powers that be" have come along afterwards and fused lies within truths causing the confusion that has led to the actual apostasy from the true message of Jesus.** This apostasy has led the people back into an institutionalized form of worship within the church. This new church has become the largest real estate owner and also one of the most if not the richest single faith based organization in the world. How much clearer can it get?

Peter has also added to the sentiment that the Gentiles can be ministered to regardless to what Jesus said. Peter in "God's" name makes this declaration.

Acts 15:7 (7) And when there had been much disputing, Peter rose up and said unto them, Men and brethren, ye know that a good while ago God made choice among us, that the Gentiles by my mouth should hear the word of the Gospel and believe. -Peter

Although it is obviously clear that Jesus says do not go to the Gentiles, Peter has avoided this instruction.

Matt 10:5 (5) Go not into the way of the Gentiles, and into any city of the Samaritans enter ye not: (6) But go rather to the lost sheep of the House of Israel. - Jesus

Peter, not Jesus, declared Gentiles worthy of hearing the Gospel. Remember this is the same person that Jesus called Satan. He also is credited as the disciple who denied Jesus before men 3 times but swore that he would die for him.

Matthew 26:34-35 69-75 (34) Jesus saith unto him (Peter) Verily I say unto thee, that this night before the clock crow, thou shalt deny me thrice. (35) Peter said unto him (Jesus) Though I should die with thee, yet will I not deny thee.

According to Jesus in the tenth chapter of Matthew whosoever denies him before men, he will deny before his father.

Matthew 10:33 (33) But whosoever deny me before men, him will I also deny before my father which is in heaven. - Jesus

Even Paul backs Jesus in regards to this point.

II Timothy 2:12 (12) If we suffer, we shall also reign with him: (Jesus) If we deny him, he will also deny us. - Paul

What makes Peter an exception? Some would say Peter denied Jesus before a woman and not a man, so technically this is why Peter was enabled to be a leader of the church. However Jesus has a rebuttal for this found in Matthew.
Here are the scriptures in the Book of Genesis Jesus is referring to.

Matthew 19:4 Have ye not read. That he which made them at the beginning made them male and female.

Genesis 1:27 So God created Man in his own image, in the image of God created he him; male and female created he them.

Genesis 5:2 (2) Male and Female created he them; and blessed them, and called their name Adam, in the day when they were created.

On the following page is an account of lip profession at its finest. Scripture informs us that Peter began to swear and curse when asked if he knew Jesus.
Matthew 26:73 (73) And after a while came unto him they that stood by, and said to Peter, Surely thou also art one of them (disciples); for thy speech betrayeth thee. (74) Then he (Peter) began to curse and to swear saying, I know not the man. - Jesus

How are we to believe a person who has shown us this type of character? Not to mention, when in secret, Peter hung from every word Jesus spoke.

Matthew 26: 31& 33 (31) The Jesus saith unto them All ye shall be offended because of me this night: for it is written I will smite the shepherd, and the sheep of the flock shall be scattered abroad. (33) Peter answered and said unto him (Jesus) Though all men should be offended because of thee, yet will I never be offended.

When asked by men (a woman) publicly, Peter acknowledges that he doesn't know Jesus; much to the like of the "Jews" who did Paul and Barnabas the same way in **Acts 13:43-45**.

Acts 13:43-45 (43) Now when <u>the congregation was broken up, many of the Jews and religious proselytes followed Paul and Barnabas</u>: Who speaking to them, persuaded them to continue in the grace of God (44) And the next Sabbath day came almost the whole city together to hear the word of God. (45) <u>But when the Jews saw the multitudes they were filled with envy, and spake against those things which were spoken by Paul</u>, contradicting and Blaspheming.

DEAF DUMB AND BLIND

While writing this book I was confronted by a man standing in the courtyard of the University of Houston. I was headed there to write and do some research when I saw him. As I came toward him to pass him, I saw him approaching, so I waived him away, and I sat on a nearby by bench. After being rejected by several university students, the man came and sat next to me and started talking about Paul. Somewhere in the conversation we began to discuss Peter, who according to the man, had repented for denying Jesus. Naturally I asked him where was this found scripturally, and he could give no answer. I then told the man according to what I had read; Peter went and wept bitterly after denying Jesus before men.

Matthew 26:75 (75) And Peter remembered the word of Jesus, which said unto him, Before the cock crow, thou shalt deny me thrice. And <u>he went out, and wept bitterly.</u>

I then gave a character assessment of Peter and before I could finish, the man jumped to the defense of Peter disregarding the scriptures altogether. The 14th chapter of Matthew shows that Peter is of little faith as he knows who Jesus is, yet he still doubts his power.

Matthew 14:29-31 (29) And he said, Come. And when Peter was come down out of the ship, he walked on the water, to go to Jesus. (30) But when he saw the wind boisterous, he was afraid; and beginning to sink, he cried, saying, Lord, save me. (31) And immediately Jesus stretched forth his hand, and caught him, and said unto him, O thou of little faith, wherefore didst thou doubt?

The water that Peter is walking on represents chaos. This symbolizes the chaos that is always around us in the world. Our elevation to a higher consciousness gives us the ability to do miraculous things (*walk on water*) which elevate us above the chaos. These miracles are only recognized by us in reference to faith.

This is said because we in our minds asked for the day we would be delivered out of this chaotic state. We get delivered because we had the sense to pray/meditate and the faith to act. When we lose sight of the fact that it is a higher consciousness that is guiding us through the tough and chaotic times (*boisterous wind*) and think it is our regular or lower selves, we fall back into the chaos. Being back in chaos, we then look to that higher consciousness to again save us from something that we have already salvaged ourselves from (*stretched forth hand*.) Looking at this passage from a literary standpoint gives us the forth sight to understand things about ourselves. These things are spiritual things, because life is, a lot of times, unpredictable and seemingly unfair. In the previous scriptures provided, Peter represents man and Jesus represents God. In all of these illustrations we keep seeing the lack of faith man has in a "*Living God.*"

When further talking to the man about the two disciples Peter and Judas I then said, "*Of the two disciples, the most devoted being (Peter) and the one who betrayed Jesus Judas; the one who betrayed him was more righteous than the one who pledged his devotion.*" When I posed this statement to the man he was stumped and asked why. I told him that upon Judas' recognition that he sinned he gave his life as a ransom for the sin that was committed.

Romans 6:23 *(23)* <u>*For the wages of sin is death*</u>; *but the gift of God is eternal life through Jesus Christ our Lord.*

The only thing Judas felt he could do to show he was truly sorry was offer his life. However when Peter denied Jesus before man and recognized he sinned he went and wept. Assessing both situations, I then asked the man of the two disciples which was more honorable. What is also a thought to ponder is that Judas actually delivered Jesus to his destiny. If he doesn't point Jesus out, the story of Jesus never gets printed because it wouldn't have happened. The irony is that Judas even in his betrayal did not commit as vile a sin as Peter in his denial because Judas actually had to **point out** who Jesus was, meaning he didn't deny his existence; he actually acknowledges his existence.

Matthew 26:47-50 *(47) And while he yet spake, lo, Judas, one of the twelve, came, and with him a great multitude with swords and staves, from the chief priests and elders of the people (48) Now he that betrayed him gave them a sign saying whomsoever I shall kiss, that same is he: hold him fast (49) And forthwith he came to Jesus and said Hail master; and Kissed him (50) and Jesus said unto him, Friend, wherefore art thou come? Then they came, and laid hands on Jesus and took him.*

The man was puzzled as to how I came to this conclusion until I further showed him that salvation was the key reason for many people coming to the Christian faith. Self-sacrifice is a theme represented within the most popular and fundamental of Old and New Testament stories. The way that God **the father*** sacrificed His Son Jesus and gave his life for mankind is in the same territory and theme as Judas delivering Jesus to his destiny by sacrificing him to the authorities.

The second is Peter was "supposedly" Jesus' most devout follower. Imagine what it feels like to be betrayed by your right hand man. Being let down by your right hand man really hurts and is different from a friend that you suspect. After making these points to the man, he went on and on about how Judas killed himself and he asked me where is that condoned in the Bible. I said that this particular reference isn't necessarily condoned however it is honorable. In the Bible there is a theme associated with sacrifice. Jesus the author of the faith himself was sacrificed by his father. Also Abraham had to sacrifice his son Isaac (*a foreshadowing to the sacrifice of Jesus*) in order to gain favor in the sight of the LORD. When I told him this, despite all evidence, he maintained his position that Judas was wrong for killing himself.

When looking closely at the scriptures, and then paralleling them with the inherent ignorance that enables man to be a non-believer, we can see which of the two disciples represented the sin and which represented repentance. Peter due to his disbelief fell in the water when Jesus was trying to lead him. Peter after also stating he would die for and never deny Jesus, denied Jesus and didn't die with him. If we apply our third eye to the situation we can see that it is Peter who all along was the worst disciple and the actual betrayer. Judas could be looked at as the most devout disciple because through tough love he has the burdening task of delivering Jesus to suffer crucifixion. This thing has to be done and even Jesus himself asked "God" if "God" would let this cup (*being crucified*) pass from him. As we gain more knowledge and look deeper into biblical stories we find points that can be argued with legitimacy. We as people have a tendency to see what we want, which is why I have used these scriptures to highlight the evidence that shows these two disciples characters in the actual light they are in; rather than how we emotionally want to see them. When I realized the man wasn't able to think along these terms I went to a passage in the book of Judges to further elaborate my points. Jephthah in the book of Judges was a man who wanted victory over his enemies. In order to attain this feat he made a pact with God. The pact stated that if Jephthah was successful in battle over his enemies and came out in one piece that he (*Jephthah*) will sacrifice whatever or whomever comes to his door step as a burnt offering to God. God came through on his end of the bargain and enabled Jephthah to defeat his enemies. It just so happened that after the victory, Jephthah's daughter showed up at his doorstep. When this happened Jephthah was very sad. He told his daughter what he had done and she told him not to worry; if he promised God this he should do it. So he sacrificed his daughter as a result of his promise with God.

Judges 11:30-33, 34-36,39 (30) And Jephthah vowed a vow unto he lord and said, if thou shalt without fail deliver the children of Ammon into mine hands (31) Then it will be, that whatsoever cometh forth of the doors to my house to meet me, when I return in peace from the children of Ammon, shall surely be the Lord's, and I will offer it up for a burnt offering (32) So Jephthah passed over unto the children of Ammon to fight against them; and the Lord delivered them into his hands. (34) And Jephthah came to mizpeh unto his house, and behold, his daughter came to meet him with timbrels and with dances: and she was his only child; beside her he had neither son nor daughter. (35) And it came to pass that when he saw her that he rent his clothes, and said, Alas, my daughter! Thou hast brought me very low, and thou art one of them that trouble me: for I have opened my mouth unto the Lord, and I cannot go back. (36) And she said unto him, my father if thou hast opened thy mouth unto the lord, do to me according to that which hath proceeded out of thy mouth: (39) And it came to pass at the end of two months, that she returned unto her father, who did with her according to his vow which he had vowed.

After the man read this from his *own* Bible, he said that he doesn't think that God approved of what Jephthah had done, and therefore it wasn't sufficient enough of a reference to be counted as evidence. I replied to him that he (*the man*) was now speaking for God. I told him what he thinks or believes isn't validated by scripture but his own emotional thinking. I went on to say that this is the problem with religion altogether. You have all of these people who read a couple of scriptures from the New Testament and then they go into the world and try to convert people based on the little information they have. Then when they are shone up by a person they least expect, rather than converting to the other person's idea or faith, they get belligerent, start making things up, and become hysterical. Their true colors are shown and they are exposed as being a part of incomplete thinking. This man after sticking his foot in his mouth then told me that you can't apply human logic with the scriptures; and only the Holy Ghost can reveal these things to people. I then responded to him that it wasn't the Holy Ghost that gave him this knowledge; he read it in a book, that book, being the Bible. If he could not read or write (*skills that are learned with human logic*) he wouldn't even be able to talk in reference to the scriptures. In other words it was his human logic that enabled him to read and process these words in an English language. So by him saying that we shouldn't use human logic was a very thoughtless contradiction. If that's the case then why not go and jump off of a building, don't use logic just jump; God will rescue you because you are one of his children. If Jesus had this thinking he would have succumb to temptation.

Matthew 4:5-7 (5) Then the devil taketh him up into the holy city and setteth him on the pinnacle of the temple (6) And saith unto him, If thou be the Son of God, cast thyself down: for it is written, He shall give his angels charge concerning thee: and in their hands they shall bear thee up, lest at any time thou dash thy foot against a stone (7) And Jesus said unto him, It is written again thou shalt not tempt the Lord thy God.

If a person doesn't use logic than they probably would jump and fall to a horrible and meaningless death. However the thought process the man had wasn't shocking to me because he was a student of Paul; and of course Paul doesn't want people to be logical because if they were logical, they wouldn't have allowed him to have a voice in regards to their religious faith. Here is a pretty logical question; why do you need Paul or Peter if you have Jesus?

Matthew 27:1 says When morning was come all the chief priests and Elders took counsel against Jesus to put him to death.

Matt 27:21 But the chief Priests and elders persuaded the multitude that they should ask Barabbas and destroy Jesus.

Matt. 27:22 Pilate saith unto them, what shall I do then with Jesus, which is called Christ? They all say unto him, let him be crucified (23) and then the governor (Pilate) said what evil hath he done? But they cried out the more saying let him be crucified.

Matt 27:24 When Pilate saw that he could prevail nothing but rather a tumult was made he took water and washed his hands before the multitude saying, I am innocent of the blood of this just person see ye to it.

The 27th Chapter of Matthew is very interesting because it lists the ones who took council to kill Jesus as the priests, leaders, and elders of the church. Wait a minute, now-a-days the main proprietors and advocates of Jesus are the church preachers/priests and their congregations. Is there any coincidence that the same is true for Paul? He was in his day one of the main proprietors and advocates of Jesus and also the person responsible for the murder, imprisonment, and persecution of the fellow believers of Christ.

Acts 22:4 & 19 (4) And I persecuted this way unto death, binding and delivering into prisons both men and women (19) And I said Lord, they know that I imprisoned and beat in every synagogue them that believed on thee. - Paul

A PAULING

No person in their right mind who was oppressed knowingly would willingly allow their oppressor to lead them spiritually. Because the average Christian is unaware this has happened, they have allowed their enemies to become their spiritual head. If Adolf Hitler after persecuting so many "Jews" was to one day fall out of his tank and say, *"Oh the lord appeared to me, only I heard his voice and he told me to go and build the Jewish Church with Peter (the same lip professing disciple who denied Jesus before men three times)* how many Jews do you think would follow him? Isn't this A (PAUL) ING. How many Jews do you think would say, *"O.K. I believe you Adolf, now lead me to salvation."* Because people get caught up in the emotion of guilt caused by their own lack of faith and disobedience and "God said" is written behind scriptures that validate their repentances; they conveniently accept whatever is read despite all of the immediate contradictions and absurdities within it.

Acts 8:3 (3) As for Saul, he made havoc of the church, entering into every house, and haling men and women committed them to prison. - Paul

Paul is the one who many preachers of today pattern their sermons after. This is because they preach the message of repentance and Paul being a persecutor of Christians is the most recognizable "poster child" for it. Many preachers today in the inner city black churches are former pimps, gangsters, and people who lived very treacherous lives prior to their conversions. In their minds because they have done so much wrong, they feel they have a duty to society to go and preach, turning those who were like them away from their destructive paths. According to the law of reciprocity though, every action has one that is equal and opposite. Jesus as an example of perfection gave his life as a ransom for many.

Mark 10:45 (45) For even the son of man came not to be ministered unto, but to minister, and give his life a ransom for many. - Jesus

How is it that the preachers or people who have done such vile acts don't use the example given by the Son of Man and give their life and become volunteers for the Red Cross or the Salvation Army? In fact even James adds clarity to what a person who is following religion or God should be like.

James 1:27 Pure religion and undefiled before God and the father is this, to visit the fatherless (bastards) and widows in their affliction, and to keep himself unspotted from the world .- James

Why do these types of preachers pay for their sins with their words instead of their actions? The answer is simple, Paul. A congregation can only grow if you're preaching to sinners, namely because who is without sin? According to Jesus, those who are whole don't need a physician.

Matthew 9:12-13 (12) They that be whole need not a physician but they that are sick. - Jesus

What Paul has done by making himself a leader of the church is made it acceptable for ANYBODY who has received a "calling" to preach the Gospel.

And for these reasons, any and every one who feels justified in becoming a preacher can become one.

II Thessalonians 3: 12-13 (12) And I thank Christ Jesus our Lord, who hath enabled me, for that he counted me faithful, putting me into the ministry. (13) Who was before a blasphemer, and a persecutor, and injurious: but I obtained mercy because I did it ignorantly in unbelief. - Paul

When did Christ accept Paul personally into the ministry when they never met physically? By Paul's own testimony it was Jesus' words he heard on the road to Damascus but this story has flaws associated with it. How are we to believe that Jesus gave him this instruction? Maybe Paul wants us to be believers in things that are faith based so we never become believers in things that are factually based. Cause if we add up all of the facts Paul should have been either executed or imprisoned for life, banished and exiled, and should have never been allowed to preach the Gospel at all. There are people who have given their whole lives to the ministry; people who have never harmed a head on any living thing. How much greater than Paul are these examples of people who are truly "Christ like." The more people that you have in your congregation the more fame and fortune you can amass. Paul's sin was that he wanted to be great; this is why Paul had so much zeal in persecuting Christians. Paul desired to be known, very well known. When he foresaw that his fame could not supersede that of Jesus, paralleled with his own convictions, he went on a reckless crusade cleverly making Jesus' Gospel his own. Though he opens all of his sermons (epistles) up with Jesus' name, it is apparent when comparing the two (Jesus and Paul's) messages, Paul's is his own, and in direct contradiction to that of Jesus. When Paul enters the fold you no longer achieve salvation by the Law (Law of Moses) or by your works; salvation through his ideology is achieved by just believing.

Galatians 2:16 (16) Knowing that a man is not justified by the works of the Law, but by the faith of Jesus Christ, that we may be justified by the faith of Christ, and not by the works of the Law: for by the works of the law shall no flesh be justified. - Paul

It seems even James had something to say about the statements made by Paul.

James 2:18 Yea a man may say, Thou hast faith, and I have works: shew me thy faith without thy works, and I will shew thee my faith by my works. - James

Yet and still Paul's message is the one that is most widely regarded; most likely because it is the most easy to do. Below are Paul's words from his own mouth, yet when we look to Jesus' words he says something completely different.

Ephesians 2:8-9 *(8) for by grace are ye saved through faith; and that not of yourselves it is the gift of God (9) not of works lest any man should boast. - Paul*

Matthew 17:27 *(27) For the son of man shall come in the glory of his father with his angels; and then he shall reward every man according to his works. - Jesus*

I ask the Christians world who are they to believe and follow, Jesus the Son of Man, who is said to be the perfected example of how humans are to be; or Paul, a former Pharisee who killed and persecuted Christians much to the liking that Adolf Hitler persecuted Jews? Even Jesus himself had to do his mission (works) in order to achieve his own personal salvation of "God" what makes man any different?

John 9:4 *I must work the works of him that sent me, while it is day; the night cometh, when no man can work. -Jesus-*

Jesus literally knows "God" and his knowledge of "God" and his relationship with him (God) being his Sun/son is not sufficient enough for him to be rewarded his place in heaven less he complete his task. Jesus himself has to complete his mission and fulfill his destiny in order to be saved, so why is it any different for man? Being that Paul is a former Pharisee it is easy to see that his bias wreaks through his message.

Acts 23:6 *(6) I am a Pharisee and a son of a Pharisee of the hope and resurrection of the dead I am called into question. - Paul*

Paul says that as a Pharisee he questioned the resurrection of Christ. Being that Paul is a persecutor of Christians who after being converted now believed in the resurrection; we can see how he has twisted the message of Jesus. Jesus says the Pharisees say and do not, meaning all they do is talk, no works. Is it coincidence this is exactly how Paul told his congregation they should be?

Ephesians 2:8-9 *(8) for by grace are ye saved through faith; and that not of yourselves it is the gift of God (9) not of works lest any man should boast. - Paul*

Jesus also says the Pharisees sit in Moses' seat; and Paul by his own admission claimed to be a Pharisee. Is abolishing the Law of Moses and making it obsolete not the same as sitting in Moses' seat? Has Paul not supplanted Moses by eradicating his Law and putting in place his own?

Matt.23:2-3 *(2) The scribes and Pharisees sit in Moses seat. (3) all therefore whatsoever they bid you observe, that observe and do: but do not ye after their works: for they say and do not. - Jesus*

Galatians 2:16 (16) Knowing that a man is not justified by the works of the Law, but by the faith of Jesus Christ, that we may be justified by the faith of Christ, and not by the works of the Law: for by the works of the law shall no flesh be justified. -Paul

Galatians 3:11-14 (11) But that no man is justified by the law in the sight of God, it is evident: for, the just shall live by faith. (12) And the law is not of Faith: but, the man that doeth them shall live in them (13) Christ hast redeemed us from the curse of the Law, being made a curse for us: for it is written cursed is anyone that hangeth from a tree. - Paul

It seems Paul has forgotten that Jesus is the Sun of Man and he is just a man.

Matthew 7: 24 & 26 (24) Therefore whosoever heareth these sayings of mine, and doeth them, I will liken him unto a wise man, which built his house upon a rock (26) And everyone that heareth these sayings of mine and doeth them not, shall be likened unto a foolish man, which built his house upon sand.

Paul's ministry lowered the standards for salvation by just simply having faith and loving Jesus' appearance. In the traditions of Paul many preachers today have become the spokesperson for God. But who other than Jesus can arrogate to a congregation what "God" has in store for them? We don't know what God may have thought about Paul. Paul could have committed such vile acts that it would take him numerous lifetimes to burn the karma off from killing and persecuting so many Christians. In 2nd Timothy however, Paul is telling the congregation that he will be preserved into the kingdom of heaven. My question is, how does he know this?

II Timothy 4:8 (8) Hence forth there is laid up for me a crown of righteousness, which the lord, the righteous judge shall give me at that day: and not to me only but unto all them also that love his appearing. - Paul

II Timothy 4:18 (18) And the Lord shall deliver me from every evil work, and will preserve me unto his heavenly kingdom: to whom be glory forever and ever Amen.

When asked a similar thing by his disciples, this is what Jesus told them.

*Matthew 20:20-23 (20) Then came to him the mother of Zebedee's children with her two sons, worshipping him and desiring a certain thing of him (21) And he said unto her **What wilt thou**? She saith unto him, Grant that these my two sons may sit, the one on thy right hand, and the other on the left in thy kingdom (22) But Jesus answered and said, **Ye know not what ye ask. Are ye able to drink of the cup that I shall drink of, and to be baptized with the baptism I am baptized with?** They say unto him we are able (23) And he saith unto them, **Ye shall drink indeed of my cup, and be baptized with the*** *baptism I am baptized with: **but to sit on my right hand, and on my left, is not mine to give, but it shall be given to them for whom it is prepared of my father.***

Below is a scripture that speaks in reference to a man who now being at the end of his life knows that he must pay for his sins.

II Timothy 4: 6 -7 (6) for I am now ready to be offered, and the time of my departure is at hand (7) I have fought a good fight, I have finished my course, I have kept the faith.

This is an indication that Paul knows what he has done and most likely is scared of what is to come in the "afterlife" by way of it. He has to basically convince himself that everything is "gonna" be alright. In the above passage Paul is counseling himself. True he went about doing "God's" work after he converted but as I stated before, we don't know exactly what Paul has done nor do we know what consequences he must pay for his actions. Just because you are forgiven of your sins doesn't mean there are no consequences for your actions. True the Bible states by Paul's own admission that he was beaten and imprisoned for promoting the message of Christ but again how can he say what is in store for him when Jesus can't tell his direct disciples what is in store for them. Jesus gave his disciple direct instructions not to go to the Gentiles.

Matt 10:5-10 (5) Go not into the way of the Gentiles, and into any city of the Samaritans enter ye not: (6) But go rather to the lost sheep of the House of Israel (7) and as ye go preach saying the kingdom of heaven is at hand (8) heal the sick, cleanse the lepers, raise the dead, cast out devils: freely ye have received freely give. (9) provide neither gold nor silver nor brass in your purses (10) Nor script for your journey, neither two coats, neither shoes, nor yet staves: for the workman is worthy of his meat.

Yet Paul's whole message of salvation and resurrection in his epistles are to the Gentiles; which is against the instructions Jesus gave to his disciples.

Ephesians 2:6 (6) That the Gentiles should be fellow heirs, and of the same body, and partakers of his promise in Christ by the Gospel. -Paul

Galatians 3:14 (14) That the blessing of Abraham might come on the Gentiles through Jesus Christ that we might receive the promise of the spirit through faith. -Paul

If there is any discrepancy about Gentiles not being able to be ministered unto by Jesus; here is another scripture that reveals Jesus' true feelings about those who are not quote on quote the "lost sheep of Israel."

Matthew 15: 22-24 & 26-28 (22) And behold a woman of Canaan came out of the same coasts, and cried unto him saying, Have mercy on me Oh Lord thou Son of David; my daughter is grievously vexed with a devil. (23) But he answered her not a word. And his disciples came and besought him saying, Send her away, for she crieth after us. (24) But he answered and said I am not sent but unto the lost sheep of the house of Israel. (26) It is not meet to take the children's bread and to cast it to dogs (27) And she said, truth Lord yet the dogs eat of the crumbs which fall from their master's table (28) Then Jesus answered and said to her O woman great is thy faith: be it unto you even as thou wilt. And her daughter was made whole from that very hour.

***Matthew 7:6** (6) Give not that which is Holy unto dogs, neither cast ye your pearls before swine, lest they trample them under their feet, and turn and rend you. – Jesus*

Paul preached to the Gentiles because he was rejected by the Jews.

***Acts 13:43-47** (43) Now when the congregation was broken up, many of the Jews and religious proselytes followed Paul and Barnabas: Who speaking to them, persuaded them to continue in the grace of God (44) And the next Sabbath day came almost the whole city together to hear the word of God. (45) But when the Jews saw the multitudes they were filled with envy, and spake against those things which were spoken by Paul, contradicting and Blaspheming (46) Then Paul and Barnabas waxed bold and said, It was necessary that the word of God should have been spoken to you Jews (47) but seeing ye put it form you, and judge yourselves unworthy of everlasting life, lo we turn to the Gentiles*

Again the Jews wouldn't accept Paul's ministry because of his past track record. Preachers who are crooked do many things that aren't scriptural in the name of "God," it happens every day. Here are just a few examples of it happening in the Bible. From these statements made by Jesus we can surmise that he (Jesus) does not wish his holy message be taught to unholy people. It is also important to notate why the sheep is used by Jesus instead of cows, goats, or any other herded animal. When we take into account that Negroes have hair that is woolly and unlike any other peoples, we get a great adjective that describes the intended "flock" for this particular messiah's message.

Paul's sin

however is out of unbelief un (belief) which means he could have believed but didn't; and ignorance which means he heard but ignored [ignore (ance)] *But I obtained mercy because I did it ignorantly in unbelief, 1Timothy 1:13.* It wasn't until Paul realized as did Judas, as did Peter, after committing the act, did he turn away from his wicked ways. Don't misinterpret what I am saying, I am all for repentance; but what I am not for is the rewarding and receiving of authoritative positions by those who have committed certain acts. For instance if a person was an admitted and convicted child molester, even after they have repented and have turned their life over to "God" and are the most devout Christian, I seriously doubt that people would allow him to be the head of *Babysitters' of America*, do you? Worst, imagine if he deemed himself most worthy based on the notion that he's best suited because as a child molester he knows the children inside and out.

Matthew 10:11-15 (11) And into whatsoever city or town ye shall enter, enquire who in it is worthy; and there abide till ye go thence. (12) And when ye come into an house, salute it. (13) And if the house be worthy, let your peace come upon it: but if it be not worthy, let your peace return to you. (14) And whosoever shall not receive you, nor hear your words, when ye depart out of that house or city, shake the dust of your feet. (15) Verily I say unto you, It shall be more tolerable for the land of Sodom and Gomorrha in the day of judgment than for that city.

What is alarming about Matt.10:11 -15 is that Jesus told his disciples if they were to encounter people who weren't believers, they should shake it off and move on to another house; why have Paul and Barnabas avoided this instruction? Mind you, this is after he told his disciples not to go into the way of the Gentiles or their cities. The answer to the question just posed is simple; neither Paul nor Barnabas would have heard this command because they were not direct disciples.

Matt 10:5-6 (5) Go not into the way of the Gentiles, and into any city of the Samaritans enter ye not: (6) But go rather to the lost sheep of the House of Israel.

Here Paul has directly disobeyed two of the things Jesus told his disciples not to do and it doesn't stop here. After viewing Paul and Peter's actions to see where they compare to that of Jesus, it is easily seen how they have done as they wished, not as Jesus wished them. This is a scary notion because anytime man has his own agenda and teaches his agenda as if it's "God's" agenda, it causes anyone who has a congregation to be the spokesperson for "God." What is equally interesting is Paul included himself with the Gentiles.

Galatians 3:14 (14) That the blessing of Abraham might come on the Gentiles through Jesus Christ that we might receive the promise of the spirit through faith.

Paul wanted very badly to be allowed in the inner circle and recognized as a disciple. The desire that Paul had caused him to delude the truth and literally becoming delusional in it, led the people to a false understanding of the scriptures. When Jesus says he is coming for the lost sheep he is talking about the people of Abraham's covenant in the 15th Chapter of Genesis.

Genesis 15:12-14. "And when the sun was going down a deep sleep fell upon Abram; and lo a horror of great darkness fell upon him. And he said unto Abram, Know of

Surety that thy seed shall be enslaved for 400 years; and also that nation, whom they shall serve will I judge: and afterward shall they come out with great substance."

The people in the previous scripture are lost because they haven't their own language, custom, or culture as they have fallen away from the knowledge of their "God" and their gods. Because Paul is reading an allegorical prophecy through the scriptures, he hasn't a clue that what he is talking in reference to about "God" and the resurrection of Christ, had not yet happened; as this prophecy is just now unfolding some two thousand years later.

Acts 7:6-7 *(6) And God spake on the wise that his seed (children) should <u>sojorn</u> in a strange land; and that they should bring them into bondage, and entreat them evil four hundred years (7) And the nation to whom they shall be in bondage will I judge, said God: and after that shall they come forth, and serve me in this place.*

However, Paul realizing he was at fault goes on a crusade to change the way the words of Jesus are taught, interpreted, and understood. When Jesus himself is with publicans and sinners he is speaking of those same lost sheep that are working in low capacities as harlots, tax collectors, and publicans, because they don't know who they are.

Matthew 21:31 *Verily I say unto you publicans and harlots go into the kingdom of God before you.*

They haven't a clue as to why they are in the condition they are in, in the foreign land they are on, and why they have been enslaved. Therefore, Jesus is their savior because he's coming to restore that which is lost, which is the knowledge of their truest selves (Astrology) and their God the LORD Adonai.

Matt. 18:11 *(11) for the Son of Man has come to save that which is lost.*

Isaiah 5:13 *Therefore <u>my people are gone into captivity because they have no knowledge:</u> and their honorable men are famished, and their multitude dried up with thirst.*

The salvation they seek is personal to *their* struggles; because the people that Jesus is restoring according to scripture are the children of the *Sun* or *God*. These people were enslaved, adulterated, persecuted, and beaten by the enemies of God. God allowed them to be taken captive by their enemies because of their idolatry and wicked ways. If God restores his children the whole world is saved because as a whole his children are the natural leaders of the world. The world follows them; so by giving them the instruction on how they can restore their condition naturally makes the world follow God; transforming the world from ungodly to Godly by bringing forth the light.

   In our lifetime today there was an artist who brought the world together (physically) to bring attention to starvation in Africa (the mother country and cradle of civilization.) Not only is he listed in the worlds Guinness Book of Records for his philanthropic contributions, but he also in the likeness of a messianic figure did like a thief in the night.

Paul or Saul knew who he was; he was a Pharisee from the tribe of **Benjamin**, who for whatever reason came to persecute those who believe. This isn't a lost person from a lost tribe; he is a person who truly just didn't believe. Paul tries to go to every nation first and pervert the Gospel before it can be realized. It is the same as a person who tells a lie, finds out that he is guilty and will be exposed; who then tries to frame the person he has lied on, before the person who has been lied on can tell the real story himself. This is the formula for every great legend that involves an antagonist and a protagonist. In any movie involving a hero and a villain, you're going to see the villain frame the hero, lie on the hero, and act as if he is the hero. It usually involves some sadistic plot where the villain tries to overtake the world based on his own selfish desire or shortcomings. Only in the end of the movie, after the hero has went through hell on earth, is he liberated from the lie of the villain. Paul being able to run amuck happened for a reason, and this reason is to see who the true believers really are. Everyone who truly has a system of belief has to *then* act upon that which they believe or know; lip profession is not sufficient. However Paul makes lip profession the only prerequisite for achieving salvation.

Roman's 4:24 (24) But for us also, to whom it shall be imputed, if we believe on him that raised up Jesus our Lord from the dead (25) Who was delivered for our offences, and was raised again therefore for our justification. - Paul

Romans 5:1 (1) Therefore being justified by faith, we have peace with God through our Lord Jesus Christ. -Paul

How absurd does professing with your lips that you believe sound? The problem with this lip profession and this false gospel is the period before the revelation. The world is in the dark ages leading up to the resurrection of the Holy One of Israel; this is a period of thousands of years. The people have grown to a very chaotic and confused state as a result of the greatest lie ever told. The fact that Paul's slick tongue is appealing to the heathen is very attractive to western society as there is no real effort or trial that has to be overcome before a person can get to "heaven." But when any person takes an adequate assessment about how things really operate here on earth, they quickly realize there's nothing on earth that can be obtained by just belief.

James 2:17 Even so faith, if it hath no works, is dead, being alone. - James

James 2:18 Yea, a man may say, Thou hast faith, and I have works: shew me thy faith without thy works, and I will shew thee my faith by my works.

This statement made by James backs up those who practice what they preach, and as a result have something to show for what they believe and know. Those who actually live in the world and do the works of "God" usually go unseen and unnoticed especially if they do their deeds not to be seen or recognized by man as Jesus informed them. Paul in the bigger sense of the scriptures is the same as Judas. By selling out Jesus he ends up fulfilling the scriptures. Because he went and educated the world in his ignorance, the world now has a generic sense of what to be looking for when *The Christ* is resurrected. Pending on which side you look from, you can see (Paul/Judas) as deceiver or deliverer.

Romans 16:17-19 (17) Now I beseech you, brethren mark them which cause divisions and offences contrary to the doctrine which ye have learned; and avoid them (18) for they that are such serve not our Lord Jesus Christ, but their own belly; and by good words and fair speeches deceive the hearts of the simple. - Paul

What is also worth noting about the scripture above is any disciple a few years back could have said the same to Paul. Jesus is with those who are lost and with sin. Paul tells the church not to be around people who are just like he was! This is further represented in the 5th chapter of 1st Corinthians.

1Corinthians 5:9 & 11-13 (9) I wrote unto you in an epistle not to company with fornicators: (11) But I have written unto you not to keep company, if any man is called a brother be a fornicator, or covetous, or extortioners, or with idolators, or a railer, or a drunkard; with such a one no not to eat.(12) for what have I to do to judge them also that are without? do not ye judge them that are within? (13) But them that are without God judgeth. Therefore put away from among yourselves that wicked person. - Paul

Paul's instructions to the church of the Corinthians are also contradictions. It seems Paul has forgotten where he has come from and who he is as the scriptures above indicate. Not only is Paul contradicting Jesus, he is now contradicting himself. How can Paul distinguish between the heathen and the lost sheep when he is giving instructions, that if Jesus would have given, Paul himself would not be permitted to socialize, teach, preach or congregate with the people who are believers? Paul says in **Romans 6:23** *(23) For the wages of sin is death: but the gift of God is eternal life through Jesus Christ our lord.* - Paul

The contradictions between Paul and Jesus don't stop here. Paul in **1 Corinthians 14:33** says *(33) For God is not the author of confusion but of peace, as in all churches of the saints.* - Paul

But Jesus says in **Matthew 10:34-36** *(34) Think not that I am come to send peace on earth: I came not to send peace, but a sword (35) For I am come to set a man at variance against his father, and the daughter against her mother, and the daughter in law against her mother in law (36) And a man's foes shall be they of his own household.* - Jesus

Matthew 13:40-42 *(40) As therefore the tares are gathered and burned in the fire: so shall it be in the end of this world. (41) The Son of Man shall send forth his angels, and they shall gather out of his kingdom all things that offend, and them which do iniquity: (42) And shall cast them into a furnace of fire; there shall be weeping and gnashing of teeth.* - Jesus

The scriptures above contradict each other. The church of today is built upon the teachings of Paul and not Jesus. If believers really believed in Jesus they would be out teaching his instruction, but then a problem arises; what instruction are they to teach? Jesus has to first resurrect before he can give the new orders as to what needs to be done. The church of today is promoting a message that it does not fully understand. If you lived during biblical times and heard about Jesus and some of the miracles he performed, you would be skeptical about whom he may be unless you witnessed his miracles yourself. When you then mention to the people of that world that Jesus was seen as a secular person, people of the church call you a blasphemer even though scriptures indicate he was always with publicans, sinners, whores, and tax collectors. They'll then try and convert you and ask you to come to their church. They forget that yeah "*they*" know that Jesus is the "son of God" because "*they're*" reading a book and it conveniently tells them so. However if a "*Christ*" were to emerge they'd be just as skeptical as the non-believers in the Bible. Many church goers have missed the message and purpose of Jesus, which as indicated by the Gospel of Matthew, is to restore that which is lost to the Lost Sheep of Israel.

Matt. 18:11 (11) for the Son of Man has come to save that which is lost.

Matthew 15:24 (24) But he answered and said I am not sent but unto the lost sheep of the house of Israel.

Those who are spiritually intact according to Jesus are fine. Jesus says he is in search for those who are the Lost Sheep of Israel. Jesus does most of his preaching and healing in the world and not the church; implying the real work is in the streets where the people who need it most are. The popular name moniker given to Jesus (thief in the night) is also indicative of how he would be missed by those seeking to see his miracles publically because he doesn't do them to display them, he does them to help those who need him. In the following scriptures, Jesus makes several references to those who do deeds to be seen in the synagogues. Though his statements are not dogmatic in the sense that a person should not go to church; there is evidence that suggests Jesus feels there's work to be done in the world. In the 6th chapter of Matthew Jesus tells his disciples they shouldn't give offerings or pray in church. He then tells them to do their offerings in secret and to go to their closets when they pray. I have yet to see one church in accordance with this instruction.

Matt.6:1-6 (1) Take heed that ye do you not your alms before men, to be seen of them: otherwise ye have no reward of your father which is In heaven. (2) Therefore when thou doest thine alms do not sound a trumpet before thee as the hypocrites do in the synagogues and in the streets, that they may have glory of men. Verily I say unto you, they shall have their reward. (3) But when thou doest alms let they left hand not know what thy right hand doeth (4) That thine alms may be in secret: and thy Father which seeth in secret shall reward the openly (5) And when thou prayest thou shalt not be as the hypocrites are: for they love to pray standing in the synagogues and in the corners of the streets, that they may be seen of men. Verily I say unto you they have their reward. (6) But thou, when thou prayest, enter into thy closet, and when thou hast shut the door, pray to thy Father in secret and Thy Father which seeth in secret will reward the openly.

Alms: (1) giving materially to another as an act of religious virtue (2) Charity

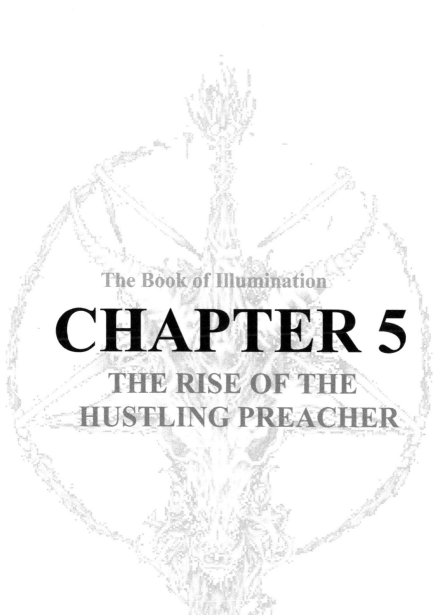

The Book of Illumination

CHAPTER 5

THE RISE OF THE HUSTLING PREACHER

The Book of Illumination

CHAPTER 5

THE RISE OF THE
HUSTLING PREACHER

THE RISE OF THE HUSTLING PREACHER

Many preachers of today love when their congregations become hysterical, which is why during the climax of their sermons, they raise their voices and ramp up the church's organs to invoke emotion. Once in an emotional state the rationalization aspect of their congregation's minds become null and void and the preacher has the ability to break the bank. This is why many preachers do not practice what Jesus preached in the 6th chapter of Matthew. If they eliminated the altar call for prayer and offering in public church, it may literally bankrupt their organizations. This way of preaching is in fact a learned art form and one that has become immensely popular within the urban sect. People tend to give more when they are convicted, and in an emotional state then they do when they are in a rational state. Preaching in public spectacles, opposed to Bible study where the people have to actually concentrate on what's being said, shows the gullibility that large congregations succumb to, even when they're hearing information that isn't correct. The reason there are so many people, namely women in the church on Sunday, is due to the high voltage of emotion and entertainment that is invoked in Sunday morning service. This entertainment factor has the same energy associated with it as concerts and musical performances, and is why women are so attracted to it. The attraction to the service is due to the woman's receptive nature and her deeply rooted connections to her emotions.

One of the greatest and perhaps the most legendary apper to date, Tupac Shakur, gave the blueprint to selling records and making money to his protégé The Notorious B.I.G. Even Tupac knew the psychology behind what draws a crowd and which sex to speak to when orating to an audience; Tupac said, "*Yo, If you wanna make your money, you gotta rap for the b@#$ es…Do not rap for the ni@#as, rap for the b@#$hes. The b@#$hes will buy your records and the N%@gga's want what the b@$%es want.*

The woman's lower anatomy shows us that she is ultra-receptive; the man's however, is projective, and is why men make exceptional preachers and rappers. In the movie *Inglorious Basterds* the Jew Hunter asks a Jewish theatre owner about the Negro she has working for her. When asked what he does within the theatre she replies, "*He is the projectionist.*" The Jew Hunter then answers her by insinuating that projection is what the Negroes do best.

101

Women anatomically are receptive, which enables them to more easily empathize with emotion. Nature fashioned them this way and their receptivity is in direct correlation to the needs of their offspring. This explains why mothers are so attentive to the cries of their newborn babies.

One Direction,

According to Fandango, the nation's leading moviegoing destination. "One Direction: This is Us" is well-positioned to top this weekend's box office. Director Morgan Spurlock's ("Super Size Me") film of the boy band's life and performances is the number one movie Fandango fans want to see this weekend, scoring 80 out of 100 points on Fandango's Fanticipation movie buzz indicator. The movie is also today's top advance ticket seller on Fandango, representing 68% of sales.

dbenson@fandango.comAccording to a Fandango survey of more than 1,000 highly enthusiastic "One Direction" ticket-buyers:

· 98% are female;

For years admittedly gay men like George Michael, have wooed women on stage and caused them to be swept away by the melody of their voices. Even though the women know these men are gay, they still fantasize about these men, and are seemingly engulfed in burning desire for them. This was epitomized within the rock & roll culture of the 80's where bands like *Twisted Sister* and *Poison*, dressed like women. The appeal these bands had over women shows us though the times change, the nature of the individual does not. I placed this piece of information to further back my point that the receptive nature of women automatically makes them irrational when watching men who project their messages emotionally on stage. Their irrational behavior is fueled by the invoking of emotion which causes them to lose their senses and accept whatever is told to them. The above information published by Fandango in August of 2013 is a testament to these facts as 98% of *One Direction's* viewing fan-base was females.

If the Jesus that people are waiting on has to come here and feed 5,000 people with five fish, raise people from the grave literally, and walk on water; then people will be waiting on a figure they may never see. The real Jesus isn't one the people have been educated to receive. What they've been taught about him is romantic; though there is a science about why he resurrects, and who he comes to "restore."

I have preached many a sermon to those of the Christian faith and what I have come to realize is that out of all the religious people I have spoken with, Christians know the least about their own God, his belief structure, and the Bible that was given to them with his instructions. Yet they are the most passionate, judgmental, and opinionated on all matters of faith and religion especially in regards to the religions of others. What is also very inconsistent is the Christians I have spoken with do not live their life according to the faith they profess to believe in. They go in search of riches rather than joining a charity cause like the Red Cross or Salvation Army. If they had faith like Paul according to their belief, then they would just exist, pray all day, acknowledge Jesus, and let God give them everything their hearts desire. If they really had passion about the Christian faith they would read and study the Bible to understand it. If they did this they would run into so many inconsistencies that it would cause them to question their faith altogether. This paragraph was not written to bash or alienate Christians; this was merely an observation I made by way of my encounters with them. I know all Christians aren't provincial and dogmatic however the Christian faith does have stipulations about the acknowledgement of other "gods" and other religions. The question I would like to ask the Christian world at this time is this, *"What if the same god has a different name in a different religion and because the language of the people is different he is referenced as a separate god?* Does the 1st commandment still apply?"

After explaining the scriptures and exposing the character types of those who built the church, Peter and Paul, the focus shifts to the churches of today. When I go to any urban neighborhood in any city in America I notice that there are 15-25 churches in a 3 square mile neighborhood. When I look at the living conditions of the people in the neighborhoods they are all dilapidated and impoverished. One would ask the question why so many churches existed; and also why there is so many of them in a neighborhood that is extremely poor. When a person poses these questions to themselves, what types of answers come to mind? For one, how do such a poor people raise the money to build a church? They live in shotgun houses that are falling apart yet they all collectively can build 20-25 churches in their immediate neighborhoods; how is this? We all know many of the neighborhoods in urban America have been destroyed by drugs. The drug trade is one of the most essential economic industries that provided what little economy these urban inner city neighborhoods at that time had. A lot of preachers in these inner city urban communities were former gang bangers, thugs, pimps, and robbers. Many of them were led into this way of life because they refused to work for someone else. They refused to be looked upon as lower or lesser and felt that in some way they had been oppressed and dealt a raw deal. Some of these preachers upon landing in prison for various criminal activities converted to Islam. This conversion made them view Christianity as the white man's religion and was further perpetuated by the Roman Catholic Church's portrayal of Jesus as a blonde haired, blue eyed white man. The Bible is written in an old English format which is why *"wherefore art thou"* and *"Verily I say unto thee"* is inscribed in it. These facts were what those former gangbangers, pimps, and thugs who came out of jail, and became preachers built there ministries from. When they came out preaching messages of Allah and a foreign god to the downtrodden and beat down Negroes, not all the Negroes accepted this "other god." The former incarcerated preacher knew of the deceit and saw the wool pulled over the eyes of the sheep. When he realized they couldn't be reformed his opportunistic intelligence made him become capitalistic allowing his lower self to perpetuate illusions to those who so willingly wanted to remain believing in something that this "enlightened" preacher considered to be false. These preachers started out preaching messages that were militant and ones that were too harsh for the masses of urban communities to follow. While these sets of circumstances lay true for the preachers who converted to Islam during their incarcerations, they also hold true for the many Christian preachers who formerly were incarcerated as well. When these preachers who started with good intent kept seeing the people backsliding, conjoined with the fact they were broke, starving, and weathered by heavy prison stints; the preachers, in the traditions of Paul, chose to give the people exactly what they wanted. Now the former hustlers and pimps didn't see the people as human anymore, they saw them as victims. Because they were already victims it didn't matter what tragedy came upon them. In the minds of these opportunistic preachers they're congregations were already deaf, dumb, and blind. These preachers felt they might as well capitalize and get there's cause a people this gullible are bound to be done in by somebody; and why shouldn't that somebody be them. This frame of mind spawned a term I refer to as Meism.

When people heard the tales of the money being made in church, many southern blacks sought out preaching as the way to the salvation of their spirits as well as their pocket books. Sensationalized by Martin Luther King and Malcolm X, this preacher became synonymous with black culture. Because the preacher himself was a former "sinner" who wanted to become rich and powerful; naturally, Paul gave him all the ammunition he would need to further justify his cause. These former pimps and hustlers, who were now preachers through the testimony of Paul, validated their lives with scripture. Jesus was becoming phased out because his message was one of Communism. After coming out of prisons, Negroes began to come together and find ways around the oppression they were up against; this was by any means necessary. Led by the former hustler turned preacher, the neighborhoods became a cesspool for prosperity preaching, as the demand for more churches and preachers increased. When this newfound mentality took rise in the Negro communities it became infectious. Anybody who saw the hustler saw a person who they envied because they weren't broke, and they were the "flyest" guys on the block. Numerous movies were made like *Superfly* and *The Mack* that showcased the mentality of the hustler. The hustler's senses heightened upon going to jail and by educating himself within its confines, he dismissed religion all together, replacing it with a new more Darwinist ideology.

Pg. 317-318 of **Malcolm X's Autobiography** [9] said that the most dangerous black person to American society was the ghetto hustler . . . "*I knew better than all whites knew and better than nearly all of the black leaders knew that actually the most dangerous black man in America was the ghetto hustler. Why do I say this? The hustler out there in the ghetto jungles, has less respect for the white power structure than any other Negros in North America. The ghetto hustler is internally restrained by nothing. He has no religion, no civic responsibilities, no fear nothing. To survive he is out there*

constantly preying upon others, probing for any human weakness like a ferret. The ghetto hustler is forever frustrated, restless, and anxious for some "action." Whatever he undertakes, he commits himself to it fully, absolutely. What makes the ghetto hustler yet more dangerous is his "glamour" image to the school drop-out youth in the ghetto. These ghetto teenagers see the hell caught by their parents struggling to get somewhere, or see that they have given up struggling in the prejudiced, intolerant white man's world. The ghetto teenagers make up their own minds that they would rather be like the hustlers whom they see dressed sharp and flashing money and displaying no respect for anybody or anything. So the ghetto youth become attracted to the hustler's world of dope, thievery, prostitution, and general crime and immorality."

In 1897 before the time of Malcolm X, **W.E.B. Du Bois** began writing about the sociology of crime in America. Right after he received his Ph.D. from Harvard in 1899, Du Bois wrote his criminology theory which contained three parts. The first was that Negro crime was caused by the strain of the 'social revolution' experienced by black Americans as they began to adapt to their newfound freedom and position in America. "*The appearance of crime among the southern Negroes is a symptom of wrong social conditions--of a stress of life greater than a large part of the community can bear 10.*" Secondly, Du Bois believed that black crime declined as the African-American population moved toward a more equal status with whites. Du Bois found direct correlations between low levels of employment and education and high levels of criminal activity. Thirdly, Du Bois held that the ***Talented Tenth*** or the "exceptional men" of the black race would be the ones to lead the race and save it from its criminal problems. Du Bois saw the evolution of a class system within black American society as necessary to carry out the improvements to reduce crime. Dubois findings expose the fact that black people became thieves, prostitutes, and criminals because of their socioeconomic statuses. The Roman Catholic Church's consent and the backing of several powerful European countries like Portugal and Rome in the removing of a people from their land in Africa, and the placing of those people in the Americas as slaves; forced those slaves who did not wish to be impoverished to seek other ways to make money. **George Herbert,** the famous poet and priest from which President G.H. Bush Sr. gets his name, has an interesting quote that is a testament to the Negroes condition in America. Herbert summed up in one sentence the information WEB Dubois outlined in his criminology theory. "*War makes thieves and Peace hangs them 11.*"

 In American society, when black men became involved in the crime syndicate, because they wanted to be providers for themselves and their families, they were shown to the rest of the world as being criminals, unscrupulous, and a threat to the civil structure of the country. When you have no other choice but to be a janitor or someone's indentured servant, what would any human being do when presented with these circumstances. The present youth have not witnessed what happened with the slave trade and the black man in America nor do they have reason to care; so they think. Malcolm X so eloquently stated the black man in America who was the most dangerous is the ghetto hustler, and now-a-days in our society, much hasn't changed. Through the popularity of movies and music the "used to be" street hustler has morphed into the "gangster" rapper or the "hustling" rapper. These gangsters and hustlers have used their art form as a way of expression and have also channeled within their music the emotion, drive, and "hard times" they experienced during their life on the streets. Because they have done it with accurate precision they have caused the youth to buy into the same "hustler" persona as that mentioned previously by Malcolm X. These "rappers" are only responding to the social and economic oppression caused by the Roman power structure here in America. Because you will be outcaste and sanctioned for any type of rebellion or unwillingness to conform to this Roman religious power structure; these rappers have went underground to the black market to make their way of living. Due to the lengthy jail sentences that come by actually living the type of lifestyle that comes with dealing in the underground black market; rappers express their stories, or the stories of others as if their own, package it up, market, promote, and sell it. Once corporate America saw how effective these rappers were at marketing this "hustler" music they in turn invested heavily to capitalize on the rapid sales and high demand. Jay – z is credited as being one of the most successful artists in the marketing of this "hustler" music. To date, Jay- z is a symbol and personification of the American Dream realized as he has made the statement from Malcolm X about the "ghetto hustler" all that much more real and prophetic.

The suburban youth who bought into the "gangster rap" images in terms of rebellion and expression may not fully understand what the gangster rappers are professing. Living with suburban luxuries alienates this person from the struggles that blacks who live in the "ghettos" experience. Because these youth are impressionable and are led by the "ghetto" spokesman they are further subjugated to participate in a never ending cycle of ignorance and anarchy. This ignorance is very dangerous because now, due to their forefather's lies, they are following the instructions of a person who is guiding them indirectly away from a lifestyle they already have. This relationship between rapper and suburban youth is one of paradox because the suburban youth are already living the life the rapper wishes he had. The rapper is making up or embellishing his lifestyle to appear luxurious, so in turn, people will feel compelled to buy and listen to his music. If he is successful he is able to make the type of money that will enable him to live like the "impressionable" suburban youth. In understanding this paradoxical relationship between impressionable suburban youth and the "gangster rap" persona's they follow; we must first take a brief look at the origins of Hip-hop to analyze how it migrated throughout America.

During the Slave trade (15th-19th centuries) there were major slave ports in the southern cities Richmond, Virginia, Charleston, S.C. and New Orleans, Louisiana. Through these 3 major port cities, slaves were distributed into the United States. Because the south is where the slave ports were and where the slaves eventually settled, it's easy to trace the musical roots of Negroes from there. The Negro hymns and spirituals were the precursors to soul and blues music and this form of music stemmed from the lamentations and hard times experienced by those who lived in the south on plantations i.e the *blues*. In this particular genre slaves and oppressed black folks often sung about their emotional experiences in their tumultuous lives. When many of the slaves began migrating north the combination of blues met with instrumentation and this mixture of Jazz and Swing music created what is known today as Rhythm and Blues. This music was the fortifying influence in the Harlem Renaissance that led a huge influx of poets to express their outlooks both socially and economically over percussion and instrumentation.

When the Great Migration took place and people from the south started mingling with people from the north, hybrid music began to form. In cities like New York there were large populations of West Indians and fugitive slaves called Marooners. Because of their rowdy and furious behavior they were left in the Caribbean and didn't make it to the Americas during the slave trade. Ultimately they had been "marooned" and this is how they got the name Marooners. It wasn't until America opened the ports at Ellis Island in New York that a surplus amount of Caribbean immigrants flooded the burrows of New York City. However these immigrants didn't come empty handed; they brought their rebellious and rowdy attitudes with them. When these attitudes fused with poetry, rhythm, blues, and the pain of the Negro struggle; a rebellion spawned within a culture we call today Hip-Hop. **H**igher **I**nfinite **P**ower - **H**elping **O**ppressed **P**eople

After the Civil War you also had many blacks (former slaves) who felt it was smart to leave the south (Great Migration) and go live in the north. There was more commerce there, and they had a chance to live in a more "progressive" state of existence. The northern blacks were generally more book educated and due to rubbing elbows with the big businesses of the cities, they after the Industrial Revolution, became more corporate and capitalistic. The blacks who migrated north due to globalization and commerce were also integrationists who became policy makers, political minded, and for the advancement of colored people. Challenging white paternalism and racism, African-American artists and intellectuals rejected merely imitating the styles of Europeans and white Americans and instead celebrated black dignity and creativity. Asserting their freedom to express themselves on their own terms as artists and intellectuals, they explored their identities as black Americans, celebrating the black culture that had emerged out of slavery and their cultural ties to Africa [11a]. Immediately after the end of slavery and Jim Crowe, these emancipated African Americans began to strive for civic participation, political equality, and economic and cultural self-determination. These ideals were the underlying themes expressed throughout the Hip-Hop culture.

The gold rush of 1849, post the Civil War, also led tons of settlers to the west coast in search of prosperity. In 1850 Abolitionists deemed California a free state and this declaration was very attractive to former slaves and those who were tired of fighting oppression in the south. The west coast didn't have the industries of the north so the people out there where more liberal, free spirited, and open minded. Because New York and Chicago were heavily populated, migrants who settled on the west coast found refuge in it's warm climate, sandy beaches, and liaise' faire attitude towards life. The west coast migrants also had a hybrid mentality that fused the southern and east coast mentalities together. They weren't integrationists like their northern counterparts because most of them being migrants from the south saw firsthand the brutality of White Supremacy; however they didn't feel it cowardice to leave a place where you were treated horribly because the color of your skin. So in a sense they took a little from both sides Yankee and Confederate, and developed a more revolutionary outlook on life. When merged with the music of R&B, and the expression through rhyme and syllable; the combination of struggle, freedom of speech, and entertainment became the foregrounds for what would become one of the biggest movements in African American History, the rise of "gangster rap."
In the beginning of "gangster rap" many of the artists who were participating in it started out as community and political activists. Their lyrics became increasingly violent when they saw how much attention being negative gets. The food drives, and the community rallies they organized got little if any press; however, as soon as someone got shot, suddenly they became celebrities overnight. As a result, rapping about this "gangsta" lifestyle became what any artist who wanted to have instant mainstream attention and commercial success talked about in their lyrics. Here is where we find a link between the frustrated

black artists who express their frustrations through their music; and the youth who use it as a fuel for their own rebellion. Because the suburban youths parents have kept them sheltered; killing, violence, and criminal activity, create excitement for the youth who are living in the suburbs (sheltered environments.) These youth feel like slaves because like slaves they have to participate in a life that is already dictated to them. These youth identify with this aspect of the music because they, like the rappers, feel they are fighting against an oppressive system. For them it is their parents, for the rapper's it is who the suburban youth's parents received their education and religious ideas from. So what started as the subjugation and control of African slaves has led to the rebellion of the very youth that these slaves were intended to serve. How ironic, by the slave masters suppression of the freewill of African slaves, the rebellious attitude within the slaves has activated within the slave master's children.

Consequently, the stories of the "streets" rappers embellish in again directly contradict those that are taught by the Mother Church, which places the story tellers in direct opposition to what the church publically promotes. The church advocates helping the weak, turning the other cheek, and becoming a servant to humanity; it then highlights and perpetuates a state of communism.

Communion: (1) the act or instance of sharing

Communism: (1) a system where goods are owned in commune and distributed.

Ism: (1) doctrine, theory (2) an oppressive or discriminatory attitude or belief

Capital: (1) relating to assets that from long time net worth of a corporation (2) A stock of accumulated good at a specified time in contrast to income received at a specified period (3) a store of useful assets and advantages

Capitalize: (1) to gain by turning something to advantage

Capitalism: an economic system characterized by corporate or private ownership of capital goods by investments that are determined by private decision, and by prices, the production, and the distribution of goods to be determined mainly by competition in a free market.

In theory capitalism is great until a person comes to realize that someone else has something they need. When America comes to these realizations she takes what she wants. She wages war on whoever has the resources she needs to further her development and living standard. I guess the question to ask is at what point do you stop capitalizing? America can now say capitalism is great because she had slaves. America was only able to build and accumulate this society's wealth due to a seemingly endless supply of slave labor; labor that if it had interest on it from 400 years of non-payment, would cause every descendant of any former slave to be wealthy beyond their wildest dreams. If you were the benefactor of this system, it would seem to be the greatest on earth; however if you are a slave in this system, it would be one of the most miserable and horrific existences known to man.

Another reason why capitalism equates to war is people develop at different times. If you had a quick growth spurt and used your size to capitalize on those who are smaller, when they grow up, a growth that took longer because they are going to be larger, they are going to capitalize on you. This perpetual state of war is what makes the world go round and also what makes the religious debate a key topic for discussion. In this scenario who the hero is, and who the villain is gets blurred. Who you view to be the hero or the villain depends on your perspective, so we have to analyze it all before we can make any true contribution towards the debate. The problems of the world to a capitalistic minded person are the ordered structure of existence which in a sense is communistic. When you limit the power of people it's difficult to get an accurate assessment of what the people have actually evolved into. Chaos is an easy unbiased way to see who is who. Take war for example…back in the days if a man didn't fight in the war he wasn't a man. This was because the survivors of the wars were the evolved elite, which is what makes a hero. The hero is the one who perseveres through all odds, the main protagonist, and the one we chant and cheer for in the movies. If a person hasn't been through the war who and how are they able to lead? Not going to war only allows a person to dictate based on perceived theory versus experienced knowledge. This is why the theme of the warrior king is the most highlighted among stories with epic or highly climactic battles. Warrior kings must conquer during immeasurable odds in order to be liberated from the oppression that has caused them to be seen in a false light. This is so because no matter how great the oppression, if the human is unable to endure it and persevere through it, it will eventually die off anyway. People become stagnant whenever you make order the way of existence; Paul deliberated about this in the 2nd chapter of Timothy.

I Timothy 1:8-10 (8) But we know that the law is good, if a man use it lawfully (9) Knowing this, that the law is not made for a righteous man, but for the lawless and disobedient, for the ungodly and for the sinners, for unholy and profane, for murderers of fathers and murderers of mothers, and manslayers (10) for whore mongers, for them that defile themselves with mankind, for mansteallers, for liars, for perjured persons, and if there be any other thing that is contrary to sound doctrine

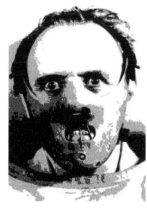

Paul says that the Law is made not for the righteous but for the lawless. Those who are of the law the law restricts. The story of **Hannibal Lecter** is a great analogy for what I am analyzing. From Hannibal's viewpoint he is a divinely appointed killer who takes the lives of people who exist in the grey areas of the law. He sees who these "people" truly are and disposes of them in the manner that is most just considering their offences. These people have evolved heightened senses but Hannibal's are even greater. They prey on the innocent which makes them the lowest of the low because they capitalize on those who have no chance, like animals. They break the law but aren't caught because the people they inflict their wrath upon; are usually social outcastes and people society doesn't care for. But in the spectrum of humanity a human is a human and "God" cares for everyone; so Hannibal is these criminals divinely appointed judge and executioner because he was appointed by nature/God.

The (law of man) says Hannibal is wrong but the law of nature makes him right. This is acknowledged because nature has a way of balancing out all life. The pesky flies that people hate so much find themselves entangled in a spider's web. The spider is a natural born killer that nature has fashioned to keep the balance of insects in any given ecosystem. The spider within this system after disposing of the flies doesn't have a judge that sanctions it to its death for ridding the world of what most consider being the peskiest of insects. However in the human realm and in the story of Hannibal man tries to arrest and label him a serial killer when he disposes of the worst humans. The masses fear Hannibal for his evolution because the fragile society they live in makes them susceptible to becoming his victims. Because they have de-evolved, they unknowingly side with the degenerate versus the superior. The degenerate is represented by the criminals Hannibal seeks vengeance upon, which the prosecutors cannot see because their dull senses have blinded them from viewing these criminals as they are. Because the people who are trying to apprehend Hannibal see themselves as potential victims subconsciously, it fuels their desire to apprehend Hannibal. They know they have been unjust in some way in previous cases, and if Hannibal judges those looming in the grey areas, they are in trouble. If the superior Hannibal is validated and rises above, and kept free, they know it is only a matter of time before they will fall below and be eliminated. So they have to eliminate the threat to their existence because they are closer to the sadistic people that Hannibal punishes than Hannibal himself. Because society can't blame itself for its degenerated (hellish) state it needs scapegoats, i.e. the DEVIL. Anthony Hopkins captured and personified this role to a tee because being a Capricorn, the astrological sign Alesiter Crowley links to the Devil, gave him the insight to channel his inner self / sol (astrological sign) to personify this character. This explains how Hopkins won the Oscar for Best Actor with less than 16 minutes on screen. The film the *Silence of the Lambs* went on to win 5 Oscars (Best Adapted Screenplay, Best Director, Best Actor, Best Actress and Best Picture) one of three films in history to do so.

The title of the movie says it all as we'll discuss later in this book in how the evolved elite prey upon the less evolved walking dead (sheep.) The account of Hannibal, who in a sense is seen in a predatory role, takes us back to the fundamental topic that started our conversation about him. When you look to nature there are animals who serve all purposes. If one animal slips another animal will capitalize, it has to, the moment it doesn't it will be consumed by something else. So the drive to capitalize becomes the drive to survive. This is the present course of the world; a course that means man has fallen from the divine state and nature he was created in, into the animalistic state that he has degenerated into.

IT DON'T MATTER IF YOU'RE BLACK OR WHITE

It is public knowledge, and also of public record, that black people in America were once hung, beaten, hosed, attacked by police dogs, thrown in prisons, and basically persecuted by the administration that at the time governed certain parts of the United States; primarily the south. George Wallace, the Governor of Alabama, even overtly displayed his racism by using his seat in public office, as a means to further suppress and oppress people of color.

In that era, the world also witnessed the **SCLC** headed by MLK, beaten and hosed on national television. I say that to say this, it was no secret, the descendants of slaves at one time weren't allowed to freely pursue education; nor were they turned onto legal avenues that would allow them to make sizeable economic gains. These people, if they got jobs, were bottom jobs, low paying jobs that kept them in a low and impoverished state. Anybody who knows anything about economics understands that in order to build wealth you must have land and a basis to build that wealth upon. In America the people who descended from the continent of Africa were the only race (in whole) that came to America against their will. Their land was taken and they were brought to the Americas to be its slaves. This means they were never thought to be included in the ruling classes of American society. In fact, during the writing of the

American constitution, of the 55 convention delegates 25 owned slaves. The 3/5's compromise was a debate of counting slaves in the population. The north was against counting slaves in the population because they felt if the slaves weren't allowed to vote, they should not be counted in the population. Allowing them to be counted in the population would give the south more representatives within the House. If the south had more representatives in the House, it would allow the south to outvote the north on the issue of slavery itself. The south wanted to keep its slaves and this is the reason why they wanted them (slaves) to be counted within their population. So as a result each slave was counted as 3/5's of a person 12. In the Hiramic legend it explains that blacks were only counted as 3/5ths of a person because they only had three of the five senses, touch, taste, and smelling; the other two, sight and hearing, are absent. According to the legend, they are missing because blacks haven't their language to hear each other properly with, and any knowledge to see each other properly with. One could argue if they had either they would be able to know when they heard God speak, or follow when they saw God leading. For these reasons blacks in America are called the deaf, dumb, and blind. I know people are going to ask what this has to do with Jesus and religion because it seems that I have diverged off topic. I had to emphasize this point so my audience is able to fully ingest what it is I am going to say next 12b. The people of the urban neighborhoods during the 1950's and 60's were given drugs to further make them subjects of the state. The rationalization for this as acknowledged in the movie *The Godfather* is that these blacks were "animals." In order to keep a people as strong as those who are natives of the continent of Africa down you would have to sedate them. If you starved them altogether they would die and you would have no slave to do all of your dirty work. Because you have given them the lowest position on the earth in relevance to salary and overall esteem of job importance, it has caused them to become very depressed. In their depression the French and Italian {*French Connection* / (Roman) "*Powers that Be*"} strategically targeted blacks and placed drugs in their already impoverished communities. They knew that this would be what the blacks turned to for their pleasure; and pleasure for a people who were in this down trodden state equaled salvation. Though crack cocaine didn't come along until the late sixties and early seventies in these communities; the rise of the Black Panthers and leaders like Malcolm X threatened the money that the drug lords could make because they were reforming addicts and cleaning up Negro communities in urban cities like Harlem and Chicago. It was at these times where the Negro communities were at their zenith. Black businesses flourished across New York City and Chicago and a new way of thinking emerged from the knowledge that blacks there had been exposed to. Queens, one of the five boroughs of New York City, still has one of the highest per capita incomes of any minority sect in America today. The knowledge that empowered the blacks to establish economic fortitude was the knowledge of the past that had been kept from them. Even if they could not accept Allah as their god, it still placed seeds of doubt within their minds that the god of their present belief, the one of Christianity, might not be the one they should serve. These seeds spawned critical thinking and led the Negroes into a mentality that is a mixture of all that we have discussed. The Negro felt since there are so many conflicting forms of thought and existence "I'ma use whatever "God" gave me legally or illegally to get mine." Once this mentality took over it was only a matter of time before the American Dream became the new standards for the goal of spirituality.

SHOULD PREACHER'S BE RICH

Should Christian preachers be rich? First and foremost I guess a person would have to look at the life and financial state of Jesus before they were to accurately give an assessment in regards to the question. If Jesus is the perfected example and he himself was not rich; how can it accurately be said without any evidence that people are to become rich as clergy men or as believers? The Bible gives many references to riches and the deceitfulness they cause, that one could say that becoming rich by preaching or believing is not why a church member or person should follow the teachings of Jesus.

1 Timothy 6:5 9&11 (5) Supposing that gain is godliness from such withdraw thyself they that be rich fall into temptation and a snare and into many foolish and hurtful lusts which drown men in destruction. But thou man of God flee these things and follow after righteousness, godliness, faith, love, patients, and meekness. - Paul
Imagine a man who is a street person, (bum) walks up in the center of the church and tells Leroy Thompson, or Creflo Dollar they are wrong for flying their leer jets, taking huge collections, and preaching about prosperity and wealth.
Imagine if he told them they have turned a house of prayer into a den of thieves. How do you think the Preachers and their congregations would respond to these allegations? How do you think they would respond to the person that is making these allegations? Jesus did something quite similar.

Matthew 21:12-13, 15 (12) And Jesus went into the Temple of God and cast out them that sold and bought in the temple, and overthrew the tables of the moneychangers, and the seats of them that sold doves and said unto them, (13) It is written my house shall be called the house of prayer; but ye have made it a den of thieves. (14) And the blind and the lame came to him in the temple; and he healed them (15) And when the chief priests and scribes saw the wonderful things that he did, and the children crying in the temple, and saying, Hosanna to the son of David; they were sore displeased.

I am quite aware the scriptures clearly state Jesus is casting out those who buy and sell in the temple, and not those who preach about wealth and prosperity.

Matthew 6:19-21 (19) Lay not up for yourselves treasures upon earth, where moth and rust doth corrupt, and where thieves break through and steal: (20) But lay up for yourselves treasures in heaven, where neither moth nor rust doth corrupt and where thieves do not break through and steal: (21) for where your treasure is, there will your heart be also.

Even Paul has something to say about those who pursue riches.

I Timothy 6:5 & 9 & 11 Perverse disputings of men of corrupt minds and destitute of the truth, supposing that gain is godliness: from such withdraw thyself. (9) But they that will be rich fall into temptation and a snare, and into many foolish and hurtful lusts, which drown men in destruction and perdition (11) But thou O man of God, flee these things; and follow after righteousness, godliness, faith, love, patience, meekness.

After reading this alongside several passages in the Bible I don't see how any preacher in the name of Jesus could preach prosperity as a reward for following Jesus, when he says his followers will be persecuted for his name.

Mark 13:9 (9) But take heed to yourselves: for they shall deliver you up to councils; and in the synagogues ye shall be beaten: and ye shall be brought before rulers and kings for my sake, for a testimony against them.

Matthew 10:22 (22) and ye shall be hated of all men for my name's sake: but he that endureth to the end shall be saved.

Another parable associated with riches is the parable of the rich ruler.

*Matt. 19:16-25 (16) And behold, one came and said unto him, Good Master, what good thing shall I do that I may have eternal life. (17) And he said unto him. **Why callest me good there is none good but one that is God: but if thou wilt enter into life keep the commandments.** (18) He saith unto him which Jesus said, **Thou shalt do no murder, thou shalt not commit adultery, thou shalt not steal, thou shalt not bear false witness, (19) Honor thy father and thy mother: and thou shalt love thy neighbor as thyself.** (20) The young man said unto him All these things have I kept from my youth up: What lack I yet? (21) Jesus said unto him **If thou wilt be perfect go and sell that thou hast and give to the poor and thou shalt have treasure in heaven and come and follow me.** (22) But when the young man heard that saying he went away sorrowful for he had great possessions. (23) Then said Jesus unto his disciples, **Verily I say unto you, that a rich man shall hardly enter into the Kingdom of heaven. (24) And again I say unto you it is easier for a camel to go through the eye of a needle than for a rich man to enter into the kingdom of God.** (25) When the disciples heard it they were exceedingly amazed saying, "Who then can be saved?"*

According to what we have just seen and heard by Jesus we can conclude that it is easier for a camel to fit through the eye of a needle then for a rich man to enter the kingdom of "God." I don't think that Jesus gave this answer in parabolic form because it is impossible for a rich man to enter into the kingdom of God. I think he is saying this to implicate the nature that man is in…meaning that it isn't possible for man because of the spiritual state man is in...but not impossible for God. If man had "God's" spiritual state, which is what Jesus represents, being rich wouldn't even be of his (man's) thought process.

Matt. 19:26 *with men this is impossible; but with God all things are possible.*

Jesus has to make this statement because if he literally says it is impossible, they will mock him and say, "Isn't your god all powerful…does your god have limitations?"

St. Matthew 13:9-11, 13, 15, 16 (9) Who hast ears to hear let him hear. (10) and the disciples came and said unto him Why speakest thou unto them in parables? (11) Because it is given unto you to know the mysteries of the kingdom of heaven, but to them it is not given. (13) Therefore I speak to them in parables because they seeing see not; and hearing they hear not, neither do they understand. (15) For this people's heart is waxed gross, and their ears are dull of hearing, and their eyes they have closed; lest at any time they should see with their eyes, and hear with their ears, and understand with their heart, and should be converted, and I should heal them (16) But blessed are your eyes for they see: and your ears, for they hear.

Matthew 13:22 the deceitfulness of riches choke the word.
How is it that Jesus is a poor man who walks around healing people and performing miracles and exposing the leading priests and high ranking elders of the church; yet now-a-days the people who claim to be his followers are rich preachers in the church who are not out in the world doing what Jesus told his disciples to do?

Matt.23:2-8 The scribes and Pharisees sit in Moses seat. (3) all therefore whatsoever they bid you observe, that observe and do: but do not ye after their works: for they say and do not. (4) for they bind heavy burdens and grievous to be borne, and lay them on men's shoulders: but they themselves will not move them with one of their fingers. (5) they broaden their phylacteries, and enlarge the borders of their garments (6) And love the uppermost rooms at feasts, and the chief seats in the synagogues (7) and greetings in the markets, and to be called of men Rabbi (8) but be not ye called Rabbi for one is your master, even Christ and all ye brethren.

I can imagine if Jesus would give this advice to a complete stranger that wanted to follow him, he would have given his own disciples a similar instruction.

Matthew 10:5-15 (5) Go not into the way of the Gentiles, and into any city of the Samaritans enter ye not: (6) But go rather to the lost sheep of the House of Israel (7) and as ye go preach saying the kingdom of heaven is at hand (8) heal the sick, cleanse the lepers, raise the dead, cast out devils: freely ye have received freely give. (9) provide neither gold nor silver nor brass in your purses (10) Nor script for your journey, neither two coats, neither shoes, nor yet staves: for the workman is worthy of his meat. (11) and in whatsoever city or town ye shall enter, enquire who in it is worthy; and there abide till ye go thence.(12) and when ye come into the house salute it (13) and if the house be worthy, let your peace return you. (14) And whosoever shall not receive you, nor hear your words, when ye depart out of that house or city, shake off the dust of your feet. (15) Verily I say unto you it shall be more tolerable for the land of Sodom and Gomorrah in the day of Judgment, than for that city.

Matthew 6:25, 31-33, 34, 35 (25) Therefore I say unto you take no thought for your life what ye shall eat or what ye shall drink nor yet for your body what ye shall put on. Is not the life more than the meat and the body than the raiment? (31) Therefore take no thought saying what shall we eat or what shall we drink or wherewithal shall we be clothed (32) for after these things do the Gentiles seek for your heavenly father knows that ye have need of all these things (33) but seek ye first the kingdom of God and all these things shall be added unto you (35) Take therefore no thought of the morrow for the morrow shall take thought for the things of itself. Sufficient of the day is the evil thereof.

According to this scripture it is very rare to find anyone living like this in America. Most preachers take the latter half of the aforementioned scriptures and say "God" provided them with all of their riches so therefore they can have them. But was it "God" that provided them with riches? In the scriptures the only disciple rewarded with riches was Judas and he was rewarded monetarily for LITERALLY SELLING OUT JESUS!!!!!

Luke. 22:3-5 (3) Then entered Satan into Judas surnamed Iscariot being of the number of twelve (4) and he went his way, and commanded with the chief priests and captains, how he might betray him unto them (5) And they were glad and covenanted to give him money.

Matthew 27:3 (3) Then Judas, which had betrayed him, when he saw that he was condemned, repented himself, and brought again the thirty pieces of silver to the chief priests and elders.

Acts1:18 -19 (18) Now this man (Judas) purchased a field with the reward of iniquity; and falling headlong, be burst asunder in the midst, and all his bowels gushed out. (19) And it was known unto all the dwellers of Jerusalem; insomuch as that field is called in their proper tongue Aceldama, that is to say the field of blood.

The above passages clearly indicate that by selling Jesus out Judas bought land. If I am looking at this literally, it says that he purchased a field. For further elaboration I will make a comparison of these events and parallel it with today's time, to see if a similar conclusion is drawn. In my example in the formulation of a modernized more relatable story, the purchase of a field represents land that can be likened to a very lucrative neighborhood that sits a mile outside of downtown lived upon by low income families. These people who live next to downtown are so close to poverty, they resemble bums. One of the impoverished locals (Jesus) service's the people of the neighborhood as a healer, spiritual advisor, and guide. Across the tracks on the other side of downtown is a moderately sized church that has ambitions of becoming larger. The particular piece of real estate the impoverished people are living on would provide the owners of the church the ability to be the biggest church in the city if they could somehow remove the people living there. The only reason the people will not sell their property to the church is because of the healer and spiritual advisor who comes to everyone's house facilitating them throughout the week. The church learns of this spiritual advisor and seeks to get rid of him so they can in turn get the property. He unlike the priests of the church doesn't charge for his service, and, the people after they hear or meet him are actually healed the same hour in which they come in contact with him. The church staff's high ranking officials (members/priests) take the money they received from many tithes and offerings from the people of the community, and go and buy the land that these people are living on. The way they acquired it was by the dope fiend son (Judas) who inherited the estate because his father was the landlord and had suddenly died. The father cast him out of the family some time before because of his drug addiction and this spited him. After his father's death he became the controller of the estate and inherited the property. The church leaders knew of the weakness of the son and when the opportunity to purchase the land came about, the church made the son an offer he couldn't refuse. The son (Judas) willingly took the money sent by the church and sold them the land. Now because the church owns the land, they can evict the one who is causing them to lose money (Jesus) and make the law to say that he is no longer allowed on their property. In Judas's mind he made a profit and in real estate the goal is such, to make a profit. Who cares about the "bums" who are living there? The fact that it is to the detriment of the lowly is not his problem. The church can now redevelop and become larger as well as build condominiums on the land and sell real estate to a wealthier clientele; which in turn, in the long run, will make them even more money. The more the people make, the more they have to give, and the wealthier the church becomes. No one outside of the people in the community knew Jesus had those types of healing skills so to them everything he's done goes unnoticed. How many people can identify personally with this scenario? This scene is so close to the norm in our society that it causes a person to readily see how easy it was in those times for Jesus to be sold out. Being that most preachers of today profess Jesus as their personal Lord and savior and follow him, they should do exactly that. The scriptures indicate Jesus had given up everything including his life; he didn't even have a place to stay.

Matthew 8:20 (20) and Jesus saith unto him <u>The foxes have holes and the birds of the air have nests but the Son of man hath no where to lay his head</u>.

I have spent a huge portion of my life in and out of the black churches of America and what I have discovered in these churches is that the people, who worship there, being poor, attribute all monetary blessings as coming from "God" and or Jesus. What was equally perplexing is that most of the people who have this particular viewpoint also had a disdain for people who were rich. The paradox within their thinking is that in these churches within these people's faith the person who they worship is Jesus. Jesus in the Gospel never once received monetary compensation for a job well done, nor has he ever blessed anyone monetarily; yet this is the person that the black churches attribute as the source of their monetary blessings. In fact Jesus speaks against riches, he says in Matthew 13:22 *the deceitfulness of riches choke the word*. Jesus tells a rich ruler to give up all his possessions and he tells his disciples to freely give when they enter the lost sheep's homes. Jesus over turns money tables in the synagogue and states that a person shouldn't build wealth on earth, but rather in heaven; and most importantly, Jesus himself is a vagabond who has no money. If I were to survey the people and ask them what they would wish for sort of like parents do their children before Christmas, what types of answers do you think I would get? If I made the wish request not related to religion or Jesus and posed the question in a mundane way, I bet what most people would wish for would be something vain or materialistic. I know a person is going to say well how do you know? The question I am posing is not for a person to tell me what I think they should ask for. I am talking about what they really want…and with the zeal as if they are "really" going to get it. Popular consensus among those who practice Christianity believes the Devil to be the ruler of the material world. Upon citing this information it isn't presumptuous to conclude that the chief Devil Satan is most likely going to be the entity who would grant the person their wish. When you look at the word Santa Claus, tell me if you can see Satan within it!? Now ask yourself why Christmas is the birthday of Jesus.

In the Qur'an they have what are called the Jinn. The Arabic root *JNN* means "hidden, concealed" as in the verb *janna which means* "to hide, to conceal" 13. The jinn or jinni is where Americans get the word genie. The word *genie* derives from Latin *genius*, which was specified as a guardian spirit presumably assigned to each person at their birth; much to the like of an astrological sign. The English borrowed the French descendent of this word, *génie* because it was similar to the Arabic word in sound and in meaning *14*. The French translated the Arabic meaning for Jinn to genie in *Arabian Nights*, the popular story of Aladdin, his genie, and his flying carpet. This use of the word was adopted in English and has since become dominant. This is why now-a-days a genie is thought to be a spirit who grants wishes, wishes that are usually personified as vain and carnal desires. In the Qur'an though jinni's can be good they are described as evil doers who possess free will.

Through the use of English and French translation we can see how something taken out of context has now misconstrued how we view desires and wishes as well as the entities that unite humans/mankind with them. These entities are their astrological signs or as the ancients wrote, *"the gods that preside over the affairs of mankind."* It is also important to notate that Solomon in Arabian legend is said to have rule and command over the Jinn. This point like many others stated within this book confirms how something can originate within one culture but when it is transferred into another culture with a different language and custom, it changes from its original intent into something grotesque and non-relatable. This is what has happened in regards to the life of Jesus as well as the message to his *"intended"* flock. In fully recognizing and comprehending this concept, it is easy to see also how a deity prophesied to come (future) could be missed by those who claim to worship him/it. In this case, perception isn't reality, or is it?

KRISHNA

The Book of Illumination

CHAPTER 6

EVERYONE ELSE
IS FREE TO GO

The Book of Illumination

CHAPTER 6
EVERYONE ELSE
IS FREE TO GO

EVERYONE ELSE IS FREE TO GO - EXCEPT YOU SLAVES

What is equally crippling in the misunderstanding of Christianity, are the people who the Bible is written about. When you overlook or do not know who the Bible's prophecies are directed to and at; it causes a false sense of religion to take place in the minds of those who are listening to the traditional information received from attending church service every week. Because the Abrahamic prophecy speaks about a *"chosen"* people of God being enslaved in a *strange* land; it's only befitting we analyze history to see where that prophecy has taken place. Many people have yet to realize the illusion America has profited from, the American Dream, is directly perpetuated from a lack of true comprehension in their religious beliefs.

In the early chapters of this book, it was stated that America was the land the Abrahamic prophecy has taken place in. The Negroes were the "sacrificial lambs" who were taken from their homeland in Africa in order to build this new kingdom in America. What people must come to grips with is the fact that history repeats itself. The orbit and plane we existence in is elliptical and moves in a circle. When time resets itself, society grows from the last cycle of history recorded. By learning from the past, planners and builders try and perfect the world and improve it from its previous condition. Their quest and mission is to achieve heaven on earth; or at least to make the cities on earth the most desirable living paradise for those who are evolved and elite. Although the enslavement of blacks happened well over 400 years ago let's look to the present to see if there is evidence that supports the notion that we have indeed perfected our world from its previous condition.

The reason that many illegal immigrants migrate to the United States is because they feel it is "heaven" on earth. They haven't necessarily come to realize they are entering a country and vying for citizenship in an already crowded arena. This is because all of the advertising America does via movies and tourism creates a "mirage." for the migrant who lives in a "desert." Once they get to America, they grow very used to the luxury the land provides and this state of luxury allows them to grow lax and forget they have become subjects of a new land. Being subjects in America is better than being nothing in their own countries; as they would rather be a slave in America than starve where they are from. This mentality mainly benefits those who are in a position to utilize them and their situations to their advantage; namely the property owners who need their land built upon, cleaned, managed, and up kept. Though this thought process could be classified as *"Jeffersonian thinking"* as he believed slavery to be a temporary but necessary evil, it is one that cannot be easily explained 12c. Most migrants who came to America when the country first began have experienced a tumultuous workload and readily understand what it was like living in a raw and un-manicured country. When new immigrants leave their land in search of America the reason stated as to why their migration has taken place is usually the hope of prosperity, wealth, and a better standard of living. Although blacks were directly targeted to be slaves when America first began, this same mentality has bled into New America and its insatiable quest for a new subservient race of people. Richard Hofstadter said in ***The American Political Tradition*** that, "*emancipation meant not merely the replacement of slave labor by hired labor, but the loss of White Supremacy, the overthrow of the caste system - in brief the end of civilization*" 12d. Being that America is looking for a new set of worker bees to improve on its vast land and real estate potential; we now have to narrow our scope to see in America where the new builders are coming from, and also, where the new build out is taking place.

Texas is the second largest state for Hispanic population with about 7.8 million Latin inhabitants. The United States has over 43 million Hispanics in it today. Though the same people inhabited Texas soil prior to the War of 1836, (*The war of the Alamo*) they are now the people sought out to be its new land builders. Texas is also listed as the only state that can succeed from the union of the United States due to its large sulfur and oil exports. It has sufficient land and climate to grow the crops that are able to feed its citizens and is a leader in the beef and cattle industry. There is also a gulf by the state, which allows the direct reception and exportation of goods to and from other countries, giving Texas direct access to global commerce and trade.

When you look at all these factors as a person who is in a ruler ship or ownership capacity would, you find out Texas has all the conditions necessary to operate as a country within a country. It is no coincidence that Texas is the home of NASA (*National Aeronautics and Space Administration*) and Fort Hood, which are the leading space exploration base and largest military base in the United States. It is also no coincidence that the 2nd father and son Presidents, mind you they both served within a ten year span of the other, are from Texas. In fact, George Bush Sr. used to be the head of the CIA (*Central Intelligence Agency*) and his son George Bush Jr. was Texas's former Governor.

 When you look at NASA and Fort Hood you can easily see how the largest military base and the space exploration program work together for the positioning of military special weapons via satellite, to facilitate covert espionage and classified military operatives. The fact that all of this activity is happening in the only state that could succeed from the union of the United States is very interesting.

NAFTA which is the (North American Free Trade Agreement), commissioned on January 1, 1994 made it possible for those who are illegal immigrants to come to the United States and obtain citizenship 15. This citizenship was allowed so they would be "legalized" in order to do the landscaping and building on the vast unaltered landscape of Texas. Though the previous statement wasn't legitimized as a declaration, reading between the lines allows a person to fully understand why it was said. Let me pose these scenarios this way. If you were a corporation and you had a slew of land to build upon, how and where are you going to get labor cheap enough that you can build, maintain the state, and turn sizeable profits afterwards? In order to successfully contract these labor positions you are going to need someone who will literally work for the lowest amount of wage for the longest amount of time. No American or unionized man is going to work for a wage that isn't to the standard set by the union. Most construction workers make anywhere from $16 to $60 dollars an hour and this doesn't include overtime pay. A usual work week on any particular construction job is 65-90 hours. If you do the math correctly that is a whole lot more than if you were to pay an immigrant $8 dollars an hour for the same work week excluding overtime pay. Positioning NAFTA was great for Texas, because Texas is right above Mexico and has all of the capabilities to become the leading superpower in terms of a "little" country within the "Big" country of the United States. To build a new huge country starting with Texas and Mexico you are going to need this million man crew to design your ultimate future living paradise.

In 1988 America and Canada had a preexisting trade agreement called the Canada-United States Free trade Agreement. When President Bush Sr. was in office is when we saw the trade agreement basically extend its arms to Mexico. Today we can see the effects of that free-trade agreement as Houston has three of the most state of the art performance arenas in the United States; all save one have retractable roofs. The names of these arenas are Minute Maid Arena, the

Toyota Center, and Reliant Arena, all built during the Presidency of George Bush Jr. Having 1.5 to 3 billion dollars floating around to build these mega-performance stadiums shows the potential of what you stand to profit by owning them.

Placing a microscopic lens on the United States most popular city, New York, a city that was formerly the "giant" in terms of commerce and influence; we saw a city wherein the Twin Towers, the leading <u>World Trade Centers</u>, were demolished. But what did this symbolize? The fact that New York is overpopulated and has no more "dream" to sell is a testament that (in whole) it has maxed out on its real estate potential. The lay people of America haven't a clue that its government's agendas are rolled out over several decades. The bigger the goal, the longer it takes for those in power to structure and run their agendas. Monarchs need their offspring to continue their agendas and legacies which is why having "heirs" to their empires is so important. In their rationale, this is the practical way of achieving immortality.

Proverbs 13:22 A good man leaveth an inheritance to his children's children: and the wealth of the sinner is laid up to the just.

America has to continue building upon its vast empire due to its population's growth. It has to seek out new territories to put the people who are coming to it from all over the world. Being that America's potential was maxed out in the busiest city for commerce NYC, there needed to be a shifting of where the money would go to develop the next viable and lucrative place for real estate. These viable places are none other than Texas and Mexico.

War stimulates economy; at least this is the general consensus among economists and those who hold high political offices. Wars and rumors of wars cause distraction. This distraction is needed because the government can't come out and broad cast to its citizens the moves it really plans to make. The expose' of the government's real agenda to the public would certainly cause civil unrest, uprisings, and chaos; which could possibly thwart the government's agendas. Overall their agendas must be met because they are the people who have an agenda to meet. Common people don't think about the rationing of resources; or where the next place of comfortable habitat will be where the elite, skilled, and resourceful of the society, can thrive and build upon the previous society. The "lay" or common people are more concerned with their television shows, what they are going to eat for lunch, and where they are going to shop. They only become excited about politics when a political issue appeals directly to them, there is a scandal, or something that happens politically that is out of the ordinary. The popular cliché that sums this paragraph up is one taken from the play *Othello* by a character named Iago, "*I am not what I am*" 12e. Man is constantly in search of a scapegoat (Devil) to blame for his/her own insecurities and short comings. The government which functions as the legislating entity within a nation is the perfect target to become scapegoats, as any person or thing of power who claims to have the answers are usually blamed for a groups/nations failures or inconsistencies; even when those who claim to have followed them went astray from the plan originally given to them by those who govern them.

For the most part I have noticed that very few people have the abilities within themselves to structure real agendas, especially agendas that cater towards the bottom line in respects to social and economic progress. Most people are only concerned with their cause directly, and like the cliché says everybody's got a cause. A person with visionary abilities isn't looking at the liabilities; they are looking at the goal. When you speak in reference to great builders of societies the common "subject" isn't something these builders can factor. This is said because the builders are looking at the goal which consists of the accommodations of millions of people. For these reasons communities are to come together to build private businesses and committees that ensure their small sects are represented in relation to the whole. This is where the special interest groups and bureaucracies develop their constituents from. A people who haven't developed the necessary psyche to have these types of conversations aren't or haven't the necessary educational levels for a government to ever factor them into their building plans; and if they are factored, they are factored into the laboring classes, which are at the bottom of the country's hierarchy. This is why slavery and the subjugation of Indians, and indigenous peoples were never thought about twice by the rulers/builders of the governing society. You can't factor what you consider low level intelligence. John C. Calhoun the first vice president after the American Revolution went on to say, *"Slavery is, instead of evil, a good – a positive good. I fearlessly assert that the existing relation between the two races in the south forms the most solid and durable foundation in which to rear free and stable institutions* 12f."* This is why even though those who build are greater physically; they haven't the visionary abilities to be perceived as being greater intellectually. You would think those who are inept physically would serve those physically adept. Yet history has shown us those with greater physicality serves those with lesser physicality; as *the pen is mightier than the sword.*

Matthew 23:11 But he that is greatest among you shall be your servant.

There wouldn't be any problem with this if the profits were equally divided. But then again the word equal describes a form of communism. Where the problem arises is that western society wants the laborer to do all of the work for inadequate compensation and the planners to reap all of the rewards. How much work does it take to build physically than to build visions? The counter argument is if the visionaries do not structure an agenda, the laborers will not

127

build on their own. This is where the great debate starts, who is greater, the one who has the initiative to think, or the one who has the ability to act? Calhoun also took into account this problem and said, '*There never has yet existed a wealthy and civilized society in which one portion of the community did not, in point of fact, live on the labor of another. It would not be too difficult to trace out the various devices by which the wealth of all civilized communities has been so unequally divided, and to show by what means so small a share has been allotted to those by whose labor it was produced, and so large a share to the non-producing class*" 12g. Now I am not one to criticize thought, as I am all for stimulated thought; however "works" are what becomes tangible and concrete. Visions, if no works are put into them, become nothing at all. Even though we know that during the building process you can't pay everyone the highest wage, you can after you turn sizeable profits, start to even out the compensation (profit sharing.) All things being equal, think about it, how is it the laborer is paid less than the planner? This question is one that shows the power of initiation as being the trait that separates the boss, who is the one who tells people what to do, from the employee, the one who is told what to do. The planners are the ones who structure the agendas, lay their blueprints, and find a means to get their constructions done. They usually after acquiring wealth sit on the money and wait for an opportunity to invest it at a profit. The laborer in general, on the other hand, is usually only concerned with his personal living space. He has no regard for anything outside of his immediate family structure and his own satisfaction. Laborers, unlike planners, typically do not have the concept of sitting on money and waiting on an opportunity to invest it at a profit. Stimulating the economy seems as simple as increasing the wages the laborers make. However, allowing the laborers to have more money would cause these laborers to spend more money; and by them spending more money, more money is circulated, thereby stimulating the economy. Only problem with this scenario is where are you going to get the money to pay the laborers... taxes....inflation? If it were as simple as stimulating the economy, this would be a readymade solution. However other factors have to be taken into account which is the common peoples disinterest in the "boredom" associated with politics, as well as their innate sense of autonomy; which pending on their level of education and evolution, can appear to be anarchy. If everyone has money the people will feel they no longer need government, as their ego's will tell them they can govern themselves. This is the first sign of ruin and the governing elite have kept the structure of the planner and the laborer this way to ensure its own survival. The American Government understands people's lust for entertainment as its 2nd leading export is film. Presidents like Ronald Reagan, a former actor and "president" of the screen actors' guild, were initiated by the American Government for this very reason. Because people pay attention to celebrities and they often overshadow political figures, as in the case of Michael Jackson, the government has now **lionized** its presidential candidates. Maybe now after reading this paragraph people will understand the rise and importance of

Americas 1st African - American President, Barack Obama who just so happens to be a Leo (lion.)

In understanding the dynamic relationship between the planner and the laborer one needs the basic knowledge of the build out. When a building plan begins, the strongest have to be utilized to build; and at every build there is a sacrifice, this sacrifice is known as the "death of the builder" in Masonry. In the case of America, the sacrifice or builders that were sacrificed in whole were the slaves who had the laborious task of the build out. However in the new kingdom, when the precession resets itself, the slaves will become the builders as their sacrifices have given them the karma to rule based on the justified law of karma and opposites which states: *everything is opposed by something equal.* In conclusion, those who promote slavery and had slaves will indeed be the slaves in the next cycle of history; and those who were slaves will be the masters. Be careful how you treat others when in power, life is a continuance that is cyclical, not linear.

The (new illegal immigrants) that have come to America have all come in search of the same thing with little regard for the people and legal migrants who have been waiting in line for their own slice of the pie. Because un-like these willing migrants, these former slaves have already worked for centuries and have not been adequately compensated for their ancestors works. What would make the (new illegal immigrants) believe they all could obtain the same goal? The answer to this question is simple, Hollywood. Again, aside from debt, the nation's number one export is film and the entertainment industry. By attracting migrants who want to live the lifestyles portrayed in the movies, these industries are the backbone for the dream that America sells to those abroad. But from this acknowledgement arises another question,

"Wouldn't coming to America to escape the reality of their previous habitat make the condition in America the same as the place they are escaping from?"

True story, when Hurricane Rita came to the gulf coast many people after seeing Hurricane Katrina on the news fled to leave Houston. What they hadn't thought about in their evacuation, is they all had the same goal and thought processes.

Because everyone left at the same time, the stampeding caused the interstates to be backed up for hundreds of miles. More people died as a result of heat stroke and automobile accidents than the hurricane itself. Likened to market saturation, this is what I meant by everyone in search of the same thing, makes that "thing" that much more un-obtainable. More degrees means the degree is worth less or "worthless." A college degree now is the same as a high school diploma, and a master's degree is now the same as a bachelor's degree. The people who are getting these degrees do not know this because they have been taught to, "Get that degree, if you want a good job!" But what job are you going to get? Jobs are created by demand, not a certificate of paper. The over population by those attending school creates a situation where those with higher educational certificates become over qualified for the jobs that do exist. Do not mistake what I am saying as if I don't understand that most jobs use education as the primary training grounds to build the skill sets of their employees. I also recognize that schooling is created for developmental purposes so the youth get a general basis for what they will be encountering when they get into the "real" world. However, nowadays many students I have interviewed and encountered say they are just trying to get a degree without any particular direction afterward. These people want the certificate of paper because they feel it will enable them to be "over" someone else. They really want to be the boss but haven't all of the mechanisms within to fully understand what that boss is.

When I surveyed the number of people in school and compare it to the number of people in the work place, it seems to serve as a buffer to keep the workplace unsaturated. Keep in mind jobs have to be created by some sort of demand. Supply and demand are the most fundamental economic principals and are comparable to cause and effect. In America, people have lost sight of these principals and are now chasing certificates as opposed to servicing the demands of the public. There are over 300 million people in America yet there aren't 300 million jobs. Faith will make a person tell themselves everything is going to be alright; fact will say that *somebody* has to have that minimum wage job. The NAFTA was passed for this very reason. The government has to maintain the standard of living for the state at all costs.

The history books will have you believe that America is this great melting pot and land of opportunity that was built by all peoples of all nations who wanted to participate in a new society; this was true on some level. There were also many migrants who came to America and worked their fingers to the bone to amass great wealth by building upon great legacies and their families fortunes; this paragraph is not for them. I am all for the legal migrant who is a hard worker that puts everything on the line to make a greater standard of living for themselves and their families; however, there is only so much space, only so many jobs, and only so many resources and opportunities.

I used the NAFTA to further highlight that slavery is a necessary evil designed to get an agenda done. This agenda has no emotion associated with the common individual as it seeks to benefit the whole as well as the ones who designed it. America's builders were only operating within their nature; a nature that is most humanistic as anyone who evolves to the higher echelons of society and walks in their shoes would do the same thing. I also felt the need to dissect the thought processes of those in power to show the difference between those who plan the build and those who labor in it. I wanted to show how the falsification of a huge portion of religion, and world history has affected the outlook of the American citizen, the Black American, as well as the "new immigrants" who seek American citizenship. Because their viewpoints have been jaded by biased information and are shaded by their personal ambitions for a better life; it has overshadowed their abilities to understand that by ignoring the plights of slaves… they have within themselves become them. A wise person once said, "Those who forget the past are doomed to repeat it."

To talk about slavery in America and not talk about the president who passed the amendment to abolish it, is like talking about basketball and not mentioning Michael Jordan. On a cosmic, spiritual, as well as physical level Abraham Lincoln has all the makings of an "avatar" who through his humanitarian exploits abolished slavery, ended the Civil War, and reunited a divided country.

Born February 12th under the sign of Aquarius most known for their humanitarianism and universal outlook; we see President Lincoln as the fulfiller of the Abrahamic covenant in the Genesis between the nation that Abraham's seed was enslaved to, and the judgment that follows. The president having the name Abraham and then abolishing slavery for an enslaved nation in a foreign land not their own, is prophetical on multi-levels. We spoke about this earlier in the beginning of the book by way of the 15th and 17th chapters of Genesis. The passing of the 13th amendment has great significance as well. In the Kabbalah the number 13 represents death. When we look at this through a historical perspective, the 13th amendment was indeed the "death of slavery" in America.

On a cosmic level we still see the relationship between the Harbinger *"one who aides and prepares the way"* (Aquarius) and the sun/son (Leo) *"the one who fulfills and completes the will set forth by the father"* in action. Illinois, popularly called the *"Land of Lincoln"* is the state where Barack Obama became a Senator. In this scenario the father was one of the *"fore fathers"* in American history (Abraham Lincoln) and the sun/son was Barack Obama. Here we find the link between the man who physically abolished slavery and the African American man who has succeeded him in becoming the 44th President of the United States.

The Lincoln Memorial in Washington D.C. shows a seated Abraham Lincoln staring at an ever erect obelisk/pillar (Washington Monument.) This is reminiscent of the relationship between Visnu and Shiva in Hinduism in how Visnu is in constant awe of Shiva. Through art and sculpting via stone masonry, those with a spiritual eye can see the universe projecting itself; which again shows the influences of Visnu and Shiva as the primary and consistent liberating forces within it.

Matthew 24:37 *When the **Son of Man** returns it will be as in **Noah's** day.*

These two movies were released a month between each other. The 1st, *Son of God* 2/28/2014, the 2nd *Noah*, 3/28/2014. As seen above, the biblical prophecy states that the Son of Man will return during the times and days of Noah. The times and days of Noah equal to that of a **flood** which, as explained several times in this book, marks the beginning of the Age of Aquarius, the water bearer.

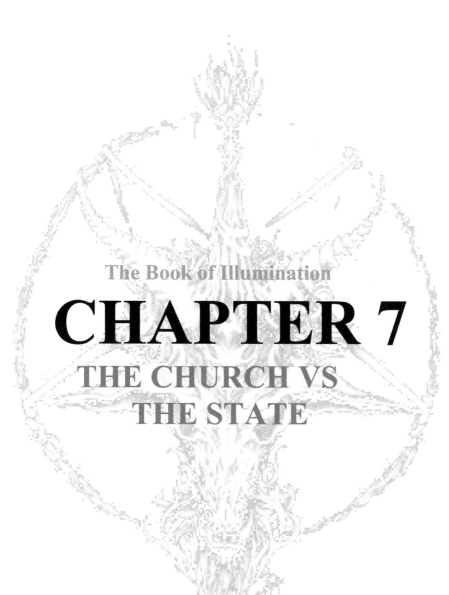

The Book of Illumination

CHAPTER 7

THE CHURCH VS THE STATE

The Book of Illumination

CHAPTER 7
THE CHURCH VS
THE STATE

THE CHURCH VS THE STATE

When analyzing the relationship between church and state, one should 1st be cognizant of what the term communism means. The reason that communism has been mentioned in this section of the book is due to the message that Jesus has given to the world as well as the way the world has shaped around it. The instructions of Jesus could very easily be seen as communistic due to the "*do unto others as you would want done unto you*" motto that is promoted within his message. When we take into account that America is predominantly a Christian nation, this acknowledgement makes us look to the economic structure of the land to see how, or if it coincides with the religious faith of the nation. Being that a person's finances generally dictate the type of household they run, in diagnosing the spiritual condition of any particular nation, one must first look at its economy.

Communism: (1) A totalitarian form of government in which a single authoritarian controls state owned means of production

Totalitarian: (1) of or relating to centralized control by an autocratic leader (2) of or relating to a political regime based on subordination of the individual to state and strict control of all aspects of life and production capacity of the nation by coercive measures (censorship and terrorism)

Autocracy: Government in which one person possesses unlimited power

Authoritarian: (1) of or relating to a concentration of power in a leader or an elite not constitutionally responsible to the people

Socialism: any of various economic and political theories advocating collective or governmental ownership and administration of the means of production and distribution of goods

.

16 The ideals of communism where everyone shares are ideals that have nothing to do with the way the former economic structure of America was governed; in fact it used to be the opposite. America has to now live up to the dream it has promoted since its inception. For reasons such as these, many people, namely those who aren't in favor of America's newly elected president, assumes the American Government has conformed at least superficially to the people's desire. A desire as stated in the introduction, for a long awaited Savior. Many political analysts feel the American public has been given one to worship

WHITE LIBERAL GUILT FINDS ATONEMENT...

FREE AT LAST, FREE AT LAST, THANK GOD ALMIGHTY, FREE AT LAST!

Obama

physically in the person of their newly elected President Barack Obama. Supporters of these cartoons through satire have covertly expressed that the separation of church and state has in a sense again become merged, due to the American public's fascination with President Obama. These analysts contend that the public at large views President Obama as a godsend that will bring economic justice (communism) to those who have been ignored, disparaged, and overlooked. Although the merging of church and state as a declaration has not been enforced or amended within the constitution; implicating it through the newly elected President, Barack Obama, holds an even greater power and effect. Because the American public has been reared in a Christian way of faith, many analysts as well as nationalists feel the American public has become gullible in their attempt to find a scapegoat (the Devil) to blame for the countries present economic situation. In implicating a villain, a hero almost always will miraculously appear. This seems to be the present viewpoint America has taken with respects to the Bush and Obama administrations 17.

With the current economic state in America being at peak lows, the American government has succumb to the same course of action as many other nations that started with a capitalistic democracy 18. Floating on the brinks of communism, Americans are now witnessing a repossession of the major money making industries that once fueled a large portion of the private sector of business in the United States. With the nations governmental buy-outs of the automobile industries, the AIG insurance companies, and the bail-outs to the banks that hold the mortgages of the countries subjects; the repossession of these industries by the government, are all examples brought forth by America's economic dilemma. The 2009 900 billion dollar stimulus bill is a great example of the government using its money to fund jobs, while simultaneously improving and innovating the countries current economic situation. When you think about why the government needs 900 billion dollars, the question people ask is where are they spending the money? The economic stimulus package of 2009 proposed by Democratic House leaders totals $825 billion and includes three large pieces: a $365.6 billion spending measure for brick-and-mortar projects such as highways and bridges; a $180 billion measure to boost jobless benefits and Medicaid; and a $275 billion tax-relief package, which includes a plan to give a $500 payroll tax holiday to all workers 19. The magnitude of the spending bill drew swarms of lobbyists who sought money and tax breaks from congress. The huge budgets had concrete companies, and cattle industries fighting over which way the money will shift. For instance the concrete and asphalt industries were battling over how the government should spend money proposed for road and bridge repairs; while dairy and beef cattle producers' feuded over speculation that the government might buy up dairy cattle for slaughter and drive up the prices of depressed milk. Concrete lobbyists want more money for long-term projects such as interstate highways, bridges and waterworks -- projects that use more concrete. The asphalt industry prefers repaving and road repair that use more asphalt. If the government ruled in favor of the concrete companies, the asphalt industry would be greatly affected. Reason being, if the concrete companies get the contracts they will be working while the asphalt companies will be at a standstill. This could be viewed as socialistic because again it is congress that is rationing out the budgets that will allow these industries to thrive and function. Though they aren't dictating this in a totalitarian sense, the companies who do not get the business will more than likely have less employment then the companies who do get the contracts. Less employment translates to unemployment, and from the bottom line means the economy suffers.

Though the government doesn't pay every citizen in its nation, it does tax the checks that are paid by employers. When a person works they receive a check; when they receive that check, they can only cash it without another tax being associated with it if they use a bank. Using a bank tracts all of the spending and places the person within a certain economic and tax bracket. This bracket has a predetermined lifestyle and fate attached to it. From the wage they receive to the house they live in, it is an already pre-designed system to keep people working as productive members of society. A person who is a blue collar wage worker hasn't a clue their lifestyles are fixed in a particular economic or tax bracket; because they have hope which is reinforced by their religious faith, and further perpetuated through entertainment. The rags to riches stories of their favorite celebrities and personas they admire most in the media, ultimately gives them the drive and inspiration to race towards their goals. This hope is what many Black Nationalists as well as some political analysts cite as the cause in the people's celebrity worship of President Obama 19b. Because these nationalists and analysts do not understand Kabbalah nor do they understand the way the elements govern the existence of people from a higher plane, they are unable to see that all the praise and adulation President Obama has received is duly deserved. According to some views exchanged within these sects, this celebrity worship, collaged with what some political analysts feel is a savior's complex, has the American citizens, namely the youth, in a state of paralysis. If at any time the youth were to take an assessment of who is strong enough and capable enough to lead America out of its present dilemma; they wouldn't be able to fathom all of the details that come with being a ruler and maintaining a state. If the youth *were* to consciously assess these things, in my opinion, they would be able to see that what they are striving for in regards to equality may not necessarily be obtainable.

Though anyone can develop any business, for that startup business to compete, it is probably going to need a loan that comes from Uncle Sam. Even if the person who is starting that business is successful in obtaining the loan; that business is going to have a very difficult time competing with all the other various businesses within the same field.

We already stated the number one export in America is debt, and the second is film. The debt comes from establishing American ideologies within other countries. This is a process in imperialism where the more advanced nation uses its finances (banks) to build underdeveloped countries. In doing so, the "dream" or the pursuit of happiness through life, liberty, and property that America promotes via film, is wholly realized and fulfilled. Common sense tells a person that if they are unable to be part of the solution, than they are a part of the problem. Those who do not willingly serve are usually in some way made to serve. The free market is becoming dissolved because of the false state of wealth that was perpetuated by the free labor slavery provided. How can you compete in this society without having some form of cheap labor? There isn't any thriving competition, more so monopolies expanded by corporate mergers. Slavery and or cheap labor are one of the fundamental ways to develop wealth in any given market or field. Your either going to have those who see the bigger picture and willingly work very hard to achieve wealth with very little initial compensation; or you'll have those who because they do not understand the way wealth is made are forced to be laborious. Either way, slavery is another necessary evil and one that cannot be easily avoided.

The one thing the elder conservative property owners never properly owned up to is going to be the thing that bites them in the back. Because they ignored slavery and never took account for the atrocities associated with it, they're offspring will become slaves to the maintenance of the future state. What started with a certain group of people, blacks, has now been perpetuated to all colors of people. Contrary to what the younger generations think, if they somehow cannot become a productive member of society they will be discarded. Anything that doesn't produce must be eradicated as resources, land, and opportunities are limited. People who aren't contributors are dependents and add to the overall debt of their country. Because they are dependents, they are taken care of at the expense of the state and its tax payers. Anytime I think on these levels it takes me to the word genocide.

Genocide: deliberate and systematic destruction of a racial, political, or cultural group

Many civil wars have taken place that deal with ethnic cleansing. A character in the movie *the Godfather* states that every few years the families have a war to "purify" those with bad blood. The Bible speaks of much genocide; however these aspects of the Bible are almost always skipped over in Sunday sermons as people haven't the real ability to accept necessary evils especially when those evils pertain to death.

Ezekiel 9:3-5 *(3) Now the glory of the God of Israel went up from above the cherubim, where it had been, and moved to the threshold of the temple. Then the LORD called to the man clothed in linen who had the writing kit at his side (4) and said to him, "Go throughout the city of Jerusalem and put a mark on the foreheads of those who grieve and lament over all the detestable things that are done in it." (5) As I listened, he said to the others, "Follow him through the city and kill, without showing pity or compassion.(6) Slaughter old men, young men and maidens, women and children, but do not touch anyone who has the mark. Begin at my sanctuary." So they began with the elders who were in front of the temple.*

II Samuel 1*: Now it came to pass after the death of Saul, when David was returned from the <u>slaughter of the Amalekites,</u>*

II Samuel 8:3-5 *(3) David smote also Hadadezer, the son of Rehob, king of Zobah, as he went to recover his border at the river Euphrates. (4) And David took from him a thousand chariots, and seven hundred horsemen, and twenty thousand footmen: and David houghed all the chariot horses, but reserved of them for an hundred chariots. (5) And when the Syrians of Damascus came to succour Hadadezer king of Zobah, <u>David slew of the Syrians two and twenty thousand men.</u>*

The American people's fear of death shows their real faith in respects to who/what they perceive as God. If everybody believes that heaven is a real place they are going to experience when they die, and they are all "saved," why aren't they lining up willingly to die to get there? This was the former question that many Black Muslims challenged the Christian world with when the Jihadists were on the speculative suicide bombing missions of 911. This sect of (extremists) who were reported to practice Islam, felt they are the "true" believers. The Qur'an uses the exact word, *"Believers,"* when speaking about those who truly walk in the faith. For these individuals jihad was merely putting their money where their mouth is. They are so ingrained in their beliefs and their god that they are willing to die to bring down the people they perceive to be his enemies.

Jihad: (1) a holy war waged on behalf of Islam as a religious duty.

People whose life experience is miserable and loathsome, who rather than killing themselves to get to a better place, sulk in their depressed life and become hecklers, cynics, critics, and judges, should take a real assessment of their faith to see how it measures up with the faiths of others. They aren't lining up to die because they know they aren't living up to the standards described in the scriptures that would enable them to be admitted within the "pearly gates" of heaven. Meanwhile they sit and blame the government for the actions it takes to protect itself from such fickle and unpredictable subjects, and for these reasons, church and state were kept separate. How does a nation as colorful as America expect its government to take on all of the misunderstanding of such a diverse amount of people?

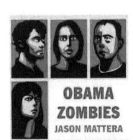

OBAMA
ZOMBIES
JASON MATTERA

How the
Liberal
Machine
Brainwashed
My Generation

The economic crisis of America 2008 - 2013 had America in disarray. With an abundance of its manufacturing and business being sent overseas, the American people were subject to whatever course of action the government had to take to ensure the nation survived. It hasn't become clear that America is becoming increasingly socialistic in the eyes of the young people, because young people have no real clue as to what the country they live in made its initial wealth from. When the youth come to the recognition that the free market they participate in is just that, "a free market," they will want the government to intercede and help them obtain prosperity. When everyone has the technology and the education to be a producer, where are they then going to find consumers? Upon this realization, the people will want to reverse the outcomes of the candidates they voted in office as they think these people aren't backed by huge special interest groups. These "subjects" feel the candidates they voted for, are his/her own independent freedom crusader, who understands their plight, and is sent to whisk them away from the "evil" dictator who previously held office. The political analysts and the Black Nationalists both agree that this is how simple the American people think in terms of their governmental candidates and how little they think about the special interest groups and bureaucracies who fund them.

No sooner than I finished this chapter in the book did I turn on the television and see the "tea baggers" a group of protestors avidly against Barack Obama. In watching the display of protest as outlined in a short documentary about the 9-12-09 Tea party, I saw the uncertainty in the eyes of those who protested. Their protest seemed to be motivated by fear more than anything else, as they had no real reason to be so against something that the documentary exposed they knew little about. I chose to tackle a lot of political issues because political correctness has caused the world to be so careful with what is said that the truth is no longer stated or even known. Anytime a political figure, or any large celebrity arises, more times than not, they are given a platform by somebody who needs them to promote their agenda. Look at the endorsements for Nike, L'Oreal, Sprite, Vitamin Water, etc. Each of the celebrities who promote these companies agendas are put there by the companies themselves. Understanding that someone has given them their platform I never look at the individual as the sole proprietor in any endeavor, good or bad. This means these companies are in tune with who the people want to see, and is why they give them the person they desire most. The fact that you have so many people against "change" in this country shows you how far it is from truly being a great melting pot where the differences of others are accepted and the lies and atrocities of the past are reconciled.

The only real belief that America's inhabitants' have is the belief of the almighty dollar. The government knows that this dollar has no real worth, which leaves the people who believe in it as expendable as the fiat substance they've pledged their allegiance to. Predominantly, much of the wealth in America has been inherited; this means that 60 to 75% of the present major corporations are built from old money; the same money collected from the direct or indirect profits received from the slave trade and all the commerce associated with it. On the flipside, having an autocratic government that rations out means of production is something that when lay people hear of (communism) they don't really comprehend. However in any family structure, business, and organization it teaches its members/employees to commune, or share, and this delegation almost always comes from the central power structure or head of the organization. In the old world this head was known as the father, i.e. Founding Fathers… now people may start to understand why the Lord's Prayer starts with *"Our father which art in Heaven."* These teachings are most fundamental because everyone having the same common goal innately understands that it is best there are public resources everyone can use and benefit from. For example:

everyone doesn't have a park in their back-yard, however there are public parks everyone can visit to facilitate their recreational activities. Taking the communal mind set and personifying it in government causes a person who desires to produce and sell at his own cost to be stifled and boxed in. This type of person wants the rewards of his harvest and hard work. Implementing a communistic form of thinking in a governmental structure is definitely thought to be the most evil of circumstances to a person with a mentality like this. When you think in terms of man as a species, a communistic government only makes it difficult for the people who haven't the ability or aren't suited for great work. Communism favors those who can work; however there is no incentive for the country to be productive. The nature of people is to do as little as they can to get by. When you couple this nature with communism it creates a state of stagnation and low productivity whereas in capitalism the more a person can work the more they can make. On the other hand capitalism in its purest form does contradict the actions of the people who pledge their allegiance to Jesus and his gospel; as again the golden rule is, *"Do unto others as you would have them do unto you."*

Matthew 22:37-39 (37) Thou shalt love the lord thy God with all thy heart, and with all thy soul, and with all thy mind (38) This is the first and great commandment (39) And the second is like unto it, Thou shalt love thy neighbor as thyself.

James 2:8 If ye fulfill the royal law according to the scriptures, Thou shalt love thy neighbor as thyself, ye do well.

Anyone who follows Jesus' instruction whole heartedly will inevitably become a communist, and becoming a communist makes you the enemy of a capitalist. I am not talking about the governmental structures of capitalism and communism; I'm talking about their root ideologies.

Ideology: (1) the integrated assertions, theories and aims that constitute a socio political program (2) visionary theorizing

If society teaches the people to capitalize but the Bible tells people to commune, how are people then able to recognize how they should be? The debate between the church and the state was one that was heavy upon the brows of the forefathers who built the American government. **Thomas Jefferson** made it a point to separate church from state [20].

Believing with you that religion is a matter which lies solely between Man & his God, that he owes account to none other for his faith or his worship, that the legitimate powers of government reach actions only, & not opinions, I contemplate with sovereign reverence that act of the whole American people which declared that their legislature should "make no law respecting an establishment of religion, or prohibiting the free exercise thereof, thus building a wall of separation between church and State - Thomas Jefferson [21].

In examining the way the founding fathers chose to separate church and state, we must first look beyond America to other countries with much older civilizations to see if they have developed similar conclusions. In ancient Israel, the priest and the king had separate roles. The priest was the head of all religious affairs and the king was subordinate to his authority as head of the state. This was because religious matters were thought to be of a higher importance because they governed the karma of the nation.

Karma: the force generated by a person's actions held in Hinduism and Buddhism to perpetuate transmigration and in its ethical consequences to determine the nature of the person's next existence

If this karma was offset there was nothing the king could do to reverse it. The king would actually rely on the priest to solve or intercede on the nation's behalf with God. Meaning if pestilence and famine were to overtake the kingdom what could the king really do? For these reasons although the king was the ruler and presided over the estate, the priest was regarded as the leader. The priests of that day were also astrologers, and they frequently advised the rulers as to what was going on in the "heavens" that would greatly affect the outcomes of the king's decisions.

Daniel 3:8-11 *(8) At this time some* <u>*astrologers*</u> *came forward and denounced the Jews. (9) They said to King Nebuchadnezzar, "O king, live forever! (10) You have issued a decree, O king, that everyone who hears the sound of the horn, flute, zither,* *lyre, harp, pipes and all kinds of music must fall down and worship the image of gold, (11) and that whoever does not fall down and worship will be thrown into a blazing furnace.*

In ancient Rome Emperors held the state's highest religious office and were commonly thought of as divine while living manifestations of God. When the people saw a political agenda associated with that of a spiritual one however, they often revolted. These are a few examples of the relations of the church and the state that show us just how difficult it is to have them separate but equal. The Bible implores its believers to be *in* but not *of* the world, yet the people of the world are whot the churches congregations are trying to reform. Society, however (*the real world/nature*) turns its citizens into people who have to capitalize if they wish to have an abundant life for themselves. This is what makes many people hypocrites. If you have a belief in Jesus and read about the parables of the rich ruler alongside several other passages in the Bible you get the sense that a person who has come up monetarily in a major way has "sold his/her soul" to get it. When you then look at these people with a microscopic lens, it's easy to find out if they did something that was directly against the spiritual laws that are outlined in the religions of Abraham. Upon the discovery that their closet isn't so clean, you now have all the ammunition necessary to caste them as unsaved and going to hell. This is what has happened recently on the internet in regards to celebrities who "*worship the Devil*" and the *Illuminati*, and as a result have grown to be rich and powerful.

James 2:6 but ye have despised the poor. Do not rich men oppress you, and draw you before the judgment of seats.

James 5:2-3 (2) you're riches are corrupted, and your garments are moth-eaten (3) your gold and silver is cankered; and the rust of them shall be a witness against you, and shall eat your flesh as if it were fire. Ye have heaped together treasure for the last days.

James 5:5-7 (5) Ye have lived in pleasure on the earth, and been wanton; ye have nourished your hearts as in the day of slaughter (6) Ye have condemned and killed the just; and he doth not resist you (7) Be patient therefore brethren unto the coming of the Lord.

The previously outlined communal mentality bred from Christianity and further perpetuated by slavery, has created a detrimental effect upon not just Black people, but society as a whole. I say this because the society in which we live is governed through a capitalistic means i.e. "*No church in the wild.*" This same society tolerates the "civil" savagery of the white collar world yet scrutinizes a milder less devastating "savagery" from those of the lower classes. Think about this, when were slaves ever in a place to capitalize, when they were brought to America as the ones to be capitalized upon. When wealth in this country is obtained by a free market capitalistic means, the people who are the subject of the capitalism are consumed *by* the capitalists.

America is a melting pot of all cultures and creeds of people. Most of those who have migrated to America have come in search of a better life for themselves and their families. When examining what they are in search of, prosperity and the pursuit of happiness, we find these 2 things embodied in what we call "*The American Dream.*" In examining this "dream" and all it entails, we must 1st explore who designed it, as well as at whose and at what expense it was created. Remember, the fundamental rule of economics is, *there is no such thing as a free lunch.* The most basic and fundamental rule of Economics has to be thoroughly investigated alongside America's origins and imperial roots to understand how this mentality has affected the current American society. When American soil was first imperialized by the Spanish and the French, history has recorded that millions of Indians (Native Americans) living holistic lives within the confines of nature were decimated in the millions. In fact, many of them were wiped out by European diseases like small pox and syphilis. Today Cancer has taken the place of these deadly diseases and is quickly becoming the main threat to all of our existences. This means the mere presence of those of European descent caused outbreaks and epidemics. When we look at the polluted world of today we have to analyze where and who this pollution came from? When we embark on a crusade to discover this we find out who the culprits are that created these conditions. Not only were the indigenous people wiped out due to illnesses, but the land they were occupying was taken from them and they were shipped off to live on reservations. The people who were capitalistic capitalized on the fact that these people had something they wanted. Markets were developing and settlers were coming from other places with money and families. So at the expense of the true American, the Native American, the current American society was formed. The movie *Avatar* is a great example of what I am referencing. You have a race of highly advanced people who are discriminated upon, taken advantage of, and their habitat and resources used as a means of commerce for the nations who are trying to imperialize and exploit them. The persons who are at the top "in the sky" (lofty positions) have no real sympathy or understanding for those at the bottom. This is how the mother brain of an entire civilization is referenced as being "just some trees." The fact that the comprehension levels of those in power and high positions (in the movie) are low, shows they haven't the ability to really understand the brilliance in which the culture they wish to destroy has. One could make an argument that if the "sky people" really did understand the indigenous culture, they would not be destroying them, rather, learning their ways. I used this point to show how differences in comprehension levels cause misinterpretations, created dogmas, and cancerous biases that ultimately lead to war and destruction.

Today America is home to people from every corner of the earth. When looking at all of the various cultures who abandoned their land in search of economic prosperity, it is a fact that the Negro was the only race that was taken and brought to America against their will. When asking one's self why these other cultures have come to America, many will say that where they came from was a third world country. In America it is no longer a dream to have running water, strip malls, and public transit systems. But let's think about this critically; why is America developed, and who developed it?

The Book of Illumination

CHAPTER 8
MASTER BUILDERS

The Book of Illumination

CHAPTER 8
MASTER BUILDERS

MASTER BUILDERS

When we think about all of the innovation that black people have done in the ancient world, we get a real picture of the biblical scriptures  and the relevance of those scriptures within American culture. When you look at the pyramids alongside the advanced civilization of Phoenicia, a city in Canaan, it is easy to see the remarkable achievements of those who lived on the African Continent. A fleet of Phoenician royal sailing ships reported to be over 5,000 years old were discovered eight miles from the Nile on December 2, 1991 by American and Egyptian archeologists. These ships were said to be burial ships, however, there were also ocean going vessels totaling 140 feet found near the Great pyramid of Giza that were reportedly capable of withstanding the oceans most powerful waves and the seas most tumultuous conditions 21d. When you combine the design of the ships with the way these (Phoenician) people had mapped out the galaxy and its stars, one can easily correlate they were perhaps, the first civilizations to circumnavigate the globe by using the constellations.

Acts 28:11KJV (28) and after three months we departed in a ship of Alexandria, which had wintered in the isle, whose sign was Castor and Pollux.

 This passage in the Bible says the way (Paul and others) knew where the isle of (Rome) was located was by way of the astrological constellation of Castor and Pollux that was above it. This is proof that sailing and navigation was indeed done by using constellations. Africans from Phoenicia also known as Canaanites had circumnavigated the world and visited every continent several times over before Rome ever existed. When you are privy to this information you get a portrait of just how advanced those ancient civilizations were.

What is even more interesting is the interpretation the NIV Bible (New International Version) gives about the account. 21b

Acts 11:28 NIV (28) After three months we put out to sea in a ship that had wintered in the island. It was an Alexandrian ship with the figurehead of the twin gods Castor and Pollux.

This passage implies the ship had a figurehead on it of the twin gods Castor and Pollux, not the constellation above the island they used to find it. This is very disturbing to witness because either the people who re-wrote the Bible think people are stupid, or they do not really understand what they are translating and re-writing. I personally do not think they are this careless or incompetent. This seems to be a ploy to cover up any evidence that would show this ancient culture to be highly sophisticated in Astrology and Astronomy to the point where they used these sciences to circumnavigate the globe. This fact is further evident in the way the retranslated biblical scriptures reference the twin constellations (Castor &Pollux) as being "gods."

After taking an assessment of the advanced technological cities of Sumer and Cairo it makes a person have to question what has been taught to them for most of their lives about the Bible, Africa, and the advancement of the inhabitants living there. When we ask the question, what are the greatest and most profound structures ever built on earth, only two come to mind; they are the Pyramids in Egypt, and the Great Wall of China. While scientists can identify the race and nationality of the people who built the Great Wall, they seem to get dumbfounded about who built the pyramids. Suddenly though all the clues are staring them in the face, it becomes a great mystery. Because it was written that blacks had no contribution toward the advancement of ancient civilization, it has caused the "Living God" to be further thought of as an unseen God. When we look at America we are looking at Egypt; the reason this is stated is both scientific and spiritual. The same people that built up Egypt and its culture are the descendants of the same people who built up America. This body can be collectively known as the body of the Most High God which literally points to Sun and Star. These are the master builders of society in the sense they are the "Godsends" and avatars who possess the talents that make it possible for everyone else on earth to live in a more "God" like "heavenly state." Through their talents "what they are born with" they upgrade the culture in ways unlike "normal" people causing the culture itself to strive for excellence. However this "heavenly state" wasn't to be lived in against the laws of nature. Going against the laws of nature actually threatens the culture built by these godsends and avatars because they were fashioned by the hand of nature itself. Nature and creation have a balance and a harmony associated with them. What I mean by this is animals do exactly what they are meant to do and nothing else. They don't go outside of how, and what they were created to be. When we look at nature we have to understand it in order to find our harmony within it. If a person has a truly whole thought, this thought will be processed three hundred and sixty degrees. Western society suffers from linear thinking rather than elliptical thinking. The ideology that it accepts views situations, energy, and life, as having ends when eastern philosophy teaches that the end of one thing is merely the beginning of the same thing. Let's take life and death for instance. When we look at life and death from a linear perspective, you live, you die that's it (YOLO.) Even though this is contradictory to what nature shows us we accept it; and this acceptance, causes us to fall in a delusion. A delusion that makes us think that we can do whatever it is we want, how we want, and when we want. While this is true because we possess freewill, also with these choices come consequences and repercussions. Upon acting in this freewill, we must first take into account the consequences that will arise because of our actions. If we do unnatural things, unnatural things are going to happen. We can't perversely manipulate nature and then think that we ourselves won't become perverted. And when we become perverted, we can't say we are "regular" because we don't want to be looked at as perverts.

By examining Roman or Greco Roman society we find that the whole culture was amerced in homosexuality. From the sculptures of Michelangelo to the Priesthood of the Vatican that has come under constant scrutiny with allegations and convictions of priests who molest boys; it is common knowledge that the culture in which I am referencing openly and freely practiced homosexuality. While everything has an equal and opposite reaction, all beings from all spectrums of life with all their respective beliefs have the right to live and practice whatever it is they want as long as it is not a detriment to the state. Even if it is a detriment to the individual one should still have the choice in how he/she will live.

In analyzing this American culture of today it has become more tolerant and now openly accepts the gay culture and is slowly promoting it as an alternative lifestyle to hetero sexual relationships. While nature has yet to condone two of the same human sexes being able to procreate, people with freewill have. The same way wars have been justified, the same way people are able to pollute their bodies with tar and formaldehyde (cigarettes.) The same way women are given a choice for abortion, and humans freely slaughter and eat other animal's shows the people who are living in this world have become bored with the regular everyday sequence of life that a "natural" lifestyle entails. The people on this earth today are seeking to explore new

151

horizons; and because they have no one to navigate them, they have to in a sense experiment and test the waters, to seek out the paths that have led to their existences. Romanticism paints the picture of the picket fence, virgin wife, well off husband who then marry, have a girl and a boy, and live happily ever after. However, this is too often not the case, and for these reasons who has the authority to tell another how they should live or be? This makes the great cliché "*do as thou will*", have such great power. By doing what it is you will, you come out with the answer that led you down your path. Every path leads to an end, and every end is a beginning. One possessing this type of mind frame inherently develops an existentialist point of view where they then become sensual, refined, and cultured by way of their experiences. They then go on to promote these experiences encouraging others to partake in all that life has to offer; the beauty, the ugliness, the pleasure, the pain, the suffering, the liberation, the death, and the rebirth. It is all a cycle and each individual is on a path of discovery.

Whenever man begins to only value that which is beautiful and becomes vain, and obsessed with himself, the people who breed within this type of mind-frame in the society will indeed breed into existence beings who only value vanity, and beauty. Thurman Fleet wrote about this when he outlined the destructive dynamics of vanity. He said, "*Whenever the desire for recognition assumes control of the psychic life of an individual, there is a constant striving for power and superiority which expresses itself in thoughts of activities which seek to display and glorify the self. Such an individual soon loses his contact with reality. Not only is the individual engaged in useless and needless efforts centered about the mere presence of things, ignoring their true nature and value, but his chief concern being the opinions and impressions of others regarding himself he loses his understanding of the human relationship.*" Vanity and beauty are both traits associated with femininity. Femininity is the most dominating energy in the universe and if unchecked has the ability to mask all signs of masculinity. Femininity becomes enhanced with luxury and domestic accommodations and causes all things masculine to become lax, and in a state where the feminine persuasion, which rules all things domestic, cancels out the masculinity.

Breeding any type of beings into existence causes those who are created in it to feel normal. They feel "God" created them just as "God" created everything else. The problem with this thinking is it isn't just God who creates humans; humans also create humans. Because most read in the Genesis that "God" created man, they accept this god as being the entity who created them, and without any real thought they have obliged to this belief pattern. This phenomenon is known as the "*willing suspension of disbelief*" and it generally works when you give a person a reasonably unreasonable world to ponder about. Man has to understand that it is his thoughts, his knowledge, and energy that are transmuted through sperm. The most powerful of his thoughts which are the thoughts he gives the most energy too, will be the one that hits the egg. In this scenario any and all types of beings have the ability to be born in the world and will eventually exist within society. For these reasons, you cannot discriminate on any one of them. What religion has tried to accomplish is the structuring and reordering of the self. If you are ordered and structured, you will have also structured your thoughts. With a little bit of discipline towards what your intended goal is, you can literally create whatever being you want through a vessel who has submitted to your thought process. This of course is from a masculine perspective but it also works with the feminine as well. Now–a–days you can't diagnose the conditions of manifested thoughts (people) that "society" has deemed to be out of nature and if you do it with accuracy, you are looked at as a hater, and a judge. This is why so many prophets of the Bible had such a hard time speaking to the people. If society had any real intelligence they would recognize that those who are preaching or teaching something that is so hated and despised have to either be very stupid or really know what they are talking about. Prophets in the Bible were people who went against the grain; in fact, many including Jesus loathed the missions they had to do.

Matthew 17:17 O faithless and perverse generation How long shall I be with you? How long shall I suffer you?

Matthew 26:39 O my father, if it be possible let this cup pass from me nevertheless not as I will, but as thou wilt.

The prophets were those who lived outside the "inn" thing and in fact did the opposite. In them going the opposite direction they were able to see why society was the way it was, and also where it was headed. These prophets were in a sense watchers and they participated in watching the fates of men. Prophets were different from godsends because godsends sometimes aren't conscious of their existence. Meaning these godsends are just functioning within their respective capacities involuntarily, unbeknownst to themselves and "they just do it." They are in certain capacities unaware of how bright and evolved they are and in many cases are unaware of who they "really" are. When I say godsends that are master builders I'm not talking about physical builders, I'm talking about people who through their monumental achievements in the arts, sports, innovation, leadership, medicine, and music that have given the American society its culture. Though the blacks who were slaves were instrumental in building this great nation we call America;

building doesn't only apply to inanimate objects. The building I'm referring to also has to do with the creation of heightened beings. Though all the people who contributed to American society's development weren't black, the ones who are prophesized about in the Bible are. I do not wish to sound fascist in the sense that I cannot recognize the achievements of those who are not black. I am merely highlighting this point with emphasis because it was said that blacks had no contribution towards the development of civilization, namely ancient civilization.

 Even in ancient Greece during the 7th century on Greek pottery the gods were depicted as black figures with engraved outlines on yellow and red clay backgrounds; these artifacts are now mostly lost but are still known through literary sources 21c.

Fascism: (1) a political philosophy, movement, or regime that exalts nation and often race above the individual and that stands for a centralized autocratic government headed by a dictatorial leader.

Inanimate: (1) not endowed with life or spirit

Remember when "God" is referenced in the Bible what is being referenced is an omnipotent physically Living God. This type of god has to be understood in this way to show that the characteristics of these people who are "animated" within this book equal to that of a "Living God." If you take the fact that this "God" is a physical living entity out, then it corrupts the language and understanding of this god and the scriptures in reference to him and his people. When the Bible is read from a logical standpoint it is easy to see how the mysteries associated within it can make the reader become atheist. This is stated due to the talking of snakes, parting of seas, and women being created from ribs; all of which have appeared in the Bible. If people had the legend behind these stories they would be able to take from them the relevance they bear. Instead, people have literally believed these things, and the literal interpretation has caused a huge imbalance in what people think and believe to be God. The god of society is the god of the people themselves. Every person you talk to has a theory of their own personal god and because they don't understand Astrology they have no clue as to what aspect of "God" (planet) rules within them. Because each person has something to say about God and is equally ignorant and passionate about it, any higher authority like the government has to learn how to separate a person's "delusion" from the actual higher power. The American Government has done so by replacing the name of the Living God Adonis or Adonai Yahweh or Jehovah and or Ba'al to GOD which is an acronym for Government of Democracy (G.O.D.) When you see IN GOD WE TRUST on money don't get so excited; just know that the God that is being referenced is everyone's own personal God at once the ALMIGHTY DOLLAR. Even this dollar has the God of Abraham and the God of Israel depicted on its back which is why there is an All Seeing Eye on one side representing the Sun who is the father, and an eagle holding thirteen arrows in his talons who is his son.

BLACK GOLD

There is a highly rich, highly imperialized area on the planet located in the middle-eastern parts of the world. Below Asia and right in the middle region of Africa, is where the most bountiful and plentiful human resource known to man once existed; untainted, untouched, and in a state of Eden-like isolation. The resource was coal black and if refined in the right manner, would revolutionize the world yielding its great energy potential. In the early 1500's the pioneers came and the extracting began. They probed very deep to find the best reserves of that pure black original substance that harnesses energy like the sun. In droves, power hungry companies and pioneers came to the place where this seemingly "black god was found." They began tearing up its habitat, separating its chemical parts, and proceeded to distribute it all around the world. The western hemisphere was industrialized as a result, and an economic boom spread throughout the western regions of the globe. The black substance I speak of isn't oil, but like oil, is the fuel that the rest of the world runs on....It's the nation God chose to be the burden bearers of Society, the niggers.

MY BROTHER"S KEEPER

In the "literal" interpretation of the story of Jacob and Esau is where we see the legacy of the older nation Esau allegorized as (Egypt) supplanted by the younger nation (Rome) allegorized by Jacob. However we have to consider the legitimacy of the event. It seems that Jacob did, according to Christian faith, something very un-godly in obtaining his brother's birth right; nonetheless the man who dwells in tents became the heir to the covenant established with Abraham according to the scriptures. The very fact the people who established this society established it as a means of manicuring (man/cure) nature, is a testament to how this mentality has bled into them also manicuring "God." 21 *"I scornfully defy all mortals with the open acknowledgement: I have stolen the golden vase of the Egyptians, to raise a tabernacle to my God far from the land of Egypt. I cast the die and write a book for the present or for posterity. God awaited six thousand years for a thinking observer."* Johannes Kepler 22.

Johannes Kepler was credited as pioneering the discovery the Earth and the other planets revolve around the Sun. Though this proclamation states that he stole it from the Egyptians, history (his/story) however, still credits him as being a primary and chief advocate of this knowledge. Here is the way that Egyptians told the same story over 3,500 years B.C. according to Graham Hancock's *The Fingerprints of the Gods* 23. *In the tomb of Unas in the Great Pyramid is a glyph of Ra the Sun God who sits upon an iron throne encircled by lesser gods that move around him constantly.* This is an obvious depiction of how the Sun is orbited by the other planets which also has been translated in the story of Jesus who is circled by twelve disciples, note disc in the word disciples. This piece of knowledge was supposedly unproven to the world until the European renaissance whereby Johannes Kepler expounding on Copernicus's heliocentric model was the "publicist "of the idea. Johannes Kepler openly admits that his god is different from the one that he has stolen this legacy from. The story of Jacob and Esau is a very good reference point that shows the true nature and thought process of the founding forefathers of America. The fact that Jacob got the birthright and blessing is a story that tells within a story how the romantics supplanted the Egyptians in matters that pertain to religion, philosophy, and science by dressing up like them and playing their role in academia and history.

24 Ozymandius a character in the movie the watchman known as *the smartest man in the world* has dressed up as an Egyptian god and also found a way to market his secret societies super powers to the world. This enables him to become a savior and a god through necessary means of genocide. The character created in *The Watchman* is a direct reflection of the founding fathers of America as they are caricaturized in the movie by **Ozymandius.** He is the embodiment of what they represent as well as the actions they have taken to build and construct this great nation of America.

*Ezekiel 3:17 Son of Man, I have made thee a **watchman** unto the house of Israel: therefore hear the word at my mouth, and give them warning of me.*

The same way the gospel of Matthew was given so the people could understand the teachings of Moses; another gospel is needed for the present time to clear up the teachings of Jesus. When one reads the Bible it is easy to see apparent contradictions. These contradictions have come about because the historical aspects of the Bible and the participants therein have indeed been falsified. Because of the falsification of the records and accounts, those who seek true enlightenment will never meet it until they are initiated in the knowledge of the occult which serves as the underlying meanings of what the scriptures superficially represent. This "world" of understanding is what Jesus was initiating his disciples into, and is referred to as *"the kingdom of heaven"* in the Gospels. Heaven as cited in the Bible is the sky. The sky is where the stars and celestial (heavenly) beings (constellations) are seen; thus the *"kingdom of heaven"* is the kingdom of the stars.

Genesis 1:7-8 *(7) And God made the firmament, and divided the waters which were under the firmament from the waters which were above the firmament: and it all was so (8) And* <u>*God called the firmament Heaven*</u>*, and the evening and the morning was the second day.*

<u>Firmament</u>: the arch or vault of heaven, sky

<u>Rapture:</u> to be swept away by the divine knowledge of the Supreme God

Though the *"kingdom of heaven"* is an astrological reference; teaching Astrology to the masses in an open forum raises many questions for those who are skeptics. For one, when people are exposed to their actual astrological signs, if they perceive them to be unfavorable, they no longer want to acknowledge what sign and energy they fall under. Most people want to see themselves in the best light possible and when this is not reflected within their signs the way they think or feel it should, they often reject them. This is why discretion is a must when teaching the mysterious aspects of the scriptures and the real walk of Jesus.

In studying Christianity, it is common to see people who congregate together in the belief that when they die they will ascend to a higher heaven in the clouds. The people who subscribe to this belief system also believe Jesus is going to descend from the clouds to earth, and whisk them away with him to heaven. They believe this to be true because of scriptures like 1st Thessalonians 4:16 and Revelation 1:7 which states *"he comes with clouds."*

Revelation 1:7 Behold, he cometh with clouds; and every eye shall see him, and they also which pierced him: and all kindreds of the earth shall wail because of him.

On Michael Jackson's *This is it* cover he is prostrated in a position as if he is being hung from a cross like Jesus. Also within the picture's background are clouds. Every eye did see Michael Jackson and all kindred of people wailed all over the earth when the entertainer mysteriously died as he is the most popular and recognizable person on the planet. In fact, the only two words that are used more, and are more popular than his name, are Coca-Cola and Amen.

1Thessalonians 4:16 (16) For the Lord himself shall descend from heaven with a shout, with the voice of the archangel, and with the trump of God, and the dead in Christ shall rise first (17) Then we which are alive and remain shall be caught up together with them in the clouds to meet the Lord in the Air: and so shall we be with the Lord.

I myself understand what it is to be from above. People with heightened mind states as well as elevated understandings in this society are most often *alienated*. When you bring into the fourfold the knowledge of the stars as explained in Astrology, as well as the elated philosophies which "*alienate*" those with these understandings; it is easy to see how someone with a layman comprehension level would caricaturize these individuals as being extraterrestrial or Vulcan. But if you asked most Christians they would tell you that *they* don't believe in (extraterrestrial beings.) The way that Paul has described the rapture would have to be something like extraterrestrials that are coming to earth to save the righteous people from the evil ones. The rapture as well as the perception of what aliens are has been so thwarted that people who haven't the ability to truly see and understand will be left behind when indeed the truth and the rapture hits the world. **Nicolas Cage** recently had a movie about the abduction of kids by extraterrestrials that included this same argument; the movie was called *The Knowing*. What was so amazing about this translation of the rapture was how the kids were taken up in an Ark and the adults were left behind. When you look at a person like Michael Jackson whose life and walk on earth in every way seemed alien and extraterrestrial, and simultaneously factor how the young people of the world were enraptured by his message and presence; it makes the imagery portrayed in the film *the Knowing* all that much more powerful. The "alien" Michael Jackson came to earth to whisk the children away to heaven, which is a place on earth that exists within a *higher* consciousness. The consciousness that creates this heaven is love, harmony, fun, responsibility, joy, praise, singing, dancing, youth, excitement, beauty, and peace; all things that Michael Jackson promoted within his music, life, and message. Many Christians today have not looked at the rapture in this way for they are caught up in emotion, and due to a lack of comprehension, they have accepted the literal interpretations of other supernatural things that are discussed in the Bible. If you don't understand what the resurrection is and what Jesus's mission is when he comes, you will take this out of context. There is no doubt that certain scriptures are written out of context because of Paul; who according to scripture, never physically met Jesus. The only time Paul met Jesus was on the way to Damascus where Paul says he saw a light others saw, but heard a voice they didn't.

Acts 22:6-9 (6) And it came to pass, that, as I made my journey, and was come nigh unto Damascus about noon, suddenly there shone from heaven a great light round about me (7) And I fell to the ground and heard a voice saying unto me, **Saul, Saul why persecutest thou me?** *(8) And I answered, Who art thou, Lord? And he said unto me,* **I am Jesus of Nazareth, whom thou persecutest.** *(9) And they that were with me saw indeed the light, and were afraid; but they heard not the voice of him that spake to me.*

What is strange about this scripture is Paul has admitted the men he was with didn't hear the voice. However Luke, who is reported to have written the **Acts**, tells a different story. The reason this raises eyebrows is if Luke corroborate Paul's story by saying the men that were with Paul heard the voice, then a person could conclude that Paul has made the whole story up.

Acts 9:3-7 (3) And as he journeyed he came near Damascus: and suddenly there shined round about him a light from heaven: (4) And he fell to the earth, and heard a voice saying unto him, **Saul Saul, why persecutest thou me?** *(5) And he said, Who art thou, Lord? And the Lord said,* **I am Jesus whom thou persecutest: it is hard for thee to kick against pricks.** *(6) And he (Saul) trembling and astonished said, Lord, what wilt thou have me to do? And the Lord said unto him,* **Arise and go into the city, and it shall be told thee what thou must do.** *(7) And the men, which journeyed with him stood speechless, hearing a voice, but seeing no face.*

This is more evidence that suggest that man has come along and tried to re-write and translate important facts out of the Bible. Most of the text that is used in this book is from the Gospel of Matthew because the Gospel of Luke contradicts itself tremendously. According to the scripture in the Book of Acts, everything Paul experienced could be of his own mind and premonition. One might wish to believe what Paul is saying if they don't know who Paul really is. In fact when Paul says he himself saw Jesus, which he didn't, (he saw a light) it causes us to readily check the validity of his whole statement. Paul saw Jesus according to his own admission when he saw a light. If Paul is validated in seeing a light that no one can disprove he saw, any and everyone who sees a light and hears a voice is valid in attributing that light and that voice as coming from God. Jim Jones heard a voice allegedly from God, and it ended up with 900 dead people poisoned from cyanide in Jonestown. David Koresh heard the voice of God and it led to the burning and deaths of dozens of people at Mt. Caramel in Waco, Texas. Could it be that suddenly within himself Paul felt convicted for all of the wrongdoings in his past? Is this a clever attempt by a Pharisee to lead the people back into the church after witnessing Jesus lead the people away from the church? Is Paul on a covert operation (under cover) to lead the people back to the institution that will indoctrinate them, making the priests and aristocrats rich? Did Paul with the priests conspire to come up with this plan after they executed Jesus? Maybe the priests thought the people's faith was unshaken in Jesus even after they killed him and they used Paul to lead the "flock" back within the confines of the church. Sounds like a conspiracy theory right? Before you dismiss this as that, think back to *Watergate, Whitewater, the Iran Contra Scandal, and 911.* Even then in the biblical times the priest used lies, deceit, and false witnesses to defame believers who were upright in the eyes of the multitudes/ masses.

Acts 6:8-12 (8) And Stephan full of faith and power, did great wonders and miracles among the people. (9) Then there arose certain of the synagogue, which is called the synagogue of the Libertines, and the Cyrenians, and the Alexandrians, and of them of Cilicia and of Asia, disputing with Stephen (10) And they were not able to resist the wisdom and the spirit by which he spake (11) Then they suborned men, which said, We have heard him speak blasphemous words against Moses and against God. (12) And they stirred up the people, and the elders, and the scribes, and came upon him, and caught him, and brought him to the council (13) And set up false witnesses, which said, this man ceaseth not to speak blasphemous words against this holy place and the law.

This scripture surely present with evidence the possibility that the "Roman authorities" could have created Paul in an espionage fashion as the person to covertly disassemble the congregation that follows Jesus. Robert Lomas seems to agree as he stated in **The Second Messiah** that, "*Gentile Christians merged myths of their old gods and the cult conceived by Paul to create a hybrid religion that had great appeal.*" He went on to further say that *Paul was never accepted by the Jerusalem church. He misunderstood their Jewish theology and turned it into a cult suitable for Romans 23b.*

I drew the same conclusion after reading the Gospel of Matthew and comparing it to the writings of Paul in his sermons to the Corinthians, and Galatians.

Matthew 21:40-41& 45 & 46 (40) When the lord therefore of the vineyard cometh, what will he do unto those husbandmen? (41) They say unto him, He will miserably destroy those wicked men, and will let out his vineyard unto other husbandmen, which shall render him the fruits in their seasons. (45) And when the chief priests and Pharisees had heard his parables, they perceived that he spake of them (46) But when they sought to lay hands on him, they feared the multitude, because they took him for a prophet.

The scriptures above indicate that even then the Jews could not harm Jesus publically for fear of the people because the people thought him to be a prophet. In order to get rid of Jesus they have to conspire secretly to come up with a plot to kill him. Realizing this and then diagnosing the social climate of America, in conjunction with the ancient world, one could see how the prophecies regarding Israel are directly related to America. If a person were to say the Americans crucified Jesus, would he be talking about the nationality of the people who actually did it or the country the people were living in when the crucifixion happened? When the scriptures says the Jews rejected Jesus, we think that it is specific to all Jews and not a basic generalization of the nationality of the people who were living in the region where all this took place. The words could easily be switched to the Americans crucified the Christ, rather than the Jews crucified Jesus. This allows us to see that it is very unfair when classifying a nationality of people and generalizing what a few have done as if the entire nation is guilty of the offense.

Many of today's Blockbuster movies have themes associated with Alien invasions. *Transformer's* and the *Avengers* are amongst the most popular titles associated to this theme. December 21, 2012 marked the Winter Solstice as well as the ending and beginning of a new age. The *"end of times"* prophecy acknowledges this date on the Mayan calendar as the ending rule of mortals into the beginning reign of the Egyptian Gods. Due to the fear of what this may "actually" mean; Hollywood through its movies have vilified these beings of higher consciousness and demonized their existences. In all actuality, Michael Jackson (Joseph) and Barack Obama (Ephraim) represent in reality the return of the Egyptian gods who have ruled the earth with their remarkable talents, abilities, and celestial makeups, every time they've existed. These "extraterrestrial" beings from (heaven) / (outer-space) have come and reshaped the American culture and as a result the world is uplifted.

The Book of Illumination

CHAPTER 9
IN CHRIST

The Book of Illumination

CHAPTER 9
IN CHRIST

IN CHRIST

The "*in Christ*" of mind and heart promoted by modern day evangelists, is very different from the Christ that is literally a man. My question to religious preachers, scholars and theologians of the world today is this, "When did the Christian world forget about the man that is Christ, and when did Paul stop becoming a persecutor?" It looks to me as if Jesus' fame and power was so immense and great that Saul/ Paul could no longer be against him publically or overtly, but covertly he could make the gospel given by Jesus his own. Saul in the times of David did something very similar to David that Paul or Saul of Tarsus (Turkey) has done to Jesus. David was promised to be the king; however Saul at every attempt tried to block David from ascending to his throne.

1 Samuel 18:6-12 (6) And it came to pass as they came, when David was returned from the slaughter of the Philistine, that the women came out of all cities of Israel, singing and dancing, to meet king Saul, with tabrets, with joy, and with instruments of musick. (7) And the women answered one another as they played, and said, Saul hath slain his thousands, and David his ten thousands. (8) And Saul was very wroth, and the saying displeased him; and he said, They have ascribed unto David ten thousands, and to me they have ascribed but thousands: and what can he have more but the kingdom? (9) And Saul eyed David from that day and forward. (10) And it came to pass on the morrow, that the evil spirit from God came upon Saul, and he prophesied in the midst of the house: and David played with his hand, as at other times: and there was a javelin in Saul's hand. (11) And Saul cast the javelin; for he said, I will smite David even to the wall with it. And David avoided out of his presence twice. (12) And Saul was afraid of David, because the LORD was with him, and was departed from Saul.

Saul or Paul of the New Testament has tried to pervert and block the message of the Son of David (Jesus) just as Saul in the Old Testament tried to block David from being the King. Paul was leading a people with a low comprehension of Jewish custom and heritage (Gentiles) to a state of spiritual confusion. The NIV translates the word Gentiles from the KJV to mean Greeks. If this is true, everything that has happened in reference to Greek culture or Greco-Roman culture is that of Gentilian influence; everything from the Vatican itself, to the Greek Pantheon of gods who preside over Mount Olympus. What is equally strange or similar, is the fact that the Saul of the OT in the Book of Samuel was of the tribe of Benjamin, just as Saul of Tarsus is of the tribe Benjamin in the NT. Seeing that I have just posted the account whereby Saul has tried to murder David, who Jesus is called the Son of, really foreshadows that Saul/Paul, who was a murderer of Christians, has done the very same thing by blocking Jesus from being seen as he is, "a man" versus as he is thought of '*in Christ.*"

Philippians 3:4-5 *(4) Though I (**Paul**) might also have confidence in the flesh. If any other man thinketh that he hath whereof he might trust in the flesh, I more: (5) Circumcised the eighth day, of the stock of Israel, of the tribe of Benjamin, an Hebrew of the Hebrews; as touching the law, a Pharisee.*

1 Samuel 9:1 *(1) Now there was a man of Benjamin, whose name was Kish, the son of Abiel, the son of Zeror, the son of Bechorath, the son of Aphiah, a Benjamite, a mighty man of power. (2) And he had a son, whose name was **Saul**, a choice young man, and a goodly: and there was not among the children of Israel a goodlier person than he: from his shoulders and upward he was higher than any of the people.*

I explained earlier how the ministry and testimony of Paul lowered the bar by making it possible for anybody to become ordained and lead the unsaved "sinners" to an unseen and unknown God. Because this has happened, a very perverse way of thinking has developed in the Christian world of today. I say this because Paul's ministry is mainly to the Gentiles. It is no secret that Paul is known as the "*Apostle of the Gentiles.*" This confusion is why the Christ of today is only relative to the point of view in which each person is referencing him, meaning that Christ changes with each different person that you ask 24.

No public man believes that the Bible means what it says: he is always convinced that it says what he means - **George Bernard Shaw** 25.

The point of view taken by many Christians leaves important detailed facts about the life of Christ out of their ministries. This in turn creates the "In Christ" mentality that changes the actual Christ, which is a sprit that resides in a human that relates to all other spirits, into just the spirit that resides in all humans. Now the man who is to come (one day) has turned into a spirit (premonition) that guides Christians every day. Christ guided his disciples in spirit, but he also was there physically. The way the world has changed a living man, into the spirit of their mind, the (in Christ) has led to a falling away of the central and original purpose of THE Christ.

Whenever you think about a super hero or super persona the next big thing has to be of greater significance or importance for it to be considered as great as or greater than its predecessor. This means that a true student/apprentice will supersede his master in his works. How then is Paul so commendable when he hasn't even scratched the surface in the magnitude of Jesus who superseded Moses? According to the Gospel of Matthew Jesus was coming to restore what was lost, as well as fulfill prophecy.

THE GOD OF IS-RA-EL

The prophecies written in the Old Testament in Jeremiah and Isaiah say the LORD of Israel in the form of a lion is coming to destroy the Gentiles.

Jeremiah 4:7 <u>*The lion is come up from his thicket, and the destroyer of the Gentiles is on his way*</u>*; he is gone forth from his place to make thy land desolate; and thy cities shall be laid waste, without an inhabitant.*

Isaiah 42 *Behold my servant, whom I uphold; mine elect, in whom my soul delighteth; I have put my spirit upon him; he shall bring forth judgment to the Gentiles.*

Isaiah 42:13 *The Lord shall go forth as a mighty man, he shall stir up Jealousy like a man of war: he shall cry yea, <u>roar</u>; he shall prevail against his enemies.*

Isaiah 10:33 *Behold, the lord, the Lord of Hosts shall lop the bough with terror: and the high ones of stature shall be hewn down, and the haughty shall be humbled.*

What we have to realize about the God of Abraham, Isaac, and Jacob is the fact the Bible speaks in reference to a <u>Living</u> God.

Jeremiah 10:10 *(10) But ADONAI, God, is the true God, the living God, the everlasting king. At his anger, the earth trembles; the nations cannot endure his fury.* – *Complete Jewish Bible*

Jeremiah 10:10 *(10) But Jehovah is the true God; he is the living God, and an everlasting King: at his wrath the earth trembleth, and the nations are not able to abide his indignation.* *- American Standard Bible*

Jeremiah 10:10 *– (10) But the LORD is the true God, he is the living God, and an everlasting king: at his wrath the earth shall tremble, and the nations shall not be able to abide his indignation.* *- King James Bible*

 The God of Israel is the God of Isis, Ra, and El. Isis has two forms, Scorpio and Virgo which represent her dual nature of femininity polarized by earth and water. This is why the glyphs in Astrology for the two signs have **M's**; the Scorpio has a devil's tale at the end of it and the Virgo's **M** forms into a fish. Ra and El which are Leo and Aquarius represent the God in both his masculine forms. You have the god of the air respective to sky and star, Aquarius; and you have the god of fire, respective to sun and

space, Ra. Ra is the god of the Sun/ Lion and El which means He/Him is the *Man*, Aquarius. Isis and her two forms of Scorpio and Virgo counter each other in several Biblical characters; Mary Magdalene and Mother Mary are the most notable. John the Baptist and Jesus counter each other as well in the forms of Leo and Aquarius. These two opposing polarities show the spectrum of being in reference to the masculine and feminine worlds. These 4 types of existences oppose each other in nature yet show the two sides of the individual self within every human (individe/dual.) Although in Astrology the fixed polar opposite to Scorpio is Taurus (ruled by Venus) the biblical scriptures have given allegorical clues that the two feminine aspects that are in opposition to one another are the two Mary's (**M's**) the virgin and the Magdalene which Libra is in between. In Astrology these three signs show how these two aspects of femininity balance each other out. In the Virgo Mary you have a mother and a lover of her man, and in the Scorpio Mary you have a lover and a pleaser of THE men. You have the man who is seen as the "God" when in his most carnal/ priestly form as the Aquarius; and Leo, who is God as a man in his spiritual/ kingly form. These attributes of king and priest are interchangeable between these signs when looking at them from different perspectives. The movie *The Watchmen* shows this theme through the *Smartest Man* in the world and *Dr. Manhattan.* Dr. Manhattan is the god in the form of a man who destroys man, and is very knowledgeable and scientific. He is so one with nature that his existence becomes involuntary with it i.e. nirvana. In the movie *The Watchmen,* Dr. Manhattan after destroying himself, recreates himself out of a triple darkness, perfecting his existence. Because he is perfect and understands life to be just that, his nirvana makes him incapable of trying to save anything, as he sees it is all part of a larger equation. Manhattan represents how the "God" who created the universe created man in his same likeness. On the other hand you have *the smartest man in the world* who through his guile, assets, and humanitarian efforts becomes a savior god. His ability to manipulate and use people according to their fundamental natures allows him though seemingly villainous to save humanity. Both use each other as opposing polarities that balance their respective destiny's and missions. These two represent the two lands of Egypt that are further explained and polarized by Judah and Joseph in this book. Whichever side of the spectrum you are looking from each can be seen as God in man or man in God. This is also depicted by the Sphinx in Egypt that stands before the three pyramids. The three pyramids behind it represent Isis, Ra, and El; again Isis has two forms, earth and water. Because the earth is 90% water, this is what gives validity to the Virgin Goddess Aphrodite (Venus) who is an "earth" goddess reported to have been born at sea. These polarizations between her dual natures again are represented by The Virgin Mary and Mary Magdalene. Because of Isis's two forms, the three gods of Isis Ra and El morph into four forming the base of the pyramid establishing a square and giving a measurement of 360 degrees.

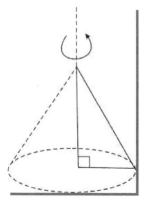

The way that man sees in planes is what made early scholars originally think the earth was flat; and why when a person looks at any window, television, computer monitor, door or screen, it is like a square or rectangle. Though your eye is circular it processes images in planes. Four right angles at 90 degrees equal 360 degrees or a square which is the same degree measurement of a circle. The "gods" and "goddesses" of ancient Egypt were said to fall under the signs of **Is**is **Ra** and **El** and the people of the nation of Israel believed in these gods. Whenever a person pledges to the god of Israel, they pledge to this belief. When they pledge to the God of Abraham, Isaac, and Jacob, they pledge belief in a "Living God."

The avatar that is the manifestation of all of these three signs (IsRaEl) is considered the all being, the Holy One of Israel, and contains all femininity and masculinity within one *plane* of existence. The Rig Veda X 90 the oldest of the Vedic scriptures, also speaks about the dis and re - member/ment of the Holy One who is said to be the archetypal man, and the giant who represents all of creation within his existence. The last (avatar) person on the planet who embodied this masculine and feminine fusion was Michael Jackson.

Ezekiel 10:14 & 20 *(14) And everyone had four faces: the first face was the face of a cherub, and the second face was the face of a man, and the third the face of a lion, and the fourth the face of an eagle.*

When the God of Israel returns these will be his attributes and some of the other beings that will surround him. In Astrology the man is the Aquarius (air sign), the lion is the Leo, (fire sign) and the Eagle is Scorpio (water sign), again the fact that the bull was left out of this description polarizes the two aspects of Isis which are the scorpion and the virgin (earth sign) or Scorpio and Virgo. Also the glyph of mercury that rules Virgo in Astrology resembles a bull and is therefore another hidden jewel that links Isis to the virgin and the bull 26. These are all indicators that will enable all four of the world's major religions to recognize their "Living Gods" upon their return.

Recently there has been a movie and cartoon called *Avatar the Last Air Bender* 25b25c. Aang is an air-bender (Aquarius) who is the embodiment of all the 4 elements of water, fire, earth, and air. Because he is the embodiment of all these elements he is the avatar who is the most powerful person on earth who removes the imperialist fire nation from their rule. In the mid 90's there was a cartoon called *Captain Planet* that was the precursor to the cartoon *Avatar, the Last Air Bender*. In the *Captain Planet* cartoon, when all the elements combined, Captain Planet was formed. He was the Great Spirit, who with the help of kids from the four corners of the earth, would crusade against the people who pollute the world. While this was as a cartoon, the actual *Captain Planet* in real life that was also an {(Elohim (Eagle, Lion, Ox & khem/him) or combination of elements animated in spirit within human flesh} was Michael Jackson.

These stories are all Egyptian stories that have to do with prophecies foretold in the Bible as well as Bhaga Vita, Rig Veda and the Kabbalah. Today those who practice Christianity, and have pledged allegiance with 'God, haven't a clue it is a "Living God" they are worshipping. Again, this "Living God" of Israel, is the one of Abraham, Isaac, and Jacob.

Jeremiah 10:10 "The Lord is the true God; He is the <u>living God</u> and the everlasting King. At His wrath the earth will tremble, and the nations will not be able to endure His indignation."

Deuteronomy 5:26 When the old covenant was given, the people "heard the voice of the <u>living God</u> speaking from the midst of the fire."

Having said this, ask any believer in any religion about the "God" they believe to worship, and they will tell you about a romanticized god, one that is unseen who exists in the sky; yet in their entire vernacular they'll use terminology in reference to the God of Israel; the God of Abraham, Isaac, and Jacob.

THE ENCOUNTER

I had several Mormons come to visit me while I was writing this book; and upon their visit they gave me a lot of information about their faith and the mission of their organization. They informed me that the founder of their faith's name was Joseph and they also have a leadership of 12 elders that preside over their congregations. Being evangelists these Mormons were here at my house because they go door to door preaching about the life of Jesus to the quote on quote "Lost Sheep of Israel." What is so ironically puzzling about this experience is after they told me about their faith, I sat them down and told them about Astrology and how it is the lost science that Jesus 's whole mission and account is about. By these Mormons taking the scriptures literally and coming to preach to me about the life of Jesus, they feel as if they are doing the "LORD's" work. The 12 elders that preside over their congregation are synonymous to the 12 disciples of Jesus. Joseph being the founder of the organization can be likened to the Joseph who was the favored son of Jacob that was the Patriarch and father to the twelve tribes of Israel. The tribes are actually the names of Jacob's sons who were birth through polygamy whereby Joseph takes the sister of his first wife Rachel, weds them both, and birth's these 12 tribes (sons) through them and their maid servants. This is why polygamy is accepted in the Mormon culture and below is the actual Biblical account.

Genesis 30:1-20 (1) And when Rachel saw that she bare Jacob no children, Rachel envied her sister; and said unto Jacob, Give me children, or else I die. (2) And Jacob's anger was kindled against Rachel: and he said, Am I in God's stead, who hath withheld from thee the fruit of the womb? (3) And she said, Behold my maid Bilhah, go in unto her; and she shall bear upon my knees, that I may also have children by her. (4) And she gave him Bilhah her handmaid to wife: and Jacob went in unto her. (5) And Bilhah conceived, and bare Jacob a son. (6) And Rachel said, God hath judged me, and hath also heard my voice, and hath given me a son: therefore called she his name Dan. (7)And Bilhah Rachel's maid conceived again, and bare Jacob a second son. (8) And Rachel said, With great wrestlings have I wrestled with my sister, and I have prevailed: and she called his name Naphtali. (9) When Leah saw that she had left bearing, she took Zilpah her maid, and gave her Jacob to wife. (10) And Zilpah Leah's maid bare Jacob a son. (11) And Leah said, A troop cometh: and she called his name Gad. (12) And Zilpah Leah's maid bare Jacob a second son. (13) And Leah said, Happy am I, for the daughters will call me blessed: and she called his name Asher. (14) And Reuben went in the days of wheat harvest, and found mandrakes in the field, and brought them unto his mother Leah. Then Rachel said to Leah, Give me, I pray thee, of thy son's mandrakes. (15) And she said unto her, Is it a small matter that thou hast taken my husband? and wouldest thou take away my son's mandrakes also? And Rachel said, Therefore he shall lie with thee to night for thy son's mandrakes. (16) And Jacob came out of the field in the evening, and Leah went out to meet him, and said, Thou must come in unto me; for surely I have hired thee with my son's mandrakes. And he lay with her that night. (17) And God hearkened unto Leah, and she conceived, and bare Jacob the fifth son. (18) And Leah said, God hath given me my hire, because I have given my maiden to my husband: and she called his name Issachar. (19) And Leah conceived again, and bare Jacob the sixth son. (20) And Leah said, God hath endued me with a good dowry; now will my husband dwell with me, because I have born him six sons: and she called his name Zebulun.

Joseph was the eleventh son born to his father Jacob by his favorite wife, Rachel. His father Jacob gave him a coat of <u>many colors</u> because he favored Joseph over his other sons. Later I will explain in depth the meaning and symbolism this coat of many colors has.

In Numerology as outlined by the Kabbalah the number 11 is a master number. This number has a very strong association to self-sacrifice for the benefit of others, as well as the transcendental number for spirituality, enlightenment, and martyrdom [27]. The name Jesus also adds up to the #11 and those born with this particular number have amazing insight into the lives of others [25a]. Again, this information is taken from the Kabbalah, which is the mystical philosophy found in Judaism that traces its origins from a 13th century collection of writings called the Zohar. This mystic system of Judaism's numbers and word equations are said to be found in earlier works called the Sefer Yetsirah, reportedly written in Palestine between the 3rd and 6th centuries [28].

In Astrology the eleventh house corresponds to the sign Aquarius. The eleventh house also emphasizes how a person relates to and engages the world. Those born in this house are greatly affected by political and social oppression and are usually humanitarians. Because those born in this house have all of these qualities they often have a knack for working with groups of people and are attracted to public offices.

In the Bible, Joseph becomes the ruler of Egypt and holds the highest seat other than Pharaoh. The foreshadowing to this event is told in the 37 chapter of Genesis whereby Joseph has an astrological vision that shows him rising to become a Ruler of the land.

Genesis 35: 2-9 (2) these are the generations of Jacob. Joseph, being seventeen years old, was feeding the flock with his brethren; and the lad was with the sons of Bilhah, and with the sons of Zilpah, his father's wives: and Joseph brought unto his father their evil report. (3) Now Israel loved Joseph more than all his children, because he was the son of his old age: and he made him a coat of many colours. (4) And when his brethren saw that their father loved him more than all his brethren, they hated him, and could not speak peaceably unto him. (5) And Joseph dreamed a dream, and he told it his brethren: and they hated him yet the more. (6) And he said unto them, Hear, I pray you, this dream which I have dreamed: (7) For, behold, we were binding sheaves in the field, and, lo, my sheaf arose, and also stood upright; and, behold, your sheaves stood round about, and made obeisance to my sheaf. (8) And his brethren said to him, Shalt thou indeed reign over us? or shalt thou indeed have dominion over us? And they hated him yet the more for his dreams, and for his words. (9) And he dreamed yet another dream, and told it his brethren, and said, Behold, I have dreamed a dream more; and, behold, the sun and the moon and the eleven stars made obeisance to me.

Here we see the relationship between the Sun the Moon and the eleven stars mentioned in Joseph's parable. In the biblical account of Joseph, he and his brothers and sister together make up the 12 tribes of Israel, however, there is a riddle associated within the twelve astrological signs and disciples. Jacob with his 12 children makes thirteen, just as Jesus with his twelve disciples makes thirteen. This thirteen represents the hidden month that is within all of the other months. 13 months x 28 days = 364 days with one day left over, the day of the dead. As you are aware there are only 28 days in a month, and there has never been an eight day week. Some months have 30 to 31 days in them. If you add up all of the days past twenty eight in all the months that extend past 28 days, you will find those extra days equals another 28 days. The thirteenth tribe which is scattered amongst the twelve is the "Lost Tribe of Israel" and when assembled back together is the body that Jesus is LORD over. This tribe is the lost tribe (sheep) of Israel who Jesus is coming to restore. Joseph alongside Jesus is paralleled, as Jesus is lord over 12 disciples and Joseph is lord over the 12 tribes of Israel. If these unsuspecting Mormons would have realized that Jesus has to first resurrect before he can give his church its instruction, than their lives and purpose may have been put into perspective when I spoke to them. If they had any deeper knowledge and knew that Jesus and the twelve people who revolve around him was a parable about the Earth and our own solar system, then they probably would no longer be Mormons.

1 Corinthians 15:13-14 (13) *But if there be no resurrection of the dead, then is Christ not risen* (14) *And if Christ be not risen, then is our preaching vain, and your faith is also vain.*

THE GREATEST OF SINS

When a person thinks about the Bible and the sins that are mentioned within it, the one that is most intriguing and sticks out the most is lust. The Bible goes on and on about fornication and condemns those who burn in their lusts and desires to a sentence of eternity in the pits of hell. Greed, sloth, envy, pride, wrath, and gluttony, are all pale in comparison to lust in terms of emphasis; but why is this? The fact that the church has replaced adultery with sleeping with another's wife is what has caused the people to have a jaded view of lust and how it relates to the other sins. The Ten Commandments has a commandment which states that thou shall not covet thy neighbor's wife, or thy neighbor's goods, but to understand what this commandment means we must 1st define the word covet.

Covet: (1) to desire (what belongs to another) inordinately or culpably

Exodus 20:17 (17) Thou shalt not covet thy neighbor's house, thou shalt not covet thy neighbor's wife, nor his manservant, nor his maidservant, nor his ox, nor his ass, nor any thing that is thy neighbor's.

Leviticus 20:10 (10) And the man that committeth adultery with another man's wife, even he that committeth adultery with his neighbour's wife, the adulterer and the adulteress shall surely be put to death.

When we look at the word covet it means to desire what belongs to another. If you cannot covet your neighbors wife what would make you think that you could sleep with her. The fact there are two commandments that essentially mean the same thing is brow raising evidence that suggests something else may have been meant when Moses gave the people the Commandment, "Thou Shalt not Commit Adultery." Adultery, according to Webster is: *to debase or make impure by adding inferior, alien or less desirable materials or elements,* which pending on what a person who is interpreting the scripture has defined the words as meaning, determines how he/she views what is being stated. What seems to me to be the 1st reported sin in the Bible is an allegory about Eve sleeping with a being (the serpent) outside of her and her husband Adam's race. This could be a clue as to what true adultery means and maybe the reason why in the Bible certain sons were prohibited from dating women from other races. Later we will discuss Eve and the serpent and analyze the scriptures for all they entail.

Mongrel: an individual resulting from the interbreeding of diverse breeds or strains

Genesis 28:1 *And Isaac called Jacob, and blessed him, and charged him, and said unto him, Thou shalt not take a wife of the daughters of Canaan.*

Genesis 28:6 *(6)When Esau saw that Isaac had blessed Jacob, and sent him away to Padanaram, to take him a wife from thence; and that as he blessed him he gave him a charge, saying, Thou shalt not take a wife of the daughters of Canaan.*

Also notice that the commandment doesn't say thou shalt not covet thy neighbor's husband. If Adultery was as cut and dry as people today have made it, sleeping with another's husband would have also been mentioned. The way the words original use has been overlooked and taught to mean a different but similar thing is understood; because whenever the Bible was written, the people that it was written for were all mixed together. If you say to an already mongrelized culture "thou shalt not sleep with others outside of your races" which the KKK did, it seems to be very racist and inhumane. In biblical times men had the right to take women as they chose and for these reasons, adultery didn't pertain to sleeping with another woman's husband.

Genesis 30:14-17 *(14) during wheat harvest, Reuben went out into the fields and found some mandrake plants, which he brought to his mother Leah. Rachel said to Leah, "Please give me some of your son's mandrakes." (15) But she said to her, "Wasn't it enough that you took away my husband? Will you take my son's mandrakes too?" "Very well," Rachel said, "he can sleep with you tonight in return for your son's mandrakes." (16) So when Jacob came in from the fields that evening, Leah went out to meet him. "You must sleep with me," she said. "I have hired you with my son's mandrakes." So he slept with her that night. (17) God listened to Leah, and she became pregnant and bore Jacob a fifth son. (18) Then Leah said, "God has rewarded me for giving my maidservant to my husband." So she named him Issachar.*

An act of polygamy as reported by the Bible is what created the twelve tribes of Israel. If adultery meant sleeping with another's wife or husband, than all the religions of Abraham are the products of adultery. Even Jesus in the 25th chapter of Matthew adds sentiment to polygamy.

Matthew 25:1-10 *(1) Then shall the kingdom of heaven be likened unto ten virgins, which took their lamps, and went forth to meet the bridegroom. (2) And five of them were wise, and five were foolish. (3) They that were foolish took their lamps, and took no oil with them: (4) But the wise took oil in their vessels with their lamps. (5) While the bridegroom tarried, they all slumbered and slept. (6) And at midnight there was a cry made, Behold, the bridegroom cometh; go ye out to meet him. (7) Then all those virgins arose, and trimmed their lamps. (8) And the foolish said unto the wise, Give us of your oil; for our lamps are gone out. (9) But the wise answered, saying,*

Not so; lest there be not enough for us and you: but go ye rather to them that sell, and buy for yourselves. (10) And while they went to buy, the bridegroom came; and they that were ready went in with him to the marriage: and the door was shut.

The above scripture is an obvious allegory about the coming of Christ for his church. Those who are prepared go with him to heaven, and those who aren't are banished from the kingdom forever. My point in citing this scripture is that Jesus would not use a reference that was outside of the people's customs. If the people of that day weren't familiar with polygamy and didn't deem it to be godly Jesus wouldn't have used this as a parable to teach with, much less liken it to the kingdom of heaven. As I said before the "God" who the people worshipped was the leader and head of the Zodiac, the Leo. When people of Israel were in a state where they weren't lost and they knew through Astrology when and where their gods would be born; as a result of this knowledge, they set up a nunnery for him as it was not good for man to be alone. Nun is the Hebrew word for Scorpio as they are the natural feminine carnal lovers of the Zodiac. When the Da Vinci code was written and Mary Magdalene was shown as the thirteenth disciple this was the foreshadowing for that story. Upon Jesus wedding Mary Magdalene he becomes the "king" of heaven because by doing so he marries the real "queen" of heaven, Venus. If you ask any man who the queens of their heavenly desires are, they may not tell you the truth, but I will. The queens of their heavenly desires are whores which is why Venus is personified as the goddess of love in mythology (Aphrodite). I'm sure many of you have heard the cliché' *everyman wants a lady in the streets but a freak in the sheets*.

Matthew 21:31 (31) *Jesus said to them, "Truly I tell you, the tax collectors and the prostitutes are entering the kingdom of God ahead of you.*

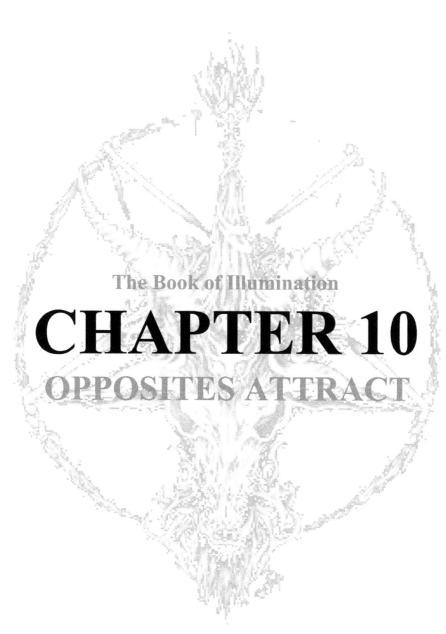

The Book of Illumination

CHAPTER 10

OPPOSITES ATTRACT

The Book of Illumination

CHAPTER 10

OPPOSITES ATTRACT

OPPOSITES ATTRACT

Since the release of the *Da Vinci code* and it's follow up *Angels and Demons*, there has been some speculation concerning the relationship between Jesus and Mary Magdalene. In the Da Vinci code, Mary is painted by Dan Brown as being the twelfth disciple after the passing of Judas. While this is not all together untrue, there are details that if explained thoroughly, the public would be able to get a more accurate view of her and Jesus' relationship. Jesus for most part of his adult life was an ascetic.

Ascetic: one who practices self-denial and mortification for religious reasons

   As an ascetic, Jesus is trying to get his disciples to understand a holistic way towards life. This spiritual attitude is one of ideal for people who are searching for enlightenment. In order to achieve this feat, a person must first step outside the confines of regular society by abstaining from it. Abstaining from it allows them to see the society's ills and all of the attachments and flaws associated with it. This bird's eye view enables the person to readily assess life's situations and by assessing these situations, it makes it easy for the person to eliminate the scenarios that would otherwise be harmful to them.

   Many ascetics practice abstinence and do not partake in worldly vices. They feel indulging in them will block the chakras that give them their insight and clairvoyant spiritual awareness's. This awareness allows them to seemingly hover above, as well as walk through life's obstacles effortlessly.
Think about when you haven't eaten for a long period of time. When you haven't eaten, it is very easy to smell all food aromas around you. When you smell these aromas, each flavor within the cooked food becomes isolated and identified. The same hypersensitivity I referenced in regard to the food aromas in how the person's abstinence from them causes a heightened sense of smell; is the same rationale used by the ascetic who becomes very sensitive to the pain and struggles people experience in the world.

   On the flipside of abstinence, imagine the thought process of a person who is experienced versus a person who isn't. The person who isn't experienced to the experienced person, looks like a sitting duck, and can easily be taken advantage of. This point relates to the elevated viewpoint Jesus's is trying to give his disciples so they won't be taken advantage of by the Pharisees and Sadducees. The only way his disciples can achieve this perspective is to physically endure the pain of living without anything but their faith.

179

Living by faith alone gives the person the opportunity to see through trial and error what is mystical from what is real. When people experience these revelations, they attribute the clarity they received by these realizations as being "God" who has "magically" shown them the way. Their newfound sense of awareness allows the individual to see just how inefficient they were prior to the clarity. When you're the person experiencing a problem or dilemma, it is often hard to see yourself, which is why many people seek out help from a counselor or a shrink. The counselors, because they are away from the problem, can easily diagnose the situation even when the person with the dilemma cannot. This is why the priests of the religious world are celibate and do not participate in sensual acts yet are considered to be the "spiritual" lovers of the world. They love people so much they have given their life in service to them. The number this selfless love is attributed to in Numerology is 11 which in Astrology is the house of Aquarius and in numerology the number of Leo. The Leo type is the most dominant, spontaneously creative and extroverted of all the zodiacal signs. They are the monarch's among humans as the lion is king of beasts. They are ambitious, courageous, dominant, strong willed, positive, independent, and self-confident. On the whole they are strongly idealistic, humane, and beneficent. They have powerful intelligence and are of a broad philosophical, sometimes religious, turn of mind. Leo's are ruled by the heart and the Sun and are a fixed masculine sign. The Aquarius is a fixed masculine air sign whose personality personifies universalism. The Aquarius polarizes the same qualities exemplified by Leo expressing them with humanitarian zeal. Though often expressed with a more mindful delivery, the Aquarius's love for harmony and peace within the social atmosphere, in terms of liberation and "fairness" for all, counterbalances the aspects that come with the gigantic and egocentric personalities of the Leo. This is why Aquarius is ruled by the planet Uranus which translates to *"the oldest inverted sun."*

While taking into the account the "signs" that humanitarianism and selfless love fall under, we also have to look at the opposing aspects of how that same love is expressed from the feminine perspective. The character in the Bible that juxtaposes this selfless and generous love carnally is Mary Magdalene. When you look at the fact that Mary was a harlot, at first glance she is judged because of this. But when you think about it with a more open ended and in depth turn of mind the question arises, *"Who services men more passionately and more submissively then whores?"* We are talking about true lovers of men, who love to please men so much that giving up their bodies has become their profession. Their whole way of existence is mastering the art of servicing men as they provide these men with carnal love. I am speaking in reference to the natural women who in today's society would be considered exhibitionists or liberals. These women seek professions as call girls and escorts because they love to give and receive pleasure. I am not speaking in reference to those who prostitute out of poverty/force or those who sell themselves because they were sexually abused as children. In the zodiac this carnal lover is attributed to the celestial sign Scorpio, however in legend these attributes were also characteristics of the goddess Venus. ♏

The Scorpio in fact is ruled by her sex organs making her a chief advocate for sex and exotic pleasures. Scorpio is the symbol of sex, is a fixed feminine sign, and is the most sensually energetic of all the astrological signs. For them, union with their lover is a sacrament. Their overriding urge in loving is to use their power to penetrate beyond themselves and to lose themselves sexually in their partners in an almost mystical ecstasy. Because they are capable of the greatest heights of passion, debauchery and perversion are always a danger, as Scorpios can become sadistic in matters of eroticism. Their feelings are so intense that even when their love is of the highest ideals, they are frequently protagonists in tragic and even violent romances. People for lack of understanding creation label these types of women whores, when in all actuality they service the world with carnal love and pleasure. So in understanding each of these signs we can readily see that the relationship between Mary and Jesus is that of a celibate man who knows and understands spiritual love consorting with a promiscuous woman who understands physical (carnal) love. They balance each other out because they both are *the* extreme lovers of the zodiac. She relieves him in ways that no one else can (physically) as fasting, meditating and abstaining from vice is his daily routine. She is his pressure release in a sense, his salvation, for what is life if it cannot be experienced. He is her guide as he shows her unconditional love despite the condition she is in and what she's done. He gives her the type of love (spiritually) that is dignified, honest, and admirable which shows her that life isn't all bad. This is her salvation because now she sees in him, God, the person whom she has been trying to find. Now the question arises; how does this relate to Mary being a disciple? That answer is as complex as it is simple.

The receptive nature of the woman gives her the capability to fully receive messages and instructions from a man, especially one that she respects and admires. Man's combative nature alongside their huge ego's, makes them incapable to a certain extent of fully absorbing instruction from other men. The only way to get a man to fully submit to another man is to whoop him in combat or kill him; which is often seen in jails. A woman's anatomy is receptive as her sex organs are that which are penetrative. A man's anatomy is projective as his sex organs are those that penetrate. Understanding this natural parallel between the unions of opposites on these very basic levels enables people to fully see the relationship between the masculine "God" and the feminine "Queen." The closeness Mary and Jesus shared is what made their relationship paramount amongst Jesus and his other disciples.

Back when most of the scrolls were written the monarchs had the knowledge of planetary alignments as well as when certain gods (embodiments of celestial energy) would be born. This was explained earlier in the example of Jesus, John, and Herod the Tetrarch. When a god would be born along with him several chaste virgins would also be raised for him to mate with. This practice is called studding today and is frequently done when breeding animals. Those priests and astrologers who were at the top of the culture practiced this process to ensure that more of the deities essence would be infused into the Universe /society. The women who accepted these commitments were considered wholly because they gave up their life and virginity to be bred with a god. It was considered the ultimate self-sacrifice and is why the women who gave their virginity in respect to this practice were so heavily adored and revered. This is where the nunnery was developed from as nun in Hebrew is associated to Scorpio, the fixed feminine sign that is "ruled" by her sex organs. Having a "virgin" who is born from the sign Scorpio again shows the dual nature of the Goddess Isis (Scorpio and Virgo) in a different form. Now due to the perversion of the language and the lawlessness that led to the enslavement of the people who held these customs you have women (nuns) who go their whole lives waiting for a "God" they will never see. Again as I have said, when you try to use the knowledge of a people that you do not understand, you usually apply that knowledge backwards, which leads too much suffering and in this case, spiritual confusion. The 25th Chapter of Matthew and the 29th Chapter of the Genesis are biblical testaments to these truths. So again why is so much emphasis placed on lust? The reason so much emphasis was placed on lust as the worst sin has to do with the (founding fathers) who never wanted the races of black and white to intermingle. Even if they had slave women, slept with them, and fathered offspring by them, publicly their messages were against integration. Senator Strom Thurmond and Thomas Jefferson are two law makers in American History who publically defended segregation but secretly integrated and had offspring with other races. Strom Thurmond, the United States Senator most known for the longest filibuster (endless debate) in the history of the United States at 24 hours and 18 minutes in protest of the civil rights act of 1957, [28a] though publicly defending segregation, fathered an "illegitimate" daughter, Essie Mae – Washington - Williams, with his family's 16 year old African-American maid Carrie Butler [28b].

Ancient World History, also, reports the Russian borderlands of the Caucasus and Georgia were an endless source of sex slaves for Middle Eastern and Mediterranean peoples. The beauty associated with the slave women from the Caucasus attributed the word Caucasian with "*enslaved embodiments of vulnerability*" 28c&d. Naturally these women being submissive were attracted to those who were dominant. When scribes were retranslating scriptures and the original historical documents, they had no idea how old the scrolls they were interpreting were. I have to use the 6th chapter of Genesis so those with lesser understanding won't typecast me as a racist, bigot, or a fascist for presenting this evidence no matter how brutal or insensitive it may seem. For fear of these "enslaved embodiments of vulnerability" becoming attracted to the "Sons of God" as indicated in biblical scriptures, the leaders of the church structured their teachings around lust to place fear in their women's eyes. This made it taboo for them to sleep with stronger or what their culture called "foreign men." They used the story of Adam and Eve as a secret underlying theme that spoke against adultery. It was all systematically designed to give inferior males breeding rights. They knew that if they did nothing to stop their women from looking and being intrigued by these powerful alphas (Sons of God) then they would be wiped from the face of the planet and considered insignificant. This is where one of the key points of this book comes into play. Because the Greco-Romans "romanticized" certain stories and beliefs from ancient Egypt, it caused, through time, the passing on of the romanticized versions, over the original versions that had oral and allegorical symbolism within the primary culture. The Roman culture, in their lack of comprehension translated what they thought was "proper" for people to know, allowing Roman culture to supplant ancient Egyptian culture. Because those who manipulate scriptures are not of the spiritual world they think they can manipulate everything physically. The culture from which this supplanting began as I mentioned earlier was a culture that was amerced in homosexuality (Greco-Roman.) Everything that happened to those cultures who were then at the state America is in now ended in ruin. If inferior males get to breed in the wild the offspring will inevitably be wiped off by something that is superior. Nature through evolution is what brings about a true king; and this again is something that is spiritual. Because males have the ability to man-ip-u-late they are able to play on the emotions of women. It is no secret that women are emotional beings who are easily persuaded by things that intrigue them whether they're right or wrong. This is also why the story of Adam and Eve was told in relation to the woman seeking what was considered taboo, (serpent/apple) and later being seduced by it. Those who are seeking to dethrone the alpha are closer to the feminine and being closer to the feminine, they understand how her lower mind (*undermine*) operates. They know that women are very jealous of one another and are always trying to show each other up. Remember **Genesis 30:14-19.** Playing off the jealousy women have for each other is how the inferior males succeed in vilifying the man (alpha) who has multiple women. The natural right of the alpha-male was turned into something sinister and evil when the inferior males saw the willingness of the women to submit to him. These inferior males inherently knew they had to do something to level the playing field. What was created were lies and propaganda to further promote a lifestyle that was more conducive towards their inferior nature. This example is best played out in the movie the *Gladiator* where Maximus the alpha is undermined and dethroned by Commodus. Note the names Maximus which is more to the likeness of alpha and Commodus which is more to the likeness of the common male or non-alpha. Thus these males introduced to society the one man one woman policy and the sanctity of marriage. In the beginning, according to the Bible when a man took a wife, they wed whenever they had sex with one another.

Genesis 24:67 (67) And Isaac brought her into his mother Sarah's tent, and took Rebekah, and she became his wife; and he loved her: and Isaac was comforted after his mother's death.

Thus marriage we can suffice to say was the child who consummates the union of the two entities of man and woman; literally the personification of "till death do them part." When the child dies their union dies as the child is half male, and half female. The persons responsible for the structuring of society, for lack of appropriate comprehension of the masses, couldn't preach this in an open forum. Only a person with comprehension could understand this, and in understanding it, practice it. Back then villages raised children and it wasn't just up to the parents, everybody took a place in rearing and raising the children as this was proven to produce more well-rounded offspring. The marriage we're familiar with today has more to do with a contract than love. The land, the estate, as well as the beneficiary of the estate are why so much emphasis is placed on the legitimacy of the union. The people who created this civil form of marriage are more concerned with their legacies and who they are going to leave everything they have worked for too. Aristocrats through imagery and folklore have subjugated the rest of the lowly people to their standards of etiquette even though the common people don't have the type of luxury, wealth, and privileges to keep up with the image the aristocrats promote. What has spawned from this manipulation is inferior male breeding. Because the inferior male can sell the woman the romantic dream that she is the only one which appeals greatly to *her* ego, she allows him to breed and his offspring to be born through her. She only realizes in the aftermath that he was just a little more skilled in hiding what his true nature is.

She was tricked and he won, because naturally, instinctively, and even subconsciously, she is seeking out the candidate with the best DNA who will ensure the survival of her and her progeny. Making the king a slave was the first ploy that enabled the Roman culture to supplant that of Egypt. If you took away the kings land, his kingdom, and all of his powers, you would be able to stand in his place and appear as being the hero, the king, and the one who is supposed to lead and rule. What is perplexing about this is the people who have done this haven't conquered and stood behind the method that got them their ruler-ship positions. Versus portraying themselves, as ruthless, liars, unscrupulous, and greedy they do the opposite exemplifying chivalry, honesty, courage, and sacrifice, all of which are kingly attributes. If they were justified in doing what they did and felt no wrong in doing it, then they would own up to it, step down and acknowledge where they got their "God" as well as their understanding of civilization from.

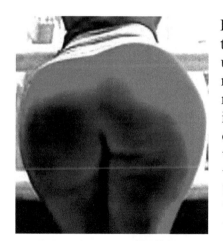

I have to again re-iterate the *kill the king* theory to better enable the reader to understand what is going on. Hearing romanticized stories appeals to the senses more so than real ones, and when you think in terms of romanticism, all possibilities occur. The popular symbol of the heart which is an obvious portrayal of a woman's voluptuousness has become romanticized to be the thing that beats between our chests. Today this heart is most recognized on Valentine's Day; where the focal point for men becomes getting some "ass."

Romanticism is why majority of Hollywood's pictures have happy endings because people generally want to believe that no matter what type of decisions they've made, the outcomes will be positive and beneficial to them. In Hollywood the deer that gets lost in the woods evades predators and ends up reunited with its mother. In reality the lost calf in the jungles is last seen dead clutched between the jaws of a jaguar. When we understand romanticism it further enables us to better comprehend the relationships between the sexes in how they

185

really feel in their natures, opposed to how they have tailored their existences because of societal pressures. Thinking with a romantic mind frame causes people to use their imagination; this use of imagination provides for them an outlet from reality. In reality evolving to the state of the alpha is one of the hardest things any being can achieve. Maintaining the position of the alpha male is equally as difficult because the alpha is usually the envy of everything inferior to him. The reality behind this topic in regards to nature is that many women instinctively flock to the alpha male because of what is in him. The essence of his nature and genetic upgrades, are what makes the women desire him; this is evolution. In today's "modern" society the take on polygamy has greatly become taboo, and is regarded as an archaic practice. Women today are detested by it but have no idea that this is the fundamental nature that a God-man is created with. Remember the song, "*Father Abraham, had many sons and many sons had father Abraham, I am one of them and so are you, so let's just praise the Lord.*" How do you think that people became sons of Abraham? Polygamy! Jacob Genesis 30:1-20

Women of modern day America also have no clue or reason as to why alpha men can have more than one woman but they (women) are looked down upon for having more than one man. This is because the practice of polygamy wasn't created it was based on natural selection.

Natural Selection: a natural process that results in the survival and reproductive success of individuals or groups best adjusted to their environment that leads to the perpetuation of genetic qualities best suited to that particular environment.

In ancient times, when a woman was born she would have to be taken care of and was considered a liability. For these reasons men who didn't have sons had to marry their daughters off, preferably into wealth or royalty. It is no different than in today's time especially within families who have built and amassed estates. Even when you look at movies with themes associated with love or money, the family is always urging the woman to use her mind and go where the money is, versus using her heart and going where the love is. In biblical times, and today in countries that still hold their traditions like India, the males would have to work for the father or present a dowry in order to buy the bride from her family. One of the main selling points was her chastity. If she was chaste she was considered untouched and pure, much too the same extent as when you buy groceries or any other products, materials, or goods; you want the ones that haven't been touched or tampered with by others.

Genesis 29:15-20 (15) And Laban said unto Jacob, Because thou art my brother, shouldest thou therefore serve me for nought? tell me, what shall thy wages be? (16)And Laban had two daughters: the name of the elder was Leah, and the name of the younger was Rachel. (17) Leah was tender eyed; but Rachel was beautiful and well favoured. (18) And Jacob loved Rachel; and said, I will serve thee seven years for Rachel thy younger daughter. (19) And Laban said, It is better that I give her to thee, than that I should give her to another man: abide with me. (20) And Jacob served seven years for Rachel; and they seemed unto him but a few days, for the love he had for her.

Dowry: (1) a gift of money or property by a man to or for his bride (2) the money, goods, or estate that a woman brings to her husband in marriage

Genesis 30: 20 (20) And Leah said, God hath endued me with a good <u>dowry</u>; now will my husband dwell with me, because I have born him six sons: and she called his name Zebulun.

Genesis 31:41 (41) It was like this for the twenty years I was in your household. I worked for you fourteen years for your two daughters and six years for your flocks, and you changed my wages ten times.

Because society caters to those at the lowest level, modern day women have listened to the inferior males and have forgotten they are naturally searching for "God" who they see in the alpha-male. Even though some women salivate at the notion of ruling men, and are fascinated by dominating a weaker man this is just a phase as they in their nature seek leadership. For a time they will be happy with the weaker male but naturally and instinctively they will always long for the "God" (good) man. Women think they are another notch on the alpha man's belt in terms of the other women that he has; and this is due to insecure thinking. Each woman has certain qualities that make her unique amongst other women. What a lot of women fail to realize is that even the weaker males secretly admire and want to be like the alpha. If they get the chance to have more than one woman believe you me they will also exercise that rite. If the right situations and circumstances permit themselves, the non-alphas will go outside of the woman they have professed their love for. Because the woman is the prize, she should recognize herself as so and choose the man who has all of the genetic qualities she needs and would like to see created within the world. The man the woman is with isn't the one that she is dreaming of. The one she is dreaming of is the one she will cultivate within her womb. This is also an underlying theme which shows the woman is really just stripping the man of his information that she will then reconfigure and shape into her vision of him. Women who look to control men usually are in search of the type of man they can manipulate; this man is usually a feminine type. Again the man being more feminized in some cases could make the woman produce more testosterone; in this event, she is the sole controller of the destiny of the offspring they would produce. The feminine type of man has much romantic appeal, as it is romance that has drawn the controlling women to him. This man woo's and worships her by telling her she is the only one. The strong-willed, masculine man is out doing what and how he pleases with women without any regard to their feelings. The controlling woman doesn't want to be another notch on his belt, and though innately she is very drawn to him, in her mind it could never be anything more than a fling. To some women, the previous notion is a stretch as these women detest these types of men and look for the softer more effeminate man to be with. It has been proven through scientific study that when women want a man just to have sex with they look for a manly man; however when women want to settle down they look for a man who most closely resembles a woman. The reason that homosexuality is so misunderstood in the United States is due to the dominance of the feminine subconscious and her ability to manifest her will in "spirit" before it manifests to earth in being. This concept was researched within female macaques and the evidence found substantiates this theory. *In female Japanese macaques, homosexual behavior appears to have evolved from female strategies to coerce reticent males to mate with them* -30b

Reticent: restrained in expression, presentation, or appearance 2.) Inclined to be silent or uncommunicative in speech

Macaque: old world monkey

Even with the legend of King Kong we see this theory examined through a slightly different scope. In the story of King Kong, the brute ape has in a sense been conquered by a petite white woman. The ape again represents the black masculine brute, and the white woman holds the key to his calmness. She seemingly is the less likely candidate that would pose a threat to a being with the physical stature of King Kong. King Kong symbolizes to the untrained eye the alpha male though dominant, who lacks the ability to think, reason, and communicate civilly which ultimately causes him to be viewed as *primitive*. This is why the black alpha male represented as King Kong is a *primate*. What has been explained through this diagnosis reflects how the non-alpha sees the alpha in his raw original form; strong, stubborn, angry, and ferocious, while lacking grace, guile, and gentleness, all feminine traits. These traits are highlighted within the persona of the white beauty, and even on this level can be seen as a female coercing a more "*reticent*" male to dominate; "reticent" defined in the sense that the ape is "unable" to speak. This examination brings to light the Romans point of view which acknowledges beauty as being paramount (dominant) over strength reversing the roles of the woman and the brute ape. The fact the ape could be conquered due to his dominance shows that his dominance needed to be integrated with those effeminate qualities previously mentioned to produce a balanced being capable of existing in the wild or a civilized society. I polarized and reversed the positions of the ape and the woman so the reader is able to see how the romantic (Roman) point of view overlooks the obvious in order to cloud its deficiencies allowing these shortcomings to go unnoticed.

In the traditional viewpoint of the alpha, as ordered by nature, the alphas numbers are limited, as there are fewer alphas than there are "recessive gene males." All the "recessive gene males" have to do is gang up to restrain the alpha to remove him (the threat to their existence) so they can freely mate. These alphas contain within their genetic make-up dominant genes that need to be reinserted in the gene pool to ensure the breed stays strong and thriving. When you take these alphas out of the gene pool all you have left are inferior genes. Inferior genes lead to sickness and eventually death. The *kill the king* theory has caused those who carry the alpha male gene and alpha male mentality to be pushed to the brink of extinction. These alphas have been imprisoned and have been castrated economically, socially, and mentally, due to societies fear that they will become what they are naturally...dominant. This castration has caused a rise in inferior male breeding. These inferior males are much weaker and are dominated by the females. This domination makes her femininity stronger than their pseudo masculinity. Now I know some people reading this may take this out of context to typecast me as fascist or a bigot; which is why I have cited scientific and pop culture reference material that bear witness to the truths reflected within this book. Barabara Ado stated, *"The driving force behind the pornography industry is the vast network of secret societies who conduct their lucrative operations legally through tax-funded intelligence organizations. Masterminded and directed by the political elect, these clandestine organizations sponsored the sexual revolution which, bankrolled by the CIA's drug running syndicate, was designed to destroy moral standards and family values, as well as fostering anarchy that would eventually lead to the elimination and distinctions of gender* 29.*"*

Upon reading this one could look at it in relation to urban and pop culture and see striking correlations. When I looked at the seemingly meteoric rise of homosexual males in the black culture, as outlined by Aaron Macgruder, founder of the *Boondocks* cartoon series, I was enlightened. Everything from the new dance crazes like the "Halle Berry" and the "Stanky Leg" (an obvious pun for a man who has just had anal sex), to popular TV and movie moguls who earned their rise to fame and fortune by dressing in drag; was extreme evidence that made Barabara Ado's diagnosis interesting. I personally have no malice towards homosexuals. I have found them to be some of the most colorful and insightful of beings; and that is an understatement. Their sensitivity to all things sensual and beautiful is unrivaled and their overall outlook on life is one that is as expansive as the universe itself. Many people in society have unorthodox lifestyles considered by some to be perverted. These perversions do not necessarily limit who they are or what they can become. More importantly, who can say they have not participated in a perverted act? The fact people consent to whatever lifestyle they have chosen for themselves is a personal choice and one they have the right to make. They should not be penalized or overlooked because of their sexual orientation.

From a Kabbalistic perspective however, the rise of those who have openly come out in the public and revealed they are either homosexual and or bisexual (*Anderson Cooper, Clive Davis*) is a direct result of the times upon us. Aquarius is the astrological sign alongside Gemini that is attributed to androgyny; and is also the astrological age the world is now in. In the Genesis, the 1st book of the bible, it crypticly informs us that the "Gene" of Isis is the Horus, which indicates to us the age of Horus, is indeed the age of Aquarius. It has been cited that in the beginning (beginning of the world/age aka the Genesis) Man was created both male and female.

Genesis 5:1 (1) *This is the book of the generations of Adam. In the day that God created man, in the likeness of God made he him;[2] Male and female created he them; and blessed them, and called their name Adam, in the day when they were created.*

This is a direct refrence to the "angellic" state spoken of in creation whereby men and women are created and love eachother equally. Translating this scripture loosely, one can see how bisexuality could be justified and validated biblically. When you then couple these acknowledgements with the life of Hermes who had a hermaphroditic son, as well as founded the prerequisites for men to become priests in the Vatican after the Nicene Council, one easily realizes there isn't a gay agenda; its more about bringing people to the understanding that homosexuality has existed since the begginnig of time and is as "*natural*" as heterosexual relationships.

In speaking in reference to pop culture and the promotion of the homosexual lifestyle within it, there was a featured segment on the Ellen DeGeneres show that highlighted Halle Berry and the dance craze that was associated with her. At first glance it seemed to be a celebration of Halle's beauty, but when I looked deeper into the matter an even greater truth was revealed. The YouTube segment that featured the "Halle Berry" dance craze video had black males doing the "Halle Berry" dance 29b. The males in this video mimic the gestures of how females put on makeup as they primp in a "make believe" mirror clutched inside their palms. Young black males behaving this way, in the video, shows a lack of "true" masculinity within their households and lives. As outlined by W.E.B. Dubois, we know that an alarming number of inner city black youth do not have fathers because many of them are locked away because they have become criminals in order to survive. These black males as W.E.B. Dubois analyzed in his criminology thesis took to a life of crime because being former slaves, they were given the "bottom of the barrel" jobs in terms of the working and social class. What makes the dance craze associated with the actress so alarming is that in 2003 Halle berry, also a Leo, had a movie called *Monster's Ball* of which she received an Oscar award for

her performance. She was the first black women in history to receive such a "prestigious" honor. The movie depicted a black woman whose husband was incarcerated and given the death penalty. The man who presided over the execution was the same man "Halle Berry" had lascivious sex with. This was highly controversial within the black community because the man was white and the black community considered Halle Berry to be one of its brightest stars. Even though she is mixed, with black and white, seeing her being "portrayed" in this manner didn't set right with Black America. In fact many blacks felt she received the award because she allowed a "white" man to dominate her sexually for the whole world to see. Black Nationalists saw this as a sign that the White Supremacists, though hidden, were sending the message they still have control and can do whatever to whomever they want. Black people were discomforted by this because it made them think back to a time when white men had in fact imprisoned black males taking their women as their own. Billy Bob Thornton (*another Leo*) was the actor who had sex with Halle Berry on screen. He portrayed the white police officer who basically presided over the town the two lived in. In the movie Halle Berry suffers much conflict because her son is a glutton who obviously has been affected by having no father within the household. The father of her child was killed by the same "justice system" that Billy Bob

Thornton (the cop in the movie) was a part of. Again the parallels between her movie role and the young black males who have popularized a dance associated with her name are remarkable as they have in common with Berry's son in the movie, *"incarcerated fathers."* Like the movie, these youth have been paralyzed by the lack of a father figure in their households and have consequently become the very *"degenerates"* their single mothers despise.

The counter argument for what many black people felt was a let down by Halle Berry's portrayal in this role is that she had to have tremendous courage to put herself out there in this way. Taking this risk on screen after being heralded as the most beautiful woman in the world could have had a negative effect on her career. The reason it didn't is because the truth that she portrayed was one that cannot be easily stated. If this truth is stated, it makes the issues become tainted as you have to segregate black and white and determine who is the oppressed as well as the oppressor. When you point this out in an open setting you become discriminate as you now have to provide evidence for your claim. However, by combining art and aesthetics you can covertly show these truths that exist within society and allow the eye of the person watching to serve as the judge for whatever was depicted on screen. What this means is, pending on how deep a person's intellect is will in turn show how much truth they recognize within the actors portrayal (s).

While further analyzing the second half of the statement made by Barbara Ado another observation was made, she said, *"Masterminded and directed by the political elect, these clandestine organizations sponsored the sexual revolution which, bankrolled by the CIA's drug running syndicate, was designed to destroy moral standards and family values, as well as fostering anarchy that would eventually lead to the elimination and distinctions of gender"* 30.

From the late 90's to 2009 there seems to be a huge influx of artists who glorify the distribution and selling of illegal narcotics on the radio airways. These artists have single handedly made most young black men aspire to be drug dealers. What I find so amazing about this is how these types of artists get the promotion they receive. It takes millions of dollars to insure that any musician becomes a household name, which means that whoever has put these artists in their respective positions wanted them there for a reason. You would think that music with this type of message would have an underground following and not a mainstream following mainly because it is rebellious and against the law. The fact the underground has made it to the mainstream shows that capitalism is the key factor that has determined who is what.

It is a fact that what is repeated over and over again will become committed to memory and is what in turn will be remembered and subconsciously sought after. When I saw the rise of these artists and this type of music it made me think to who bankrolls them and for what purpose? Circa 2000, among the urban sect, can you name one popular rapper who hasn't directly profited from the glorification on record of drug usage or drug trafficking? At the same time, you have paralleled by this a disproportionate number of black masculine heroes, television personalities, as well as movie stars. The heroes in the biggest movies are always depicted as being white men. If you look closely, out of all the roles that leading black men get, most of them are comedic roles where they are shown as buffoons. You will always have exceptions to each rule however for the most part this is the case; and for every one exception, there are twenty that apply.

As I stated with the Hannibal Lecter theme earlier in the book, most people aren't superior in the sense of superiority. What I mean by this isn't money, I mean genetics. Genetically more people are have-nots then haves, and for these reasons society sides with those who are more like those who have not than those who have. What democracy has been so masterful at creating is the illusion of the have and have not. It has transformed Darwinism into Social Darwinism and made those who have of the genetic pool inferior to those who have not. I'll use the example of any team owner to that of its franchise players; think about who would be the alpha and who would be considered the inferior genetically. If you do this with accuracy, then you have all the answers that you'll need to understand.

Darwinism: (1) a theory that inherent dynamic forces allow only the fittest persons or organizations to prosper in a competitive environment or situation (2) a theory of the origin and perpetuation of a new species of animals and plants that offspring of a given organism vary, that natural selection favors the survival of some of these variations over.

Social Darwinism: (1) a sociological theory that socio-cultural advance is the product of intergroup conflict and competition and the socially elite classes (as those possessing wealth and power) possess biological superiority in the struggle for existence.

 *The Incredibles* 31 is a very fascinating animated epic about a Superhero, Mr. Incredible, who due to the jealousy and overzealous fanaticism of a degenerate admirer, has to retrain and resurrect himself from his washed up state, to battle against a foe whose covetous heart has caused him to go on a crusade to remove the

world of all its pre-existing superheroes, so he himself can appear to be one.
You mean you killed off real heroes so you could pretend to be one - Mr. Incredible 32

33**Syndrome** is this character's name and he only wants to be the hero because
he desires the fame and honor Mr. Incredible has.
In fact the movie states that Syndrome has created technology to
level the playing field between the superheroes and the regular
people so that no superhero will be able to exist.

*"I'll give them heroics; I'll give them the most spectacular heroics anyone
has ever seen. And when I'm old and had my fun I'll sell my inventions so
that everyone can be superheroes, everyone can be super, and with
everyone super no one will be."- Syndrome* 34

The problem with Syndrome's mentality and a point the movie showcases is
the only reason that Mr. Incredible is incredible is because of his superior
moral belief and his actions within that belief structure. Mr. Incredible wants
the best for his family and will go to great lengths to ensure their survival
even if it means sacrificing himself. If you were to look at the world today
and attribute a superhero to a being, what being would it be? If you were
honest with yourself and looked at all of the super human feats of the past
century an easy conclusion can be drawn. One reading may ask how this
relates to the Bible and its characters. The comparisons are further
acknowledged in the Bible in the story of Jacob and Esau. Jacob who was
coerced to supplant his masculine brother with the help of his mother is the
one in the Bible who through manipulation received his brother's birth right
and blessing. Jacob was not the stronger brother yet he was the one who
through his cunning ability received the inheritance. This story is significant
for a number of reasons. The first of which is the direct symbolism of the
manner in which he exists. Though Jacob isn't more powerful than his

brother (the alpha)
physically he uses power of
mind via manipulation to
conquer those who are
stronger. This is an
example of deceptive
intelligence; that of which is
considered paramount in
western society. Two other
characters who represent these opposing entities are Magneto and Professor X
of the X-Men 33b.

Professor X in the comic book *The X-Men* is handicapped and telepathic. This allegorically represents how when a person loses a sense, a limb, or any voluntary bodily function, it causes their other senses to become heightened. These "heightened" senses have enabled Professor X to see from the perspective of the coach or overseer (officer.) Because he hasn't the ability to move around physically he can show those who have remarkable abilities how to use their abilities more efficiently. The fact that he is paralyzed from the waist down shows his impotency as Professor X seeks harmony with mankind. Being physically inferior and in direct opposition to Magneto, Professor X sees how (mankind) is inferior to Mutants (humans.) In all of Professor X's attempts he is seeking unity with mankind because ideally, he himself realizes that everything that isn't dominant doesn't need to be destroyed or enslaved. Like those who lack mutant genes, Professor X, is an example on how mankind can use their minds to compensate for what their genes do not. Magneto on the other hand is a telekinetic super mutant (superhuman.) Because he is superior to mankind and humans he feels that he should rule them. Magneto wears a protective helmet so that his mind cannot be penetrated by Professor X; this is to protect his ego and shows he is phallic. Without his ego he would be unable to have the drive to use his uncanny abilities to oppress and destroy mankind. Mankind has yet to recognize that Mutants (humans) are more evolved then they are so (Magneto) being preeminent among the mutants and mankind feels it is his place to overthrow them by setting right what is out of place. Mankind is threatened by the rule of mutants (humans) because mankind is inferior to them. This inferior nature causes them to protect themselves and makes their mentality one of paranoia. Mankind has to survive and take all precautionary measures to make sure they are able to keep their way of life and is why they are warmongers. They need the comforts and luxuries of living in the pleasant places and because their physically weaker than mutants, they need sheltered and protective environments. As internalized by the mind of Magneto, (mankind) has yet to understand their boundaries as they wish to do as they please with no regard for anything or anybody. When one assesses the mentality of mankind through the point of view of Magneto, comparisons are easily drawn with it and the mentalities of infants. The infant wants what it wants when it wants with no regards to anything else. Magneto recognizes that mankind is in an infantile state in regards to evolution and looks at them as a retarded species of degenerates who for lack of evolution need to be overthrown and eradicated from the ruling classes. The only problem with this is star players have proven they are unable to be great coaches. Because they coach other players with fewer abilities then they have as if the players have their abilities, it

195

prohibits the players to maximize the abilities they do have. This is why a person with the stature of a Magneto if in a position to rule would inevitably become an authoritative dictator, the enemy of a democracy.

 Coach Mike Krzyzewski popularly called Coach K, is the most winning coach in the history of men's NCAA Basketball. Born February 13th under the sign Aquarius, with the name Michael, he epitomizes the role of the overseer or coach who doesn't have the abilities of the star players but has found a way to become the most successful person in one of the most recognized collegiate programs in history.

Democracy: a government in which the supreme power is vested in the people and exercised by them directly or indirectly through a system of representation usually involving periodically held free elections

Dictator: one ruling absolutely and often oppressively

What the lay people don't understand about democracy is everybody can't rule at once. There has to be subjects in order to have rule. Those who are in a democracy do not wish to be ruled, they wish to rule themselves. But how can one rule if one doesn't know or study the nature of the individuals or people they are governing? One thing about people is they haven't the ability to see themselves, yet they see everyone else crystal clear. The government looks at people based on the nature in which they exist, not in the nature they profess to exist in. Anything that is perceived as stronger or has the ability to remove the government from their position, the government must eradicate. This is one of the fundamental rules of government as the state has to protect itself from all forms of anarchy and overthrow. This is broken down further as the difference between order and chaos. Civilizations remain "civilized" by maintaining order, which again is the state's highest objective.

If you gave everyone their own personal platform to lead and govern themselves, it would still end in chaos. If you do not believe what I am saying log onto YouTube and look at some of the comments that appear on the bottom of any given video page. When you look at these comments you get a clear assessment of what you would have if you gave any and every body a platform to speak from. It's not about freedom of speech, it's about those who have the insight and knowledge to say something that has merit and is backed with fact, versus those who haven't and base what they say upon their own emotions. The illusion the ego creates tells each and every person they are the one who is the supreme ruler and authority. This goes back to the point made about the individual god of our ego as the one that we are serving. People don't realize this because they haven't stepped outside of themselves to recognize their limitations and their short comings. Professor X had to do it because of his paralysis. If people understood Astrology then they would see what "god" they draw their perspective from. Those who are of the governing elite have been through a hazing process; processes that are unimaginable to the common citizens of the state. The type of mind development activity they have been through has caused them to step outside of themselves and recognize who and what is the real authority. Though this group is small and confined to a very minute clique, it rules and governs the world.

In the story of Jacob and Esau, like Professor X, Jacob triumph's because he realizes his limitations and through his submission to the dominance of femininity, he is able to find a way to become king even though it is the natural birth right of his brother Esau. Understanding this will enable the reader to see why Professor X leads the X-men and also how those with romantic influence were successful in creating a doctrine that has amassed the largest influence over religion in the western world.

Genesis 25:23&25-26 (23) and the lord said unto her, two nations are in thy womb, and two manner of people shall be separated from they bowels; and the one people shall be stronger than the other people; and the elder shall serve the younger (25) And the first came out red all over like a hairy garment; and they called his name Esau (26) and after that came his brother out, and his hand took hold on Esau's heel; and his name was called Jacob: (27) And the boys grew: and Esau was a <u>cunning hunter, a man of the field</u>; and Jacob was a plain man, <u>dwelling in tents</u> (29) And Jacob sod pottage: and Esau came from the field and he was faint (30) and Esau said to Jacob, Feed me, I pray thee, with that same red pottage; for I am faint (31) And Jacob said, sell me this day thy birthright (32) And Esau said behold I am at the point to die: and what profit shall this birthright do to me? (33) And Jacob said, Swear me to this day; and he sware unto him: and sold his birthright unto Jacob.

Briefly, in the last paragraph, we spoke about the dominance of femininity. When you dissect the word divine you'll find the root of this word is Diva.

<u>Divine:</u> of, relating to, or proceeding directly from God or a god

<u>Diva:</u> Italian, literally, goddess, from Latin, feminine of *divus* divine, god

In Spanish the word Deva is attributed to the astrological sign Virgo, which is why the Virgin (Virgo) Mary has so much emphasis within the world of religion and divinity in Latin culture. It is also important at this time to again notate the astrological sign of Michael Jackson was Virgo. Many problems in society arise because people are unable to recognize superior beings within it. Because of the awareness's of these superior beings, they aren't governed the same as the lay people. This causes much dissention because the laymen have a communistic mindset in regards to the equality of people. Royalty and sovereigns are "supposed" to be sent from the heavens or the "stars" which make them free from the prison that confines everyday people to mundane existences. The talent levels of these "royals" provide them with a life wherein they live like the "gods" themselves. These "royals" or "stars" are born through alignments which in turn give these beings higher senses of awareness. This awareness was deemed by the Mother Church as "witchcraft" and "wizardry" and anyone who was believed to have superior awareness or senses were burned at the stake or stoned. Most people cannot really grasp these concepts because they are surface dwellers that deal in black and white and the carnal realm. The only way a person can get outside of this realm is to abstain from certain worldly vices as described earlier in the breakdown of asceticism. This practice allows the person to recognize certain spiritual phenomenon's that are invisible to others whose temples have been dulled by carnal activities. Celibacy and asceticism weren't supposed to be lifelong practices; they were merely exercises that enabled the person on the journey to distinguish between the carnal and spiritual realms. When you have not thoroughly thought out or comprehended this level of understanding it leads to great suffering and misapplied knowledge. For instance the woman being the superior and most dominant being has to understand and recognize that it is her and only her who can be the vessel for a higher being to be cultivated and manifested to earth through. She alone contains the ability to go in her mind and conjure (God) into existence. She is the most dominant because of her potential to evolve through creation and childbirth. A male once in his physical state, has no chance of becoming greater; he is in a sense "stuck" and has to again revisit the womb in order to evolve. This why Jesus says if you want to enter the kingdom of "God" you must first be born again.

John 3:3-6 *(3)Jesus answered and said unto him, Verily, verily, I say unto thee, Except a man be born again, he cannot see the kingdom of God. (4)Nicodemus saith unto him, How can a man be born when he is old? can he enter the second time into his mother's womb, and be born? (5)Jesus answered, Verily, verily, I say unto thee, Except a man be born of water and of the Spirit, he cannot enter into the kingdom of God. (6)That which is born of the flesh is flesh; and that which is born of the Spirit is spirit.*

What I mean by this is the alpha male is actually the evolution of the woman. If she births a daughter there is no progression, rather another cycle repeating itself. In dissecting and presenting this theory the audience has to keep in mind that the goal for spirituality is the realization of the self, i.e. who you were in your past as well as who you are in your present life. When I said, "*If the woman has a girl there would be no progression*" that was stated in the context that becoming the alpha male is the goal. If the woman births a male however, she will have de-evolved. This is the great mystery of sex and also with it where the unwanted population called the *varna-sankara* in Hinduism find their origin. The *varna-sankara* is the unwanted population that disturbs the peace of the general society 35. This comes about when a person is born and doesn't have good genetics and is in a hellish state because of the way people treat them. This with the fact they cannot live their life with the same fullness as those who have good genes is what further leads to their dissatisfaction. The way they come about this conclusion is by looking at others and desiring what others have which is considered being envious or covetous. Becoming the alpha is the way the woman can get to her highest state of evolution, but this takes a true submission of herself to do so. It may take a woman several lifetimes to ascend to higher states within her femininity. Carnal women cite beauty as the most coveted feminine desire, making it in their reality paramount and the epitome of femininity itself. In this case, for the majority of women who have this mind frame, they may have to come back more and more beautiful to rid themselves of the beauty complex before they are able to ascend to higher levels of consciousness. Becoming more beautiful may cause them to have the experiences that liberate them from those desires. By ridding themselves of their desires these women grow to levels where they become beautiful unbeknownst to themselves. Once this consciousness has taken shape within them; the vanity, the arrogance, and the selfishness fades away and are replaced with innocence, love, and sensitivity to others sufferings. When you look at the word consciousness it speaks about having awareness, this is directly related to how a thing is perceived and because it is perceived at such a level the actions of those who have gained the perception begin to shape their world as well as the world around them.

In the book *Understanding Human Behavior - a successful guide to Human Relationships*, Sigmund Freud's theory of penis envy was cited. Freud in his studies concluded though most women enjoyed being women, if they had the choice they'd rather be men 35a. This presents evidence that women subconsciously desire the presence, the power, or the position men have which adds more relevance to the statement made in regards to a woman's highest evolution as becoming an alpha male. Because women aren't necessarily conscious of the differences between the males, the females, and men they believe they can do what they see men doing. What they haven't realized is they are really comparing themselves to males and not men. This is a very hard to distinguish topic because on the surface males and men appear to be the same. The acronym for M.A.N. is (Master Able Noble) and is used to distinguish those males who have evolved to a higher state of consciousness and being. Though women are a higher creation than males they are still subordinate to "God" which is the alpha functioning in his highest "spiritual" state. The fight is between the alpha and the male for breeding rights. The woman is often in conflict between the two because one usually has money and the other has superior genetics. The fact that women were seen as subordinates to men in biblical times further fuels Freud's theory of penis envy.

1 Corinthians 14:34-35 (34) Let your women keep silence in the churches: for it is not permitted unto them to speak; but they are commanded to be under obedience as also saith the law. (35) And if they will learn anything, let them ask their husbands at home: for it is a shame for women to speak in the church.

Being seen as "lesser than" in society would automatically make any one desire the opposite. The question I have to ask is how is it girls develop penis envy before they are ever relegated by society as being subordinate to men? Men are the personification of the building by the builders themselves and represent the temple or the body. The woman is the entity that births the builder of the buildings. Although she herself in the physical doesn't naturally build anything nor does she have the desire to build anything, these factors have to be looked at and examined when speaking in reference to creation and the sexes. When we take an assessment of roles between men and women to see who is best suited for what position, we find nature dictates who is what. However in a domesticated society again the men aren't easily separated from the males, and because they look the same superficially, subconsciously and unknowingly, the woman because she is dominant has a tendency to try to dominate them both. The war that started in the beginning was the war of the sexes. In the beginning, the black was the feminine light, and the white was the masculine dark. This is stated because once in the masculine realm all traces of potential are now finite. The feminine realm is where an infinite range of possibilities and potentials occur. Albert Einstein's quote *"Imagination is greater than knowledge"* is a testament to this truth.

In the feminine realm even though all possibilities are already accounted for, whenever the cycle resets itself, the evolution of the resetting of a cycle will bring about a different interpretation of the same cycle. An example of this is the cycle of numbers of 1 to 9 back to 1 again. 10 equals the upgrade of the same cycle of 1 which was personified at 9. The 1 equals the mutation that enables it to be different and the zero indicates that it is a replication of the same thing only enhanced. This is the way that numbers tie into the realm of masculine and feminine parts. When analyzing masculinity versus femininity the inevitable question arises, which is the most dominant, the one that possesses the beauty, or the one that possesses the brawn? These are the questions that lead to a true understanding of creation and all of the various points of relativity that are directly personified through it. Let's say a woman has a husband that is very cunning and controlling and she herself cannot match his intellect or his physical prowess. Because of this, she uses his genetics in order to birth a son. She does this because she can fashion (her son) to be better in an abstract form which enables the son through the will of the mother to conquer the man in her way. The abstract form the son is born in would be classified as "spiritual" and would be looked at by those in the society that have consciousness in this way. This is where the name Herman /Hermes comes into play and is why he is the author of many esoteric writings; this is his secret. But when you factor in the resetting of the cycles of life, orbits, death, and creation even though the father is out of the way, the woman will still have to deal with him through the son. To put it in layman's terms when you're dealing with the son, you're still dealing with the father. Pending on the level of relation between the two, man and woman, will determine how that conquering son will manifest into the physical realm. He may be a total opposite of his father in the rebellious sense. He may be more handsome and able to amass wealth because of his looks versus his strength. We never know exactly how the son or child will develop within this scenario, but we do know the mother will be instrumental in his overcoming of the father, and this again is due to evolution. Alexander the great is a story that has this as its underlying foundation so does Jacob and Esau. When you look at the power of the woman it is unprecedented here on earth. Traditionally men conquer through barbarianism and war, whereas women fight mentally and subconsciously. Women operate in the subconscious unknowingly which is why when they are in an emotional state it is seemingly uncontrollable. Though women are dominant, they aren't really aware of their power. Being unaware of their power is why men place them in positions where their power can be utilized and further refined to the fullest.

Domestic: (1) devoted to home duties and pleasures relating to the household

The woman's rule over all things domestic is what gives her the power over the circumcised male as his lower anatomy is also that which is domestic. The woman being immensely powerful mentally has to be given busy work to occupy her subconscious mind, which naturally makes her exceptional when structuring and ordering the lives of toddlers who are highly energetic and impressionable. Being rooted in the subconscious, women use that energy to nurture in ways that are unbelievable, unseen, and amazing. The woman being the more dominant of the sexes has the patience and mental capacity to deal with children and accommodate them in special ways. This is why the Supreme Lord and the Supreme Being in Hinduism are called Isvara and Krishna. If you look at the ends of their names they end in a's which show feminine correspondence.

The hierarchy in terms of the sexes both begins and ends with the alpha male or "*all female*." The woman and the man are eye to eye and lastly you have the males; this is the hierarchal structure of natural creation. Certain negative factors like fornicating outside of certain cycles of nature bring about all sorts of beings who are mixtures of masculine and feminine energies. The west (American society) further creates these conditions the more it changes the landscape and the way in which wealth is built. For instance credit is something that every American practically lives their life from. This system of credit is where you get a line of debt to pay off debt as you go. The more debt you pay off the more debt you are able to have. This means that you make money through a regulated or fixed salary, acquire what it is you need, and pay as you go. With credit you buy your house, your car, all of its amenities and over a period of 20-30 years, you pay all of these things off. This system of credit is a system that has been extremely beneficial to inferior males. I say this because the woman would not think to create credit for herself because being the more dominant of the sexes she would just seduce men to get whatever she wanted. It wouldn't necessarily matter to her who was in rule the alpha male or the inferior male. An alpha male is going to work for what he is due and will out work the competition thereby getting ahead in the field in terms of farming, agriculture, or whatever respective business he is in. This was the model of the old world, the same world that produced the alphas who built the very society people live in today. The Kennedy's did it with bootlegging; the Bushes did it through espionage, and warfare. The Jackson's did through music and entertainment. An alpha will produce sons that enable him to build upon his empire. These sons do not require him to pay them salaries because they are of his household, taken care of, and accounted for. If the father had to outsource his business to other employees he would have to create a salary that was conducive towards compensating that employee for all their expenses like house, car, and living. Employing his sons saves him money and allows him to build upon his fortune. Credit has the potential to perpetuate a false system of commerce. It is advantageous for those who have accumulated wealth, as they can use money which isn't theirs to make more.

Now that the fundamental building processes are through in America the manly men are no longer needed and are more of a threat to domestic rule. After any kingdom is built what is most sought after are beautiful women. The kingdom can only be maintained through peace, and this peace is what attracts beautiful women to it. Because a heightened society has these types of women, it develops to the point where the arts and entertainment thrive. This is why the Muses are regarded as being feminine; nine sister goddesses in Greek mythology who preside over song, poetry, the arts and sciences. The culture that houses these (muses) then refines around their women and begins to project an aesthetic exterior. The women want a more comfortable way of life so they naturally seek men who are able to give it to them. In today's time women do not really get to see what type of man they are with because now wealth is built from groups of males getting together and teaming up behind a cause. The cause for the teaming up and the person(s) they are teaming together to defeat is the alpha. By these males merging together, once their agenda is complete, they "appear" to their women to all be of a certain cloth. So we can still surmise the fight is between the woman who evolves into the alpha and the woman who degenerates into a male. The ancients hid the realization of this information in the name of Eve as it is short for evil or *evolution.*

I guess to accurately understand what is meant by inferior males we have to present a definition as well as a balanced interpretation of what type of male this would be. In western society, capitalism accurately gives us the ability to see who has what talent. By looking at the various types of people that have all sorts of talents, how would we know who would be considered the alpha? This would be increasingly difficult in trying to determine when you have so many people who are passionate about diversity. This passion is the driving force that makes these people constantly yearn for something new and different. Prime example is whenever you have a lot of strong men they will in themselves war with one another. This barbarianism when unchecked becomes less and less of what is desired. So when a softer or a more effeminate male is shown to the women, those women who once were attracted to the ultra-masculine men will inevitably flock to the change just because it is a change. The story of Helen of Troy depicts this theme with Paris being the man of her choice over her more barbaric and masculine husband Menelaus. How can we accurately within so much diversity see who is the superior and who is the inferior in regards to individuals who are mixtures between masculinity and femininity? What is the criterion that makes these distinctions known? American society as a whole is a melting pot of so many different kinds of people and genes that we cannot accurately say that a particular set of genes lie within any specific people. We can only postulate on the pure breeds to see what or who indeed is the carrier of what such genes.

The Olympics are today, the purest form of sport and testing grounds that enables the fit and more dominant people to be seen by the entire world. Though some would argue that the games are limited, their arguments often dismiss physicality as being the main criterion or prerequisite to dominance. The speculation that is aroused from this mentality usually includes the countless other categories that are not displayed at the Olympic Games; and is used by the person with the counter argument who says the games do not provide a legitimate assessment for defining what an alpha is. Because certain professions require skill sets that have nothing to do with a person's physical makeup it makes it that much more difficult to develop definitive proof when categorizing people under this criteria who deal in professions like commerce, business, or finance, which do not require the person to be physically fit. What western society has been masterful at creating is counter intelligence versus evolved intelligence. This has to do with a person's ability to counter that which already exists in its perfection. Counter intelligence stems from replication. This means that a person is constantly studying a subject unbeknownst to the subject studied, to figure out why it works, and what are its flaws. This counter intelligence finds a way to humble the most seemingly evolved of beings. Once those who counter find out how these "evolved" beings work, they are no longer considered preeminent amongst the rest of the beings in creation. Whereas the old world might have classified a certain animal as being the end and be all of existence; counter intelligence relegates it from being paramount, to just one of the elite. Having many elite, who would be able to say what is the most elite. How this train of thought relates to spirituality is also the underlying point of view expressed in this book with the question, "Is there only one living god or many?"

Anytime you tell someone that they are inferior you spark within them the ability to supersede that which you think them to be. Something in them channels the energy just to disprove what you have said; this is the classic theme of the underdog. As long as these discussions remain in the raw and un-suspected by those it claims to expose, it is the truth. But once you diagnose a certain people as having superior or inferior genes, those who do not agree actively work to show you the inconsistencies within your theory. As long as it never comes to a mental/physical confrontation, people will always be able to manipulate the situations. Pending on how the situations are manipulated, a person can appear to be something they are not; which was once again personified in the story of Jacob and Esau. Even Jacob knows the superiority of his brother and we see it as he calls him master. He is fearful of his brother Esau and acknowledges he is his brother's servant.

Genesis 32:3-7 (3) Jacob sent messengers ahead of him to his brother Esau in the land of Seir, the country of Edom. (4) He instructed them: "This is what you are to say to my master Esau: 'Your servant Jacob says, I have been staying with Laban and have remained there till now. (5) I have cattle and donkeys, sheep and goats, menservants and maidservants. Now I am sending this message to my lord, that I may find favor in your eyes.' " (6) When the messengers returned to Jacob, they said, "We went to your brother Esau, and now he is coming to meet you, and four hundred men are with him." (7) In great fear and distress Jacob divided the people who were with him into two groups, and the flocks and herds and camels as well. 8 He thought, "If Esau comes and attacks one group, the group that is left may escape."

When referring to the Bible we have to recognize that it is an old world model that we are looking at. When they saw an alpha male, he was considered a man's man much to the like of a *Ben Hur* or any other heroic figure that is beyond the measure of regular men.

One of the bigger issues in society and an even bigger issue in the world of religion is how women are in a sense vilified and also seemingly left out of the conversation in regards to God. God is always referred to as masculine and a goddess aspect is only seen in the Hindu, Semitic, and Egyptian religions. *The social and legal position of an Israelite wife was inferior to the position a wife occupied in the great countries round about. The wife addressed her husband Ba'al or master; she also called him adon or lord; she addressed him as a slave addressed his master or subject, his king.35b*

The conversation of the misogynistic treatment of women has baffled the world of science as scholars have conjectured about there ever being a female

205

prodigy like Mozart or Michael Jackson 34a. Seemingly the most phenomenal occurrences that have hit the globe in epic splashes have always come in a masculine form. Aristotle contended that women exist as natural deformities or imperfect males and also Socrates' insisted that men surpass women at any task that both sexes attempt 35c. Though you have women who are stronger, faster, and more skilled then men; when you compare the fastest or strongest woman to the fastest or strongest man the gaps between their abilities are very wide. To state the obvious seems chauvinistic but I had to make this conversation readily available to the audience because of the way I have referenced the alpha male within this book. Man as a whole is both male and female and everyone comes from a man and a woman. To classify them as separate, from a holistic perspective, is no different than separating black and white, and God and the Devil. The more you calculate and look into a thing, the more everything blends together as one. The differences and biases stem from what you think is greater, what appeals to your sense of self more. Think about it like this, what is more abundant on the planet's surface than water? Then imagine what it would be like without air. Take away the light in the sky or the earth that we stand upon and see what type of world we would have. Everything and everyone has their place and also the potential to do something great in the world; time and chance govern it all. Once we open our eyes to the reality all around us is when we will realize the value in everyone's contribution. Most people in the world will be forgotten even the ones considered to be great. The ones who are written in the book are the ones who have taken a stand to make their presences known and also felt. Their lives also seem to be a fixed part of the world as we know it and predestination plays the role of the master of ceremonies. In the words of the great playwright, *the world's a stage* it's "stars" recurrent and everlasting.

The Book of Illumination

CHAPTER 11

THE SUN OF GOD

The Book of Illumination

CHAPTER 11

THE SUN OF GOD

THE SUN OF GOD

Due to mankind's unrelenting egoism and infantile understanding of 'God, a (Sun) avatar is sent into the world to teach mankind about the nature and true potential it possesses. Man's possibilities are greater than his attainments 36. Being that man is one of the highest creations, he has one of the highest potentials. I am talking literally about powers, ascensions, and greater evolutions within man's spiritual awareness. Mankind will never be able to fully assess the damage it's done to humanity unless it is truthful about the things in history that have happened, like the holocaust of the dark people from Africa, and the birthright that was supplanted by romantic imagery. Until these things are brought to the forefront and given the proper attention, many of the world's problems will never truly be solved.

When you talk about the Christ, you're talking about someone who is fighting against oppression; namely an oppressive system of religion, biases, and ideologies. When I look at the Gospels and the story of Jesus, I see for lack of understanding, mankind trying to humanize what they perceive to be "God." In order for people to truly relate to someone they have to have experienced or went through the same thing. This is a primitive way of relating, but nonetheless it is the way that people draw their associations. If what people are analyzing isn't like them, they cannot fully accept and follow it. Because "God" is unfathomable to most people, humanizing him is the only way people relate to his/its existence. The scriptures indicate "God" is aware of this dilemma and as a result manifested to earth as a *Sun* in human flesh to teach the people how to become more godly (civilized.) When I speak about Jesus and the gospel, I am looking at it from a literary point of view first. I am reading it as if it were any other great work of literature as opposed to the almighty and encompassing word that "God" wrote himself through divinely inspired authors. Imagine that all the knowledge that exists within the Bible has a science associated with it. He who knows the science knows what was written by THE LORD and what was written by man. When I read the Bible, I read it from a literary standpoint first. Looking at the Bible from this point of view makes the stories in it even more humanistic.

Celestial: (1) of or relating to heaven or divinity (2) of or relating to sky

Disciple: (1) one who accepts and assists in spreading the doctrines of another

LITERARY NOT LITERALLY

Reading the Bible from a literary standpoint gives me the insight to connect any and all points that are relative.

Literary: (1) of, relating to, or having the characteristics of humane learning (2) of or relating to books

When reading the Bible and referencing other literary works with it, it is easily recognized that the stories that are translated within the Bible, are stories from older cultures and sources. The conception story of Jesus comes from the Egyptian stories of Horus, Set, Osiris and Isis. If you never went outside of the Bible to see where the origins of these stories lie, you would place the origins of the stories as coming from the Bible itself. Remember *Biblos* means the *little books*, and the Bible again is a compilation of ancient books and manuscripts. What is equally intriguing about cross referencing other stories with those of the Bible; is that you don't have to go outside the religions of Abraham to find out the stories in the Bible are always in a continuance. Looking at biblical stories from a literary perspective further allows the reader to see what is figurative, what is literal, what is historical, what is allegorical, as well as what is embellished. Reading from this perspective allows the consciousness of the reader to become more broadened and enlightened to the truths the stories are reflecting. For instance Samson shows the way beautiful women manipulate strong men to their demise. The true power of the woman is demonstrated when Herodias's daughter danced for King Herod and pleased him so much he granted her whatever she wanted; it just so happened she asked for the head of John the Baptist.

Matthew 14:6-10 (6) But when Herod's birthday was kept, the daughter of Herodias danced before them and pleased Herod (7) Whereupon he promised with an oath to give her whatsoever she would ask. (8) and she, being before instructed of her mother said, Give me here John the Baptist's head in a charger. (9) And the king was sorry: nevertheless for an oath's sake, and them which sat with him at meat, commanded it be given her. (10) And he sent and beheaded John the Baptist.

A dance was all it took for the "*greatest born of women*" to be beheaded.

Matthew 11:11 (11) Verily I say unto you, Among them that are born of women there hath not risen one greater than John the Baptist: not withstanding he that is least in the kingdom of heaven is greater than he.

Scriptures like the one's just referenced put into perspective what sex truly has power. The illustration of these points within passages from the Bible, allows one who is reading from a literary perspective, to gain a true perspective of what is being taught through the allegories expressed therein. The fact that throughout the Bible women are shown manipulating men and getting them into trouble is a constant underlying point of emphasis represented from the Book of Genesis with Eve and Adam, all the way to the Gospel of Matthew with Herod and John the Baptist. Because women can manipulate men with their beauty, women on the eastern side of the world are covered up. This is done to eliminate this manipulation from happening as well as keeping other men from lusting after women who have husbands.

1 Corinthians 11:5 But every woman that prayeth or prophesieth with her head uncovered dishonoureth her head: for that is even all one as if she were shaven

How will a man ever respect a woman for her mind if what he is attracted to is her body? All he will do to win her favor is tell her whatever she wants to hear so he can obtain that which he wants. Usually if the woman's body is what he has seen; it is probably what he is after. All a woman has to possess is beauty. Her beauty is so powerful that it humbles the most savage of tyrants. King Kong is the story that personifies this relationship. When looking at these parallel's one can readily comprehend how an all-powerful alpha that has conquered the world, slain thousands of men, and participated in hundreds of wars, would kneel to give all his spoils to a beautiful woman. The woman's power is unprecedented in terms of the sexes as physical strength has only one rival; beauty.

Adam and Eve
Genesis 3:6 (6) And when the woman saw that the tree was good for food, and that it was pleasant to the eyes, and a tree to be desired to make one wise, she took of the fruit thereof, and did eat, and gave also unto her husband with her; and he did eat.

Abraham and Sarah
Genesis 16:2 (2) And Sarah said unto Abram, Behold now, the Lord hath restrained me from bearing; I pray thee, go in unto my maid; it may be that I may obtain children by her. And Abram hearkened to the voice of Sarah.

Rebekah and Jacob

*Genesis 25:28 (28) And Isaac loved Esau, because he did eat of his venison but Rebekah loved Jacob **Genesis 27:1-18** (1) And it came to pass that when Isaac was old, and his eyes were dim so that he could not see he called Esau his eldest son and said unto him Behold here I am (2) And He said behold I am old now I know not the day of my death (3) Now therefore take I pray thee thy weapons thy quiver and thy bow, and go out to the field and take ne some venison (4) And make me savory meat, such as I love, and bring it to me that I may eat ; that my soul may bless thee before I die (5) And Rebekah heard when Isaac spake to Esau his son. And Esau went to the field to hunt for venison, and to bring it. (6) And rebekah spake unto her son saying, Behold I heard thy father speak unto Esau thy brother saying (7) Bring me venison, and make me savory meat that I may eat and bless thee before the Lord before my death (11) And Jacob said to Rebekah his mother Behold Esau my brother is a hairy man, and I am a smooth man (12) My father peradventure will feel me, and I shall seem to him as a deceiver, and shall bring a curse upon me, and not a blessing (13) And his mother said to him, upon me ne thy curse my son only obey my voice and go fetch me them (14) and he went and fetched and brought them to his mother and his mother made savory meat such as his father loved (16) And she put the skins of the kids (goats) upon his hands and upon the smooth of his neck (17) And she gave the savory meat and the bread that she prepared , into the hand of her son Jacob (19) And Jacob said unto his father I am Esau thy firstborn; I have done according as thou badest me arise I pray thee sit and eat of my venison, that thy soul may bless me.*

Samson and Delilah

Judges 16:18-19 (18) And when Delilah saw that he had told her all his heart, she sent and called for the lords of the philistines saying, come up this once for he hath shewed me all his heart. Then the lords of the Phillistines came up unto her, and brought money in their hand (19) And she made him (Samson) sleep upon her knees and she called for a man, and she caused him to shave off the seven locks of his head; she began to afflict him, and his strength went from him

Herod and John the Baptist

Matt.14:6-10 (6) But when Herod's birthday was kept, the daughter of Herodias danced before them and pleased Herod (7) Whereupon he promised with an oath to give her whatsoever she would ask. (8) and she, being before instructed of her mother said, Give me here John the Baptist's head in a charger. (9) and the king was sorry: nevertheless for an oath's sake, and them which sat with him at meat, commanded it be given her. (10) And he sent and beheaded John the Baptist.

It is more important to see what about the human condition these stories are telling us, versus are they in themselves holy or literally true. They are holy but not in the sense of "*Holy*" rather wholly in the sense of whole. A person reading the Bible from a literal standpoint most likely will miss the underlying pretenses translated in its scriptures because of the allegorical style the scriptures were written with. There are certain people who have gifts of translation and can see through the scriptures and if they have focused meditated and paid attention to the patterns of life and nature, their translation will be very acute.

Preachers of today mistake the preaching of Jesus and John to be like their own, which is a misconception, because Jesus and John were both resurrected. This means they were conscious of their past lives and have instructions for mortals who are not conscious at all. Who would have a better understanding then them? Listening at a mere mortal in reference to the life of Jesus can only cause confusion. Imagine if you died… Now think about a friend who knew you. How might a person who knew you and studied your life reference you to others? How could we trust their testimony about you to be accurate? What might they say in reference to your memory? I'm asking you to do this because this is what has happened with the Bible in regards to Jesus and who has reported his life story. Luke, John, and Mark were all fellow colleagues of Paul and through their gospels they have written about the life of Jesus.

In today's society the media gossip on the most trending blog sites often displays the dirt about public figures written by people who do not know them personally. While these gossipers will elaborate on the person's life, they somehow forget to mention what the person being written about is reacting to. This same rationale can be applied to the people listening at preachers rather than waiting on the messiah they been taught to worship. What man can really say that he is worthy enough to stand on a pulpit and preach to people as if he really knows what is going on with Christ or God? For one, the person who is leading the flock may not have a clear perspective to teach them with. If the congregation is caught up in the way the preachers deliver their messages, this can distract them from what is actually being said in the preachers sermon. There are often times delivered by the preacher in their grandstanding, irrelevant scriptures citing the words of Jesus. Once the preacher's passion invoking sermon is fused with a choir and a band, it enables the preacher to establish an emotional connection with the congregation. Now connected, the preacher is able to convict the congregation based on the fundamental nature they were created with, which is lust. But after the emotional rant, misapplied Bible verses, and passion invoking music, what has a person genuinely come away with? I always use the story of the physician when speaking in reference to this topic. When a person is sick, they go to the doctor and get diagnosed. Upon the doctor figuring out the problem, the patient is treated, given medication, and then sent back out to society. In the church however, if a person is spiritually sick, they don't get treated because there often is no one on one diagnosis for the individual. There are no priests to diagnose them, and if there is a priest there, he usually isn't the same person that is preaching to them and giving them their instruction. Unlike a hospital, the person stays at the place where their sickness is supposed to be treated for their entire life in an endless cycle; and they still have to pay each and every time they come. The question I often ask is, where's the real healing? After the people have attended church service and have to go back to reality, there is only more confusion which causes them to have to keep attending. Who stays at a hospital their entire life?

While the church has been instrumental in divulging a lot of scriptural Information it has equally done the same with scriptural and spiritual confusion. Insanity is classified as doing the same thing over and over again expecting different results. If people were taught more about themselves, and the Bibles stories were used as the basis, a great transformation will start to take place within the individual. However when a person references the Jesus and the "*In Christ*" of the mind, without bearing witness to the Jesus who is a living person, this is sacrilegious. Namely because only the one who the world has been waiting to see (The *Sun* of Man) has the truth, the rest are just those with hypothesis's or for the un-learned, educated guesses.

The institution of the Mother Church as well as the American Negro churches seems to be headed towards reform; but before you can reform or rebuild, something has to be destroyed. I don't want to sound too critical or come down too harsh upon the church. As I stated before, the Bible is full of contradictions and even the Gospels including the story of Jesus Christ are different pending which one is being referenced. Who is able to distinguish what part of the text are man's words, apart from those that are "God's" words? And for these reasons we should first look at what the scriptures say literarily before we dive in head first accepting them on a literal basis.

What I have learned about faith, and Paul is an example of this, is that with it you can (move mountains) and achieve great things, even if they be in falsehood. Most of what people believe is just that, a belief; not everything is proven with fact. However when talking about the scriptures, Jews, and the Christ, there is definitely evidence that suggest that what the world has been given by way of the scriptures, lacks in detail what it needs to fully understand the life of Christ, immortality, and the promises foretold within the Bible. As the Masons say, the true WORD has been lost and the world has spiraled into an abyss of confusion and delusion because of it. Obviously the people who invaded Israel and Judah went through great lengths to destroy the old records that would give the world the clues needed to return it to a golden age. For these reasons scholars, theologians, historians, and anthropologists have been searching for the lost Ark, the Holy Grail, and the lost Logos for quite some time; and they haven't a clue they are all one in the same. When you look at this from a carnal standpoint you have to ask yourself, "Why would someone go to these lengths to destroy the truth?" Two words come to my mind when confronted with this question, power and control. Most of what people experience in life is an illusion. Because they can't fully comprehend life they use imagination to fill their intellectual gaps. For instance when you ask a person what color was Jesus, they respond, "*Well that's not important, the important thing is that he died for our sins and through our belief in him we are saved.*" Another response might be "*He is all colors because he is God.*"

Revelation 1:13-15 (13) And in the midst of the seven candlesticks one like unto the son of man, clothed with a garment down to the foot, and girt about the paps with a golden girdle (14) <u>His head and hairs were white like wool</u>, as white as snow: and his eyes were a flame of fire; (15) And <u>his feet like unto fine brass, as if they burned in a furnace</u>; and his voice as the sound of many waters.

My point here is to acknowledge there is some indication as to what color or race Jesus may be according to the description given in the 1st chapter of Revelation, which describes him as having hair like wool and feet as if burned in a furnace. My next question is why the Catholic Church hasn't put forth this evidence when making an image of him, (*which is forbidden in the Law of Moses to do.*) Yet they promote this image of Jesus (below) even though scripturally there is no evidence to support it.

Exodus 20: 4 (20) Thou shalt not make unto thee any graven image, or any likeness of anything that is in heaven above, or that is in the earth beneath, or that is in the water under the earth.

<u>Jewish</u>: of, relating to or characteristic of the Jews; *also*: being a Jew

<u>Jew:</u> (1) a member of the tribe of Judah (2) Israelite (3) Semitic

<u>Semitic:</u> (1) of, relating to, or constituting a subfamily of the **Afro-Asiatic** language family that includes Hebrew, Aramaic, Arabic, and Amharic (2) Jewish

<u>Israelite:</u> a descendant of the Hebrew patriarch Jacob

LIP PROFESSION

Matthew 15:7&8 (7) *You hypocrites! Isaiah was right when he prophesied about you (8)'These people honor me with their lips, but their hearts are far from me.(9)They worship me in vain; their teachings are but rules taught by men.*

The story of Moses to most people is a great story about the heroic faithful servant of "God" who through his convictions about his lineage leads his people out of bondage and into a promised land. Along the way this servant of "God" suffers many hardships and obstacles, that when paralleled to our own lives, gives his story personal significance to us. However objectively looking at this story, rather than subjectively paralleling ourselves to it, allows an even greater lesson to be learned. The way most people have been taught to look at this story was in the performance given by Charlton Heston in the movie *The Ten Commandments*. The way this story has been depicted has forever left an imprint upon the minds of all those who viewed it because an interpreted image of the story has been stamped on the viewer, locking the viewer into that interpretation. That interpretation, may blind those viewing from seeing an actual occurrence in the life they are living today. This is why you have people walking around praying to statues, and thinking the coming of the avatars, or "godsends" to be like the movies, while simultaneously minimizing the actual avatars and not fully crediting them for their monumental achievements and abilities when they incarnate to the planet.

When dissecting the account of Moses, there are two interpretations that come to mind. The first is a man who through his naive understanding of the human condition leaves the royal house of Pharaoh (which he is already and heir too) only to wander in the wilderness for 40 years and never see the *Promised Land* for himself. In diagnosing the story through this point of view a person arrives to the logical conclusion that Moses, if he wanted to be in control of the fates of the Jews, could have waited it out in Pharaoh's house. Pharaoh favored Moses over his own blood son and would have made Moses ruler over all of Egypt when he died. Once Moses became leader he could have done whatever he wanted as Pharaoh. But, because Moses feels that Pharaoh is neglecting the Jews who he (Moses) has discovered are his people, he gets convicted, and leads a crusade against Pharaoh...ultimately causing the people to abandon Pharaoh as their ruler. Though hindsight is 20/20, Moses then spends 40 years in anguish only to find out what Pharaoh already knew.

Pharaoh was hard on the people because he knew their hearts; he knew they really had no belief in anything. In his reckoning, a people like this deserve to be subjected to whatever rule comes over them. Moses being naïve to this understanding only finds out in the end why Pharaoh was the way he was from the beginning. When Moses had to kill 3,000 men because they were idol worshippers, I bet secretly he was thinking about Pharaoh.

Genesis 32:22-28 (22) And Aaron said, Let not the anger of my lord wax hot: thou knowest the people, that they are set on mischief. (23) For they said unto me, Make us gods, which shall go before us: for as for this Moses, the man that brought us up out of the land of Egypt, we wot not what is become of him. (24)And I said unto them, Whosoever hath any gold, let them break it off. So they gave it me: then I cast it into the fire, and there came out this calf. (25) And when Moses saw that the people were naked; (for Aaron had made them naked unto their shame among their enemies :(26) Then Moses stood in the gate of the camp, and said, Who is on the LORD's side? Let him come unto me. And all the sons of Levi gathered themselves together unto him. (27)And he said unto them, Thus saith the LORD God of Israel, Put every man his sword by his side, and go in and out from gate to gate throughout the camp, and slay every man his brother, and every man his companion, and every man his neighbour. (28)And the children of Levi did according to the word of Moses: and there fell of the people that day about three thousand men.

Moses spent countless hours trying to civilize a people who at the drop of a dime would change their minds about the god they served and the way they worshipped him. It's plausible to surmise that the wickedness of the people's hearts is what led them to having a leader that was best suited to counter their type of mentality (Pharaoh.) The people in the Book of Exodus, as regarded by the Bible, wished to do as they wanted, when they wanted. After being delivered from the clutches of Pharaoh, which can be likened to the people of today who in the guise of freedom practice anarchy under perceived governmental control; the people still fail to acknowledge the person who physically delivers them. When you take into account the nature of these people the scriptures indicate they are by design wicked and rebellious. Moses, if he so chose, could have easily let the people go after becoming Pharaoh. Why couldn't he foresee this? Was it because he was naïve or was he simply blinded by his ego? He was in denial about the character of the people he was dealing with; and caught up in his emotions. He lost his woman, his position, and his chance to see the *Promised Land* for a wicked and rebellious people; a people who after his demise still ended right back in captivity. When I take into account the story of Moses from this perspective it further allows me to see why *Jews* do not believe in a savior; for who can really save YOU but yourself? This also validates the notion why the *Jews* closed their Torah with this last lesson, and further employs within them a realistic mindset towards life and spirituality.

The second interpretation of the story of Moses is one that is found when you look deeper within the scriptures to define the meanings of words and use the meanings of the words to give you the actual lessons. For instance: Moses in Arabic is spelled Musa, which is where the root of the words muse, Moslem and Muslim come from. A Muslim is defined as one who submits his soul to do the works of God.

John 6: 38 (38) For I have come down from heaven not to do my will but to do the will of him who sent me. - Jesus

Muse: (1) to become absorbed in thought; *especially*: to turn something over in the mind meditatively (2) any of the nine sister goddesses in Greek mythology presiding over song and poetry and the arts and sciences (3) a source of inspiration; a guiding genius

Museum: (1) Latin *Museum* place for learned occupation, from Greek *Mouseion,* from neuter of *Mouseios* of the Muses, from *Mousa* (2) an institution devoted to the procurement, care, study, and display of objects of lasting interest or value

In today's society, the person who fits the mold as the muse's muse is Michael Jackson. Michael's life, like the story of Musa, can be looked at as the cultivation of an uncivil and low level society to the culmination of a heightened society brought forth by a muse, whereby heavenly attributes are expressed through the arts. This is stated because through musing or meditation, the muse hears the instructions of their highest self (god). The muse then uses these instructions to transform the society into the thought process of its "higher" self. The muse's gift is the translation, or the tongues they speak with. This "tongue" touches the god energy (Namaste) within the people and makes them march in the direction of the astrological self which literally is the (higher being) that is influencing the muse. In the case of Michael Jackson his "higher being" /astrological self is (Virgo) which translates in Latin to Deva or Diva. Here is where we find the mystic link between him, his artistry, and the "divine." Virgo is ruled by the planet Mercury which in the Zodiac controls communication. These "God-given" attributes are what enabled him to became the greatest artist of all time. Michael Jackson was a muse whose life was the physical living canvas that illustrates the supplanting of the original face of the Egyptian gods to the commercialized face of their romantic counterparts.

"Art has as its ultimate goal the union between the material and the spiritual, the human and the divine." – Michael Jackson

Michael's life represents the story of how a young black boy, who started out saving his village in Egypt, was transformed into a white man who dies trying to salvage humanity. He went from being black to white in a single lifetime bringing together a divided nation of races with a natural religion (music.)

Michael's greatest musical accomplishment was a song where he danced alongside zombies; as it is written the disciples of Jesus, would raise the living dead, freely give, and heal the sick.

219

Matthew 10:8 Heal the sick, cleanse the lepers, <u>raise the dead</u>, cast out devils, freely ye have received freely give.

His most famous dance was the moon walk, where in the likeness of Jesus, he glides across stage as if *"walking on water."* One of his most heartfelt and inspirational messages was when and wrote and performed *We are the World;* a song that featured the most influential artists of the time to draw attention to starvation in 3rd world countries. He was a "savior" in the sense that he gave millions of dollars for the medicines and vaccinations that preserved the lives of millions of kids in Africa. Michael is also listed in the Guinness Book of World Records for giving to the most charities; it is estimated he gave over $500,000,000 million dollars.

Paul the leader of the church as well as the author of many of the NT books had this to say about charity in Corinthians 13:13

1Corinthians 13:13 And now abideth faith, hope, and charity but the greatest of these three is charity.

Michael was a healer as he invited kids to his house who were sick and needed his energy to strengthen and liberate them from their diseases and ailments. Many people will say, "Well, why was he climbing trees, having amusement parks at his house, and having sleepovers with kids." Here is your answer found in the 18th and 19th chapters of Matthew:

*Matthew 19:13-14 (13) Then little children were brought to Jesus for him to place his hands on them and pray for them. But the disciples rebuked those who brought them. (14) **Jesus said,** "Let the little children come to me, and do not hinder them, for the kingdom of heaven belongs to such as these."*

Matthew 18:1-5 (1)At the same time came the disciples unto Jesus, saying, Who is the greatest in the kingdom of heaven? (2)And Jesus called a little child unto him, and set him in the midst of them,(3) And said, Verily I say unto you, Except ye be converted<u>, and become as little children, ye shall not enter into the kingdom of heaven.</u> (4) Whosoever therefore shall humble himself as this little child, the same is greatest in the kingdom of heaven. (5) And whoso shall receive one such little child in my name receiveth me.

Michael Jackson's antics seem strange until an assessment of scripture is taken whereby people can attest that he is literally following the instructions given by Jesus; which consist of humbling oneself and becoming like a child. Michael Jackson is also the single most influential person to date in relation to pop culture. When blacks couldn't get on MTV he was the first to give them a culture they could participate in and make tons of money through. Before

Michael Jackson, there were no endorsement deals or mega million dollar opportunities for blacks in pop music, because the genre of music known as pop didn't exist until he sold out those concerts and record stores.

The younger generations have not experienced racism in the way their parents and grandparents did, and haven't a clue in regards to its severity. They don't whole heartedly believe in the Bible. This point is expressed because the world is expecting a returning savior. But how will the world recognize him if they don't have any indication of what he may look like?

The younger generations have also already risen above racism but the older generations do not know to what extent. These youth bond together with common interests and social mediums such as music and pop culture. Because the music and the artists they like are the same, they don't see color they only see talent. For these reasons, the youth now more than ever are cliqued based. They group together from common interests and are more attracted to pop cultured lifestyles. When the previous generation, (those who are 40 and above) were growing up, the social climate in this country was shifting. Michael Jackson was instrumental in the integration of an American culture that was once divided. Michael united a whole generation of different people through music, as he is the most recognizable and popular artist and person to date. Born on August 29th 1958, a few years before the decade that would permanently alter American politics; we witnessed the great violence of that decade that spawned songs like *Can You Feel It* from The Jackson Five. In late November of 1963 President Kennedy was assassinated, two years later in 1965 Malcolm X met his death at the hands of an assassin. In 1968 both Martin Luther King and Robert Kennedy, the brother of JFK were assassinated as well. Here in this decade you had a president, a senator who just received the Democratic nomination as the candidate for presidency alongside two of the most prominent civil rights leaders the world has ever known, all assassinated. So when you hear a mega-hit song like *Can you feel it*, with Michael chanting *"all the colors of the world should be loving each other wholeheartedly, Cause we're all the same yes the blood inside of me is inside of you"* 37b you get a feel for what fueled his artistry.

When internalizing the story of Musa (Moses) and paralleling aspects of that story to modern day America, I know a lot of people are asking what the story of Moses has to do with Michael Jackson. In analyzing the word Musa and then looking at the world's greatest muse parallels between the two can be easily drawn. One of the parallels between Michael and Moses is the story of the golden calf. At face value this calf seems to be just that, a golden bull; but when analyzed further we can see how this bull is still relative today.

Exodus 32:1-4 *(1) And when the people saw that Moses delayed to come down out of the mount, the people gathered themselves together unto Aaron and said unto him, Up make us gods, which shall go before us; for as for this Moses, the man that brought us up out of the land of Egypt, we wot not what has become of him (2) And Aaron said unto them, Break off the golden earrings, which are in the ears of your wives, of your sons, and of your daughters, and bring them unto me. (3) And all the people brake off the golden earrings which were in their ears, and brought them unto Aaron (4) And he received it at their hand, and fashioned with it a graving tool, after he had made a <u>molten calf</u>: and they said these be the gods, O Israel, which brought thee up out of the land of Egypt.*

Merrill Lynch

38 When opening up the story of the Golden Calf found within the Book of Genesis, we have to realize that this story, like several other stories in the Bible, is allegorical and represents something a little more provocative. A bull, in biblical times, was the ultimate symbol of wealth and economic prosperity because it was the main source of business and livelihood for the family. It is still used today by major investment banks like **Merrill Lynch**. The bull was considered holy, sought after, and prayed for because if you had a bull, you could breed him and make more bulls. More bulls meant more plows, more cows, and more meat. The more cows a person has, the more milk they could sell. The more plows a person had the larger crop they could plant and harvest. An abundance of crops, meat, and milk was considered wealth in those times. So when the people who were led out of bondage attributed their liberator to being a golden calf rather than Moses, it is no different than today when people attribute money to being their savior rather than the person who paved their way to freedom. For example, the generation that follows the Michael Jackson Pepsi generation are the hip-hoppers /rappers who express emphatically through their music a culture that acknowledges *cash* as its *king*. The two leading record labels who have the most urban/ commercial influence are *Roc-a-fella Records* and *Cash Money Records*. Both have to do with money, as *Cash money* is self-explanatory, and the *Roc-a-fella* reference is an obvious play on the Rockefeller family that is regarded as being if not the wealthiest, one of the wealthiest families in the world. This generation was the 2nd generation of hip-hoppers and the first to see the shift in economic prosperity go from people who lived in the suburbs to people who were born in ghettos. In this *rag to riches* era, those who were born of the most humbling of circumstances, through rap music, could grow into huge moguls. I know you're asking the question, what do the calf and Moses have to do with Michael Jackson? What Michael was singing about and fighting for was

equality of race and harmony within humanity. He stressed the coming together of rich and poor people of all nationalities and creeds. Michael single-handedly desegregated the world globally, and was basically fighting for everything that would liberate the human people from their bondage to an oppressive system of ideology; yet now he is despised, ridiculed, and considered a horror story for the rest of man and mankind.

Michael Jackson, one of the richest black men in America who was the most famous person in the world for 40 years of his life does not have a song about how much money he has; yet by paving the way for African Americans to get on music television, (MTV) which can allegorically be synonymous to *"parting the red sea,"* the music culture of today is now dominated by artists that glorify material wealth. If we were paralleling Michael's life and compositing it with the time of Moses with relevance to what is going on in pop culture today; we could easily make the argument that what is happening today is no different than what happened then with the golden calf. A people who were delivered from an oppressive state attributes that to which saves as *"money/golden calf"* versus the person who under the authority of a "higher being" literally delivered them from their bondage. When this period of history is recorded in history's books, Michael Jackson could very well be looked at in the same light as Moses.

What makes the story of the golden calf even more prophetic is the bull in ancient times actually had a cult associated with it. On the surface, it appears this cult worships the calf because of the various necessities a bull provides for everyday farm life like milk, meat, and the labor associated with plowing crops. However, this particular "bull" has relevance to the indigenous peoples of Egypt and India and has an underlying astrological significance directly related to Michael Jackson. This is a topic that will need an elaborate explanation, one that will be further discussed in latter chapters.

Coincidentally, in this new generation, there was another Michael of monumental significance who wore the symbol of the bull upon his chest. The peoples' fascination with the individual Michaels and not the power or sources of knowledge behind their personas only makes the people strive to be like them superficially. In doing so, the people are always looking to the end of the story and leaving out the particulars and the details, which are the main ingredients to the lessons and allegories therein. Because these two Michaels have become billionaires due to them harnessing the energy of the Godhead, people look at becoming multi-millionaires rather than trying to harness the energy or spirit that made these two magnificent individuals into who they are today. The focus of the lay people is no longer on the spiritual aspect that enables the being to evolve to a state where it alone creates its wealth. The people have skipped this step and degenerated into worshipping the money and the material itself; the same way they did in biblical times when they worshipped the golden calf. This is also why in the Bible men were not supposed to make graven images of God. If man is fixated on that which the "Living God" used to look like; when the "Living God" changes his physical appearance, man will be unable to see him in his altered form.

The two Michaels, Jordan and Jackson, literally led a people who had been oppressed out of bondage by musing and entertainment. Endorsement deals, TV time, and sold out arenas found their birth within the rise of these two heroic individuals.

Revelation 21:7-10 (7) And there was war in heaven: Michael and his angels fought against the dragon; and the dragon fought and his angels, (8) And prevailed not; neither was their place found any more in heaven. (9) And the great dragon was cast out, that old serpent, called the Devil, and Satan, which deceiveth the whole world: he was cast out into the earth, and his angels were cast out with him. (10) And I heard a loud voice saying in heaven, Now is come salvation, and strength, and the kingdom of our God, and the power of his Christ: for the accuser of our brethren is cast down, which accused them before our God day and night.

39 In the 90's Michael Jordan was said to have generated ten billion dollars in the American economy as well as a trillion dollars to the city of Chicago; a trait that is indicative of Taurus (the Bull) as it symbolizes wealth and prosperity. A very interesting characteristic to note about Michael Jordan is his highly competitive spirit and combative nature. This trait enables him to virtually "annihilate" all competitors in his path on the basketball court. The birth date of Michael Jordan is February 17th; which is also the day the Hindi religion celebrates the birthday of Kali, the goddess of annihilation 39a. The astrological sign Aquarius is depicted in the tarot as a serene woman sitting naked by a lake. Both Michael Jordan's astrological sign as well as tarot card indicate he is an Aquarius, which again is depicted as a woman even though Aquarius is a masculine sign. Look at the goddess Kali's tongue on the picture next to Jordan; in every depiction of her, we see her tongue stretched forth which was also the trademark of Michael Jordan 40.

Though Kali, in Hinduism, is often referred to as a goddess, this can be likened to the fact, as explained earlier, that Aquarius is seen in the tarot as being a woman. Kali is the wife of Shiva the Sun. This is a relationship that best describes the marriage between sun and star or Leo and Aquarius. Aleister Crowley defines the two entities as Nuith and Hadit in his Thelema religion. Kali in Sanskrit literally means "Black" and in understanding that, look at how dark Michael Jordan's complexion is. I placed this information in the book so the naysayers who think all of these findings are coincidences are forced to look at what aren't just striking similarities but also striking parallels. If gods are immortals, why would they not live amongst humanity eternally? Why wouldn't they be unrivaled and epic in their achievements? If they weren't, how would people be able to recognize them?

In Roman mythology, Michael Jordan would be known as Achilles, the

great Trojan War hero who was unconquerable in battle. The fact that his shoe is the most popular selling shoe and he's born on the day of *the battler*, again relates Michael Jordan to Achilles 37c. This comparison is made because Achilles was the ultimate battling warrior in his time as Michael was when on the basketball court. Michael's shoe is the symbol that links him and Achilles together from times of antiquity to the present. When much of the history was being assembled into the books we read today, certain legends would be merged with other legends when they had similar attributes that link two contemporary astral deities or gods together. For example, Achilles dies in the same manner as Krishna, by being shot in the foot, and Achilles, like Krishna, is unconquerable in battle. The name Krishna, like Kali, also corresponds to black, and when we look at the two, Michael Jeffery Jordan and Michael Joseph Jackson, both of their names have the same initials, MJJ. That alongside the fact they are both related to a "Bull" and have fathers who are Leo's shows how both characters' lives when being assembled into a legend, could have easily been mistaken for one another and then printed into texts as the same person. The people who were breaking down and translating these legends of the gods from ancient manuscripts didn't have television nor could they see what an actual god physically looks like. They could only hypothesize and make evaluations from the text itself which as I previously stated, when translating, can be misleading especially when you do not have a visual record to go by. Today we have television and visual records that enable us to see exactly who is who. This gives us the ability with clarity to understand the pantheon of gods we read about in legend and composite them with accuracy and precision with people of monumental and astronomical importance and influence today.

Michael's Jordan's father James R. Jordan was born on July 31st making him a Leo and an emperor by way of astrological and tarot interpretation. The merging between the two astrological angles of Leo and Aquarius, gives Michael Jordan a Heru/ Achilles alignment. The numbers He (4) and Tzaddi (17) correspond together as the Tzaddi or Star (17) is also the Sun (Leo) who is the King (4.) The more that we think things change, the more that we see they remain the same. This is why a complete understanding of planetary alignments is the ultimate source as to what & who really governs this world.

ALLEGORY

Allegory: a form of extended metaphor, in which objects, persons, and actions in a narrative are equated with the meanings that lie outside the narrative itself. The underlying meaning within the allegory has a moral, social, religious, or political significance, and its characters are often personifications of abstract ideas

The definition of allegory defined above indicates that a symbol has significance and can represent a truth that may be hidden from someone who is looking at the same thing literally. Allegories are literary devices that have a moral, historical, and spiritual significance and were often used to hide the real meaning from the enemies of a particular nation so that only those who were initiated through the customs and conditions of that nation would be able to understand and comprehend the meaning of the allegories fully.

Another Biblical story that directly relates to that of Michael Jackson through allegory is the story of Joseph, which is also found in the Book of Genesis. Michael Jackson, like Joseph, wore the "*coat of many colors.*" In the story of Joseph the ruler of Israel, this coat was given to him by his father Jacob as Joseph was the favorite son of Israel [41], [42].

Genesis 37: 3-4 *(3) Now Israel loved Joseph more than all his children, because he was the son of his old age: and he made him a coat of many colors.(4)And when his brethren saw that their father loved him more than all his brethren, they hated him, and could not speak peaceably unto him.*

In the case of Michael's Jackson, the *"coat of many colors"* is reflective of the mentality he possessed in relation to all races loving one another in harmony; a trait in Hinduism that is indicative of the peacock. This *"coat of many colors"* was also projected through Michael's skin complexion as his skin went through many "transformations" and "colors" within his lifetime. Witnessing Michael's *"coat of many colors"* reigns true on so many levels, from the literal JACKETS Michael wore, to his literary and figurative skin changing metamorphosis.

Isaiah 52:13-15 *See, my servant will act wisely: he will be raised and lifted up and highly exalted. (14) Just as there were many who were appalled at him his appearance was so disfigured beyond that of any man and his form marred beyond human likeness(15) so will he sprinkle many nations, and kings will shut their mouths because of him. For what they were not told, they will see, and what they have not heard, they will understand*

43 When further anatomizing the story of Joseph, the Bible indicates he was thrown into a pit by jealous siblings. This was fueled by his father Jacob's enduring love for him and also the dream he had which his siblings took to mean, Joseph would enslave them.

Genesis 37:5-10 *(5)And Joseph dreamed a dream, and he told it his brethren: and they hated him yet the more. (6) And he said unto them, Hear, I pray you, this dream which I have dreamed: (7) For, behold, we were binding sheaves in the field, and, lo, my sheaf arose, and also stood upright; and, behold, your sheaves stood round about, and made obeisance to my sheaf. (8) And his brethren said to him, Shalt thou indeed reign over us? or shalt thou indeed have dominion over us? And they hated him yet*

227

the more for his dreams, and for his words. (9) And he dreamed yet another dream, and told it his brethren, and said, Behold, I have dreamed a dream more; and, behold, the sun and the moon and the eleven stars made obeisance to me. (10) And he told it to his father, and to his brethren: and his father rebuked him, and said unto him, What is this dream that thou hast dreamed? Shall I and thy mother and thy brethren indeed come to bow down ourselves to thee to the earth? (11) And his brethren envied him; but his father observed the saying.

At face value, the above scripture seemingly has nothing to do with Michael Jackson. But when we analyze the relationship between Michael and his siblings Jermaine and Latoya, we see how the story relates to Michael's Life.

Genesis 37: 17-20 *(17) And Joseph went after his brethren, and found them in Dothan. (18) And when they saw him afar off, even before he came near unto them, they conspired against him to slay him (19) And they said one to another, Behold, this dreamer cometh. (20) Come now therefore, and let us slay him, and cast him into some pit, and we will say, Some evil beast hath devoured him: and we shall see what will become of his dreams.*

As a child it was no secret that Michael was a prodigy, and the talents he demonstrated stirred envy amongst his siblings LaToya and Jermaine. In fact LaToya went public to tell the world she thought Michael was guilty of the 1st child molestation charge. The rumor mill has also circulated that Jermaine wrote a book proposal about Michael before Michael died entitled "Legacy." MSNBC "reportedly" obtained excerpts from the book proposal and below is a quote from that report. *"My brother is not what the world thinks he is; he's not what we've always told you he was either. My brother is a superstar, yes. My brother is wealthy. He owns shares in Sony music. He drinks, he does drugs, he lies, he cheats, he changed his skin color and mostly, he's human"* 43a. As a result of the hidden jealousy of these siblings, Michael was often left in isolation. This "isolation" is synonymous to being "thrown in a pit." When Michael separated from *The Jackson Five* to pursue a solo career, the revelation of the dream Joseph had also played out in Michael's personal life; as he went on to become music's all-time highest selling artist. Just as Joseph grew to be the ruler of Egypt because he could interpret dreams; Jackson's *Thriller* album, in the likeness to that of Joseph, was an artistic "vision" whereby Michael as the Canaanite wolf resurrected the living dead. This "vision" is a direct reenactment of the occult Osirian resurrection story where Osiris the "wolf" is resurrected from death by his consort Isis. Through the artistic interpretation of *Thriller*, we get an accurate portrait that displays Michael's dynamic ability through art to showcase his visions like that of Joseph. These abilities enabled him to be the King of Pop like Joseph's abilities enabled him to become the Ruler of Israel.

Another direct and shocking parallel that ties the life of Joseph and Michael together has to do with an altercation Joseph had with Pharaoh's wife.

Genesis 39:7-10 *(7)And it came to pass after these things, that his master's wife cast her eyes upon Joseph; and she said, Lie with me. (8)But he refused, and said unto his master's wife, Behold, my master wotteth not what is with me in the house, and he hath committed all that he hath to my hand; (9)There is none greater in this house than I; neither hath he kept back anything from me but thee, because thou art his wife: how then can I do this great wickedness, and sin against God? (10) And it came to pass, as she spake to Joseph day by day, that he hearkened not unto her, to lie by her, or to be with her. (11) And it came to pass about this time that Joseph went into the house to do his business; and there was none of the men of the house there within. (12)And she caught him by his garment, saying, Lie with me: and he left his garment in her hand, and fled, and got him out. (13) And it came to pass, when she saw that he had left his garment in her hand, and was fled forth, (14) That she called unto the men of her house, and spake unto them, saying, See, he hath brought in an Hebrew unto us to mock us; he came in unto me to lie with me, and I cried with a loud voice.*

Again this reference seems to be off base to the life of Michael Jackson until we look at the 1st number one single from the album *Thriller*, **Billy Jean**. *"Billy Jean is not my lover; she's just a girl who claims that I am the one"* 44. In paralleling the life of Joseph, the ruler over the 12 tribes of Israel to Michael Jackson, the King of Pop, it is evident their lives indeed are parallel. The fact that Joseph dreamed the Sun and the Moon and the other eleven stars were bowing to him is also a very profound astrological clue. When this clue is taken and paralleled to the life of Michael Joseph Jackson, one can make the claim that every other "star" in Hollywood, no matter how large, no matter what genre of entertainment, all "bowed" to Michael and acknowledged him as the King. Madonna representing (*Leo/Sun)*, Quincy Jones representing (*Pisces*), Diana Ross (*Aries*) Stevie Wonder (*Taurus*), Paul McCartney (*Gemini*), Princess Diana (*Cancer/Moon*), Beyonce Knowles (*Virgo*), Jesse Jackson (*Libra*), Tatum O'Neal (*Scorpio*), Berry Gordy (*Sagittarius*), Muhammad Ali (*Capricorn*), and Ronald Reagan (*Aquarius.*) Michael's middle name Joseph and last name Jackson, a variant Hebraic form of Jacob, serves as a direct in your face clue which makes this information even more plausible. Who can deny clarity at this level? Owning the world's most lucrative and valuable music publishing catalogue only adds more evidence to Michael's executive and ruler ship abilities in the present as it proves Michael is indeed a king. The publishing company Michael Jackson owned contains the music of the Beatles and Eminem. The Beatles are the most successful group in the history of music and Eminem is the most successful rapper in the new millennium having sold over 30 million records to date. Michael Jackson shattered records with the highest selling album of all time called *Thriller*, which is speculated as having sold over 110 million copies. Michael has sold over a billion albums worldwide and is the highest selling and grossing artist of all time. Michael Jackson sold out for seven nights at Wembley Stadium, London, England in the summer of 1988 where a total of 504,000 people saw him perform on July 14-16, 22-23, and August 26-27. Michael is also credited as having the highest music contract ever totaling $890 million (Sony Music Contract), with prospective earnings of $1 billion 45. What this information is telling us is something of monumental and epic significance. The Joseph of the Bible and Ruler of Israel, the "*Holy Land*" the world is fighting over, was Michael Jackson. This means that all prophecies related to Joseph and Israel in the Bible are related in this time to America making Michael Jackson the former King of Israel. Israel corresponds to a "nation" of people not just a land mass and country.

Just as I have paralleled the life of Michael to Moses, and Joseph, I can also directly parallel his life to the Archangel Michael described in the Bible. Here are a few indicators that metaphysically as well as physically link one of the greatest angels to the person we know today as Michael Jackson. For starters his name is Michael Joseph Jackson which says a lot as it translates to **Michael** (*who is like God*) **Joseph** (*the father*) **Jackson** (*God's son.*) Michael dad's name is the same as the father of Jesus and in the Kabbalah has a strong correlation to the word "father." Joseph Jackson's astrological sign being Leo makes him the monarch/king of the Zodiac providing a link between the father and the "son of the father" witnessed in Michael and Joseph's kabalistic relationship. Michael's mother however, falls under the astrological sign Taurus and is represented by the great Mother "Cow" (ox) in the celestial heavens. Katherine, the name of Michael's mother in the Kabbalah, is equivalent to "pure" and is synonymous to what Christians acknowledge as being virginal or chaste. Both Michael's mother and father being (angles) or "*angels*" that are fixed (*Leo* and *Taurus*) allows Michael to demonstrate that angelic influence received from his parents celestial makeup's by manifesting that energy through his music for the people on earth in epoch proportions.

The Book of Illumination

CHAPTER 12

LOS ANGELES

The Book of Illumination

CHAPTER 12

LOS ANGELES

LOS ANGELES

Speaking in reference to Michael Jackson and the Kabbalistic pedigree that showcases scientifically why he is called an archangel, namely the Archangel Michael; let's now examine literarily how these mystical beings called angels came into existence.

THE CHERUB OF EZEKIEL

<u>Cherubim:</u> an order of angels in the celestial hierarchy [46]

Ezekiel 10:14 & 20 *(14) And everyone had four faces: the first face was the face of a cherub, and the second face was the face of a man, and the third the face of a lion, and the fourth the face of an eagle. (20) This is the living creature that I saw under the God of Israel by the river of Che'bar and I knew that they were the cherubims.*

<u>Cherub:</u> an order of angels in the celestial hierarchy

<u>Celestial hierarchy:</u> a traditional hierarchy of angels ranked from lowest to highest into the following nine orders: angels, archangels, principalities, powers, virtues, dominions, thrones, cherubim, and seraphim

<u>Angel:</u> a person having qualities of beauty, purity, or kindliness (2) a supernatural being in humanoid form.

Both definitions of angel fit the persona of Michael Jackson to a tee. The picture above is a caricature describing the creature in Ezekiel's vision. In Freemasonry, the creature containing, the Lion, Eagle, Ox, and Man represent the *Royal Arch* coat of arms. These four quadrants symbolize the four fixed signs of the Zodiac which are the angles of the arch {Royal Arch (next page.)}

"Freemasonry is the place where people who are still in a natural state of religion, pagan or otherwise marked by their belief in a supernatural Supreme Being are introduced into towards monotheism. But the secret of this can be only found through the super structure of the "Royal Arch" Alexander Piatigorsky [52a].

233

THE ROYAL ARCH

If you understand what Alexander's quote represents, all the answers are before you. The natural religion was music; the supernatural Supreme Being was Michael Jackson himself. The validation is the Royal Arch coat of arms of which the Leo (lion) and the Taurus (ox) represent the Royal *angels* at the top of the arch. These two *angels* of Leo and Taurus are the birth signs of Michael's parents. Many may wonder why I attributed the astrological signs of Michael's parents' as being angelic. In the image of Ezekiel's wheel, according to his description, the creatures (cherubim's) that he saw under the God of Israel were a man, a lion, and an eagle around the face of a cherub. The fact that <u>angels</u> are distinguished as having these characteristics isn't that farfetched as we can see they all are <u>angles</u> in reference to the zodialogical cross of masculine and feminine astrological (signs) as seen in the Royal Arch above. Notice the play on words from angels to angles. The fixed signs of the astrological model are just that, fixed as they cannot change what they are. This same language is what has been used to describe the nature of the angels of God, as angels reportedly do not to possess free will. Angels in romantic legend also are known to have androgynous qualities 47.

<u>Androgyny:</u> having both masculine and feminine characteristics

Fixed: (1) having a final or crystallized form (2) not subject to change

Another peculiar OT story that deals with angels is the story of the LORD God of Israel who manifests with a company of angels during his incarnations to earth. This gives rise to what is called the Elohim or (E) eagle, (L) lion, (O) ox, and (Him) which is Man. Again, the four fixed signs of the zodiac are Leo, Aquarius, Scorpio, and Taurus.

Elohim: (1) the God of Israel in the Old Testament. (2) A plural of majesty

In The URANTIA Book, the New Age Morontia Foundation promotes that the "Archangel Michael i.e. St. Michael, is the Archangel of Cosmic Justice, and the spiritual force which moves that justice throughout the universe. *The Archangel Michael's mission is to alert all souls to the changes in the coming new millennium. The mission of Michael's ministry is to teach each one of us how to raise our consciousness in preparation for the coming changes and to align us with the energy of the new millennium to achieve our greatest prosperity, abundance, joy and true love* 48b. When we look at what Michael Jackson has done in respect to eliminating racism and promoting a message of love and peace to humanity we can readily see how in today's time his message has indeed resonated through the hearts and minds of the citizens of this world. America now has a president who like Michael Jackson defines to a tee that it doesn't matter if your black or white, and like Michael he is both. I would say that Michael Jackson has indeed promoted cosmic justice throughout the world in the 50 short years that humanity got to spend with him. Below are lyrics from *Another part of Me* 49

We're Takin' Over	*The Planets Are Linin'*	*Part Of Me…*
We Have The Truth	*Up*	*A Revelation*
This Is The Mission	*We're Bringin'*	*Fulfill The Truth*
To See It Through	*Brighter*	*The Final Message*
Don't Point Your	*Days*	*We'll Bring To You*
Finger	*They're All In Line*	*There Is No Danger*
Not Dangerous	*Waitin' For You*	*Fulfill The Truth*
This Is Our Planet	*Can't You See . . .*	*So Come Together*
You're One Of Us	*You're Just Another*	*We're Meaning You*

Citing beliefs from other cultures to those in the western world who hold the religious point of view traditionally given by Christianity takes them outside the main source for what they believe their religion speaks in reference to. In this book all religious practices and beliefs are used to show that regardless to the culture or belief Michael Jackson fits the mold as the person who those religions worship as their deity.

Daniel 12:1-2 (1) *And at that time shall Michael stand up, the great prince which standeth for the children of thy people: and there shall be a time of trouble, such as never was since there was a nation even to that same time: and at that time thy people shall be delivered, every one that shall be found written in the book. (2) And many of them that sleep in the dust of the earth shall awake, some to everlasting life, and some to shame and everlasting contempt.*

In the book of Daniel it says that Michael the great prince of the people will stand up for the children of Israel. Michael's Jackson's love for children was really inherent in his nature and philanthropic endeavors. The fact that Daniel is an apocalyptic book that speaks about eschatology and end time scenarios makes apparent the comparisons between the prophetic Michael of the book of Daniel, and the Michael Jackson we saw with our own eyes. Michael Jackson loved the children and in fact said, "*What's wrong with sharing your bed.*" The lay people however interpreted this with a perverted mind state and trumped up charges against Michael tarnishing his legacy up until his acquittal in 2005 and death in June of 2009. Here are a few more heart felt lyrics from Michael Jackson; at the end of the song he literally encourages man to stand up and make a change.

I'm Gonna Make A Change, for Once In My Life It's Gonna Feel Real Good, Gonna Make A Difference Gonna Make It Right . . . If You Wanna Make The World A Better PlaceTake A Look At Yourself, AndThen Make A Change 50.

Michael the Archangel of the Bible is considered by the Jehovah's Witnesses to be Jesus Christ. This is explained in their book, *Aid To Bible Understanding* 51. According to the research of the Watchmen Fellowship Expositor, "Jesus of the Watchtower" is not God but an archangel. If this doesn't shock you maybe this will, Michael Jackson grew up a Jehovah's Witness. Urantia also teaches in the URANTIA book that Jesus was a created angelic being called Michael.

In *The Merovingian Dynasty the Satanic Bloodline of the Antichrist & False Prophet*, Barbara Ado lists a number of references about the coming Christ as well as all the occult knowledge surrounding his life and legacy 52. The above material as well as other references and excerpts that she used in her works have been placed within this book to show the legitimacy of the claim about Michael Jackson being the Archangel Michael. Although in Ado's works she has attributed this archangel to be persons other than Michael Jackson himself, I have used her research to highlight and clarify the point that Michael Jackson has every trait suitable to be considered the reincarnation of the Archangel Michael who many cultures believe is the Supreme Being. This is evidence that provides relevancy to the theory that the "messianic" figure who is Jehovah's witness has possibly came and left the earth yet the religions who claim to be its/his servants have yet to acknowledge his/its existence. The fact that they have made and worshipped graven images **Exodus 20:4** is why they have lost the ability to recognize a Supreme Being when he comes to the earth, despite how monumental and undeniable his presence is. Being this is the case, the person who they are looking for, and in church listening to their preachers about, isn't the savior. The savior is long gone, The messiah, or rather the ONE WHO IS TO COME, is the one who is sent to destroy and rule with an iron fist.

Revelation 19:13-15 *(13) And he was clothed with a vesture dipped in blood: and his name is called The Word of God. (14) And the armies which were in heaven followed him upon white horses, clothed in fine linen, white and clean. (15) And out of his mouth goeth a sharp sword, that with it he should smite the nations: and he shall rule them with a rod of iron: and he treadeth the winepress of the fierceness and wrath of Almighty God.*

Rudolph Steiner speaks about this in a significant way in the course of a lecture of 1 August 1924 (GA 237.) Sergei O. Prokofieff gives us the details on pg. 114-116 of *The Twelve Holy Nights and the Spiritual Hierarchies* 53. There, Steiner describes how in the circle of other Archangels who have "resigned" themselves to the fact of man's fall from the spiritual world through the influence of the "Ahrimanic" and "Luciferic" powers. *Michael alone refused to submit', he felt that mankind can come to earth to embrace the Divine in a wholly sinless form'* 52. Michael-Christ's aim is to lead humanity beyond the confines of the astrological world, and thereby to a conscious union with the forces of the `Mystic Lamb' represented by (B.H.O.) 52b

Oriphiel, the Demiurge and "evil" counterpart to Michael, wants to lead humanity back to full subjection to cosmic necessity, as was ordained in old times by God 52c. "Mankind cannot become divine" is the view of Oriphiel. However it seems his stance is taken in the sense that it isn't impossible, but mankind will not do it because it is out of his nature to be divine, sort of like turning a lion into a vegetarian. Michael's unending faith in humanity is what causes him to intercede on their behalf, as he feels mankind can rise up and become godly-in contrast to Oriphiel. This display of cosmic quarreling was depicted in the movie the *Transformers Dark of the Moon* where Sentinel Prime fails in bringing Cybertron "the heavens" and former home of the fallen "alien" Transformers, to earth. Optimus Prime obstructs his plan and restores peace and tranquility to earth allowing the people their continued freedom as Sentinel Prime would have enslaved them.

The aforementioned excerpt taken from Rudolf Steiner was written in 1924, and scholars have yet to acknowledge that everything they have seen and studied has indeed come true except the rise of Oriphiel. Michael Jackson indeed came to earth and tried to unite humanity through musing and entertainment, however the deification of Michael Jackson during his lifetime was rejected, ridiculed and overlooked, by many people here on earth. It seems the point of view given by Oriphiel was indeed true as mankind has turned their backs to the evolutionary insight that was given by Michael Jackson. Michael pled with the people to turn away from their wickedness and hatred of one another in terms of race and social status. The people then in turn chose to view Michael as a sick and crazy child molester who bleaches his skin and pops pills. The popular name given to Michael was Wacko Jacko, and when asked by many people is he the Christ or messiah, they disagree with an emphatic No, despite his monumental achievements, talents, abilities and godly lifestyle. This gives rise to the position of Oriphiel who said that mankind always and will forever be corrupted and therefore must be ruled with an iron fist. There is indeed a need for a new world order.

This information recorded 34 years before the birth of Michael Jackson serves as a literary reminder that the prophecies written about in the scriptures are both real and in turn validates the notion there are beings of higher consciousness and planes of existence living in the world today. Even the names of the two spiritual Archangels (Michael and Oriphiel) bear witness to the difference between their spiritual activities in our cosmos. When translated from the Hebrew, the name `Oriphiel' means `My neck [is] God'; *for Oriphiel directs his gaze wholly to the planetary world (Astrology) (to the past) and apprehends the working of the starry Spirits of Wisdom only as a `memory' of the Old Sun condition of the earth* 52d. The *Old Sun condition* was connotes Saturn; meaning the original constellation the Sun rose in was first recorded in the constellation of Capricorn/Saturn. This means that when Oriphiel rises it is through his words that he reorders the universe. He will put what is out of alignment into alignment by "speaking it into existence" the same as the craftsmen (Demiurge), and patron of the city of Memphis, Ptah. *Timaeus* in Plato's the Socratic dialogue in 360 BCE refers to the Demiurge as being the entity who "fashioned and shaped" the material world. Timaeus describes the Demiurge as unreservedly benevolent, and desirous of an ideal world 52e.

Demiurge: craftsman" or "artisan

 Through the neck is also where the Great Hindu God Shiva has a link to Oriphiel. Shiva swallowed the poisons of the world to save it from annihilation and is characterized by having a <u>blue neck</u>; this imagery relates the two entities (Oriphiel and Shiva) together 52f. Also the Great God Shiva wears upon his neck a serpent, the King Cobra. Shiva to the Hindus is the wild god of ecstasy and tantra who births the world's savior and demon's destroyer through his virginal goddess Parvati, who has a link to other Semitic goddesses such as Sekhmet, Isis, and Anat. Shiva, like the Demiurge, is also known to be very gracious and benevolent; in Hinduism, Shiva was also the god Krishna prayed to when he wanted boons of glory, children, and honor.

The Mahabharata, Anusasana Parva Section XIV 53

"We know, O Krishna, that Thou, O slayer of foes, art filled with the greatest devotion towards us. Do what is for Thy good. My love and affection for Thee is very great. Do Thou ask for eight boons. I shall verily give them unto Thee. O Krishna, O best of all persons, tell me what they are, O chief of the Yadavas. Name what Thou wishest. However difficult of attainment they be, Thou shalt have them still". The blessed Krishna said: "Bowing my head with great joy unto that mass of energy and effulgence, I said these words unto that great Deity, with a heart filled with gladness, -firmness in virtue, the slaughter of foes in battle, the highest fame, the greatest might, devotion to Yoga, Thy adjacence, and hundreds upon hundreds of children- these are the boons I solicit of Thee"."So be it" said Sankara, repeating the words I had uttered. After this, the Mother of the universe, the upholder of all things, who cleanses all things, who is the spouse of Sarva (Siva), that vast receptacle of penances said with a restrained soul these words unto me; "The puissant Mahadeva has granted Thee, O sinless one, a son who shall be named Samva. Do Thou take from me also eight boons which Thou choosest. I shall certainly grant them to Thee."

Oriphiel is the angel linked to Osiris, Ptah, and Shiva. To Oriphiel's credit, the fact that Michael Jackson has done on the earth what has been documented in times of antiquity shows that even though Michael looks to what can be, what can be has already happened before. As his view isn't that things are created rather things are discovered. This being the case, what was is, and what can be has already been, therefore, the alignments of the original Zodiac and the Sun's revolution through the constellations will always be the original and fundamental concept that orders the existences of people on earth even though the customs, values, societies, and the rules men structure will change.

"If a religion wants to be not only universal (ubiquitous) in space but also eternal, then we have to admit together with the royal arch companions that it is god as sun or Osiris (not as supreme being) who was the demiurge and word long before we arrived at the third stage of religious consciousness manifested in Christ" 54.

This quote taken from Alexander Piatigorsky may be the first encounter where readers have heard "God" mentioned as Osiris. In Egyptian legend, Osiris is the original "Sun" whose story passed down through oral tradition, became the myth of the Jesus of Nazareth people worship and revere today. By breaking down and decoding the lives of actual deities and separating the legends that were merged together by scholars and scribes; upon defining the meanings of words and biblical terminology, we begin to understand what exactly happened with relation to religious records and events. When Alexander Piatigorsky says that it was Osiris that was the Demiurge and word long before the arrival of the Christ, one can only understand what is being said if he has studied ancient religious manuscripts. In Hinduism there are two factions and cults that have prominence, they are the cults of Vishnu and Shiva. In Egypt these two are known in the legend of Osiris and Set, and in the Bible they are known as Jesus and John the Baptist. Because the Sun moves counterclockwise through the constellations in its revolution around the earth; the beginning becomes the end and the end becomes the beginning. Osiris is the original story of the Sun in its original orbit in the constellation of Capricorn/Saturn. The arrival of the Christ is the manifestation of the Sun in its final orbit before the Great Age resets itself. Osiris was the original manifestation of the Sun and the Hormus (Michael) was the final manifestation of the Sun, both deities are contemporary but only one is fully conscious of the other, that one being the elder. In the chapter entitled Avatar this will be explained in further depth as we explore the Matsya Purana which is the oldest story in Hinduism that bears a striking resemblance to the story of Noah.

In Hebrew Kabbalah, according to Eliphas Levi, Oriphiel like Saturn, is also known as (Pan) and is referred to as the angel of the wilderness 54a. St. Mark 1:2-4 cites John the Baptist as the one in the wilderness who prepares the way of the LORD.

Mark: 1-2-4 As it is written in the prophets, Behold, I send my messenger before thy face, which shall prepare thy way before thee. The voice of one crying in the wilderness, Prepare ye the way of the Lord, make his paths straight. John did baptize in the wilderness, and preach the baptism of repentance for the remission of sins.

When we acknowledge that the Egyptian God Ptah is located in the constellation of Pan (Capricorn/Saturn) just as Jesus is located in the wilderness with John; these are clues that link these stories together making John Pan and Jesus Ptah. The only difference between the Egyptian, Indian, and romantic accounts is translation. We also cannot ignore the fact that the Demiurge as regarded by Hinduism is known as the Shaivite Trimurti where

Shiva (Sun) manifest in triune form with Vishnu and Brahma 54b. This is the same "LORD" that manifests in triune form as an Elohim in the 18th chapter of Genesis upon whom we spoke about earlier in the beginning of this chapter.

Genesis 18:1-3 (1) And the LORD appeared unto him in the plains of Mamre: and he sat in the tent door in the heat of the day; (2) And he lift up his eyes and looked, and, lo, three men stood by him: and when he saw them, he ran to meet them from the tent door, and bowed himself toward the ground, (3) And said, My LORD, if now I have found favour in thy sight, pass not away, I pray thee, from thy servant.

Several deities were mentioned in this book that may be unfamiliar to most people. Because I have introduced this foreign religious material, I have cited it for cross reference and further study in the bibliography. Osiris, Ptah, Sehkmet, and Anat are all Egyptian and Semitic deities who laid the blueprints from which the stories of Jesus and Mary we're created. In varying cultures each represent the same exact stories, themes, and outcomes though some have a little more details than others. Anat like Isis avenges her husband's murder and pieces back his dismembered body. Ptah with Sekhmet creates Atum (Adam) and divides the two lands of Israel. Osiris is resurrected by his son as Jesus is the resurrected son sent from the father. In whole, these acknowledgements expose the scholars and scribes who retranslated the scrolls from ancient scripts, were translating the lives of these deities and placing within the texts the mathematical correspondence for what their names meant. This gave the same deity a different name that corresponds to what their actual names meant numerically. For example Jesus is equivalent to a master number in nomenology, and numerology that equals eleven. Eleven is the number of self-sacrifice. Though Jesus' name isn't Jesus rather Immanuel, the scribes translated his self-sacrificing quality because he's born on a day that equals eleven. This is to highlight his self-sacrificing trait as being the one that dominated his persona. All of the masculine deities that were mentioned above were absorbed within the LORD of Israel's personality. These legends are different legends about the same deity; each story giving detailed aspects of the deity's life and character. When these books were compiled together, the layman (even though considered by their communities as scholars) thought these were different people and different legends. In all actuality, these legends were a compilation of the deities' lifetimes throughout hundreds of thousands to millions of years of existence. Again, this is why the scriptures indicate "there were giants in those days" because literally having a constellation fall to earth would make its presence humongous.

Barbara Thiering, an expert on the Qumran (Dead Sea) scrolls and Greek New Testament, outlines in her book "*Jesus and the Riddle of the Dead Sea Scrolls*" that the scriptures are written in a "pesher" code where one word stands for another. This "pesher" technique was reportedly developed by the scribes of the Qumran community that authored the Dead Sea Scrolls. Thiering's conclusion says the crucifixion did not kill Jesus. It also speculates there were no miracles, and no real resurrection from the dead as these events were all described symbolically, in code, in the Gospel's manuscripts 54c.

I used the above, as well as majority of the references in this book so those reading, through the use of these references, may see the truth. People in this world have biases, and from their biases they create beliefs. Because of these biases, they are unable to see people in their truest light, which is why this society has such a hard time accepting Michael Jackson as a messiah. A person can reject what I have stated only so long before they mature and begin reading the theories of scholars who have PH. D's and countless hours of study with regards to religion. Once they've grown past their own biases and begin to tackle the "god" complex, as well as the creation of life and the universe; they'll then pick this book back up and bear witness that the theories of the scholar's they revere, have been mastered and debunked within its ciphers. When they see the limits of what has confined these scholars shattered by the clarity apparent in each chapter, then and only then will they understand how magnificent the "Living God" truly is. In this book I've shown you how those scholars erred in translating scripture because they've ignored black people and their positions in the pantheon of the elder Egyptian gods. This has caused "scholars" to have a jaded viewpoint in regards to the scriptures they've read; which warps the scriptures they have translated, even though their translations come from a seemingly high intelligence.

For instance, in the Qur'an, Iblis is punished for not prostrating to Adam, the perfect human. The Iblis is considered a manifestation of Melek Taus also known as Vishnu in Hinduism. Melek Taus as well as the Iblis are called the peacock of the angels in legend; this peacock is the symbol that links Michael Jackson to Krishna, Vishnu, and the Iblis. In one of Michael's poems *Are You Listening* - he refers to himself as the Iblis. *Immortality's my game - From Bliss I came, In Bliss I am sustained, To Bliss I return - If you don't know it now, It's a shame - Are you listening?*

The Book of Illumination

CHAPTER 13

THE GOD THAT DOES EXIST

The Book of Illumination

CHAPTER 13

THE GOD THAT
DOES EXIST

THE GOD THAT DOES EXIST

In Roman Catholicism they worship Jesus as the "Sun" in spirit. However again, Peter is considered the earthly leader of the disciples. As stated earlier, Peter is one of the two people credited with starting the religion of Catholicism. The Catholic Church, known also as the Roman Catholic Church is the world's largest Christian church, and claims over a billion members. Peter is widely regarded by scholars and theologians as the disciple who was the closest to Jesus (SUN of man). Because Jesus only incarnates every 25,920 years, the Sun of Man and the Christ is hidden for that amount of time. During that huge amount of time the Sun of Man and the Christ are worshipped in spirit by the Pope who acts in the stead of Peter.

Because the Romans didn't fully comprehend precession and astrological alignments they could not teach outwardly (to the masses) that God (literally) is walking the earth physically; which makes it even harder for them to admit that the Great Architect of the Universe is another name for the God of Abraham, Isaac, and Jacob 58a. The way they chose to translate this was through the story of Jesus the "heavenly father's" son. The "heavenly father" in Astrology is ascribed to the 5th house, the house of Leo which is ruled by the SUN. The eighth month in our calendar today is attributed to this sign as well (Leo.)

I Kings 6:38 (38) And in the <u>eleventh</u> year, in the month <u>Bul,</u> which is the <u>eighth</u> <u>month</u>, was the house finished throughout all the parts thereof, and according to all the fashion of it. So was he seven years in building it.

The above scripture is taken in reference to the building of Solomon's Temple. The sign of the lion and the bull have a reoccurring link throughout all Egyptian culture and will be explained further after we've covered the basic instructions needed to comprehend the more complex chapters ahead. In our time today the eighth month is regarded as Leo but as you can see from the Book of Kings, the eighth month in ancient times was regarded as the month of the Bull.

By breaking down the word Jupiter we find the annunciation to be pronounced as Jew/ Peter or Jew/Ptah. Being that the establishment of the Mother Church was founded from Peter covertly conveys the Roman power structures inner relation with Jupiter in regards to the SUN. It is public knowledge that Michael Jackson identified himself with the character Peter

Pan or as we have just annunciated Ptah/Pan. When we further study the Egyptian Gods to see where they are similar and how they are different from the Roman gods, we come across a slew of differences and coincidences. The most notable is the fact that the stories from the Egyptian pantheon are older yet they have the same information carried over to the Roman pantheon of gods. Note the word Pantheon {(PAN) (THEO) N} or PAN and GOD.

Pantheon: (1) the gods of a people; *especially*: the officially recognized gods

The goddess NEITH, the Weaver.

OSIRIS, judge of the dead.

The goddess SEKHET, the Sun-flame.

HĀPI, the god of the Nile.

PTAH, the Creator.

AMEN, father of the gods.

RĀ, the Sun-god.

THOTH, scribe of the gods.

Ptah, was the pre-dynastic Egyptian god of craftsmen, pottery, creation, and the patron of the city of Memphis. Egyptians believed Ptah was the god who created everything from artifacts, to the world {(orphic) egg,} to the other deities themselves. The Opening of the Mouth ceremony performed by him whereby he raises all the dead souls in the awakening is eerily reminiscent of the rapture spoken of by Christians where Jesus returns to raise the dead from their graves. Ptah created the universe by speaking words through his tongue and by thoughts coming from his heart (linked to Horus the Elder). Through the heart and tongue Ptah commanded into being Atum, the Egyptian version of Christianity's Adam 58d. As regarded by Dr. James Anderson, the writer of the Masonic Constitution, the creation of Atum by Ptah performing the Opening of Mouth ceremony of Osiris is the same as the Great Architect of the universe who created MAN (Adam) 58e. Ptah's consort Sekhmet, the warrior Goddess with a lion's head, has a direct correlation to the goddess Kali found in Hinduism and Anat found in Egypt. Kali, is regarded as the wife of Shiva the Sun, Isis is the wife of Osiris the Sun, and Anat, is the consort of the "LORD" Ba'al, also known as Melkart the master of the Furnace (The Sun.)

Ptah, was 1st cited in the Egyptian pantheon of gods in the constellation of Capricorn/ Saturn (Pan), and is where the character Peter Pan finds its origin. Though Ptah doesn't directly relate to a Roman god like Thoth does to Hermes, he does have attributes comparable to the god of all gods in Roman Mythology called Zeus known as Jupiter. The American statue of the Oscar is a modernized version of the Egyptian statue of Ptah. Ptah was the first to create and craft the legends of the gods in ancient manuscripts and these stories have endured throughout time. This is why in the likeness of Ptah who has immortalized the gods, actors are given an Oscar (statue of Ptah) to symbolize that like the gods, they also will be immortalized forever. I used this reference to explain that older gods in Egypt are only transferred into newer gods, as historians and scribes piece together histories records.

Just as the archangel Oriphiel (original Sun) is an angel ruled by the planet Saturn, so does Ptah (the Sun) find himself in the constellation of (Pan) (Capricorn/Saturn.) If the Romans were identifying "God" as the SUN in the heavens, we can see how Jew/Ptah (Jupiter) would be the 1st representative who occupies the position of the Sun during his absence namely because Jupiter is the largest planet in our solar system next. Due to Romans mimicking what they found in hieroglyphs and ancient scrolls; they then worshipped (Jupiter) as the earthly representative of their god instead of the SUN itself because (Jupiter) described as atmosphere, clouds, storms, and thunder in legend, provided them shelter and protection from a Sun that would surely scorch and destroy them via famine and drought (desert.) Though subconscious and unknown until now, this is the reason that Peter (the Pope) is thought to be the earthly liaison between the Church and "God" (the SUN) in the absence of Jesus (Sun of Man) as Jesus is no longer a man but worshipped as a spirit.

Zeus as described by Astrology in the Roman pantheon is known and ruled by the planet Jupiter. The Sun of Man and the Christ are living entities that have been translated into a premonition of the mind rather than physical beings that walk the earth. A great example of how the Roman world totally minimizes the Sun and the values and talents it has within its human incarnation is best noted in the legend of the Titan Hyperion. The Titans according to legend were overthrown by their offspring which were the Gods of Mount Olympus who again had Zeus as their leader 59a. When we look at the values of the Roman world they differ from the ones in the Egyptian world in that the Egyptian world values knowledge and wisdom over the Roman world which values conquest and warfare. **Hyperion** which in Greek translates as the "High-One" was the "Sun of Uranus" lord of light, and the Titan of the "east." This description parallels Hyperion to being the Sun of an Aquarius, likened to the Egyptian God Osiris and the Sphinx, which is a combination of Leo the lion and the Aquarius also known as the Man. Hyperion was referred to in early mythological writings as *Helios Hyperion* 'Sun High-one. Hyperion was also described as having the epithet the 'God of Watchfulness and Wisdom', while Helios became the physical incarnation of the Sun. According to historical documentation, Hyperion plays virtually no role in Greek culture and little role in mythology except for his role as one of the twelve Titans 59b. Later, however the Greeks stated this of Hyperion: "*Of Hyperion we are told that he was the first to understand, by diligent attention and observation, the movement of both the sun and the moon and the other stars, and the seasons as well, in that they are caused by these bodies, and to make these facts known to others; and that for this reason he was called the father of these bodies, since he had begotten, so to speak, the speculation about them and their nature*" 59c..

The incarnation of the Sun (Hyperion/Helios) making known the movements of the Sun and Moon as well as the other planetary alignments of stars and the seasons, is another indication of the Demiurge known as the SUN or Osiris/Ptah who names and builds the legends of deities (gods) according to observation and meticulous attention to detail. This description also directly parallels Hyperion to the author of this book and Solomon whose name literally if broken up annunciates the word <u>Sol</u> (Sun) <u>o</u> (of) <u>mon</u> (man.) Notice the correlation to Astrology found in the scripture below. *Note the parallels between the 12 signs of the Zodiac and the Sun of Man, Solomon*

***1 Kings 4:**7(7) And Solomon had <u>twelve</u> officers over all Israel, which provided victuals for the king and his household: <u>each man his month in a year</u> made provision.*

It's always interesting to see how you're referenced by others, especially when they think your existence to be a myth. When we factor in how the Roman Church follows Peter as its pope we can correlate this to mean the church is still governed by Jew Ptah (Jupiter) which is none other than (He' Zeus.) Again not understanding precession and the fact that immortals reincarnate to the earth in the physical flesh, the people are stuck worshipping the last incarnation of the "god" and the images and legends they've created about him/them. Because they worship him superficially in the form of the image they have created of him and not (W) holistically; when the same "god" resurrects to earth, the people kill and crucify him. If they truly worshipped this deity they would assist him when he descends back to earth. The Tibetan culture understands this and as a result raises the (Dalia Lama.)

I referenced Astrology as it pertains to the culture of the Romans and Greeks to show the reader what role Astrology played in Greco Roman society. I also thought it necessary to show why the Romans worship God as Jupiter rather than the Sun. This "leader" of the Roman Gods (Jupiter/Zeus) falls under the sign of Sagittarius in the Zodiac; while the leader of the Egyptian Gods better known as Ra or Re is a Sun god who falls under the sign Leo the (Lion.) Though the Sun is usually not regarded as a planet, in our immediate solar system, it is the largest and most brilliant object in the sky. What makes this information worth evaluating is next to the Sun, Jupiter is the largest planet in the Solar system; yet due to the way its attributes block the sun rays, and provides favorable weather conditions for Romans, and the nature in which they exist, they worship its God Zeus, rather than the Sun.

Since we have begun to talk about Jupiter and its place amongst the gods theoretically, let's take a look at how Jupiter looks when he manifests to earth in human form. Jay –z was born on December 4th under the sign of Sagittarius. Sagitarrs are known in mythology as centaurs. In Roman Mythology the king of the gods again is Zeus and "Jovial" is a word that describes those born under this sign 59d. In many of Jay- z's songs he often refers to himself as Jay – Hova or Hov. If we were looking at the romance languages namely Latin and Spanish J's are pronounced like H's; an example of this is the name Jose. When we look at this with a meticulous scope we can see that Jay –z is aware of who he really is as he refers to himself as the god "Jove" - Jovial being the adjective that describes the planet Jupiter which the

Roman god Zeus presides over. 60a 60bOn the other hand we have his wife Beyoncé, who was born on the 4th day of September, the sign in astrology that is ruled by Virgo (the Virgin), on the day that is ruled by Ares/ warfare in the tarot. When we look at the legend of Athena we find she is the virgin goddess who was born fully armed for warfare and who was known for standing up against her father 59h. Athena was also the patroness of embroiders, spinners, and weavers in legend who turned Arachne into a spider after being outclassed in a weaving/embroidery competition 59j. What makes this reference to Athena who is the patroness of spinners, weavers, and embroiders parallel to Beyoncé Knowles; is in 2011, Beyoncé publicly fired her dad as her manager "standing up to her father."

The name of Beyoncé's mother Tina, is closely associated to Athena, and the two have a clothing business named *House of Dereon.* The name of the clothing line Dereon is taken from the grandmother of Beyoncé, Agnez' Beyince, who Beyoncé was named after (Agnez' DeRouen-Beyince) Mrs. DeRouen was a seamstress which links her profession to spinners, weavers, and embroiders 59g. What gives this legend even more validity is the fact that Athena in Roman Mythology tamed a vicious and irrational centaur 59f and at her birth she had a cry so loud that it made the earth tremble and raised the waves of the sea 59i. This cry is an allegory that describes the loud and powerful voice of Beyonce, highlighting her singing abilities. What makes the taming of the centaur reference credible, is the fact that the husband of this "living" virgin goddess is Jay –z; a "centaur" who in one of his biggest hits "*Big Pimpin*" has boasted he will never give his heart to a woman. "*Me give my heart to a woman/ not for nothing never happen I be forever mackin.*" These lyrics in conjunction with other songs and lyrics from the rap icon allow us to see how he has matured from his old self and become more refined and civil (tame) "*I don't got the bright watch, I got the right watch, I don't buy out the bar, I bought the night spot, I used to let my pants sag not giving a f$%k but baby boy now I'm all grown up.*"

While Jay-z' lyrics have toned down and been refined over the years (*Suit &Tie*) his wife Beyoncé's have grown more boisterous and imperial. She started out with songs like *Bills, Bills, Bills* where she asks the man courting her, can he pay her bills. Another popular song was *Bug-a-Boo*, where Beyonce rants about the guy courting her being a pest. The pop star then transitioned to songs like *Independent Women,* and (*Single Ladies*) *Put a ring on it*, to *Who run the world – Girls,* all titles that are self-explanatory. When looking at the lyrics and lifestyles of the two media icons, we can see how like the legend of Athena the goddess of crafts, embroidery, and weaving, Beyonce has indeed tamed a centaur, making her husband's popular slogan "men lie, women lie, numbers don't" all that much more prophetic.

The alter ego of Beyoncé personified as a warlike, powerful, and domineering femme fatale named Sasha Fierce is how Beyoncé expresses consciously that she is a deity. Though subconsciously she may not be aware she is Athena, the character Sasha Fierce lays sway that Beyoncé is aware of her powers, as well as functioning consciously with use of them. Remember in the Chapter entitled *Master Builders* we discussed as stated by Alexander Piatigorsky, that, "a *myth may or may not be conscious of itself as related to a ritual or other myth.*" In seeing how Beyoncé is regarded as a modern day goddess, but is not necessarily conscious that she is Athena reincarnated, gives understanding to the quote above given by the author of the book, *Freemasonry.*

I think at this time the mentioning of Thomas Jefferson as a prophet is a befitting term because he predicted in 1823 in his letter to John Adams that Athena would be compared to Christ, *"And the day will come when the mystical generation of Jesus, by the supreme being as his father in the womb of a virgin will be classed with the fable of the generation of Minerva (Athena) in the brain of Jupiter* 59j. While his prediction was seemingly off based then, Athena known in Rome as Minerva in this book has been used/animated alongside the Christ Michael Jackson to prove that deities do exist outside of the most popular deity, Jesus, who as regarded by Paul, is the only one (person/god) with immortality. Beyoncé's 2013 Super-Bowl performance solidified her immortality when she asked the audience to give her their energy; as a result, the 1st ever power outage took place at a Super-Bowl game.

*The people who constructed the Bible knowingly or unknowingly were passing down information found in the hieroglyphs of Egypt. These hieroglyphs contained within them all the information about the past incarnations of the gods/ (astral deities/stars) and the Egyptian societies built shrines and monuments to mark the descents of these celestial beings.

Another modern example of this is the Japanese anime called Saint Seiya. The story follows five mystical warriors called saints who fight wearing sacred armor named "cloths" formed from various constellations. The characters have also adopted their destined guardian symbols powered by a mystical energy called "Cosmo." The saints have sworn to defend the reincarnation of the Greek Goddess Athena in her battle against other gods 4446. The strongest of the saints is Tauro who is also known as *Aldebaran*, which as explained later is the star that marks the birth of Krishna. Tauro, along with the other (five) mystical warriors is another parallel to Krishna and the Five Pandavas, and Michael Jackson and the Jackson five. This legend was constructed in an anime created in 1986. What makes it serve as prophetical is due both to the signs/*cosmic cloths* of Michael and Beyoncé (Virgo), their prodigious backgrounds, and Beyoncé's confession in a tribute letter that Michael *"changed"* her by giving her soul (sol) 4447.*
Again, Kabbalah is the mystical system of words and their numerical

equivalents, and in Judaism, it is the deepest and most hidden meaning of the Torah, and the Bible. Through the ultimate knowledge and mystical practices of it, one can reach the highest spiritual levels attainable. Although many people rely on belief, faith, and dogmas in pursuing the meaning of life, the unknown, and the unseen, Kabbalists seek a spiritual connection with creation, so that the strange becomes familiar, and faith becomes knowledge. To understand Kabbalah it takes a great deal of study and discipline. Once the discipline is achieved, the person is given the type of clairvoyance that enables them to see beyond the limiting scope the other five senses promote. Seeing beyond the five senses develops the person's **sixth sense** and once that has matured they are able to see things they normally couldn't see which brings new meaning to the phrase, "*I see dead People*" **The Sixth Sense**

Since the Kabbalah was deemed heretical by the Catholic Church, sciences like Astrology and the tarot were thought to be mystical by those who didn't understand them. In Revelation 2:7, there is a reference that states Jesus will give those who "overcome" fruit from the Tree of Life.

Revelation 2:7 *(7) He that hath an ear let him hear what the spirit saith unto the churches; <u>to him that overcometh will I give eat of the tree of life</u> which is in the midst of the paradise of God (8) these things saith the first and the last which was dead but is alive.*

Again, the **Tree of Life**, also mentioned as Jacob's ladder in the Old Testament, is sacred to the Jews and their mystic system of "God."

Genesis 28:10-12 *(10) And Jacob went out from Beersheba, and went toward Haran. (11) And he lighted upon a certain place, and tarried there all night, because the sun was set; and he took of the stones of that place, and put them for his pillows, and lay down in that place to sleep. (12) And he dreamed, and behold <u>a ladder set up on the earth, and the top of it reached to heaven: and behold the angels of God ascending and descending on it.</u>*

In the *Book of Thoth*: *Tarot of the Egyptians* written by Aleister Crowley, he outlines some very important facts about the tarot and the respective manifestations that incarnate to the earth as beings on certain days. These discoveries are realized and are paraphrased on the next page. Although Crowley does not have a physical face that he assigns these manifestations to, I have paired them together and animated these beings and brought them to life in the flesh using the Tree of Life. To Crowley's credit he did acknowledge the coming age as the age of the Leo and the Aquarius and he was also correct when he said the BEAST would be the new priest and ruler of the Aeon to come. The age we are leaving as regarded by Aleister Crowley is the Age of Isis the "Virgin" which in Astrology is polarized by Pisces. Michael Jackson again was born under the sign of the "Virgin/Virgo" on August 29th 1958. This 29th day corresponds to the 2nd card in the tarot of the Egyptians and symbolizes the High Priestess. The High priestess in the tarot is the first card that connects the father in his highest aspect, and the son in his most perfect manifestation. This conversation within the Kabbalah served as the blueprints from which the ideology and story of the Christ was developed. This card also represents the most spiritual aspect of the virgin [61]. In this card, that most spiritual aspect (the manifestation of the feminine) takes on a masculine form. When we think in terms of Michael's mother and the value of her name meaning "pure" we can see how through Michael, Katherine's influences are also felt. VAU, [63] which is the Hebrew name for the letter 6 corresponds to Taurus in relation to the Zodiac, as does Michael in relation to the dominion of angels. In the prophecies of Isaiah according to the Kabbalah, when VAU is lifted up to He' which corresponds to the Emperor card in the tarot, Israel will be lifted out of the dust, meaning, the God of Israel in an Elohim form, will rise from the grave and walk the earth once again. The birthday of Katherine Jackson is May 4th. We also see the purity of Katherine personified physically because Michael sign is Virgo or the "virgin." The virgin in the tarot is indeed a woman and through Michael we see how this woman has literally taken a masculine form *"The Messiah will draw to him the whole world; it shall be so to the end of the century; and then the VAU will be united with the He [62]."*

Joseph Jackson, Michael's father, was born on July 26, 1929. This 26th day corresponds to the 8th card in the Egyptian tarot called Justice. This card is represented by Libra which is ruled by Venus. Libra is said in this tarot to be the partner of the fool and is represented as a young slender woman poised upon toe-tip. Here is the logo for MJJ music below which highlights Michael dancing upon his toe tips [61b]. The woman is masked (masculine) and her

expression shows her domination of every element of disequilibrium in the universe. The woman goddess is Harlequin, she is the many colored, many willed ultimate illusion which is manifestation, dancing showing how the harmony of beauty causes all things to cancel out. When we look at Michael Jackson, he is literally posed dancing upon toe-tip. Through his music he is expressing the disharmony and imbalance that has affected the earth and humanity [64].

When you factor the kabalistic inner selves of the two individuals destiny's (Michael and Joseph) we see through the son, (Michael) the most spiritual aspect of the virgin personified through the highest aspect of the father (Joseph, The sun, Leo) making Michael literally "the son of the father." Masked and represented by the many colored dancing fool for love, this slender woman who is portrayed in dance upon toe tip, as "Michael himself" takes a masculine form and shows her dominance over disharmony within the universe promoting justice and equality (balance.) Note also the reference to "many colors." We saw this in the story of Joseph known as Israel and we'll further analyze later how it correlates to the Supreme Being in Hinduism.

In summary of the chapter we have just read it is very important that we conclude it by referencing the end of the chapter before it. In that chapter we learned *the original constellation the Sun rose in was first recorded in the constellation of Saturn.* When we link this with the fact Aquarius was originally "ruled" by the planet Saturn, it further shows where we are presently in relation to the stars. Anytime a major turn of events happens on Earth we should look to the heavens or the "stars" to see exactly where we are in terms of our planetary position. The two biggest "stars" on the planet presently are President Barack and his wife Michelle Obama. With her speech at the 2012 DNC, she has become a modern example of the true power of femininity. By acknowledging the original SUN was 1st recorded rising upon the constellation of Capricorn/Saturn, also where the 1st point of "consciousness" was cited; we can now look to that same set of "stars" on Earth as a reference to validate our findings. Barack Obama, a Leo, born in the sign of the Sun, is married to Michelle Obama, a Capricorn ruled by Saturn. Both the 4th day He' and the 17th day Tzaddi (their Kabbalistic birthday numbers) also correspond with one another in perfect alignment. Being the world has *"started over again"* as the world changes ages, we now find ourselves in the Aquarian/ Leo age after leaving the Piscean /Virgo age. Because Aquarius was originally ruled by Saturn, we know that *-the oldest inverted sun, Uranus* is actually Saturn. This means Saturn is on the opposing side of the SUN in relation to Earth. Understanding this correlation enables us to see why the *"Devil"* rules the material Earth lives in the hottest place, Hell, and has an association with fire and light – LUCIFER. This is also why Christmas (Winter **Sol**stice) is celebrated on December 25th in Capricorn/Saturn and also why Saturday is followed by Sunday at the weeks end. In observance to this ancient celestial knowledge many people get the weekend off from work.

Genesis: translated from Hebrew: בְּרֵאשִׁית, Bərēšīṯ, "In the beginning"

As stated several times throughout this book, the present age we are now in is the Age of Horus also known as the Age of Aquarius. When we talk about this age we have to also discuss with it, its characteristics. Each age or constellation the Sun rises in projects the energy of the constellation onto the Earth. The age of Horus is most recognized by the Eye of Horus which is known as the All Seeing Eye. When we factor this information and composite it with what is going on in the world circa 2013, we get a real profound sense of how Astrology and the constellations "the Heavens" have influence over the people of the Earth. The Internet, high definition television, and movies with CGI graphics are most indicative of the *"sign of the times."* The scope and sharpness of today's camera lenses are remarkable as now the lines between fantasy and reality are seemingly non-existent.

The age of Horus in legend and biblical scriptures always marked the "beginning" of a "new" world. In ancient times the word for world and age were synonymous. This is how people today mistake the end of the world with the end of the age. In the Book of Genesis there is a story of Adam and Eve, which in this specific translation represents the whole of man and mankind. In the scriptures of Genesis, the serpent tells Adam & Eve when they eat of the fruit (APPLE) they will be as gods knowing good and evil. Being today how APPLE computers is on the verge of being the world's 1st trillion dollar company, it is easy to recognize that the prophecy of mankind eating the fruit (Apple) and becoming as "gods" "in the beginning" has just taken place. Since technology has leveled the playing field, everything is now global, and everyone is connected through the Internet. Social media sites have empowered the average human, giving them god-like access to all information through the All Seeing "Eye" Phone (IPhone.) It's important to cite that Siri backwards is Iris which is the part of the eye that controls how much light goes to the retina. Two of the IPhone's key components are its talking robotic built in computer Siri and its retina display screen. Keep in mind, matter is neither created or destroyed it just **changes** forms, *"there is nothing new under the Sun."* With that, remember, Dr. Dre is an Aquarius. Dre's 2014' unprecedented multi-billion dollar merger with **Apple** is another *"sign of the times"* that indicates we are indeed in beginning of new Age, The Genesis.

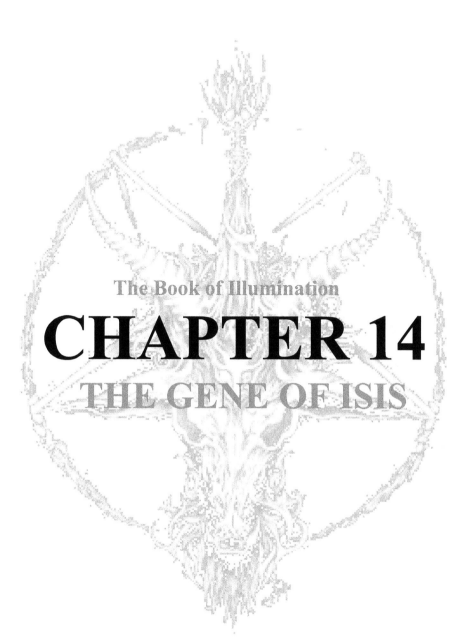

The Book of Illumination

CHAPTER 14

THE GENE OF ISIS

The Book of Illumination

CHAPTER 14

THE GENE OF ISIS

THE GENE OF ISIS

65 The Egyptian legend regarding the (Gene of Isis) or the son of Isis, the earth mother, was transformed into the conception story found in Christianity where the Virgin Mary (Isis) birth's the Christ, Jesus. In *Isis Unveiled*, H.P. Blavatsky wrote: "...*Cyril, the Bishop of Alexandria, had openly embraced the cause of Isis, the Egyptian goddess, and had anthropomorphized her into Mary, the mother of God* 66. When we look at this story on the surface, it makes us think about a literal virgin giving birth to a savior. In Egypt however the constellations themselves represent actual people similar to how the "gods" are portrayed in Roman Mythology. Only those who are initiated into the greater mysteries of heaven and earth get a clear perspective for what is actually being translated. Being born of the Virgin Mary could easily mean being born under the sign Virgo, Mary the virgin being the "celestial" virgin. It is also believed that Virgo, the Virgin, "...the constellation Virgo, is the first sign of the coming Christ because she holds a branch which is a familiar Old Testament name for the messiah. Many Old Testament scriptures bear witness to the fact that Jesus is 'The Branch.'

Zechariah 6:12-13 (12) *And speak unto him, saying, Thus speaketh the LORD of hosts, saying, Behold the man whose name is The BRANCH; and he shall grow up out of his place, and he shall build the temple of the LORD: (13) Even he shall build the temple of the LORD; and he shall bear the glory, and shall sit and rule upon his throne; and he shall be a priest upon his throne: and the counsel of peace shall be between them both.*

Zechariah 3:8 *(8) For, behold, I will bring forth my servant the BRANCH.'*

Isaiah 4:2 *(2) Also 'In that day shall the branch of the Lord be beautiful and glorious.'*

Bishop Rudolph Graber, wrote in his book ***Fatima Advancing Rapidly Towards Final Fulfillment*** *"In conclusion, we greet Mary (Virgo) as the great sign in the heavens which precedes the coming of her Son, because the mother always precedes the son. We greet her as the one who at Fatima wanted to bring peace to the world if we fulfilled the demands of her maternal heart... We greet her as the Victor in all the battles of God, and as the Mother of the Church who will bring the Good Friday of the Church to an end and give it a new Easter"* 67.

Michael Jackson born of a (Virgin) under the sign Virgo is the Son of God (Leo) "named Joseph" who embodies all of these qualities. It is also important to note that the Arch Angel Michael is regarded as being ruled by the sign Leo in Astrology 67b. The glyph for Virgo in Astrology is an M with a fish; the sign most Christians reference Jesus by 67cc.

Here is a glyph for the word Ormus (OR♍US.) This symbol incorporates the glyph for Virgo which is placed inside the word orus which according to *the Merovingian Dynasty and Satanic bloodline of the false Prophet and Anti-Christ*, is a corrupted form of Horus, and is used in Crowley's 5th Degree Ritual for the OTO and stands for IACCHUS, ASI, and ORUS. The origin of the Ormus dates back to ancient Egypt and is found in the legend of Hathor. Hathor is the mother "Cow" goddess who sits upon a throne as the goddess of music, dance, foreign lands and fertility 67c. The husband of Hathor was a

solar deity name RA/Re who is often referred to as the Sun God or "father" of the Gods 67cd. IACCHUS is an obvious play on the Roman deity BACCHUS who is also known as Dionysus 67d.

Dionysus's most notable trait is that he is described as being "*man womanish*", and makes people break out into wild uncontrollable orgies. Orgies as described by Webster are frenzied outburst of energy whereby people are mad and drunken with ecstasy. If you've ever been to a Michael Jackson concert you'd understand what is meant by describing the behavior of his fans as orgiastic as they appear to be "*drunken with an ecstatic spirit*." Lisa Marie Pressley in an interview with Oprah Winfrey in 2010 said that being around Michael was the most "*intoxicating*" feeling she's ever had; and her dad was Elvis Pressley.

Orgy: secret ceremonial rites held in honor of an ancient Greek or Roman deity and usually characterized by ecstatic singing and dancing

Ecstatic: Being in a state of ecstasy; joyful or enraptured

It is also important to notate the difference between sexual orgy and the orgy described by Webster. The root of the word ecstasy is also found in the word ecstatic which to most people, means highly joyful and enraptured. Though many people use the word ecstatic they never make the correlation between this word and the word ecstasy which hints to sexual pleasure as it is used in the descriptive context in the word orgy.

When we factor in the inner astrological gods/selves within the mother of Michael Jackson we see that she is a Taurus born on the 4th day. The fourth day as defined earlier corresponds to the emperor, which in the tarot sits upon the throne of He. The Taurus again as regarded by the Royal Arch sits

opposite the Lion which corresponds to Leo, and again is the astrological sign of Michael's father, Joseph. In the Egyptian myth Michael Jackson would be considered a son of Hathor and Ra making him the reincarnated pharaoh "The Hormus" spoken about in the ancient Egyptian myths. Michael left evidence to the fact that he was an ancient Egyptian reincarnated deity in the music video *Remember the Time*.

In Astrology Taureans are noted as being the most musical of all the signs 67e. Recognizing that Michael Jackson was the god of music in real life, and Hathor is the goddess of music in Egyptian mythology, brings us to the conclusion that these myths are indeed real. When looking at the painting on the previous page that depicts Michael in the likeness of the Roman deity Dionysus, a number of hidden realities come to life. The black Cherub is on the ground asleep with his back turned to Michael while the other white Cherub's are flying around him in awe of his presence. This is directly related to the fact that Michael Jackson was rejected by people of color as being divine or the messiah; while people who are white accepted and embraced him wholly in his royal and divine form.

Ichthys from Greek ἰχθύς is the ancient and classical Greek word for "fish". This symbol was used by early Christians as a secret symbol for the Christ and is now a colloquialism for the "sign of the Jesus fish." Notice how close ichthys resembles Isis. The use of the Ichthys symbol by early Christians (*Ichthy*) can be read as an acronym. It equals to "Jesus Christ, God's son, savior," in ancient Greek language.

Iota (i) is the first letter of *Iēsous* (Ἰησοῦς), Greek for "Jesus".
Chi (ch) is the first letter of *Christos* (Χριστὸς), Greek for "anointed".
Theta (th) is the first letter of *Theou* (Θεοῦ), Greek for "God's", the genitive case of Θεός, *Theos*, Greek for "God".
Upsilon (y) is the first letter of *yios* (Υἱὸς), Greek for "Son".
Sigma (s) is the first letter of *sōtēr* (Σωτήρ), Greek for "Savior" 68.

Remember, the Gene/isis or "Gene of Isis" marks the beginning of the new Epoch. An Epoch is a new age where the Sun rises in a different set of constellations, and the energy of that constellations takes precedence in the moods and understandings of the people on earth. Earlier we spoke in reference to the Horus, who originally was named Heru, is where Hero gets its meaning and connotation from in the chapter entitled *Genesis*. Again, the arrival of the Horus indicates the end of an age has occurred and the beginning of the Great Age has begun. *The *ALS Ice Bucket Challenge* is another "*sign of the times*" and testament to this truth. It's participants, Michael Jordan, George Bush Jr., Bill Gates, and Lebron James, to name a few, drench themselves with buckets of water, in the same likeness as the *Water Bearer*. This *Water Bearer* is attributed to the sign Aquarius in astrology, as he pours a pitcher of water 68e.

During the Age of Aquarius, it has been prophesied that the avatars of God will reincarnate to the Earth to return it to a golden age. Every 25,920 years there is a full rotation that causes the Sun to orbit through each astrological constellation for a period of 2,160 years. There are twelve of these periods and each period is marked by an astrological sign. The rotation goes counterclockwise from Pisces all the way to Aquarius. At the end of the rotation each fixed backdrop or constellation will have been moved through by the Sun similar to how in a year the Earth moves through the seasons. The Sun will rise at the vernal equinox in each of the twelve astrological signs within this 25,920 year period.

THE COMFORTER

When we take into account that we are headed out of the Piscean age and into the Age of Aquarius we have to look at the astrological glyphs to determine where we are in terms of our spirituality and consciousness. This in congruence with biblical scriptures marks what deities and avatars we should expect to find in the coming age. When we look at ancient stories and texts there is a story about a great flood found in the Bible. This flood was said to mark the destruction of an old world, and the beginning of a new one.

Genesis 6:7 (7) And the LORD said, I will destroy man whom I have created from the face of the earth; both man, and beast, and the creeping thing, and the fowls of the air; for it repenteth me that I have made them.

Genesis 7:24 (24) The waters flooded the earth for a hundred and fifty days.

Genesis 9:1 (1) Then God blessed Noah and his sons, saying to them, Be fruitful and increase in number and fill the earth.

Genesis 5: 28-29 (28) And Lamech lived an hundred eighty and two years and begat a son (29) And he called his name Noah, saying, This same shall comfort us concerning our work and toil of our hands, because of the ground which the lord had cursed.

I highlighted comfort because when the scripture above is joined with John 15:26, it indicates to us the coming avatar sent after the Christ of the Piscean Age is the one spoken of in the days of Noah because the fish precedes the flood, or that Pisces precedes Aquarius in the constellations.

John 15:26 (26) But when the comforter is come, whom I will send unto you from the father, even the Spirit of truth, which proceedeth from the father, he shall testify of me.

The Christ spoken of by St. John says the avatar who is coming after him is the *Spirit of Truth* who will testify of him just as I have testified that Michael Jackson was the messiah of the Piscean age. The flood or "great deluge" is what the Egyptians called the time period between the Piscean and the Aquarian ages.

THE FLOOD

The story of the flood in the Bible references Noah and his three sons Ham the "Black" son, Japheth the "white" son, and Shem the "mixed" son as Semi/ means half. This story like others discussed within this book, is also another allegory that describes the beginning of the world. That beginning, as I have reiterated several times, translates to the beginning of a new age. In this parable, Noah represents the avatar that is in an ark which is symbolic of the *Ark of the Covenant*. This Ark is also the vessel containing the complete knowledge of the **Zodiac** (*circle of animals*), which is why people believe all the animals were in it. Again, allegories disguise truth within myths.

Semi – (1) precisely half of

When the world has multiplied and mixed itself to the point where it has forgotten the LORD and the knowledge and covenant he instituted on Earth in his last descent upon it; this delusion, created by adultery, fornication, and over population is what causes the LORD to destroy it.

By analyzing the story of Noah we can conclude that Hinduism was the religion of the time because the religions of Judaism, Christianity and Islam had not yet occurred. These three religions spawned forth from Abraham who was a descendant of Noah. In the Hindu religion the great god Shiva, known as the LORD in Judaism, incarnated to earth to birth the human race with his three wives Durga, Gauri, and Parvati. This was done in the same likeness to Noah who gave birth to the new human race with wives of whom he had three sons. Hinduism is viewed by today's western world as polytheistic; however historically, Hinduism is the world's oldest religion. A person may ask how I came to the conclusion that Hinduism was the religion being practiced at the time of Noah; and like many other questions that are posed within this book that answer too is also simple. In Hinduism there are many gods, and the people of the Hindu faith readily keep their god's in their houses; the most notable are the statues of Krishna, Shiva, Ganesha, and Vishnu. Below in 31st chapter of Genesis is a testament to these facts.

Genesis 31:31-32 & 35 (31*) Jacob answered Laban, "I was afraid, because I thought you would take your daughters away from me by force. (32) But if you find anyone who has your gods, he shall not live. In the presence of our relatives, see for yourself whether there is anything of yours here with me; and if so, take it." Now Jacob did not know that Rachel had <u>stolen the gods</u>.(35) Rachel said to her father, "Don't be angry, my lord, that I cannot stand up in your presence; I'm having my period." So he searched but could not find the <u>household gods</u>.*

The scriptures indicate the people of that time in the Bible kept their gods in their households, again, a practice that is indicative of Hinduism. Christianity is a religion that has borrowed nearly all of its theology from Hinduism and this is expressed through its triune deity represented in one Godhead known as God the father, the Son, and the Holy Spirit. This three in one trinity exposes that the Christian religion isn't monotheistic. When we add the words of Jesus found in the 10 chapter of John in the 34th stanza it totally contradicts the monotheistic principals Orthodox Christianity promotes.

John 10:34-36 (34) Is it not written in your law, I said Ye are gods (35) If he called them gods, unto whom the word of God came, and the scripture cannot be broken (36) Say ye of him, whom the father hath sanctified, and sent into the world, Thou blasphemest, because I said, I am the Son of Man

If this isn't clear the 1st chapter and 26th verse of the Genesis may clear up matters even further.

Genesis 1:26 (26) And God said, Let us make man in our image, after our likeness: and let them have dominion over the fish of the sea, and over the fowl of the air, and over the cattle, and over all the earth, and over every creeping thing that creepeth upon the earth.

The religious people of the American society today view themselves as being created directly from God; which in a sense would make them gods as well right? In fact, if you asked most Christians, they would say they are a "child of God" the same as when Jesus was told by perpetrators they were "sons of Abraham" in John 8:41. The only reason that most Christians have accepted the false notion of monotheism is that it was promoted to them for centuries by the establishers of the church. Constantine mandated that monotheism be taught and slew any who opposed this doctrine. He in the likeness of Akhenaton outlawed polytheism and went on a crusade to make sure the people's faith remained monotheistic. The 6th chapter of Genesis however, states the *Sons of God* with a big G and sons in the plural sense and is yet another direct polytheistic reference found within the Bibles scriptures.

What makes the Hindu religion unaccepted by the western world is the way the aspects of the one God are broken up into gods and worshipped. But think about American society; one of their most popular shows is American Idol. Every year the people elect their idol and this person becomes a "star." Also with that, the most coveted trophy in American culture today is an Oscar which is also an idol.

<u>Idol</u>: (1) a representation or symbol of an object to worship

You haven't become successful in the world of film (America's # 2 export) unless you've won this prestigious award. People in the world of drama portray whatever type of character in order to achieve this trophy (idol.) But think about whenever a person is admired by another; the first thing that person says about the person they admire is, "yeah that's my idol." The idol worshipping of the western world is just as much a part of American culture as polytheism is to India. As previously stated in the Hindu religion there is a trinity of Gods called the Trimurti; their names are Brahma the creator, Shiva the destroyer, and Vishnu the preserver. The worshipping of the animals as deities themselves are what made foreign invaders think that the indigenous people of Northern Africa and Asia were polytheistic pagans. An example of this is the worship of the Bull. The western way of thinking is this, "Yes a

bull is an animal, but what makes it more sacred than a horse?" Min the Egyptian god of fertility was described as a bull. The bull was the ultimate symbol of virility, strength, and wealth, as wealth was determined by sons in the ancient world. So by Indian people literally worshipping the physical bull westerners think they have fallen away from worshipping the God of Abraham, Isaac, and Jacob. However the procreative God of Abraham is worshipped in the aspect of the Bull in Hinduism's and is known as the potent god of sex and fertility named the LORD Shiva who rides a bull. Shiva is one of the most powerful gods in the Hindu Trimurti, and represents for Hinduism what Min does for China and Osiris does for Egypt 67f. Aang the avatar who rides astride a white bison is a modernized form of the Hindu (Indian) avatar Shiva.

If we look deep enough we can still see that these Hindu's are worshipping the same gods as those of the Bible; just in a more holistic and natural form. When a person thinks about embodying something the mind is only limited by what it is able to imagine. If the Hindu people go to the limits of their mind to personify and impersonate the legends they've read about in their ancient scriptures, why are they regarded as being pagan? Because the Hindu culture worships animals in this way they seem to be of low intelligence. Their way of worship is merely an advanced system of thought expanding past the acknowledgment that all people and creatures come from God making them all his children (gods) as well. In their view of "God" he is the author of all creation, not just man. Man thinking he is the highest in terms of all creation to them is an opinion. This is said because all animals have characteristics that differentiate themselves from other animals making their form of existence unique and respected just as man is. Hindus recognize that everything that has a human exterior doesn't mean that it is human. This is why Hindus view all of creation as God's children, whereas the religion of Abraham teaches that man is the highest creation fashioned in the image of God; both are right, it is perspective that creates the bias. This bias is further enabled by the education the common people have been given in the western world which discourages wholistic thought. This education keeps them in a certain state of mind; a state of mind that allows them to be bred and viewed much like the cattle the Hindu's worship. Because the westernized masses are kept in a "cattle like" state, they are the fuel that feeds the people who have evolved out of that particular mental state. These evolved people usually find themselves atop the food chain in positions and seats of power like executive offices and governing bodies. These cattle like masses are preyed upon by the evolved elite for several reasons. For one the evolved elite have already come to the people (herd) and told them the truth. The truth they told the people, the people didn't believe, in spite of all the evidence that was supported with it. So after much strife, contention, and quarreling these evolved beings became the ones who feed upon the walking dead "cattle-like" "goyim" people. This is symbolized by the vultures on the headdresses of Egyptian monarchs. Rather than keep bumping their heads to give the people the truth, they gave them what they wanted. In giving the people what they wanted, the evolved elite's view of the people diminished and they no longer cared for the fates of the people because the people in their eyes were the walking dead. They just used whatever means necessary to ensure the flock doesn't go outside of the fence. If the herd (people) gets outside of the fence they have an opportunity to become a threat that could possibly fracture the civil structure of the land; a structure that took years to assemble but will take seconds to destroy. Because structures are easily destroyed and harder to build, the state has to take every precaution in managing itself from the chaotic subject who has a great potential to create and build, but also has an even greater potential to destroy and rebel.

When we look at evolved beings, evolved beings are almost always atop the food chain. People who are of the governing elite have been trained to be orderly and apart from the chaotic nature the subjects they rule are in.

AVATAR

Consider the idea that at the end of an (age) the freewill of mankind has destroyed the innate balance of the (righteousness) in that cycle of time. Therefore to sustain the world, the creator incarnates in worthy vehicles (avatars) to not only correct the imbalances, but to bring to a close one cycle of time so that another may begin.

The story of Noah was 1st recorded by the Hindus in the Matsya Purana. We spoke about this earlier in reference to the god Osiris who was as explained by Alexander Piatigorsky, the WORD long before the arrival of the Christ of St. John. The **Matsya Purana** is the first and the oldest of all the Puranas and Hindu scriptures. It is primarily the story of the first Avatar of god Vishnu, in the form of a fish. These Hindu Scriptures have predated Christianity by an estimated 3,000 years [69].

The Matsya Avatar Satyavrata, who later was known as Vaivasvata Manu, was a pious and righteous king. Once as he scooped water from a river a tiny fish came along with the water. He was about to return the fish to the river when it asked for protection from the larger fish in the river. Satyavrata put the fish into his urn but overnight it grew big and asked for a larger container. This happened night after night and the king moved the fish from pond to lake to the ocean. Then he realized that the fish could be no ordinary fish but had to be God incarnate. He offered his salutations and begged resolution of the mystery. The fish told him that in due course the earth would be inundated and all life would be destroyed. Satyavrata was asked to collect the seeds and animals required for life to begin again and wait for the fish. When the deluge began the fish appeared with a boat in tow and Satyavrata got in with the seeds and animals. While the flood lasted the fish kept the boat afloat on the water and also narrated to Satyavrata the contents recorded in the Matsya Purana [69b].

Avatar: (1) The descent of a deity (2) incarnation of a god

Matthew 24:37 *But as the **days of Noah** were, so shall also the coming of the **Son of man** be.*

THE AGE OF AQUARIUS

One of the earliest references to avatar is in the Bhagavad Gita (c. 3138 BC) which describes the typical role of an avatar of Vishnu—to bring dharma, or righteousness back to the social and cosmic order: *Whenever righteousness wanes and unrighteousness increases I send myself forth. In order to protect the good and punish the wicked, In order to make a firm foundation for righteousness, I come into being age after age 69c.*

Michael Jackson known as the *Hor*M*us* and the avatar (Krishna) was sent to bring balance to the world at the end of the Piscean age. Racism at that time was the imbalance and evil of the day. Michael was the avatar sent to earth to warn the people why they need to heal the world, respect each other's race's,

and love the children. As diagnosed throughout this book in countless examples and references, the story of the Flood found in the Bible was taken from the account given by Hindu's in the Matsya Purana. Because it is the oldest story found in Hindu legend is why it was placed at the beginning of creation within the Bible where Noah births the new race of man and mankind. The precession shows us the earth is now in the exact same place where the "Baptist" can be seen in the heavens as the Aquarius is the only fixed constellation that is a man in the zodiac. Again, known as the *Water Bearer*, the Aquarius holds a pitcher of water, pouring out that water from the heavens to the earth below. *ALS Ice Bucket Challenge 2014*

This Age of Aquarius is the age of spiritual enlightenment where people become awakened about God, both the one of themselves and the one they have been taught to worship. This is what is meant by the dead shall rise and walk again on earth. The (avatar) or Christ of the Aquarian age is the 1st one awakened and is here to awaken others. This awakening causes the people to become more spiritually inclined and less given to dogma and superstition. The reason this comes about is the constellation in the heavens has moved positions from the fish (Pisces) into the constellation of Aquarius (Water Bearer.) The energy of the constellational shift has set the tone for the events we've been witnessing here on earth. It is no different than the seasons, as in summer it is hot and in winter it gets cold. When people think of the end of the world it is merely the end of that age 70. This is why we are seeing circa 2010 all forms of androgyny, gay marriages, as well as **pan**demonium on earth. The flood gates (*PANdora's box*) have been opened and with the opening of the "eye", aka the *sun in a new constellation*, all manifestations of the star energy brought forth by the cosmic constellational shift, has caused the universe to project these energies to us in physical form. The internet is the physical portal they project through, as it is the gateway that shows everything happening in and around the world as related to the universe.

James Cameron, the director of one of the highest grossing films of all time entitled *Avatar,* was born under the sign of Leo on the 18th day; the day of the moon in the tarot. While this piece of information doesn't strike a chord initially, when one thinks about the solar deity that has been mentioned in this book, and all of the information regarding the religious works ascribed to him; it is easy to see how large in scale this solar deity's presence is. Just as Shiva and Krishna in the Hindu pantheon of gods are blue, in the movie, the avatars are also blue. This reverses the role of them being "God" incarnates in "earthly" vehicles to being earthlings in "godly vehicles. The movie the *Avatar* is the most popular movie of all time just as Krishna is the most popular Hindu avatar of all time, and Michael Jackson was the most popular icon of all time. Both the movie (James Cameron's the *Avatar,* and, the *Book of Illumination,*) the book about avatars, have been brought to light by Leo's; showing the SUN is at work even in the subconscious realm. This realm, governed by the moon however, is still projecting the "Sun" just as it does in nature. The universe is alive…

The Book of Illumination

CHAPTER 15

NEW WORLD ORDER

The Book of Illumination

CHAPTER 15

NEW WORLD ORDER

NEW WORLD ORDER

Due to Earth's orbital precession, which occurs every 25,920 years the prophetic Egypt & Israel are presently located in North America. This means the position of the Sun and the constellations of Orion and Ursa Major in relevance to the Earth are now over America; in ancient times they were over Egypt/Israel; which makes America prophetically Egypt/Israel. Many of the Egyptian prophecies regarding Israel were presages directed at foreshadowing the place where the "gods" would reappear in the flesh. This place again due to precession is America making it the prophetic Israel spoken about in the Bible. So when the prophecy states that Joseph was a Ruler of Israel, we can take that to mean Joseph is a ruler in America through the person of Michael (Joseph) Jackson. Thus the resurrection of the Jesus of Nazareth spoken of in **Matthew 22:29-30** is the precession when the immortals walk on Earth again as avatars; literally dead people rising from their graves.

Precession: (1) a change in the direction of the axis of a rotating object. (2) a change in direction of the rotation axis where the second Euler angle is constant.

When I state that ancient Egypt is presently America it means that America is the place where God is seen both figuratively through stellar constellations and literally through human embodiments called avatars. One of the other recorded existences of this phenomenon whereby immortals walk the earth in the flesh was reported in a country in Africa called Ethiopia which translates to (Theo = God/ Opia = Eye) Making Ethiopia the place where "God" Sees everything (ALL SEEING EYE/THE SUN.)

Again, the place where people see God is the "sky" where the "stars" are located; and in ancient times, the "heavens" were the celestial civilizations that housed the gods. These stars which form constellations in ancient times were also called "gods" as well. However when the people worship the stars in the sky they are unable to recognize the avatars that are the embodiments of the stars themselves on earth. Imagine the star itself is literally in human form on earth yet the people ignore (it) to go and kneel before the stars in the sky.

Zephaniah 1:4-5 (4) I will destroy every remnant of Baal worship in this place, the very names of the idolatrous priests, (5) those who bow down on the roofs to worship the starry host, those who bow down and swear by the LORD and who also swear by Molek.

The Hollywood star walk is supposed to document the stars of the "heavens" that fall to the earth in epic forms; which is why it is located in Los Angeles, literally, the "city of Angels." People who represent these qualities of the gods (not embodiments but aspects) usually end up in HOLLYWOOD where through movies; they project the lives of the deities to mortals.

Fanatics are attracted to Hollywood because it provides a romantic escape from the ills experienced here on earth. These depictions are acted out by people who literally represent the "stars" from the heavens on screen. Because art imitates life, the actors become immortalized in their roles once seen by hundreds of millions of people on screen. When the life begins to imitate the art, the future generations now looking at what was seen on screen, begin to mimic it, creating warped renditions of it. These renditions become more general and less detailed. The less detailed, the less amount of information is transferred. The less amount of information that is transferred, the fuzzier the picture; and when the picture becomes fuzzy, that means there is need for an upgrade.

In Hollywood you also have people who represent the gods acting in god-like roles, which for regular people is very appealing and intriguing. This intrigues them because in their minds, this is an easy way to become immortalized; where they can "live forever" like the gods in heaven and legend. (This also contributes to why film is the country's second leading export.) However, when a true god/goddess arises he/she will manifest in the physical with paramount achievements and talents like Michael Jordan, and

Michael Jackson. These gods are the people you read about in all esoteric books about gods, like Heracles and Hermes and are the people who are living in the kingdom/country where the planets and constellations are in alignment. Most people do to the distorted and perverted images the media and society has produced throughout time would think these (gods) to be aliens due to their insufficient knowledge, and pending on how you look at it, they are. In Fact William Cooper in his book *Behold a Pale Horse* is quoted as saying on page 73 *"The initiated elect communicate directly to the Gods [Aliens?]The elect are given knowledge of the Mysteries and are illumed and are thus known as the Illuminated ones, the guardians of the secrets of the ages 72."*

When we look at the word illuminate, if forces us to readily assess in nature the things in it that are illuminated. Within our immediate solar system, the Sun, Venus, the Moon and the stars are the objects that are illuminated, with the Sun being the most illuminated. In Astrology the Sun is unanimously labeled as a fire sign. The fire that corresponds to the earth is the volcanic type, which erupts and destroys everything in its path while creating a new fertile landscape. This is what parallels the volcanic aspect of the fire sign to masculinity and the phallus itself as its eruptions are similar to ejaculations. The fire signs are also the signs that are the most logic/ rash and on the opposite ends of the spectrum in regards to signs that represent emotion (Pisces, Cancer, and Scorpio.) Because the fire sign which houses the Sun is more rash than emotional, it is considered to be alien (outer worldly) rather than human (earthly). The outer-worldly and rational personality of the fires signs were personified in a character named Doctor Spock. Dr. Spock's ability to rationalize with logic enables him to become the "conscious" of the starship enterprises leader, Captain Kirk. What is interesting about Dr. Spock is the V gesture that he makes with his hand which is indicative of Venus and the Semitic god Min. This hand gesture symbolizes the highly phallic nature of the Star trek character who originally received his energy through a plate in his stomach where the "fire" chakra is located. In Star Trek the Motion Picture, Spock also sacrifices himself in order for the ship and the crew to be saved. He then is resurrected in the next Star Trek, *Star Trek III: The Search for Spock* with the "genesis machine." All of these correspondences liken Spock the alien as being self-sacrificed, resurrected, and fiery just like the solar deity described within this book.

History repeats itself; but then again why wouldn't it, the earth moves in orbits which are circular and elliptical. Those master builders and Masons laid within their framework a map that would enable them to see when and where the gods would manifest next. Again due to precession they knew the land the gods would manifest in would be where the stars or constellations aligned; this land happens to be America. The divinely inspired plan to build another portal for the celestial beings to manifest to earth through was part of the divine plan to teach all of creation that an All-creator exists. The fact that he exists is what the people after so much time between his manifestations have fallen away from. This falling away is the result of the out of sight out of mind paralysis that occurs with mortals between Great Ages which are 25,920 years apart.

The factions of people, who hold high seats in the religious and political world that aren't aware that God is real, have turned the world into what it is today. *It has served us well this myth of Christ"* Pope Leo X, 73. Corruption and greed are now norms within American society as an all-out apostasy from spiritual mores and ethics has taken place. The ruling classes of both government and church have yet to acknowledge the mistakes their forefathers made in regards to how religion is taught to the masses. It's the same as when "THEY" said the earth was flat, or when Columbus's pelagic exploits led to the erroneous branding of Native Americans as Indians due to thinking he was in India. This lack of acknowledgement to past errors has caused the crippling of morality within the earth. The apocalyptic doomsday theory, cultivated through oppressive religious dogma, has become the theory that has now ended the present world as we knew it. As the world by way of an unadulterated, technically enhanced global reckoning, has now been liberated from the shackles of ignorance. The end of the world as prophesized in eschatological studies is actually the ending rule of those who have abused their power and caused these atrocities to exist on earth. The passing of the torch from mortals back to the gods is what the Age of Aquarius represents as the 6,000 year prophecy has ended.

Wherever the alignments of the celestial stars are, is where the original immortals will manifest in flesh and being. When these "stars" align the dead shall rise. This means that the gods who once lived on earth will reform themselves upon it and the god of the aeon, Horus the resurrected Osiris, who has uncanny scientific knowledge and abilities, will begin to preach his message of the mysteries of "God."

In each surrounding age of 2,160 years there is a person/ avatar who comes during the age that embodies the energy of the age. This star is the persons whose accomplishments and feats are greater than anyone else's in respect to the age. Pending on where the stars align will in turn be the location where this avatar is born. When these avatars hit the scene they usually greatly advance and upgrade the culture. These avatars are also attributed to being gods or godsends and all have the same bizarre set of circumstances surrounding their births. When we read about epic legends from historical books they don't display the scientific knowledge within them overtly the way reference books do. Instead they infuse scientific knowledge within the story itself, replicating the patterns that exist with every precession. This is why many of the stories written in ancient epics have heroes with virgin births.

Earlier in the book we spoke of Michael Jackson being the instrumental force in creating the integrated society in America we love today. Michael Jackson was born under the sign of Virgo to a father named Joseph. Again the fact that the story is translated literally may in turn steer us from a revelation that is right in our face. Imagine if the Bible is a book of Astrology and all the information in it is to lead the reader to certain understandings about

astrological signs and the way these signs relate to one another through allegory? This would be considered the ultimate guide to understanding God, which as we have discussed, is the god of our own individual interpretation and conscious 74, 75. The High Priestess tarot card as outlined by Robert Lomas and Christopher Knight on pg. 90 of the *Second Messiah* stated *"The card that was most immediately offensive to the (Catholic) church was the high priestess"* 74b.

277

When you factor a real Christ or Christ like figure descending to earth in the physical flesh this would be highly offensive to a church that promotes the IN Christ, the Christ of everyone's mind and hearts versus, the God/man who comes to the earth to show it how it can improve and become more spiritual. Notice at the bottom of the card is a camel, the same animal seen in the Statue of the Archangel Michael at St. John's Cathedral in New York City. This statue found at St. John's Cathedral is another direct clue to show that the particular messiah that is being referenced is the Christ of St. John, also known as Michael Jackson.

Beside the camel on the previous page stands a large statue of Michael the Archangel destroying a great Dragon. Also in the statue, the Archangel Michael is standing on top of a large crab while petting a camel. The crab is the symbol for the sign of Cancer in Astrology. Being that Michael Jackson died on 6-25-09 during the period that cancer ruled in Astrology as well as the day Cancer ruled in the tarot, shows those with the spiritual eye what age we are headed into as well as the age we are leaving. This would mean that his death marks the end of an era and the beginning of the era by which the great Mother Church is held accountable for all of the lies and romanticism that has caused the world to de-evolve spiritually into a dark age. The high priestess card is the tarot card that Michael Jackson was born on. The high priestess card represents the moon Goddess who rules Cancer, and controls the tides of the water (masses.) The fact that Michael Jackson is known for the moon walk, and controlled the most people at a concert in Wembley stadium (500,000) further admonishes that he like the moon controls the chaotic water represented as the masses of people. The wild uncontrollable outbursts of energy seen within the crowds attracted at Michael's concerts enables a person to comprehend the meaning of the word "lunatic" which is defined as insane or wildly foolish and has the word lunar at its root. Look at the picture on the following page and tell me who the true controller of the masses is?

I have placed these references within the book to add evidence that the literal aspect in which the Bible is read from is blinding people from the literary nuances that give a very colorful and meticulous assessment of the scriptures and the characters represented within them.

Now that we have a better understanding as to why Michael Jackson has been called or likened to the Christ, we can see at this time how other cultures view Jesus as well as why they have come to their own particular understandings about certain messianic figures.

The High Priestess card in the tarot is symbolized as being the moon and "Moon-goddesses often have association with bears. The bear is like the primal mother, and will defend her cubs against all forces to the death 76."

In the occult underground, in various schools of esoteric teaching, they break down the astrological associations that are subtly placed within the Bibles scriptures. Rosicrucian symbolism represents Jehovah as a *bear*. According to Peter Dawkins esoteric book, *Arcadia; The Ancient Egyptian Mysteries*, "*Ursa Major* and *Ursa Minor* are the celestial signs, or symbols for Jehovah 77." Other biblical scriptures give rise to astrological associations with bears. Below is a scripture that refers to the Egyptian Sun God RA likened to Vishnu, who Egyptians believed traveled across the sky in a solar boat.

Job 9:8-9 (8) He alone stretches out the heavens and treads on the waves of the sea (9) He is the Maker of the Bear (Arcturus) and Orion, the Pleiades and the constellations of the south.

Pleiades: (1) a conspicuous cluster of stars in the constellation Taurus that includes six stars in the form of a very small dipper

Mazzaroth (1) Hebrew; meaning The Constellations of the Zodiac

According to *The Power of Birthdays, Stars and Numbers*, the star that influences those born on August 29th between 1930 and 2000 is the star called Alioth. Alioth is located in the constellation Epsilon Ursa Major and is a blue white star found in the tail of the Great Bear [78]. The tail of the Great Bear Constellation has 4 stars within it, they are—Alioth, Alcor-Mizar and Alkaid. According to Hastings' *Dictionary of the Bible*, these stars are the sons of the Great Bear *Ayish*. The 'sons' of *Ayish* are spoken of in Job 38:32, and are regarded as the three stars in the tail of the bear [79].

Job 38:31-33 (31) Canst thou bind the sweet influences of Pleiades, or loose the bands of Orion? (32) Canst thou bring forth Mazzaroth in his season? or canst thou guide Arcturus with his sons? (33) Knowest thou the ordinances of heaven? canst thou set the dominion thereof in the earth?

The new international version of the Bible translates Arcturus as *bear*. King Arthur a form of Arcturus is associated with "bear" in that his name comes from the constellation of the Greater Bear, which was also known as 'Arthur's Plow [77b]. Note the (Arc) or Ark in the front of his name which is an obvious allegorical clue that relates Arthur as the one who travels in the boat, just like the Egyptian Sun God Ra, The Hindu Deity Vishnu, and Noah who was also in an ark..

Job 38:31-33 (31) Can you bind the beautiful Pleiades? Can you loose the cords of Orion? (32) Can you bring forth the constellations in their seasons or lead out the Bear with its cubs? (33) Do you know the laws of the heavens? Can you set up God's dominion over the earth?

Bible commentaries seem to agree that the previous verse is a reference to the constellation of the Greater Bear. In the book the *Hiram Key* Robert Lomas and Christopher Knight attribute the Templar Knights at discovering the star that they called L'america. which was the star presiding over the land that "bears" its name 80. America was designated as the place and the Star of L' America could have been mistaken for the star of Merak which is located in the constellation Alpha Ursa Major or the Big Dipper and is most commonly referred to as the Greater Bear. "Merak" comes from an Arabic description that means "the flank/loin of the Greater Bear 81. If a person has a hard time believing this, the capital of America, Washington D.C. which was built by Masons, again is a direct replica of the city of Memphis in Egypt. The Big Dipper is among the most recognized constellations and a small part of the ancient figure of Ursa Major, the Greater Bear..." "*The name Ursa Major, according to The New English Dictionary, 'appears to arise out of the verbal association of the star named Arcturus. In Welsh lore, the constellation is seen as a symbol of the Celtic King Arthur; his name, it is claimed, is derived from Arth-Uthyr, 'the wonderful bear'* 85. Furthermore it is suggests that the Zodiac, with its circular route, is what led to the round table. When we look at the story of King Arthur in further depth we find he was appointed king because he was the only one who could pull the sword from the stone. He was also mentored by Merlin, a wizard who wears upon his hat a star and a crescent moon. This symbolizes the underlying astrological associations with the story which like other great literary works places a master with an apprentice. This relationship is exploited in Star Wars with Anakin and The Emperor, the Matrix with Neo and Morpheus, as well as in the Bible with Jesus and John the Baptist. The Arthur or avatar, society is looking for in the new Age, (Age of Aquarius) is the person who has the ability to put together all of the lost information in regards to religion. "*The elect must hope always for the coming of the man of holiness, He is the man in transcendence, the man who is allocated in one place to the sephira Chockmah (wisdom) He is the man more precious than fine gold who is mentioned by Isaiah* 86." This man is the king of the occult knowledge here on earth as regarded by those who practice Christianity, Judaism, Hinduism, and Islam. The piecing back together of all the lost information is known to the Egyptians as the piecing back the body of Osiris and to Masons as the piecing back the body of their Master Builder Hiram.

The 147th Psalm is a great testament to the infinite understanding of the LORD / "God" that names and numbers stars as well as gathers the outcastes of Israel as he rebuilds its temple.

Psalm 147: 1-5 *Praise ye the* LORD: *for it is good to sing praises unto our God; for it is pleasant; and praise is comely.(2)* <u>*The* LORD *doth build up*</u>

281

Jerusalem: he gathereth together the outcasts of Israel. (3) He healeth the broken in heart, and bindeth up their wounds. (4) He telleth the number of the stars; he calleth them all by their names. (5) Great is our Lord, and of great power: his understanding is infinite.

THE LION AND THE BULL

The 'Unification of the Two Lands' in Ancient Egypt (Israel and Judah) is most notably symbolized by the Sphinx, this symbol and these "lands" marked the start of the first cycle of pharoanic dynasties that began with the commencement of the astrological Age of Taurus, *c.* 3,240 BC [82]. It is known that Aldebaran, the star that presides over the birth of the Hindu deity Krishna, is said to be the eye of the bull or Taurus. We've already concluded that Michael Jackson was the reincarnation of Joseph in Israel. When we link the eye of Taurus, the lives of Joseph and Krishna, and composite those incarnations within the life of Michael Jackson, we can then take historical prophecies with reference to the stars to find out what should happen next on earth.

The two constellations, which determined the whole length and course of the first cycle of Egyptian pharoanic civilization, were Ursa Major, the Greater Bear, and Leo, the Lion. These astrological ages were recognized by the Egyptians, and their civilization adapted accordingly. Leo and Ursa Major were considered by the Egyptians to be the magical 'thigh' (or right foreleg) of Taurus, the latter symbolizing the illumined mind and is referred to as the 'Eye' of Horus. With this 'thigh of the Eye of Horus' *Ptah* (the Creator god signifying the Voice of God) 'opened' the mouths of divine entities and the souls of the dead [83]. Later in the Swedenborg concordance we will be confronted again with how this (magical thigh) relates to the Bible and the relevance it bears within creation and the mystical Tree of Life.

1 Kings 6:38 (38) And in the eleventh year, in the month Bul, which is the eighth month, was the house finished throughout all the parts thereof, and according to all the fashion of it. So was he seven years in building it.

Earlier in the book we discussed Ptah's role in the creation of the world and Atum with the opening of the mouth ceremony of Osiris. Ptah is also responsible for the dividing of the two lands of Upper and Lower Egypt between Set and Horus. Again this links him with the "LORD"/Ba'al as described in the 37th chapter of Ezekiel. The upper region attributed to Set /Joseph the lower region attributed to Horus/Osiris/Judah. "*I have separated Seth from the houses of the above because of the Elder who was with him [82b].*"

1 Chronicles 5:2 And though Judah was the strongest of his brothers and a ruler came from him, the rights of the firstborn belonged to Joseph.

Michael relating himself to Ptah or Peter Pan is huge because we saw (Michael) in the tradition of Ptah open his mouth and the souls of the dead arose in the most popular video, album, and song to date, *Thriller*. Just as Joseph rose to prominence and power by interpreting visions from God, Michael did also. This symbolizes the foreshadowing of the awakening of all the dead gods that awaits in the coming Age of Aquarius by the next avatar, the Sun of Man, making Michael Jackson in the tradition of The Kingdom Hall, Jehovah's Witness. The opening of the book by the Lion of Judah has taken place with the writing of this book whereby the revelation of all scriptures are wholly realized bringing another grand cycle of history to a close.

There is a prophecy in the 37th chapter of Ezekiel that states Joseph and Judah should be placed together under one nation, one King, and one God.

Ezekiel 37:19-23. (19) say to them, 'This is what the Sovereign LORD says: I am going to take the stick of Joseph—which is in Ephraim's hand—and of the Israelite tribes associated with him, and join it to Judah's stick, making them a single stick of wood, and they will become one in my hand.' (20) Hold before their eyes the sticks you have written on (21) and say to them, 'This is what the Sovereign LORD says: I will take the Israelites out of the nations where they have gone. I will gather them from all around and bring them back into their own land. (22) I will make them one nation in the land, on the mountains of Israel. There will be one king over all of them and they will never again be two nations or be divided into two kingdoms. (23) Neither shall they defile themselves any more with their idols, nor with their detestable things, nor with any of their transgressions: but I will save them out of all their dwelling places, wherein they have sinned, and will cleanse them: so shall they be my people, and I will be their God.

Judah is known as the southern kingdom of Israel and is regarded as being a lion. Judah is where the name and religion Judaism comes from.

Genesis 49:9 *Judah is a lion's whelp: from the prey, my son, thou art gone up: he stooped down, he couched as a lion, and as an old lion; who shall rouse him up?*

This same "Lion" called Ja, the Iron Lion of Judah, the ruler of Ethiopia has been popularized by the legendary singer, Bob Marley born February 6th under the sign Aquarius. On Carlos Santana's *Supernatural* album, of which he won a Grammy, Lauryn Hill boasts these lyrics on a song entitled *Do You Like the Way "Through Zion we marching through like African Mayan's Conquering Babylon with the heart of a lion.* The Mayan culture of which Lauryn Hill speaks gets their name from the mother of Krishna, Maia. Ethiopia again is "the place where GOD SEES; the ALL SEEING EYE/THE SUN." As implied earlier, Ethiopia has nothing to do with the geographical region the country is located in. The merging of the two tribes of Joseph and Judah symbolizes the fusion of two types of Christ figures; Horus the son of Osiris and Isis, and Hormus the son of Hathor and Ra. The two figures are personified by humanitarian and peaceful aspects seen on the right hand of God, and vengeful warlike and revolutionary aspects seen on the left hand of God. Perhaps this is why the Jesus of Nazareth's life has both aspects of Joseph (Krishna) and Judah (Shiva/Isvara) fused together in one individual. For this fusion would represent the one God (the Holy One of Israel) who rules over both nations which in Judaism are known as the tribes of Joseph and Judah or northern and southern Israel. In Hinduism these two entities are known as the cults of Krishna (Vishnu) and Shiva. The two cults have gained tremendous popularity in the world of religion as together they represent the whole five billion followers of all the four major religions of the world. Even the major television networks like CBS and NBC uses their symbols as their logos.

We've already established who Joseph is and with the promotion of this book and the visuals that aide it, the world will soon know the Judah and man of transcendence it has so anxiously been waiting to see 87. **CBS** uses the All - Seeing Eye, which traits are taken from the Hindu God Shiva represented in Judaism as Judah. **NBC** uses the peacock which is the ever popular symbol of Krishna represented by Joseph in Judaism. The cult of Krishna personified through Joseph and Michael have to deal with the universal (catholic) aspects of the faith as it pertains to the virginal (feminine) and the purity associated with "God" fellowship, and harmony. This side doesn't deal in specifics, rather the overall mood and feelings associated with sensation and the stimuli of the senses in motion, as in "wow that song was great; that whole experience was invigorating," This side has to do with the natural fellowship like singing, dancing, joy, and expression that comes with revival.

Judah deals with the specifics, the hidden yet actual side of "God" as it's discriminating, rational, (masculine) and all-encompassing, showcasing all sides of positivity and negativity within it. This side is more like the revelation, the story in whole, and the epiphany whereby meticulous attention to detail brings to life understanding through "eureka" and animation; more like Bible study than revival - covering details in solitude (JUDAISM.) Each are aspects that together represent the whole combination of masculine and feminine energies; the example of which is (Krishna) and the truth and knowledge of (Shiva) behind the visual display Krishna's life represents.

It is important to note that the Bhagavad Gita says the system of Yoga, and the Bhagavad Gita itself was 1st spoken to the Sun God, and it is this same Sun God personified as the LORD (Adonai) who must speak it again as the world has lost the translation of what the word means 87a. This is similar to the *Recitation* of the Qu'ran given by Gabriel to the prophet Muhammad. Both Hindu cults together represent the Sun and Moon, the Sun having a duality or as what Aleister Crowley describes as Nuith and Hadit; the whole star Nuith, and the point within it, Hadit 88. Because it is harder to ascend into the realm of the higher nature and most beings function in a / their lower nature, the left side of God cannot be taught in an open forum to the masses. The teaching and practices on the left side are only for the adept/ or highly intellectual, experienced, and spiritual; comparable to explaining child birth and sex to a toddler. For these reasons the right side (universal/catholic) or generic (vulgate) /is the side the masses easily recognize and identify with as the left side seems a way to justify evil, chaos, and the giving in to the primal instincts and urges (archaic.)

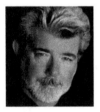 George Lucas, who was born under the sign Taurus the bull, and famous for directing the epic Stars Wars had a very profound state of mind; he said, "*I came out of film school, I looked at the world and said well this isn't the way they told me it was going to be this is terrible we aren't what we thought we were --it's like hey it isn't a wonderful place it's a horrible place and so you spend a lot of your time saying I'm going to spring this on the rest of the world but really anybody over 30 is well aware of what kind of world this is --I've discovered in my making movies that they don't help society very much ultimately. What helps is to sort of promote the human spirit to say let's think of ourselves as those good people that we were brought up in the fairy tale of adolescence of childhood to believe we were and let's promote those ideas and believe in that*"88c.

Michael Jackson was the personification of this profound wisdom and state of mind that George Lucas so eloquently defined in the quote above. Michael's love for all things magical, and his sensitivity for humanity caused him like Lucas to look to adolescence and the fantasy and wonderment associated with childhood.

In amassing knowledge from all of the various schools of philosophy and religion there seems to be a pattern and a war between gods and men. This war has been a constant theme throughout all mythology. The heavier the course of study, the more the person reading realizes the "Gods" in all the four major religions are all the same. The only differences are the names they call them, the slightly different translations of what they come to do, and the culture barriers that make the lay people unable to make the correlations they have the same God as everyone else. This is why the universal message of come together and love one another is paramount, because people in a sense all come from the same place. If people listened at the actual commandments given by Jesus they would have no need to listen to their preachers because like Jesus said himself if you can't understand the law or the prophets love "God" and do unto others as you would want done unto you.

Matthew 22:36-37, 39-40 (36)*"Teacher, which is the greatest commandment in the Law?" (37) Jesus replied: 'Love the Lord your God with all your heart and with all your soul and with all your mind.' (39)And the second is like it: 'Love your neighbor as yourself.'(40) All the Law and the Prophets hang on these two commandments.*

CONCLUSION

When they write about Michael Jackson in the next cycle of history they will say he walked on the moon, and was transformed from black to white in a single lifetime. They will say that millions of people were energized by his mere presence and that some even died upon looking at him in person. When it is all said and done he will be written of again as a god. The fact that his nose has eroded the same way as the sphinxes shows the correlation he has in relevance to it. Because Michael Jackson has been vilified for what he has done, it has erased his legacy in the minds of the American public and though he hasn't been convicted of these things in a court of law, public opinion believes he is guilty; even when it was proven the people who brought these allegations against him were liars and after his money. This is what often happens in terms of history when it comes to powerful men and where their

287

places are in it. All of their magnificent glory is stripped away from them when the people who are lesser then they are mob together and formulate stories and opinions about them that are not factually based. The people who bring these allegations are jealous and want to find fault within the icons.

They do this because they in themselves are nobody's and the world will never know who they are or for that matter care 89.

Michael Jackson who descended to earth in the personification of Lord Krishna – the Supreme Being has come and left and nobody seems to have a clue as to what this signifies. Krishna in the Hindu Pantheon is the Supreme Being and is worshipped as an avatar of Vishnu just as in the Jehovah's Witness faith the Archangel Michael is worshipped as the Supreme Being. Krishna is

said to be the only fully human incarnation of Vishnu who was aware of his godly powers from infancy which again is likened to Michael Jackson who was a child prodigy with tremendous powers and abilities.

Janmashtami, 90 the birth of Krishna, is celebrated between August 14th and September 1st in India during the same time as Michael Jackson's birthday which is August 29th. Krishna comes from krsta which in Sanskrit means <u>all-attractive</u> 86. When assessing Michael's artistry, persona, and message he's attracted the most people on earth to his movement causing him to literally be "all attractive." Anyone who can put 500,000 people in one concert, another Guinness book world record, has to be all-attractive. Krishna's symbols are the cow and the peacock. The peacock represents the many colors of the

rainbow as its tail overtly displays a plethora of colors. The cow is indicative of Krishna's mother often referred to as Maia, which is synonymous to the month of May, as Michael's mother was born on May 4th. The star that marks the birth of Krishna in Hinduism is Aldebaran which again is located in the eye of the great bull (Taurus.) The legend of Krishna is recorded in the Bhaga Vita a book that is as holy to India as the Bible is to Christians. When we examine the actual birthplace of Michael we discover yet another clue that further defines just who Michael Jackson was. Michael Jackson was born in Gary, Indiana. While this doesn't light a fuse initially, probing deeper into it, we find the terrain from which Michael was born, named Indiana translates to "*Land of the Indians*." Each of these parallels only solidifies that Michael was the reincarnation of the deity Krishna, as matter is not created or destroyed it just changes forms. It is also worth noting that America was originally a land of Indians and is why those who inhabited the country prior to British and Spanish Colonialism were Indians called Native Americans.

Many people also refer to Krishna as Hare Krishna, a distinction according to Gaudiya Vaishnava theology, is an incarnation of Vishnu that designates the self's original consciousness and goal for life as being the pure love of God 86a. It is no secret that Michael Jackson's artistry was all about love, peace, and humility. It is also important to note again that many ancient languages like the romance languages sometimes pronounce its G's like H's; an example of this is the Spanish word *gente* which means people and the Italian word *lasagna* where the <u>ag</u> in the middle is pronounced like an <u>ah</u>. So when a person says Gary using a romance tongue it can easily be pronounced Hary. Though seemingly far-fetched, this is a clue that designates Michael Jackson as being the personification of Hare Krishna.

In a recent interview Deepak Chopra was quoted as saying, "*You know Michael was a Krishna archetype. He was ambiguous about his sexual identity he had both aspects to it, he was an amazing dancer, musician, etc. So you think, oh – and when I first went to his house, I saw little Krishnas all over. And of course I said, "What's that?" He said, "Hare Krishna."* 89b. I know everybody reading is saying wait a minute is he Moses, is he Joseph, is he the Archangel Michael, Dionysus or is he Krishna?

By studying different religions you are able to make direct comparisons and parallels between the characters represented within them when you obtain the knowledge and clairvoyance given by Kabbalah. We also can never forget that wars and biases have caused people to believe and worship in different ways. The ways in which people comprehend are usually what limits them from understanding all of which they study and profess to know. What they know isn't the truth at all, rather a version they can understand that they've submitted to and created for themselves. It is more important a person is given knowledge or that they receive information they can understand verses information they can't. I mean, how valuable is quantum physics to the masses? Now ask yourself how valuable is basic arithmetic? I wrote these things in this book so the person who is studying or reading from a limited knowledge base, will think twice before trying to convert others to a limited way of thinking based on the limited piece of information that person was given. Romanticizing biblical stories has caused a great imbalance within the world because there are beings in the world with higher levels of consciousness, intellect, and strength. The world relegating these beings to myths has caused the masses to think everybody is indeed regular or mortal; while simultaneously believing the myths to be fairytales. For these reasons I've used science, history, and all the universe's major religions and philosophies to prove the myths within them are real. I used the Hindu scriptures because Hinduism is one of the oldest religions in the world and also Krishna is cited as being a Supreme Being in it. When we look at Michael Jackson he was no different; he represented all things to all people and is why he is the highest selling, grossing, most sought after and loved person this cycle of history has yet to witness. The supremacy of his being and legacy can be refuted by no one, as he is man, woman, child, black and white and represents all spectrums of being for humanity. The fact that he is the eighth child (look it up Marlon had a twin that died at birth,) parallels him to Krishna. If you look at his videos as well as the *Destiny* album cover with his brothers, you will see Peacocks which are the favorite birds of Krishna. The Jackson's music production company called Peacock productions is a further distinguishing characteristic that parallel's Michael Jackson's life to the life of

Krishna as does the flute which symbolically highlights that Krishna like Michael, was also a musician. The word Krishna also translates to *the Black one*. Michael and Krishna look alike, and both Krishna and Michael died eerily similar deaths. Krishna was shot with an arrow while resting; Michael was shot with a needle while resting. Krishna and the five Pandavas were the only surviving warriors between the Pandavas and the Karauvas. In this cycle of history Krishna or Michael Jackson is still with those same five Pandava brothers represented by the Jackson Five. When reading an account versus seeing it, reading allows us to use our imaginations. Using our imaginations causes us to be limitless in our thoughts about what a thing could be versus how it actually is. Because of this, perversion is always a huge threat. When you actually see something, even though you have the use of your imagination, that image in your mind has to shape around what you've have just seen; this limits the type of perversions a person can have.

Many Hindi scholars believe the death of Krishna marks the beginning of the Kali Yuga Age. It is also believed that Krishna is the GREAT sign of the coming Messiah who is to rule with an iron fist and vanquish all the unrighteousness from the face of the earth. This is stated because the Virgin (Virgo) precedes the Sun (Leo) in the heavens. The notion that there are multiple messiahs is one that A.E. Waite explains in depth in his translation of the Kabbalah on page 320. He broke down the possibility there are several messiahs. The 1st is the son of Ischai the master of all, who through him, the earth is nourished. The second is the son of Ephraim who will be driven back

from Rome. The third is the son of Joseph, and the fourth is the son of David. According to Waite, the 3rd and the 4th are one and the same as the son of David will be brought together with the son of Joseph under one house. We spoke of the "sun of Ephraim" Barack Obama on pages 34-36. What makes this theory of Barack Obama being the son of Ephraim even more plausible is the prophecy A.E. Waite acknowledged in his rendition of the Kabbalah that states *"the son of Ephraim will be driven back from Rome."* On May 21, 2012, 43 Roman Catholic dioceses filed a lawsuit against the Obama administration on its stance towards contraception. Amongst those who filed suit were the Archdiocese of New York, Washington and St. Louis; the Diocese of Dallas, Fort Worth, Pittsburg and the Catholic University of America. 90b

The celestial beings that manifest to earth in the forms of avatars each have different fronts they fight on in route to winning the war between the gods and the demons. Krishna was a great sign and a messenger warning humanity that if it isn't careful it would face its impending destruction. He was the ambassador who interceded and sacrificed himself for mankind in order to turn mankind from their destructive ways into creative ways. Michael Jackson in his epic thriller says *"There's no escape from the jaws of the alien this time."* He also went on to say *there is no second chance to kill the creature with the 40 eyes.*

Revelation 4:6-9 (6) *And before the throne there was a sea of glass like unto crystal: and in the midst of the throne, and round about the throne, were four beasts full of eyes before and behind .(7) And the first beast was like a lion, and the second beast like a calf, and the third beast had a face as a man, and the fourth beast was like a flying eagle.(8) And the four beasts had each of them six wings about him; and they were full of eyes within: and they rest not day and night, saying, Holy, holy, holy, Lord God Almighty, which was, and is, and is to come. (9) And when those beasts give glory and honour and thanks to him that sat on the throne, who liveth forever.*

In regards to Michael Jackson being the messenger who comes to earth to warn the people of its impending doom and destruction, this aspect is played out in the two characters named the *Silver Surfer* and *Galactus*. Michael Jackson's astrological sign being ruled by Mercury signifies his herald and "mercurial abilities." Michael being the world's brightest star can be likened to the silver skin of the surfer that makes him also shine brilliantly.

 Galactus' characteristics are most like the Hindu god Shiva. Known as the destroyer in Hindu legend, like the blazing desert Sun, he is a terror walking with destructive functions. He like the LORD, Adonai as referenced on pg. 233 may actually be the "BEAST" from Ezekiel's vision with the 40 eyes Michael warned the world was "about to strike" in his epic song and video, *Thriller*.

The scholars who have cited this information about Krishna and the coming Yuga (age) have no idea Michael Jackson was Krishna himself; the same as theologians in biblical times didn't know John the Baptist was Elijah. Many interpreters of Hindu scriptures believe the earth is currently in the age of darkness. Kalki, the last avatar of Vishnu, is coming to return the world to a golden age much like the rider of the white horse in the Book of Revelation.

Revelation 19:11-16 *(11) And I saw heaven opened, and behold a white horse; and he that sat upon him was called Faithful and True, and in righteousness he doth judge and make war. (12) His eyes were as a flame of fire, and on his head were many crowns; and he had a name written, that no man knew, but he himself. (13) And he was clothed with a vesture dipped in blood: and his name is called The Word of God. (14) And the armies which were in heaven followed him upon white horses, clothed in fine linen, white and clean. (15) And out of his mouth goeth a sharp sword, that with it he should smite the nations: and he shall rule them with a rod of iron: and he treadeth the winepress of the fierceness and wrath of Almighty God. (16) And he hath on his vesture and on his thigh a name written, KING OF KINGS, AND LORD OF LORDS.*

The Mahabharata Vana Parva and the Bhagavat Mahapurana gives the descriptions of what the people on earth should see when the Lord Kalki, i.e. the Destroyer avatar of Christ appears before them. *And the clouds will commence to shower seasonally, and the stars and stellar conjunctions will become auspicious. And the planets, duly revolving in their orbits, will become exceedingly propitious. Commissioned by Time, a Brahmana of the name of Kalki will take his birth. And he will glorify Vishnu and possess great energy, great intelligence, and great prowess. And vehicles and weapons, and warriors and arms, and coats of mail will be at his disposal as soon as he will think of them. And he will be the king of kings, and ever victorious with the strength of virtue. And he will restore order and peace in this world crowded with creatures and contradictory in its course. And that blazing Brahmana of mighty intellect, having appeared, will destroy all things. And he will be the Destroyer of all, and will inaugurate a new Yuga* 91.

The Bhagavat Mahapurana: *In this way, when the Kali age, whose influence is so severe on the people, is well-nigh past, the Lord will appear in His divine form (consisting of*

Sattwa alone) for the protection of virtue. Lord Vishnu, adored by the whole animate and inanimate creation and the Soul of the universe, appears (in this world of matter) for protecting the virtue of the righteous and wiping out (the entire stock of) their Karma (and thereby liberating them). The Lord will appear under the name of Kalk. Riding a fleet footed horse named Devadatta (because it will be presented to Him by the gods) and capable of subduing the wicked, Lord of the universe, wielding the well-known eight divine powers (Anima and so on) and possessed of endless virtues and matchless splendour, wearing the insignia of royalty, he will traverse the globe on that swift horse and exterminate with his sword (weapon) tens of millions of robbers. Now when all the robbers are (thus) exterminated, the minds of the people of the cities and of the countryside will become pure indeed because of their enjoying the breeze wafting the most sacred fragrance from on the person of Lord Vasudeva. With Lord Vasudeva, the embodiment of strength in their heart, their progeny will grow exceedingly strong (as before). When Sri Hari, the Protector of Dharma, appears as Kalki, Satyayuga will prevail (once more) at that time and the progeny of the people will be of a Sattvika (virtuous) disposition. When the moon, the sun and Jupiter rise together in one zodiacal house and the Pusya constellation is in the ascendant, then it will be known as Satyayuga 92.

In accepting the revelation of Michael Jackson being Krishna, we also have to realize that in the Jewish Kabbalah, the Jesus of Nazareth is said to be both a son of Joseph, and a son David. As hard as this is to understand, dissecting this prophecy allows us to readily see the creation of the Jesus of Nazareth in the Gospels was done with a tremendous amount of editing. Why do I say this? Krishna precedes the coming of Kalki who is the second coming of the *Christ* Jesus of Nazareth. If Michael Jackson was Krishna then it only means that the coming destructive messiah has yet to walk the earth or make himself known to the rest of the world. The fact that the Jesus of Nazareth in the Bible has aspects of Shiva's and Krishna's life, shows that scribes and those who have constructed the Bible made the messiah to come, one they've created and already given to the masses in the 4 gospels of the New Testament. They in a sense have merged the lives of (Krishna {the healer and meek shepherd} and Shiva the destructive and vengeful wandering ascetic}) together creating the life of Jesus of Nazareth. By merging the two Hindu God's stories they have mimicked the purpose and fundamental process by which Masonry was created to do, which is the "naming and building of a legend." In this book I pointed out certain references that would enable the reader to understand the last world and cycle of history that was lived in. Because history has been known scientifically to repeat itself, these topics discussed within this book will always be in a continuance. The alpha is the omega, and the beginning is the end. Death isn't the last stop rather another resetting of the cycles. Pending on how you lived, treated others, and the "credit" that you established within the universe, determines how, where, and to what level of being you will be in your next lifetime. I know after reading this book most people will ask the question, "*If God is a physical being, who is it I have been praying to?*" .

Meditation, popularly called prayer in the Christian world, is the process by which you center your most coveted and desired wishes. When you pray or meditate about these things your reality begins to shape around them. This shaping of your reality can only be recognized if you are aware of what it is that you really desire. Once a person becomes awakened to the point they are able to shape their reality, the person then becomes responsible for putting all of the pieces together themselves. Prayer and meditation merely attracts all of the pieces to you; it is up to you to recognize these pieces by fashioning them into living constructs, making your wishes or desires come true. Most people attribute their desire as something that is out of their hands which leaves them looking for someone outside of themselves to intercede and show them the way (genie.) The greater the clarity the more empowered a person will see they are. In discovering this they will in turn see the "God" they thought they were praying to was the channeling and invoking of the energy that is within themselves. When you were created, the essence of what you know to be "God" already factored how and where you would be. Of course you can choose to do other than that which you were meant but in doing this the level of talent and stature that you will have will be nothing in comparison to if you found yourself and your calling. Another question asked is, "What if you do not have a purpose or calling?" Even the smallest living things have purposes. Roaches eat nasty bacteria, spiders eat pests like flies and beetles; earthworms till soil, birds regulate how many insects are in any given ecosystem, and the list goes on and on. Life will bring you back through the same situations and circumstances regardless if you're conscious or not. Pending on what a person has done, and the level of knowledge they have attained will then formulate into how much energy they are able to manifest. The level of energy they are able to manifest will in turn transform them into that level of being physically.

1 Kings 4:30-34 (30) And Solomon's wisdom excelled the wisdom of all the children of the east country, and all the wisdom of Egypt. (31) For he was wiser than all men; than Ethan the Ezrahite, and Heman, and Chalcol, and Darda, the sons of Mahol: and his fame was in all nations round about. (32) And he spake three thousand proverbs: and his songs were a thousand and five. (33) And he spake of trees, from the cedar tree that is in Lebanon even unto the hyssop that springeth out of the wall: he spake also of beasts, and of fowl, and of creeping things, and of fishes. (34) And there came of all people to hear the wisdom of Solomon, from all kings of the earth, which had heard of his wisdom.

In the movie, *The Life of Pi,* the story of the Matsya Purana is reenacted. I brought this back up at this point in the book, because in this chapter, we discussed in depth that Krishna, the most popular deity in Hinduism, was Michael Jackson. Being that we have started to talk about Hinduism in depth, I felt the need to reference an Academy Award winning movie that highlights one of Hinduisms oldest and well known stories. *The Life of Pi* is a story that discusses how all

religions come from one source; (Krishna) and the source for understanding these religions all lies within the journey of the self (Shiva/Sun.) The movie depicts this artistically as the main character's name is Piscine which is the French word for fish but also is an allegorical clue that hints towards Piscean, as in Piscean Age. 3.14, the number of Pi, physically takes place during the lunar month of March of which the constellation

"Pisces" is at work. Michael Jackson (Krishna) was the avatar of the Piscean age. In the previous chapter we learned that the Matsya Purana is the oldest story in Hinduism. This story features an ark, and a man as well as a fish. In Hinduism it is a popular notion that Shiva and Vishnu, who Krishna is a manifestation of, are one in the same. This is why the cults of Joseph/ Krishna and Shiva / Judah are often placed together. It is also no secret that the God Vishnu/Shiva travels in an ark or a solar boat and is often seen prostrating on tiger skin. In the movie *The Life of Pi* Piscine is ship wrecked in an ark full of animals which is indicative of the Zodiac. We know that between the Piscean and Aquarian ages a FLOOD takes place because the Zodiac moves counterclockwise. This, as previously stated, shows us the Age of the Fish (Pisces) precedes the Age of the Flood (Aquarius) linking the avatars of Shiva the (Sun) and Krishna the (Moon) together through Vishnu.

The Book of Illumination

CHAPTER 16

DID JESUS
FAKE HIS DEATH

The Book of Illumination

CHAPTER 16

DID JESUS
FAKE HIS DEATH

DID JESUS FAKE HIS DEATH

I felt it necessary to save this part of the book to be the last chapter before I picked back up with the Genesis. Reason being, after witnessing what has just been explained within the previous chapters, one begins to understand why the truth of man's creation has been falsified and kept hidden from the world. If Jesus as an avatar came to earth and said the things I've written to the Christian world today, how do you think the people would respond? I'll tell you how…they would crucify him once again and cite the reason for doing so because he perverted the scriptures. Does this sound like something we have seen or heard before?

Rejecting what I have written doesn't make it untrue; it just makes the person who doesn't agree either uniformed, or unable to recognize the truth. When a person is unable to recognize truth, it only means they have receded further into a lower form of existence. Before you rebuttal look at the people in life with real abilities and ask yourself how you rank among them. This will tell you where you are in respects to greatness and also put into perspective what you need to do in order to "ascend" to a higher state of being. Jesus's whole mission as an avatar is to restore what has been lost to a lost people. As regarded by the scriptures, what these people have lost is the knowledge of their gods. This knowledge as prophesized in all 4 major religions will be brought back to a "chosen" people by a Sun God, who is the personification of the WORD itself manifested in a human form.

I've made it a point to show the reader there's a lot of information that has been distorted due to translation errors, language barriers, and lack of proper comprehension. For example, in the Bible, it is written Jesus was crucified on the cross, and the popular belief is that he died and resurrected on the third day. When Jesus went into the wilderness to be baptized by John, the baptism gave him the knowledge on how he was to complete his mission. The mission that Jesus was on would require that he have the discipline and the training to endure the torture that came with crucifixion. John the Baptist's was also known as John the harbinger.

Harbinger: one that pioneers in or initiates a major change

Is it farfetched when I say that John was in the wilderness showing Jesus how to use the powers of asceticism to develop the skill he would need for the illusion he would use in regards to his crucifixion? When you look at ascetics of the eastern world it is easily recognized they have tremendous physical and mental abilities; they can exist in the harshest of circumstances and are capable of enduring immense pain. Some can do handstands with two fingers; others can walk on fire, make their body temperatures higher or lower, as well as make their pulse disappear. When Jesus went to John perhaps these are some of the things he was given in the "baptism." In movies like the *Karate Kid*, there is a theme that involves a hero who is schooled and taught by a master teacher (harbinger.) The master gives him all sorts of tests and trials that he must complete if he is to achieve his goal. If John the harbinger is one who prepares the way, why would his role be any different to that of Jesus? Jesus was strengthened and changed by the knowledge of the harbinger. This knowledge gave him the fortitude as well as the courage to be placed on the cross and endure the hardship and pain that was associated with crucifixion. It is stated that before Jesus gave up the ghost and died on the cross, he shouted at "God." When he shouted at "God" he called for Eli, which most people took to mean he was shouting for Elijah. If Elijah was John the Baptist Jesus is asking John who has also been killed why has he forsaken him.

Matthew 27: 46&47 (46) And about the ninth hour Jesus cried with a loud voice, saying, Eli, Eli, lama sabachthani? that is to say, My God, my God, why hast thou forsaken me? (47) Some of them that stood there, when they heard that, said, This man calleth for Elias.

Elijah also raised a man from the dead, parted a river, and ascended to heaven without dying a physical death on earth. Could Elijah be the "father" /master who resurrected back to earth to guide the Sun on his spiritual mission to transform the people of the world; much to the same extent as Merlin led King Arthur to regain his kingly throne?

Eli or El in Hebrew is a Canaanite deity who is known as the father of the gods 92a. El or Eli is often depicted as having two lions by his side in ancient hieroglyphs and artwork. These two lions are synonymous to the double pillars of Jachin and Boaz, built by Hiram in Solomon's temple as well as the Hindu trinity of Vishnu, Shiva and Brahma, whereby the destructive and creative pillars are two figures who Vishnu is in between 92b.

In the Masonic texts, Melkart is said to be a son of Venus and a "sun" of El. Melkart is the same name attributed to Baal which is a title meaning "Lord" or "Master craftsman." The Demiurge is also a word that links the "Builders of Legends" with the same person responsible for creating the universe as being Melkart and the logos, Jesus. The Jesus of the NT who is initiated by Elijah or John the Baptist is said to be the son of a carpenter or master craftsmen.

Matthew 13:55 (55) Is not this the carpenter's son? Is not his mother called Mary? and his brethren, James, and Joses, and Simon, and Judas?

When cross referencing the origins of these legends we can see how El being the "father of the gods" initiates Melkart as his "Sun" making his "Sun" in his likeness, also a master craftsman, and the person for which he erects a temple. The "Sun" reinforces the fact though EL is the master of the craft; the "Sun" has in a sense perfected the craft so much that, the master becomes the pupil, and the pupil becomes the master. Melkart is also symbolized as being the "master of the furnace." It is here where we have two other biblical references involving furnaces, associated with the Son of God, and the Sun of Man that link the "master of the furnace" and the Sun of man together.

Revelation 1:13-15 And in the midst of the seven candlesticks one like unto the Son of man, clothed with a garment down to the foot, and girt about the paps with a golden girdle. (14) His head and his hairs were white like wool, as white as snow; and his eyes were as a flame of fire; (15) And his feet like unto fine brass, as if they burned in a furnace; and his voice as the sound of many waters.

Daniel 3:23 -25 (23) And these three men, Shadrach, Meshach, and Abednego, fell down bound into the midst of the burning fiery furnace. (24) Then Nebuchadnezzar the king was astonished, and rose up in haste, and spake, and said unto his counsellors, Did not we cast three men bound into the midst of the fire? They answered and said unto the king, True, O king. (25) He answered and said, Lo, I see four men loose, walking in the midst of the fire, and they have no hurt; and the form of the fourth is like the Son of God.

Again being able to sustain the hardship of being thrown in a furnace is another clue that points to asceticism and also Satan as he resides in the fiery pits of hell. The story of Melkart who is also referred to as Baal is also a story about the "LORD" who engenders with a virgin queen Anat, a great hero. This story of Ba'al in Hebrew legend has elements of the Osiris and Isis story found in Egypt whereby the virgin warrior goddess enraged at her lover's murderer, murders him and erects through the corpse and phallus of her murdered husband a successor to his plan. This "LORD" is the same LORD who visited Sarah in the account of Abraham. This "El" is the same El/ Eli who is the harbinger to the Messiah that comes as the Hierophant to unearth and reveal the hidden knowledge awakening the "spiritually dead" people on earth; while simultaneously bringing to life the other resurrected "gods" who have literally "risen from their graves." This is the "priceless" man of wisdom and transcendence that A.E Waite speaks of on page 317 of the Holy Kabbalah, *"who is more precious than fine gold."* The edited version of these stories takes place in the piecing together of the Jesus of Nazareth story in which God and the Virgin Mary, who is the wife of Joseph, birth a son who will be the savior of the world.

DEATH HOAX

Machiavelli in ancient Rome was said to have promoted the staging of one's death to expose his/her truest enemies. Here is a comment from him in one of his most revered works, *The Prince. "Any man that has a great undertaking of mind must first make all necessary preparations so that when an opportunity arises he is able to put it in execution according to his design."*

Think about it, after Jesus was betrayed by his closest and most devout follower (Peter) and seeing that his disciples didn't have the ability to be believers, why wouldn't Jesus pull a tremendous stunt in order for his disciples to acknowledge a higher power? Jesus says in *John 4:48 Accept ye see signs and wonders ye will not believe.* Knowing this about the conditions of man we can readily bring into the argument that Jesus may have faked his death on the cross to inspire his believers to *BE* believers. This is still the ultimate self-sacrifice because being as gifted and enlightened as Jesus was he still had the passion to be crucified in order to teach others about their higher natures. Who else would willingly suffer crucifixion in order to teach unrighteous, ignorant, and hypocritical people about God, but the "Sun" of God? There is a movie that has this same theme associated with faking ones death to avenge one's self; is there any coincidence it's called *The Count of Monte Cristo*?

The Book of John indicates the soldiers broke the legs of the other two criminals who were crucified next to Jesus; but the legs of Jesus were not broken. If Jesus' legs would've been broken then how would he have been able to physically walk after the crucifixion?

John 19:32-33 (32) Then came the soldiers and brake the legs of the first, and of the other which was crucified with him (33) But when they came to Jesus, and saw that he was dead already, they brake not his legs.

Scriptures like the one previous cited raise questions that cause us to look at the crucifixion with an open eye. This alongside several other coincidences gives rise to several theories; one has to do with the person who was supposed to die in place of Jesus, his name was Barabbas.

The so-called mystery of Barabbas refers to some puzzling similarities between the released prisoner and Jesus himself; and the most striking similarity concerns their names. Some ancient Syriac copies of Matthew, and a few other ancient sources, call the freed prisoner Jesus bar Abbas. The name Barabbas can be obtained from this by dropping the name Jesus and changing bar Abbas to "Barabbas. Furthermore, the phrase bar Abbas can be translated as "son of the Father" which is an obvious notion that the "messiah" that is being referred to in this account is the "son" of the father. The father of the gods in Egyptian legend as explained earlier is known as the sun God Ra. Remember the name Joseph in the Kabbalah has a strong correlation to the word father. The father of the Gods in Canaanite legend is El or Eli. From this evidence, many scholars have concluded that Barabbas' original name was "Jesus bar Abbas." Other evidence indicates that this name was intentionally altered by later Christian writers. The gospel of Mark says that Barabbas had been imprisoned for taking part in a revolt, and his popularity with the crowd suggests that he had been one of its leaders. In our lifetime today the "son of the father" who had "popularity" within the crowds that was imprisoned, acquitted, and crucified in the media was Michael Jackson.

Stories merge every time a grand cycle of 25,920 years occurs and the gods reappear on earth. Their last incarnations are added to their present incarnations and the same account is told over and over again from slightly different perspectives. For example in Semitic legend Uranus also known as El, is the Egyptian sky god who was absorbed into the Roman God Zeus, which is why Zeus adopted the symbol of the eagle or falcon when in Astrology it is obvious he is a centaur. This is why Rome is called Rome – because the place in which the gods appear and reappear is always different, the culture in itself roams from place to place and at the end of the cycle the history is reordered and rerecorded.

Mark 15:7 And there was one named Barabbas which lay bound with them that had made insurrection with him, who had committed murder in the insurrection.

Insurrection: an act or instance of revolting against civil authority or an established government

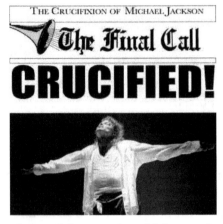

The Final Call

CRUCIFIED!

Another possibility in the case of Jesus versus Jesus Barabbas is that the insertion of Barabbas could be an indication that the real Jesus, the rebel leader, was indeed let go and the "son of the father" went in his place to be crucified. This particular view is held by many Muslims. The fact that Jesus was a revolutionary and the whole of society and the church not preaching this further shows how the Mother Church, and those who support her, or are supported by way of her romantic interests, have indeed changed the way in which people view spiritualism and the life of Jesus. What is equally important and profound about the life of Jesus and the resurrection is the fact that the resurrection doesn't only pertain to him. This particular piece of evidence is found in the 22 chapter of Matthew.

In *Matthew 22:24-32 (24) Saying Master Moses said, If a man die having no children, his brother shall marry his wife, and raise up seed to his brother. (25) Now there were with us seven brethren: and the first, when he had married a wife, deceased and having no issue left his wife unto his brother. (26) Likewise the second also, and the third, unto the seventh. (28) Therefore in the resurrection whose wife shall she be of the seven for they all had her. (29) And Jesus answered them; ye do err not knowing the scriptures, nor the Power of God. (30) For in the resurrection they neither marry nor are given in marriage, but are as the angels of God in heaven (31) But as touching the resurrection of the dead, have ye not read that which was spoken unto you by god saying (32) I am the God of Abraham, Isaac, and Jacob? God is not the God of the dead but the living.*

The first point that solidifies my claim is that the resurrection was known by the Pharisees and the Herodians and it mentioned others besides Jesus, who would be able to partake in it. This totally shatters the notion that only Jesus was resurrected and that he alone is immortal. The second point is that Jesus stresses a "Living God." If we look at this in a literal context, what would it mean? John 10:34 gives us clues about the acknowledgement of who the "Living God" or gods may be.

John 10:34 (34) Is it not written in your law, I said ye are Gods? (35) If he called them Gods, unto whom the word of God came, and the scriptures cannot be broken: (36) Say ye of him, whom the father has sanctified, and sent into the world, Thou blasphemest: because I said, I am the son of God?

Sanctified: (1) to set apart to a sacred purpose or to religious use (2) to free from sin

<u>Blaspheme:</u> (1) the act of insulting or showing contempt for God

In the last scripture referenced Jesus says, *doesn't it state in the law (Torah) that ye are gods. If the Torah says this, and the scriptures are true and cannot be undone why do you say I am a blasphemer because I said I am the Son of God?* The scripture that Jesus was referring to was the one found in the 3rd chapter of Genesis.

Genesis 3:5 *for God doth know that in the day that you eat thereof, then your eyes will be opened, and ye shall be as Gods, knowing good and evil.*

Genesis 3:22 *(22) And the Lord God said, Behold, <u>the man is become one of US</u>, to know good and evil, and now, lest he put forth his hand and take also the tree of life, and eat and live forever.*

When you put both of the scriptures above together it states that basically man has become one of (us) the entity that is speaking as the (us) is the LORD God who is the chief speaking amongst the other gods. We can conclude that the people of that time could not recognize the intellect of Jesus and their refusal to acknowledge his seat as the natural king is what has fueled them in their denial. Just as I have made known the gods in this society in this book think of how people will vilify what I have written based on what they have been taught by those who promote romanticism. When Jesus is said to be king against "Rome" this is an implication that he is paramount and "King" over all things romantic because like Ptah, he brings to life the "word" or "legends" / gods and shows them to the lay people in real life. This animating talent is further supported by the Kabbalah, the ancient esoteric writings of the Jews.

In the gospel of Luke the chief priests are said to have persecuted Jesus for "perverting the masses" with all forms of "Jewry." I think revealing the Kabbalah to the masses could be considered a form of Jewry, do you?

Luke 23:5 *(5) And they were the more fierce, saying, He stirreth up the people, teaching throughout all Jewry, beginning from Galilee to this place.*

Luke 23:2 *(2) And they began to accuse him, saying, We found this fellow perverting the nation, and forbidding to give tribute to Caesar, saying that he himself is Christ a King.*

In this book I have used multiple biblical references so people who haven't read or cannot comprehend the Bible will be able to understand the symbolic meanings behind the literature. I have also brought to light with clarity the true meaning of resurrection combining all 4 major religions of the world including Roman mythology, Egyptology, Kabbalah, Thelema, Astrology as well as Freemasonry. If people want to continue to believe that snakes talk, seas part, and dead people are raised from the dead literally, then you as sound minded people have every right to ask them to show you proof for where they are getting their knowledge besides the allegories written in the Bible. Something that was written in allegory to show the world the symbolic significance of what happened in history has been turned into something very grotesque and misleading. This is the true vice of romanticism and this romanticism has led to the idle (idol) worship seen in regards to the present deluge of the world. This reminds me of the tower of Babel in how people became so lofty in their *IDEALS/IDLES/IDOLS* they grew delusional about the word of God to the point where their speech, prayers, and acknowledgements about him were turned to worthless babbling. Note how close the word ideal is to idol and idle. When people become so "ideal" in their thoughts and interests about how or what something should be like, they become delusional and are taken over by romanticism, falsehood, and lies.

Genesis 11:1-9 (1) And the whole earth was of one language, and of one speech. (2) And it came to pass, as they journeyed from the east, that they found a plain in the land of Shinar; and they dwelt there. (3) And they said one to another, Go to, let us make brick, and burn them thoroughly. And they had brick for stone, and slime had they for morter. (4) And they said, Go to, let us build us a city and a tower, whose top may reach unto heaven; and let us make us a name, lest we be scattered abroad upon the face of the whole earth. (5) And the LORD came down to see the city and the tower, which the children of men builded. (6) And the LORD said, Behold, the people is one, and they have all one language; and this they begin to do: and now nothing will be restrained from them, which they have imagined to do. (7) Go to, let us go down, and there confound their language, that they may not understand one another's speech. (8) So the LORD scattered them abroad from thence upon the face of all the earth: and they left off to build the city. (9) Therefore is the name of it called Babel; because the LORD did there confound the language of all the earth: and from thence did the LORD scatter them abroad upon the face of all the earth.

Again, I have placed these references within this book to show how the literal translation of the Bible people have accepted, has blinded them from the literary nuances that give a colorful and very meticulous assessment of the scriptures and the characters represented within them. Egyptians understood the relationship between cosmic energy and material energy and used

Astrology and the Kabbalah (mathematics of existence) as a means of documenting this phenomenon. They also had a profound understanding of masculine and feminine energies and how they relate as well. We know this because each astrological sign has a masculine or feminine significance attached to it. The Egyptian god (Osiris/Ptah) upon constructing the world knew if (he) wanted to create a man he would first need a female for him (the man) to be born through. This is symbolism showing the allegorical relationship of the first (man) that was created from Isis, that man again being Horus. However this man wasn't a man in the sense of a male, it was a man in the sense of a being containing both masculine and feminine parts {Eve and Serpent.} This story was first cited in Egypt whereby God (Sun) and the earthly fashioned (goddess) (Virgo) gave birth to what is known as the divine androgen i.e. the Hero/Heru also known as Horus, the double eagle (Man) a combination of the Scorpio (eagle) and the Aquarius (eagle.) Remember, in the Beginning, (Genesis) man was both male and female and "his" name was called Adam; a clue that highlights man's androgynous beginnings (dual nature) and speaks directly to the Age of Aquarius.

Genesis 5:2 *(2) Male and Female created he them; and blessed them, and called their name Adam, in the day when they were created.*

307

The Book of Illumination

CHAPTER 17

WHOLIER THAN THOU

The Book of Illumination

CHAPTER 17
WHOLIER THAN THOU

WHOLIER THAN THOU

Look at the image of King Tut. The picture below it shows how the original image over time has been romanticized and changed, though the symbols of the shepherd's staff and the snake (hood) were carried over with it. The new Sun of Man versus the ancient Sun of Man has two distinct contrasts. The new Sun of Man is white and is obviously displayed humbly as a plain shepherd; whereas the ancient Sun of Man is displayed as a king whose vesture is crafted and dipped in pure gold. With this in mind, the

bottom image is the image romantics have given blacks of their former king, which in turn detaches any notion of black people identifying themselves with richness and valor; attributes commonly associated with Egyptian culture. Images like the one below have been literally resurrected in place of the original by way of Rome and other prominent European civilizations. Promoting a white Jesus to the masses as it's figurehead not only replaces the image of the Sun of Man's grandiose, kingly, and opulent status; but ultimately cultivates a white supremacist mindset within the already over exploited, socially repressed Negro. Because Tut's image has been erased from the minds of blacks even though NT scriptures denounce materialism, blacks glorify material wealth because they innately know deep down they came from a culture that was as rich in knowledge as it was in treasures. Because of this falsified image, the world sees no true association between King Tut and the Jesus they profess to love and worship today.

Exodus 4:2-5 And the LORD said unto him, What is that in thine hand? And he said, A rod. ³And he said, Cast it on the ground. And he cast it on the ground, and it became a serpent; and Moses fled from before it. ⁴And the LORD said unto Moses, Put forth thine hand, and take it by the tail. And he put forth his hand, and caught it, and it became a rod in his hand: ⁵That they may believe that the LORD God of their fathers, the God of Abraham, the God of Isaac, and the God of Jacob, hath appeared unto thee.

311

In the Genesis as regarded by the Kabbalah, by A.E Waite, the serpent is the name given to classify the (God) that Eve slept with. "*She cohabitated with {the serpent} who corrupted her and by him she became with child bringing forth Cain. The serpent had "criminal relations" with her and injected his defilement into her* 94. We speculate that this serpent is an Egyptian God because Egyptian monarchs (Gods) wore snakes (uraeus's) on their heads to show they are divine manifestations of deity; or basically, they are gods in an elemental/corporeal form. The snake is a symbol of regeneration and supreme wisdom due to the fact that snakes can shed their skin, synonymous to the way the Egyptian monarchs shed lifetimes. The reason that a negative connotation is given by the Kabbalah in regards to the "*criminal relations*" the serpent had with Eve is due to the biases the Roman world has towards Egypt and anything that comes from the indigenous cultures of melanated people.

Uraeus: A representation of the sacred asp upon the headdress of rulers in ancient Egypt symbolizing supreme power. 2. Cobra

In the traditional solar system model the SUN is the entity the other (planets) revolve around. The sign the Sun falls under in Astrology is Leo. The glyph associated to Leo also resembles a snake. The Hebrew word for Leo is *teth* and means serpent. This makes what we read in the Genesis have a totally different interpretation. Combining these meanings and then linking them with other symbols like the shepherds staff, gives us a clearer view of what is being communicated through ancient language and symbolism. 95a

Psalm 23 (1) *The* **LORD** *is my shepherd; I shall not want. (2) He maketh me to lie down in green pastures: he leadeth me beside the still waters. (3) He restoreth my soul: he leadeth me in the paths of righteousness for his name's sake. (4) Yea, though I walk through the valley of the shadow of death, I will fear no evil: for thou art with me; thy rod and thy staff they comfort me.*

The LORD "Adonai" who visits Abraham is the God that is being exalted and lifted up through these scriptures. The shepherd's staff that comforts David in one of the most popular Psalm's in the Bible, indicates those passages are clues that link the LORD to the Comforter, who is known in the legend of Noah, as the *Spirit of Truth* sent from the "Father.

John 15:26 (26) But when the comforter is come, whom I will send unto you from the father, the Spirit of truth, which proceedeth from the father, he shall testify of me.

Looking at the image of King Tut, it is apparent he holds the shepherds staff within his hand and the eagle and the snake upon his head. These three symbols together link him to the God of Israel; an acknowledgement that places him far beyond the pharaoh he is historically known to be. Both figuratively and literally he is the most popular Egyptian Pharaoh and through his monuments we see his mastery over the afterlife. His understanding of it (afterlife) has enabled him to conquer time and death, making him famous eternally paralleling him to Osiris, the Egyptian God of the dead.

In the third chapter of John, Jesus compares himself to the serpent that was lifted up in the wilderness by Moses. According to the passages below, the serpent and the Son of Man are one and the same.

John 3:14 (14) And as Moses lifted up the serpent in the wilderness, even so must the Son of man be lifted up.

Numbers 21:8-9 (8) And the LORD said unto Moses, <u>Make thee a fiery serpent</u>, and set it upon a pole: and it shall come to pass, that every one that is bitten, when he looketh upon it, shall live. (9)And Moses made a serpent of <u>brass</u>, and put it upon a pole, and it came to pass, that if a serpent had bitten any man, when he beheld the serpent of brass, he lived.

If we then take the scriptures of Genesis 3:4-5 and analyze them further, we find out that (LEO) the God of Israel, is also the serpent who says, *"When you eat of the fruit (tree of Life) you will become as gods knowing good and evil."* I can testify that this acknowledgement by the serpent is real because I have eaten fruit from the "tree of life" and by way of it, have made known the appearances of gods who walk about the earth in human flesh.

John 10:34-36 (34) Is it not written in your law, I said Ye are gods (35) If he called them gods, unto whom the word of God came, and the scripture cannot be broken (36) Say ye of him, whom the father hath sanctified, and sent into the world, Thou blasphemest, because I said, I am the Son of Man.

Next we'll discuss how this serpent is viewed in other ancient writings. Not only will we discuss its personality in detail, we'll also show why its identity has been masked, kept hidden, and disassociated to anything deemed righteous or Godly.

THE FIERY DRAGON

In the Book of Enoch, Gabriel, who is considered to be the Chief Archangel, was said to have dominion over <u>serpents</u>, paradise, and all things powerful,

Enoch: XX. Names and Functions of the Seven Archangels 20:8 *Gabriel, one of the holy angels, who is over Paradise "The 'Ikisat " (the fiery serpents) serpents and the Cherubim.*

When Mary the Mother of Jesus is visited by an angel, Gabriel is that angel. **(Luke 1:26–38)** When the mother of John the Baptist, Elisabeth was visited by an Angel, Gabriel was that angel. **(Luke 1:5–20)**

In the Kabbalah translated by A.E. Waite, Cain was said to have resembled those above, not those below as Eve is recorded to have said: "I *have gotten a man, an angel of Jehovah"* 95b. Anytime the most important women in the New Testament are bearing "God's" children, Gabriel is the archangel that visits them. If Gabriel is indeed over serpents and fiery serpents and he is the one visiting barren and chaste women before they get pregnant, then we can make a correlation between him as the same entity that visited Sarah in the 18th chapter of Genesis before she bore Isaac, as well as the Virgin Mary who birthed Jesus. Seraphim's which are the highest in the order of angels in the Christian faith are said to be fiery serpents as well.

<u>Seraphim:</u> A member of the highest orders of angels

Making this assumption to most Christians would be considered sacrilegious due to the fact that it exposes their doctrine as being misinterpreted. The composers of the Bible we read today couldn't print that God physically impregnated Mary because being virginal and chaste are key tenets in the Christian Faith. The authors of the Christian faith wanted to make it congruent with its key tenets of belief so they replaced what actually happened by disguising truth with myth. Rather than having "God" physically impregnating Mary they wrote an angel visited her and upon him leaving she was pregnant. This is the same as when parents tell their kids stories about storks to hide the unpleasant realities of child birth and sex.

Ancient symbolism was the way older cultures preserved their knowledge as their "people" became integrated with migrants and other nations. They developed an advanced system of communication by way of it and used it to pass on information that could not be spoken in public.

The name Joseph in Hebrew also means "lingam" and as previously stated bears a strong connection with paternity and fatherhood 95c. A lingam is a very large shaft or (phallus {Washington Monument, church steeples etc.}) A large phallus indicates that the holder of the phallus has the alpha or (God) male gene, as this lingam or (obelisk) is what the God of the old world, (The omnipotent highly procreative fertility God) was defined by.

Lingam: A phallus, symbol of Shiva.

Phallus: a representation of the penis employed in the art and religious practices usu. a symbol of male regenerative powers.

Most old buildings or ancient monumental structures have an (obelisk) or phallic symbol associated with them. These Obelisks are Egyptian monuments that through artistic expression show the omnipotent aspect of "God" that gives him his highly potent, procreative, and regenerative abilities. These abilities were spoken of in the Old Testament with the story of Abraham, God, and Isaac in the 18th chapter of Genesis. Theologians and scholars have had the hardest time covering up the humanistic aspect associated with procreation and God. If you look at Jesus as the Son of God, this must mean that he was birthed by a "God" who was also on the earth physically.

The serpent, the shepherd's staff, the phallus, and the Sun are all symbols of the ancient God known as Shiva in Hinduism. Shiva also goes by the name Isvara, its shortened form is Isa …or as the Bible reveals Esau. Here is where we discover the truth about the real identity of the LORD.

Genesis 18:1&2 (1) *And the LORD appeared unto him (Abraham) in the plains of Mamre: and he sat in the tent door in the heat of the day; (2) And he lift up his eyes and looked, and, lo, three men stood by him: and when he saw them, he ran to meet them from the tent door, and bowed himself toward the ground,*

315

Genesis 18:13&14 (13) And the LORD said unto Abraham, Wherefore did Sarah laugh, saying, Shall I of a surety bear a child, which am old? (14) Is anything too hard for the LORD? At the time appointed I will return unto thee, according to the time of life, and Sarah shall have a son.

Genesis 21:1&2 (1) And the LORD visited Sarah as he had said, and the LORD did unto Sarah as he had spoken. (2) For Sarah conceived, and bare Abraham a son in his old age, at the set time of which God had spoken to him.

The actual word used in the Hebrew Scriptures is (*paqad)* which in Hebrew means to "*visit*" in the sexual sense 101. So by this indication we can see that the LORD has come in the place of Abraham an engendered a son with his wife Sarah. If one is talking about the God of Abraham, Isaac, and Jacob, one is referring to a physical and tangible God, not an unseen unknown God (microcosm.) If one is looking at the whole of creation including the stars, the moon, sun, planets oceans, earth animals etc. one is talking about the All God (macrocosm.) The microcosm is a smaller version of the macrocosm; which means that the "God" of the earth is the equivalent of the "God" that is represented in the universe. *See Dr. Manhattan.* When you think in reference to the "God" who created everything, the All God, the one of the sky who most people believe has an unfathomable form, it is easy to see how upon reading the OT, most people would deny that "God" would exist in a human body. This is where the confusion about "God" in regards to religion has taken place. It is only when you understand Astrology and the Kabbalah do you see the aspects of the universe in conjunction with the elements and planets which serve as the blueprints to the actual makeup of the God of Israel.

Acknowledging the God of Abraham, Isaac, and Jacob, was the omnipotent regenerative Sun God (Shiva); who engenders sons with hidden "Queens" would also make his offspring have the abilities of "God" their father. When we analyze the New Testament with that of the Old Testament scriptures, we can take these same acknowledgements and replace the Old Testament characters with New Testament characters. If the name Joseph was translated in the Kabbalistic sense, it would describe the spiritual character of Joseph defined as "lingam" as a distinguishing characteristic that links him to the alpha male, Shiva aka Isvara. The alpha male is what the people in ancient times considered to be a god among men; which is why the scriptures are stated like this in the 6th Chapter of Genesis.

Genesis 6:1-2&4 (1) And it came to pass, when men began to multiply on the face of the earth, and daughters were born unto them, (2) that the <u>*Sons of God saw the daughters of Men that they were fair:*</u> *and* <u>*they took them wives of all which they chose*</u> *(4)* <u>*There were giants in the earth in those days,*</u> *and after that,* <u>*when the sons of God came into the daughters of men, and they bare children to them, the same became mighty men which were of old, men of renown*</u>

<u>Renown</u>: widely acclaimed; highly honored.

The following scriptures again, appear to have been edited for discretionary reasons. I say this because <u>Isaac</u> being the first "Son of God" is said to have loved Esau.

Genesis 25:28 (28) And Isaac loved Esau, because he did eat of his venison but Rebekah loved Jacob.

However when you read Malachi 1:2-3 It states that the Lord hated Esau.

Malachi 1:2-3 (2) I have loved you saith the Lord. Yet ye say wherein hast thou loved us? Was not Esau Jacob's brother? Saith the Lord: yet I loved Jacob (3) And I hated Esau, and Laid his mountains and his heritage waste for the dragons of the wilderness.

If Isaac is the Son of the LORD who visited Sarah in the 18th chapter of Genesis; in The LORD's absence, Isaac would then become the rightful heir to the LORD's almighty throne. How can Isaac the son of the LORD love his son Esau but then the scriptures turn and say the LORD hated Esau? What is even stranger is that the Bible rewards Jacob for stealing the birthright and blessing from Esau. Could this be because the same faction of people who wrote this in the Bible, are guilty of stealing the birth rights and lineages of other nations, by claiming to be "God's" chosen people? Once again man is changing the view of the Bible and using "God's" name to do it. These contradictions are why there is a need for the truth to be told. Isaac's son Esau is said by Jacob to have resembled the face of "God" which is apparently contradictory again with the passage of Malachi.

Genesis 33:1& 10 (1) And Jacob lifted up his eyes, and looked and behold, Esau came, and with him four hundred men. (10) And Jacob said Nay, I pray thee, if now I have found grace in the sight then receive my present at my hand: for therefore <u>*I have seen thy face, as though I had seen the face of God and thou was pleased with me*</u>

317

The Bible tells us the God of Abraham is the God the Christians follow.

Matthew 22:32 (32) *I am the God of Abraham, and the God of Isaac, and the God of Jacob? God is not the God of the dead, but of the living.* - Jesus

This passage in Matthew **22:32** comes directly from the LORD "God" who in the 18th and 21st chapters of Genesis came in the flesh, as an actual person who walked, talked, ate and drank, as well as impregnated Sarah to create a godly lineage through her. This LORD was so virile and potent that he was able to impregnate Sarah who was very old. Again the 6th chapter of Genesis stresses the existence of a "living God." It also links the phallus as the main tool of the God of Abraham, Isaac, and Jacob making him the Alpha- male, who through use of it (phallus) births "superstar" offspring.

Hero: (1) from Greek hērōs: the offspring of a deity and a mortal

Lebron James' physical specimen is a testament to what is being explained here in the 6th chapter of Genesis. In comparison to the woman he is holding, who by the way is 5'10, he in every way appears to be a dominant giant. This is why he is referred to as King James, "King" being synonymous with the ONE or the alpha 102. Look at the way that Lebron James is holding Gisele Bundchen. This is a real depiction of an allegory told and shown in the story of King Kong and in the Genesis. You have the massive black alpha, "god" and the petite white (fair) beauty. Again you couldn't shout out to the masses that these huge athletes are descendants of gods the same way you couldn't say that obelisks, pyramids, steeples etc. are depictions of large penises. "*Giants in the earth*" is also an astrological reference that indicates the gods have fallen to earth, and are again the huge "stars" that are seen manifested in human forms. If you could see their heavenly forms you would understand why they were called giants and gods. Their splashes upon the earth are so epic; they often are recorded as separate people in different legends. For instance Michael Jackson is so gigantic he has elements of Moses, Joseph, Krishna, Jesus, Dionysus, and the Archangel Michael, all within his personality making him literally THAT gigantic. These acknowledgements are key factors that add explanative evidence to the attraction that dominance creates and the beings of less dominance that are attracted to it. We could also parallel this with a hypothesis as to why homosexual men revere manly men.

Homosexual males relate more with femininity and are also in search of "God" and or the alpha male. This explains why they marvel over the dominance and physical prowess the alpha male has by displaying this fascination within the physique of their male statues; as they are attracted to what epitomizes the height of even their existence. Because the Greeks and Romans were known to be lovers of men they expressed their homosexuality in art, sculptures, and also in their Roman Mythology. Homosexuality dominated their culture and is spoken against in the Bible.

Leviticus 18:22 Thou shalt not lie with mankind, as with woman kind, it is an abomination.

Romans 1:27 (27) And likewise also the men, leaving the natural use of the woman, burned in their lust for one towards another; men with men working that which is unseemly, and receiving in themselves that recompense of their error which was meet.

Genesis 19: 24 (24) Then the Lord rained upon Sodom and upon Gomorrah brimstone and fire from the Lord out of Heaven.

Abomination: (1) Extreme disgust and hatred (2) severely unpleasant

Sodomy: (1) Homosexuality (2) anal or oral copulation of the same sex

The title the LORD was inserted into the King James Bible in place of the Hebrew equivalent Adonai who is called Adonis in Greek Mythology and often depicted with his consort Venus (Aphrodite) as a perfectly sculptured man. Adonis represents how the Greeks chose to show what the omnipotent god looks like when he walks the earth as he represents the perfect *"Temple"* of God.

1 Corinthians 3:16 (16) Don't you know that you yourselves are God's temple and that God's Spirit dwells in your midst

I placed this point within the texts to show there are deeper meanings associated within the stories of the Bible. If "God" is an alpha male his natural opponent would be a homosexual male. Homosexual males in the truest sense do not love or want to have children with women. Thus we can

319

say they by definition are not potent; but rather impotent. This impotency is what makes them the opposite of omnipotent. So in nature (*the alpha and the homosexual male*) are in opposition of each other, meaning placed on opposite ends of the spectrum. We saw this aspect personified in the *007* film *Skyfall*. James Bond had sexual relations with both women (below) in the film demonstrating his alpha male and ubiquitous persona. Later we'll talk more about the masonic meaning of 007 known as the two-ball cane, the penis.

The initial books that were placed in the Bible come from older works and knowledge's created in older cultures. The information that was passed down through these cultures was the knowledge of how a kingdom is built and maintained. The Bible that people have deemed a holy book today was originally a book about kings. The alpha male superiority reflected within the characters represented in it (Bible) is what enabled their kingdoms to thrive and flourish. Adam, Noah, Abraham, Isaac, Jacob, Joseph, Moses, David, Solomon, and Jesus were all kings; which makes the Bible extremely biased against homosexuals, and women, and is the reason behind why its stance deems homosexuality as an impermissible and abominable lifestyle.

Potent: (1) Having or wielding force, authority or influence (2) able to copulate, usu. used in reference to males

Impotent: (1) not potent lacking power, strength or vigor (2) sterile

Omnipotent: (1) having virtually unlimited potency (2) Almighty

Speaking of unlimited potency and virile power, in relation to the strength and the dominance of the alpha male; we again see this same set of patterns represented through Gabriel, most noted as the chief archangel whose name means "Strength of God" or "God is my strong Man/Hero." If this Gabriel who comes in the guise of a man has the omnipotent abilities to impregnate barren women and is also the head of the Seraphims, the serpents, and paradise, then all of the aforementioned information links the highest archangel with that of a serpent, a lion, and a bear; making Gabriel himself the "God" of Israel and Aleister Crowley's tarot deck with the card *strength* entitled *lust*, the most powerful, prophetic, and enigmatic tarot deck of them all.

In Aleister Crowley's tarot card decks he has a card formerly called "*strength*" in the major arcarna that he renamed "Lust" 103. On this card is a seven headed lion with a woman riding upon his back. The lion's seven heads are seven different characters, a *saint*, a *man of valor*, a *poet*, an *adulterous woman*, a *martyr*, an *angel* and a *lion serpent* 104. This is the Beast of Revelation, and the heads on it represent its past seven incarnations. Crowley in *Tarot mirror to the Soul* attributes this tarot card as being the most powerful in its deck. It's found on the 11th card which is a master number in Numerology and also attributed to the sign Leo.

The woman on the back of the beast is reportedly the scarlet woman (Venus.) This card bears reference to the seven headed lion and the scarlet woman as being bearers of lion serpents. I used Crowley's deck because his interpretations aren't filled with the romantic imagery that clogs the realistic associations in regards to sex and procreation that is apparent within the Bible and other religious works.

Crowley refers to the woman as Lady Babylon 103a. This is a very interesting and key piece of information because the Babylonians under the Lordship of Ba'al (The LORD) were the first culture to reference Astrology. BABA - according to Webster's Dictionary means peasant girl and can be likened to maid or maiden – which in the ancient world, was synonymous to (Virgo) virgin. Lon is an obvious association to Lion. When we look at the combination of servant girl lion we in a sense see the Goddess Sekhmet the consort of Ptah as well as Anat the wife of Melkart appear. Again, these are Egyptian and Semitic deities that existed in works several thousands of years older than the Bible.

The imagery and allegory that implicates the Archangel whose name means "Strength of God" or "God is my strong Man/Hero" known as the "left hand of God" represented on the 11th card in the major arcana that Aleister Crowley appropriately renamed lust; is only fully realized when you combine scriptures of the Old and New Testaments. In the 17th chapter of Revelation we are given the account of this scarlet woman in another form.

Revelation 17:3-6 (3) *Then the angel carried me away in the Spirit into a desert. There I saw a woman sitting on a scarlet beast that was covered with blasphemous names and had seven heads and ten horns. (4) The woman was dressed in purple and scarlet, and was glittering with gold, precious stones and pearls. She held a golden cup in her hand, filled with abominable things and the filth of her adulteries. (5) This title was written on her forehead: MYSTERY BABYLON THE GREAT THE MOTHER OF PROSTITUTES AND OF THE ABOMINATIONS OF THE EARTH. (6) I saw that the woman was drunk with the blood of the saints, the blood of those who bore testimony to Jesus.*

The reason they call the Scarlet woman (adultery) the mother of all whores is because she in the tradition of Bathsheba, in the tradition of Eve, in the tradition of Sarah slept with and bore sons from a man/ "God" other than their original husbands. Jesus ultimately follows in the same footsteps with the offspring he had with the Magdalene as she was a harlot and women were forbidden for "priests" to have. The blood of the saints spoken of in this excerpt from the Book of Revelation represents the blood from Kali, or Anat who viciously murders her husband Osiris/Ba'al's (THE LORD's) murderers. She resurrects through him the son that will avenge his death restoring the body of knowledge that was dismembered and scattered through the 4 religions of the world. As you look at Kali you see symbolism that reflects a woman astride a man (beast/god) like the picture that Crowley designed for his lust card. The man she has mounted is the Beast of Revelation, Shiva. Note the parallel to the beast being a leopard and look at the loin of the Great Hindu God Shiva that Kali is atop. The Beast that the woman is astride in Crowley's tarot card is described in the 13th chapter of Revelation.

Revelation 13:1-4 (1) *And I saw a beast coming out of the sea. He had ten horns and seven heads, with ten crowns on his horns, and on each head a blasphemous name. (2) <u>The beast I saw resembled a leopard, but had feet like those of a bear and a mouth like that of a lion.</u> The dragon gave the beast his power and his throne and great authority. (3) One of the heads of the beast seemed to have had a fatal wound, but the fatal wound had been healed. The whole world was astonished and followed the beast. (4) Men worshiped the dragon because he had given authority to the beast, and they also worshiped the beast and asked, "Who is like the beast? Who can make war against him?*

There are two things that are very interesting about these scriptures in Revelation. The first of which is the description of the Beast as being a leopard, a lion, and a bear. In the 13th chapter of the book of Hosea which is a prophetical book of the OT, it states that "God" will come to judge the Israelite tribe of Ephraim for their worship of idols as a "Beast" that is like a lion, a leopard, and a bear. It is important to notate both these scriptures appear in the 13th chapters; 13 being a scared number in Jewish mysticism.

Hosea 13: 1-8 (1) *When <u>Ephraim spake trembling, he exalted himself in Israel; but when he offended in Baal, he died</u>. (2)And now they sin more and more, and have made them molten images of their silver, and idols according to their own understanding, all of it the work of the craftsmen: they say of them, Let the men that sacrifice kiss the calves. (3)Therefore they shall be as the morning cloud and as the early dew that passeth away, as the chaff that is driven with the whirlwind out of the floor, and as the smoke out of the chimney.(4)But I am the LORD your God, who brought you out of Egypt. You shall acknowledge no God but me, no Savior except me. (5) I cared for you in the desert in the land of burning heat. (6) When I fed them, they were satisfied: when they were satisfied, they became proud; then they forgot me. (7) <u>So I will come upon them like a lion, like a leopard I will lurk by the path.</u> (8) <u>Like a bear robbed of her cubs,</u> I will attack them and rip them open Like a lion I will devour them; a wild animal will tear them apart.*

The other description is given in the New Testament in the Book of Revelation written long after the Book of Hosea under questionable Roman authority. Though Revelation is a prophetical book, it is easily seen that in the OT the same description was given to describe "God."

Here, also found in the Book of Hosea, is a rivalry between Ephraim and Ba'al who we have decoded is the LORD aka the God of Israel. According to Ezekiel 37 Ephraim was the tribe that had the tribe of Joseph in its hands. The Bible indicates the LORD will take the stick of Joseph (Michael Jackson) which is now in Ephraim's hands (Barack Obama) and join it with the stick of

Judah. We already stated in the preface that Saul was made king by way of the king making ritual of the Hebrew people after their urbanization. Barack Obama was also a judge who was made king at Oprah/Ephraim in the same likeness to Saul during the urbanization of the Jews of America in our time presently. It is very important to note that Saul was elected king because superficially he had all the characteristics an ideal king would have. He was tall, handsome, and eloquent; however David who was small in stature (from humble origins) who plays the harp, symbolizing he's a musician, became the king and ruler over Israel upon his defeat of Goliath.

1 Samuel 9:2, 9:15 10:1, 17-27: (1) There was a Benjamite, a man of standing, whose name was Kish son of Abiel, the son of Zeror, the son of Bekorath, the son of Aphiah of Benjamin. (2) Kish had a son named Saul, as handsome a young man as could be found anywhere in Israel, and he was a head taller than anyone else. (15) Now the day before Saul came, the LORD had revealed this to Samuel: 16 "About this time tomorrow I will send you a man from the land of Benjamin. Anoint him ruler over my people Israel; he will deliver them from the hand of the Philistines. I have looked on my people, for their cry has reached me."

1 Samuel 10:1 (1) Then Samuel took a flask of olive oil and poured it on Saul's head and kissed him, saying, "Has not the LORD anointed you ruler over his inheritance

1 Samuel 17:37 (37) David said moreover, The LORD that delivered me out of the paw of the lion, and out of the paw of the bear, he will deliver me out of the hand of this Philistine.

Ezekiel 37:19-23. (19) say to them, 'This is what the Sovereign LORD says: I am going to take the stick of Joseph—which is in Ephraim's hand—and of the Israelite tribes associated with him, and join it to Judah's stick, making them a single stick of wood, and they will become one in my hand.

The tribes of Judah and Ephraim are similar in likeness (lions.) They both represent the same thing (kingship) and according to the Bible, they're rivals.

Isaiah 11:13 The envy also of Ephraim shall depart, and the adversaries of Judah shall be cut off: Ephraim shall not envy Judah, and Judah shall not harass Ephraim

BEAUTY AND THE BEAST

It is in the 'lust/strength" card shown on page 321 where we get a clear understanding of the trinity as well as the relationship between opposites. Here beauty and the beast find themselves madly in lust for one another; their agonizing lust brings about the birth of a Hero.

The popular story of Beauty and the Beast is where we see beauty and strength polarized. On page 255 of the Kabbalah by A.E. Waite, on the sixth node of the sephiroth, it lists the name Michael as the sixth archangel whose name means "like unto God" as corresponding to Tiphereth, which is beauty. It was here where strength has only one rival and the story of Jacob and Esau points this out to us. This is the reason for the fusion between beauty and beast and is what the hero is a combination of; for what is a beast to look at that is hideous, and frightening? Think about Joseph Jackson - Leo/king of beasts; now imagine a beast cloaked in beauty, (Michael Jackson,) this is evolution. An evolution so powerful, that it's the consummating factor that ties romanticism and realism together in all stories and epics of antiquity. The (beauty) romanticism draws you in enough to get your attention, and then the truth, is that (beast) that makes you hate what it is you just professed to believe. Understanding "God" and the virgin, beauty and the beast, alongside angelic intervention allows a person to make the link between "God's" "left hand" and the earthly sons that are born of him.

Many people skip over the fact that Gabriel is called the "left hand of God." They suffice this to mean he stands on the left side of "God." Being a "leftist" or being placed on the left handed side of God, only means he is on the "secret" side rather than the right handed or "ideal" side of God. This makes him a secret agent super stud like o7o James Bond.

Isaiah 45:15 (15) Verily thou art a God that hidest thyself, O God of Israel the Savior

The left handed side of God is where forbidden things like Astrology, tantra, and the occult are permitted and practiced regularly. The leftist's concede that man has a nature to do that which is unlawful or forbidden, and by exhausting his desires is the only way to make him become upright. Abstaining from them causes dissention, and a more coveted desire to do them. These desires can push a person to addiction and ultimately catastrophe.

Many people try to discredit the divinity of Michael Jackson solely based upon his addiction to prescription pain killing medicines. These addictions spawned from a Pepsi commercial Michael was burned in, in 1983-84.

In the book entitled *the Secret Language of Birthdays* it states that those who are born on August 29th have a sensitive nervous systems and are prone to addictions. It further states that if they do not maintain a healthy balance in their personal lives, their life can become chaotic and ultimately end in addiction 106d. Everything in the physical realm is governed by the rules of its existence. If this wasn't so, Jesus upon being crucified wouldn't have felt pain. The fact that Michael became addicted to prescription pain killing medicine was attributed to the energy of the day he was born on. I wrote this about Michael and Jesus to show how even deities are restricted and governed by the laws of their existences even though they possess supernatural powers.

Another very interesting account is the one given in the *Homeric Hymn of Dionysus no. VII* recounted by Ovid were Dionysus was abducted by Tyrrhenian Pirates. Dionysus asked them to take him to Naxos and when they refused he caused wine to gush inside the boat and transformed the oars to serpents. He then transformed himself into a terrible lion and caused a bear to appear in the center of the ship. The pirates who tried to abduct him were thrown from the ship into the sea where they became dolphins 105.
Anybody that has studied Dionysus knows that he is the god of wine and orgies. This links him to the Hindu God Shiva and also links him to Osiris in Egypt, as Osiris was said to be the inventor of the vine, and was hailed as the great phallic god who the goddesses adored. When compiling the imagery portrayed in these accounts, it paints a portrait that shows in it, all the images of the SUN of Man. Jesus turned water into wine, which is symbolic of Dionysus. God judging his people in the form of a lion and a bear is symbolic of the LORD of Israel and Judah. Everywhere we look we find this imagery. So in reading these stories we can see how through them this same "God" appears over and over again. Even with the name El Elyon we see the word

El which means man or he, synonymous with God and the word Lyon or lion. Thus man and Lion equal El Elyon which again is the "Most High God" represented as Father and Son. This Man and Lion are represented by the great statue that sits outside the three great pyramids, the Sphinx 106.

Here, is another depiction whereby a woman astride a beast creates a child with heroic and superhuman abilities. In Egypt (left) the woman that rides the lion is called Isis. She resurrects through Horus, Osiris who is the Egyptian God of the dead. In this story is where we find the 1st example in history of a Son (sun) resurrecting the father (El). The Bible that we read again comes from older stories that were broken down and retranslated to pass on the meaning of certain esoteric knowledge's. This knowledge would only be recognized by the "God" who spiritually was alive when it was 1st contextualized. Only He would be able to read and decipher these meanings and teach them correctly as HORUS is the only god capable of piecing back together the body of "Osiris" which is the source/body from which all religions come. *The Egyptian Book of the Dead* is a hieroglyph that chronicles his journey upon his resurrection from the afterlife to the present life. The afterlife is the future life he will live when the stars realign. The last time he lived was roughly about 77,760 years ago 107.

According to Alexander Piatigorsky in his book entitled *Freemasonry*, on pg 141, it states, "*It was Osiris the sun considered as the demiurge who made the world under the direction of the Supreme Being*" 108. He went on to say, the primary state of natural religion that came before the time when the god of Abraham, Isaac, and Jacob was worshipped was the religious cult of Osiris.

"If a religion wants to be not only universal (ubiquitous) in space but also eternal, then we have to admit together with the royal arch companions that it is god as sun or Osiris (not as supreme being) who was the demiurge and word long before we arrived at the third stage of religious consciousness manifested in Jesus Christ and saint John" 109.

The two things that have caused the people to forget their deities are time and their worship of graven images. The masses have yet to prove they really understand "God" and the way he manifests to earth. They either worship him in spirit (the unseen - son and the "stars" themselves) or in the form of an idol (inanimate/statue/image.) This means, each time the circular revolution of the Sun through the constellations occurs, the people are worshipping the stories of the god(s) subconsciously, rather than consciously worshipping the actual living manifestations of the god(s) (avatars) that are on the earth.

Here is a scripture that says the virgin of Israel is fallen and shall no more rise.

Amos 5: 2 (2) The virgin of Israel is fallen she shall no more rise: she is forsaken upon her land; there is none to raise her up.

 However she (virgin of Israel) arose again in the personification of Mary the virgin who is the mother of Jesus of Nazareth. This shows that the prophecies given in these books have been misinterpreted or not properly understood. Being that the Bibles books were selected (canonized) we can see how some of the texts contradict that which happened on earth. Today the Virgin Mary is one of the most worshipped archetypes in the Catholic religion, a religion that has one sixth of the earth's population as its members. If you asked me that virgin has again risen in worship. On a conscious level, the fact that Michael Jackson was born under the sign of the virgin (Virgo) and was the most revered person on the planet, further disproves the statement made in the Book of Amos… And with that, the danger of the {**Roman**(tic)} religion again is that it worships idols. The Pope easily will kiss and revere this statue of the Christ and his mother but wouldn't bestow the same honor to Michael, Katherine, or Joseph Jackson.

The conclusions people have drawn from misinterpretation and comprehension error has caused them to profess a faith they really have no knowledge about; and because they have done so, they really don't know who is who. This means the Gentile can no longer be classified as a particular race or set of people because the cultures today have mongrelized themselves and become all mixed together. Because this has happened the uneducated masses act and perform as the Gentiles in the Bible did, (again prophetic) making them the new Gentiles who ultimately will be consumed and destroyed by the truth expressed in this book.

Jesus in the 24th chapter of Matthew states that you will know the end of times when the prophecy of Daniel begins to reenact itself on earth.

Matthew 24:14:21 And this gospel of the kingdom shall be preached in all the world for a witness unto all nations; and then shall the end come. (15) When ye therefore shall see the abomination of desolation, spoken of by Daniel the prophet, stand in the holy place, (whoso readeth, let him understand.

In the Book of Daniel it states Michael will stand for the children of Israel.

Daniel 12:1-2 (1) And at that time shall Michael stand up, the great prince which standeth for the children of thy people: and there shall be a time of trouble, such as never was since there was a nation even to that same time: and at that time thy people shall be delivered, every one that shall be found written in the book. (2) And many of them that sleep in the dust of the earth shall awake, some to everlasting life, and some to shame and everlasting contempt.

We just witnessed Michael (Joseph) Jackson stand for the Children of America, which as previously mentioned, is the prophetical Israel. In the accounts below, Gabriel is saying that he will be assisted by Michael in fighting against the Princes of Greece and Persia.

Daniel 9:21 (21)Yea, whiles I was speaking in prayer, even the man Gabriel, whom I had seen in the vision at the beginning, being caused to fly swiftly, touched me about the time of the evening oblation.

Daniel 10:18-21 (18)Then there came again and touched me one like the appearance of a man, and he strengthened me, (19)And said, O man greatly beloved, fear not: peace be unto thee, be strong, yea, be strong. And when he had spoken unto me, I was strengthened, and said, Let my lord speak; for thou hast strengthened me. (20)Then said he, Knowest thou wherefore I come unto thee? and now will I return to fight with the prince of Persia: and when I am gone forth, lo, the prince of Grecia shall come. (21) But I will shew thee that which is noted in the scripture of truth: and there is none that holdeth with me in these things, but Michael your prince.

Grecia is the ancient name of the Greeks, the same people that the NIV version of the Bible translates as the *Gentile* nations. The Persians in ancient times were thought to be comprised of the Germans, the Greeks, as well as the Latins. Modern day Persia is represented as Afghanistan and Iran; people who all have Aryan descent. Based on the consistency of what I have been reading and speaking about, it is very clear as to whom the archangel Gabriel is coming with Michael to avenge and destroy. The war that Michael and Gabriel are fighting against these nations however, is an ideological one. When we take an assessment of what these nations have historically done to the Jews, and the Egyptian people; the prophecies recorded in these ancient texts become all the more real and three dimensional. Germany is where we saw 6 million Jews executed at the hands of Adolf Hitler. Greece is where we saw Roman Mythology emerge with the shifting of the gods from Egypt being transformed into those of Greek origin in legend. The Aryans, historically, were the conquerors of ancient Vedic Brahmanism where Hinduism was the main religion; it was here were the stories of Egyptian origins were 1st transformed into romantic fairy tales 109a. The Latin and Roman cultures have further perpetuated these images/idols and romanticized all religion itself which has de-generated the thought patterns of the people, and has caused our world to descend back into the dark ages.

Just as I have explained how scribes and editors have come along and retranslated scriptures to turn the God (Christ) who will chastise the Roman, Grecian and {Latin} nations into the {anti-Christ} by the creation of the Jesus of Nazareth, which was a myth constructed in the four gospels by merging the lives of Krishna (Joseph) and Shiva (Judah) together. So have these Masons and practitioners of the occult and ancient texts done so by waging war upon the nations of the Middle East, with the" *War on Terrorism"* as Afghanistan and Iran are modern day Persia. Because they mimic prophecy, they have waged war with the nations that have romanticized and stolen the knowledge and prophecies of the Hindu and Canaanite people, by passing it off as their own. *I.S.I.S. is the *"new"* terrorist organization that threatens America in 2014. While this is largely perpetuated by the media, the war America engages in against **ISIS** is really a marker that shows we have ended the Age of Isis (Piscean/Virgo Age) and entered the age of Horus (Leo/Aquarian Age.)

Being that all of these things correlate together, it is not strange to presuppose that it was Gabriel who was the Archangel aspect of God who came to earth to father these God men i.e. Jesus, Isaac, Solomon and Cain. I'm sure this indication seems blasphemous to most Christians however to literally believe that a snake can talk isn't something that readily makes sense.

The reason that a person believes this is because it was taught to them as children, when their minds were impressionable. Because no one has ever questioned this, the people go about their lives as if it doesn't matter. They brush it off, and place it to the back of their minds as one of the many things man can't fully understand, like the origins of the races.

Reading the account of the Genesis literally would make a person conclude that "God" through genetic manipulation created a whole new race of people. However, when you combine this information with romanticism and then factor the low comprehension levels of the masses, it causes the type of "mass" confusion we see today. Again, in the Old Testament, during the times of Abraham, it states that "God" literally came down, and physically spoke with Abraham, as well as had sexual intercourse (*paqad*) with his wife Sarah 101. Is this not God in the flesh coming down to man an engendering a son with a woman? The God of Abraham physically coming to earth and birthing a son with a queen makes the son he had with the woman a son of God, right? The name of this "God" engendered son was Isaac, and the root of his name Isa is another name of the great and highly procreative Hindu phallic God, Shiva aka Isvara. Shiva carries with him, a trident, symbolizing the trinity. He also has a King Cobra around his neck; in Hinduism, he's known as the Supreme Lord and in Christianity he is known as the Baal.

The Book of Illumination

CHAPTER 18

THE LIVING GOD

The Book of Illumination

CHAPTER 18

THE LIVING GOD

96 As I stated earlier, the reason a lot of religious and historical records were deleted is due to a dark secret. A secret that if exposed would in a sense cause the world as most people know it to end. When cross examining color as it pertains to genetics it is a scientific fact that all colors originate from black. It is also a fact that all people originate from Africa (mitochondrial Eve.) The world recently witnessed this by way of the black British couple that gave birth to a white baby girl who is blonde haired and blue eyed, but is not an albino. This piece of information is critical in examining the origins of the races and how they pertain to the creation story of the Genesis, whereby God is the creator of the new species of man. This is why I said the gods who created man were located in the place where the "stars" were in alignment; because life and energy as well as thought travel's in light. Thought manifests to flesh and this process is comparable to sperm which are thoughts, meeting flesh which is the egg/matter. The pinnacles of the pyramids, like phalluses, were markers for the place where the light/energy of Orion's (Osiris') belt would be felt and harnessed. This made it possible to locate the city/place where these celestial (energy/ beings) would manifest in embodiment form on the earth.

Again, this alignment of stars (Orion's belt) created a "gateway/portal" and marks the spot geographically where these astral deities in relevance to the Sun came into being on Earth. Though you have celestial gods like Venus, Mercury, Jupiter, and Mars which represent the celestial gods in heaven (the planets); you also have these gods, and goddesses manifested in the flesh on the Earth. The Earth is the planet where all things are made manifest. It's sort of like the eyeball, when your eyes are closed and there is no light, there appears to be nothing there. Just because you can't see something doesn't mean that it isn't there, it just means that you haven't enough light or the ability to see it. The Earth being like the eyeball, when it is open, all things in creation are able to be seen.

Humans are embodiments of light; expressed as moving planets; and a planet is a star. This statement is represented scientifically by the five pointed star, a symbol that represents the 5 points of the human body. The light from the Sun we look at is the opening to the outside realm that shows us the light from the constellation it is revolving through. In the Earth is a Sun (core) and in the Sun is an Earth (nucleus); thus Isis buried the penis of Osiris to resurrect him as Horus in legend.

We learned earlier that an obelisk is a representation of a large shaft. This phallic symbol promotes dominant male or alpha male superiority. The 32nd chapter of the Genesis gives us a detailed account about its power.

Genesis 32:24-32 (24) And Jacob was left alone; and there wrestled a man with him until the breaking of the day. (25) And when he saw that he prevailed not against him, he touched the hollow of his thigh; and the hollow of Jacob's thigh was out of joint, as he wrestled with him. (26) And he said, Let me go, for the day breaketh. And he said, I will not let thee go, except thou bless me. (27) And he said unto him, What is thy name? And he said, Jacob. (28) And he said, Thy name shall be called no more Jacob, but Israel: for as a prince hast thou power with God and with men, and hast prevailed. (29) And Jacob asked him, and said, Tell me, I pray thee, thy name. And he said, Wherefore is it that thou dost ask after my name? And he blessed him there. (30) And Jacob called the name of the place Peniel: for I have seen God face to face, and my life is preserved. (31) And as he passed over Penuel the sun rose upon him, and he halted upon his thigh. (32) Therefore the children of Israel eat not of the sinew which shrank, which is upon the hollow of the thigh, unto this day: because he touched the hollow of Jacob's thigh in the sinew that shrank.

Sinew: (1) tendon (2) the chief force

I used the above scripture to show subtly how the pineal gland located at the top of the head (Kether) is connected to the crown chakra, and the "hollow" of the thigh, the "sinew that shrank" the penis. This is how "God" connects the head above with the head below, which is necessary when harnessing energy to birth powerful offspring. I also wanted to show through scriptures, how the crown chakra, light, the pineal gland, and the penis are all connected both physically and metaphysically in the account given in the Genesis whereby Jacob wrestled with an angel. Remember as we stated earlier, the unification of the two lands' in ancient Egypt (Israel and Judah) is most notably symbolized by the Sphinx, which marked the start of the first cycle of pharoanic dynasties that began with the commencement of the astrological Age of Taurus, *c.* 3,240 BCE 82.

Again, the two constellations, which determined the whole length and course of the first cycle of Egyptian pharoanic civilization, were Ursa Major, the Great Bear, and Leo, the Lion. These astrological ages were recognized by the Egyptians, and their civilization adapted accordingly.

Leo and Ursa Major were considered by the Egyptians to be the magical 'thigh' (or right foreleg) of Taurus, the latter symbolized the illumined mind and is referred to as the 'Eye' of Horus. With this 'thigh of the Eye of Horus' *Ptah* (the Creator god signifying the Voice of God) 'opened' the mouths of divine entities and the souls of the dead."

The acknowledgement of these two lands, though seemingly a geographical reference, connects the eye of the mind with the eye of the penis. It is also why Leo represented by the (all Seeing Eye/pineal gland) and the bull (the phallus itself) are also connected in the heavens. This again can be illustrated in the life of Michael Jackson in how the "bull" Cow/Katherine is connected to the phallus (Joseph) who is also the lion (Leo.) This fusion created the most powerful being in the universe Michael Jackson who was known for "grabbing" his crotch; just as Jacob, the father of Joseph, wrestled with the angel where the "sinew" shrank in the Bible. The eye of the "mind/head" opening, and the dead coming to life, is an easy correlation to ejaculation; where thoughts as sperm, which were once in their graves, (testes) are shot out through the vaginal cavity onto the egg matter (earth) to birth life. The same way as when the eye of Horus opens the light hits the matter of creation (Earth) illuminating everything on it including the gods, causing everything and everyone literally to "come" to life.

The **Swedenborg concordance** also bears witness to the connection between the pineal gland and the conjugal love associated with the human love muscle the penis.

The hollow of Jacob's thigh is where conjugal love is conjoined with celestial love and natural good - Swedenborg concordance 97.

Conjugal: to join, unite in sex

Remember there is a Sun within the Earth's (core.) The friction from sex is what releases the woman's "earth oil" in "Zion" (water) which then mixes with the man's (semen.) The combining of the two fluids represent the water of life and the Milky Way - literally (Milky-Way), the way god manifests on Earth as being. By harnessing the light from the Sun, the "God" channels his most powerful thoughts through his pineal gland. This is the gland that secrets melanin, the substance that harnesses and pulls the light within his mind from the Sun. The actual thoughts (sperm) then travels down to the testes where they gather nourishment, and are then ejaculated within the host or vessel (vehicle) the woman. The violent act of sex and the powerful back and forth motion is what is known as the "*Big Bang*" where the large shafted man enters the woman through the act of sex. The Sun god is the procreative god whose physical makeup embodies this understanding because of his proximity to the Sun itself. The Sun is what gives the power to the thoughts, which are again sperm. Being that we are in the Godhead (universe) every star represents a point of reference in the mind of the "All" much to the like as dendrites do in our own brains. Since every star is a place of knowledge think of them as the places in the mind where the answers to what is unknown has been discovered; or the Y's (why?) that solves the X's (unknown.) The blackness that exists in the solar system is the space between the places or points of reference in the "All" mind. They represent potential un-harnessed, stagnant, and untapped energy in our own brains as well. The Universe is "THE MIND" of that which we call "God" and everyone is connected in it, and through it. There are over 102 billion gods which are known as stars. When the Sun rises in a new constellation all of the stars in that constellation are magnified and fall to the Earth during that period of 2,160 years. Depending on what level of being you are, how far you have ascended through birth, and the number of dendrites you've connected together, will ultimately determine what type of being you are able to harness from the heavens and birth to the Earth. However certain practices and vices block this star energy from being harnessed and when that happens a person is born purely carnal, meaning that they come from below (lower mind only) and not above from the high mind (which when activated through meditation is connected to the heavens. Jesus speaks about this in **St. John 3:6**

St. John 3:6 *That which is born of flesh is flesh that which is born of spirit is spirit.*

It can take several lifetimes and births to ascend to a higher consciousness. It all depends on the level of existence each individual is trying to achieve and create. The meditations are what bring power to the thoughts. It is this practice that chisels, refines, structures and orders thoughts; these thoughts again, are what sperm are made of. Usually the most powerful thought manifests. The difference between the meditated thought and the loose thought (in sperm) is likened to the stick figure and a sculpture done by Michelangelo. Those people who structure their thoughts and lives before creation create high level beings; those who don't leave it to chance, and with that chance, enables the varna-sankara (*unwanted population*) a greater chance of being born.

In reading and examining these scriptures below it is easily seen that this is an earlier account of God sleeping with a woman to birth a king.

Genesis 18:1-4 9-10,12,14 &17 Genesis 21:1 *(1) And the Lord appeared unto him (Abraham)in the plains of Mamre and he sat in the tent door in the heat of day; (2) And he lift his eyes up and lo three men stood by him: and when he saw them, he ran to meet them from the tent door and bowed himself towards the ground (3) And said, My Lord, if now I have found favor in thy sight, pass not away, I pray thee, from thy servant: (4) Let a little water, I pray you, be fetched, and wash your feet, and rest yourselves under the tree: (9) And they said unto him,* **Where is Sarah thy wife**? *And he said behold in the tent. (10) And he said (God)* **I will certainly return unto thee according to the time of life; and lo Sarah thy wife shall have a son.** *And Sarah heard it in the tent door, which was behind him. (12) Therefore Sarah laughed within herself, saying, After I am waxed old shall I have pleasure, My lord being old also (14) And the Lord said* **Is anything too hard for the Lord? I will return unto thee according to the time of life; and Sarah shall have a son.**

Genesis 18:17 *And the Lord said, Shall I hide from Abraham that thing which I do?*

Genesis 21:1-2 *(1) And the lord visited Sarah as he had said, and the Lord did unto Sarah as he had spoken (2) For Sarah conceived and bare Abraham a son in his old age, at the set time of which God had spoken to him.*

Sarah in Hebrew means queen 98 and we can take from this story the mythology associated with "God" and a queen birthing an heir to a godly lineage. The name Sarah in its Kabbalistic interpretation also is equivalent to forbidden 98. It is a known fact that kingship was passed down through the genealogy of the mother due to scientific discovery of mitochondrial DNA 99. While Indo-European peoples mainly were patriarchal and patrilinear, certain ancient myths have been argued to expose ancient traces of matrilineal customs that existed before historical records. Two ancient historians, Herodotus and Strabo are cited by Robert Graves in his translations of Greek myths as attesting to that while the royal function was a male privilege, power came through women; namely because the future king inherited power through marrying the queen heiress. Think about it, if kingship was determined through patrilineal descent, than Abraham would have HAD to birth Isaac himself like he did Ishmael. The fact that the covenant is established through the son that Abraham's wife "The forbidden Queen" had with (a) or (the) God places emphasis on the notion that the woman decides who, why, and what type of king will be born. Jesus being born through Mary again shows the relationship between the matrilineal descents that kingship was determined by.

Matrilineal: relating to, based on, or tracing descent through the maternal line

Patrilineal: relating to, based on, or tracing descent through the paternal line

Maternity: the quality or state of being a mother

Paternity: the quality or state of being a father

The way that masculinity is personified in its most brutal and warrior form seems archaic and primitive to the feminine psyche; and the image of the cave man beating the women over the head with a club is a great way to look at how the woman sees the man when in his rawest form. The way the delicate woman rationalizes not killing a sickly child because of her emotional attachment to it seems to be a weakness to the masculine man as the sickly child will hinder the movement of the whole group. The man looking at the woman's emotional condition makes it hard for him to allow her to be a leader or decision maker. When the two breed pending on how much she uses her subconscious mind, how much she has submitted to his will, and how many qualities that he has that she is stimulated by; will in turn factor into what type of being is created through their union. If you took notice, I didn't use the man's dominance as a prerequisite to the type of being that will be produced.

The popular theory is that a father determines the sex of the child because males can donate both an X and a Y chromosome, while females can only donate an X chromosome to their offspring. However if a woman during her pregnancy is producing abnormally high quantities of testosterone, even though the fetus is of XX genetic make-up, the mother's hormones can influence it to develop into a male, even without a Y chromosome. On the other hand, if an XY fetus cannot produce enough androgens to cancel out the estrogen and progesterone being produced by its mother (either because the fetus simply isn't producing adequate androgens or because the female is producing unusually high levels of feminizing hormones) it can develop into a perfectly normal female, despite having both an X and Y chromosome. This is a direct scientific explanation that supports the true dominance of femininity [99]. Again, it is no secret that in ancient time's kingship was established through the woman by matrilineal descent. This is also illustrated in the Homeric myths where the noblest men in Greece vie for the hand of Helen (and the throne of Sparta [100].) It was also evident in the Oedipian cycle where Oedipus weds the widow of the late king at the same time he assumes the Theban kingship. Matrilineal descent takes place when the conquering hero weds the daughter of a king; and upon doing so the hero is crowned as the successor to the former King's kingdom. A more recent example of this is when Michael Jackson married the daughter of Elvis Presley. Michael was vying for his position as the king upon the throne of music and rock and roll i.e. KING OF THE MUSES. Elvis was the former King and in fact was called simply "The King." His daughter Lisa Marie Pressley, was the heir to that throne. By Michael Jackson wedding Lisa Marie Presley, he further solidified his place as the undisputed King of Pop, and Rock and Roll music. [101a -101b]

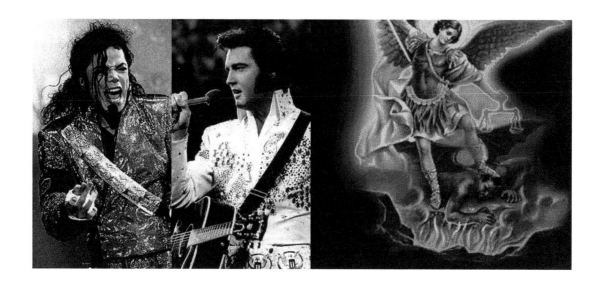

When animating the story of Michael Jackson and his place in history and comparing it to the life of Elvis Pressley; another epic tale is revealed before our eyes. Michael Jackson and Elvis Pressley arguably are the two most iconic musicians of all time. The two men are often compared posthumously as the public wants to know who the undisputed King of Pop and Rock and Roll music is. When we look at Elvis Pressley's birthday it is on January 8th which according to the Kabbalah is regarded as the month of Capricorn who in urban legend is referred to as "the Devil" or "the goat man." Elvis Pressley was born on the 8th day which is the day of Saturn; and again where the term Satan finds its origin. If we were to look at these two individuals based on their inner selves and their life missions, by using the Kabbalah, we clearly are shown how a title match that headlines as, "The son of God /Archangel Michael Jackson vs. The Devil of Satan, Elvis Pressley" could easily be promoted. The victor of this epic bout is crowned as the undisputed champion who ultimately gets worshipped in the great book written at the end of the age. When you add up the fact that Michael Jackson has the highest grossing album of all-time as well as numerous world records for charity and popularity, it is easily seen how one could write in an epic legend how God/Archangel Michael indeed defeated Satan on earth and reclaimed his kingdom and place upon his heavenly throne. On the flipside to this conversation when looking at the character of Elvis Pressley it was reported that he quote on quote "stole black people's music" and got rich from emulating their styles. Little Richard, for instance, was once quoted as saying, *"Elvis was paid $25,000 for doing three songs in a movie and I only got $5,000, and if it wasn't for me, Elvis would starve."* And, after hearing Presley's version of the song "Trouble," blues legend Muddy Waters said Quote" *"I better watch out - I believe whitey's pickin' up on things that I'm doin'"* 101c. This is what Elvis himself had to say in regards to the matter "*The colored folks been singing it and playing it just like I'm doin' now, man for more years than I know. They played it like that in the shanties and in their jukee joints and nobody paid it no mind 'til I goosed it up. I got it from them..."* 101d

What also makes these two figures lives parallel are the rumors surrounding their sexual relationships. Michael, who was framed as being a pedophile, was vindicated on all charges of child molestation. Elvis Pressley according to some accounts had sexual relations with Priscilla Pressley when she was fifteen years of age while he was twenty five. It has even been reported that Priscilla said Elvis raped her 101e. Elvis and Priscilla eventually married one another, and though Elvis was never seen as a pedophile or rapist in the eyes of America or the world, according to some accounts, he was 101e.

In the December issue of *People Magazine* 2010, under the "star revelations" section, the doctor that presided over the death of Elvis said that "the singer's death in 1977 was actually caused by severe constipation and not heart failure" 101f. If a person was looking at this from an ironic or dark satirical standpoint one could say that Elvis literally died "full of shit." I have no disdain for Elvis, nor is this a particular view that I hold. I am just showing with factual evidence how the viewpoint and disposition of the person who is writing the legend, can affect how the person in the legend is viewed by those who are reading it.

We have to keep in mind the Bhaga Vita, the Torah, the Bible, the Qu'ran as well as mythology's characters are actually celestial energies embodied in human flesh, that upon their descents to earth, become the "stars" that are revered today. For instance Elvis Pressley shares a birthday (January 8th) with Robert Kelly, a multiplatinum music composer and performer whose career was ruined because he was caught on tape having

sex with a minor. In the likeness of Elvis he was also speculated in the late 90's to have married a 15 year old R&B songstress named Aaliyah Haughton. In fact, Aaliyah's debut album *Age Ain't Nothing but a Number* co-written by R. Kelly is an obvious testament to the truest mentality that R. Kelly represents. Looking at the character of Pan in the picture above, and what he represents within ancient legend, this seems to be a reoccurring theme in how he entrances young girls with his intoxicating music, gaining their trust and their affection. Pan in Astrology is attributed to the sign Capricorn of which Elvis and R. Kelly were both born under. At any rate, the account of Michael Jackson versus Elvis Pressley further polarizes "good" and "evil" with a textbook analysis, allowing the audience to view for itself which of these two men would be perceived as godly and which would be perceived as satanic. These facts could not be taught to the masses due to the information they've been given for many years. Back when these stories where written the level of education and comprehension was just pictorial, and the people of that day lacked the ability to photograph the actual manifestations of the deities who were referenced within the ancient scriptures, statues, and glyphs. The way they chose to record this information was within the totems of ancient Egypt and the hieroglyphs. Because they were factoring the energies within deities; statues, glyphs, and paintings later became the standards for recording a history that otherwise only existed in an oral form. Now that we have HD television and movies that are in 3D, we have the clarity and the ability to see these stories acted out today "literally" on the stage. Remember, matter isn't created nor destroyed, it just changes forms. If we are mindful with the way we look at things portrayed in religion like angels with wings, and a red devil with horns, our intellect would tell us these types of beings cannot or do not exist in real life today. However when we put an image to their characters based on the lack of technology we have at the time, as well as place value in the idol we have created over the physical living god we are looking at; societies then lack of recognition to the living manifestation causes people to call into question religion altogether. Seeing the archangel Michael defeat Satan in this way seems frivolous right, but now ask yourself how frivolous the drawing of the archangel and Satan looks in comparison to the picture beside it. Both are true, but ask yourself which example is more vivid and alive. Do you like the more primitive drawing or the 2013 version? The fact that Michael died across the street from where Elvis Pressley lived is a testament to the contemporary lives these two entities have when they manifest in physical forms, as well as the constant competition between them. Even if people do not accept this view formally, the Kabbalistic mathematical breakdown behind both these individuals is undeniable. One could easily rationalize that people are going to do and continue to believe what they want anyway. If they come to the realization that what they believe isn't true, they usually dismiss the entire belief before seeing what in it is valid. This is what gives rise to the disposition of the atheist as well as what creates the catalyst that activates the anarchist to destructive behavior patterns. The rivalry between Michael Jackson and Elvis Pressley in relation to pop culture reveals in the most epic way the truth behind these two energies personas in how they play out when seeing them in their actual physical forms.

Anytime you see a person with superior abilities know that these persons have lived and perfected levels of existence prior to the one they are living in now. There are many levels and it is all situational as no two scenarios in creation will be the same though some will have similar outcomes. When I first started writing in this book the topic of mind was change and to "think a new thought." Then I realized that nothing really changes which made me readily assess who and what humanity has become as a whole.

THE FOOL.

One of the greatest cliché's "there is nothing new under the sun" appears to stem from the same philosophy that promotes that nothing really does change. It is more about when a person starts paying real attention to life that they see the more things change, the more they stay the same. Once this train of thought is examined and well thought out, then true enlightenment will occur. This conversation is further explained in the name, Percival, who in the tarot is the Fool. "Perceival" is depicted as wandering near a cliff. His leap of blind faith is what leads him to enlightenment, or in layman's terms, the understanding of himself and his surroundings. Percival's name in conjunction to how he is depicted in the tarot is indicative of how a person's "perception," can lead to their condemnation or salvation. The way we perceive a thing can err in how we see it and ourselves; and the misdiagnosis of these things which we "perceive to be" are what leads to the biases and dogmas that have caused confusion in the world of religion, science, politics, and literature.

In taking an assessment of these things it is important to note that some people do not wish to be awakened. Some people only want to awaken to the point where they can look at others and not themselves. All in all everything is perfect in creation, and everything in the end balances back out. We have people on this earth whose understanding though limited is right, for they are reacting to something that we may not be aware of. I am not a Universalist in the sense that I think all people are created equal. I am universal in the understanding that creation dictates all of this to man and in the end it all evens out. Free will is instrumental in determining what universe people live in. Because the universe in which we live is so vast many people are unable to see that even though they think they are different and apart from it, they are as typical as any other part in it. The word is universe which translates to one verse. Although this one is a single entity, within it is everything that can possibly exist, so in the one you have the all. Understanding this brings us to the point of collective consciousness. This collective conscious is the point where everyone functioning involuntarily brings us all back to the point of recognizing who we are as a whole. Some people are meant to be servants, others rulers. Some women are supposed to be whores, others mothers. We

345

only judge because we within ourselves are scared to think beyond the limits of what keeps us bound to our own personal belief systems, prejudices, and comfort zones.

Jude 1: 10 (10)Yet these men speak abusively against whatever they do not understand; and what things they do understand by instinct, like unreasoning animals—these are the very things that destroy them.

Usually the person who has the most or heightened power is the one who will be vilified. The witch hunt starts within the group of individuals who are less evolved. This hunt usually involves those who are less enlightened lynching the people who are more enlightened. The real war between the have and the have not started with creation, evolution, and karma. This war was determined when one child was born with beauty, intellect, and charm and the other wasn't. This war started way before money was ever created and will continue to take place until people no longer exist. It is the way that the species thrives and keeps evolving, and the way that the universe expands, and contracts. It is the way that people learn and process information; and the way that beings are born into the physical plane. Everything is relative within creation; and in this creation is the ultimate truth. All a person can do is get glimpses of that truth and from those glimpses formulate their own particular theories of life. Many people have fought to understand themselves and others. Many who fought weren't necessarily liberated from the ignorance they fought for. Some people have to be negative and be conquered so other people have examples to learn from. Because survival is the most fundamental and lowest level of intelligence that exists, it inevitably becomes the central focus for all life. Babies are born cute and cuddly so they in turn can have all of their needs met. If they were hideous and were not able to be looked at with compassion their parents wouldn't respond to their every beck and call. If their needs weren't met the babies would not survive. Some women who are very voluptuous are filled with so much lust and passion that they cannot help but to exude that passion in a sexual way. If they tried to be with one man and one man only it would inevitably lead to their unhappiness and demise. Other women because they are intimidated by the voluptuousness of these types of women call her names and make her out to be a spell caster because their husbands desire her. I challenge the reader to look in the mirror and see who they are. Not the person that they think they are; the person before the make-up, before the gut is sucked in, before the chest is stuck out, before the clothes are put on, and their hair is made up. I employ each individual to really look at themselves and take an assessment of their lives to see exactly where they stand; not according to any religious judgment, but to the standards that they hold others to. When people begin to do this they will be able to see the truth; and this truth, will no longer need to be stated.

Western society enables people to rally behind causes that are based on prejudices by allowing groups of individuals to influence the masses even when their causes have obvious biases. If most people were able to look within the spiritual realm, which is the realm prior to manifestation, they would be better prepared for what happens physically to them. Moving towards this collective consciousness is the intended goal and also why this "America" was built in the first place. Society wanted to know as well as witness for itself if all that it once knew to be true still holds to be true today. We've seen all that there is to see, except one thing. There is only one thing that the world is anxiously waiting to witness; and that is its own destruction; some call it Armageddon, others call it the rapture.

Another popular cliché often used by old folks is, "*be careful what you wish for because you just might get it.*" The world is yearning for a messiah and they received one. The world has yet to acknowledge a lot of its past atrocities, and these atrocities though covered up will come to light. The book has been opened and the die has been cast. All those who can understand will those who don't, "will" be left behind. I hope that you will take these things with you as they will be what will assist you in obtaining consciousness in the next plane of time.

RACE RELATIONS

According to the Genesis, whether it was a spontaneous mutation birthed by the goddess that upon the G.O.D's recognition of it they replicated more of the same kind by using the gene; or, it was by a direct cloning of a gene into a man that caused a race of individuals to be created. In the time of Adam, there were great distinctions between gods and the newly formed race of man that was created.

Genesis 1:26 And God said, "Let us make man in our image after our likeness."

Adam and Eve respectively show the fall of man from the image of "God."

Genesis 1:27 So God created man in his own image, in the image of God created he him; male and female created he them.

347

When I say fall it signifies a downgrade or a distinction showing "God" to be superior/higher than his creation. Gene/isis or Genesis is the book that indicates the beginning of mankind. However the title in itself tells an even greater story. The term Gene /Isis could be looked at as a correlation to Mitochondrial Eve. Mitochondrial Eve is the name given by researchers to the woman who is defined as the matrilineal most recent common ancestor for all currently living humans. This DNA is handed down from the mothers to their children. -- Mitochondrial Eve's DNA is the mitochondrial DNA found in ALL living humans, which means every mtDNA in every living person is derived from hers. She is believed by scholars to have lived about 170,000 – 200,000 years ago [110]. This places her in a period significantly earlier than the out of Africa migration some 60,000 years ago, and close to the first appearance of archaic *Homo sapiens* whose remains were found in Ethiopia. Being that Mitochondrial Eve lived in Africa, she is sometimes referred to as African Eve.

In understanding the scripture below, it implies that the command to stay out of the garden bearing the tree of knowledge was both given to Adam and Eve. We know this because Adam represents the race of man, not just the male. When Eve is talked to by the serpent, this is a very edited and romantic way of translating that Eve was slept with by the God/serpent. This produced a seed known as Cain, the first murderer, but again a person may ask how do I know this?

Genesis 3:2-5 (2) And the woman said unto the serpent, We may eat of the fruit of the trees of the garden: (3) But of the fruit of the tree which is in the midst of the garden, God hath said, Ye shall not eat of it, neither shall ye touch it, lest ye die. (4) And the serpent said unto the woman, Ye shall not surely die: (5) For God doth know that in the day ye eat thereof, then your eyes shall be opened, and ye shall be as gods, knowing good and evil.

In the Kabbalah it is stated that eve cohabitated with the serpent and the union of their cohabitation brought forth Cain. Notice it says in **Genesis 3:15**"*And I will put enmity between thee and the woman, and between thy seed and her seed it shall bruise thy head and thou shall bruise his heel.*"

Here, "God" draws a direct distinction between Adam's seed, and his woman's Eve's seed, indicating that her (Eve's) seed is not his, (Adam's) seed. (Cain) was the first bi-product of the first record of adultery (race mixing/lying with a woman who belongs to another race.)

<u>Adulterate:</u> to debase or make impure by adding inferior, alien or less desirable materials or elements

If "God" is pure and unadulterated, mixing himself with a lesser substance, as man was described to be, (next to God) would fit the definition of adultery to a tee. Thus Cain was different from Abel because Abel wasn't mixed nor did he possess the power of the gods. This clue again takes us back to the difference between Isaac and Ishmael as Isaac was the son of the LORD and Sarah given to Abraham because of Abraham's good nature.

Genesis 18:18&19 *(18) Seeing that Abraham shall surely become a great and mighty nation, and all the nations of the earth shall be blessed in him? (19) For I know him, that he will command his children and his household after him, and they shall keep the way of the LORD, to do justice and judgment; that the LORD may bring upon Abraham that which he hath spoken of him.*

The comparison here is between the serpent and Eve and The LORD and Sarah; the bi-products between their unions are Cain and Isaac. Isaac was sacrificed by his <u>father</u>, The LORD, and given to Abraham. Cain was also sacrificed to be the servant of servants by his (grand<u>father</u>) Noah. Jesus was sacrificed by his <u>father</u> for the remission of sins for the people on earth. When you put all of this together, it basically tells you the story of how "God" falls to earth, engenders a son who has to go through slavery or become sacrificed in order to rebuild and purge himself to inspire the rest of the world to become whole. This explains why religion takes precedents over every other thing in the lives of the people on earth. The religions of Abraham provides substantial evidence that the same LORD /God through lifetimes descends to earth to work his agenda; which is the continual perfection of being or what is called in Masonry, the building of the unfinished Temple. The story of Adam and Eve as told by the Bible and believed by Christians; is the story of the first man and woman born to this earth who bore the new race of man. According to biblical record, in the time of the Genesis, gods existed and were separate from man. These gods were celestial beings that manifested through the ethereal planes into flesh and being by way of the Sun. Though we do not get a direct record of this account, the Genesis gives us the account of angels referred to as the Sons of God who came from "heaven" to procreate on earth with women. Enoch confirms this calling the sons of god fallen angels.

Genesis 5:1 & 2 *(1) This is the book of the generations of Adam. In the day that God created man, in the likeness of God made he him; (2) Male and female created he them; and blessed them, and called their name Adam, in the day they were created.*

Genesis 6:1 & 2 & 4 *(1) And it came to pass, when men began to multiply on the face of the earth, and daughters were born unto them, (2)That the sons of God saw the daughters of men that they were fair; and they took them wives of all which they chose. (4) There were giants in the earth in those days; and also after that, when the sons of God came in unto the daughters of men, and they bare children to them, the same became mighty men which were of old, men of renown.*

Enoch VII. *and all others (angels) together with them took unto themselves wives, and each chose for himself one. and they began to go into them and defile themselves with them, and they became pregnant, and bare great giants whose height was three thousand elles. Who consumed all the acquisitions of men and when men could no longer sustain them. The giants turned against them and devoured mankind.*

In the book *Fingerprints of the Gods*, an Egyptian record keeper and Priest named Manetho confirmed these findings. He acknowledged that gods existed in a period on the earth dating back over 36,000 years. The primary gods Manetho referenced we're Osiris, Ra, Isis, Shu, Tefnut, Geb, Nut, Set, and Nephthys. Manetho's records indicate these gods ruled Egypt for 18,000 years before mortal Pharaohs ever ascended the throne [111]. If this is true this means the 6,000 year period scholars predict to be the origins of all creation is the period at the end of the grand cycle whereby mankind was created and able to rule on earth. The Qu'ran gives us more insight about the Genesis.

Qur'an al araf 7:10 *It is <u>We</u> Who have placed you with authority on earth, and provided you therein with means for the fulfillment of your life: small are the thanks that ye give! And made in it means of livelihood for you; little it is that you give thanks.*

Qu'ran al araf 7:11 *It is <u>We</u> Who created you and gave you shape; then <u>We</u> bade the angels prostrate to Adam, and they prostrate; not so Iblis; He refused to be of those who prostrate. 7:12(Allah) said: "What prevented thee from prostrating when I commanded thee?" He (Iblis) said: "I am better than he: Thou didst create me from fire and him from clay."*

Here is an instance cited by the Qur'an whereby the Iblis of God created out of pure fire will not bow to MAN. When I think about what would cause man to continually be perfected by The LORD or why an entire race would need to be created, a plethora of theories come to mind. When I then look to older works that have themes associated with "God" and the creation of races it causes a plausible explanation to form in my mind. Each and every encounter with this subject brings me back to the same conclusion that suggests a primary race was threatened by their own offspring. The Titans and the gods of Mt. Olympus, Beowulf, King Arthur, Alexander the Great as well as Oedipus are all legends that have themes with offspring uprooting their monarchal Fathers, which also played out in the life of Michael Jackson.

In my hypothesis of how legends as well as the races were created, the reason the Adamic race was made was to control the lesser gods (angels) who were threatening the rule of the higher gods. I used the Qur'an in my example because it gives a detailed description of what is discussed in the Book of Genesis and Enoch from a slightly different perspective. Many of the stories in the Bible are found in the Qur'an, the only difference is interpretation. Since interpretation is the reason that most Christians dismiss the Qur'an altogether, it made me decide to use it, as interpretation is what has caused so many different sects and creeds within the Christian faith. Being that Christianity has so many different sects and viewpoints that stem from the inconsistencies written in the Bible, the Qur'an has just as much validity as any other sect within it. Let me clarify this point a little further; when we read the Bible from a literary standpoint, one of education, there are a lot of puzzling details that if misdirected could lead a person to an understanding that could clinically be diagnosed as insanity.

Insanity: (1) extreme folly or unreasonableness (2) something utterly foolish

The Qur'an's instructions are practical and basic and are regarded by many scholars as being mathematically perfect. Because of the Qur'an's basic structure and the many biblical stories that are in it, Islam, the religion the Qur'an represents, is quickly becoming the fastest growing religion in the world. It is believed in Islam that the Qur'an was revealed to Muhammad by the angel (Gabriel) from 610 CE to his death in 632 CE. Imagine what we've just examined about what and who the angel Gabriel secretly may be. Followers of Islam further believe that the Qur'an was written down by Muhammad's companions while he was alive, although the primary method of transmission was oral. It is maintained that in 633 CE, the written text was compiled, and in 653 CE it was standardized, distributed in the Islamic empire, and produced in large numbers 112. Many of the same characters stories in the Bible are found in the Qur'an. Abraham, Mary, Gabriel, Isaac, Ishmael, Jacob, Jesus, and Moses all have stories within it. I could devote a whole chapter to the differences between the Qur'an and the Bible but there are many other books that illustrate those points. The Islamic faith stems from the 16th chapter of the Genesis when Sarai told Abraham to take her maidservant to be his wife. Arabs claim their descent from Hagar and Abraham; Jews claim there descent from the LORD Sarai and Isaac.

Genesis 16:1-12 (1) Now Sarai Abram's wife bare him no children: and she had an handmaid, an Egyptian, whose name was Hagar. (2)And Sarai said unto Abram, Behold now, the LORD hath restrained me from bearing: I pray thee, go in unto my maid; it may be that I may obtain children by her. And Abram hearkened to the voice of Sarai. (3)And Sarai Abram's wife took Hagar her maid the Egyptian, after Abram had dwelt ten years in the land of Canaan, and gave her to her husband Abram to be his wife. (4)And he went in unto Hagar, and she conceived: and when she saw that she had conceived, her mistress was despised in her eyes. (5)And Sarai said unto Abram, My wrong be upon thee: I have given my maid into thy bosom; and when she saw that she had conceived, I was despised in her eyes: the LORD judge between me and thee. (6) But Abram said unto Sarai, Behold, thy maid is in thine hand; do to her as it pleaseth thee. And when Sarai dealt hardly with her, she fled from her face. (7)And the angel of the LORD found her by a fountain of water in the wilderness, by the fountain in the way to Shur. (8)And he said, Hagar, Sarai's maid, whence camest thou? and whither wilt thou go? And she said, I flee from the face of my mistress Sarai. (9)And the angel of the LORD said unto her, return to thy mistress, and submit thyself under her hands. (10)And the angel of the LORD said unto her, I will multiply thy seed exceedingly, that it shall not be numbered for multitude. (11)And the angel of the LORD said unto her, Behold, thou art with child and shalt bear a son, and shalt call his name Ishmael; because the LORD hath heard thy affliction. (12) And he will be a wild man; his hand will be against every man, and every man's hand against him; and he shall dwell in the presence of all his brethren.

Getting back to the central point for this chapter takes us back to the Book of Genesis which states "let **US** make man." When looking to the Qur'an at a similar passage it says, "it is **WE** who created you." Many other ancient stories like the stories of Enki and Enlil which predate biblical scriptures by over 2,000 years paints a picture that the race of mankind who was created on the earth was originally created to be a subservient race for the gods. These stories date back to ancient Sumer and their remnants are seen in the story of the Genesis in the Bible.

Enki was a god in Sumerian mythology, later known as Ea in Akkadian and Babylonian mythology. He was the deity of crafts mischief; water, seawater, and lakewater intelligence and creation. Considered the master shaper of the world, god of wisdom and of all magic, Enki was characterized as the lord of the Abzu the freshwater sea or groundwater located within the earth 112 b. Enki explains that Enlil is unfair to punish the guiltless Atrahasis for the sins of his fellows, and secures a promise that the gods will not eliminate humankind if they practice birth control and live within the means of the natural world. The threat is made, however, that if humans do not honor their side of the covenant the gods will be free to wreak havoc once again 112c.

Enlil the ancient earth god of Sumer, is worshiped in Babylonian religion with the sky god Anu and the water god Ea who form the great divine triad. Enlil, also referred to as Bel, could be hostile or beneficent. He was responsible for the order and harmony in the universe, but as a god of storms and winds he brought terrible destruction. According to legend, the other gods rebelled against Enlil because he made them work too hard. As a solution, the gods decided to create humans to labor for them. This seemed fine for a while, but as the human population increased, their noise kept Enlil awake at night. Angered by this disruption, Enlil sent disease, drought, and a great flood to reduce the number of people on the earth 112d.

If the word Gentile is broken down it literally translates as obtained or produced by a gene. See also German /Germ/Man

Gene: a linear sequence of nucleotides along a segment of DNA that provides the coded instructions from synthesis of RNA, which, when translated into protein, leads to the expression of hereditary character

Tile: obtained by, or produced by

Germ: (1): a small mass of living substance capable of developing into an organism or one of its parts (2) something that initiates development or serves as an origin

In the Qur'an the Iblis represents the same energy/ spirit as the Lucifer in Christian Mythology. Lucifer according to Islamic Mythology was the perfect angel. It has been said that he was "God's" highest creation and when man was made, God wanted Iblis to bow to him. Iblis refused because he felt that he was of a more pure substance than (man.) He also felt no one served "the Father" with the zeal and tenacity he had. Being he was made of pure fire, and considered to be "God's" perfect creation, he refused to be subordinate to beings he considered inferior. I feel the need here to play devil's advocate so the reader can look from a perspective that is most like their own. When anything that we read has a negative connotation or stigma associated with it, the people reading conveniently jump on the side of the victor, which in the biblical sense is "God." I don't think it arrogance to presuppose that the reader not being "God" or a god would be able to relate to "God" in matters of judgment. Because people usually rebel against authority, I am playing devil's advocate so the reader can see from a perspective that is most "humanistic" and like their own. The Bible also gives an account whereby Lucifer revolts against God and is sent to the underworld.

Isaiah 14:12-15 (12) How art thou fallen from heaven, O Lucifer, son of the morning! how art thou cut down to the ground, which didst weaken the nations! (13) For thou hast said in thine heart, I will ascend into heaven, I will exalt my throne above the stars of God: I will sit also upon the mount of the congregation, in the sides of the north: (14) I will ascend above the heights of the clouds; I will be like the most High. (15) Yet thou shalt be brought down to hell, to the sides of the pit.

The account above is taken from the Book of Isaiah and is written from "God's" perspective and not Lucifer's. But think about it, if you were made from the essence of the Sun/ fire and energy itself, what would make you bow to clay. If you were looking at "God" you may start to think that he's senile or that maybe because he is excited about his new creations it has caused him to err in his judgment. To you, it may seem as if his ego has gotten in the way of him recognizing who is who. If your dad did you like this, how would you react? I put it in these terms because "God" to Lucifer is like his father. If Lucifer didn't have the power to rival "God" would there be a story? A worthy adversary has to be able to rival his opponent. You wouldn't want to see Mike Tyson in his prime fight Floyd Mayweather right? You want to see a heavy weight fight someone who is equally proportioned or matched. If Lucifer didn't stand a chance in raising opposition towards "God" what would be the point in making him "God's" chief adversary? What we also have to realize about the story is again it is printed, and anything that is in print is subject to edit. If the people who gave the present world its knowledge about "God" (*even in that he's referenced by God and not his actual name*) how would people know who they say is "God" really is God?

The story of Iblis not bowing could really be about how people in power forget about the people who worship and serve them the most; and when the new person comes along how the (devout servers) are made to serve them after they've given years of service and have done extraordinary works. In many cases it is usually the under bosses who do all of the tedious yet cardinal work to keep a business or organization functioning. These under bosses from their perspectives are overworked and not appreciated for "holding things down." They see the rulers as becoming soft, aged, arrogant and dull. When the under bosses feel they are taken for granted they become passive aggressive and a revolt usually in some way will occur. This may be THAT story, but because aristocrats, and scribes have put the stories together, we may have received a translation that suited their perspective. This is a very critical perhaps even perverse way of looking at these scriptures, however I felt the need to literally play "Devil's" advocate to show how people conveniently jump on the side of "God" even though in their lives they are clearly on the opposing spectrum. Here again I am just giving this story a realistic back drop so the reader may get a different perspective of the events foretold. The fact that *The God* everyone is referencing has all of these human characteristics yet no one can see him or has seen him is very puzzling as well. However if this "God" does walk the earth and indeed has these human characteristics then the question would be is what separates the God(s) from the men? Many points that I make within this book are relative to each other and the deeper you get into the book the more you see these points come together. One of those points mentioned is that people only ride with "God" because they are scared of evil. Because people don't really understand evil, they make it out to be the worst thing that has ever taken place on earth. The paradox to this is most people have to act good. I say this because they eat other animals, wear their skins, they litter, poison and pollute their environments, kill each other in wars both foreign and domestic, and cannot get along with one another. They do all of these things continually yet they all say and feel they are good and are going to heaven. If this is the upside down perspective that people have taken let's look at good and evil through this perspective as well. Maybe the god that is easiest to serve is the god of evil…And maybe this god of evil is what scares people because they realize that something and someone more evil then they are will dominate them and have no mercy on them just as they have no mercy upon life forms they've deemed inferior. When people come to this point in their minds it makes them construct within it a merciful counter to that aspect of themselves that will do the easiest thing. It is only when they foresee their own destruction do they look at what is perceived to be "God." This merciful counterpart is the God that is acknowledged only after the realizations of what a person has done and is why Adam and Eve turn back to "God" after realizing they have eaten the forbidden fruit.

One of the reasons the "gay" culture has become dominant in all aspects of corporate and private business is they own up to their lifestyles, and they face them with pride and vigor, as they have accepted who they are. They lack the "God" complex previously referenced and because they are highly sensitive, and receptive, they very easily can recognize something is wrong. In their recognition, they aren't afraid to explore or revel in the other side. They don't care about being perceived by those who practice religion as the Devil or evil because they see the evil men do every day and also how these men (people) justify it in the name of "God." And if what these "justifiers" say is God, is God, the Devil then doesn't look so bad. The "gay" culture is courageous enough to admit something is wrong and they live with it regardless to the outcome. They are the true messengers and their lives are beacons that reflect the conditions in a society that appears to be good and upright but really is numb and turns a blind eye to its own hypocritical origins, concepts, ways of existence, and laws. This is a critical examination that explains the ideology and meteoric rise of the artist known today as Lady Gaga.

When you think about life and what type of lifestyles the masses desire, everyone wants to "ball till they fall." Look at the word live or lived backwards and what do you get, evil and the devil. If you gave a person a choice of living in an honest farming and agricultural country where they had to exist in the confines of nature and till the soil; or a country that manipulates everything, has strip malls and air conditioned housing, where do you think people are going to live? If you have any problem finding your answers just look at America. My point here is that people have to first ask themselves what it is they are analyzing and from that point make a solid judgment with knowledge and study to get closer to the truths they have placed their beliefs in. In my theory I reckon "God" to be a physical entity that walks the earth. One, because all the books that reference a "God" refer to him as having a physical form, the other because scientifically and physically no being can exist in the earth realm without taking a material or elemental form. So if people have written about "God" and he has never taken a material form, than everything written about him in this way IS and HAS TO BE FALSE. When many atheists say they don't believe in "God" they may believe in a higher power, just not the power that man has written about in the New Testament of the Bible. If a person cannot understand this point they might as well stop reading this book right now.

What we are reading through the stories of the Bible, the Bhaga Vita, and the Qu'ran, are attempts to explain events that mankind cannot fully articulate or understand. The reason being is explaining it will ultimately cause destruction. This is said because in the explanation is a very deep and dark secret that will be revealed. The revelation of this secret causes those who are culprits of it to reject it. Being of lower intelligence, upon rejecting it, they will do so in a war-like fashion. They will want to tear the world up. They will be so mad and angry that they won't want anything or anybody to live which is why the Book of Revelation precedes the Armageddon.

Those who do not wish to be exposed by the lie they have perpetuated, have used the media, like a weapon to assassinate the characters of those who do have "star lined" destinies. Rather than rounding all of the scholars and leaders of the world together in a public forum, and pulling out all of the ancient texts to see who and what is this physical "God" that everybody is talking about; they further perpetuate the lies and ignorance that keeps the masses distracted and satisfied. I think an important fact to note is it wasn't until 1979 that the Roman Mother Church formally accepted Galileo's heliocentric solar system model. What is also important to remember is the Bible is a compilation of stories that show aspects of the lives of the "gods" lifetimes recorded through written text. These "gods" again are embodiments of celestial energy i.e. (star energy) and when they come to earth, they take human forms. Most scholars and people who have written about or compiled this evidence DO NOT understand this fully. The ones who do have clues understand the comprehension level of the masses and due to this; they keep the knowledge hidden and esoteric. In fact this is directly related to the charge of Adam and Eve to stay away from the tree of knowledge. Because people who aren't supposed to rule wish to rule and control other people, they distort reality so the people aren't able to see they are imposter's (*The Wizard of Oz*) Simultaneously, you have people who have fallen or have not accomplished certain goals in their life, and due to bitterness they want to bring the people who strive for excellence down where they are. We saw this with the life and trial of Michael Jackson. When you put the ruling priest imposters, with the people who have fallen and are bitter together; what you have created is a rink whereby the ruling priest imposters promote the agendas of degenerates, who in turn know they wouldn't have the positions for any other reason than being a tool. These tools follow suit with the agendas of those on top to suppress the real hero who will inevitably emerge. This was seen in the Movie *300* when the hunch back was promoted and initiated by Xerxes to expose the whereabouts of the Spartans. The same people who wish to control the masses have done so by making the person (s) who has no star lined destinies into a "star" and have kept hidden from the world the person(s) who is/are actually the stars written in the "books of antiquity." In doing so when the person who is destined to come arrives, the people who so desperately tried to stop him will become obsolete, much to the like that Jesse Jackson did at President Obama's 1st Electoral College victory.

RACE RELATIONS RELOADED

When we began talking about the Genesis and the races that were created in it, we must 1st have a basic understanding of genetics and what part they pay in ancient literature. If we study genealogy and look at dominant and recessive genes in races of (Homo sapiens), how would we find out who possesses the superior or more dominant genes? For these reasons there would have to be some game or sport "divine play" that would peacefully determine who the most evolved is. These games performed in ancient times were called the Olympics, conveniently named after the "gods" who presided over Mount Olympus.

In today's time the dominance of Negroes in any field of sport is extraordinary. Whether it is soccer, (Pele) Golf (Tiger Woods) American football (Jerry Rice) baseball, (Barry Bonds) tennis (Serena Williams,) track and field (Usain Bolt) boxing (Floyd Mayweather Jr.) blacks are amongst the most dominant of the players. Once again we would have to use a sport that combines strength, speed, ingenuity, endurance, and team involvement to determine who out of all participants has the most evolved genetics. Let's use the sport of basketball since it combines speed, strength, endurance, and team involvement. The most prolific figure in sports history is none other than Michael Jordan. Michael Jordan gives us an un-tampered, unbiased view of the black gene in the gene pool, and through his reign we can see just how dominant this "dark" gene is.

Look at Michael Jordan when on the basketball court, doesn't he appear God-like. He flies through the air, conquers all in his path, and does inhuman feats on the court with a basketball. If you were a spectator or fan, how do you think that you (that fan) would describe Michael Jordan to other people who weren't there?

You would probably describe him as superman or as a god. In fact Larry Bird is quoted as calling Michael Jordan "*God in a pair of basketball shoes*" 112dd. I included this modern day quote from Larry Bird so people can understand the way the term/word/noun/adjective (god) was used in the time when the hieroglyphs were written is no different than the way (god) is used today.

Daniel 3:25 (25) *He said, "Look! I see four men walking around in the fire, unbound and unharmed, and the fourth looks like a <u>son of the gods</u>."*

But even if a person where to take an assessment of Michael Jordan and his characteristics, again the being that he represents *spiritually,* would make people readily understand that he was more than a man. Michael Jordan was born on February 17th in the sign Aquarius, known in Astrology as a fixed

(angelic) masculine air sign. The popular title given to Michael Jordan was "Air Jordan." When Michael was drafted to Chicago, the "windy city," the elements and energy of that city enhanced his abilities exalting him to his position as the "god of air," which is reflected by his logo which allegorically represents a man (Aquarius) reaching up and touching the Sun.

At this time, I'd like to point out the geographical city and area that propelled Michael Jordan to his destiny. Chicago, the 3rd largest city in America, is located in the Midwest and in a sense, is the central point of America. Likened to the eye of a storm the "windy city" is home to the Sears Tower, once the largest building in the world. This tower touches the "heavens" and is a magnetic harvesting center designed to attract major celestial energies which in turn attracts trade, money, people, and commerce. This would explain how 3 gigantic icons of this time, Michael Jordan, Oprah Winfrey, and Barack Obama all rose to prominence in this city. Another important fact to notate is Gary Indiana, the birthplace of Michael Jackson, is 35 miles from the cities center. If Indiana was located inside Illinois, it's close enough to be considered one of Chicago's suburbs. Each of these icons also has a connection with the Leo and Aquarius energy, which as we have discussed, is the Sphinx and key to mysteries as well as the riddles of the gods.

When the original earth inhabitants first physically walked the earth they were unadulterated and contained a very pure hue. Think about how strong coffee gets when you use a whole lot of coffee beans. The significance here is found in the word strong. This isn't strong in the physical sense like having muscles; it is strong in the sense of being concentrated or unadulterated, i.e. pure. This is where we begin to understand how the word "strong" is used in association with "God."

As previously stated, when Eve slept with a "black god" the bi-product was Cain, known as the first Jew. This mixture symbolized the integration of god and man and birthed a different outlook and interpretation of life itself for the newly created being. The birth of Cain is the first account on why the one who is called Christ would be a (Jew) or an Asiatic/Black Semite. Cain having committed the "murder" was marked by his skin. This marker is also an allegorical clue that highlights the dominant nature and genes of the beings that were born of the Serpent and Eve. At that time Cain was of a brown color as he was a mixture between "God" and man, black and red. He easily stood out because of his mixture and because he committed the murder, he was cursed. The curse was the bi-product of the prophecy stated by "God" that there would be strife between Eve's child and Adam's child. Later in the Bible we see this same clutching of the heel with Jacob and Esau. By taking an in depth look inside the story of Cain and Abel, the translation of the children fighting in the womb can be looked at as a direct allegory related to the strife and natural opposition that both white and black energies have for one another. If these energies are reflected within people, than the people will have the same type of conflicting and quarreling relationship. Fighting in the womb is an allegory synonymous to fighting in the MOTHERLAND. The motherland is Africa and when you look at its history and how the continent has been war ravaged between Jews, Arabs, Europeans, and Africans you see just how prophetic this statement is. Naturally the black represents the feminine which is the most dominant form of existence; however it is also the most un-stable and chaotic. The white is the more docile of the two, and is more rational and calculating. Black and white have always existed together eternally just as masculinity and femininity has. Even before they were polarized between two separate entities the masculine always existed within the feminine and the white always existed within the black.

Cain, the dominant son's, murder over Abel, the docile son, is one of great controversy. The seed of Adam was proven to be more docile than the seed of EVE AND THE SERPENT. Cain perceiving his brother Abel as being docile (gentle/Gentile) murdered the weaker link. This is a customary practice as the weak or sickly child in a village was often killed or banished because if it gets sick it will infect others causing the whole village to perish. For these reasons, human sacrifices to Molech were a part of ancient Semitic customs.

Leviticus 18:21 (21) And thou shalt not let any of thy seed pass through the fire to Molech, neither shalt thou profane the name of thy God: I am the LORD.

Adam and Eve sleeping with one another produced a "physically weaker" child as those of recessive genes together in nature will do. The child again was named Abel. So Cain's murdering of Abel could be perceived as instinctive intuition, versus a malicious attempt to get rid of his brother due to jealousy. This story depicts the first account of Darwinism, and the interpretation of this story uses a very basic and carnal example. When looking at this story through nature's scope, it seems justified that Cain murdered Abel. Think about it in terms of your life and reality today. Anything that people feel isn't human like rats, snakes, roaches, and rodents they will kill in an instant. In fact this was the very justification that Romans used when they killed and enslaved people and the same rationale used in *Inglorius Basterds* by the character known as the "Jew Hunter." People who hunt often kill instinctively. Imagine if you were a god and were crossbred with another form of being different and inferior to you. What do you think psychologically that would do to you? It probably would make you into a beast and beasts kill any and everything they deem weaker then themselves.

Genesis 3:4-5 *For God doth know that in the day that you eat thereof, then your eyes will be opened, and ye shall be as Gods, knowing good and evil.*

Enoch VII. *and all others (angels) together with them took unto themselves wives, and each chose for himself one. and they began to go into them and defile themselves with them, and they became pregnant, and bare great giants whose height was three thousand elles. Who consumed all the acquisitions of men and when men could no longer sustain them. The giants turned against them and devoured mankind.*

Few people who are apart of society, and the lies therein, have the ability to understand beyond the limiting scope of what they can physically see. This is due directly to their ability or inability to face truth. Most people when coming into an understanding either face the facts or they do what is easiest for them. Often times the truth hurts and is so painful that people would rather live in the delusion than face the reality. For these reasons, Rabbi's and high religious leaders who constructed the Bible gave the people watered down versions of religion. They kept things generic in order for those who have low comprehension levels to understand the basics.

ILLUSION

The delusion that these people live in is (Maya.) This is the place where they have to constantly be distracted and entertained to keep their thoughts and minds from chaos and destruction. This entertainment is through cable television programs, games, sports and basic media in general. Because the individual chooses not to objectively pursue the truths that he/she sees is in front of them, they are often distracted by things that entertain them. If what they are entertained by is perversion they will become perverts. In a society like America there are so many things that a person can be entertained by. Companies who wish to sell products to people research what people are most stimulated by. Young people especially, have a knack for participating in all things forbidden and taboo; because their curiosity and inquisition is so high the industries that have labels like **XXX** and **PARENTAL ADVISORY** on the packaging of their product usually sell big.

The things that people distract themselves with usually pull them further astray from who they are. The prophets and godsends have through time given the people certain knowledge's to ensure that they get the information on how to stay connected to the truth that will keep them healthy "in a heavenly state." These knowledge's have been recorded in the holy books, the Bhaga Vita, the Torah, the Qur'an, and the Bible. However the more that people disbelieve in the basic truths, the more people become susceptible to follow a lie. The more the people follow the lie, the more the lie becomes a reality. I said all that to say this; because for so long humans have strayed away from the truth about their existence and the nature that they exist in, they have forgotten the very sciences of pyramids, the celestial bodies (gods) and how, why, and when they manifest on earth.

SONS OF GOD VS THE NEPHILIM

In the kingdom of earth you have 4 quadrants. These four quadrants consist of the four elements, fire, earth, air, and water. Water and earth are on the surface and fire and air are above it. The fire and air represents the higher portions of the kingdom and the earth and water represent the lower portions of the kingdom. Lower is mentioned because again water and earth are on the planet's surface. The higher portion of the "Kingdom of Israel" is attributed to the sky and light. This is why in the Bible they say that "God" is coming from the sky because water, air, and light all comes from the sky. The combination of all three of these substances is why the Roman's worship the god of storms which is regarded as being Zeus in their mythology. We discussed the relationship between Zeus (Jupiter) earlier in how the Romans worshiped this planet over the Sun. This is further demonstrated when we think about how atmosphere (clouds), and storms block out the rays of the Sun giving mankind below tolerable and pleasant weather as well as volatile and horrendous tempests. If you were a layman then you would think that this god of storms has the power to rival the Sun. In Masonry Gabriel is said to have a red square banner with an eagle and the sign of the planet Jupiter, all symbols and aspects of Zeus *113.* If the Sun god of the east known in Egypt as Heru was combined with the Roman god of thunder and storms in the west Zeus, what you would have in that combination is He/ Zeus or Jesus, a combination of the fiery serpent the lion and the eagle in the form of a man.

Again, in Astrology fire and air are attributed to the mind and intelligence. When the chroniclers and writers of Egyptian legend were translating these stories from ancient Egyptian hieroglyphs they put the higher aspects of "God"/creation into beings that had these attributes. The bottom part of the kingdom of Earth is where they placed the carnal or "lower" aspects of God. The water signs in Astrology represent emotions, and Scorpio the fixed water sign, is influenced by the sexual organs. The earth signs are called the sensual signs, but this isn't meant in the sexual sense. Sensuality in this sense pertains to all things described in these signs that relate to the senses and the carnal world. These four elements represent the Kingdom of Israel; again, the bottom portion is earth and water, the higher portion is fire and air.

When the gods fall from heaven to earth, from a carnal/elemental perspective, it is felt through lighting, rain, and the Sun's rays. This is why this romantic imagery has been expressed in poetry and ancient literature. So if the Sun god (Heru) through thunder (Zeus/Thor) strikes the earth (Virgin/Virgo) and a Hero (Man) is born, we can see how these myths were formed from elemental truths in nature. In the Egyptian model the SUN occupies a position that is higher than the sky, and is only affected by clouds, air, and atmosphere on the earth. This Sun in regards to the other corresponding celestial planets, is the Most High God as it is the one seen the clearest and most brilliant in the heavens (sky.) If I were to create a "literal" story about the origins of creation in relevance to man and "God" based on these aforementioned acknowledgements; I would associate the high gods with the gods of fire and air and lower gods with water and earth. In Israel the northern part of the kingdom is Israel and the southern part of the kingdom is Judah. Judah as regarded by the Genesis is a Lion's whelp and Israel is succeeded by Joseph.

Genesis 49:9 (9) Judah is a lion's whelp: from the prey, my son, thou art gone up: he stooped down, he couched as a lion, and as an old lion; who shall rouse him up.

Being that the sphinx is a symbol in Egypt that is half man, half lion, we can use this symbol in making an evaluation in terms of Israel and Judah. Since the higher aspects of "God" are attributed to air we have to attribute the southern part of the kingdom to Israel which is the "all god" containing the spiritual and astrological energies of (EL) (Aquarius/MAN) (RA/Sun Leo/ LION) (ISIS/ the virgin/Virgo) and the northern part solely to Judah or Leo. The northern kingdom is attributed to Leo/lion because the light that hits the planet comes from the Sun. Upon this "Let there be Light" phenomenon, that shines on the planet Earth, all elements of earth, air, and water are seen and are now visible showcasing everything that is living in it. Because fire and air travel together as air strengthens fire, both of these elements are in a sense one in the same, making the full spectrum of the Kingdom of Israel a link between Man and Lion or Leo and Aquarius. This is why Horus is also the patron of Upper Egypt and the Holy One of Israel. Isis, Ra, and El rule the entire nation of Israel that was desegregated between upper and lower regions by the god Ptah. Even though Judah is popularly regarded as the southern kingdom, and Israel the northern kingdom, these two kingdoms flip and change places with each precession making them interchangeable, pending on what aspect there being judged by. Michael Jackson being born in Gary Indiana again would make the northern part of Israel that of Northern America and Judah being from the Southern region of America, Texas, where Nasa and the largest Army Base Fort Hood are located, are indications that the northern and southern tribes of Israel have gods born from these regions in America.

In understanding Masonry and all its aspects, the central theme associated with it is that of naming and building legends. *"The word by its very being makes everything be furthermore the naming side of the word entails the naming of actual men and turns them into the protagonists of a legendary plot, thereby building up a legend."* Alexander Piatigorsky 112e.

Here is an example of how a legend can be assembled when the person building the legend has esoteric information about the characters, the plot and the theme associated with the myth. This example will include allegory as well as pertinent historical information that relates directly to the race the gods created and the result that ended in the fall of "God" to Mankind. In this example, keep in mind, when any one person is referenced they represent a nation of people and beings.

A Sun is born in a new galaxy and the light from it is now penetrating the dark areas of space. When the light hits the matter of space the energy within it takes a material form. This material formed beings that represented the energy the light was made of. They took shape upon the new matter (earth), and formed the original gods. They were equally yoked and separated by masculine and feminine qualities and in turn were attracted to one another. The first to manifest on the surface of the matter was the light itself who was the one chief who became the leader and the most powerful. The second was air, the third was water, and the fourth was earth. Each God that manifested had aspects of the other thus you had four beings each in every element that existed. You had the fire fire, the air fire, the earth fire, and the water fire. There was also the air fire, the air air, the air earth, and the air water. This continued with the earth fire, the earth air the earth earth and the earth water and continued with the water fire, the water air the water earth and the water water. The High gods were the double gods of fire fire and air air, and their counterparts were the double goddesses of earth earth and water water. These gods now started to build a kingdom and they ruled for thousands of years with peace and prosperity. The double gods because they were more concentrated and powerful became the monarchs and the original light, the chief, ruled over them. However the other gods who weren't as concentrated as the high gods felt they being also "original" should have the right to be in the high council. They proposed this to the high gods and the high gods demonstrated their power over them showing them who was boss. The other gods seeing they were no match for the unadulterated gods began to consort with one another. They figured if they bred, by sheer number, they would be able to overthrow the unadulterated gods. So they left the abode for the wilderness or unshaped parts of the new matter and began to mate with one another. When they felt satisfied that they had sufficient numbers they marched back into the kingdom where the unadulterated gods were and a war broke out. Many of the offspring were slaughtered but because there were so many other gods, the high gods were overthrown from their kingdom. This is when the high gods in defeat figured if they were to survive they would need to retreat and formulate a plan. They took council and decided to also mate together, but when they could not procreate at as rapid a pace as their enemies they decided to clone and cultivate beings from their DNA. When their numbers were sufficient, they would then be able to march back in and rightfully regain their positions as the rulers of their kingdom. So they too retreated to the wilderness and the first and chief double fire god mated with the double earth goddess and produced a Super god who was more powerful than any being that existed. He alongside the offspring of the unadulterated gods and the clones went back into the kingdom where the other gods where leisurely existing allowing the kingdom to fall into ruin. They dethroned and slew many of the other adulterated gods that had existed in the land. The high gods regained their position however now because the son of the double earth and double fire god and goddess had done such an admirable feat all of the other high gods and their offspring now worshipped him instead of the double fire god.

This legend that I am building is based on the Genesis whereby man was said to be made by the gods to rule over the kingdom of earth. When the scriptures say "let us make man" this is a reference that the "God" and "Goddess" (queen) have decided to copulate to bring about a hero in the body of a man. The reason for their copulation was because the sons of fornication, which were created because the gods had many consorts, had basically taken over the kingdom where the gods were supposed to rule. These "sons of fornication" were the offspring created by the high gods having sex outside of the proper season(s) i.e. fornication. Once the gods began copulating idly, their offspring (lower gods /angels) began to multiply beyond their control running amok in the holy land. The unwanted offspring are what we call today demons. Demons are *"what is left behind"* and represent the child or children who in the creation process lack the overriding genetic upgrade, or "good genes." These children will fight the one who has the good genes and will always attempt to thwart and set those with good genes on destructive courses. This was seen in the Genesis in the story of Joseph, and also in **John 8:40-42**

John 8:40-42 **(40)** *But now ye seek to kill me, a man that hath told you the truth, which I have heard of God: this did not Abraham. (41)Ye do the deeds of your father. Then said they to him,* <u>We be not born of fornication</u>; *we have one Father, even God. (42)Jesus said unto them, If God were your Father, ye would love me: for I proceeded forth and came from God; neither came I of myself, but he sent me.*

This conflict between the have and havenot of the genetic world is where the division between higher gods and lower gods began and also where 'human sacrifices' found their origin. The gods being unable to control their sexual urges began to have many children born out of their signs in respect to masculine and feminine properties. Sacrificing their unwanted (offspring) became as much a part of their lives as living itself. Remember the gods were omnipotent highly regenerative sexual beings. –Back to the Legend-

After the ostracization, when the high god set out to create a man or a son, he took into account everything that son would need genetically in order to conquer the land and terrain that was now threatened by the unruly offspring of the adulterated gods. Before the high god ever manifested in the matter he separated his masculine and feminine selves so when he landed upon the matter (earth), he now had to find the feminine aspect of himself which was the goddess. Upon locating the goddess as he was now on a lower plane, (the matter itself) through her he created a being whose sole purpose was to be the slayer of all the (demonic) and unruly adulterated gods offspring. The being he created had a survival based mentality and also had the dexterity of the high god and the deviant nature of the demon fused together within his being. This happened because he was birth by way of the high god descending to a lower nature (earth) in order to bring about his, (man's /Adams) existence. So when the other angels fell to earth to produce through themselves powerful offspring to rival the high god, the high god himself created from a goddess and birthed through her a supremely powerful being. This being was purely Arien/ war driven and his name was Adam.

Those who robbed the tombs and hieroglyphs, to pass it off for their knowledge, associated the Flood, which symbolizes the Age of Aquarius and the beginning of the grand year where the Sun moves through all the constellations; to be the beginning of the physical material world itself. However this Age of Aquarius marks the beginning of the world that is conscious of itself. *"Let there be light"* means this point in the constellation marks the time in which a supreme consciousness gave shape and construction to everything unconscious in the material world around it. This supreme consciousness was known in ancient Egypt as Ptah and is known in the literary world as the Demiurge or Logos. This is particularly significant because the being known as Logos was conscious of everything, but not everything was conscious of him/it. He /it has to be man's/Earth's architect, for only he knew the origins of what exists in it. If Egyptians gods were the founders and the people who birth civilization, then it would also hint to the notion they also created it. When you factor life is neither created nor destroyed, with reincarnation between lifetimes, what you have is people either ascending to higher states of consciousness, or lower states of consciousness. The lower states are states that are not conscious of the previous levels, which would make one who is conscious of all the other levels the supreme conscious of consciousness.

I broke away from the legend to have a conversation regarding the knowledge and information behind it that serves as its basis. In order to keep track with the legend I've constructed, it is important to give the reader additional information that enables them to better understand what the Genesis and Flood actually represents. - Back to the Legend-

The son of the double fire and earth god and goddess known as the MAN had no restrictions and grew to be very coveted by the lower gods. To be able to live a life and do whatever you wanted appealed greatly to them (lower gods). The man in their eyes was seen as having a perfected existence because he truly had freewill. Freewill is what the lower gods wanted because they were restricted by the laws of Ma'at. The high gods knew that the laws of the Universe would bring about certain consequences for certain actions. Some actions lowered their birthright. If they did lowly things they understood they would come back in a lower form. As a result the lower gods figured if they could rid themselves of the Ma'at complex then they would have the ability to truly live as a high god, which in their view was a being that encompassed all power, even the power to do so as it pleased. Their interpretation was, "If you were a high god, then why can't you do whatever you want?

Ma'at: the Ancient Egyptian concept of truth, balance, order, law, morality, and justice, regulating the stars, seasons, and the actions of both mortals and the deities who set the order of the universe from chaos at the moment of creation.

The Book of Enoch sheds light on this subject, and though it is an apocryphal book, its contents are still relevant in exposing the relationship between fallen angels, God, and the rest of humanity and mankind.

VI-XI. The Fall of the Angels: the Demoralization of Mankind: the Intercession of the Angels on behalf of Mankind. The Dooms pronounced by God on the Angels of the Messianic Kingdom-- (a Noah fragment) - Enoch 7:1 (1) And all the others together with them took unto themselves wives, and each chose for himself one, and they began to go in unto them and to defile themselves with them, and they taught them charms (2)and enchantments, and the cutting of roots, and made them acquainted with plants. (3) And they became pregnant, and they bare great giants, whose height was three thousand ells: Who consumed (4) all the acquisitions of men. And when men could no longer sustain them, the giants turned against (5) them and devoured mankind. And they began to sin against birds, and beasts, and reptiles, and (6) fish, and to devour one another's flesh, and drink the blood. Then the earth laid accusation against the lawless ones.

Here again is where the mystery begins. The Bible gives a completely different interpretation of the events entailing angels who consort with women. Here is the account of these same events as told by the Genesis.

Genesis 6:1-4 (1) *And it came to pass, when men began to multiply on the face of the earth, and daughters were born unto them, (2) That the sons of God saw the daughters of men that they were fair; and they took them wives of all which they* *chose. (3) And the LORD said, My spirit shall not always strive with man, for that he also is flesh: yet his days shall be an hundred and twenty years. (4) There were giants in the earth in those days; and also after that, when the sons of God came in unto the daughters of men, and they bare children to them, the same became mighty men which <u>were of old, men of renown</u>.*

The 15th chapter of the Book of Enoch may have the explanation we are looking for.

***XII - XVI. Dream -Vision of Enoch:** his Intercession for Azâzêl and the Fallen Angels: and his Announcement of their first and final Doom.*

15:3-6 (3) for you: Wherefore have ye left the high, holy, and eternal heaven, and lain with women, and defiled yourselves with the daughters of men and taken to yourselves wives, and done like the children (4) of earth, and begotten giants (as your) sons? And though ye were holy, spiritual, living the eternal life, you have defiled yourselves with the blood of women, and have begotten (children) with the blood of flesh, and, as the children of men, have lusted after flesh and blood as those also do who die (5) and perish. Therefore have I given them wives also that they might impregnate them, and beget (6) children by them, that thus nothing might be wanting to them on earth.

Men of renown and honor are what the people of the old days called their heroes; the Book of Enoch paints them as monstrous. Though the Book of Enoch is usually regarded as being part of the Apocrypha, which are a compilation of books left out of the Bible, it is still relevant when comparing the Bibles contradictory viewpoints. It is very bizarre that the Bible has so many different books that contradict one another and add so much confusion to "God's" holy words.

What stands between a legend and the history proper is a text. If that text has a credible history provenance and is not an invention, it is history proper. And if that text does not survive in its original form it was largely invented… So history in this instance must also include the invention of history" 114.

I placed this quote within the book at this time because anytime history's records are lost or unknown a history is created in place of the lost knowledge. Countless stories that we see today were constructed by Masons, as Masonry again consists of the naming and building of legends. Many of the comic book characters, as well as cartoons referenced in this book were all created by Masons. Because Masons have physically built the monuments and cities as well as the legends and myths that have influenced all of pop culture only adds legitimacy to why they call or worship the Supreme Consciousness and reference him as being the Great Architect. Alexander Piatigorsky who wrote the book *Freemasonry* explained what happens when the history isn't there when a legend is being constructed. He said the history in regards to the legend is then created to go along with the legend. This *"made up"* history is what may have caused the inconsistency within the Bibles scriptures as indicated within this book. This information was cited as a rebuttal to the question of why so many books in the Bible contradict each other. One of the most plausible explanations is because the Bible had many writers. Those writers translated and interpreted scriptures in different ways, not to mention they went as far as retranslating certain things to hide knowledge from people with low comprehension. This is why in Masonry you have knowledge that is exoteric and available to the masses and knowledge that is esoteric which is only viewable/ knowable by the initiated elite.

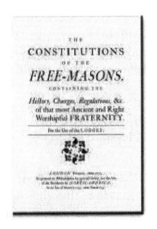

Dr. James Anderson, a Freemason, was the master of a Masonic lodge, and Grand Warden of the Grand Lodge of London and Westminster. He was commissioned in September of 1721 by the Grand Lodge to write a history of the Free-Masons, and it was published in 1723 as The Constitutions of the Free-Masons 115. In the constitution, Dr. Anderson states, *"being a mason is being the natural state of man at his creation by God, the great architect of the universe"* 116. The most natural state of an individual is their inner truest selves which points to Astrology. Being that which is within you, at the time of your creation is what in a sense the author of the Masonic constitution states, is being a Mason. Again these Masons mimic and discuss all of the things in relation to the architect, or Supreme consciousness that created ADAM/Atum/Atem. Dr. Anderson went on further to say that, *"Masonry is the name of the mythological elite, the existence of which had always guaranteed the perpetuation of civilized societies"* 117. The mythological elite are those astral deities like the ones mentioned in this book who are present in their myths the same way they are in their actual lives. For these reasons everyone living in a civilization has associated the MAN who was created to civilize and rule a kingdom on earth, as THE MAN who they were in a sense, the offspring of (Adam.) This is found in the commentary spoken of in the 8th Chapter of John in the Bible. The reason people feel this way about this subject, is it was taught to them by The Roman Catholic Church. Those who wished for their own political agendas to be orchestrated used the church as a means to *civilize* the masses with these teachings. Because mankind has attributed their God to being the creator of Adam; it has caused many who have converted to this idea to become perverted in their imaginations about what, where, how, or who this God may be when he walks the earth. Understanding this takes us directly to how the accounts of myth can have truths and falsehoods side by side. It is only when looking at the complete history that the truth separates from the myths.

Myth: a traditional or legendary story, usually concerning some being or hero or event, with or without a determinable basis of fact or a natural explanation, esp. one that is concerned with deities or demigods and explains some practice, rite, or phenomenon of nature.

Legend: a non-historical or unverifiable story handed down by tradition from earlier times and popularly accepted as historical

When analyzing the building of a myth and piecing together information between what seems to be a record of the same myth with different interpretations; it then causes us to examine both texts to see where the consistencies lie within them. Earlier in the book, with the explanation of the Royal Arch, I revealed how in legend angels were created from the Arch's angles. These angles again point at Astrology which causes us to look at Astrology when making an assessment of both the scriptures in the Book of Enoch and the 6th chapter of Genesis.

In the Book of Enoch the mountain the fallen angels landed on was called Mount Hermon or Armon.

[I Enoch VI.6, vs.1-5] *And the angels, the children of heaven, saw them [handsome and beautiful daughters] and desired them... And they were altogether two hundred; and they descended into Ardos, which is the summit of Hermon. And they called the mount Armon, for they swore and bound one another by a curse"* 118.

When taking into account the place where these fallen angels landed was Mt. Hermon, at first glance, leaves little clue in solving the mystery about why the angels fell and how it relates to Astrology. However when we look at Hermes, a variant form of Hermon/Herman/ who as regarded by legend, knows the sacred rituals that invoke other gods, we find he may have been responsible for "invoking" them to earth. This statement is further supported by the fact that these angels (gods) landed on a mountain named after him. Hermes in masonic legend was a guide for and assisted dead souls to the afterlife. Hermes is also credited as being thrice great (Trismegestis 119a) as he knows the knowledge's of alchemy, invoking, and Astrology.

As we'll analyze later, during the Nicene council after Athanius defeated Arius over his view of God, Athanius then went to teach asceticism and monasticism in Rome and Greece. Hermes Trismegestis was noted to be the founders of the sect of monasticism Athanius was teaching after the council, whereby a prerequisite for the priesthood was celibacy 119. From then until this day is why the men who head the churches of the Roman and Greek cultures are celibate. Hermes also fathered a hermaphroditic son and is responsible for many writings as well as the monasticism practiced today in Christianity. His symbol, the caduceus, is the same symbol, *"the serpent upon the pole"* that Moses lifted up in the wilderness.

Numbers 21:8-9 *(8) And the LORD said unto Moses, <u>Make thee a fiery serpent, and set it upon a pole</u>: and it shall come to pass, that every one that is bitten, when he looketh upon it, shall live. (9)And <u>Moses made a serpent of brass, and put it upon a pole,</u> and it came to pass, that if a serpent had bitten any man, when he beheld the serpent of brass, he lived.*

The relationships between these SUPERSTAR offspring created by gods or angels consorting with women found in the 6th chapter of Genesis are the same people throughout the Bible the masses have been taught to worship i.e. (Jesus, John, Enoch, Isaac.) Again, these cross-bred offspring between "God" and mortals are known in the literary world as being heroes. Though Cain is a bi-product of "God" sleeping with an earthly queen, he is not popularly believed to be a hero, but a villain.

<u>Hero:</u> (1) from Greek hērōs: the offspring of a deity and a mortal

This same relationship is explained through the lives of some very popular movie characters. In occult legend the unrelenting inner man crossbred with a god is known in his dual nature as the "Wolf." This wolf is synonymous to Osiris as well as the land of Canaan "Canine" or Cain. **Conan** (Canaan) **the Barbarian** featuring Arnold Schwarzenegger was a movie depicting the story of the Canaanites. In this legend, Conan was a bi-product of the War driven (man) /mortal and the omnipotent (God) / (The Serpent) played by James Earl Jones. Because Conan was crossbred between them, he had a power that would eventually rival them both.

Another popular character that depicts the Canaanites inner Adam man is **Wolverine,** the X-Men character. WOLVERINE annunciated (Wolve) arine (arien) has an (**ADAM/MAN**/TIUM) indestructible skeleton. The inner Adam man's indestructible skeleton represents the created aspect of himself that was made like a machine. I've used this example of how a myth is created to show how the power of words lays shape to defining the universe around us. *In the Beginning was the word… and the WORD was God* **John 1:1**

This same (Adam Man)/ (Atom Man/see Dr. Manhattan) was created and made for the sole purpose of being the ultimate weapon in combat as well as a ruler and vicegerent for the higher gods of the earth 120.

Now that I have elaborated, we can now get back to the legend I'm building that shows how legends are constructed.

Adam, the son of the double fire and earth gods, now was the ruler of the Kingdom; and as its king, his subjects addressed him as Cain. Cain took consorts of all kinds and his numbers eventually increased because all the goddesses wanted to possess his "heavenly" powers. In the kingdom you now had the Sons of Cain, the higher gods, the offspring of the higher gods, the lower gods, and their offspring. The adulterated gods had been driven out and forced to live in the deserted regions of lower Africa. The sons of Cain were able to overpower the offspring of the adulterated gods, because they possessed the same mind and warrior ethic but had superior strength. Cain wasn't as restricted by Ma'at as the high gods which gave him the tenacity to conquer to an even greater degree than gods or their offspring. Cain was able to rival the gods because he had a mind that made him insensitive towards the plane of the soul. The restrictions the gods had towards karma and laws didn't necessarily apply to Cain. This was stated because he was created on the matter and didn't manifest to the matter's surface as the original unadulterated gods had. The fact that he had the strength and knowledge of the gods made him invincible... Over a period of thousands of years the war between the quarreling races settled and a great migration occurred. The sons of Cain later drove the offspring of the high gods out of civilization of Mesopotamia and into Asia and the Caucuses where they later settled into Europe. The Canaanites that didn't leave to go to the Caucuses who stayed became the people the gods mixed with. These Canaanites along with the gods mixed their customs and became known as the Egyptians. Because they varied in so many different hues it was very difficult for outsiders to tell some of the original Canaanites from the original gods. Eventually you had Canaanites mixing with the same gods who had been driven into other regions like Asia. This is where all of the races of the earth spawned forth from. Through years of these races evolution and adaptation to climate, vegetation and living standards, they eventually all ended up in different parts of Asia and the eastern world with different customs, races, hues and creeds. All of the different races and colors of man came about by way of the mixing and migration between gods and mankind – This took place over thousands of years, each precession causing the same manifestation of deity to reincarnate in the new place the migrations had occurred. -End of the Legend-

I created this legend as an attempt to show the reader how when compositing a legend; historical, allegorical, as well as figurative language and examples are used to pass along the factual basis for events that cannot be explained in an open and public forum. Some of this information would be very offensive in the eyes of those written about, and for these reasons, much of the historical information is omitted from scriptures by scribes so the stories can be universally accepted. For example, according to Edith Sanders, the 6th Century AD Babylonian Talmud states the descendants of Ham/Canaan are cursed by being black and are sinful with a degenerate progeny (offspring.) Slave holders, slavery defenders and racial theorists used this information alongside biblical scriptures to justify black slavery in the Americas 119b.

Genesis 9:25-27 and he said, "Cursed be Canaan; a servant of servants shall he be unto his brethren (26) and he said, blessed be the Lord God of Shem; and Canaan shall be his servant. (27) God shall enlarge Japheth, and he shall dwell in the tents of Shem; and Canaan shall be his servant."

This particular viewpoint suited the ideological interests of the European elite; especially as the chief enemy of Christianity was Islam, which dominated North Africa. Popular belief holds that Islam originated with the Semitic Arabs, however as I have hypothesized in this book, the angel Gabriel is indeed the LORD who comes and engenders sons with women and delivers messages to mankind. This "God" as we have discussed as an avatar (Gabriel) brought his teachings (Qur'an) to a race of men that were Semitic Arabs as again Jibril (Gabriel) revealed the Qur'an to the GREAT prophet Mohammed. This is eerily similar to a man named Quetzalcoatl also known as Viracoacha, and Kukulkan, the fiery Serpent, who was a master builder that brought Mexico civilization, science, the calendar, writings, pyramids, and the secrets of Masonry. Quetzalcoatl was a lawgiver, a protector of craftsmen and the patron of healers, diviners, and all the arts. In the likeness of Vishnu, Quetzalcoatl also made his departure from the earth realm as he sailed away on a bed of serpents 119d. The reference to Quetzalcoatl like the mentioning of other foreign deities in this book is further evidence that shows the same being (deity/ serpent) has again reincarnated on earth to every culture and creed to re-teach and re-promote literally the knowledge of the gods. Every place this Ark/serpent lands marks the place where the stars realign when the constellations reset themselves and the serpent (kundalini) as an avatar, is brought forth to birth civilization. Whether you're in India and knew him as Shiva, China were they knew him as Min, Canaan where they knew him as Solomon, Rome where they knew him as Jesus, ancient Egypt where they knew him as Osiris, England where they knew him as Arthur, Greece where they knew him as Hyperion or America where your reading this book. A person inquisitively turning each page may not realize the significance of Quetzalcoatl until they come to know he founded the Mayan culture that has the world's largest pyramid (Kulkan) as well as the most famous calendar in regards to all the new age prophecies. This calendar marks the destruction of the present world/age, setting the date as December 21, 2012 during the Winter Solstice.

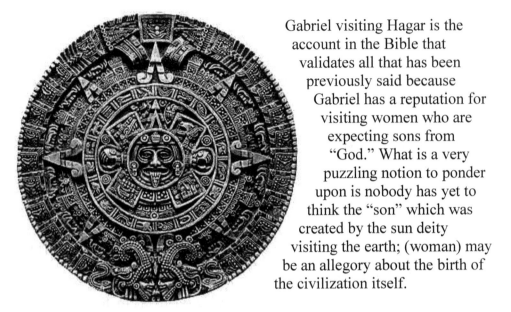

Gabriel visiting Hagar is the account in the Bible that validates all that has been previously said because Gabriel has a reputation for visiting women who are expecting sons from "God." What is a very puzzling notion to ponder upon is nobody has yet to think the "son" which was created by the sun deity visiting the earth; (woman) may be an allegory about the birth of the civilization itself.

Genesis 16:7-15 (7) *The angel of the LORD found Hagar near a spring in the desert; it was the spring that is beside the road to Shur. (8) And he said, "Hagar, servant of Sarai, where have you come from, and where are you going?" "I'm running away from my mistress Sarai," she answered. (9) Then the angel of the LORD told her, "Go back to your mistress and submit to her." (10) The angel added, "I will so increase your descendants that they will be too numerous to count." (11) The angel of the LORD also said to her: "You are now with child and you will have a son. You shall name him Ishmael, for the LORD has heard of your misery. (12) He will be a wild donkey of a man; his hand will be against everyone and everyone's hand against him, and he will live in hostility toward [b] all his brothers." (13)* <u>*She gave this name to the **LORD** who spoke to her: "You are **the God who sees me,**"*</u> *for she said, "I have now seen the One who sees me." (14) That is why the well was called Beer Lahai Roi, it is still there, between Kadesh and Bered. (15) So Hagar bore Abram a son, and Abram gave the name* <u>*Ishmael*</u> *to the son she had borne.*

This passage informs us that Gabriel/Jibril visited Hagar, who according to Christian and Muslim religions is the mother of the Arabs. Gabriel visiting Hagar, and then later revealing the Qur'an to the prophet Muhammad, is evidence that Islam originated long before even the creation of the Arabs. The word Qur'an means *recitation* which proves that the true WORD of "God" had been lost and therefore had to be re-cited. This same "recitation" happened in India where the system of Yoga and the Bhagavad Gita was 1st spoken to the sun God who recited it back to the Indian people. *4445*

CANAAN - THE WOLF MAN

Cain, known as the wolf, is where occultists get the term werewolf from. Romantic imagery often stressed the blackness of the Islamic Moors and associated them with the cursed sons of Ham 119c. Later, with the emergence of the slave trade, it justified the exploitation of a ready supply of black African labor which classified blacks as being savage beasts and animals.

Traditionally, it is held that Ham was the son of Noah who moved southwest into Africa and parts of the near Middle East. He is unanimously believed to be the forefather of those nations. The Bible refers to Egypt as "the land of Ham"—whose grandson was called Canaan. This is where we find the correlation between blacks, called beast-like, and the term Canaan which is a term referring to Osiris also known as the constellation, the Dog Star Sirius.

In Canaanite tradition, the Moon was symbolic of the rib or gene (man) that came out of the body of the earth (Eve) in order to make a being that would protect the Gods (Sun) from their enemies. It was once speculated that the circumference of the earth was 35,000 miles in diameter and after the blasting of the moon (rib) from the earth it dropped to 25,000 miles in diameter. This is why it is said it takes a little over 25,000 years for the Sun to move through all twelve constellations. There is also another occult legend of the moon being blasted out of the earth tipping over and spilling the water seen in the Pacific Ocean back on the Earth.

Water in Egyptian folklore again represents the feminine or chaotic nature of the hu/man masses. This chaotic nature brings out the beast (emotion) within the human making him uncivil, unpredictable, and irrational. Again, the werewolf represents the hu/man whose feminine nature has overtaken him and the Moon is what in occult legend causes the wolf to transform. Michael Jackson's *Thriller* depicts the Wolf/Beast who walks with the living dead at the end of time. His tarot card *"High Priestess"* as we've learned is also known as the Moon Goddess. Since the Moon controls the waters of the earth this means it also controls the masses of people. Remember Michael Jackson put a half a million people in one concert reacting ecstatic in "Dionysian fashion," which reiterates that Michael is the true controller of the mass (*masses*) not the pope.

In another Greek legend the figure who is associated as being the bringer of light to mankind is Prometheus. Prometheus who is known for his mercurial intelligence in legend was a champion of human-kind, who stole fire from Zeus and gave it to mortals 121. Zeus then punished him by having him bound to a rock while a great vulture ate his entrails every day only to have it grow back to be eaten again the next day. The author *Jacolliot*, referring to the "Bhagavad-Gita and Brahminical traditions in Hinduism," states that the body of Krishna: "*was suspended to the branches of a tree by his murderer, that it might become the prey of the vultures* 122. In the legend of Prometheus and the legend of Krishna, their carcasses are hung out and vultures are eating their entrails. These are all allegories that describe avatars who were born during certain star alignments and sent to certain unrefined cultures (Gentiles) to civilize them.

There was a recent movie called the *Underworld* that depicts the legend of the werewolf and the vampire. The vampires are beings who get burned by the Sun and can only come out at night; the prey upon people and drink their blood in order to survive. If we are to look at who physically these vampires would represent it would definitely be the embodiment of white supremacy which is personified through the movie as being the old Roman Catholic Church. The Lycans however, who were created by Lucian, are a breed of Werewolves. These werewolves are "savages" and are very emotional with superior-strength to that of the vampires; they would allegorically represent black slaves.

Acts 14:11-12 (11) And when people saw what Paul had done, they lifted up their voices, saying in the speech of Lycaonia, The gods are come down to us in the likeness of men (12) And they called Barnabas, Jupiter; and Paul, Mercurius, because he was the chief speaker.

Notice that these "pagans/savages of Lycaonia as acknowledged by biblical scriptures, had Astrology as a system of belief.

Again, these pagans of Lycaonia (Lycans) would represent Africans or blacks in the movie the *Underworld*. The same word "pagan" used by the Mother Church to describe the people of African descent who held beliefs in Astrology is used indirectly when the monsters are called Lycans in the movie. The vampires fear the Lycans because of their chaotic nature. Even though the vampires are monsters, they see themselves as being civilized and because they are *civilized* they feel they are better than the Lycans and view them as savages. This particular point in the book brings me to the word genteel which is another variant of the word Gentile that describes the way in which vampires are most often depicted (gentle.) Their *civilized* manner makes them "think" they are more distinguished than other life forms and is very similar to how upper society views poor people. The way in which the word *Genteel* is defined reflects the correlation between the symbolic character of the vampire in the movie whose Victorian principles make them identifiable with the Roman Church, and the rich subjects that serve the church under its present doctrines.

Genteel: (1) marked by false delicacy, prudery, or affectation (2) having an aristocratic quality or flavor (3): of or relating to the gentry or upper class (4): elegant or graceful in manner, appearance, or shape (5): free from vulgarity or rudeness

In the movie the *Underworld* Lucian was the first Lycan (werewolf) who was able to take human form. This symbolizes that he was a black person who was able to speak, act, and demean in the manner of white people or (vampires.) Lucian represents the carrier of the mutated (alpha) gene much like Noah. Being that he was an anomaly, the aristocracy of the vampires wanted to make him into a slave because the strength that the (werewolves) had was remarkable as they could work all day within the Sun. Making Lucian a slave would allow the vampires to breed him, and in breeding him he would be able to make more beasts, who like Lucian, could remain in their human form and not be the uncivil beasts the vampires couldn't control. Because they get burned and meet their death if they are in the Sun, the vampires need the "beasts" with superior strength to work during the day when they cannot. In the movie, Lucian's right hand man was a black man which further implies the werewolves represent the chaotic blacks.

Lycaonia: An ethnic district in south-central Asia Minor traversed by the main east-west trade route from Asia Minor to Syria. It bordered the plains of Galatia and Cappadocia on the north and east and was bounded by hills on the west and south. Acquired by Rome in 190 B.C., it was divided among three Roman imperial provinces by Pompey in 64; the west went to Cilicia, the east to Cappadocia, and the north to Galatia. Eastern Lycaonia became independent of Cappadocia in 25 B.C. The mixed population included the native "pagan" Lycaonians, for whom the territory was named

HUGH JACKMAN   KATE BECKINSALE

VAN HELSING

There was another blockbuster movie in recent times that linked the Canaanite (wolf) with the angel Gabriel, who comes to slay the Great Dracula. The name of this movie is *Van Helsing.* In the movie, Van Helsing, is a reincarnation of Gabriel who has to transform into a wolf if he is to destroy Dracula. Previously we discussed the relationship between vampires, and werewolves in how they are clues and allegories that represent races and natures of people. The fact that Gabriel is a vampire hunter in the movie is another interpretation that if linked with all the other previous stories gives us a very detailed hypothesis. Van Helsing's first name was Abraham; this is to imply that he has a covenant with Abraham or that he is of the offspring of Abraham who had the covenant with God in the 17th chapter of Genesis. His transformation into a wolf shows he is a Canaanite and a murderer of Gentiles. Again Dracula represents the Vatican (Gentiles) though in the movie they have Gabriel fighting for the Roman Catholic Church. Because the true Catholic Church or (Universal Church) as Catholic means Universal, has been overtaken. Gabriel must fight with Michael (the wolf) to bring it back to its rightful position. We've already linked Gabriel to serpents and the sign of the serpent which is Leo the "Beast." In understanding all of this, in the movie, Van Helsing as Gabriel the archangel, turns into a (wolf/Canaanite under the promise of Abraham) to slay the great Roman (Dracula.) He does so with the help of his consort and fulfills the ancient prophecies, by restoring the worship of the most High God, destroying those who have corrupted and romanticized his word and legacy.

The Book of Illumination

CHAPTER 19
SIBLING RIVALRY

The Book of Illumination

CHAPTER 19
SIBLING RIVALRY

SIBLING RIVALRY

In this book we've briefly discussed the murdering of Cain and Abel. In discussion of these events though elaborate, we've lacked great detail in the exploration and explanation of the genealogies of these characters. Here below are a few scriptures that when looking at with a microscopic lens shows some rather "peculiar" editing.

Genesis 4:16-18 *(16) And Cain went out from the presence of the Lord, and dwelt in the land of Nod, on the east of Eden (17) And Cain knew his wife; and she conceived and bare* Enoch: *and he builded a city, and called the name of the city, after the name of his son, Enoch (18) And unto Enoch was born* Irad: *and* Irad *begat* Mehujael *and Mehujael begat* Methusael *and Methusael begat* Lamech.

Notice that both Enoch and Lamech flow from the lineage of Cain. Enoch was said to have never died but ascended to heaven just like Elijah and Jesus and was also given the book that recorded the sleeping of angels (lesser gods) with women. Lamech was said to have been the father of Noah. Noah was the chosen righteous seed that "God" left on the earth as a remnant after he destroyed the world because man had grown increasingly wicked.

Genesis 6:5 *(5) And God saw that the wickedness of man was great in the earth, and that every imagination of the thoughts of his heart was only evil continually. (7) And the Lord said* **I will destroy man whom I created from the face of the earth** *(8) But Noah found grace in the eyes of the Lord.*

Here is where the story gets fuzzy. When we read Genesis **4:16-18** we see the descendants of Cain, the cursed and wicked seed, has the same bloodline line that produced Abraham, Noah, Moses, David, and Jesus.

Genesis 5:1 & 9-12-15-18-21-24- 25-28-29 *(1) This is the book of the Generations of Adam in the day that god created man in the likeness of God made he him; (9) And Enos lived ninety years and begat* Cainan *(12) And* Cainan *lived seventy years and begat Mahalaleel (15) And Mahalaleel lived sixty five years and begat Jared (18) And Jared lived a hundred and sixty two years and begat Enoch (21) And* Enoch *lived sixty five years and begat* Methuselah *(24)* **And Enoch walked with God and he was not for God took him** *(25) And Methuselah lived a hundred and eighty seven years and begat* Lamech *(28) And Lamech lived an hundred eighty and two years and begat a son (29) And he called his name* Noah, *saying, This same shall* **comfort** *us concerning our work and toil of our hands, because of the ground which the lord had cursed.*

However in the example given about the genealogy of Adam, it is "*heir apparent*" that the names have been falsified and switched due to the recognition of the error of placing all of the biblical heroes under the cursed genealogy of Cain. Cain is lengthened to Cainan, Methusael, is changed to Methuselah, and Irad is changed to Jared. The Hebrew language having no J's in it would make Jared sound like Irad. This is an attempt to supplant and make the people of the Bible and their influences come from the genealogy of Adam and Eve versus that of a "God" (Serpent) and an earthly queen (Eve.) Here the story of Eve and the serpent again is the foreshadowing of God/gods coming down from heaven and engendering sons with man.

In the first account given in Genesis 4:16, Cain's son Enoch fathered Lamech, who fathered Noah, who built the Ark. Later the covenant was established through Abraham from Shem who was one of Noah's sons. Noah was the only righteous person living at the time according to the Bible. Cain was the son born from Eve and the serpent. If you know about eugenics or race mixing when the genes are spliced and you have the recessive mixed back in with the dominant genes, these genes become hybrids between the two taking many forms. All other types of lighter hues and shades will appear if no other dominant colors are introduced. Meaning if you mix a black dog and a red dog, a brown dog will be produced. If that brown dog mixes with another red dog, a lighter (orange) dog will be produced. This is what was happening on the earth at that time. You had all races of men created from the *gods consorting with the daughters of men.* This took place until the days where there were all types of colored people on earth. Because dominant genes attract everything inferior to them, the fairer skinned women had a natural attraction to the Black Gods; i.e. Eve sleeping with the serpent.

Genesis 6:1 *"And it came to pass when men began to multiply on the face of the earth, and daughters were born unto them. That the sons of God <u>saw the daughters of men that they were fair</u>; and they took them as wives of all which they chose. (4)* ***There were giants in the earth in those days*** *and also after that, when the sons of God came unto the daughters of men, and they bare children to them, the same became mighty men which were of old men, men of renown.*

Fair: (1) of a light hue, not dark. (2) Pleasing to the eye

Renown: widely acclaimed; highly honored

Hero: (1) from Greek hērōs: the offspring of a deity and a mortal

Notice it said when MEN began to multiply on the face of the earth not gods; gods already existed. *"There were Giants in the earth in those days."* The mixing of gods and man produced humans; this is where the term Hu/man comes from as Hu means colors.

I have within this book offered a theory, a theory I think may explain all of the events foretold within all ancient scriptures and texts. It deals with the intermingling of the black gods with a race they created. This theory is an attempt to explain the fighting between the different races on the earth, and in it are references from occult sciences, other ancient texts, as well as modern day comic book characters who I feel were created allegories to represent these heavy themes. As I stated in the opening chapter of this book, the story of Adam, Eve, and the serpent, is a conception story that again marks the beginning of a new world and a new age. The *"Let us make man"* is the God and the Goddesses attempt to perfect themselves through blissful union and cohabitation. This act of tantra is one of thought and precision as the God and Goddess look to produce through Adam/Atum, the perfect man to rule over mankind because mankind has degenerated to the point where they have become cancerous and are rapidly destroying all of creation and humanity. Because the "Gods" eventually ascend back to their celestial home (heavens/stars), in the periods between their descents to the earth plane, the ruling mortals in their stead mimic their actions in what is called (magic) in hopes of becoming deities themselves.

While in the middle of this chapter we learned the genealogy and bloodline of the prophets was switched in the story of Cain and Abel. The story between the two brothers takes us directly to another account of two other siblings, who like Cain and Abel, had a pretty contentious relationship. The account is about Jacob and Esau and in it is a wide array of allegorical information that gives us further insight in regards to the (Adamic) race that was created in the Garden of Eden by "God" and also the legacy that was supplanted by a younger nation standing in place of an older one.

ISRAEL AND ESAU

The 30th chapter of Genesis is a great example of a race of cattle being genetically altered by Jacob to bring about a stronger and better breed of cattle. This is also synonymous to the mixing of the gods and man who brought about the birth of Cain and the Canaanites. It has been studied in certain small esoteric circles that during the African slave trade, the slaves who were all mixed up produced stronger slaves. The rationale that explains their strength has to do with them having melanin from all over Africa within their DNA; versus the other Africans who only have strands of melanin from their own country. Having these variations coded within their DNA made them a race of "super" hybrids which enabled them to ultimately endure and grow very powerful from the effects of slavery.

Genesis 30:31-43 (31) And he said, What shall I give thee? And Jacob said, Thou shalt not give me any thing: if thou wilt do this thing for me, I will again feed and keep thy flock. (32) I will pass through all thy flock to day, removing from thence all the speckled and spotted cattle, and all the brown cattle among the sheep, and the spotted and speckled among the goats: and of such shall be my hire. (33) So shall my righteousness answer for me in time to come, when it shall come for my hire before thy face: every one that is not speckled and spotted among the goats, and brown among the sheep, that shall be counted stolen with me. (34) And Laban said, Behold, I would it might be according to thy word. (35) And he removed that day the he goats that were ringstraked and spotted, and all the she goats that were speckled and spotted, and every one that had some white in it, and all the brown among the sheep, and gave them into the hand of his sons. (36) And he set three days' journey betwixt himself and Jacob: and Jacob fed the rest of Laban's flocks. (37) And Jacob took him rods of green poplar, and of the hazel and chesnut tree; and pilled white strakes in them, and made the white appear which was in the rods. (38) And he set the rods which he had pilled before the flocks in the gutters in the watering troughs when the flocks came to drink, that they should conceive when they came to drink. (39) And the flocks conceived before the rods, and brought forth cattle ringstraked, speckled, and spotted. (40) And Jacob did separate the lambs, and set the faces of the flocks toward the ringstraked, and all the brown in the flock of Laban; and he put his own flocks by themselves, and put them not unto Laban's cattle. (41)And it came to pass, whensoever the stronger cattle did conceive, that Jacob laid the rods before the eyes of the cattle in the gutters, that they might conceive among the rods. (42) But when the cattle were feeble, he put them not in: so the feebler were Laban's, and the stronger Jacob's. (43) And the man increased exceedingly, and had much cattle, and maidservants, and menservants, and camels, and asses.

 The story of Jacob, the son who also stole the birthright of his brother Esau, has a very controversial back-story that Black Muslims cite as being the way the white race came into existence. Because the Hebrew Language does not contain J's, everyplace there would be a J, would be replaced with a Y. In Hebrew, Jacob isn't Jacob, rather Yakoub, or as the story is told by Elijah Muhammad, Yakub. Yakub was said to be an evil scientist with a very large head who had a heavy interest in playing with metals. At six years of age Yakub discovered the laws of magnetism and repulsion by playing with magnets made of steel. This realization spawned his plan to create a new race of people as at that time dissatisfaction among the people of Mecca was 30%. According to Elijah Muhammad, Yakub saw an unlike human being, made to attract others, who could, with the knowledge of tricks and lies, rule the original black man. Yakub would later come to discover that the "original black man" contained both a "black germ" and a "brown germ." Upon this discovery he developed a way to separate the "brown germ" from the "black germ" and in turn grafted whites from the "brown germ," in a process that took 600 years to complete. Elijah Muhammad further adds that Yakub discovered that the "white …was the weaker of the black germ" and they were made to be the ruler over the black race for 6,000 years 124.

When we parallel this story to that of Jacob's in the Bible in how he bred the strong speckled cattle and brown cattle/sheep to produce a superior head of cattle, we can see correlations between his story and Yakub's. The Jewish word *goyim* is used to describe the non-Jewish "masses" of people as "cattle" which again makes the two stories that much more comparable. However one cannot say with accuracy if the account is all fact, based on the limited knowledge the culture has in regards to race, and an unclear perspective to look from with regards to what may be allegory or embellishment in the account. Because of insufficient data, we do not know what in the Yakub story is true apart from what is allegory. The truths that are reflective in it are that recessive genes do come from the dominant genes. As it pertains to the Bible there was a process whereby Jacob "Yakub" did genetically alter the natural course of how the cattle would breed; and these cattle and sheep are said to have been speckled, spotted, and brown. Also, Jacob stealing the birthright from his brother Esau and supplanting his legacy paints the character of Jacob or Yakub as being a trickster and a liar.

A person would ask why I have put this in the book. The answer is to encourage people to look at things wholly to see where they are in it. There is no problem with war if we know what it is we are fighting for. If we are fighting because a people are jealous of another than that isn't necessarily a just cause for war. I am trying to get to the bottom of the lies that have been perpetuated within the world for the last two thousand years. If the Yakub story is reverse racism lets analyze it and cross-reference it with a similar story to see how it compares. If it is hogwash then just disregard it, and put it next to all the other conspiracy theories and exploitative racial propaganda.

In the chapter *My Brother's Keeper* is where we 1st spoke in reference to the story of Jacob and Esau. The story of Jacob and Esau has another interpretation which examines the lives of two brothers who are twins and identical in likeness from an animated and astrological celestial perspective. This "likeness" is only understood when further analyzing the inner Kabbalistic selves of the two identical twins that Jacob and Esau allegorically and symbolically represent. When comparing Michael Jackson's life to the story whereby Yakub/Jacob grafts a devil by slowly transforming its skin color from black to white; we can also see this parallel through his life. Michael's skin after his accident in a sense was grafted or changed. Through this change, Michael went from being black to white the same as the infamous Yakub's or (Jacob's) creation. The Jacob of the Bible was said to have done this with a herd of cattle, and is also the father of Joseph, who like Michael wore the coat of many colors. Cattle / *goyim* again are known symbolically to represent the unenlightened masses of people who are in a sense food for the evolved elite. Krishna aka Michael Jackson was known as a cow boy as this recognition of being a cowherd is a distinguishing characteristic ascribed to him because his mother Maia is the great celestial cow 124c. In the eyes of the Black Nationalist Michael wouldn't be accepted as their messiah because among them there is popular consensus that he was a traitor and a person who turned his backs on blacks, while simultaneously hanging around whites, marrying their women, and in their opinion having his kids grafted to be white as well. Though this view point is one that comes from those who do not believe in integration; from a universal standpoint, it has little if any merit. This is stated because no matter what color you are, everything originates from the same source. In matters of race this means all colors come from black, and in matters of religion all people come from "God." Michael constantly talked about this in numerous songs like *Another Part of Me*, *Black and White* and *Can You Feel it.*

On Michael's *History* album he has the 777 upon his armband which is a mystical Kabbalistic number that points to the house of Jacob, also called the House of Israel 124b. His last name *Jack* (son) is a variant form of Jacque which according to the Kabbalah equals Jacob. On the other end Esau is another name for Isa named after his father Isaac, who was conceived when the "LORD" "visited" Sarah. As we analyzed earlier, Isaac's name is a direct correlation to the Hindu god Shiva also known as *Isvara*. Shiva again is referred to as the Sun in Hinduism; a distinction that points to the astrological sign Leo as well as the Tribe of Judah and Gabriel. In the account of the Bible, Esau was despised because he took women who were forbidden for him to take 124d.

Genesis 28:6-9 *(6) Now Esau learned that Isaac had blessed Jacob and had sent him to Paddan Aram to take a wife from there, and that when he blessed him he commanded him, "Do not marry a Canaanite woman," (7) and that Jacob had obeyed his father and mother and had gone to Paddan Aram. (8) Esau then realized how displeasing the Canaanite women were to his father Isaac;(9) so he went to Ishmael and married Mahalath, the sister of Nebaioth and daughter of Ishmael son of Abraham, in addition to the wives he already had.*

This is indicative of Shiva as Shiva lost his phallus in Hindu legend, as well as the house of Judah as Judah took a prostitute Tamar, who he conceived twins by in the 38th Chapter of Genesis. Shiva's/Judah's/Gabriel's tantric philosophy in regards to sex and creation causes those who are on the right to cringe and further reject that he could be the messiah in whom they are to worship. The pattern of taking the forbidden woman is a theme we explore constantly within this book in the stories of Abraham, David, Solomon, and

389

Eve and the serpent. When we look at the word Jacob it means to supplant or take the place of. The fact that Jacob dressed up like his brother Esau "Osiris" – who is older - is an allegory that possibly represents the way Michael through his interpretation and artistic vision "*dressed up*" like the messiah who is to come that is prophesied to raise the dead from their graves through resurrection (animation), and make the blind see through revelation of the scriptures. This has "*in a sense*" visually supplanted the "*hidden*" messiah who embodies all of these things; making Krishna (Michael) the messiah of the masses verses Shiva/Judah representing "Osiris" who is the messiah of the occult or (hidden) world. This particular theory is further admonished in the *Simulacra and Simulation* where Baudrillard explains the phenomenon of how the simulated copy supersedes the original object. So when you hear the phrase Michael Jackson was YOUR Jesus, know that he is the messiah that stands for humanity that raises the conscious level of the world as it heads into a new age.

Isaiah 45:15 *Verily, Thou art a God that hidest Thyself, O God of Israel, the <u>Saviour.</u>*

Ur on the end of *saviour* indicates the biblical verse is referring to the elder Horus and hidden messiah Osiris/Shiva. The Osiris conception story was the 1st story of the Christ whereby the Horus avenges his father's murder after being birth from his virgin mother Isis. It furthers discusses the re-member-ment of the All God, Osiris/Ra Atum who is resurrected in his son Horus. However the tremendous decent of Krishna/Hormus is where he was entered into the pantheon of Hindu and Egyptian Gods as the Supreme Being due to the enormous popularity of his presence, the love and peace he bestowed upon the earth, as well as his uncanny attractive abilities. Now that we know who Krishna is, Michael Jackson, we can now formulate that the story of Krishna or the Hormus which came after the story of Osiris was accepted by Christian culture and interwoven within the story of the Jesus of Nazareth. Though they are of the same spirit, it was here where the Christ and Holy ONE of Israel were mistaken to be the same person. Looking at the gospels with this additional knowledge and eagles eye perspective, we can see how the younger "twin" who "stole" the birthright under "feminine" authority, became known in the public's eye as the Supreme force of the Universe based on what is universal (feminine) and how this universal interpretation became printed within the Bible in the story of the Jesus of Nazareth. This would represent the right hand of God as Michael/Krishna/Joseph is on the right side of God. Gabriel /Shiva/ Osiris/Judah would be considered the left side of God. Though Shiva/Judah's story is most accurate to the Jesus of Nazareth written in the gospels, it would only be known to those in the occult world who have the initiation and understanding of esoteric knowledge. This is why their symbol is the All Seeing Eye because it sees everything, all the way down to the most meticulous detail and reflects a life, religion, and culture though seemingly masculine, which encompasses it all.

1 Chronicles 5:2 And though Judah was the strongest of his brothers and a ruler came from him, the rights of the firstborn belonged to Joseph.

Joseph is older than Judah in the sense of "physical age" because he was born before Judah. Joseph represents the avatar of the Piscean age though at the end of time, comes before the beginning of time which is represented by the Age of Aquarius. Because the ages move in circles and the constellations move counterclockwise, from Aquarius to Pisces, it makes Judah the elder because the story of the flood found in the Matsya Purana is the 1st legend in Hinduism that predates that of Krishna and represents initial creation. This makes Judah the elder "spiritually" as he was 25,000 years older before the

Sun reached the constellation of Pisces. One represents the beginning, the other represents the end; together both represent the eye. The point at which light enters (Sun) and the point at which it projects (Moon) making the total sum of the two halves/twins, the alpha and the omega, beginning and the ending. This is a very deep interpretation of the accounts written in the Bible through these characters and their allegories. Although everything does not match dead on we can take key moments in the lives of those written about and composite those against the stars/beings of today to see in a sense who is who. Upon doing so we realize that the characters represented in the Bible and other religious works are really just aspects of the same spirits lives. This is why in ancient Egypt as well as other indigenous cultures they have totem poles. These totem poles show you the various stages in the evolution of the being through the beings various lives and existences. This is how I can reference Michael's life through the likeness of Krishna, Jesus, Joseph, Israel, Archangel Michael, Dionysus and Moses. Each account represents an interpretation of the same set of events whereby the ONE individual's life is broken up into different segments which represent the point of view of those speaking about him. For example the aspects of a person's character its enemy sees are a lot different from the aspects seen by that same person's friend. Imagine if what was written in the Bibles stories has aspects taken from many people writing about the same thing unbeknownst to each other or

391

the subject who is being written about. When the people who gather these scrolls come along millenniums later interpreting them and putting them together in religious works, the one person written about gets dismembered into many persons each having a part of the legend that is being spoken about and examined as if it were its own separate story. I am looking at all of the stories to separate what is fact from fiction, what is truth from falsehood, on both sides. In my quest for truth I have no regard for emotion or feeling because in order to travel where we are going, we have to suck it up, face the facts and then use what we have learned to rebuild and restructure the governing aspects of ourselves as well as our present world. The person who wants a tan is no different than the girl who wears a weave. If you encourage people to be real and you are wearing eyelashes that aren't yours, what you are saying is a contradiction. My whole point is let's stop being so sensitive, and look at these topics of race, religion, sex, and politics to understand where they come from so we can better understand why people are the way they are, and why they fight for the things they believe in.

I illustrated the story of Jacob and portrayed it in this way as well as other stories in this book so people may see from an animated perspective. Reading an adulterated version of something verses seeing it, has led to the type of religious dogma and confusion the world is experiencing today. The Yakub story found within the belief of the Nation of Islam has some heavy science associated with it. This science is very unsettling and unpleasant to those who are non-black. Because recessive genes come from dominant genes is cause for anyone who learns these truths to question the origins of the races. It is equally understood why anyone trying to stand in the place of a legend about a particular race of people would also keep this type of knowledge from being public knowledge. When we take into account these sciences and this knowledge we can now look back to the origins of the Bibles stories to see where these sciences are applicable. This may provide even more clues in route to our enlightenment in regards to the religions of Abraham and the creation of man.

In the example given in the Genesis, it says the gods created the race of man or Adam. Like I said earlier the creation of a race could have occurred naturally and upon this spontaneous occurrence many more of the same "*kin*" were genetically bred into existence like the ring-straked cattle in the 30th chapter of the Genesis. Either way there is enough evidence that suggests one of the two if not both happened during the beginning of creation.

Time is a great hindrance when we try and place all that has been written within the 6,000 year period projected by Scholars. Because it takes 25,920 years for the Sun to move through all 12 constellations shows that the time that scholars have factored these events in, has to be incorrect. Their projections are off by many thousands of years. What is also strange about the Bibles language is the Bible says that God made Adam 1st before Eve.

Genesis 2:7 And the Lord God formed man from of the dust of the ground, and breathed into his nostrils the breath of life; and man became a living soul.

Genesis 2:22 And the rib, which the Lord God had taken from the man, made he a woman, and brought her unto the man.

Now this scripture is saying he made them both and called **their** name Adam.

*Genesis 5:1&2 This is the book of the generations of Adam, in the day that God created man, in the likeness of God made he him: Male and female created he them: and blessed them and **called their name Adam**, in the day they were created.*

This is most likely to satisfy the argument for how Cain found a wife. The argument was that if Adam, Eve, and Cain were the only people living at the time, then how did Cain go to another place and find a wife? Either scribes came along later to piece together the story making Adam a race instead of just a man or Adam was a race that was created by G.O.D. or a "God" who physically walked the earth and existed with others.

In the genesis, the forbidden fruit that has traditionally been accepted by society is the apple. However when we employ a Kabbalistic interpretation of the same events, the tree of life, subsequently becomes that fruit. The serpent tells Eve that once she eats of the fruit she will obtain the knowledge of good and evil, and shall be as the gods. The knowledge the Black Egyptian Gods had was both supported and mathematically probable by the laws of physics. The Egyptian gods knew that matter was neither created nor destroyed it just changes form. Knowing this law, they understood when they returned from death they would live again. Death for them was merely the period of time in which it took the precession to again reach the same point and constellation they had lived in before. This is the reason they are considered immortal. They hadn't conquered death in the sense of not dying. Death according to how they exist is just a phase. However how they manifested in the afterlife was also determined by how they lived in their present life. Every action has a reaction that is opposite and equal to the action, so they were encouraged to live holistic "do unto others" types of lifestyles; which was expected to ensure they obtained an equal or greater form in the next life existence. This is why Pharaohs in Egypt buried in their tombs, their treasures, servants, and everything else they would need in the afterlife with them. Their logic told them if matter is neither created nor destroyed, when they lived again, the matter they buried with them would somehow take form. The form the buried objects would take, according to their math, would serve as an equal purpose to that which it held in the previous life. This meant when the Pharaoh lived again he should have his treasure, his staff, and the knowledge to regain the position he had in his former life, which was a ruler of a kingdom. This is what the Egyptian *"Book of the Dead"* is about and the reason the Jesus of Nazareth is on a mission to regain his kingdom on earth.

Whenever the spirit reincarnates to the earth, the incarnated spirit uses its knowledge of metaphysical symbols "in the physical" to lead them back to who they were spiritually, in their past life. The Sun of Man is the awakened one, meaning that he is the first who comes into knowledge of his immortality (truest self.) This is the true message of everlasting life that Jesus Christ is preaching in the Gospel. So the resurrection preached about by Jesus is really the time period where the Sun of Man resurrects in embodiment form on the Earth; and the period in which this happens is the Age of Aquarius. "*When the moon is in the seventh house, and Jupiter aligns with mars, then peace will rule the planets, and love will steer the stars* 125." This law of Karma is why Jesus preached the golden rule, "Do unto others as you would have done unto you," because everything that you do comes back to you. If you had to live for eternity then all the sins that you commit are going to forever be with you. Sins are no more than negative experiments that draw you further away or closer to who you are. Pending on your level of comprehension you will either evolve or de-evolve by way of them. The way to burn off bad karma and sin is by doing good deeds, selfless acts of benevolence, and helping others along their own spiritual journeys. This is truly the reason why the non-violent approach taken from the civil rights era in regards to slavery was so appealing to the American Negro. The Negro had a subtle spiritual understanding of the consequences that will arise if the war of racism was won by force. If you live by the sword you will die by the sword.

Matthew 26:52 Put up again thy sword into this place: for all they that take the sword shall perish with the sword.

Here is the example of the sacrificial lamb. The example is a replica of the biblical story of the "lamb of god" who is sacrificed in-order for the whole "nation" to be saved. This lamb in this cycle of history was MLK. In OT biblical times the sacrificial lamb was symbolically linked to Abram's seed Isaac, and in the NT the lamb was linked to the son of Mary and Joseph, Jesus. MLK represented for the (civil rights era) the lamb (Capricorn) that was sacrificed, deified and given to the Negro people as a saint, a martyr, and the epitome of non-violence during a very violent and tumultuous time period. This was done in order to turn Negroes away from their destructive thoughts of revolution. The fact that MLK was assassinated on April 4th – both the day

and the month of the ram/lamb in Astrology and the tarot, shows it was a ritual and blood sacrificial murder. Barack Obama is the resurrected Lamb (RAM) in America's post-civil rights struggle who exemplifies the triumph over opposition in a refined genteel revolutionary persona. The inauguration of President Obama's 2nd term took place on January 21, 2013 - the day that also commemorates Martin Luther King. The *"powers that be"* today understand that the lesser gods or "matter" (of the Negro people) are idol worshippers *Exodus 32:1-4*. Countless times throughout history the "indigenous" people have always been idol worshippers; and through the (governors) understanding of this they give the people LIVING idols to worship. (Note the photo The Living King.)

MLK (above) who was a Capricorn born on the 15th day is sporting a Rolex watch worth anywhere from $10,000 - $50,000. This form of materialistic expression goes directly against the meek and humble teachings promoted by those who advocate Christianity.

Matthew 6:19-21 (21) *Lay not up for yourselves treasures upon earth… For where your treasure is, there will your heart be also*

<u>Panorama</u>: from <u>Greek</u> πᾶν "all" ὅραμα "sight" = all sight.

THE DEVIL

Pan and the Ram together represent having (all sight) a trait indicative of Masonry and the All Seeing Eye placed in the forehead of Baphomet. Capricorn is one of two signs in the Zodiac that embodies materialism, and materialism in the Bible was known to be a form of idol worship. What is also a very interesting correlation to MLK was the day he was born on which as regarded by the major arcana (tarot) and Aleister Crowley is the day of the Devil. The Devil in the Kabbalah represents people's dependency upon material things as he ensnares them by way of their desires for them.

These ruling (Masons) have learned, by talking and consulting directly with the "Living God" that the indigenous peoples are unable to worship the one true "God" who is a living spirit within a man. They can't fathom worshipping this living spirit because the only spirit they can relate to is the one within themselves. The spirit within them is only an aspect of the one that encompasses it all; and the one that encompasses it all, manifests in the flesh to earth as an avatar to bring the fallen away people back to the knowledge of the "Living God." The people themselves again are but aspects or projections of God. They have forgotten what aspect/projection of God (Sun) they are which is why they don't know who "God" is. The one that encompasses it all and manifests to earth as an avatar is known as the Christ; and this Christ comes in many different forms. This is that universal all-encompassing spirit known as the Holy ONE of Israel who returns to earth to bring about the knowledge of the gods to a people who are lawless. Their lawlessness has caused them to be enslaved which forced them to go through a purging process known as the "circumcision." However perversions of the mind, and the (other reincarnated gods) who are consciously aware they are not the one (high god), causes these individuals who are waking up to be very destructive. This is represented by Neo's counterpart, Smith, in the movie the Matrix.

If people had the understanding "God" has, they wouldn't be destructive because it only lowers their existence from the realm of the human into the realm of the animal. When Abram was told by "God" that his seed would be enslaved in a foreign land, it was foreshadowing to the sacrifice of his son Isaac. This is said because the sacrificial lambs (lost sheep/Isaac) are who represents Abram's seed. These enslaved descendants of Genesis 15 were given as a hu/man sacrifice to build a new society. In our time, the sacrifice of the lamb (MLK) was a ritual performed in order to maintain the present ruler ship (Masonic order); which opposes the uncivil characteristics of the indigenous people, that the "goyim" or *unwanted population* represents. This point is further backed by looking at the effects of what MLK's efforts have produced. The urban youth within not only the city of Atlanta, but the world as a whole, have taken the freedom fought for by people like MLK and used it to "idly" express themselves in ways that are looked at by the government as chaotic and animalistic. When we factor in the Kabbalistic pedigree of MLK again we see he is born on the day of the "Devil" in the month of Capricorn, also known as the goat man. If we are looking at this from a top down unbiased view, it can be argued that MLK opened the flood gates of "hell" in liberating all the "devilish" forces the "G.O.D." was trying to contain. This analysis makes those who are looking at all sides empathize with the position the American government took in regards to the treatment of the Negro masses prior to their liberation by the civil rights struggle. Today these rights have extended past the Negros and have further liberated other socially outcast subcultures like the gays. We spoke about this earlier in the introduction, and with the recent proposition of gay marriage being legalized by President Obama; it further corroborates all that has been previously said.

Remember, Richard Hofstadter stated in **The American Political Tradition** that, *"emancipation meant not merely the replacement of slave labor by hired labor, but the loss of White Supremacy, the overthrow of the caste system - in brief the end of civilization"* 12d.

So like the rulers in Egypt who buried their treasures with them due to their understanding of the way matter changes form; the same are the rulers of today who are devout followers of the Bible by way of religious ritual and reenactment. They act out in ritual the things that took place in the last cycle of history to further ensure "G.O.D.'s" covenant is with them in this cycle of history. Remember, in the Bible, the lost children of Israel were led into bondage because they forgot their <u>God</u> and did not keep his commandments.

Another great example of this ritualistic magic via reenactment is the Moon walk. On July 20, 1969 it was publicized to the world that man had walked on the Moon. What is intriguing about this day is that 69 is the glyph for Cancer in the Zodiac, and the sign of Cancer is also ruled by the Moon. Cancer as regarded by Astrology is the sign whose period in the year comes between June 22nd and July 22nd. July, the 7th month, holds the greatest number of days where the constellation of Cancer's influence is felt.

The 20th day in the tarot deck symbolizes the Day of Judgment. Notice on the card there is a figure in the sky who is executing judgment by sounding a horn from the heavens to the people below. This figure is traditionally believed to be Gabriel as he is the archangel who sounds a trumpet upon bringing the end of times revelation to the world. So, on this 20th day of July, the high Masons knew and understood that if they were going to pull off a great feat such as making people believe man has walked on the Moon, this was the day the energy of the universe would make it possible. I know this seems like a farfetched notion, but when you take into account the power of Astrology, numbers, and the association of these energies in the personalities of people; it makes one acknowledge that these energies on these days are indeed real. Here are a few excerpts given from President Nixon after the Moon landing that was broadcasted to over 400 million people on earth. *"This certainly has to be the most historic telephone call that has ever been made. I just can't tell you how proud we are of what you've done. For every American this has to be the proudest day of our lives. Because of what you've done the heavens have become a part of man's world. For one priceless moment in the whole history of man all the people on this earth are truly one. One in their pride of what you've done it inspires us to redouble our efforts to bring peace and tranquility to earth.*

1 Thessalonians 4:16 For the Lord himself shall descend from heaven with a shout, with the voice of the archangel, and with the trump of God: and the dead in Christ shall rise first.

In the guise of Gabriel, President Nixon used his words (*shout of the trumpet*) to induce the feeling that the moon landing was the most historic event that has ever happened. The heavens becoming a part of man's world and the invoking of peace and tranquility as the intended goal of the moon walk, shows how the moon landing was the foreshadowing for an actual occurrence which would take place 13 years later.

On March 25, 1983 Michael Jackson moon-walked his way into national stardom at Motown's 25th anniversary. The 25th day of the month and the 25th anniversary of the celebration again bears witness to the power of the tarot, Numerology, and Astrology because 2+5 equals seven. The seventh card in the major arcana tarot deck is called *the Chariot,* of which Aleister Crowley in *Tarot Mirror to the Soul,* has cited as the card that Cancer rules. The sign Cancer in Astrology, as previously mentioned, is also ruled by the moon 126.

The moon is reported to be 250,000 miles from the earth, again another important numerical clue that highlights the number 7. Michael Jackson's life and legacy on earth universally was the greatest demonstration of peace and tranquility from one single person the world has ever seen. The fact that Michael Jackson "moon-walked" into stardom is another way of showcasing how the universe operates with use of avatars that are fallen "stars" from the "heavens" who bring about peace and prosperity through the arts to the people on earth.

The Priests of antiquity were astrologers who advised the rulers and kings by foretelling events by using the stars. This fortune telling was critical to the legacies of the kings and rulers because the kings were very subconscious with how they would be viewed in the afterlife. They treated these holy men with the utmost respect because harnessing the power and energy of the stars could heighten or destroy their reputations as rulers in respects to their legacies and their overall places within history.

Isaiah 47:12-13 (12) keep on, then, with your <u>magic spells</u> and with your <u>many sorceries</u>, which you have labored at since childhood. Perhaps you will succeed, perhaps you will cause terror (13) All the counsel you have received has only worn you out! Let your <u>astrologers</u> come forward, <u>those stargazers</u> who make predictions month by month, let them save you from what is coming upon you.

Considering this new found knowledge, and seeing the accuracy in which these concepts play out, allows us to look within our society today to see if there are correlations between numbers and significant events. 9-1-1 is the popular code for emergency here in America. On 9-11-2001 the twin towers came crashing down. Knowing what I have just explained to you in detail about the significance of numbers and how they parallel to events that have the same energy associated with them; is there any speculation that these two incidences are coincidental? Again, high ranking Masons that hold high political positions have re-enacted through ritual these "stunts" / "magic spells" in-order to keep the established order on top. Another example of a ritual that was reenacted was the cloning of the 1st sheep. In order to bring about the existence of the "*Lamb of God*" a ritual in the cloning of a sheep was done. Remember, the first man who was made was created Arien in nature. Aries is the animal in Astrology that represents the ram or lamb/sheep. These Ariens are war driven and said to be natural born leaders because the Ram is the actual leader of sheep. So when you hear stories of the first clone being a sheep you can make the correlation that those (Wizards/Masons/) are trying to reenact the circumstances that brought about Adam's existence. In doing this they feel they are paying homage with the entity that gave man life (God/Sun) while simultaneously making sure they rule based on their understanding of the true and "Living God." These individuals have changed the form from a man/Aries, (He/MAN) being created from a goddess (ISIS), to the real life recreation of a man/ram via a king making ritual... The deaths of Muammar Gadhafi and Osama Bin Laden under the Obama administration acting as Commander in Chief are all examples of this "Ram's" *Arien* abilities.

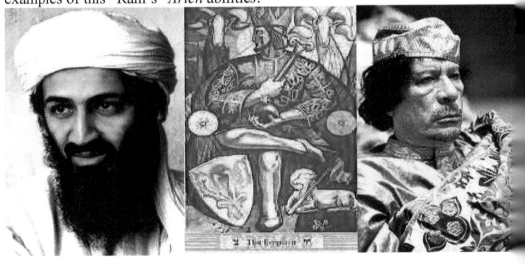

The Book of Illumination

CHAPTER 20

A LINK TO THE PAST

The Book of Illumination

CHAPTER 20

A LINK TO THE PAST

A LINK TO THE PAST

Upon studying ancient civilizations, the second oldest to that of Africa and Mesopotamia, are the Asian dynasties. When looking at Asia and evaluating the culture that exists there, one can hypothesize that the Asian civilizations were spawned from the first, which were located in Africa. The word Semitic which also classifies the Jew and the Hebrews is a term that designates a people of Afro-Asiatic descent. The fall of man from Egypt to Asia can be seen in the way that the Asian culture has existed and held its place as the Mecca of eastern religion and philosophy. Even if we do not accept the story of the Genesis as the birthplace of creation, we know through historical and factual evidence the Asian dynasties are the second oldest civilizations on the earth. Just as the prophecy of the 400 year slavery is as applicable today as it was when first written; so are the other civilizations that were spawned by the original cultures like Canaan, Sumer, and Phoenicia who migrated to other places on the globe. This is how we can look to a prophecy like the one in the Genesis that describes the fall of man and liken it with the fall from Africa to Asia where the gods became humans carrying over the same customs and traditions held in their original civilizations.

Mongol: A member of a pastoral people or group of peoples of Mongolia prominent in Medieval Asian history under Genghis Khan and his successors

Mongolia: region E Asia E of Altai Mountains; includes Gobi Desert

Mongolism: of, relating to, or affected with Down syndrome

Mongoloid: of designating or characteristic of one of the traditional racial divisions of humankind, marked by yellowish complexion, prominent cheekbones, epicanthic folds, and straight black hair including the Mongols, Chinese, Japanese, Siamese, Eskimos, and in some classifications Native Americans

When studying the term Mongoloid, a term once used to classify Asians, we also find within that word, the word Mongol; which is the name that designates those who have the nationality from the country Mongolia who were conquered by one of the greatest empire builders in history, Genghis

403

Khan. Genghis Khan was born *Temujin* which means *"iron worker"* and was the founder, and emperor of the Mongol Empire, the largest contiguous empire in history. He came to power by uniting many of the nomadic tribes of northeast Asia. Genghis Khan started the Mongol invasions and raids of the Kara-Khitan Khanate, Caucasus, Khwarezmid Empire, Western Xia and Jin dynasties. His descendants went on to stretch the Mongol Empire across most of Eurasia by conquering and or creating vassal states out of modern-day China, Korea, the Caucasus, Central Asia, as well as substantial portions of Eastern Europe and the Middle East 126b. I went into the history of Genghis Khan to place emphasis on two things: the 1st is to highlight that the Asian dynasties are the second oldest in reference to humankind; and the 2nd to illustrate the alpha male superiority of the Asian ruler Genghis Khan.

Recently, an international group of geneticists studying Y-chromosome data have found that nearly 8 percent of the men living in the region of the former Mongol empire carry Y-chromosomes that are nearly identical; which translates to 0.5 percent of the male population in the world, or roughly 16 million descendants living today. Geneticists attribute the spread of these y chromosomes to natural selection, where an extremely fit individual in this case, Genghis Khan, manages to pass on some sort of biological advantage to its offspring. This is the first documented case where human culture has caused a single genetic lineage to increase to such an enormous extent in just a few hundred years 126c. Because Genghis (Cain's) numbers were so many, the term Mongol was given to all people who had Asian features like slanted eyes. Historically Mongols were classified as having down-syndrome (Mongolism) which serves as an allegorical term for what the *"fall of man"* actually signifies.

The question to ask is why have scientists called Asians with Egyptian features Mongoloids or the Mongoloid race? Due to Genghis Khan conquering most of Asia and spreading his seed throughout the land is why a large population of Asians today are somehow related to him directly or indirectly. This alpha male-like display of procreative tenacity is very similar to the characteristics of the omnipotent Egyptian God Khem known in Asia as Min; thus linking the two cultures together, the Egyptian black and the Asian yellow.

Genesis 4:22 *and Zillah she also bare tubal Cain, and instructor of every artificer in brass and iron.*

The name Tubal Cain here has great significance for a number of reasons. For one, Tubal Cain is listed as the offspring of Cain and his wife Zillah in the Bible. Secondly this story bears reference to the highly procreative powers of the Egyptian God who like the one mentioned with the Mongol empire is so potent that his offspring are too numerous to count. As stated earlier in this book Khem was the name for Egypt. Due to sound change, and the change in language between Egyptian and Hebrew people, Ham most plausibly was a name derived from Khem (Egypt.) Khem was sometimes used as an epithet for Min, the god of fertility, and was shown as a human male with an erect penis. In Egyptian times, he was usually an ithyphallic bearded mummiform man, standing with both legs together, an arm raised holding his symbol or a flail, and wearing the same low crown with twin plumes as Amen. (The way he holds his flail is symbolic of sexual intercourse - the flail forms the V while his upraised forearm seems to thrust inside the V.) The Egyptian paintings and reliefs on tomb walls and temples didn't show Min's other arm, but the statues of the god show him with his hand encircling the base of his penis. The V symbolizes Venus as he is a great lover of women.

... Min, Bull of the Great Phallus...
You are the Great Male, the owner of all females.
The Bull who is unites with those of the sweet love, of beautiful face and of painted eyes, Victorious sovereign among the Gods who inspires fear in the Ennead....
The goddesses are glad, seeing your perfection 127,128. See – Exodus 4:2-5

In China, the Ming (Min) Dynasty was responsible for succeeding the empires of the Mongols and building the Great Wall of China. Not only does the culture of the Asian dynasties pay homage to Egypt's in the form of Masonry; (building) Min's characteristics are so similar to that of Genghis Khan that we have to ask was he and Genghis Kahn the same person. Is this an indication that the god of fertility (Min) has been reincarnated in the flesh of Genghis (Khan/Cain?) Once again one could liken this to theory or one could say that symbols and customs analyzed together gives an account of what allegories are being written and represented through scriptures and artifacts. I made a point earlier that Masons use allegories and mix truths within falsehoods to show distinctions between Masonic degrees. When the Mason learns that the key to the warrior is the proper application of living power, he has learned the mastery of his craft. Before he may step or move up in degrees, he must prove his ability to properly apply energy. He must follow in the footsteps of his forefather, Tubal-Cain, who with the mighty strength of Thor (Zeus) hammered his sword into a plowshare 129.

For Masons who wish to conceal their membership from non-Masons, but still advertise it to their lodge brothers, there is a special pin they wear. It looks like an upside down golf club with two balls near the top....Many people assume the person is a golfer, but it is actually a visual Masonic pun with a sexual connotation associated with Tubal Cain. This is called the "**Two Ball Cane,**" 129b and is the secret password of a Master Mason, as well as a very obvious pun on the 'god' of Masonry, the male reproductive organ, the penis (also lingam/ Isvara). The code of secrecy and alpha male superiority Masons swear to uphold is personified in the character of o7o James Bond.

The large shaft that Min is holding is instrumental in creating the man – child because the woman's body will naturally attack male sperm that are ejaculated within the vaginal cavity. Male sperm aren't as strong as female sperm, and they don't live as long, however they swim much faster. Because of this phenomenon a large penis was needed to ejaculate inside of the woman's vaginal cavity close to the uterus to ensure a man-child was born. It is also important to note, the woman's body does not attack female sperm; this is also why there are more women in the world than men.

"If the woman emits seed 1st a male-child will be born" 129a.

All of this information allows us to again make the correlation that the builders of the Great Wall and the Asian dynasties of China were also the descendants of those who built the pyramids. (Note the word descendants)

Descend: (1) to pass from a higher place or level to a lower one (2) to lower oneself in status or dignity (3) to worsen and sink in condition or estimation

Descendant: (1) moving or directed downward (2) proceeding from an ancestor or source

This would satisfy the notion that the second dynasty (Asian) came from the first (African) and the Afro-Asiatic mixture is what created Jews.

Semitic: (1) of, relating to, or constituting a subfamily of the Afro-Asiatic language family that includes Hebrew, Aramaic, Arabic, and Amharic, Jewish

 In 1897, **WEB Dubois**, sociologist and historian, said, "*the final word of science, so far, is that we have at least two perhaps three, great families of human beings -- the whites and Negroes, possibly the yellow race* [he calls this "Mongolian" later]. "*Negroids and Mongoloids are primary, with Caucasoids listed as a type between these, possibly formed by their union, with bleached skin and intermediate hair.*" 130

Du Bois was considered the most prominent intellectual leader and political activist on behalf of African Americans in the first half of the twentieth century. Du Bois entered Harvard College in the fall of 1888, upon which after receiving a scholarship, earned a bachelor's degree *cum laude* in 1890. In 1892, he attended the University of Berlin for graduate work. While a student in Berlin, he traveled extensively throughout Europe and this is where he matured intellectually. While studying with some of that nation's most prominent social scientists, like Gustav von Schmoller, Adolph Wagner, and Heinrich von Treitschke, Dubois developed remarkable insights about race and religion 131.

Cum laude: with distinction

In 1895, Du Bois became the first African American to earn a Ph.D. from Harvard University. What is ironic about Dubois's philosophy is he developed these theories about race and the source from which they come while studying with Germans and Europeans. One would think that a person would have to be biased or a Black Nationalist who because of scorn, would take the approach to make the white inferior to the black solely on the basis of reverse racial discrimination. What is equally alarming is that many of the things that W.E.B. outlined 120 years ago are still in practice today, particularly with his take on criminology in America and how this crime directly relates to blacks in their struggle for economic and civil justice.

GOD AND SCIENCE

The living omnipotent procreative God of Abraham, Isaac, and Jacob, has a HIGH science associated with him. When speaking about the lineage of God we still have to take in account humanistic sciences in relation to procreation. Bringing this evidence into the fourfold will allow us to wholly or fully process the scriptures and nature, and balance them with our own personal views of God. Note: *The God of your conscience, the one of your mind, is not the same god as the God of Abraham, Isaac, and Jacob.*

Remember, science tells us that the females' body naturally rejects male sperm. This was understood in biblical times but was not explained in a scientific way. People back in that time saw the difficulty it took to have a male child and as a result they had to pray to the LORD *(the omnipotent ithy-phallic fertility god)* in hopes that a male child be born.

Genesis 25: 21 (21) Isaac prayed to the LORD on behalf of his wife, because she was barren. The LORD answered his prayer, and his wife Rebekah became pregnant.

This is why you have stories in the Bible that relate to these truths like Sarah, Elizabeth, and Rachel all of which at some point in time were barren and needed "God" (phallus) to intercede so they could have children. When you have a true agricultural way of life, or a way of life that is governed by hunting and farming you need strong men in order to maintain the living standards of the village. Men were needed at that time to protect the family and property of the father, carry on his name, and help him build upon his fortune. Women were to be taken care of so they were considered a liability and a luxury. Not a liability in the sense of being negative, but they were supposed to be served and pampered and this took fortune. So the fathers wanted males to help them build their fortunes. It wasn't until an alpha male was born of the (males) that the culture developed the kingly standard, and through legend passed down stories of the alpha who had tremendous power. This was done by the elders of the cultures who watched and passed down these stories to the younger generations living in the village. The elders saw that in comparison to the alpha, some males had degeneracy. These degenerate genes led to their insecurities, and their insecurities, caused them to develop traits like jealousy, envy, hatred, and spite. Even though they were male they weren't really powerful enough to organize and maintain the village. The king was an alpha and through evolution was naturally smarter, stronger, and wiser than the other males in his clique. The alpha had a square jaw line, broad shoulders, natural muscle tone and an elongated penis. This is why the king was given the women with the best genes to produce more beings like him. The more beings that were produced like him, the more likely the village or tribe would be strong and successful. Again, polygamy originated within this thought process and is nothing more than a form of natural selection.

John 3:6 *(6) That which is born of flesh is flesh, and that which is born of spirit is spirit.*

If a man is born of a spiritual essence; he will be just that, spiritual. The spiritual essence has everything to do with the submission of the woman to the alpha male in which she is relaxed enough to let him enter in fully. This allows for the intercession of "God" which is the perfect spiritual blending of the alpha and the woman, water and spirit. The submitting of the woman is a spiritual act, one the alpha has an edge on getting the women to fully commit to. Once she comes into contact with this spiritual presence she feels things that she never felt before and this isn't all physical. A lot of it has to do with the mind, which in Hebrew, is connected to and viewed as the spirit.

Cheating creation is what leads to the perversion of the sexes. It is only through spiritual ecstasy which is followed by sensual death that a person will be able to fully recognize their state and position in their life. This will give them clues as to what sign and person is compatible with them. What I am explaining is the centering and finding of one's self as well as what other chemicals/ traits or genes are needed from the opposing sex that once bonded with, will enable the individual to ascend to a higher level of creation and consciousness. Meditation is the only practice that will enable the individual to bond with that other part which is the mate who has all of the qualities the individual needs to ascend to higher levels spiritually physically. It takes a tremendous amount of effort and an honest assessment of self before any major results will occur. Most people go through an initiation, one preceded by nature and guided by the depths of their own minds and imaginations. Basically, it is however deep they are willing to go, to discover a thing, to bring about a desired result. This is a very powerful concept and like any other powerful thing it takes meticulous attention to detail in order to bring about the structured being. In talking about creation, every aspect plays its own unique part in developing and producing heightened levels of consciousness. This is why fornication was so despised. When beings are born through acts of fornication they usually do not stem from a structured thought. However when they are born from fornication they have ego's that tell them they are the one, **John 8:40-42.** This is very dangerous because the unstructured thoughts usually will rival the offspring who were structured thoughts. Thus you have a struggle between the ordered and the chaotic of the genetic world which occurs within nature. The fight is between civilization and the wild. Those who represent chaos are a detriment to the state, and because of this, they are heavily monitored, oppressed, and ultimately terminated.

No one is ever going to say they were the product of alcohol, a lonely night, and the back seat of a Chevy. They will hide the origins of their creation so they won't be looked down upon by society. You also have those who are very powerful thoughts that are born from heavy spontaneous acts of lust which usually are perpetuated by the phases of the moon. Those who are conceived during full moons, when the woman's mind is fully open and able to draw in energy associated with clairvoyance, and clairaudience, are individuals who too will have uncanny talents and abilities.

Truths placed against historical backdrops based on factual evidence validated by scientific evaluation have been dissected in this book. These truths seem very inhumane and have to be transformed into allegories so the people who can truly see will draw distinctions between the truth that is hidden and the fluff that is all around it. These principles and truths can't be taught to the masses because the masses often times cannot see themselves. Therefore one who is weak would not know of his weakness until he truly met someone who was strong. He may have a personality like Judas but because Jesus is socially acceptable he will say he's a Christian. Lip profession is ramped when dealing with religion because everyone wants to do what they want to do and also be perceived as righteous. No one wants to be scum. Even the villains have twisted outlooks where they view themselves as the heroes. So allegories have to be written to pass down the true translations to the people they were written for; while simultaneously hiding the true meanings from those who would use the knowledge to capitalize.

CAPITALIZATION

The following biblical passages are what were used to excuse the enslavement of the American Negroes during the slave trade. While this topic provides the undertone and central theme for this book, it has been overstated because many of the problems that we face in the present world stem directly from it. Acknowledging it brings no solution; however admitting there is a problem is the first step to getting on the road to recovery.

Genesis 4:9-12 *"And the lord said unto Cain, Where is Abel thy Brother? And He said I know not: am I my brother's keeper? And He said, what hast thou done? The voice of thy brother's blood crieth unto me from the ground, and now art thou cursed from the earth, which has opened her mouth to receive thy brother's blood from my hand. When thou tillest the ground, it shall not henceforth yield unto thee her strength.* <u>*You shall be a fugitive and a vagabond shoult thou be in the earth.*</u>

Genesis 9:25-27 *and he said,* **"***Cursed be Canaan; a servant of servants shall he be unto his brethren (26) and he said, blessed be the Lord God of Shem; and Canaan shall be his servant. (27) God shall enlarge Japheth, and he shall dwell in the tents of Shem;* <u>*and Canaan shall be his servant*</u>*. "*

The recent recession that America was in, according to President Barack Obama was due to credit schemes and what he called *"paper champions."* When we think about credit as it pertains to currency, no real money is even exchanged as money has now become credit. Paper currency has no real worth, and is only a means to transfer debt, not resolve it. American dollars are just promissory notes a person exchanges as a measure of good faith until they pay the debt off. The reason that paper money was used is because gold and silver (legal tender to pay off and satisfy debt) was too heavy to lug around all of the time. Not to mention if a person was caught on the open range lugging all their heavy gold around, they could be robbed and have all of their gold taken from them. As a result, the people who had gold kept it in banks, and in return they were given promissory notes or paper money.

<u>Promissory note:</u> a written promise to pay at a fixed or determinable future time a sum of money to a specified individual or to bearer

Whenever people who had gold were doing business they exchanged promissory notes in place of their gold as a promise to pay for whatever they were buying at the time. However, gold was no longer considered legal tender to pay debt in 1971 and this standard was created by Richard Nixon.

In 1971, the Vietnam War increased domestic spending acceleration and inflation caused the United States to run not just a balance of payment deficits but also a balance of trade deficit. For the first time in the 20th century America was faced with this type of crisis. The turning point came in 1970, when a foreign arbitrage of U.S. currency saw U.S. gold coverage of the paper dollar deteriorate from 55% to 22% [133].

<u>Arbitrage:</u> (1) a nearly simultaneous purchase and sale of securities or foreign exchange in different markets in order to profit from price discrepancies (2) the purchase of the stock of a takeover target especially with a view to selling it profitably to the raider

This deterioration, in the view of American economists, represented the point where holders of the dollar had lost faith in the United States ability to cut its budget and trade deficit; because assets totaling $22 billion left the United States. More and more dollars were printed and then sent overseas to pay for the nation's military expenditures and private investments. Because of the excessive printing of paper dollars, and the negative balance of U.S. trade, other nations were increasingly demanding fulfillment of America's "promise to pay." They wanted payment in the form of gold, not paper dollars. On August 5, Congress released a report recommending devaluation of the dollar in an effort to protect the dollar against foreign price-gougers. This was done to stabilize the economy and combat runaway inflation. On August 15, 1971, President Nixon imposed a 90-day wage and price freeze, a 10% import surcharge, and "closed the gold window," making the dollar nonconvertible to gold directly, except on the open market 134. Today America is in a similar crisis as many of its jobs are going overseas. What most people do not understand about the current American economy is that its money is no longer in the country. Hypothetically, for the sake of the example, let's say there was a trillion dollars in circulation in America, whereas now 35% of that trillion is in the banks of foreign nations. With these dollars out of circulation, the 350-400 million people in America are now operating on only 65% of the total budget which has caused a major pinch in the lifestyles the American people were once accustomed to having. America is a consumer nation which means most of its money is spent overseas in foreign exports. The money it spends overseas stays overseas because Americans do not produce and export enough goods that peak the interests of the countries it imports from. If America did, these other countries would import from America spending back the money Americans spend with them.

The solution has always been to print more money but that causes inflation and the money ends up right back overseas. America has grown lax, lazy, privileged, and pompous and is now being invaded by what it calls "aliens." These "aliens" aren't from outer space but from other countries. The original customs that were laid by the ancients were set in place to keep the nation strong against foreign invaders. America has perceived its enemies to be barbaric and carnal and has bulked up its military thinking this is the strategy that will eliminate the threat of it being conquered. However this is a very primitive way of thinking because wars are fought through ideology and strategy, i.e. the pen is mightier than the sword. Your enemy wears a smile, shakes your hand, and sits across from you every day at work. The day of the enemy showing up to your doorstep with a gun and saying come out and fight has long gone. This is paralleled to how America won its revolution against Great Britain. The Red coats wanted the Americans to do what was proper and come out and combat them face to face. The Americans however used strategy, ambush, and more cunning ways to beat the Brits even though they were outnumbered and out financed. Again, I know a person is going to ask what does this have to do with the Bible in relation to religion and sex. I placed the reference of currency within this book so people could get a very adequate view of why the people of the old world worshipped the alpha male (Phallic God/Adonai) and translated his triumph through tribulation in their stories. When you cater to the weak or a weakened mind state you inevitably become weaker. When you kill the strong because you are intimidated by them, you allow something or someone weaker to fill its place. What isn't realized on the opposing end of the weakness is the recession, which means the further weakening of what you replaced the dominant with. All the decisions made by the weaklings trickle in weak thought causing the whole to become crippled which is what has happened to America's economy. When you make a "Living God" a premonition of mind versus a real life physical person, you have just forsaken the natural evolution process that causes genetic upgrade. Lebron James is not Michael Jordan, and Justin Beiber is not Michael Jackson. When you function in a mind state that does not clearly indicate who is who then what you have done is set a stage whereby anybody and anything can lay claims to being "God" himself, god's messenger, god's disciple, and gods servant. This is what has happened in the word today and unless the nation of the gods acknowledges this, everything within it and around it will face certain destruction. The creation and election of Barack Obama shows the current nation is aware of these things, but there still exists within the country a rebellion towards these acknowledgements. Because American money is in these other countries banks, it has no choice but to expand into a one world government, whereby a new realized religion is set in place to ensure the nation remains functioning and powerful. This serves as a reminder that the "Living God" is real and also sets an evolutionary ladder and hierarchy in place for those who love and cherish civilization.

Here in the world today everyone is only concerned with what directly affects them. They haven't a clue as to what indirectly affects them even when it has a potential to be more devastating than a direct hit. They aren't concerned with anything until it shows up at their door step personally. This nihilistic approach at life has caused people to worship things in vain idly that they don't understand; they just merely do it because everyone else is doing it. **Stevie Wonder** said *when people believe in things they don't understand they suffer*. This mentality has led to the present state of false worship, false impersonation, and falsification of "God" in western society. If I show you that money has no real worth and that you can't satisfy but only transfer debt with it, what does this really mean? To the average citizen who is trying to escape a third world country it doesn't mean anything. They would prefer a system that is easy for them to adjust to that will allow them to start participating in the luxuries that America provides, and rightly so; who wants to struggle? However for the person, or descendants of the people who created these knowledge's and systems of religion and ways of existence, it is counterproductive towards the custom that enabled them to evolve into self-sufficient beings in the 1st place. What if you do not want to go to the super market and get groceries and you want to grow your own? What if you do not want your kids to grow up with the present education in America and you want to teach them yourself? What if you have developed to the point where you do not need currency to live and would rather farm? When a person sees what they are up against in terms of debt, ownership of land, and turning real profits from being self-employed, these will become the questions they will ask. When these questions are responded to is when a "living god" will be sought after and very much desired. Now the only real purpose the American dollar holds is the worth that its people think it has; this is where the term fiat comes from.

Fiat: money (as paper currency) not convertible into coin or specie of equivalent value

Today people kill over a substance that has no real worth, and go against a lot of the "do on to others as you would want done unto you" teachings in order to satisfy their own personal lusts of the flesh. Money is almost always the reason that people compromise themselves in this way. The movie *Avatar*

is the highest grossing film to date because it exposes this truth. I wonder what people will say when dollar bills are piled up in the streets because inflation has caused them to have no worth. People who haven't studied history may laugh until they realize this happened in the 30's in Germany and was one of the reasons Hitler was able to come into power. *Private currency speculators caused the German mark to plummet, precipitating one of the worst runaway inflations in modern times. A wheelbarrow full of 100 billion-mark bank notes could not buy one loaf of bread* 134d.. Because money is fiat, it has no real worth, and for these reasons now everything is placed on a debit card. This debit card really is a socialistic form of doing commerce. I say this because no money is even being transferred just 0's. Again dollars are promissory notes, not a legal tender that will satisfy debt. Because the youth who are very impressionable are preyed upon, they will already be ruined before they arrive at these conclusions in their adult life. The language and culture barriers in America make it easy for the person who is for the self to achieve satisfaction with little regards to how or who they infringe upon to obtain it. These selfish tendencies will lead them to justify any means of existence.

Matthew 19:33 then said Jesus unto his disciples, Verily I say unto you, That a rich man shall hardly enter into the kingdom of heaven.

Since wealth is no longer determined by birthing strong sons or "heirs" as it was in biblical times, due to credit; it only seems befitting that the church do away with the old teachings. However the church knows it is only a matter of time before nature brings about the events that causes the world to see the truth. This is why on the 13th card of the Tarot in the major arcana; the pope is kneeling before the man of Death (Daath) who rides the white horse, begging him for mercy and or intercession.

135 Credit allows any person who can understand the system and how it works to be enabled to prosper over those who may be superior genetically or physically. This is stated because in today's times, *"perception is reality."* A person who may be outworked physically can use the means of money that he

415

has not yet earned to advance him in his economic conquest over the person who is diligently working hard to achieve his economic goals. A person with good credit can purchase a business by way of it, and pay someone without it (good credit) a wage. Since the wage worker is paid less than the planner this system of unearned wealth creates a situation where the worker is at a great disadvantage. Being that the workers are those of the minority class, you can see how the imbalance of wealth and work is disproportionate within the system of debt and credit. What credit does, is, it allows those who understand its system to purchase for themselves a lifestyle they may be unable to afford. As long as they appear to have money they can mask their actual worth and pass within society as having it "all together." In this society those who are perceived as being wealthy get preferential treatment opposed to those who do not. Because no one wants to be frowned upon, they all accept "the loan" in order to "keep up with the joneses." Their lifestyles are then driven and predicated by "trending topics" gossip, and vain glorious posing, as each person involved talks up their new toys, new houses, and new fashion, with a "look at me I've got it all together" attitude. If for any reason they lose the job that provides them income, they will be in danger of forfeiting over everything that was bought with credit. The person who has no credit but is willing to work for whatever he obtains has no idea that most of the wealth in America is a perpetrated illusion, as majority of the people are living by means of unearned wealth. The banks have purchased their cars, their homes, as well as the degrees the people have obtained to get a good job. In fact, many people in America who aren't really wealthy but appear to be wealthy use their house as their bank. Because they have credit and a decent job they are able to get approved for a $500,000 house. This house is what they spend majority of their salary on and by the time they are willing to sell it, if they've invested properly and surveyed the housing market correctly, it has doubled its present value. The credit they were able to receive because they had a great job over a thirty year period enables them to sell the property at a very sizeable profit; whereas a person who doesn't have credit can only rent. Renting means the person does not have ownership. The money they are paying to live goes in someone else's pockets. Because it is in someone else's pockets the renters are getting rich from the rent the tenants are paying. If you can't somehow find your way outside of paying rent, in twenty to thirty years you will have nothing. So your children will have no inheritance and like you they will have to use their present life to pay for a house instead of building a fortune upon that foundation the house provides. The descendants of the people who were made to be slaves in whole are at a great disadvantage in terms of credit, housing, and the receiving of good jobs. In a system like the current one in America they are commonly found at the bottom of the economic scale. This has nothing to do with working or building upon something concrete, it has to do with the structuring of a certain system that requires a certain level of education to understand it and another level of inheritance to build into and maintain it. The notion of getting something before you have earned it to the descendants of slaves is a policy that most do not really understand. Because these people have been functioning in a "slave" mentality as a whole many have no idea how simple and easy the credit system is to use. Only the most trained of mind and disciplined of character are able to understand credit, banking, and government. Because lower level intelligence also exists in humans, provisions have been made so those who operate in higher mind states will not be held hostage by those who operate in lower mind states. Overthrow and anarchy aren't options for the state and those who seek this path, seek destruction. Credit on the other hand is a great resource for those who build empires and have the understanding as well as the discipline to execute their plans. Those who complain about it have not evolved to the point where they really grasp why credit was designed and why it has been instrumental in the building of the New World.

Edwin Griffin in his book a *Creature from Jekyll Island* outlined what he perceived to be the corruption administered within the Federal Reserve System. Griffin said that the Federal Reserve is a cartel designed to make the tax payers bailout banks when other countries that the banks have lent their money to can no longer pay. These tax payers' dollars ensure that the banks still operate when the money they have lent out is spent and is not able to be paid back. He went on to say the Federal Reserve is a silent partner in the cartel of privately owned banks that uses the law to regulate the interest rates that the banks have on their loans. Because the bankers have come together with the help of "The Feds" a monopoly is formed whereby the government facades ownership of the banks and poses as the humanitarian establishment to the people.

But again, even if Griffin's words are true, most people have no concern culturally for those who have been made to serve. There is so much distance between the people in America culturally that they view each other as alien. In the Q&A forum held after the state of the union address by President Barack Obama in his 1st term, we saw just how much America is still divided. Viewing each other as alien only "alienates" people from the things that make them similar. Most people do not even think about other people's cultures and how the ignorance of not having an understanding about the cultures of others limits the scope of their own individual consciousness. This ignorance in turn hinders their social awareness and creates a state of prejudice and bigotry, whereby they classify these alien cultures according to their stereo-types rather than their character types. Though certain stereotypes may be true they often stem from somewhere and there is usually an unseen or unrecognized schism within a cultures makeup and way of life that causes them to have a character trait that when highlighted appears to be a character flaw.

136 Our society today operates in opposition to nature; it punishes the strong and rewards the weak. *"It shoots eagles and feeds pigeons."* It punishes the dominant ones for fear of its own safety not knowing the more it kills the dominant the more it as a society dies. The more it fears polygamy, the more weaker males are encouraged to breed. The alpha male has evolved to maintain breeding rights among those un-evolved, to ensure the species not only survives but excels. Again the evolution of the woman is the alpha male and this is why he attracts so many women. Who would know best how to treat a woman than an evolved woman in her highest state? The more of "God's" essence a man has within him, the more women will be attracted to him. (This is supported by the life of MJ & the great King Solomon who had wisdom that exceeded all who lived in Egypt so much that he had a 1000 wives and concubines as a result of his godly essence.) Telling women the truth seems harsh and inhumane, yet it is what is needed. The weaker males

tell her what she wants to hear and still have their women or men on the side. These romantic instances show how people want to be lied to. When the world wants to believe that "God" is a blonde haired blue eyed male with no supporting evidence aside from paintings done by Michelangelo, it further shows how people are more inclined to believe something that is made up versus something that is the truth; especially when we now know the origins of all people come from Africa through Mitochondrial Eve.

On June 5th 2010 the 89-year-old Hearst Newspapers columnist and white house press icon Helen Thomas made remarks that earned her the label of being anti-Semitic. These remarks forced her to resign from a job she held for over 60 years. She said, Jews should *"get the hell out of Palestine"* and *"go back home to Poland,*

Germany, America and everywhere else" 136b. Her "jaw-dropping words" sparked a firestorm of controversy in the media; but one may inquire as to why her words caused such a huge ripple in mainstream news and journalism? When we look at the word Semitic is translates as a branch of the Afro-Asiatic family comprising a number of ancient and modern languages of Southwest Asia and Africa that includes Akkadian, Hebrew, Aramaic, Arabic, and Amharic. Nowhere does it say those of Germanic, or Polish descent. One theory as to why her words were piercing and intolerable is that the people now living in these areas of Palestine and Gaza are not the people of original "Semitic" descent. The people who are living in Palestine now, who Thomas was describing, have ancestry that lies in Germany, Poland, and other European countries. When the scriptures were written and the Bible was constructed the scriptures were talking about the original inhabitants of the land. People today, who do not know their history, think the people now living in those areas (Palestine) are the direct descendants of the God of Israel and Abraham; this is where the great confusion lies. To bring this point to a more conclusive end, imagine if the prophecies were about the original Americans, (the natives or Indians) but everyone who has migrated from other nations to America, are acting like the prophecies are about them. A journalist comes along with sixty years of expertise in her field of research and makes a statement routed in truth and it ends her sixty year career as a journalist and white house press correspondent. Because she stated, *"they should get the hell out of Palestine"* probably was enough to lose her job. Being at that high a level one would think a person would know how to express themselves. Because she was the leading expert in her field, her emphatic statement showed bias, and though her statement may have had truth routed within it, the way she went about it obviously was interpreted as unprofessional. Though good journalism is unbiased and a presentation of facts, I was once told that if you threw a rock at a pack of dogs, the one who cries is the one who gets hit. As stated in this book earlier, the prophecies regarding that region are related to America which makes all the fighting over the holy land today really obsolete and out of date. What those people are laying claim to is something that happened thousands of years ago and is now happening again in America. This example shows you how people can wander into delusion further causing them to lose their eyesight which paralyzes their intelligences and recedes their comprehension levels to the point where it becomes non-existent. This is what reverses the upright stance that people have evolved into and causes them to descend downward back into the animal nature where they walk on all fours instead of two. This is what I call de-evolution.

Romantic: (1) Imaginary not based on fact (2) Marked by the imaginative or emotional appeal of what is heroic, adventurous, remote, mysterious, or idealized

Allegory: a story in which the characters and events are symbols that stand for truths about human life

   Though the heads of the false religious systems are the beneficiaries of the lies, the people of the Abrahamic covenant today (descendants of slaves) who profess to believe in a "Living God" are the same as the people in the Bible who turned their backs on Moses, Jesus, and the rest of the prophets. This is stated because if we were to composite the life of the people here today and place society as a whole within the Bible, these same people who know what is in the Bible and can readily comprehend it choose to idolize materialism, all forms of romanticism, and secretly and covertly promote anarchy under the guise of freedom; which is the exact thing that happened in the Bible according to the Book of Isaiah.

Isaiah 30: 8-13 to Egypt, whose help is utterly useless. Therefore I call her Rahab the Do-Nothing. (8) Go now, write it on a tablet for them, inscribe it on a scroll, that for the days to come it may be an everlasting witness. (9) These are rebellious people, deceitful children, children unwilling to listen to the LORD's instruction. (10) They say to the seers, "See no more visions!" and to the prophets, "Give us no more visions of what is right! Tell us pleasant things, prophesy illusions. (11) Leave this way, get off this path, and stop confronting us with the Holy One of Israel!" (12) Therefore, this is what the Holy One of Israel says: "Because you have rejected this message, relied on oppression and depended on deceit, (13) this sin will become for you like a high wall, cracked and bulging, that collapses suddenly, in an instant.

Naturally if you have a class of citizen on the top you'll have a class of citizen on the bottom. But any person black, white, red, or yellow that climbs to the higher echelons of society will inevitably face the same conclusion, which is ruin. Once you've hit the top the only place to go is the bottom. This is the great way in which the universe operates; destruction and creation, contraction and conception, youth, old age, life and death.

In looking at the condition and mind-state of the people here on earth, it is imperative the state uphold order at any cost. When the ruler-ship of a nation is shown to have flaws or kinks, the people with the undeveloped conscious and mind will trample over the order in the civilization. Once this occurs, the likelihood of the civilized state becoming a third world country increases. Edwin Griffin the author of *The Creature of Jekyll island* also said that, "*a grouping of financial, political and industrial interests at the very top of the world's economic and political power pyramid" have "created a popular climate of bias that makes scientific objectivity almost an impossibility.*" I placed this quote here again because the truth is so absent from the society we live in today that one would conclude it (the truth) is something that people in power do not want people without power to know.

While writing this book I had the notion that the questions people aren't asking are the ones that will give them the answers to the questions they think they know. What I mean by answers are not rebuttals; I am talking about the real solutions to the real problems. When I think about race and religion in the world and how it relates to America, several questions come to mind. The first, is why would the people who have written and arranged the Bible and taught it under its present pretense, never acknowledged that they wrote and taught what was suitable for them and their culture? Secondly is why the intellectuals of the scholastic world would refer to blacks as being apes? Here we have Romans who have now printed their own Bible as well as Romans on the opposite end of that spectrum in the scientific world both making claims that black people should be slaves due to their animalistic and pagan natures. This is a very puzzling notion as it would hint to a typecasting of an entire race of people based solely on color and physical stature.

In August of 2009 a story broke out about a Costco doll that was black. The reason the story received so much press is the doll which was sold by the Costco Company, came with a monkey. The doll holding the monkey is wearing a skull cap with the words, Lil monkey on it 137. It was no secret that blacks in America used to be called porch monkeys, and were depicted in minstrel shows and cartoons as such. Though blacks are no longer taunted with the words "porch monkey" as they once were, this thinking is still a part of the psyche of some racist and bigoted individuals who have positions of power within American corporate media.

137d Assessing stories like these and further researching the origin of racial slanders and slurs, I decided to look back to the origins of human existence from not only a biblical standpoint but also a historical point of view as well. Upon doing so, I discovered that Africa is the "cradle of civilization" and is where ALL people originated from. Researching Africa caused me to inquire about the origins of the major races of the world. I've already given details about the Asian dynasties being the eldest next to those of ancient Africa, so naturally I looked to the origins of those with European and Caucasian ancestry. This caused a whole slew of questions to be asked. The first of which is, "Why would the Romans falsify the origins of blacks as if it is the origins of their race? And what would make a culture stand in place of another culture and emphatically preach that the other races culture is their own? What is it in their own culture they are running from? What are they trying to hide?" The answers to these questions are the key to the religious debate in the world as well as America. Why have these people done these atrocities? Either they don't know where they come from, or the origins from which they come stem from a very bizarre set of circumstances. Circumstances that if the public knew would cause these Europeans to be looked at much like the blacks who some scholars have typecast as the descendants of apes.

The Book of Illumination

CHAPTER 21
PLANET OF THE APES

The Book of Illumination
CHAPTER 21
PLANET OF THE APES

PLANET OF THE APES

138 In American literature there is a very popular story involving an ape who is named King Kong. This is the portrayal of a big black ape, who is a god to its inhabitants on its own land away from everything and everybody. In this story European opportunists stumble upon this huge ape residing in his natural habitat. They come to the conclusion that if this huge black god "ape" was brought over to the United States, it could make a lot of money and attract a lot of  spectators. This opportunistic thinking led to them enslaving the black god "ape" where they then brought him to the United States on a ship to be their entertainment. While over in the United States the black ape and a white woman developed a special type of relationship and a natural fascination with one another... She understood his dominance and was the only person able to tame him; while he showed her that no one on earth could protect her and

 worship her with more admiration than him. The movie the *Blindside* starring Sandra Bullock further exploits this aspect of the relationship between the big black (ape /Michael) and the beautiful petite white woman. In fact Sandra Bullock, another Leo, won an Oscar for her portrayal in this movie. However unlike the movie the *Blindside*, in the story of King Kong, the black ape grows tired of entertaining settlers, and when he revolts the society conspires to kill him. In the end of the story the ape takes the white woman and climbs a tower (phallic symbol) to show he is preeminent even in his death. He climbs all the way to the top of the tower and beats upon his chest before he is executed; showing the world that he is the most dominant and evolved being in it. When I parallel this story to black males in America the similarities are shocking. Quentin Tarantino seems to think the same thing and in his movie ***Ingloriuos Basterds*** he scripted a dialogue about it. *"My native land is the jungle but my visit to America was not fortuitous to me...When I went from the jungle to America did I go by boat, against my will? On this boat ride did I go in chains? When I arrived was I displayed in chains? Am I the story of Negros in America? – Well I must be King Kong"* 138a.

425

I referenced the story of King Kong in this manner to show the power of allegory to those who have not the ability to recognize it in their own religious faith. By looking at the story of King Kong and paralleling it to black males, maybe someone who was unable or un-willing to see the points I am making in regards to religion, will be able to open their eyes and take a closer look at what is being said within this story about the American culture of today.

Dragon Ball Z, the world's highest grossing Japanese anime, has become a

hit sensation within the American world of cartoons. In the Dragon ball Z cartoon, there is depicted, a representation of how huge apelike beasts turn into Asians that morph into blonde haired, blue eyed warmongers.

When the moon is full these *Saiyans* transform into huge ape like destructive beasts. One of the final stages of the Asian Saiyan's transformation is when they morph into Super Saiyans. This is when they become the blonde haired, blue eyed, nearly unconquerable warriors who get stronger after every battle. Goku, the main hero of the saga, gets his name from Gokul, India, the birthplace of Krishna. When I compare this cartoon with the race theory proposed by W.E.B. Dubois, two plausible explanations occur. The apes either represent the black race that the Asians and Caucasians came from, or it is an aspect that hints to the complete nature of the Caucasian man as being a Neanderthal/ape man, [(Cauc) Asian] who eventually ended up blonde haired and blue eyed. Many reading may ask how I've come to this point. M. Knight Shymalan delivered through Samuel Jackson a heavy monologue in the movie **Unbreakable.** Jackson's character, Elijah said, "*I've studied a form of comic books intimately I spent a third of my life in a hospital bed with nothing else to do but read. I believe comics are our last link to passing on* *ancient knowledge and history. The Egyptians drew on walls, in countries all over the world to pass on knowledge through pictorial forms.*"139 In the Movie **Unbreakable** Samuel Jackson's Character, Elijah, who initiates the son of David (Bruce Willis) is an obvious allegory that represents a more realistic interpretation of the biblical story of Jesus and John the Baptist. The quote taken from the movie *Unbreakable* is evidence that ancient knowledge's are passed on through pictorial forms, and those with illuminated crown chakras can see what the characters in them are representing. Before comics were invented, there were hieroglyphs and these hieroglyphs are what the stories in the Bible are comprised of. The new pictorial forms of the 21st century are movies, and for these reasons I have used many in this book.

*"If it were not for the fact that White and Black can procreate together…there would be two quite distinct species. The Negro would be to man what the donkey is to the horse, or rather, if the White was man, the Negro would no longer be man but an animal of another species like the Ape." -**George Louis de Buffon*** 140.

141 **George Louis de Buffon** published *Histoire Naturelle* (Natural History) in 1749. In it, Buffon theorized that African skin tone was a result of the intense tropical sun and also considered the similarities between black people and apes hinting at the possibility of a common ancestry between them. Since many scholars and scientists attribute evolution as the way life started on earth this would be an interesting discovery because Mr. Buffon's hypothesis would inevitably link black people as the first Homo sapiens next to their "hominoid ancestors." In this train of thought, European Scholars linking blacks to apes adds legitimacy to the theory to blacks being the original people. This is stated because in Darwin's theory of evolution he attributes man's existence as coming from apes. If apes are the original species man evolved from, by Mr. Buffon's categorization of blacks as coming directly from them, he is acknowledging that blacks are the original people of the earth. Romantics who were ethnocentric and naïve in their descriptions printed these views within their textbooks; but what is of particular interest about Mr. Buffon's theory is that he could say that black people came from apes but could not say that white people came from blacks.

In the 18th century for the most part, people acquired their information about Africans and Indians in North America, not from direct experience with these nations, but rather primarily from those involved in the slave trade. J.F. Blumenbach, a German physiologist and anthropologist, born in Gotha,

Germany in 1752 divided humanity, into five races: 1) Caucasian or white; 2) Mongolian or yellow; 3) Malayan or brown; 4) Negro, Ethiopian or black; and 5) American or red.

Blumenbach thought the origins of white Europeans geographically were near the Caucasus Mountains, and referred to them as "Caucasian" 142a. The term *Caucasian* originated as one of the racial categories recognized in the 19th century and is derived from the region of the Caucasus Mountains located in the middle of the Eurasian plate between Europe and Asia. The term Caucasus from which the racial epithet Caucasian originates also refers to the Caucasus Inducus, a mountain range stemming from north-western Pakistan to eastern and central Afghanistan also known as the Hindu Kush. The Caucasus had an attraction to scholars of the 19th century, because of its proximity to Mount Ararat, the tallest peak in Turkey where Noah's Ark was speculated to have landed. That alongside the famed beauty of Caucasian women was more than enough to examine it with a thorough scope for 19th century philosophers like Blumenbach 142.

Genesis 8:4 And the ark rested in the seventh month, on the seventeenth day of the month, upon the mountains of Ararat.

143 Kim Kardashian, one of the most beautiful women in the world today is of Armenian descent, a country located in the Caucuses. Her attraction to men of color and former relationship with Reggie Bush, a pro athlete/gladiator with the physique of a "god" has always baffled people in the mainstream media like Howard Stern. Her recent *marriage to Kanye West a professed "god" is more evidence that validates how Caucasian women and *"the sons of god"* share a mutual attraction for one another. This relationship, like many others in this book, was prophesized in the Book of Genesis; bearing more evidence that we are indeed, at this present time, back at the beginning of a new age.

Genesis 6: 1 That the sons of God saw <u>the daughters of men that they were fair;</u> and they took them as wives of all which they chose.

When speaking in reference to this new age, knowledge and information are the key words that describe it best. In this book I've made known the existences of deities by using sacred geometry and supreme mathematics. On a milder note, both Kim Kardashian and Amber Rose, the former girlfriend of Kanye West, share the same birthday. This shows his adoration for these types of women stems more from an energy stimulus than it does from the women themselves proving once again numbers don't lie.

Getting back to the reason I say "speculated" biblical accounts in regards to Noah's Ark is due to the allegorical style the Bible was written in. When taking into account the Matsya Purana in seeing that a (Hindu) legend existed prior to Noah's ark about a flood; and then further looking at the allegories represented therein. The landing of Noah's Ark in the Caucasus Mountains most likely is an allegory about the <u>carrier of the covenant,</u> {the ARK itself, i.e (NOAH)} and the new place the WORD or LOGOS was in when the world started over during the Age of Aquarius. Looking at the allegory within the story makes the ark itself "the boat" fictitious in the sense that Noah was the "ARK" that carried the ancient and sacred knowledge and COVENANT of the "Living God." The last place this remnant (Noah the Ark) was deposited were the Caucasus, just as the new place the ARK is being deposited in this cycle of history is America. This Logos as described by ancient philosophers is synonymous to the Demiurge of Freemasonry that creates the universe through naming and building, i.e. animating; "*let there be light.*" What makes this Logos or Demiurge so significant is that civilization doesn't exist until He/It reincarnates to reorder it. The "entity" who reorders and renames the universe is also the consciousness that "created" it. His/ its existence has been recorded since the beginning of civilization and again is called Isvara.4444

<u>Logos:</u> the divine animating principle pervading the Universe. 2.) Jesus Christ

According to the Bible, Japheth and his two brothers formed the three major races. The tribe of Japheth was supposed to have originated in the Caucasus, and then spread north and westwards. Japheth is one of the three sons of Noah in the Bible. He is most popularly regarded as the youngest son of the three. For those Jews, Muslims, and Christians who take the genealogies of Genesis to be historically accurate, Japheth is commonly believed to be the father of the Europeans. The link between Japheth and the

Europeans stems from *Genesis* 10:5, which states the sons of Japheth moved to the isles of the Gentiles, commonly believed to be the Greek isles although some theories suggest the British Isles.

Genesis 10:1-5 *(1) Now these are the generations of the sons of Noah, Shem, Ham, and Japheth: and unto them were sons born after the flood. (2) The sons of Japheth; Gomer, and Magog, and Madai, and Javan, and Tubal, and Meshech, and Tiras. (3) And the sons of Gomer; Ashkenaz, and Riphath, and Togarmah. (4) And the sons of Javan; Elishah, and Tarshish, Kittim, and Dodanim. (5) By these were the isles of the Gentiles divided in their lands; every one after his tongue, after their families, in their nations.*

Japheth, the son of Noah, had seven sons: Below are the peoples/races that scholars attribute to be his progeny.

(1) Javan: Greeks (Ionians)
(2) **Magog:** Scythians, Slavs, Hungarians
(3) Madai: Mitanni, Mannai Medes, Persians Indo-Aryans, Kurds
(4) **Tubal**: Tabali, Georgians, Italics, Illyrians, Iberians, Basques
(5) Tiras: Thracians, Goths, Jutes, Teutons
(6) **Meshech**: Phrygians, Caucasus Iberians
(7) Gomer: Scythians, Turks, Armenians, Welsh, Picts, Irish, Germans 144

<u>Caucasus</u>: Region in SE Europe between the Caspian Sea divided by Caucasus Mountains (2) Caucasia

<u>Caucasians</u>: consisting of or characteristics of a race of mankind native of Europe, Southwest Asia, and classified by physical features of having light skinned pigments and of European descent.

The Qur'an makes mention of those who transgressed against Allah as de-evolving and turning into apes.

The Qur'an (al Araf) 7:166
And then, when they disdainfully persisted in doing what they had been forbidden to do, We said unto them "Be as Apes despicable.

The Qur'an (al Maeda 5:60
Say: "Shall I tell you who, in the sight of God, deserves a yet worse retribution than these? They whom God has rejected and whom He has condemned, and whom He has turned into apes and swine because they worshipped the powers of evil:" these are yet worse in station, and farther astray from the right path [than the mockers].

This particular scripture from the Qur'an provides evidence that a group of people who transgressed against the teachings of "God" where outcaste and transformed into apes. Making sense of all that we have speculated upon really becomes tangible when we take into account that an Ice Age occurred around 11000 B.C. Since ancient cultures passed on knowledge in pictorial forms such as hieroglyphs and writings on the walls of their temples, this is more evidence in support of the race theory W.E.B. Dubois hypothesized about. If a people were driven out of the land between the Tigris and Euphrates rivers into various regions of Europe before the Ice Age; that Ice Age extending through several millenniums could have confined them to their own habitat and region. This confinement could have easily changed their appearances making them lighter in hue due to the cold and intense climate. In this theory they may have never came in contact with their original people; and if after being isolated for many thousands of years they were to see their original people, they may become frightened, threatened, and disoriented.

Adolf Hitler who was the Fuher in Germany during WWII is said to have hated Jews and Negroes. Being a devout studier of the Occult he is said to have waged war with these people as a result of what he studied and how he was treated as a child. Hitler represents for my example the fundamental truth that showcases the natural paranoia between the [germ/man (not those of Germanic nationality] but the ({primitive mind-state} of the Neanderthal personified) and his feelings towards the original (black God) and his mixed kinsman the (Semite)

Neanderthal: a sub species from the genus homo Sapien neanderthalensis known from skeletal remains in Europe that lived about 30,000 years ago

The Neanderthal is a small valley of the river Düssel in the German federal state of North Rhine-Westphalia, located about 12 km (7.5 mi) east of Düsseldorf. The Neanderthal was named after theologian Joachim Neander, who lived nearby in Düsseldorf in the late 17th century. "Neander" is a form of the common German surname Neumann. In turn, Neanderthals were named after "Neander Valley", where the first Neanderthal remains were found 145.

Earlier in the book we discussed the relationship between Magneto and Professor X of the X-men. In the most recently released epic about the two entitled *X-Men 1ˢᵗ class*, we saw the origins of Magneto's and Professor X's friendship develop from its inception. In the story of Magneto we learned he was a Jewish exile whose mother had been executed and experimented on by German scientists. Magneto is on a mission to execute the German scientist who killed and experimented on him and his mother. This, as implied in the movie, is the only way to liberate Magneto from the misery and humility faced while living on the concentration camps. The movie also has an undertone that hints to the opposition between mutants and mankind. Magneto fights on the side of the natural born mutants who are discriminated against by the rest of the layman society. The German scientist Magneto is in opposition with gains his mutant powers by experimenting on (mutants) in inhumane ways, in order to figure out what their powers are, so he himself can obtain them. If we acknowledge what has been mentioned within this book and parallel the characters in the movie to it, all of the answers instantly jump out in front of us. WWII pitted the German (Nazi's) under the authority of Adolf Hitler against the Jews. The Neanderthal's origins as just explained are from Germany. In the prequel *X-men 1ˢᵗ Class* there was a statement made about the "Neanderthal" being on the run, and towards the end of the movie, the Neanderthal is executed by the Jewish Magneto whose name, Eric means Ruler or King and in the kabbalah in Hebrew is spelled Aryk which again hints to the Ark of the Covenant [145a].

Germ: (1): a small mass of living substance capable of developing into an organism or one of its parts (2) something that initiates development or serves as an origin

Mankind: (1) a bipedal primate mammal (*Homo sapiens*) that is anatomically related to the great apes but distinguished especially by notable development of the brain with a resultant capacity for articulate speech and abstract reasoning, is usually considered to form a variable number of freely interbreeding races, and is the sole living representative of the hominid family

Mankind is distinguished from the rest of creation by having society as its form which is, in itself good but unenlightened – Alexander Piatigorsky.

Early interpretations of the Bible led many Western scholars to believe that all of humanity was descended from Noah; I personally have discovered these stories written in the Bible are allegories that tell us pertinent historical information. According to Manetho, a priest and scholar of the ancient world, at the time Neanderthals were roaming around the country where their origins lie, Germany, civilizations in Africa were flourishing and at their zenith. If the modern world knew this about the two cultures, it would in a sense cause the world to end as everything that has been taught in the present American society would have to be reexamined. This information is coded within the Bibles scriptures, their titles, the name of the characters, as well as the regions the characters are from. Chapters 9 and 10 of the Book of Genesis deal with the breaking up of Noah's sons into the world. The name of Cush, Ham's eldest son, means 'black' in Hebrew, and "Canaan" means 'lowland. In the Genesis Noah does not curse Ham, but curses Canaan, saying that he and his descendants would be a "servant of servants."

Genesis 9:24-26 **(24)** *And Noah awoke from his wine, and knew what his younger son had done unto him.(25)And he said, Cursed be Canaan; a servant of servants shall he be unto his brethren (26) And he said, Blessed be the LORD God of Shem; and Canaan shall be his servant.*

When we refer back to the story of Cain and Abel we see Cain who was also referred to as "Cainan" was cursed just as Canaan in **Genesis 4:8-12.** This is further foreshadowing that "Canaan" is supposed to be cursed throughout the Bible, similar to how all three wives of the sons of Abraham were barren. (Sarai , Rachel, Rebekah.) The same sets of recurring circumstances appear again and again in the Bible, which makes us look to the patterns rather than the stories themselves.

Genesis 4:8-12 (8) And Cain talked with Abel his brother: and it came to pass, when they were in the field, that Cain rose up against Abel his brother, and slew him. (9) And the LORD said unto Cain, Where is Abel thy brother? And he said, I know not: Am I my brother's keeper? (10) And he said, What hast thou done? the voice of thy brother's blood crieth unto me from the ground. (11)And now art thou cursed from the earth, which hath opened her mouth to receive thy brother's blood from thy hand; (12) When thou tillest the ground, it shall not henceforth yield unto thee her strength; a fugitive and a vagabond shalt thou be in the earth.

In the Old Testament in the Book of Ezekiel it states the Son of Man should turn his face against Gog the land of Magog and prophecy against him. It goes further to state the LORD, God is against him (Gog). The land of Magog is the land of one of the sons of Japheth who is a Gentile. Gog is "supposedly" a prince occupying the lands throne; Gog alongside Meshech and Tubal are "reportedly" all sons of Japheth.

Ezekiel 38:2-3 (2) Son of man, set thy face against Gog, the land of Magog, the chief prince of Meshech and Tubal, and prophesy against him,(3) And say, Thus saith the

Lord GOD; Behold, I am against thee, O Gog, the chief prince of Meshech and Tubal.

However, when we look at the New Testament scriptures regarding what seems to be the same events we get an entirely different interpretation.

Revelation 20:7-8 (7) And when the thousand years are expired, <u>Satan shall be loosed</u> out of his prison, (8) And shall go out <u>to deceive the nations</u> which are in the four quarters of the earth, <u>Gog, and Magog, to gather them together to battle</u>: the number of whom is as the sand of the sea.

I underlined certain pieces of the scripture so we can get a more accurate portrait of what they are saying which is, "*Satan shall be loosed to deceive the nations of Gog and Magog to gather them together in battle and prophecy against them.*" So now, not only do we have Jesus who in the Gospels tells his disciples not to go in the way of the Gentiles in the NT, (matt. 10:1-5) and later states that he will be delivered unto the Gentiles to be crucified (Matt. 20:18-19), we also have the LORD himself declaring war against the Gentiles in the OT, however again, the New Testament calls him Satan.

Matthew 20:18&19 (18) Behold, we go up to Jerusalem; and the Son of man shall be betrayed unto the chief priests and unto the scribes, and they shall condemn him to death, (19) And shall deliver him to the Gentiles to mock, and to scourge, and to crucify him: and the third day he shall rise again.

Isaiah 42:1 (1) Behold my servant, whom I uphold; mine elect, in whom my soul delighteth; I have put my spirit upon him; he shall bring forth judgment to the Gentiles.

Joel 3:9-12 (9) Proclaim ye this among the Gentiles; Prepare war, wake up the mighty men, let all the men of war draw near; let them come up: (10) Beat your plowshares into swords and your pruninghooks into spears: let the weak say, I am strong. (11) Assemble yourselves, and come, all ye heathen, and gather yourselves together round about: thither cause thy mighty ones to come down, O LORD. (12) Let the heathen be wakened, and come up to the valley of Jehoshaphat: for there will I sit to judge all the heathen round about.

These aren't the only indicators that enable us to understand that God is waging war continuously in the Bible with certain nations. Again here are other clues that when connected together we get a greater sense of what the Bible is saying in reference to the nation(s) the "Living God" despises.

Jeremiah 4:7 (7) The lion is come up from his thicket and the destroyer of the Gentiles is on his way; he is gone forth from his place to make thy land desolate; and thy cities shall be laid waste, without an inhabitant.

Isaiah 42:13 (13) The Lord shall go forth as a mighty man, he shall stir up Jealousy like a man of war: he shall cry yea, roar; he shall prevail against his enemies.

Isaiah 10:33 (33) Behold, the lord, the Lord of Hosts shall lop the bough with terror: and the high ones of stature shall be hewn down, and the haughty shall be humbled.

Amos 9:13 (13) behold, the days come, saith the lord, that the plowman shall overtake the reaper, and the treader of grapes him that soweth seed; and the mountains shall drop sweet wine, and all the hills shall melt.

Each of these references about Gentiles being judged is found in the OT. Even the 46th chapter of the Book of Enoch supports the OT.

XLVI. The Head of Days and the Son of Man. *Enoch 46:2-6 (2) And I asked the angel who went with me and showed me all the hidden things, concerning that (3) Son of Man, who he was, and whence he was, (and) why he went with the Head of Days? And he answered and said unto me: This is the son of Man who hath righteousness, With whom dwelleth righteousness, And who revealeth all the treasures of that which is hidden, Because the Lord of Spirits hath chosen him, And whose lot hath the pre-eminence before the Lord of Spirits in uprightness forever. (4)And this Son of Man whom thou hast seen Shall raise up the kings and the mighty from their seats,[And the strong from their thrones]And shall loosen the reins of the strong,And break the teeth of the sinners. (5)[And he shall put down the kings from their thrones and kingdoms]Because they do not extol and praise Him,Nor humbly acknowledge whence the kingdom was bestowed upon them. (6) And he shall put down the countenance of the strong, And shall fill them with shame.*

Remember **Ezekiel 38:2** says the Son of Man should turn his face against Gog and Magog and prophecy against them to gather them together to battle. In Jeremiah the destroyer of the Gentiles is listed as a lion. And in **Isaiah 42:13** the Lord is said to be a mighty man who will stir up jealousy like a man of war roaring and prevailing against his enemies, yet in the 1 Epistle of Peter the (roaring) lion is called the Devil. *The devil is in the details...*

1 Peter 5:8 (8) Be sober, be vigilant; because your adversary the devil, as a roaring lion, walketh about, seeking whom he may devour.

In Genesis 49:8-9, as well as Revelation 5:1, the Lion is regarded as being praised by the other tribes of Israel as well as being the only entity who was able to loosen the seals of the Book of Life. These scriptures coupled with the fact that in Astrology the Leo (short for Leader) is ruled by the Sun and is depicted as a lion illustrates to us that this lion is a very key and significant figure throughout many of the Bible's prophecies.

Amos 3:8 (8) The lion hath roared, who will not fear? The lord God hath spoken, who can but prophecy?

Hosea 11:10 They shall walk after the LORD: he shall roar like a lion: when he shall roar, then the children shall tremble from the west.

Micah 5:8 (8) And the remnant of Jacob shall be among the Gentiles in the midst of many people as a lion among the beasts of the forest, as a young lion among the flocks of sheep: who, if he go through, both treadeth down, and teareth in pieces, and none can deliver.

Again when you take the scripture Micah 5:8 and put it with Matthew 20:19 and Genesis 15:13-15, it basically states that the root of Abraham through Jacob whose ancestors were enslaved for 400 years will be a lion who will be delivered up to the Gentiles to be crucified. After that crucifixion, he will return to deliver his lost people by bringing judgment to the nation they were afflicted by, and then he will ascend to his kingly throne. It seems to me, and again I am just speculating, that the nations of the Gentiles (Romans and Greeks) who wrote and comprised the Bible in its present form(s) added these new chapters in the NT as they deciphered OT scriptures.

As their studying became greater and more advanced, they tried within the Bible to translate out the fact that the nation the "Living God" would judge would be the Gentile (Greco-Roman) nations and because they were Gentiles, they tried to create in the latter half of the Bible through Paul and Peter an outlet that would enable them to twist the facts and make themselves appear to be the nation (Church) that "God" was with. Remember the pledge stated in the 15th chapter of Genesis that says that God will judge the nation that the children of Abraham served.

Genesis 15:13-15 (12) As the sun was setting, Abram fell into a deep sleep, and a thick and dreadful darkness came over him. (13) Then the LORD said to him, "Know for certain that your descendants will be strangers in a country not their own, and they will be enslaved and mistreated four hundred years. (14) But I will punish the nation they serve as slaves, and afterward they will come out with great possessions. (15) You, however, will go to your fathers in peace and be buried at a good old age.

Continuing past the Genesis we get into the Exodus which is a book that examines the exit of the Hebrew slaves from the rule of Pharaoh. It also entails an in depth story of a Canaanite (avatar) who leads a revolt against an oppressive Egyptian government. If we are looking at this story as an allegory that has within it the details that tell us prophetically what would happen to the enslaved seed of Abraham after they were led out of bondage; we can then composite this story in relevance to the American Negros of today. It says here in the Book of Exodus that the Egyptians made the children of Israel serve with rigor.

Exodus 1:11-12 (11) And the Egyptians made the children of Israel serve with rigour (12) And they made their lives bitter with hard bondage, in mortar and brick, and in all manner of service in the field: all their service, wherein they made them serve, was with rigour.

Rigour: a condition that makes life difficult, challenging or uncomfortable

Acts 7:6-7 (6) And God spake on the wise that his seed (children) should sojorn in a strange land; and that they should bring them into bondage, and entreat them evil four hundred years (7) And the nation to whom they shall be in bondage will I judge, said God: and after that shall they come forth, and serve me in this place.

Acts 7:34-36 (34) I have seen the affliction of my people which is in Egypt, and I have heard their groaning, and am come down to deliver them, And now come, I will send thee into Egypt. (35) This Moses whom they refused, saying Who made thee a ruler and a Judge? The same did God send to be a ruler and a deliverer by the angel which appeared to him in the bush (36) He brought them out, after that he had shewed wonders and signs in the land of Egypt and in the red sea, and in the wilderness forty years.

In this account of the Exodus Moses or Musa in Hebrew rises as the heroic figure that becomes a "god" and leads the people of Israel out of bondage from the Egyptians.

Exodus 7:1 And the LORD said unto Moses, See, I have made thee a god to Pharaoh: and Aaron thy brother shall be thy prophet.

146 Avatars as regarded by the scriptures are born of water, which is an indication they come from chaos. Joshua the son of nun, Jesus Christ, and Solomon were all born of water. The water birth of Moses was attributed to his mother rapping him in swaddling garments and placing him in a basket where he later was discovered by Pharaohs daughter. (Note all of the godsends endure through times of chaos which water represents. All remain a float with the help of the ark, which is the WORD that carries them through times of tumult as they are the holy vessels of/ for "God/good.") Above is Vishnu who floats on an ark made of a bed of snakes, he is the first "original" avatar in Hinduism.

John 3:5 *"Verily, verily I say unto, except a man be __born of water__ and of the spirit, he cannot enter into the kingdom of God."* (***Jesus***)

Exodus 2:3 *And when she could no longer hide him, she took for him an __ark__ of bulrushes, and daubed it with slime and with pitch, and put the child therein; and laid it by the flags in the __riverbank__.* (**Moses**)

2 Samuel 12:24 *And David comforted __Bath__sheba his wife, and went into her, and lay with her; she bare a son, and he called his name Solomon, and the Lord loved him.*

The Ark represents the (order) out of water (chaos.) This chaos is the state of the world when it is in flood. The order from the Femi (nine) chaos is the mascu (line) sun/son. All the stories of Avatars depict this pattern as it is the (order from chaos) pattern that marks the prophet which is personified by the mystery number 19. Moses in the account of the Exodus is credited with being a deliverer for the Hebrew Israelites from an oppressive Egyptian Government; he was an Asiatic/Semitic avatar and was sent to remove the children of Israel from bondage. Moses being a high ranking general in the Egyptian Army as well as a member of the royal family indicates that he was an army man as well as a king (Warrior King.) This is the highest seat a ruler can occupy upon a throne. This symbolism also shows that he is revolutionary because he wishes to place the proper royals upon the throne (the Jews of Abraham's covenant.) He does this aggressively in a warlike fashion while his counterpart Jesus does it in a diplomatic fashion. These two conflicting ideals of mental diplomacy as well as physical combative revolutionary tactics show the relationship of the Holy One of Israel as having a dualistic nature associated with him. This dualistic nature indicates though he has a diplomatic nature and can fight mentally, he also excels at combat and can bring about the revolution physically; this explains why both Jesus and Moses were transfigured with Elijah. Elijah is said to be the guide/mentor/harbinger to the Sun of Man and Moses and Jesus both reflect and represent his (messiah's) active and passive qualities. The messiah is able to do and be both. We spoke earlier about Michael Jackson being looked at like Moses. Michael came from a Royal family, (see Royal Arch) *The Jackson's,* and wishes to place the proper royals upon the throne *"This is our planet we have the truth, the final message we'll bring to you."* –Another Part of Me. Michael's soft speech and humble nature when he's not on stage, showcases his ability to be diplomatic. However, when he's on stage, we see the warrior come out of him in its purest most unadulterated form. The fact that Moses murdered an Egyptian soldier is how he is marked as being a descendant of Cain; (a murderer) just as Michael Jackson in *Thriller* morphed into a canine/Canaan/werewolf; all of which point to Sirius short for Osiris which is the Great Dog Star also known as the Black Sun.

Exodus 2:11-12 (11) And it came to pass in those days, when Moses was grown, that he went out unto his brethren and looked on their burdens and he spied an Egyptian smitting an Hebrew, one of his brethren (12) And he (Moses) looked this way and that way, and when he saw that there was no man, he slew the Egyptian, and hid him in the sand.

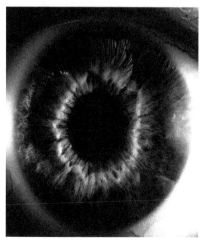

The Black Sun (Osiris {iris} is the All Seeing Eye itself though when allegorized the "Black Son" also represents the Messiah Isa/Esau. When we understand that through the black of the eye all colors, shapes, and images are seen; it proves to us that blackness draws in light. Melanin, secreted from the pineal gland, brings this point to a close as the 3rd eye is what allows spiritual vision giving sight to the unseen. This eye sees everything under the Sun; it records all the energies that exist and renders karmic judgment based on the choices that were made by the individual.

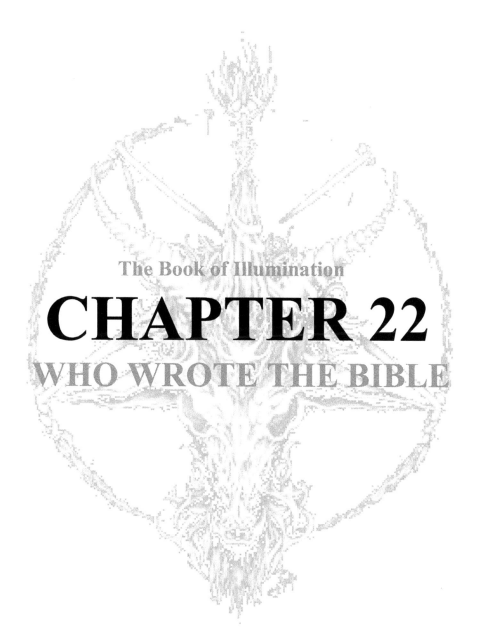

The Book of Illumination

CHAPTER 22

WHO WROTE THE BIBLE

The Book of Illumination

CHAPTER 22

WHO WROTE THE BIBLE

WHO WROTE THE BIBLE

I've spent countless conversations in this book about how much the Bible has been edited; and I've also shown many of these edits found with my own research and due diligence. But what hasn't been shown in this book is the historical account of how these books have been edited and who these books have been edited by. This is why this next chapter is so important because in it I've referenced just how the Bible that we read today came into existence.

The Septuagint was the original collection of Hebrew writings that Jewish rabbis converted into Greek scriptures. These scriptures at a later date were then voted into what we call the Canon. The Canon is the 46 books that are found in the Old Testament that a particular set of religious leaders of the world at the time thought necessary to be printed in the Bible. The Apocrypha are the remaining books that are in the Septuagint and Vulgate but have been left out of the Bible we read today. Most Christians seem to think the current Bible they read from has existed since the beginning of time. However the Bible that most Christians read from each and every day was indeed put together by mortal men. The word Canon refers to the divinity of a specific set of writings that these mortal men deemed publishable. The books that are considered canonical and the ones that aren't has been the subject of debate among Jewish and Christian leaders for the last two thousand years.

Septuagint: (1) a Greek version of the Jewish Scriptures redacted in the third and second centuries B.C. by Jewish scholars and adopted by Greek-speaking Christians

Canon: (1) an authoritative list of books accepted as Holy Scripture (2) a regulation or dogma decreed by a church council

Apocrypha: (1) books included in the Septuagint and Vulgate but excluded from the Jewish and Protestant canons of the Old Testament

Vulgate: (1) a Latin version of the Bible authorized and used by the Roman Catholic Church (2) the speech of the common people and especially of uneducated people

Revelation, James, Hebrews, Peter, 2 Peter, 2 John, 3 John, and Jude were all books that were once left out of the Bible. These Books are now accepted by Christians, but for many years they weren't. Judith, the Epistle of Barnabas,

The History of Susanna, The Prayer of Manasseh, Ecclesiasticus, 1 Esdras, 2 Esdras, 1 Maccabees, 2 Maccabees, 3 Maccabees, 4 Maccabees, 5 Maccabees, are all books that have been left out of the Canon but are found in other ancient writings and documents. The only books in the Bible that are considered "divinely inspired" by all Jews and Christians are the first five books of the Old Testament known as the Pentateuch or the Torah.

There are many lost books, which if included into the Canon would give Christians a completely different view of the religion they so faithfully profess to serve and believe in; here is a list of some of these books: (The) Book of Enoch, Book of the Wars of the Lord, Book of Jasher, Book of Gad, Book of the Covenant, Visions of Iddo, Book of Nathan, Book of Samuel, Prophecy of Ahijah, Acts of Uzziah, Acts of Solomon, Three Thousand Proverbs of Solomon, A Thousand and Five Songs of Solomon, Chronicles of the Kings of Israel, Chronicles of the Kings of Judah.

The canonized Bible of today is minute in comparison to the vast number of unpublished books that were left out of it. On the following pages are timelines that allow the reader to fully assess what happened in history in reference to the books originally written to go inside the Bible. These timelines show how and why the Bible has been edited into the versions we have presently.

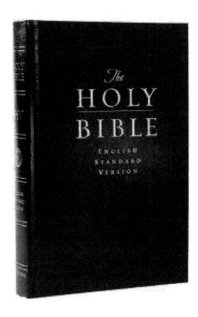

1000-50 BC:
The Old Testament (OT) books are written.
C. 200 BC:
Rabbis translate the OT from Hebrew to Greek, a translated version called the "Septuagint" is created (abbreviation: "XXI"). The XXI includes 46 books.
AD 30-100:
Christians use the XXI as their Holy Book, this enrages the Jews.
C. AD 100:
Jewish rabbis meet at the Council of Jamniah under Roman authority and decide to include in their canon only the 39 books that were written in Hebrew.
C. AD 135:
Hadrian rebuilds Jerusalem and bans Jews from entering the city for 500 years renaming the providence Syria, Palestinea and the city Aelia Capitolina.
C. AD 400:
St. Jerome translates the Bible from Hebrew and Greek into Latin, this version is called the "Vulgate." Jerome limits the OT to 39 books at 1st but the Pope, Damasus wants all 46 traditionally-used books included in the OT, so the Vulgate has 46.;
AD 1096:
Crusades begin under the tutelage of Pope Urban II and Christian Knights form an army and crusade the Holy Land, fighting with Moors.
AD 1536:
Martin Luther translates the Bible from Hebrew and Greek to German. He assumes that, since Jews wrote the Old Testament, theirs is the correct canon; he puts the extra 7 books in an appendix that he calls the "Apocrypha."
AD 1546:
The Catholic Council of Trent reaffirms the canonicity of all 46 books

Although this gives an indication on why and what was contained in the Old Testament Canon the New Testament's Canon was something that was entirely different and almost completely constructed by the Catholic Church.

C. AD 51-125:

The New Testament books are written, but during this same period other early Christian writings are produced, the Didache (c. AD 70), 1 Clement (c. 96), the Epistle of Barnabas (c. 100), and the 7 letters of Ignatius of Antioch (c. 110).

C. AD 140:

Marcion, , teaches in Rome that there were two Gods: Yahweh, the cruel God of the OT, and Abba, the kind father of the NT. Marcion eliminates the Old Testament as scripture and, keeps from the NT only 10 letters of Paul and 2/3 of Luke's gospel. The 1st NT was Marcion's "New Testament" which forced the mainstream Church to canonize the four gospels and letters of Paul in it.

C. AD 200:

The canon is not yet determined. According to one list, compiled at Rome c. AD 200 (the Muratorian Canon), the NT consists of the 4 gospels; Acts; 13 letters of Paul (Hebrews is not included); 3 of the 7 General Epistles (1-2 John and Jude); and also the Apocalypse of Peter.

AD 325:

Council of Nice; Athanasius's view of Christ is published, and the debate over the deification of Christ is settled. He is considered God in flesh. Nicene Creed is also adopted.

AD 367:

The earliest extant list of the books of the NT, in exactly the number and order in which we presently have them, is written by Athanasius, Bishop of Alexandria, in his Easter letter of 367.

AD 610

The Qu'ran is revealed to Mohammed by the angel Gabriel

AD 904:

Pope Damasus, in a letter to a French bishop, lists the New Testament books in their present number and order.

AD 1442:

At the Council of Florence, the entire Church recognizes the 27 books, though does not declare them unalterable.

AD 1521:

Martin Luther is ex-communicated by Pope Leo X for not recanting 41sentences including his 95 theses

AD 1536:

In his translation of the Bible from Greek into German, Luther removes 4 NT books (Hebrews, James, Jude, and Revelations) from their normal order and places them at the end, stating that they are less than canonical.

AD 1546:

At the Council of Trent, the Catholic Church reaffirms once and for all the full list of 27 books as traditionally accepted.

In the time line between 200 B.C. and AD 30 we can get a clear view of what may have happened in regards to the scriptures. The Jesus of Nazareth at the time of his walk is exposing certain knowledge's that enable the people and the elect to know he is the one who has been prophesized to come. The reason they don't believe him is because what he is proposing, seems preposterous. That along with the fact that the knowledge they are professing to have, they aren't acting in accordance with. Because the people in power are using the knowledge base that stems from ancient Egyptian customs, Jesus is the reincarnated past king who is exposing those who are using the knowledge and customs to make money. Imagine a reincarnated Egyptian King in today's time that comes to Las Vegas, sees the Luxor pyramid, and obtains his recollection and memory. In his day, these pyramids were a sacred holy ground used for worship and to collect souls who sought spiritual enlightenment. Jesus comes to the Luxor Casino in Las Vegas and sees gambling, prostitution, and pandemonium. When he goes and talks to the owners of the establishment they say they are Jews. He then says, "If you are Jews, why have you desecrated my Holy symbol and temple?" They look at him crazy in bewilderment. He persists and goes on and on and on and eventually files a lawsuit against the owners. They go to court, and while in

court, he explains with the use of the Kabbalah; that he was the king that owned the original Pyramids and thereby exercises the rights to sue any and all who exploit his symbols and knowledge's for monetary gain. He further admonishes that all the rights to the use of the Egyptian symbols and temple are his." He then pulls out the mystic knowledge of the Kabbalah and says LOOK, here is my birthright. The owners of the casinos who are Jews look at him crazy like what are you talking about? After Jesus loses the case in court the headlines in the Newspaper read. CRAZY MAN CLAIMING TO BE THE MESSIAH LOSES LAWSUIT.

Acts 23:7 & 8: For the Sadducees say there is no resurrection; neither angel nor spirit but the Pharisees confess both.

Sadducees: (1) a member of an ancient Jewish sect consisting mainly of Priests and Aristocrats that differed from the Pharisee especially in its literal interpretation of the Bible and its rejection of oral laws and traditions

Pharisee: (1) a member of an ancient Jewish sect that differed from the Sadducees chiefly in its strict observance of the religious practices, liberal interpretation of the Bible, and adherence to oral laws and traditions

As I stated earlier, the Sadducees didn't believe in the resurrection from the dead in the way the Christians do. This is probably what upset the Jews when the Christians, after the descent of the Christ of St. John, used the Septuagint, the version that was edited for the Greeks, as their book. These people not being of Jewish custom or origin could not readily digest the complex system of scriptures and words; and therefore they accepted certain things that were figurative literally, and other things that were literal figuratively. Regular laymen didn't have the Jewish system of Kabbalah. At that time, there was a very minute circle of men who were initiated into the mysteries of it. The way that initiation works in the Masonic order is by way of degrees. This means that though a person can be of high rank or degree, that rank or degree is only a superficial ranking. This is done in order to protect the agenda of the order. You could have a high ranking master but it wouldn't necessarily mean that he would know the "real" secrets of the order. The Sun of Man being the reincarnated "Ethiopian" king Osiris, who created the customs whereby these initiated men were permitted to study, can pick up the book (Bible) open it, and interpret what it truly means; this is what separates him from all other gods, priests, clergymen, scholars and scribes. This is the true meaning of pulling the sword from the stone. Because man has so perverted the teachings, upon his (Sun of Man's) return the Priests and elders will be against him, AND they will be trying to convince HIM about something that he himself created long before they existed.

John 8:56-58 (56) Your father Abraham rejoiced to see my day: and he saw it, and was glad. (57) Then said the Jews unto him, Thou art not yet fifty years old, and hast thou seen Abraham? (58) Jesus said unto them, Verily, verily, I say unto you, Before Abraham was, I am.

Jewish Kabbalah and mysticism isn't something that the laymen of that day would have been able to understand. It is like teaching someone who doesn't understand addition and subtraction, trigonometry and algebra. When you talk about the resurrection from past lives you virtually open up a Pandora's Box to a plethora of other questions, and usually these question stem from a perverted place. The Rabbis and members of the Jewish Elect gave the lay people a subscript or a watered down version that corresponded with the comprehension levels of the people. Remember at the council of Jamniah Jewish rabbis under Roman authority and control canonized only the 39 books that could originally be found in Hebrew. Also later in the 1st century A.D. is where the stories of Jesus were compiled by those who were not of Jewish descent. This would be the same as people from England coming to Texas and trying to tell Mexicans about the battle of the Alamo. Because there is so much confusion and the time period between the resurrections is so long and vast, man has tried to take it upon himself to keep retranslating the Bible according to his own biases and comprehension levels. This is why there were ultimately four gospels written and why the Bible was edited into the version known today. Even the Vulgate is derived from the word vulgar and when defined states, *the speech of the common people and especially of uneducated people.* In understanding this we can conclude that the heavier associations in the Bible were never meant to be taught to the masses because of their "suspected" low comprehension levels.

Hosea 4:6 (6) My people are destroyed for lack of knowledge: because thou hast rejected knowledge, I will also reject thee, that thou shalt be no priest to me: seeing thou hast forgotten the law of thy God, I will also forget thy children.

When the Bible was being constructed, you had at that time many religious zealots and people whose unending searches led them into certain discoveries. Upon discovering certain information they took this "knowledge" to the masses. When the masses got a hold of the knowledge it didn't change them and when they overthrew the dictators, they became them. There is a saying that "power corrupts absolutely" and "either you die a hero or live long enough to become a villain." This dilemma is what the men who had the arduous task of compiling the Bible had before them. Everyone is different in the dark then they are in the light. Think about how different you are when no one is looking at you; now think about how you change when in public. People have always been known to do whatever they want to do. Those who are able to take advice, apply it, accepting coaching and criticism usually become champions; and those who can't often become losers. The fact that Christians believe that when Jesus died he resurrected immediately again is a very hard notion for the Jews to swallow, and because the lay people believe this, the Jews have no mercy in regards to how these same people are accommodated. They are in charge of managing a people with what they perceive as having low levels of comprehension and existences; so to them that type of resurrection of Christ is just a myth. The actual "Sun of Man" is exposing these religious scribes in the 23rd Chapter of Matthew for corrupting the knowledge that started in "Ethiopia." These "Jews" that Jesus is tongue lashing are really Romans, who are posing as Jews, much to the like as Paul a Bejaminite posed as a Christian. This is why Jesus is calling them a synagogue of Satan. When I say Roman I am speaking in reference to romanticism and the ideology of the people who function in it, not the nationality. Many people adopt romantic views as indicated earlier with the example of the heart and the butt; and these views are so jaded that it makes them unable to see truths that are right before their eyes. This is why in the Bible there are so many references and parables to those who can physically see but are still blind.

Matthew 13:13 (13) *Therefore speak I to them in parables: because they seeing see not; and hearing they hear not, neither do they understand.*

The blindness that Jesus is speaking in reference to has nothing to do with not being able to see at all (literally) it has to do with not being able to see with the mind's eye, the third or spiritual eye. This is why the leaven of bread example is given in the Bible to highlight this very point.

The Bible was written over a period of 1400 to 1800 years by more than 40 different authors and is a compilation of 66 separate books, divided into two primary divisions: the Old Testament (containing 39 books) with the deleted book called the Apocrypha and the New Testament (containing 27 books.) Genesis, Exodus, Leviticus, Numbers, and Deuteronomy all are attributed to have been written by Moses in 1400 B.C. These first five books of the Old Testament (known as the Pentateuch to the Greeks and the Torah to Jews) was written by Moses during the forty years that the children of Israel wandered in the wilderness (1450 - 1410 B.C.) The twelve historical books of the Old Testament continue to record the history of the people of Israel under the leadership of Joshua, through the period of the Judges and the reign of the kings of Israel. The books of Ezra, Nehemiah, and Esther record the history of Israel following its period of captivity under Babylonian rule. The historical books span the history of Israel from 1050 - 465 B.C. The books of Job, the

Psalms, the Proverbs, Ecclesiastes, and the Song of Solomon are considered the poetical books of the Old Testament. Scholars have been unable to determine with any specificity when Job was written but most say it is one of the oldest books in the Bible. Based upon the manners and customs recorded in the text, many believe the book was written during the time of the Patriarchs of the Faith. The individual Psalms, comprising the entire collection, were written from the days of Israel's Exodus to its restoration after the Babylonian captivity. Many of the Psalms were written by King David during his reign over Israel and the entire book was compiled between 1000 - 300 B.C. King David's son, Solomon is credited with writing Proverbs, Ecclesiastes, and Song of Solomon, during his reign (971 - 931 B.C.) The seventeen prophetical books of the major and minor prophets span Israel's history from 700 - 450 B.C. and 400 years after the writing of the Book of Malachi, the Old Testament was closed. It is generally agreed that the Book of Matthew was the first Gospel written and that it was written between A.D. 50 and 75. Of the four Gospel's, John's is considered to have been the last one written, around A.D. 85. The Book of Acts, a historical account of the establishment of the early Christian church, is believed to have been written by one of the Apostle Paul's associates, around A.D. 62 (near the end of Paul's imprisonment in Rome.) The Pauline Epistles (the Apostle Paul's letters to the early church) were authored between A.D. 50 - 67. The author of Hebrews is unknown, but the book is commonly thought to have been written around A.D. 70. The epistles of the other Apostles were written between A.D. 48 - 90. The Book of the Revelation of Jesus Christ is believed to have been penned by the Apostle John between A.D. 70 - 95 [149].

Now that we have been briefed on who actually wrote the Bible, let's examine the account as to why Jesus reprimanded those posing as Jews. The popular belief is that Jesus was killed for saying that he was the Son of God however this isn't supported by scripture.

*Luke 23:2,3 (2) And they began to accuse him, saying, We found this fellow perverting the nation, and forbidding to give tribute to Caesar, saying that he himself is Christ a King (3) And Pilate asked him, saying, Art thou the King of the Jews? And he answered him and said, **thou sayest it.***

John 18:37 (37) Pilate therefore said unto him, Art thou a king then? Jesus Answered,, Thou sayest that I am a king. To this end was I born and for this cause came I into the world, that I should bear witness unto the truth. Everyone that is of the truth heareth my voice.

Mark 15:1,2 (1) And straightway in the morning the chief priests held a consultation with the elders and scribes and the whole council and bound Jesus, and carried him away, and delivered him unto Pilate (2) and Pilate asked him, Art thou the King of the Jews? And he answering said unto him, **Thou sayest it.**

Matt 27:11 (11) And Jesus stood before the governor: and the governor asked him saying, Art thou the King of the Jews? And Jesus said unto him, **Thou sayest it.**

The gospel of Luke gives us an indication as to why they may have crucified Jesus; one of the reasons given, was that he was quoted as perverting the nation; but with what? What teachings did Jesus have that were so perverse that it caused them to sentence him to death? It wasn't because he said he was the Son of God because he never admitted this at his trial. If a person were to literally ask themselves who is *The God, w*ould that all powerful being that may have no shape or form be able to engender a son? Does the all-powerful essence that created everything just have man as a son? Is the whole creation not his child? Seeing that this may have been a trick question posed by Pilate to test the sanity of Jesus, we see how Jesus avoids giving him a truly perverse and illogical answer by saying *Thou sayest it* 149cde. When looking at the scripture that states that Jesus was the Son of Man or Son of God I like to pull this analogy into today's time. Michael Jordan who is seen as the greatest

person to ever play basketball is quoted by Larry Bird as being *"God in a pair of basketball shoes"* 112dd. -- Michael dominated the game with so much ferocity and was the perfected example of competition and mastery in its purest human form. Anyone who watches Kobe Bryant can see that he is the true offspring or "sun/son" of Michael Jordan because his game is patented after Michael's. Though physically Michael has sons who aren't Kobe Bryant; on the court and in the mannerisms in which Kobe expresses himself, we can say spiritually that Kobe Bryant is Michael Jordan's son.

Michael Jordan is an Aquarius born on the Piscean cusp on February 17th and Kobe Bryant is a Leo born on the cusp of Virgo August 23[rd.] Both are 180 degree polar opposites which further mathematically make them in essence father and son, teacher and disciple, master and apprentice. Michael Jordan was quoted saying this about Kobe in an interview with Ahmad Rashad, in February of 2013. *"He's cursed as much as I am."* If you understand my analogy you can see how Jesus being the "son of Joseph" can also be called or looked at as the "Son/sun of God." This is further realized as Jesus' spiritual father was Elijah who was resurrected as John the Baptist whose "water bearing" Baptist qualities make him likened to an Aquarius. Jesus being a "Sun" is attributed to the sign Leo. Jesus again was harbinged by John the Baptist which makes him the "son" of Elijah. This relationship also parallels to the relationship between Shiva and Vishnu in the Hindu scriptures.

Matthew 27: 46&47 (46) And about the ninth hour Jesus cried with a loud voice, saying, Eli, Eli, lama sabachthani? that is to say, My God, my God, why hast thou forsaken me? (47) Some of them that stood there, when they heard that, said, This man calleth for Elijah.

The universe projects itself in mathematical ways; though to the uninitiated, these ways seem mysterious and unknown. Again, the Hebrew word for Leo is teth and means serpent. Kobe Bryant being born under the Leo/Virgo cusp shows us what energy is functioning within him, as he is known to the world under the alias, **The Black Mamba** a serpent. One of the fundamental teachings of Kabbalah is that there are no such things as coincidences. Earlier we spoke of Michael Jordan being an Achilles archetype. Kobe Bryant's 2012-2013 season ending Achilles injury further likens him to his spiritual father, Michael Jordan. Another interesting point to note about Kobe Bryant was the day he had the best performance of his already legendary and illustrious NBA career. On 1/22/06 during the constellation that houses the zodiac sign Aquarius, Kobe Bean Bryant scored a whopping 81 points in a single game 2nd only behind Wilt Chamberlain, another Leo born two days before Bryant, who scored 100 points in a single game.

The same rationalization used in the Kobe/ Jordan example can be said about Justin Beiber. Born on the 1st day of March (Pisces); Beiber is the direct polar opposite of Michael Jackson born August 29th under the sign of Virgo. When looking with the 3rd eye we can see how the name given to his followers "beliebers" is associated directly to MJ. Michael Jackson is Justin's "true" father, reminiscent of the relationship between Optimus Prime the "immortal" (as 29 is a prime number) and Sam Witwicky his "mortal son." -See chapter 25 - Recently Justin Bieber became the most popular person on Twitter

with well over 40 million followers. In the likeness of MJ, the former 'King of Pop", Beiber has now taken over that title as well.

We've all heard that everything exists within its opposite. The universe is no different in how it projects itself to us. Later, in the conclusion of this book, I explain how Hollywood decodes through movies this esoteric knowledge. Ran by the people who are devout studiers of the occult, numerology, and the Kabbalah, Tinsel- town has been the single most influential media conglomerate in the rolling out of this Occult information. The crippling in understanding this complex system of mathematics lies in a person's inability to look beyond the surface. Remember, the people that have been written about in ancient legends are deemed to be "supernatural." Look at the word again "SUPER" natural; which means there's something so very natural that it exists easily in a super/superior form. When we look at the way astrological signs play out not only in ancient scriptures/mythologies, but in today's time, it allows us to see just how precise the universe is. Because we've been taught to call it GOD though we are speaking in reference of a higher being; we can't help but to associate that being as having a likeness to ourselves. This explains how a mortal, in the absence of an immortal, can imitate him becoming like a "god" by portraying the gods likeness.

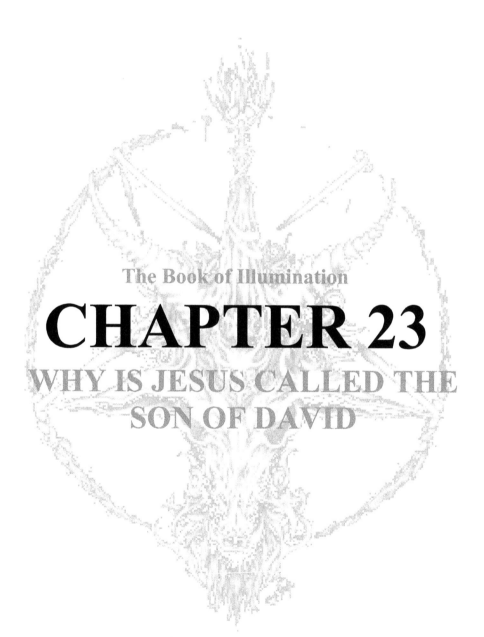

The Book of Illumination

CHAPTER 23

WHY IS JESUS CALLED THE SON OF DAVID

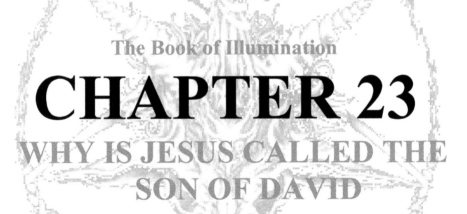

The Book of Illumination

CHAPTER 23

WHY IS JESUS CALLED THE SON OF DAVID

WHY IS JESUS CALLED THE SON OF DAVID

In Matthew - chapter 1 we are given the genealogy of the Christ it states

Matthew 1-16 (1) the book of the generation of Christ the son of David, the son of Abraham. (2) Abraham begat Isaac; and Isaac begat Jacob; and Jacob begat Judas and his brethren; (3)And Judas begat Phares and Zara of Thamar; and Phares begat Esrom; and Esrom begat Aram; (4) And Aram begat Aminadab; and Aminadab begat Naasson; and Naasson begat Salmon; (5) And Salmon begat Booz of Rachab; and Booz begat Obed of Ruth; and Obed begat Jesse; (6) And Jesse begat David the king; and David the king begat Solomon of her that had been the wife of Urias; (7) And Solomon begat Roboam; and Roboam begat Abia; and Abia begat Asa; (8) And Asa begat Josaphat; and Josaphat begat Joram; and Joram begat Ozias; (9) And Ozias begat Joatham; and Joatham begat Achaz; and Achaz begat Ezekias; (10) And Ezekias begat Manasses; and Manasses begat Amon; and Amon begat Josias; (11) And Josias begat Jechonias and his brethren, about the time they were carried away to Babylon: (12) And after they were brought to Babylon, Jechonias begat Salathiel; and Salathiel begat Zorobabel; (13) And Zorobabel begat Abiud; and Abiud begat Eliakim; and Eliakim begat Azor; (14) And Azor begat Sadoc; and Sadoc begat Achim; and Achim begat Eliud (15) And Eliud begat Eleazar and Eleazar begat Matham and Matham begat Jacob (16) <u>And Jacob begat Joseph the husband of Mary of whom was born Jesus the Christ.</u>

In the scriptures above Jesus is referred to as the son of David. This is because the bloodline of Abraham came through the line of David. The bloodline of David was a lineage of kings that were direct descendants of the LORD who in place of Abraham, was the true (Patriarch) of modern religions such as Judaism, Christianity, and Islam. The Book of Kings pays homage to David and gives reference to the fact he was a great king for Israel. David's son was none other than Solomon {Sol/ sun-/o/of/- mon/man} this literally translates to Sun of Man or son of Min who as explained earlier was the great phallic god of the orient also known as the great bull. Because the Sun is the chief life giving force in our solar system they called Jesus the Sun of Man or the Sun of God. It wasn't Son as in s-o-n it was Sun as in s-u-n. This is an astrological reference meaning that he was born under the sign of the Sun, which is the sign, ruled by Leo. This is why you hear about the Lion of the tribe of Judah; who in the scope of the twelve tribes of Israel (Astrology) is represented by Leo the lion in Revelation 5:1-5 and Genesis 49:8-9. Again, the Sun is the leader of the Zodiac, so when Jesus called himself the Sun of Man he was technically correct. This solves the argument as to why Muslims and Jews don't believe he was the Son of God. In their logic, if he was the Son of God and people are all "God's" children (creation) what makes Jesus more of a son then any of them? This Son of God/ Sun of Man is a play on words and an allegorical riddle. This riddle was written only to be interpreted properly at the end of time by the person who was its true author. Only "God" himself could define its truest meaning. So when Muslims say they don't believe that Jesus is *The Son* of *The God* they are merely using plain logic; that logic being based from a literal interpretation of ancient texts and writings like the Zohar and the Torah. If they were true initiates in the understanding of the mysteries and divine esoteric knowledge's they would have a more enlightened perspective for what these terms mean.

As stated in previous chapters, in the Hebrew Kabbalah, the name Joseph is equivalent to "lingam" which as we defined earlier by way of Webster is a phallic symbol of the Hindu God Shiva, known also as Ba'al & the LORD

149b. Shiva, in Hinduism, is known for his lingams which are all over India. In fact in the *Padma Purana* Shiva was turned into a phallus because he ignored the Brahmin Brighu and persisted to make love to his wife 150. This story reflects an obvious allegory that shows just how concentrated and omnipotent Shiva is in regards to sex and procreation. If Joseph were translated in this sense as "lingam" it would change the translation of the father of Jesus to being a "Phallus" which when translated with Kabbalah is indicative of the LORD Shiva. The boy praying to the statue in honor of Shiva is why the scripture below is directed toward the worship of Ba'al in the Bible.

Zephaniah 1:4 (4) I will destroy every remnant of Baal worship in this place, the very names of the idolatrous priests.

In Hinduism, however Shiva and the virgin Goddess Parvati birth a savior son named Karttikeya/Kalki who is known as the vanquisher of demons. His symbol is also the peacock as his birth was the combination of the elements of earth, fire, water, and the Pleiades of air and cosmic space making him like the avatar Aang (*The Last Air-bender.*) Note: Aang rides a white air bison just as Shiva rides a white bull.

Karttikeya in legend was also said to have been given six heads to please the six Pleiades which are the six points of Ursa Minor…or the little dipper. This is also similar to the creation of Adam who in the translation of the Kabbalah written by A.E. Waite, was to rule over the six directions of space 150a. This would further the notion that Jesus being called the Son of David and the Son of Man make sense in relevance to Solo-mon (Sun of Min) who was the richest, and wisest of all the kings in Israel who was phallic in the sense that he had 1,000 wives and was figuratively the son of David and figuratively the son of Joseph (lingam.)

When we look at the prophecies of Ezekiel 37:22, Joseph and Judah are placed under one stick. Though they in essence seem to be two different individuals, in order to verify the sacred texts, we'll have to look at these stories with microscopic lenses. When we look at the offspring of Jacob, we find that Joseph is the son of Israel, and Solomon is the son of David. To understand why the Jesus of Nazareth as regarded by the Kabbalah is acknowledged as being both, we must look back at the story of David 151. The story of David like the serpent in the garden, and The LORD who appeared to Abraham and visited Sarah, resembles these accounts in that he took a queen that belonged to another man (*a forbidden woman*) to produce by way of her, an heir to a godly lineage. The key words again are Ur as Abraham was from the city of Ur, just as Ur/iah was the husband of Bathsheba, and the Ur in Uraeus, which represents the serpent that cohabitated with eve. The coming messiah is said to be both a son of Joseph (lingam) and a son of David Sol/o /Mon which scripturally makes him a son of Shiva and the ruler of the coming world /age/ aeon.

Ur: a combining form meaning "earliest" or "original" 2. S. Iraq

Once again what people are reading is written, and because it is written the use of words and allegories through literary elements is what gives these stories the three dimensions to captivate its readers. This captivation is what causes the reader to be engulfed in the underlying spiritual information that is received subconsciously. The recession of this spiritual knowledge invokes a cathartic feeling, and this emotion creates the "eureka" like experience which enables the reader to relate to the wisdom hidden within the religious texts.

Once entranced in this emotion, they then associate the magical feeling to epiphany whereby they link everything they experienced in that moment as being the unseen silent demonstration from "God."

People who lived in ancient times didn't have the technological advancements of today, and would cherish the Bible and the information in it as being something that only a superior intellect could write, translate, and understand. Pending on their level of knowledge in turn determines what level of intellect they believe wrote it. If their intellect is low then they'll perceive this to be the divine knowledge of *the* God. If their intellects are high then they'll still be able to recognize that it was a superior intellect that wrote it, but not necessarily the "God of all creation." When we are reading the Bible, the "God of all creation" is walking the earth as a man. This man speaks with Abraham, and establishes a covenant with him. A person has to believe the god they pray to can physically walk the earth before they can fully pledge allegiance with the God of Abraham, Isaac, and Jacob. If a person is viewing the "God of creation" who may be bigger than our solar system itself, then the vernacular that is used to describe god to them in the Bible would seem vulgar, or like a cute story meant to inspire faith in man. This is the extent that a person who views "God" in this sense would have. Yet when you implore Astrology and understand celestial ascensions and descents you'll realize the same Sun that rules our solar system also falls (descends) to earth just as the stars do. This is what the Jesus of Nazareth represents and is why the whole world has submitted to his doctrine. The God of Abraham Isaac and Jacob is the god of the Sun. This makes sense when you acknowledge the region where these stories originate has the largest desert in the world, the Sahara; a desert so large that you could fit the entire United States within it.

The goal of religion is to get people to understand the patterns that follow life i.e. you reap what you sew. Falling in line with the energy that is going to keep you salvaged as well as propel you to your destiny is the most fundamental aspect of faith. If you aren't going to be delivered somewhere what is the goal of having faith? What is the path less traveled? Why even attend church? There are many reasons that people attend church service each and every Sunday. One of the reasons when asked why, is people want to make sure they have some insurance in the life here after. Life is so unstable at times that people can't tell their right from their left. Certain things that are in peoples respective paths are hindrances, others are blessings. The stories in the Bible reflect all of the scenarios of life which is what makes them brilliant, and able to inspire the reader. The inspiration the reader experiences again is spiritual. This spiritual energy makes the person feel good, and more secure about what it is in life they don't understand. As previously stated, the Book of Job is said to be one of the oldest books in the Bible. Job's story is one of extreme faith through the most trying of circumstance as he is stripped of everything in the most inhumane way imaginable. In the end, Job's unrelenting faith caused him to be blessed ten times over making his account the ultimate story of sacrifice, faith, and triumph. When capitalistic men saw the faith the story of Job and those like it inspired within the people, they through religion made these stories more general by commercializing them to make a profit. These generalizations robbed the stories of the esoteric richness hidden within their subtexts and through time, the passing on of the generalities lead the people away from the central purpose for why the stories were selected to go in the Bible. The people became so indoctrinated in how having faith would benefit them, that they were given over to delusion. Due to man's egomaniacal thought processes, the material presented to him became warped by his perverted mind state which lead to people having faith without works, causing them to become superstitious, ignorant, and lazy; all things which have plagued black people in America.

Romans 1:21 *(21) Because when that they knew God, they glorified him not as God, neither were thankful; but became vain in their imaginations, and their foolish heart was darkened.*

 Once perversion occurs, a person will twist everything that is said out of context. They will see what they want to see because they desire to do as they wish. Because mankind wants to be the author of the brilliant knowledge that stems from the stories about the gods themselves in the Bible; he has discredited the very people that it came from, so he as "God" could stand in their place to be viewed and seen as a deity in the flesh. This book was not written to discredit organized religion. The religion people have been forced to believe in encourages people to accept things literally that are humanly impossible. With regards to the religion of most of America, pretty much everything that is seen or known about "God" paints him as a white man with a beard on a cloud. If I'm looking at the "God" that is promoted to me literally; he would be the all-powerful white men over the course of history that created the {Government of Democracy (G.O.D.)} If you don't comply with what the all-powerful white men of the all-powerful

461

democracy say, you'll end up in jail or exterminated; which has been too often the result of many black men in American society.

In the movie *The Transformers Revenge of the Fallen* a great example of standing in the place of "God" to appear as "God" was shown when an Ivy League professor is teaching the class about physics and astronomy. Because the students in his class have little knowledge about the subject he is teaching, he appears to be a god among them. Shia Labeouf's character Sam Witwicky is actually anointed by the gods (the transformers), and he demonstrates this when he gets on the professor's stage and completes the equation the professor was hypothesizing about. Because the professor is upstaged by the youth, he kicks Shia's character out of his class.

Another great story that encompasses this as its theme is the story of Mozart who was a child prodigy and a much better musician than his nemesis Anthony Salieri. However Salieri's jealousy of Mozarst left him unable to appoint Mozart at the royal court which would have provided Mozart with the financial means to sustain himself. However, due to Salieri's jealousy of Mozart they both fall to ruin. The opposing nature of both individuals Salieri and Mozart is highlighted through their relationship as Mozart was an Aquarius and Salieri was a Leo. These two examples show us the contentious relationship between the truly ordained versus the learned practitioners, and can be likened to the people who stole the knowledge of the Egyptian people, put their face on it, and taught it to the world in a perverted way by standing in the place of the true embodiments of the scriptures. This is why the Davidic lineage has to be revealed to further show that those who are pretending to be divinely appointed can be exposed as liars. For these reasons we must examine the lineage of Jesus to see if we can find a link between him and Solomon. If Jesus wasn't Joseph's son there is no way he could be a blood heir from the line of David because the line of David descended through Joseph. I know that Jesus and John the Baptist were related through Elizabeth and Mary which could technically make him a blood heir that way, but why would the scriptures not indicate this clearly? Why do the scriptures say that *Jacob begat Joseph the husband of Mary of whom was born the Christ*?

Matthew 1:16 (16) *And Jacob begat Joseph the husband of Mary, of whom was born Jesus, who is called Christ.*

Again, Joseph of the OT is linked with the Joseph of the NT in that they both represent the same thing in different ways. How do we know this? The father of Joseph in the OT was Jacob; the father of Joseph in the NT is Jacob.

This shows the correlation between both Jesus (Judah) and Joseph as they represent the same spiritual energy and like missions. Joseph wears the coat of many colors symbolizing that he is universal and has every color of man within him. Jesus being the Sun of Man is the light that shines through all of humanity. Both Jesus and Joseph go through trying circumstances and ascend to kingly thrones. These themes are highlighted through glyphs to illuminate that the two messiah's Joseph and Jesus (Judah) are reconfigurations of the same spirit which are identical yet different.

Jesus is called the son of David because David was known as the giant slayer. **1 Samuel: 17:50** gives the vivid account of David slaying the Giant Goliath.

1 Samuel: 17:49-50 (49) And David put his hand in his bag, and took thence a stone, and slang it, and smote the Philistine in his forehead, that the stone sunk into his forehead; and he fell upon his face to the earth. (50) and there was no sword in the hand of David.

According to scripture, David slew the giant by hitting him in the middle of his forehead, the place of the pituitary gland and brow chakra. The brow chakra's primary function when developed is clairvoyance and selfless acts of benevolence and community service. The very fact that Michael Jackson the son of Joseph has given the most money to the most charities is the same as figuratively hitting the giant in the forehead (pituitary gland) with a stone. By Michael giving so much to humanity, it constitutes as a selfless act of benevolence, which again is a trait that is indicative of the brow chakra, the same place where the giant Goliath was struck. This selfless act as well as many other humanitarian feats has solidified Michael's place in history as the greatest philanthropist the world has ever known.

Given the analysis and scriptural breakdown one has to consider the reality that most of what has been written has been coded with pertinent esoteric information. This information as stated repetitively in this book is only understood by those with high IQ as those with low comprehension levels develop the thought processes like that of the Pharisees and Sadducees and teach the scriptures as doctrine from a literal interpretation. The great house of David was the line of kings who were small in stature but brought down mighty armies for the house of Israel. Jesus was called the son of David because he was of that same lineage; small in stature, with the power to bring down a great institution.

Matthew 22:42 -45 *(42) What think ye of Christ? Whose son is he? They say unto him, The son of David. (43) He saith unto them, How then doth David in spirit call him lord, saying (44) The Lord said unto my Lord, sit thou on my right hand, till I make thine enemies thy footstool? (45) If David then call him Lord, how is he his son?*

This passage proves the title given to Jesus as being the son of David isn't literal but a distinction to classify him as being of the line of Judah and David.

Genesis 49:8-10 *(8) Judah, thou art he whom thy brethren shall praise: thy hand shall be in the neck of thine enemies; thy father's children shall bow down before thee. (9) Judah is a lion's whelp: from the prey, my son, thou art gone up: he stooped down, he couched as a lion, and as an old lion; who shall rouse him up? (10) The scepter shall not depart from Judah, nor a lawgiver from between his feet, until Shiloh come; and unto him shall the gathering of the people be.*

This line of Judah is the line that was prophesied in Isaiah as being the destroyer of the Gentiles, and the son of David was Solomon as described in the previous example. Solomon was the great (alpha) who had 1000 wives and concubines and was said to be the most intelligent and wisest king in all of Egypt. The fact that he had 1000 wives and concubines again is another allegorical reference to highlight his omnipotent and super phallic powers just like the "Living God" of Abraham, Isaac, and Jacob. Solomon prayed for understanding to judge the people and as a result he was given riches that exceeded every other king before him.

1 Kings3: 9-13 *(9) Give therefore thy servant an understanding heart to judge thy people that I may discern between Good and bad: for who is able to judge this thy so great a people. (10) And the speech pleased the lord, that Solomon had asked this thing (11) And God said unto him, because thou hast asked this thing, and hast not asked for thyself long life; neither hast asked riches for thyself, nor hast asked the life of thine enemies; but has asked for thyself understanding to discern judgment. (12) Behold, I have done according toothy words: lo I have given thee a wise and an understanding heart; so that there was none like thee before thee, neither after thee shall any arise like unto thee.*

1Kings 4:29-34 *(29) And God gave Solomon wisdom and understanding exceeding much and largeness of heart, even as the sand is on the seashore (30) And Solomon's wisdom excelled the wisdom of all the children of the east country, and all the wisdom of Egypt. (31) For he was wiser than all men; that Ethan the ezrahite, and Heman, and Chalcol, and Darda, the sons of Mahol: and his fame was in all nations round about.*

At this time in Egypt none had exceeded the Wisdom of Solomon. He was the great king, the alpha, and son of David. Being that Solomon was so great in wisdom and understanding he was the highest (most high) that a man could look to be in the carnal sense. Jesus is called the son of David because being a son (descendant) of David (sol/sun o/of mon/man) he would carry on the legacy and task of destroying a giant (*which translates to the now Roman Catholic church*) while simultaneously being an alpha male with exceptional wisdom and riches. So when we combine the line of Joseph (Israel) and the line of David (Judah) we see through the blending of these two lineages the true nation the gods will descend to earth to rule over as prophesied in the 15th chapter of Genesis. Michael Jackson, the Krishna, the all-attractive Supreme Being and Shiva Mahadev the Supreme Lord and great god of wisdom will together flourish in one house (cult) to solidify the covenant with the Most High God on earth by destroying all forms of idol/idle/ideal worship from the face of the planet. The two work side by side in the guises of Michael and Gabriel to bring about the construction and finishing of Solomon's Temple

In today's time the seed of Abraham was prophesied to be enslaved in a land that is not theirs in a foreign country for 400 years. As previously stated in **Genesis 15:12-14**; Ham was the (proposed) black son of Noah which is why his name was changed from Abram to Abra**ham**. This is another allegorical clue that suggests that America is the nation (African/Black) that is being spoken of in the above scripture. Jesus is a bloodline descendent of Abraham/David whose lineage would flow through this prophecy. The American Negros are the "Jews" who are spoken of in these prophecies and Jesus is the "Sun" who is sent back to deliver them their true teachings by exposing the liars of the Mother (Church.) This is what Jesus is doing in the Bible. The last Christ that Jesus was referencing was Moses, so when the next Christ comes he will be referencing the words and life of Jesus. The Jesus of Nazareth is the lowly plain son of a carpenter who is coming to slay the great church; the same church that killed and persecuted the very indigenous people that these biblical stories come from. This Catholic Church is the same church that says Astrology is satanic and paints all of the Jewish and Egyptian heroes as being white which causes me to ask the question, "Is falsifying biblical records not the same as deceiving the whole world in that even the very elect will be deceived?" The picture on the following page is of the Sistine Chapel, the official residence of the Pope. It is important to again notate that "Romans" in culture as well as in mythology were described as "Lovers of Men." It's common for men to have pictures of naked women on their walls (posters.) The pope has pictures of naked men…you do the math.

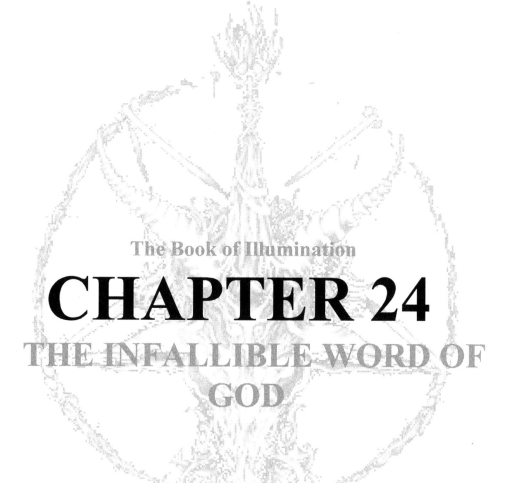

The Book of Illumination

CHAPTER 24

THE INFALLIBLE WORD OF GOD

The Book of Illumination

CHAPTER 24

THE INFALLIBLE WORD OF GOD

THE INFALLIBLE WORD OF GOD

Infallible: 1. incapable of error; unerring

I stand on the point I made earlier in the chapter entitled *Who wrote the Bible* that there is substantial evidence that shows that the Bible has been tampered with. Whether through translation or a covert operation to falsify the origin and knowledge of the "Living God" it is apparent that man has placed his hands all over it. One would ask themselves, why are there so many books written about the exact same thing; where was the divinely inspired plan in that? Only a scholar would know the gospel of Matthew was the 1st gospel written in Ad 60 and for the Jews. The Gospel of Mark was written for the Gentiles in AD 63 by Mark who obtained his knowledge from Peter. The gospel of Luke was written for the Greeks by Luke, who was a Gentile by birth and under the guidance of Paul. And last but not least the Gospel of John was written for all mankind in AD 85. This would explain why certain things are changed within the Gospels. For example, the relation of John the Baptist and Jesus is only discovered after reading the Gospel of Luke and even then one would have to make the comparisons on their own to discover that Jesus could be a blood heir because Mary and Elizabeth are cousins. As I have also stated the Gospel of Luke was written later and under the tutelage of Paul. The Gospel of Matthew doesn't give you the whole story of John the Baptist, but Luke does. In the Gospel of John, Joseph of Arimathea gets the body of Jesus before his legs can be broken. The Book of John contradicts that of Matthew, the Genesis, Isaiah, and Kings. Here are a few examples of these contradictions.

John 3:13 (13) And no man hath ascended up to heaven but he that came down from heaven, even the son of man which is in heaven.

2 Kings 2:11 (11) And it came to pass as they still went on and talked that behold, there appeared a chariot of fire, and horses of fire, and parted them both asunder; and Elijah went up by a whirlwind to heaven.

John 6:38 (38) For I came down from heaven, not to do mine own will, but the will of him that sent me.

John 5:45 (45) Do not think that I will accuse you to the father: there is one that accuseth you, even Moses, in whom ye trust.

Matthew 10:33 (33) But whosoever deny me before men, him will I also deny before my father which is in heaven.

John 8:15 (15) Ye judge after flesh; I judge no man.

Isaiah 42:1 (1) Behold my servant, whom I uphold; mine elect, in whom my soul delighteth; I have put my spirit upon him; he shall bring forth judgment to the Gentiles.

Isaiah 42:13 (13) The Lord shall go forth as a mighty man, he shall stir up Jealousy like a man of war: he shall cry yea, <u>roar</u>; he shall prevail against his enemies.

John 13:16 (16) Verily, verily, I say unto you, The servant is not greater than his lord; neither he that is sent is greater than he that sent him.

John 15:20 (20) Remember the word that I said unto you, The servant is not greater than his lord.

Matthew 23:11 But he that is greatest among you shall be your servant.

John 12:49 (49) For I have not spoken of myself; but the father which sent me, he gave me commandment, what I should say what I should speak.

The Jews have instructions that are most mathematical and make the most sense with the Book of Matthew. This is why I used the Book of Matthew the most when analyzing scripture, because this book is of Hebrew (Jewish) origin and this account of the Gospel is probably the most pure. The Gospel to the Greeks, the Gentiles, and mankind would probably be less concentrated as the people of non-Jewish origin would not understand the Jewish customs. All the other Gospels save that of Matthew would most likely be inferior to Matthew because the secrets the Hebrew people know are not to be thrown to those with lesser understanding. If this wasn't true, different gospels wouldn't be written just translated into different languages?

TRUTH OR FALSEHOOD

Due to the play on words in which wholly, a reference to looking at something from a three-hundred and sixty degree perspective has been changed to holy; there is no a doubt in my mind the information presented in this book will be considered blasphemous. Instead of wholly or fully processing a thought from beginning to end, people have for a lack of understanding, mystified the word "holy" and with it, mystified the "Living God."

John 4:12 No man hath seen God at any time. If we love one another, God dwelleth in us, and his love is perfected in us.

The scripture above is a direct contradiction between the Old and New Testaments. John has stated that no man at any time has seen "God." Yet Abraham is said to have talked with "God" gave him something to eat, and asked him to wash his feet.

Genesis 18:1-4 (1) And the Lord appeared unto him (Abraham)in the plains of Mamre and he sat in the tent door in the heat of day; (2) And he lift his eyes up and lo three men stood by him: and when he saw them, he ran to meet them from the tent door and bowed himself towards the ground (3) And said, My Lord, if now I have found favor in thy sight, pass not away, I pray thee, from thy servant: (4) Let a little water, I pray you, be fetched, and wash your feet, and rest yourselves under the tree.

When we have contradictions like these it is no wonder that Jews would dismiss certain practices the Christian faith acknowledges. The terminology and the way that "God" is referenced has changed from a physical being to a being of mind. John who is writing this book seems to be sadly mistaken. If he is wrong on this point how many other points may he have erred in? Are we to question the legitimacy of his other writings? John's Gospel was the last to be written in about 85 AD. He was the youngest disciple and the fact that his Gospel came last is why so many of the questions/ statements in it are more in depth. It has been proven that when a story has errors or pertinent (heavy) information in it, usually those who are responsible for the editing process remove, re-write, or retranslate the errors/pertinent "heavy" information out of it. Any person that has worked within any particular field that deals with production, writing, film, and storytelling knows the story is told on the editing table. Most actors who have been on movie sets and movie roles know just how much their performances are minimized by editing. Everything has to follow a script and a pattern. This pattern is determined by the director and the person responsible for editing.

Edit: (1) to prepare as literary material for publication or public presentation (2) to assemble by cutting and rearranging (3) to alter adapt or refine especially to bring about conformity to a standard or to suit a particular purpose

Heavy: (1) having great weight (2) hard to bear (3) of serious importance

Scribe: A member of a learned class in ancient Israel through New Testament times studying the scriptures and serving as copyists, editors, and teachers

Matthew 23:23 *Woe unto you, Scribes and Pharisees, hypocrites! For ye pay tithe of mint and anise and cumin, and have omitted the* <u>weightier</u> *matters of law, judgment, mercy, and faith: these ought ye have done, and not to leave the other undone.*

If a person can understand what the definition of editing means one could also understand what I mean when I say the Bible has indeed been edited or altered to bring about conformity to a standard. But what standard of conformity has this editing process led the people to? When reading the New Testament books namely those after the Epistles of Paul we get a sentiment that those who were in power translated their political agendas within a spiritual agenda; here are a few verses that indicate this.

Hebrews 13:17 *Obey them that have the rule over you, and submit yourselves: for they watch for your souls, as they that must give account, that they may do it with joy, and not with grief: for that is unprofitable to you.*

Hebrews 23:24 *Salute all them that have the rule over you, and all the saints. They of Italy salute you.*

Colossians 3:22 *Servants obey in all things your masters according to the flesh; not with eye-service as men-pleasures but in singleness of heart fearing God.*

These verses seem to be more politically driven than spiritually driven. If Moses or Jesus were to have abided by these rules, how could they have delivered a people from Pharaoh and the corrupt Pharisees? These constant contradictions between Old and New Testaments prove there is an agenda the Bible has been orchestrated to carry out. This realization is scary to most people because where do they go from here? If what they have been taught is a lie, what should they now believe? For these reasons I have felt the necessity to show what has been covered up and why.

Matthew 24:24 *for there shall arise false Christ's, and false prophets, and shall show great signs and great wonders insomuch that, if it were possible, they shall deceive the very elect.*

Many of Jesus's humanistic characteristics in the translation of the Gospels were omitted at the Nicene council by the Emperor Constantine. Constantine himself was a non-Christian who upon being on his death bed converted to Christianity. He was also a brutal ruler of Rome and upheld his rule with the sword and an iron fist. In order to fully understand what has just been cited I have pulled into reference the happenings of the Nicene council. This council is a factual historical occurrence that tells us which theory of Jesus was taught and why. Though this reference isn't my own, what is expressed through it serves to make what I have written even more significant. I have done this to further illustrate my point about the aspects of black culture in the ancient world that are left out and the lack thereof in understanding it by those of Roman interest and influence. Even the monasticism that found a home in Roman Catholicism originated from the asceticism that was prevalent in Egypt, dating back to the time of Hermes Trismegestis. Hermes who is known as Thoth in Egypt became the prototype of the 'hermit' monk. This "monk" is who many friars emulate in their monasteries today. Because this is the case Jesus was depicted as a monk for all of his life rather than a monk for a period of his life. Again 18 years of his life were omitted from biblical record; and due to the manipulation of historical facts, the Roman Church only published the parts of his life that were suitable to their agenda [152].

Monasticism: of or relating to monasteries or to monks or nuns

THE NICENE COUNCIL

The purpose of the Nicene council pronounced naisi/n (note the parallel in pronunciation to Nazi) was convened by Constantine in the summer of 325 AD. Bishops of all provinces were summoned to Nicaea and attended from every region of the empire except Great Britain to resolve disagreements arising from within the Church of Alexandria over the nature of Jesus in relationship to the Father; in particular, whether Jesus was of the same substance as God the Father or merely of similar substance. The controversy was a dispute about the Christ that began in Alexandria between the followers of Arius (the *Arians*) and the followers of St. Alexander of Alexandria, Athanasius. Athanasius and his followers believed that the Son was of the *same substance* as the Father, co-eternal with him. The Arians believed that they were different and that the Son, though he may be the most perfect of creations, was only a creation. The council decided against Arius overwhelmingly. Of the estimated 250–318 attendees, all save two voted against Arius. Much of the debate hinged on the difference between being "born" or "created" and being "begotten." Athanasius' sect believed that to follow the Arian view destroyed the unity of the Godhead, and made the Son unequal to the Father, in contravention of the Scriptures (*"The Father and I are one"*, John 10:30). Arians, on the other hand, believed that since God the Father created the Son, the son then must be less than the Father and since the

473

Son was created afterward could not be eternal. The Arians used Scriptures from John 14:28 to corroborate their case. *"The Father is greater than I."* Athanasius's sect countered the Arians' argument by saying the Father is eternal and because the Father was always a father, the Son always existed with him. The Council decided that the Father and the Son are of the same substance and are co-eternal, basing the decision in the claim that it was a formulation of traditional Christian belief handed down from the Apostles. This declaration is why people of today view Jesus more as a spirit than a person 153. At the council of Nicea the Catholic Church adopted its primary belief from what is called the Nicene Creed, It states:

I believe in one God, the Father Almighty, Creator of heaven and earth, of all things visible and invisible. And in one Lord Jesus Christ, Son of God, the only-begotten, born of the Father before all ages. Light of light, true God of true God, begotten, not made, of one substance with the Father, through whom all things were made. Who for us men and for our salvation, came down from heaven, and was incarnate from the Holy Spirit and Mary the Virgin, and became man. He was also crucified for us under Pontius Pilate, and suffered and was buried. And He rose again on the third day, according to the scriptures. And He ascended into heaven, and sits at the right hand of the Father. And He will come again with glory, to judge the living and the dead, and of His kingdom there will be no end. And in the Holy Spirit, the Lord, and Giver of life, who proceeds from the Father, who together with the Father and the Son is worshipped and glorified, Who spoke through the prophets. In one holy, catholic and apostolic Church. I profess one baptism for the remission of sins. I expect the resurrection of the dead; and the life of the world to come. Amen 154.

The Council of Nicaea in 325 A.D. was also used by Athanasius to incorporate in the canons of the Church the requirement of celibacy for Christian leaders. Following his victory over Arius and the Arians, Athanasius traveled throughout Europe promoting monasticism and asceticism. He is credited with introducing monasticism specifically to the Romans and Germans.

If you look at the traditional father and son relationship, (in the successor model) usually the son is expected to succeed the father but not necessarily be greater than the father, because "greater" is a matter of perspective. Example: even though Solomon was the richest and wisest king in the Egypt, his father David slayed the giant Goliath *and* created (him) Solomon. The strength and courage it took to pull off slaying this giant was one that at that time was the most extraordinary thing that was seen. Only "God" himself in the flesh could have done it. However the fame, fortune and wisdom that Solomon had was so great that he in himself grew to be viewed as a great king as well. Looking at the relation between David and Solomon, we can see how the understanding between "God" and his son could be misconstrued and misunderstood. It all depends on what you view as bigger, what appeals to your sense of what is greater. Remember, when you are talking about the God of Abraham, Isaac and Jacob, you are talking about a god who literally came in the flesh to produce a son in the lineage of Abraham, leaving the question of which is greater; the "Living God" who has been mystified, or his son who the world worships.

The main theological issue and focus of the world had always been about Christ. Since the end of the Apostolic Age and beginning of the Church Age, saints began questioning, debating, fighting, and separating over the question, "Who is the Christ?" Is he more divine than human or more human than divine? Was Jesus created / made or begotten? Being the Son of God, is He co-equal and co-eternal with Father God, or less and lower in status than the Father? Is the Father the One and only true God, or are the Father, the Son, and the Holy Spirit the One true God?

As I researched the Nicene council what I found when referencing and reading it, is a group of scholars that have gathered together to try and make sense of what and whose god is greater. The fact they are trying to see if the son is greater than the father, and is the trinity one or all three beings, shows that what they are looking at are the gods from the Hindu and Egyptian Pantheons. Vishnu, Shiva, and Brahma are the original trinity expressed in the oldest religion. They alongside Krishna are considered the highest of all the gods. As stated on pg. 74, in *The Second Messiah* by Christopher Knight and Robert Lomas, *"Gentile Christians merged myths of their old gods and the cult conceived by Paul to create a hybrid religion that had great appeal"* 155. The great debate in Hinduism, the world's oldest religion, was always over who was the most powerful God, Vishnu, who is said to be personified as Krishna or Shiva the god who is referenced as the all god having no beginning or end. Shiva, in the Hindu religion, is the wild god of power and ecstasy. He represents the tantric and sexual magic that brings about the creation of the human, mankind, and the universe. He is also an ascetic who is a person that practices asceticism, and would be considered on the left side known as the hidden and secret side of "God." This aspect is seen in the life of Jesus as a wandering ascetic who reveals sacred mysteries and precedes a baptism by Vishnu known as John the Baptist. The other half of the life of Jesus whereby he has mystical powers as a child, walks on water, and is a healer who is the perfected example for man to follow would represent Krishna and the right hand of "God." Both of the cults of Krishna and Shiva together represent the cults of Judah and Joseph (Israel) who are to be placed under one stick and ruled by a new "God." The actual "Jesus of Nazareth" known as Kalki in the Hindi religion, is to rule over the two cults in the present age the earth is entering which as I have previously stated is the Age of Aquarius.

As I've reiterated before, there is also a conception story that dates back as far as the origins of creation that speaks in reference to a Sun who resurrects the all god or the god of the dead. This is told in the Egyptian story of Osiris, Isis, and Horus. These three represent the other "original" trinity (Sun, Earth, Man.) expressed through the formulation of the pyramids. Horus is the Sun god, who resurrects the father (All God.) This notion is puzzling to scholars because the sun/son is resurrecting the father; and is why they argue over Jesus versus his father, "God" as well as hypothesize about who is greater. In the 27th verse of the 1st chapter of James, God and the "Father" are listed as being separate entities. This is indicative of the relationship between Shiva known as the LORD God and Vishnu his harbinger and mentor / "Father."

James 1:27 *Pure religion and undefiled before* <u>*God and the Father*</u> *is this, To visit the fatherless and widows in their affliction, and to keep himself unspotted from the world.*

The story of Jesus is the story of Horus found in ancient Africa. It was retranslated using a new language in order for the "Living God" who resurrects to piece the WORD who was literally his son back together. When the trinity of Hinduism is combined with the trinity of ancient Egyptian (Israel) we get Solomon's seal; two equilateral triangles ascending and descending into one another. On Solomon's seal on the following page, notice how the snake and the eagle encompass the seal and also how within the seal, there are glyphs associated to astrological signs. These signs are the Sun, Moon, Mercury, Venus, Jupiter, Saturn, and Mars, and again symbolize the God of Israel who is personified symbolically as a snake & an eagle 162.

John 15:26 (26) *But when the comforter is come, whom I will send unto you from the father, even the Spirit of truth, which proceed from the father, he shall testify of me.*

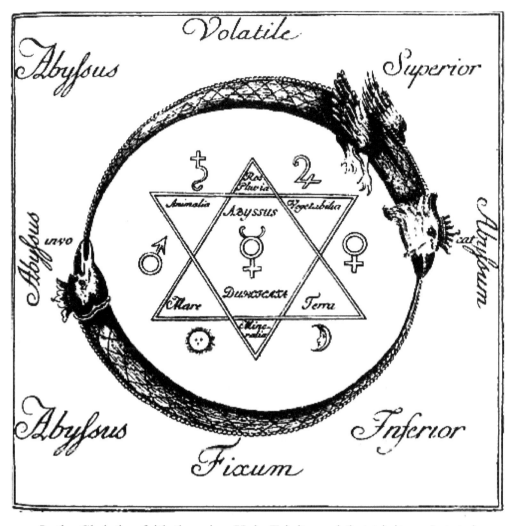

In the Christian faith there is a Holy Trinity and that trinity as I stated consists of God the father, God the son, and the Holy Spirit. The Sun of Man is the Spirit of Truth, who is sent as a Comforter to the people from the "father" in the gospel of St. John. This is similar to the Hindu religion where it is prophesized that a son of Shiva-Mahadev or Isvara will be the one (Sun) that is sent to earth to restore it back into its Golden Age.

The same as Elijah who is the "Father" of Jesus is coming and restoring all things before his "sun" Jesus can come and destroy the present system of false god and religion. In ancient Phoenicia Eli – points to the Father of the gods known as Uranus /Aquarius. Jah is the name of the Sun god or the lion/Leo that is also known as the "father of the gods" in Egypt. The reason for both Uranus and the Sun being considered the father of the gods in varying ancient

Semitic religions has to do with precession when the north and south poles on the globe exchange positions. Because Aquarius and Leo are polar opposites, when these poles exchange positions, these signs also exchange positions and literally become each other. If Elijah is represented by the coming together (fusion) of these energies of both Aquarius (Eli), and Leo (Jah) that would mean that the son of Elijah would also be the Holy ONE of Israel who is both "the almighty father" Uranus, the glorious sun of Leo and the Holy Spirit through Shin that connects all three beings in one Godhead 162a. This is the three in one entity known as the Jesus of Nazareth, whose father is known under several different titles like Jehovah, the LORD, Adonai, and Shiva. In Freemasonry the Supreme Being is represented symbolically by a Sun at the head, a ruler for the arms and chest, the Holy Bible for the abdomen, the twin pillars of Jachin and Boaz as his legs and feet, with a globe beside the seven luminaries inside of a crystal ball at its loins. The seven luminaries inside of the globe are Osiris, Set, Isis, and Horus, Ra, Hathor, and Hormus. This totem represents The HOLY ONE of Israel and is the God of Israel, and the present age, the Age of Aquarius. Again what is left out to the people's understanding of "God" is that "God" is in the flesh physically walking the earth. We know this because he physically has to create a son who represents elementally everything that can exist in creation in one being. This being is who the present church and all system of religions have been taught to worship. This is why he has more importance and relevance then the "god" that fathered him. The "god" who delivers him is the vessel or the carrier of spiritual essence and knowledge which is why Vishnu of the Hindu scriptures as well as the solar deity Ra of the Egyptian hieroglyphs travels upon the cosmos in an ark 157. The father again is not listed in the Christian gospels as having a mortal body precisely due to the Nicene council. This is why scholars that the Nicene Council were trying to figure out who came first the father or the son. These stories they received at the council were originally found in Egypt where the god was Osiris and his son was Heru or Horus. Leaving the fact that they got this information from Egypt and reconstructing it as their own has bred confusion in the minds of the people of the Christian faith. Osiris was **dis**membered and his (body) of work was spread out into fourteen parts; the "Sun" of Man has to find those parts and reassemble them. These are the parts and aspects of himself that were broken up and scattered amongst all of the religions of the world, Hinduism, Judaism, Christianity, and Islam. Upon doing this, the God then finds the Goddess (Isis) who contains the ability to "Supe him up" transforming him through her womb into his re-membered self who has all power. In this story the "Sun" resurrects the "father" or the Leo resurrects the Aquarius. This is why in the Christian faith people don't really understand what these aspects of the resurrection truly mean. A true son will resurrect the legacy of the father, this is common knowledge and the part that anybody can relate to and readily see; a great example of this is Floyd Mayweather Jr. However when talking about Osiris we are talking about a "Living God" that has existed since the beginning of time as we know it; and with him exists Isis and his son, Heru or Horus. The son is the "father" and the father is the *Sun*.

Psalms 119:130 (130) *The unfolding of your words gives light it gives understanding to the simple.*

In lieu of all the complex breakdowns of the previous paragraph we'll summarize the latter by saying this, the Sun was sent to earth to resurrect the father or "all God" on Earth. He resurrects the father by finding the goddess who is on earth disguised as a servant girl; much like Hagar in the Bible and also like Sarah. These two stories of Sarah and Hagar are written to show you the dual nature of the "Queen of heaven" who like Cinderella, is a queen disguised in humble obscurity as a servant girl as well as the "God" of gods who is on earth disguised in mortal skin as a man. Digesting this material is a very hard notion to ponder for those who have simply went to church and lived their lives by faith alone. This book though easily read and comprehensive, has been tailored towards scholars and those theologians with extensive knowledge about the Bible and the ancient cultures from which it spawns. But even if a person was not a scholar and wanted general information about the Bible and the life of Jesus, how can anyone accurately hypothesize about his life if they do not have the whole record? Both the NIV and King James Bibles have left out over eighteen years of his life. Jesus is seen as a boy of twelve and then it skips to when he is thirty years old.

Luke 2:40 & 42 (40) *And the child grew, and waxed strong in spirit, filled with wisdom: and the grace of God was upon him. (42) And when he was twelve years old, they went up to Jerusalem after the custom of the feast.*

Luke 3:23 (23) And Jesus himself began to be about thirty years of Age, being (as was supposed) the son of Joseph which was the son of Heli.

Heli in the passage above points to Helios (Sun)

Also, it is no wonder that upon this time the people of the earth in this spectrum of the world can't really say they know anything about the happenings on the eastern side of the globe because they leave out the existence of black people. It's no mystery why the bishops, rulers, and people of Roman influence cannot understand the phenomena associated with the scriptures. By omitting black people's existence from the history books in relation to world history, they have closed themselves off from any real truth in regards to the religion they profess to believe in. This is why publications like the April 1st 2011 edition of *The Watchtower,* a newsletter of the Jehovah's Witnesses since 1879, can acknowledge that the Supreme Ruler of the Universe is Jehovah, who has a real government and kingdom in "heaven," that will bring an end to all wickedness and transform the earth into a paradise. Yet, they are unable to comprehend that the "heavenly kingdom" they are referencing points to Astrology, and the new "Sun" personified in human flesh is the LORD Jehovah himself, who alongside his son will be the new "Rulers" of the world to come.

THE LIBRARY OF ALEXANDRIA

The loss of the Library of Alexandria, the ancient world's single greatest archive of knowledge, has been lamented for ages yet how and why the library became lost is still a mystery. The library of Alexandria was founded in Egypt by Alexander the Great, and the museum was a shrine of the Muses modeled after the Lyceum of Aristotle in Athens. It was also a place of study which included gardens, lecture areas, a zoo, and shrines for each of the nine muses as well as the library itself. It has been estimated that at one time the Library of Alexandria held over half a million documents from Assyria, Greece, Persia, Egypt, India and many other nations. Over 100 scholars lived at the museum full time to perform research, write lectures, or translate and copy documents. The library was so large it actually had another branch at the Temple of Serapis. The first person blamed for the Library's destruction was Julius Caesar. Supposedly in 48 BC, Caesar was pursuing Pompey into Egypt when he was abruptly confronted by an Egyptian fleet at Alexandria. Being severely outnumbered in enemy territory, Caesar ordered the ships in the harbor to be set on fire. The fire spread and destroyed the Egyptian fleet, and it also reportedly burned down the part of the city where the Library of Alexander was at 156. The second story of the Library's destruction is said to have been done by Theophilus who was a Patriarch of Alexandria from 385 to

412 A.D. During his reign the Temple of Serapis was converted into a Christian church. The Temple of Serapis was estimated to have held ten percent of the overall Library's holdings. A Christian proselyte was publicly killed by order of Orestes and riots broke out. Orestes was said to be under the "spell" of Hypatia, a female philosopher. Some hypothesize that the death of Hypatia caused the Library of Alexander to be destroyed; others blame Theophilus when he raided the Temple of Serapis prior to making it a Christian church 156a. The Moslem Caliph Omar was the final individual blamed for the destruction of the great library, and in 640 AD, the Moslems took the city of Alexandria after discovering it was the world's largest and most prestigious library. The Caliph has been quoted as saying the Library's records would contradict the Qur'an, So, allegedly, all the books and records were destroyed as a result.

Here, another instance of Romans erasing records has been cited to show the historical significance behind the stolen knowledge and legacies of the world's ancient and original civilizations. Again when I say Roman I am not speaking necessarily about those who are from Rome or European ancestry. When I say Roman I am speaking about anyone who takes romanticism over reality. When I look at the western world it is consumed by fantasy; I understand why because reality is boring. Reality is the given and in life people need entertainment and want to see beyond the limiting realities their lives are prison to. Truth makes people miserable. The people in this present American society have fallen so far away from it not because they don't want it, truthfully, they can't handle it. This is why people have created all of these perceived and romantic ideals. They are just trying to spice up their lives and find a moment of happiness in all of the turmoil and uncertainty. The only problem with this is at whose expense has the lie and life of happiness infringed upon. Having the type of person in office like Barak Obama is the only necessary diplomatic approach in mediating the race relations in America without having to own up to all the lies the media has further perpetuated. If the current rulers of American society are sincere in their intent we should see a great transformation that extends past the superficial display of change. The change will be one of impact, relief, and restoration, not of ideal and theory. Those who have been left out, wronged and unjustly cast as the burden bearers for American society will be liberated in the sense they are able to live and function according to their nature and not a system. The truth will set the world free from the bondage of ignorant men who wish for their own selfish motives to rule the world and run it into the ground based solely upon a legacy stolen from other ancient cultures.

THE YIN AND THE YANG

The universal law states that every action has one
that is equal and opposite. So naturally if God had
an opposite that opposing being would be equal.
The opposing being would have to be the Devil,
which according to this Law of physics makes
them two aspects of the same one; sort of like a
coin. But let's think about this critically. If
humans are both God and the Devil fused together
in one being (individuals) wouldn't this give rise
to the theory of yin and yang; one light and
masculine the other dark and feminine? This is an interesting concept and one
that is explored as well as depicted in Masonry. Its name is Baphomet and it
alone represents this juxtaposed counterpart to what Christians know as God.
When we look at the image of Baphomet we see it has mammary glands like a
woman. It is also winged and has the five pointed star upon his forehead,
symbolic of man. There are two moons beside its hands, one on the left, above
that is white representing masculinity; and another below that is dark
representing femininity. Baphomet has the goat upon its head which is
indicative of Pan or (Saturn) and it is prostrated in the Sukhasana position
which shows its enlightenment. Referred to as the Sabbatical Goat, Baphomet
represents the true Sabbath, as Saturday is the day most people do their carnal
deeds before repentance and a return to holiness on Sunday. For Freemasons,
Baphomet represents the union of opposites in its "wholistic" form which
causes all masculine and feminine energies to merge within one being creating
an enlightened life form from the recognition of these acknowledgements.

Baphomet in whole represents the "Baptist" the inverse of what is
considered to be right, good, and God. The universe works in oppositions and
polarizations as well as projects assimilations of the actual manifestations in
like characters. Example, in today's time Kim Kardashian is considered a
goddess due to her uncanny beauty and physical attributes, but according to
the kabbalistic breakdown of Beyonce's character, she is an actual
reincarnated deity. Though Kim isn't written in the ancient books as being a
goddess one can argue that she's has now become one.

BAPHOMET is made up of a reverse of three abbreviations. **BA – PHO – MET** which reversed are **TEM – OPH – AB**. **TEM** = Templi or Temple. **OPH** = Ominum Pacis Hominum **AB** = Abhas - Together equaling TEMPLI OMINUM HOMINUM PACIS ABHAS which translates in Latin to THE GOD OF THE TEMPLE OF PEACE AMONG ALL MEN - I.E. - KING SOLOMON'S TEMPLE. If the name Solomon is the name describing the SUN – the inverse of that SUN again would point to URANUS. From the Greek translation we have **BAPHE** which = TO DIP/ DYE OR BAPTISE **METIS** = MATH/METRIC. Under this translation BAPHOMET = TO BAPTISE IN THE KNOWLEDGE WISDOM & UNDERSTANDING OF MATH. In Egypt there is a different spelling which also adds another corresponding clue. **BA** = SOL /IMMORTAL/ ESSENCE - **FA** = TO CARRY/BORN/LIFTED **MAAT** = ORDER/ JUSTICE/ TRUTH - under this translation **Baphomet** = THE IMMORTAL ESSENCE BEING LIFTED AND BORN IN TRUTH.

When those of Roman origin read and deciphered the scrolls and scriptures they took light for white and dark for black. In reading this in this way they didn't understand that it is vice versa and the roles are reversed. Things that are black attract light and pull light in; and things that are white refract light and push light away. Think about your eyeball, the pupil is solid black yet when you look out of it you don't see darkness, you see light. The white part of the eye (sclera) reflects light. Having this understanding they took everything at face value and rationalized that since dark people are dark, they must be evil; and because white people are white or light as in hues they must be godly and pure. If they were looking at the color black they would find that things that are black are lit up and full of light, and things that are white reflect and are void of light.

White: (1) free from spot or blemish: (2): free from moral impurity: innocent

Black: (1) thoroughly sinister or evil: wicked (2) connected with or invoking the supernatural and especially the devil

In taking into account the way roles are reversed in how we think about black and white as they pertain to race; when analyzing the truth about race and masculine and feminine energies through a scientific scope, we come to the word individual, which is something that has two parts that isn't divided individe (dual.) This fusing of the two natures of black and white / masculine and feminine energies together is what makes and creates balance within the universe. One side is different from the other yet it is the same entity; you have Sun and Moon, masculine and feminine, yin and yang, black and white.

It is of popular belief the Devil is the opposing entity to God; which is why the Black Nationalist, particularly the Black Muslims, polarized this acknowledgement as the Black Man "God" versus the White man "Devil." God has power over the physical realm were reality is paramount, and the Devil has power over the imaginary world were romanticism is paramount. Depending on what perspective you are looking from either one can appear as God or the Devil. The same goes for masculine and feminine energies; but because "God" doesn't have a negative stigma associated with him like the Devil does, both of the sexes view themselves as God rather than the Devil. The same mental thought process is evident in white and black people. Black people's belief that humans carry animal energies associated within them seems very devilish to white people. Also Polygamy seems to be inhumane and satanic from their (Roman) viewpoint as well. To the hu/man it is the natural order of things, and the way they are created in nature to be. On the flipside, the way the Roman culture openly embraced homosexuality to the alpha black man is seen as an abomination. This "romantic" man in his religious beliefs practices chastity and views sleeping with women a defilement of the flesh. The reason this is so is because his nature and origin has been hidden from him. He heard the story of Cain but wasn't made aware that the serpent wasn't a snake, it was a large black gods "phallus." Because he isn't connected to the spiritual world he is made to believe that the act of sex itself was the defiling act; so he requires facts and proof with sight in order to validate his theories. But as far as his limited knowledge reaches, he is right in his belief.

Revelation 14:4 No one could learn the song except the 144,000 who had been redeemed from the earth. (4)These are those who did not defile themselves with women, for they kept themselves pure.

The Book of Noah gives us more clues as to what took place in the Genesis. It also adds clarity as to why those who advocated for a Jesus, or a "God" that was white, felt completely just in making pictures that depicted the "God" in this way. In the Book of Noah, it states that when Noah was born he came out looking different than expected. If we're translating the Genesis with a literal interpretation, during the times of the flood, the earth had started over where everyone except Noah and his family were obliterated from the earth.

Book of Noah CVI-CVII (1) *And after some days my son Methuselah took a wife for his son Lamech, and she became pregnant by him and bare a son (2.). And his body was white as snow and red as the blooming of a rose, and the hair of his head and his long locks were white as wool, and his eyes beautiful* 157.

By this indication is seems possible that Noah could have been an albino. If the world started over with him and his seed this would serve as a clue as to why Romans have depicted the chosen people of God's covenant as being a people with fair skin who are white. Since the Bible states the world started over after the flood ended, I take this to mean the Age of Aquarius was the beginning of the new world/age; and upon the world falling into its deluge (flood), Noah was the Avatar/Christ/Horus that was the progenitor of the people who had a covenant with the God of Isis Ra and El. This is further evidence that exposes why the Bible says all of the races of man came from Noah and his sons, Ham, Shem, and Japheth. This also adds explanative evidence that links the Demiurge (Osiris) who creates the new universe by "naming" and "building," to Noah, who as the new Adam, animates creation by naming the animals and everything in it. - Genesis 1:20.

Genesis 1:20 *And Adam gave names to all cattle, and to the fowl of the air, and to every beast of the field; but for Adam there was not found an help meet for him.*

Remember in that time it says the sons of God came into the daughters of men; the Sons of God where black and the daughters of men were fair, lightly complexioned red or white. How do we know this? Let's add up all the facts. Even if Noah was an albino he would still be considered African or black racially although he was white physically. This could be why the people of Roman descent do not feel they are wrong for the mishandling or misinterpreting of certain biblical scriptures and depictions. The Book of Noah was taken out of the Bible alongside several other books including the Book of Enoch yet most Christians who have a King James or an NIV version aren't even aware these books exist. Because they do not have these books to read from, they have developed a theology for themselves that has a lot of holes in it when looked at from a logical or an intellectual standpoint. Having these records to reference gives the individual a more in depth perspective to draw their conclusions from in regards to their beliefs. Presenting orthodox Christians with this information most certainly will be seen as devilish. Because the Mother church has taught as dogma the present view of Christianity and labeled these occult teachings as satanic, it has corralled the world into an unenlightened belief in regards to the Bible and its scriptures.

Genesis 6:1 *"And it came to pass when men began to multiply on the face of the earth, and daughters were born unto them. That the sons of God saw the daughters of men that they were fair; and they took them as wives of all which they chose.*

Noah's color would indicate that he was a hu/man and being albino would render him capable to produce all other colors in regards to race. Every color originates from black, and we can trace Noah's lineage back to Cain who was the first crossbreed. If you could get black from white then this theory about Noah being an albino would have little if any merit. But because you can get white from black this makes this particular theory all the more plausible. Knowing this, Noah would have to be of black origin and a [CARRIER/ (ARK)] of the dominant (black/alpha gene) even if his skin wasn't. We know this because he fathered a black son (Ham.) Joseph the father of the Christ was also a [CARRIER/ (ARK)] of the alpha gene 158. Earlier in this book when I said the Gentile was produced or obtained by a gene I said that it could have been a point where a "mutation" occurred and upon the recognition of this occurrence an entire race sprang forth from it. If any of that theory has truth to it, we can take this to mean that Noah and his descendants upon being set in an ark to repopulate the Earth were sent to another place as in a "foreign" land to repopulate the landscape with the (Ark of the Covenant.)

Genesis 8:15 -17 (15) Then God said to Noah, (16) Come out of the ark, you and your wife and your sons and their wives. (17) Bring out every kind of living creature that is with you the birds, the animals, and all the creatures that move along the ground so they can multiply on earth and be fruitful and increase in number upon it.

Hypothetically, imagine if Africa was overrun by blacks because they had multiplied and mixed themselves to the point where they were no longer in the form they once existed in; and having so many different dominant beings all

 fighting and vying for the throne left their civilization in ruin. A mutation occurs within a black womb and the being that comes from it is very different from the ones that were seen in that particular area. Say that same being within his DNA carried the alpha genes that would one day be responsible for a whole nation of people; yet the people overlooked him to due to his outward appearance. This would be the ultimate way for the universe to bring about change by hiding the "king" in plain sight, reminiscent of the thief in the night persona that "God" disguises himself with when he descends to earth. This change of pigmentation could also be looked at as the mark of Cain, a

distinguishing characteristic that separates the carrier/Ark from the rest of the lot. Remember in those times alphas were dominant and able to breed with many females, this again was to ensure more of their kinds essences were infused within the society/village.

In this same example, let's also suppose that the foreign place or "new world" these alpha genes were deposited at was America; and due to what the gods/elders saw in the last "world" they lived in, gave them an edge on protecting the new world they were trying to reform and create.

Genesis 6:11-13 (11) Now the earth was corrupt in God's sight and was full of violence. (12) God saw how corrupt the earth had become, for all the people on earth had corrupted their ways. (13) So God said to Noah, "I am going to put an end to all people, for the earth is filled with violence because of them. I am surely going to destroy both them and the earth.

If this is the case, it makes sense as to why the "powers that be" would not want the Hamites (blacks) to breed within and integrate in their society. In fact some White Supremacists sects did breed the Africans with their (white) blood to produce crossbred slaves that were more controllable. Again, this crossbred slave was looked upon by the rest of the more unadulterated slaves as being the "house/weak" slave who was privileged with living in the house while the dark slaves lived in the outhouses or the fields. Recognition of these facts allows us, if we have a truly unbiased open mind, to see the reasoning as to how slavery was justified in the Americas. When we factor the scriptures states the LORD abandoned his children, leaving them to be imperialized by their enemies, it all makes sense.

Hosea 4:6 (6) My people are destroyed for lack of knowledge: because thou hast rejected knowledge, I will also reject thee, that thou shalt be no priest to me: seeing thou hast forgotten the law of thy God, I will also forget thy children.

Pending on how far we are looking back, and whose point of view we are looking from, the bible gives us clues as to why the dark people of the world went into bondage and were discriminated against in the Americas of today. Even in the legend of Noah, his grandson is cursed for taking a forbidden woman which again lays hold to the claim that the "dark gene" being dominant is in a sense, predisposed to following laws. In the ninth chapter of Genesis Ham's descendants are cursed because once again the gene of Cain was present. One of the blacks, "descendant of the (gods)" slept with a woman that was off limits to him. This time it happened to be Ham; before, it was Eve sleeping with one of the "gods" the (Serpent). The woman Ham slept with was one of his father (Noah's) wives. How do we know this? When we parallel two scriptures together we can begin to paint the picture as to why a man would be cursed to be a slave because he saw his father's nakedness. After all, seeing your father naked doesn't warrant you being a slave for all eternity does it? Here once again the curse is placed on the Black (god.)

Leviticus 20:11 (11) <u>and the man that lieth with his father's wife hath uncovered his father's nakedness:</u> both of them shall surely be put to death; their blood shall be upon them.

Genesis 9:22 (22) and Ham, the father of <u>Canaan, saw the nakedness of his father,</u> and told his two brethren without.

Genesis 9:25-27 (25) and he said, "<u>Cursed be Canaan; a servant of servants shall he be unto his brethren</u> (26) and he said, blessed be the Lord God of Shem; and Canaan shall be his servant. (27) God shall enlarge Japheth, and he shall dwell in the tents of Shem; and Canaan shall be his servant."

After putting the two of these scriptures together we can conclude that Ham the black god again was cursed for sleeping with the wife of his father Noah; which proves a number of things. The first of which is the connecting pattern which is sleeping with another's wife (*forbidden woman*) that was done by (The LORD) in the account of Sarai and Abraham, the Serpent in the account of Adam and Eve, and David in the account of Uriah and Bathsheba. If we

look into these matters deeply to see what it is they may be saying we can draw conclusions that give us very different outcomes then the ones that are traditionally accepted. Michael Jackson also expressed this theme in his *Remember the Time* video where he seduces the wife of Pharaoh as well as his real life where he weds Lisa Marie Pressley causing her to leave the husband she had at that time.

Dominance attracts everything that is inferior to it. Look at all the (players) and people who wear Michael Jordan's shoes in admiration of him. This dominant gene when unchecked is the cause of attraction and the rise of envy, strife, and dissatisfaction amongst those who are inferior to it. In nature it is simple, the dominant genes have to be reintroduced into the gene pool to ensure the species and the race thrives, as the more recessive genes lead to sickness and death and the dominant genes ensure survival and strength. Look at animals, in most cases, the dominant males are the only ones who get to breed and the females won't breed with a weaker male. If for some reason she is overtaken by a weaker male and he is able to impregnate her, she will eat her offspring when they are born. In humans the weaker males are almost always driven to acquire money and wealth in unscrupulous ways. They then use their money and wealth as a manipulating tool to give them the upper hand in the mating game. The weaker male is no match for a dominant male by himself; he needs a yacht, a huge house, and a fancy car to inspire the same emotion in a female the alpha would get by taking off his shirt. If the dominant males revel in the same tactics to acquire their wealth, they weaken as it goes against the very thing that gives them their strength. This is why in the story of Superman kryptonite, the glowing and green substance which allegorically represents money, is his ultimate weakness. Superman has a suit that is red, gold, and blue symbolizing fire and air (Leo and Aquarius, the Sun and the father.) The gold **S** upon his chest is symbolic for where he gets his power which is the Sun. He has x-ray vision, which figuratively represents his clairvoyance and (3rd eye) perspective. He also has superhuman strength, and he can fly faster than a speeding bullet which represents the rapid IQ that allows him to "travel" spiritually, the same "traveling" associated with Masonry. His arch nemesis is Lex Luther a wealthy and ruthless businessman who at every attempt tries to monopolize every situation. One would ask how a man who hasn't any physical power could ever rival the most powerful being in the universe. The reason is the development of the other senses has heightened in the weaker males because their mind has to compensate for what their bodies will not allow them to do. The weaker male's minds are strengthened and they find ways to man/ip/u/late situations so they can appear as dominant. This is the classic villainous image portrayed in stories that have a hero and a villain. Note, most of the successful pioneers other than those who had inheritances come from impoverished backgrounds; and their tremendous drive and sense of survival is what ultimately gives them their strength. One of the principal reasons as to why the world is not operated the way that it should be is because the natural born leaders as in the case of Mozart and Maximus are always obstructed by a "spoiled" ruling class of aristocrats whose rule usually ends up running the people into the ground. Knowing they are the natural leaders who were fashioned by the hand of God/nature itself, the "spoiled" aristocrats will not let them rise to power because it will put an end to their corruption and greed.

Isaiah 10:33 Behold, the lord, the Lord of Hosts shall lop the bough with terror: and the high ones of stature shall be hewn down, and the haughty shall be humbled.

This same scenario can be likened to the "God" in America who went through his rights of passage (slavery) and has the right to rule based on the conquering of himself in the most harshest and unforgiving terrain. He has yielded in his understanding and knows the weaker male is constantly trying to dethrone him; so he has placed himself in the most tumultuous of climates (slavery) in order to gain the mental strength needed to rival his opponents. Practicing asceticism, fasting, and an all-out denial of self, through (Yoga) is what makes him obtain and uphold his position as well as keeps in check the very thing that has caused his pain and suffering. The black man's libido is the reason he was enslaved, and castrated. It is easy to see how those who were rulers of Rome have used the curse of Canaan to justify slavery, and later discrimination against blacks, arguing that Ham was the one who actually committed the sin, and since he is the father of the black race, all of his descendants (not just those of his son Canaan) were cursed. We also know this to be accurate because Noah cursing Canaan doesn't make sense at the time of the curse because Canaan hadn't yet been born. Inferior beings not really understanding nature take offense to dominance and natural kingship. They become jealous, and spend every effort in enslaving the king/alpha to try and control him.

In the chapter entitled *Who wrote the Bible,* we briefly discussed that Jesus was exposing the corrupt priesthood because they perverted the Egyptian system of knowledge that we know today as Kabbalah. When we link the God of the Genesis to a physical person walking the earth, and make known he is an Egyptian god, it makes the whole story of what Jesus is speaking in reference to, in the Book of John come to life.

John 8:39-44 (39) If ye were Abraham's children ye would do the works of Abraham (40) But now you seek to kill me a man that has told you the truth, which I have *heard of God: This did not Abraham (41) Ye do the deeds of your father. Then said they to him, We be not born of fornication; we have one father, even God (42) <u>If God were your father, ye would love me: for I proceeded forth and came from God;</u> neither came I of myself, but he sent me (43) Why do ye not understand my speech? even because ye cannot hear my word. (44) <u>Ye are of your father the devil, and the lusts of your father ye will do.</u> He was a murderer from the beginning, and abode not in the truth, because there is no truth in him. When he speaketh a lie, he speaketh of his own: for he is a liar and the father of it.*

When Jesus says if God were your father you would love me for I proceeded forth from him, he is literally saying that he is a bloodline descendant of the God who birthed Isaac through Sarah. The fact that in the account the "Jews" here are saying their father is Abraham shows they don't know that Abraham didn't father Isaac; they are just lip professing. These people have read the scriptures and are able to pass as sons of Abraham to uneducated people but are easily exposed by a true blood heir, which Jesus represents.

 **John 8:39-44** is telling us the covenant was made with the Jews (Israelites) who were Afro/Asiatic -Black-Red mixed = (Brown) which again are the Negroes of America. Thus the sacrificed Ram (Black Sheep/lamb of God) becomes a Hu/man. The Black nation of enslaved sheep who were mixed with their racial opposite was the sacrifice made in order for that same nation to be made into Hu/mans; Hu/man meaning half man and half god which is why Jesus is viewed to be half God, half man, (Heru/hero.) This story in whole could also be seen as "God" sacrificing his son (black children) to suffer crucifixion, (slavery) only to be chastened, purged and refined, so they arrive in his kingdom (America) as the new royals and heirs to his godly throne. Christians are those who are descendants of this phenomenon; they are not a church or a pledged religion. They are the body of people that this crystallization (Christ/a/lization) process has occurred in. Now just because a person is an American Negro doesn't automatically mean they are Christian, the true Christians shine; meaning their levels of talent and contributions to society are immeasurable. They are the diamonds that shine through the rough. The rough organic matter (carbon) *"lesser gods" / varna sankara* represents the masses that went through the slavery process, "the Negroes themselves" who didn't evolve. The diamonds or "Christians" are the ones who were changed and crystallized by way of the slavery process.

<u>Carbon</u>: a non-metallic element found combined with other elements in all organic matter and in a pure state as diamond and graphite.

The Star of David is nothing more than a diamond. Diamonds are precious stones that are found in pressurized carbon. Carbon is the earth's (black) element that contains the other three elements, hydrogen, nitrogen, and oxygen within it. When this earth matter is put under highly intense pressure, a diamond is formed. The diamond is said to be the purest state of the carbon which is synonymous to the fifth element, spirit. 159, 159b, 159c

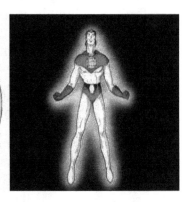

The pressure for the Negro (carbon) was again slavery, and the four elements together when compressed form a diamond which corresponds to that 5th element, again known as the spirit. The elements themselves are what the 4 quadrants of the Astrological signs fall under and since the Negroes are the people of the Sun, Astrology is the science that governs them. The spirit rising above the four elements of earth, fire, water, and air form a square and is the basis for what the pyramids symbolize. We talked about this earlier in the Captain Planet example where when the four elements combine the spirit rises above them. This is the five pointed star personified through man and the five points of his body are represented in the acronym ALLAH which stands for {(A) rm (L)eg (L)eg (A)rm (H)ead or (I) (S)elf (L)ord (A)m (M)aster. The Hebrew people associate the spirit and the mind as being one which is why the spirit is located atop the star "head" in the diagram above.

The "circumcised" negroes who understand why they were held captive also understand what changes they needed to make to crystallize into the aspect of themselves that are truly brilliant. The mixed (Semitic/Jews) who went through the slavery process, [CIRCUMSION (where musing/Islam was used,)] were mixed this time with European blood, in order to fashion and fuse the nature of God and man in one entity; changing their form from "inanimate matter", represented as (carbon) into a crystallized diamond that shines reflecting light from all the colors of creation. This is the rainbow that Michael Jackson frequently associated himself with, as he was the living embodiment of it.

 Ab/ram on the other hand connotes that the man that was made from the rib would be a Ram or a HE, a ruler of the 4 elements of the material world. Aries is an astrological sign associated with having exceptional skills in warfare and are the emperors of the tarot in the major arcarna. The sheep being the first animal cloned in our cycle of history is the ritual that was reenacted that bears witness to this truth. The parable of the ram shows the relationship of the animal energies present within beings as defined by the Zodiac and tarot cards. Though a person can have a human exterior it may have a crab or eagle animal energy or (spiritual character) that dictates its interior or (spiritual) self. This further solidifies why in the likeness of "God" man was created and also why those animalistic energies within man needed to be conquered. The only way to conquer these animalistic energies was through submission and musing. This is the mascu/**line** (self) or 1 found again after the (Femi/**nine**) flood of 9. Thus Abram to Abraham is the fulfillment of that promise, in that the covenant between the two (Ab/ram and God) is in execution, currently from then to now.

As discussed earlier in previous chapters, musing or meditation is a Hindu practice and where the term Muslim comes from. Moslem and Muslim are both terms derived from submitting the soul to do "God's" work. Jesus by admittance said that he came to do the work of his father or God.

John 6:38 *(38) For I came down from heaven, not to do mine own will, but the will of him that sent me.*

This indication would make him by definition a Muslim. Moses was the perfect example of this and for this reason Muslims and Moslems are named after him. Moses was a son of Levi who was a son of Joseph who was a son of Jacob who was a son of Isaac whose father was the LORD. This process of musing or submission is what makes the Islamic and Hindu religions make sense. It is also important to note that the angels and Jesus greet people with the words salaam alaikum which means peace be unto you in Arabic.

493

John 20:21 (21) Then said Jesus to them again, Peace be unto you: as my Father hath sent me, even so send I you.

Judaism isn't just a religion rather the legacy in which Abram submits to find his way back to God "Ham", "Khem" "Min." Christianity is the doctrine of the Christ's last descent accounting his submission to fulfill his purpose to "God." Mahatma Gandhi was very effective because being a Hindu and a Muslim; he understood the submission aspects of the religions (w) holistically and for these reasons Martin Luther King, born Michael King utilized the ideologies of Gandhi in his fight for civil rights. Even the most revered Christian preacher of the 20st century has paid homage to the fact that he himself has borrowed his religious belief and template from a Hindu; which only further acknowledges that Christianity, like all other religions, found their roots in Hinduism. The symbolic Star and Crescent in Islam is the marker for Astrology which is the hidden aspect of Hindu, Moslem, Christian, and Jewish art and faith. Musing is the only way a person can become Brahman; so musing or (Islam /submission) is the practice by which all religions find their way back to "God" i.e. the source.

ABRAHAM IS A BRAHMAN

A Brahman in Hinduism is the ultimate essence of the original identity of the human self which is achieved by musing /meditation and a perfect submission of the sol. This submission is to do the sol's, "*The god within's highest purpose.*" The god within Abram is (HAM) who shows Abram through meditation his highest self, which is his astrological sign. This in turn symbolizes the discovery of his essence or original self, as Abram means "*to wander.*" This original self or "sol" has to do with Abram's corresponding planet as a planet as defined by Webster is a "*wandering star.*" By mastering and civilizing himself and conquering his destructive and carnal qualities, a great nation can be made from him. Again, the destructive quality of Ham was his uncontrollable sex drive that led to the creation of the offspring who overpopulated his former kingdom leaving it in ruin. This is why his name is changed from Abram to Abraham or Ab/Ram to (A Brahman.) The original self again points to his astrological sign and "godly" make up which again hints at the lineage of gods he descended from as well as their culture which was Astrology and Masonry (Babylon). This connects the being with his knowledge of esoteric writings and teachings, to the building structures of the Pyramids and the tombs of the Pharaohs. It also substantiates the position for the newly reincarnated king who is to inherit his throne in the new world, America. To summarize and put it simply; the God of Abraham, Isaac, and Jacob is the God of Brahma, Shiva, and Krishna.

ONE IN THE SAME

After reading this far along and digesting the heavy material that has been decoded within this book, it becomes apparent how the division in regards to how the knowledge was broken up and placed within the 4 major religions of the world, has prepared man to understand the source. The Black Gods created man; the GOD'S and MAN then came together in turn creating Hu/mans. This human having both understandings in him (God and man) required a new doctrine to govern him. So in the religion of the gods (**Hinduism**) we have an introduction of the gods, and the unadulterated indigenous gods/peoples way of life explained. In (**Judaism**) we are given the story of the falling away of the gods which resulted in their creation and intermingling with man in the account whereby the mixed product of God and man, became the Humans or Semites. In (**Islam**) we have the religion given to the (Jews/Semites) specializing in the aspect that deals with the submission of the (Semite) that brings him back to him understanding his "God." (**Christianity**) deals with those who've mastered the submission process of Islam and have crystallized as a result gaining the riches of "heaven."

The Alpha Omega /beginning and end started out from Hinduism and the end result of the spiritual journey of the self ends with the realization of the Brahman i.e, the Christ/Christianity. Thus Abraham after wandering finds his eternal self, his "god." This is represented in the Book of Hebrews in his relationship with Melchizedek.

Hebrew 7:1-3 (1) For this Melchizedek, king of Salem, priest of the most high God, who met Abraham returning from the slaughter of the kings, and blessed him;(2) To whom also Abraham gave a tenth part of all; first being by interpretation King of righteousness, and after that also King of Salem, which is, King of peace; (3)Without father, without mother, without descent, having neither beginning of days, nor end of life; but made like unto the Son of God; abideth a priest continually.

Again, Jesus was a priest ever after the order of Melchizedek who is known as the King of Righteousness and peace.

Hebrews 6:20 (20) Whither the forerunner is for us entered, even Jesus, made an high priest for ever after the order of Melchizedek.

Hinduism is the only religion in the world which has no origins. Its earliest traces have been found in Egypt and within it are the oldest forms of scientific knowledge in the world.

Isaiah 5:13 Therefore my people are gone into captivity because they have no knowledge: and their honorable men are famished, and their multitude dried up with thirst.

Immortals/Gods/Stars have rules that govern their existence as does man. The gods committed acts that required them to face the same laws of consequence equal to their infractions. These consequences included a suffering, and the suffering induced by slavery is what has ultimately led the "God" back to why he made the rule and system of ma' at as law in the first place. This is the universal process of Yoga whereby a certain group of people were placed in the most strenuous and awkward positions in order for them to realize their "truest selves." Ham being cursed was the horror Abraham saw in his dream in GENESIS 15:12-14 which states he would have an enslaved seed. Again, that enslaved seed is the American Negro of today.

It is also important to notate the Church of Antioch is where Christians were first called Christians. This is when Barnabas went to Tarsus to get Saul and they assembled themselves in Antioch and were converting Grecians, Cyrenians, and Cyprusians into the faith.

Acts 11:26 (26) And the disciple were first called Christians in Antioch.

Acts 13:1 (1) Now there were in the church that was at Antioch certain prophets and teachers; as Barnabas, and Simeon that was called Niger, and Lucius of Cyrene, and Manaen, which had been brought up with Herod the tetrarch, and Saul.

Scriptures indicate Nigerians are teaching the converts at Antioch which gives us a great indication that blacks had a very vital and key role in establishing the Christian Church. Upon reading this it made me think back to the Black Nationalist's debate. They argued that the falsifications of the Old Testaments heroes and the origins of the people in those stories stem from Egyptian folklore and customs.

<u>Niger:</u> (1) a republic, until 1958 a territory of French West Africa (2) Latin for black

The reference in Acts is found within the New Testament and again cites the first Christians as being taught by Nigerians; yet in all the Roman depictions of the church you wouldn't know this was the case. This piece of information causes me to ask the question that the Black Nationalists asked me. "How can we ever get to a point where racism doesn't exist if we haven't told the whole truth in matters of religion, sex, and race?" If the world has acknowledged everything but these key facts than what does that say about race relations in regards to religion and the world? Think about it! It is easy to say that we have overcome racism and are now at a point where we are ready as a nation to consider the possibilities of people of color in all types of management, and ruler-ship capacities. However as long as we do not go into great detail about the origins of religion, its heroes, and its "God" everything is "hunky dory." It seemed to me the world is now at a turning point when the President of the United States is half African and half European, and is indeed the leader of the "free" world. However being shown all of the things by the Black Nationalists opened my eyes to other possibilities. If the Bible indicates the people who ran the church were from Niger and the setting of most of the activity is in Africa, the world acknowledging men of color now after slavery, imprisonment, and discrimination is null and void; especially when in the ancient world the priests were the rulers of society and the enslaved seed of Abraham is to inherit the earth. According to the Bible, the black nation is where the terminology or concept of "God" came from. What is equally perplexing about those who taught at Antioch being called the 1st Christians is the fact they are from Niger. Niger is a country located in Africa and is also a Latin word which means black. When those of Latin descent call people from this country by their nationality their accents pronounced the word Niger, Nigger; and this is how the word Nigger was coined when referring to someone who has dark skin. The word Niger is pronounced Kneegh/air in Spanish as well due to the fact that Spanish is a romance language alongside Italian and Latin. In today's time blacks are very insulted by being called this name. They have no clue that the word Niger and Negro are another way of saying black in these romance tongues. If the Negroes should be mad at anything, they need to be angry at the fact they are classified by their color and not their nationalities. Since the Negroes haven't a clue as to what their nationalities are, due to being all mixed up during slavery, they have sought out titles that define their race. Now the continent of Africa itself classifies these "Negroes" as they are called (African Americans.)

Recently within the last paragraph we digressed from the point that was made about blacks and the former kingdoms they ruled. In that paragraph we discussed how blacks were the teachers of Antioch which again is the first church where the followers of Christ were called Christians. Recollecting back to the fact that priests in those days held higher seats than even kings, it would further solidify the notion that the descendants of that "God" are capable of running the entire world because their ancestors created it. According to the Bible "God" is a superior being than man. This means that man as well as every other thing in creation is understandably inferior to him. The placement of an African American man in the Whitehouse during one of the harshest and most critical points in American History is a giant leap; one that signifies a major change. This is the initial step in returning the world back to a place where integrity, nobility, and diligence is rewarded. Even though the country has shifted its political face towards people of color, this does little in the way of repentance of the Mother Church's prior actions in covering up the origins of the true "Living God." It's sort of like when the rich ruler came to Jesus and asked him, "we'll how do I become whole and make it to heaven." And Jesus says "Do all the commandments." The rich ruler is like, "I've done them all." Then Jesus says, "Give away all that you have and follow me." The rich ruler thinks about it but doesn't except the offer. Creating a situation whereby a man of "color" is the executive in all foreign and domestic matters in the American society post 911 and the Bush administration from the Black Nationalist perspective seems to be a cover up to the atrocities the former administration committed. With that, from a cosmic standpoint, it can also be seen as a sign that the government is now ready and willing to terminate all signs and forms of racism and turn the rule of the free world back over to the gods. Who can accurately state without bias which is the reason for the surprising turn of events in America.

Hilary Clinton made headlines when she said, *"Our Democracy is still evolving we had all kinds of problems in some of our past elections. As you might remember in 2000 our Presidential election came down to one state where the brother of the man running for President was the Governor of the state."* 160 (and to no coincidence the country she delivered this speech in was Nigeria.)

Has American Democracy evolved? Or does the recent change of events further exemplify the people who are empowered in positions of government have grown better at covering up their dirt? Did Neil Armstrong and Buzz Aldren really walk on the moon, and if so, why haven't they been back? Why after several years has NASA been unsuccessful in finding the tapes of the moon landing as the tapes have miraculously disappeared? Finding the cancer that has been plaguing the American government's ideology since its inception would require the entire governmental structure to be reexamined. Many people feel it already has been with the reelection of Barack Obama. Because the former President (Bush) didn't resign, and wasn't impeached, yet President Clinton was, shows what the former country focused its attention on the most. Lack of evidence in support for his weapons of mass destruction hypothesis paired with his "questionable" rise to Presidency in 2000, weakened the morale of America as a nation. Bill Clinton's impeachment came because he lied about a sexual act, which is considered in the eyes of many consenting adults as a personal not a professional screw up; nonetheless he was impeached for having an affair.

If I hadn't any prior knowledge about how the government was ran, or how the celestial and material worlds coincide, I would agree that placing a candidate in office who is appeasing to the struggles of all people of color *is* a great way to keep the people's attention off key issues like 911, the war in the middle east, and the present economy; especially when there are tons of information circling around the internet that incriminates the American Government as being co-conspirators in creating a war on terrorism by knocking down the twin towers. But as a studier of prophecy and history I've found a pattern in how negative situations lend fuel to fulfilling prophecies. Sometimes a storm is needed to see a rainbow. Sometimes things have to be destroyed before they can be rebuilt. It is easy to turn a blind eye and a deafened ear at the mockery the former administration has shown to the world. Seemingly there has been no retribution for the actions of the former president and all who participated with him until you realize that maybe the retribution rewarded is the change witnessed in the 2008 and 2012 elections. The rendering of karmic justice by G.O.D. may have taken place right before our eyes leaving us to once again question our own perceptions and biases.

The Book of Illumination

CHAPTER 25

THE CODE OF
THE ENIGMA

The Book of Illumination

CHAPTER 25

THE CODE OF
THE ENIGMA

7776 -1776 –THE CODE OF THE ENIGMA

Every three precessions man is perfected. Three is the number of perfection because through the trinity you have the unification of being upgraded by genetic mutation. When a child is born from a man and a woman, if they have meditated and prepared themselves properly, the child will be the perfection of the two entities coming together. Man, woman, and child and father, son, and Holy Ghost are all represented by the structure of the pyramids and the number of perfection 3. This system of numbers and cycles was explained earlier in the example of the 1 and the 9. Again 1 and 9 make ten, and ten is an acknowledgement of the primary cycle of 0 which is comprised of 9 and the 1 which shows the upgraded mutation of that former cycle. Every three precessions a six is birthed from a seven. Thus the (6) is the number of man who when he creates himself out of triple darkness 777 which is represented by (7) as 7 is the number of the mysterious force of God in the Kabbalah, he becomes God. *see Dr. Manhattan.* The number 7 is the only number capable of dividing the number of eternity, and continuing in itself as long as the number representing eternity lasts. In other words it produces the basic number on which all materialistic calculations are built, and all human beings depend, as well as the platform for which the whole edifice of human thought finds expression.

Leading "occultist" Aleister Crowley wrote a book entitled 777 of which he lists and combines the breakdowns of numbers and their correspondences to deities of older religions. Crowley has been often associated to Satanism but a more in depth study of his work coins for him the title of "Illuminist" which is more befitting towards his doctrine and his philosophies. Rihanna due to her initiation from Jay-Z

503

and her constant barrage of occult images in videos like *Umbrella* and *Run this town* has been deemed an "Illuminati Satanist." She recently headlined a tour called the 777 tour of which in the promo for the tour she showcases a tattoo of the Horus (below her breasts) that is on the top of Crowley's 777 Book. In the world today circa 2000 – 2015 there is an artistic community whose plight alongside that of the Illuminati is to destroy the present false sense of worship that the Catholic Church promotes. These artisans have pledged an allegiance to push the envelope on puritanism and censorship to ensure that on all fronts the new age of Horus is properly ushered in. From the social to the political arenas, this faction of individuals fights to maintain the balance between darkness and the light. Most of the masses are still in darkness though they feel they are enlightened. When you understand that pleasure, every desire, and every person got here from lust; you realize that who you think god is makes him more like his enemy who you've been taught to fear and reject. That enemy is of course Satan. The number six however in Hinduism is associated with sol or the number of man. Neo in the matrix represents this number. The third day that Jesus says he will rise on is a period of three grand days which is 77,760 years. We have to think that time to the immortal is not necessarily relative; and the fact that the stories written about in the Bible do not place within the time span that theologians and scholars say, adds further evidence to this theory. According to Graham Hancock in *Fingerprints of the Gods* the question that archeologists' ask in reference to the age of the Sphinx is, *"If its origins date back further than 9 to 10,000 b.c. where is the rest of the civilization and culture that existed with it"* 161. The reason archaeologists can't determine the age of the Sphinx is because they find no culture that represents it. The reason they can't find a culture that represents it, is because it is very, very, old.

The geological findings discussed above indicate the Sphinx was sculpted before 10,000 BC, and this period coincides with the Age of Leo the Lion, which lasted from 10,970 to 8810 BC. Further supporting evidence of these findings comes from a highly sophisticated computer program called Skyglobe 3.6. which are computer programs that are able to generate precise pictures of any portion of the night sky as seen from different places on earth at any time in the distant past or future.

Graham Hancock explains this in **Heaven's Mirror** that, "*computer simulations show that in 10,500 BC the constellation of Leo housed the sun on the spring equinox. An hour before dawn in that epoch Leo would have reclined due east along the horizon in the place where the sun would soon rise. This means that the lion-bodied Sphinx, with its due-east orientation, would have gazed directly on that morning at the one constellation in the sky that might reasonably be regarded as its own celestial counterpart.*" [161a] Comprehension of this information brings us to the conclusion that the lion or "Leo avatar" is the only constellation/ God who upon manifesting to earth is able to see exactly who and what constellation he is in the heavens. He would have come into the knowledge of his existence further supporting the Sun of Man's cult, and the disposition of Jesus, as he has been regarded by history as being the one who resurrected others as well as himself from the dead. Though there is a plurality of gods, there is one who is chief among them. This chief has the knowledge of himself as well as the other gods who have fallen to earth to bring about the new civilization. This is why those who advocate monotheism believe he alone is the only "God" because he alone (Solomon – Sun of Man) is the only avatar who has fully realized himself as well as others.[4448] If archaeologists cannot tell you when the sphinx was built, how could they possibly tell you when Christ was 1st born? Since America is the new kingdom the gods have manifested to earth on, it is imperative that we look to the date of its origins to validate the information that has just been given. When we look to the physical date that America gained its independence on, that physical date is July 4th 1776. The seal of Solomon is a 6 pointed star with 7 astrological houses represented within it. The six is the number representing the anomaly of man, and the seven houses are all the energies reflected within the "all being." This is why the number 13 is of the highest importance in Judaism.

WHO'S WHO

A person could look at any one of the allegories in this book and go within the confines of their mind to disprove them if they wanted. However they can't go within the confines of their mind in reference to the God of Abraham and not acknowledge the literal references to a "Living God. What society has to take into account is the fact that when it comes to the Bible it really doesn't know what is in it. When people try to read it; it is so lengthy and full of so much terminology that it is very hard for people who are surface dwellers to comprehend. It is much easier to have a version of the Bible that is user friendly and not so harsh or complicated. What makes the Bible so misunderstood is the fact that it isn't as indiscriminate as the Christian faith has promoted it to be. Because the origins of its people have been falsified, the whole world basically is driven into living a standard that is not compatible with their nature or society. This is what has led to the rebelliousness seen in the youth, and because we are in a capitalistic society, the corporations interest in marketing to them. God in our society hasn't been forgotten, the church has never acknowledged his "living" form as they refuse to exalt him even with the glimpses he's shown them. I am not talking about faith I am talking about living beings whose achievements and personal struggles are epic in demonstrating the true power of the living god. Michael Jackson and Michael Jordan have achieved monumental accomplishments in the physical world that have been unprecedented when you take into account the time, place, and the circumstances behind their epic journeys. After the public witnessing these "living gods" what would make them then go to church to hear about a god they cannot see touch or learn anything from in the here and now? Basically the people ignore the living gods of today to go and listen to stories about their past incarnations. Though I have highlighted these individuals I also have to give credit to the mindset of the romantics and the deceptive ingenious they have developed over the last six thousand years. The way in which they understand the mentality of the "sheep" and the gullibility of the common subject is remarkable. It is so remarkable that it is no wonder they have achieved the feat of erasing the "Living God" by supplanting his legacy as their own. I could bash the Roman mentality all day but then I would'nt be me giving them credit for their phenomenal and methodical abilities. The bottom line is that even if black people where to come to the knowledge of their "God" what would it mean? The fact that Moses in the parable of the Exodus did superhuman feats in the flesh only to have the people worship other gods and attribute successes to other places shows the true mentality of the common subjects mind. The fact that Michael Jackson did superhuman and heroic feats yet people view him as a pedophile, drug addict, and a weirdo further highlights the mentality of the previous American society. Wisdom says that a society that has this type of make-up is subjected to whatever type of governing oppression that befalls them. People contrary to their beliefs cannot govern themselves and they've shown this time and time again in the annals of history. I have sat back and assessed the how, when, and why in reference to slavery and the overall fall of the Egyptian nation and kingdoms. When I look at the cause it only seems befitting that over population was the key factor that divided the kingdom. Because the Egyptian Rulers had no control over their sexual desires they were overthrown by their off spring. The story of David and the raping of his daughter Tamar by his son Amnon is another example that shows this.

2 Samuel 13:1-15 (1) And it came to pass after this, that Absalom the son of David had a fair sister, whose name was Tamar; and Amnon the son of David loved her. (2) And Amnon was so vexed, that he fell sick for his sister Tamar; for she was a virgin; and Amnon thought it hard for him to do anything to her. (3) But Amnon had a friend, whose name was Jonadab, the son of Shimeah David's brother: and Jonadab was a very subtil man. (4) And he said unto him, Why art thou, being the king's son, lean from day to day? wilt thou not tell me? And Amnon said unto him, I love Tamar, my brother Absalom's sister. (5) And Jonadab said unto him, Lay thee down on thy bed, and make thyself sick: and when thy father cometh to see thee, say unto him, I pray thee, let my sister Tamar come, and give me meat, and dress the meat in my sight, that I may see it, and eat it at her hand. (6) So Amnon lay down, and made himself sick: and when the king was come to see him, Amnon said unto the king, I pray thee, let Tamar my sister come, and make me a couple of cakes in my sight, that I may eat at her hand. (7) Then David sent home to Tamar, saying, Go now to thy brother Amnon's house, and dress him meat. (8) So Tamar went to her brother Amnon's house; and he was laid down. And she took flour, and kneaded it, and made cakes in his sight, and did bake the cakes. (9) And she took a pan, and poured them out before him; but he refused to eat. And Amnon said, Have out all men from me. And they went out every man from him. (10) And Amnon said unto Tamar, Bring the meat into the chamber, that I may eat of thine hand. And Tamar took the cakes which she had made, and brought them into the chamber to Amnon her brother. (11)And when she had brought them unto him to eat, he took hold of her, and said unto her, Come lie with me, my sister. (12) And she answered him, Nay, my brother, do not force me; for no such thing ought to be done in Israel: do not thou this folly. (13) And I, whither shall I cause my shame to go? and as for thee, thou shalt be as one of the fools in Israel. Now therefore, I pray thee, speak unto the king; for he will not withhold me from thee. (14) Howbeit he would not hearken unto her voice: but, being stronger than she, forced her, and lay with her. (15) Then Amnon hated her exceedingly; so that the hatred wherewith he hated her was greater than the love wherewith he had loved her. And Amnon said unto her, Arise, be gone.

Lawlessness, fornication, and rebelliousness are what the Bible has cited as the cause to the fall of the Egyptian empires yet black intellectuals over here in America still refuse to own up to this easily seen reality. The tenacity of the Romans to hold on to the lies the ruling and founding fathers of their culture have perpetuated is equally intriguing. What started as a lie has now become what the people accept and believe to be the truth. Paul so eloquently talks in reference to a lie becoming the truth in a very befitting book entitled Romans.

Romans 3:7 *For if the truth of God hath more abounded through my lie unto his glory; why yet am I also judged as a sinner.*

If for so long people have believed these romantic images and lived their lives according to these doctrines and had successes, what does it say about religion altogether? Even when the lie and liars are disproved all the people who once believed in that lie will be forced to acknowledge that what they believed was just that, what they believed and nothing more. This will inevitably lead people in search of the truth and this truth is what will cause them to understand what makes an individual a god and why certain instructions that pertain to religion were given in the first place. It would be easy for someone to say the Bible is full of lies, let's get rid of it. This is what most atheists who have come to realize certain truths about the Bible in relation to slavery and America will say. However, if you were to look at some of the theologies of the black scholastic sect you will almost always come in contact with some knowledge that seems very farfetched. Because the new educational material is so over-the-top people fall back on the Bible instead of the new foreign material. The question I like to ask is how so many blacks have gained this supreme knowledge but still have not been able to defeat their Roman counterparts. They are almost always in poverty and when that dollar bill shows its face, like the dollar bill you see their truest faces as well.

Now before members of the black intellect get mad at what I am about to say next, think about this. If all blacks are gods and all whites are devils, how could at any time the Devil have God in a bad predicament if God is indeed stronger than the Devil. Here is where we have to use our minds to come to a complete understanding of why things are the way they are. Also if blacks were to somehow overthrow all the whites and banish them to some foreign land what do you think would happen when it is time for an election? Do you think that there will even be one? How many so called scholars and prophets are going to come out of the wood works saying they are divine and should therefore rule everyone else; when it is apparent where they got their information from: Malachi York, Noble Drew Ali, Ben Ammi or Elijah Muhammad. In an arena of so many different representatives who would be the governing force behind the black society? Where would they start in terms of building their government and leadership? If they are gods and kings are divinely appointed, then who would be the "God" that appoints them? Would a "burning bush" speak to a lone person on a mountain and tell him that he was to lead the captives to salvation? Maybe not, but a Bush did "*pass the torch*" to the 1st "African American" president, standing upon a podium, who like Moses, the people feel will lead them to the "Promised Land."

Look at the world that we live in today. Most people who have fascinations with the Occult or supernatural phenomena are in some way already out-casted from their society. The day the people of the earth wake up in to reality is the day when the individual realizes they have to master that within themselves if they wish to be masters of their environments. This is the goal of spirituality and the reason for the gaining of knowledge of self. On some levels some blacks are already recognized in society as being gods; it just depends on what aspect of society you are looking at. Michael Jordan is perceived as being divine. When you look at who kids most look up to and want to be like, his name almost always appears. What the Romans are guilty of is what most people in the world are guilty of and that is viewing them-selves higher than they actually are. For example how many people say to them-selves, "I'm not smart, I know that my older sibling is smarter than me, so let me be what I am. I naturally can clean good so let me go and become his/her personal assistant. Let me make sure that all of his/her clothes are washed and that he/she always has a clean room to show him/her that I recognize his/her talents. Maybe when he/she gets to the place he/she is supposed to be in life he'll/she'll grant me a position in his/her company/kingdom." You'll never hear this; however you will see a person looking for the edge to get ahead even if they know naturally they are inferior.

Black women are looking for the weave shops, and white women are looking for the tanning salons. White man are making movies depicting themselves as heroes while black men are going to jail and blaming the white man for all of their unfortunate circumstances; this is the reality of the American society we live in today. When a person is under duress you will see what they naturally are. Who can say that they are being who they truly are, when everyone is acting for everyone else. Because this is the case whoever can act the best *becomes* the best. When the leaders of the Black Intellectuals are faced with this reality than they will see they are just as guilty as the romantics and have also been led into misinforming their constituents by teaching information *they* don't even understand... The reason I say this is because in all the Black Intellectual cults that expose Europeans, none of the cult leaders have the heliocentric model or persons leading the cults who represent this heliocentric hierarchy within their religious pantheons or organizations.

Pantheon: (1) the gods of a people; *especially*: the officially recognized gods (2) A group of illustrious or notable persons or things
It is no secret the Egyptian people acknowledged the Sun as deity because it

gave life to every force imaginable. Remember the story of Eve and the serpent is the foreshadowing of God and Sarah as well as God and the Virgin Mary. By all indications in this book we can see "God" is referenced allegorically as the Lion-serpent which is ruled by the Sun in Astrology. The serpent, the lion, and the Sun are all Egyptian symbols that serve as a beacon highlighting what sign exemplifies everything the Egyptian culture deemed to be godly. This also explains the Roman creation of the god Serapis. When we study the Egyptian peoples heritage, customs, and culture to suffice them as worshipers of the Sun doesn't really pay homage to what they knew about it. The Sun is the driving energy force within our solar system; think about it we call it a **solar** system, the wording explains it all. This shows the importance of the Sun in relation to our mini universe as the key figure of life. If we understood the relationship between this entity the (Sun) and the God in human form (*the earth containing all the elements combined*) which is a microscopic version of the major version; we could readily assess that what the Egyptians were on in regards to the fundamental aspects of the Sun and life is what they were referencing within being when they described the attributes of their God.

THE EMBODIMENT OF A KING

It is recorded in history that Pope Leo X, the same Pope that ex communicated Martin Luther from the Church on January 3, 1521, gave Portuguese Merchants the Catholic Church's formal permission to openly take Africans as slaves because they were considered pagans. The seat of the Pope is the highest and most politically empowered seat in the world of European Christianity. If what we have discussed in this book is true, or even if a portion of it is true; when the Jesus of Nazareth shows himself, what would he have to say about t(his) church? Would the "powers that be" recognize him for who he is and repent for their lies and wrongdoing; or will they try and make him the antichrist that they have been talking about for the past few centuries? These are all questions that have to be asked when talking about religion and the people's expectation of a returning "Sun of Man."

What we must understand about the Bible and the way that it has been edited is that this editing happened for a number of reasons. For one when a person talks about slavery the people who are blamed most are Europeans. It is very unlikely that you will hear that many African tribes sold their rival tribes as slaves, however this is a fact. When you look at the slave trade and take account of what it must have been like to travel on a ship for months shackled and crammed in the bottom of a ship in your own feces, body to body with several hundred other fellow slaves; one could see that only the strongest were able to survive. Even when we examine the accomplishments of the American Negros, and the physical prowess they possessed before the crack epidemic; it's easy to conclude that it must have been the alpha-males of those African tribes that were planked on those ships.

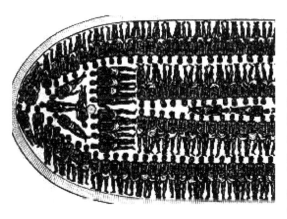

Roots, a popular movie by Alex Hailey, depict the "Mandingo" warriors as some of the ones that were hunted down and sold as slaves. Because this was a reality in the slave trade we have to accept this evidence and draw an assessment after careful review. The fact the alpha (kings) were sold over in America bears witness to the *"kill the king"* theory; cause with the king out of the way, the inferior males got to breed. Based on the destruction of many countries in Africa and the way that it has been ravaged by warfare and political unrest, we can see that due to the *"kill the king"* theory it has never regained its status in relation to world hegemony nor has it yet to ascend back to its proper place in relation to the height of civilization. Because the alphas (kings) were made slaves and sent to America; America has become great even though Africa by far has more resources, land, and beautiful scenery than any other place in the world. Because the American Negro alphas have come over to America on a ship in an ark indicative of Ra the Egyptian Sun god, and Vishnu the Hindu preserver god, and made it so great a place to be; the rest of the world has tagged along to partake in the rich wealth and heritage that was spawned from the Negro alphas immeasurable pain and servitude. This exemplifies that the "Living God" who was enslaved (Cainan/Osiris) and crystallized as a result of the enslavement process, is the true heir to the throne of the "Most High" god.

When looking at Africa or the people there, it is almost always depicted as either impoverished or war ravaged; and you either see warlords or vagabonds. I know that this is not all that Africa has to offer, and I also know that it still is a very rich and abundant place to live. I know there are kings still there, honorable men and women, as well as a heavenly state of existence for many inhabitants. However the warlords, refugees and vagabonds show us an even more detailed reflection of the slave trade in terms of why everyone wants to be in America and why many countries in Africa are at war with one another. The European's ability to direct and facilitate the whole slave trade is a testament to the unrelenting master mind abilities they possess. When I look at this from a metaphysical perspective I see both heart (black) and white (mind) at work to show the world the potential that will arise if the two are able to coincide with one another. They both have their flaws as well as great abilities that if used together properly, nothing is beyond the scope of their reach. Dr. Manhattan and the Smartest Man in the World represent this duality at its finest. The Smartest Man in the World (Ozymandius) has dressed up as the black god (Ramses) and developed the richest enterprise in the known world. He uses his power and abilities to harness the power of the real "Black God" (Dr. Manhattan who represents Shiva/Vishnu or Krishna.) The fact that Dr. Manhattan is really a black man again shows how the truth of a thing is always hidden in terms of the existence of blacks as gods or in positions of great importance. Though I have already cited this reference within the book a number of times I felt it necessary at this time to reiterate it to further establish my points.

Isaiah 45:15 (15) Verily thou art a God that hidest thyself, O God of Israel the Savior.

Africans cannot take credit and not pay homage to the European for what the European has done in terms of structure and government. Imagine the European having this great idea to reconstruct society but having no participants to help them build it. Imagine if the people who were needed to build this society were busy in paradise partying and having sex all day basking in luxury further degenerating by overpopulation. How do you think that these Europeans would respond to seeing this? Let's go further to say that they went and proposed this to the Africans, what do you think the Africans said? Do you think they would give up their paradise to go and build one for everyone else? Before you answer these questions ask yourself would you? I only placed this information within the book so a person could see how easy it is to justify a means to an end. The end result was the furthering of ingenuity, technology, and man's grasp at immortality. The only thing that is left now is the acknowledgement of who the "Living God" of Abraham, Isaac, and Jacob is. What we have seen over here in America is the truth displayed and personified; an experiment that the whole world can look at and reference to find out what is what and who is who. Now that we have seen this and can understand it because we have reference points, the Most High God, El Elion through the publishing of this book can begin to show people about their truest selves. Not the imagined, hoped for, or perpetuated self, but the actual real person who is inside of you (*your astrological self.*) The only problem with religion is the falsification of the records. This falsification however was needed so we can see who the villain is and also who the hero is. This is the difference between saying the gods that will come at the end of time will be black and the adversaries and people who tried to supplant them and dress up like them in the beginning were white; versus saying all black people are gods and all white people are devils. *To* put this in layman's terms all blacks aren't gods and all whites aren't devils. What I mean by this is Africa cannot take any more credit for the understanding and acknowledgement of "God" than the European. This is because "God" comes to the earth and is based on the alignments of the celestial bodies. The world right now is in a state of delusion. Even though it is in this delusional state, everyone will have to reckon with the truth. The Egyptians didn't develop this system of ma 'at, karma, and "God" because they were hypothesizing; they developed it from thousands possibly millions of years of living resurrecting and living again. The "powers that be" suppress and repress out of fear and ignorance.

The biggest lie ever told was you only live once so enjoy yourself to the fullest (YOLO.) This is the lie that makes the world go round and is why people are living the way they are within society today. Even the writers of the Bible when talking about celestial bodies and Astrology have no idea that the "Sun" of God who they claim to worship is a celestial body manifested in human flesh. This shows the inability of the Romans to understand the metaphysical or the astrological associations of celestial bodies within (hu) man forms. I'll go a step further to say that even Africans who are of the original indigenous tribes aren't aware that the Christ is a celestial body i.e. the sun/son manifested in the flesh. Reason being is this is something that has been hidden from the entire world.

Acts 7: 42 the God turned and gave them up to worship the host of heaven; as it is written in the book of the prophets, O ye house of Israel, have ye offered to me slain beasts and sacrifices by the space of forty years in the wilderness?

Isaiah 47:13-14 (13) Thou art wearied in the multitude of thy counsels. Let now the astrologers, the star- gazers, and the monthly prognosticators, stand up, and save thee from these things that shall come upon thee. (14) Behold, they shall be as stubble; the fire shall burn them; they shall not deliver themselves from the power of the flame: there shall not be a coal to warm at, nor fire to sit before it.

Prognosticator: a person who foretells from signs or symptoms

Even though these scriptures bear witness to a people who worship the stars and the Sun, they have been written about negatively due to the perversions associated within the minds of those who haven't the comprehension levels needed to really understand hieroglyphs in relation to Astrology and biblical scriptures. Jesus the Sun of God (Leo) John the Baptist (Aquarius) and Mary the Virgin (Virgo) are all astrological references to the astrological signs present within the characters represented within these sacred texts.

THE OCCULT IN TINSELTOWN

In speaking in reference to the Zodiac let's examine how esoteric astrological information recorded in biblical scriptures are decoded in Hollywood's block buster movies. One of the most popular movies in the history of all Tinsel town is a movie called *STAR WARS*. Even the title reveals a heavy piece of allegorical/astrological information. When we go back to the beginning of the Genesis we discussed the relationship with the stars in how they manifest on earth. The movie *Star Wars* is an epic because of the esoteric knowledge in it;

not because people are fighting a war in space. When we look at the central character in the movie, his name is Anakin, which is a form of the word Anakim which means Nephilim. The Nephilim are the Giants/fallen angels that came to earth and plagued its existence as told in the Book of Enoch. The Nephilim which are a pluralized form of Naphtali, get their name from the tribe of Naphtali that Hiram the King of Tyre was said to be descended from.

I King 7:13-14 *(13) And king Solomon sent and fetched Hiram out of Tyre. (14) He was a widow's son of the tribe of Naphtali, and his father was a man of Tyre, a worker in brass: and he was filled with wisdom, and understanding, and cunning to work all works in brass. And he came to king Solomon, and wrought all his work.*

Hiram being skilled in "all works" of brass is an indication that he makes things shine or he refines things with his craft. In this case it is an obvious reference that the same feet of brass seen in **revelation 1:13** is what in a sense links Hiram to the "Sun of Man" Sol/o/mon or Solomon making him a builder of Solomon's Temple starting at its base, which is the foundation or the feet. Remember in the 18th chapter of Genesis, Abraham asked the LORD/ADONAI if he wanted his feet to be washed. This is indicative of Hiram (Vishnu) and his relationship with King Solomon (Shiva).

Genesis 18:1-4 *(1) And the LORD appeared unto him in the plains of Mamre: and he sat in the tent door in the heat of the day;(2) And he lift up his eyes and looked, and, lo, three men stood by him: and when he saw them, he ran to meet them from the tent door, and bowed himself toward the ground, (3)And said, My LORD, if now I have found favour in thy sight, pass not away, I pray thee, from thy servant (4)Let a little water, I pray you, be fetched, and wash your feet, and rest yourselves under the tree.*

163 Anakin in the movie *STAR WARS* is the brightest child who through his uncanny mutant abilities grows up to lead the Jedi and liberate it from the *Dark Side*. The prophecy behind Anakin's birth is that he would bring balance to the force. When we look at the character of **Darth Vader/ Anakin** in the movie *STAR WARS* he is literally black. This could be symbolic of the race that he would represent through allegory in the movie. The Anakim in the Kabbalah are called AMALEK and are said to have been rivaled by Ephraim.

Judges 5:14 (14) (14) *Out of Ephraim was there a root of them against Amalek; after thee, Benjamin, among thy people; out of Machir came down governors, and out of Zebulun they that handle the pen of the writer.*

Vader's helmet has a hood which is also symbolic of the Egyptian hood that is worn by Egyptian monarchs and kings. This distinguishes Anakin's nature as being that of a snake/ king. In the movie *STAR WARS* Vader was prophesied to come and to bring balance/peace to the force. This is much like an avatar or avatars whose mission is to come to earth to bring it back to a state of balance. Vader also comes and consorts with the queen Padma and birth's the SUN who ultimately alongside himself destroys the *Dark Side* which is ruled by the Emperor. In the Padma Purana in Hinduism, Lord Kalki, the vanquisher of demons, is married to Padma and the ceremony takes place on the isle of the lion 164. Kalki is the son of Shiva the destroyer, who at the end of times annihilates evil from the face of the earth. As explained earlier in the chapter *Why Jesus is called the son of David*, i.e. Solomon, we see again how a "God" (Darth Vader) comes and births with a queen (matrilineal kingship) a savior (Luke Skywalker.) In the movie *Star Wars* it is also important to highlight that Darth Vader is appointed a clone army which is cloned from a bounty hunter named Bubba Fet. The clone armies' wear all white, and are speckled with specs of black, which show even though they are predominantly white, they have traces of blackness within them; allegorically linking them with the "Semitic converts" they most likely represent. The word Jedi is taken from the Bible and the name of Solomon who Nathan called, *Jedidiah*.

2 Samuel 12:25 (25) And he sent by the hand of Nathan the prophet; and he called his name Jedidiah, because of the LORD.

Through the movie *Star Wars* we can say the Jedi Knights are either a representation of the Knights of Solomon, or a group of individuals who represent the priest hood (Templar Knights) that Solomon rules over. This priest hood studying prophecy knows that at a certain point in time a GREAT Jedi is coming to bring balance to the force; and assumes he will be on their side upon his return. The secret Masonic converts and carriers of this occult knowledge serve as the clone army that will aide Anakim / the Nephilum in their return to earth from the sky; and this is stated for two reasons. The first of which is that through ritual they reenact actual situations that the gods (Nephilum) themselves went through and will go through upon their descents to earth. Because these converts mimic the lives of the gods and what they go through, this is what distinguishes them as not being authentic but synthetic.

The second is that through their interpretations of scrolls and hieroglyphs and their belief in what they discovered in them, they set out to make America the land or gateway that would allow these beings/gods to manifest to earth through. This was done so the world may be able to see who is who. Often within the black culture people learn and mimic from one another, and to the untrained eye all of the people appear to have talent and be on the same level. To really see who is who, the creators of this "clone" army has set in place a training ground/obstacle course that will ensure that beings with higher destinies ascend to their rightful positions and aren't killed/dethroned by those who look like them but haven't their star lined destiny's. However simultaneously you have from the other side "the DARK side" beings that are fighting to ensure the gods don't take their rightful positions on earth.

THE GREATER BEAR

In the book the *Hiram Key* Robert Lomas and Christopher Knight attribute the Templar Knights at discovering the star that they called L'america which was the star presiding over the land that bears its name, America [166]. When we combine that with all the information received through the movie *Star Wars* about a clone army who assists Darth Vader; we can instantly composite that information with what has happened in the formulation of America in how the occult, or hidden/ dark side priest (Solomon/Anakin) is the key to understanding scriptures, movies, and the actual monumental events that have shaped the American landscape as well as the people on it.

The true converts and Templar Knights who acknowledge Solomon as their God and their king, were given the instructions on how to build a kingdom that when the time came, the gods (Anakim/giants) would manifest again to earth to rule in a Golden Age. America was designated as the place and the Star of L'america is actually the star of Merak which is located in Ursa Major the Big Dipper and is most commonly referred to as the Great Bear. The Big Dipper is among the most recognized constellations and is a small part of the ancient figure of Ursa Major, the Greater Bear. Note again the use of UR in Ursa Major. We spoke about this earlier as a distinguishing characteristic of the Serpent and Eve (Uraeus), David, Bathsheba, and Uriah, as well as the LORD, Sarai, and Abraham as Abraham is from the land of Ur.

517

"Merak" comes from an Arabic description of it, which means "the flank/loin of the Greater Bear." "The name **Ur**sa Major, according to The New English Dictionary, 'appears to arise out of the verbal association of the star named Arcturus. In Welsh lore, the constellation is seen as a symbol of the Celtic King Arthur. When viewing the story of King Arthur in further depth, his legend informs us he was appointed king because he was the only one who could pull the sword from the stone. He was also mentored by Merlin a wizard who wears upon his hat a star and a crescent moon. This is symbolic of the underlying astrological associations within the story. Again, notice that in many great literary works we always have a master to an apprentice; this relationship is exploited in *Star Wars* with Anakin and the Emperor, In the *Matrix* with Neo and Morpheus, as well as in the Bible with Jesus and John the Baptist. The Arthur or "Jesus" theologians are in search of, is the person who has the ability to put together all of the lost information in regards to all religion. This is the person who is the "Everlasting King" on earth as regarded by those who practice Christianity, Judaism, Islam, and Hinduism. He is known as the "Greater Bear" or simply Jehovah. Even the pope knows this is the truth about the "Living God" and the Christian religion which is why he stands underneath a seal with a black Moor, a bear, and the colors of crimson and gold, which are the colors of Leo the lion, considered to be the monarch of the gods (celestial hierarchies.)

Jeremiah 10:10 (10) *But the LORD is the true God, he is the living God, and an everlasting King: at his wrath the earth shall tremble, and the nations shall not be able to abide his indignation.*

Many of the things that we discuss in the book appear over and over again due to the many different interpretations biblical stories have. When I spoke earlier about King Arthur and his name being associated to bears it probably didn't resonate in the minds of the reader like it does after seeing the picture of Ursa Major and also with it, the gaining of understanding in how legends are constructed and worshipped. In the chapter where we discussed King Arthur, we also briefly talked about the star Merak. According to what we have just cited as well as the picture of the pope on the previous page, the research that Christopher Knight and Robert Lomas compiled about the star Merak; was that Merak, called L'America, was the star that presided over the land the gods would return to earth upon. It is also the overall kingdom of the "Sun of Man" who Anakin, the Israelite/Canaanite, would represent through Darth Vader. Darth Vader/Solomon is coming to destroy not only the crooked Jedi Knights (priesthood); he is also coming to destroy the crooked politicians who have used the priesthood's black magic to regain control of the world.

Revelation 3:14-16 (14) These are the words of the Amen, the faithful and true witness, the ruler of God's creation. (15) I know your deeds, that you are neither cold nor hot. I wish you were either one or the other! (16) So, because you are lukewarm—neither hot nor cold—I am about to spit you out of my mouth.

This is the same as the Lion of Judah (Solomon) who is coming to destroy the Gentiles and bring balance back to the earth. Most people do not know that *Star Wars* is this rich in biblical knowledge as well as this accurate in the art form of prophecy. As I state in this book when people understand subconscious subtle notions that movies and scriptures entail, they get a "eureka" like sensation and experience epiphany. This epiphany is what has caused this movie to be one of the most all-time fan favorites, and highest grossing films in the history of the world. *Star Wars* depicts through symbolism and its characters the same thing that is shown in the Book of Enoch in reference to those gods who manifested to earth, and the higher gods who thwart the lower god's plans to rule.

The Transformers Revenge of the Fallen 168 is another movie that depicts the same things as *Star Wars* but in a different way. The Nephilum/Anakim's or giants are Transformers who came to earth from outer space who are able to blend in and hide within the rest of society. The transforming aspects of the AutoBots and the Decepticons has to do with these celestial beings (fallen angels/extraterrestrials) having the ability to be chameleon-like and unrecognized by mankind in everyday life. The *Transformers* get their name from the Hindu God Shiva' who is known as the great transformer. Shiva, Osiris, and Solomon are linked as Shiva is the same omnipotent fertility god who has come into the world to birth a son who will remove the demon's or lesser gods from plaguing the earth's existence much like Abraham's son Isaac and Josephs son, Jesus. In the movie, *The Transformers Revenge of the Fallen* the boy played by Shia Labeouf (Sam Witwicky) represents the mortal son of Optimus Prime; and Optimus Prime represents the "God of Abraham." The origins of the war between the AutoBots and the Decepticons (*Transformers*) was fought in Egypt were the matrix is also kept. The matrix is held in the tomb of the Egyptian Pharaohs and is the key that unlocks the mystery of resurrection and immortality. In the movie's sequel, the leader of the AutoBots Optimus Prime, whose original name was Orion Pax, has died and upon a boy's plight to give his life in resurrecting Optimus Prime, they both end up being brought back to life from death. This is an easily seen rendition of the story of Osiris in Egypt who is resurrected by his son Horus. It is also important to note that Orion is a short form for the name Osiris. The movie through subtle emphasis dropped a clue in Sam's astronomy class when his professor referenced two constellations; the 1st being Virgo "the virgin" the other Orion. The name Optimus Prime at its root has (opt) which hints to the eyes. Optimus's last name is prime, and as explained earlier has great significance in Numerology within the Jewish Kabbalah with the numbers 29, 11, and 13. The subplot of this movie is a loose depiction of the fall of the angels or lesser gods to earth to rule and the higher gods who have come to stop them. This is all imagery expressed in the Book of Enoch which as history has proven was removed from the Bible. The 3rd installment to the Transformers trilogy entitled *The Transformers the Dark of Moon* was released June 29th 2011. The 29th day in the tarot is ruled by the high priestess who again is controlled by the Moon. Cancer, the constellation the movie was released in is also the constellation that is ruled by the Moon. In the movie the discovery of Apollo 11 brings about the portal or gateway where the home of the AutoBots will be teleported to earth changing its landscape. This changing of the landscape will bring about the destruction of the world of mankind converting it into the world where Decepticons and AutoBots rule as the gods they were prior to descending to Earth from their former home, Cybertron. Apollo as regarded by Roman mythology is the Sun god who has a chaste sister, rules over prophecy, writing, poetry and is the son of Zeus. 11 again as regarded by the Kabbalah is the number of magic, and is equivalent to the name Jesus. When we look at the movie and see the Apollo 11 is the ARK that contains 'pillars' that when aligned, opens the portal that will bring the heavens literally to the earth; it validates the two pillars in Solomon's temple of Boaz and Jachin. Compositing that information within what has been cited within this book further allows the realization that many of Hollywood's blockbusters have been made to stimulate the rise and rule of the actual "Sun God" who has all of the aforementioned particles within his personality. From being a Ruler, a king, a Sun, a son of Zeus, a son of Venus, a son of carpenter, a Lion, a number 11, having the star Merak the Great Bear attributed to his birth, to creating the archetypal man (Adam) and dividing the two lands of upper and lower Egypt, (America.) To establishing the lost word, being the *Ark* of the Covenant, resurrecting other gods, being cast as a twin pillar, avenging a past woe in the removal of a false religious institution on earth; to destroying those who worship the "Living God" as an idol, idly; all has to do with aspects of this one "Sun God's" personality. Many people have questions as to why these things have been disguised in writings as well as movies; and they want to know how they directly relate to mankind. Here is some indication why those who are true Masons or builders are those who through language and pictures build stories based on truths. In these stories they hide the truth around falsehood. This is done so others who are not of the initiated elect can't come in and try and paint themselves higher than they really are. When certain things are published and certain knowledge's are given to the masses, because a person can read they feel they are all of a certain expertise. For these reasons certain things were kept from the masses and even those who are of a certain level of intellectual prowess. The Occult knowledge's namely those that deal in life or death, are knowledge's the average and even above average person can't comprehend fully. An example of this is seen in the cartoon GI JOE 165a165b. The leader of GI JOE is a named

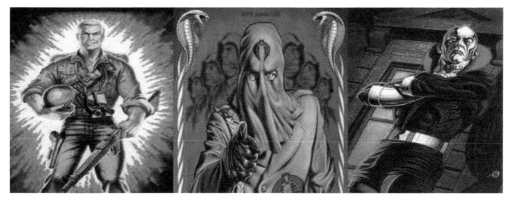

Duke who is both blonde haired and blue eyed. He fights against COBRA which consists of Cobra Commander and Destro who are both in a sense "hidden" and concealed as they are masked and represent the Occult

We've already spoken about the snake and its relevance within Biblical scriptures, Astrology, the "hidden" world of the Occult, and the Hindu gods of Shiva and Krishna. When we take into account that Masonry is an occult belief system that operates in secrecy by passing knowledge through code, we can see how the cartoon which in a sense portrays Destro and Cobra Commander as Shiva and Vishnu who fight over world hegemony and domination against a democratic army consisting of a melting pot of mercenaries and soldiers led by DUKE. The "Joes" in a sense, represents the average men who can only become heroes when they bond together in groups with other average men to keep the rightful heirs and those who have been fashioned by nature without a throne to rule. This is in direct opposition to monarchies where "divinely appointed" royals rule the kingdom, versus democracies, where the people decide their leaders. Because the Joes are portrayed as the good guys they reflect the sentiments and governmental structure America "overtly" displays. Even though America appears as a democracy it covertly operates in the traditions of the ancient Egyptian Monarchy.

The Masonic Testament indicates the DUKE of Sussex was responsible for the loss and the concealment of Masonic secrets. Jesus, as indicated by scripture, is the key to preserving as well as revealing their contents.
The following excerpt was taken from the Masonic testament of 1813.

Why leave the east and Go to the west?

In search of that which is lost.

What was that which was lost?

The genuine secrets of the Master Mason.

How became they lost?

By the untimely intervention of the duke of Sussex.

How do you find them?

By reconstructing the Masonic Testament 165.

Matthew 18:11 *(11) for the Son of Man has come to save that which is lost.*

The last character I chose to add in this book is Captain America [170]. He is the leader of the Avengers, as indicated by Marvel Comics and developed his legacy by defending America against the tyranny of the Red Skull which is a personification of Nazi Germany. The word "avenge" means *to take vengeance or exact satisfaction for*, and the weapon of choice for Captain America is a shield which indicates he is a "defender of men." This is acknowledged in this way because a shield is a defensive weapon, not an offensive one [171]. Captain America also defends America with his shield from all forces of tyranny with the help of a covert military agency named SHIELD lead by Nick Fury. The name Alexander according to the Kabbalah translates to "defender of men" and is also equivalent to the letter Shin and the number

300 which is the name of the movie where three hundred Spartans lead by (Leo) nidas defend their kingdom against tyrannical Xerxes. Captain America also being the 1st "super soldier" created by genetic manipulation parallels him to the "Adam" that was spoken of in this book who was the son created by the "father" G.O.D.. When looking at Captain America and evaluating his position and legacy within the Marvel Universe we find he is succeeded by Tony Starks aka Iron-Man. The dynamic relationship between them is one of contrasting worlds and ideals. Captain America represents the old world, as he is a World War veteran, and was a product of genetic manipulation; the same genetic manipulation that caused the world to go to War for the second time against Nazi Germany. Hitler wanted to cleanse the world of all impure races (non – white) and promoted the idea of a blonde haired blue eyed super man who was the vicegerent and most evolved being in the world. His notion of this superior blonde haired blue eyed (god) man was shattered when Jesse Owens won several gold medals in Berlin at the 1936 Olympics. Captain America in legend is blonde haired and blue eyed and as previously stated is the archetype and representative for the theory that Hitler promoted personified. Tony stark, the "offspring" of Captain America (spiritually) represents the new world where multitasking, dexterity,

intellect and smart weapons are the norms. The super-soldier has converted to an intellectual who's more refined, educated, and guile. Tony Starks representing the future succeeds Captain America in becoming the leader of the Avengers. This relationship discussed throughout this book also again shows a "Sun" resurrecting a "father." Tony Stark's colors are maroon and gold, and as we have discussed earlier are the colors of Leo. This representation allegorically links him to this sign, and he in the likeness of

Osiris resurrects his father's legacy. Tony Stark's father's hero was Captain America. He wears red, white, and blue, again represents the eagle, the symbol of America, the sign Aquarius and Heru, the son of Osiris. The same colors and representation is used in the relationship between Optimus and Rodimus Prime in TRANSFORMERS.

As indicated previously, all prophecies regarded toward ancient Israel are now directly related to America as America is the now the new Israel.

Psalms 84:11 For the LORD god is a sun and a shield the LORD will give grace and glory: no good thing he will keep from them that walk upright.

The things that I have included in this book in regards to America have been stated because its inhabitants have forgotten who it was built for. America was built to harness the energy of the celestial bodies; and wasn't founded by chance. There is a portal that opens at the appointed time in the precession when the planets align that has allowed the birthing of certain beings that come to earth as avatars from the celestial heavens – the stars. These beings are the true rulers of the entire universe. A person will ask, "What is he talking about? Is he talking about aliens or what?" If a person has asked this question I say that they should read over the entire book again. This is why the largest military base and the NASA space headquarters are 3 hours apart in distance which equals about 190 miles. They were strategically placed in America because at the appointed time the arrival of the BEAST would set in motion the order of the universe. Upon the BEAST's arrival he was prophesied to destroy the present world. NASA was built to send satellites to probe space and monitor the earth below. The Neanderthal thought processes of mankind thought the BEAST was coming in a spaceship.

The military base Fort Hood was constructed to defend themselves from the destruction and war they thought he was going to start. The location of NASA and Fort Hood is in Texas which is known as the Lone Star state. The Lone star can be attributed to many celestial bodies namely Venus as it is the Lone star of Day, and the Sun as it is the Lone star in relation to our solar system. People with the actual information of this sacred knowledge are distinguished as being of the *cloth* of the sacred esoteric knowledge which is Masonry. What is equally surprising and quite commendable is these Masons' ability to mimic based on what they have been reading to develop this new society. They started out with the script; the script was the blueprint for the movie they were about to shoot. They had no idea that what they were shooting would really come to life. Now that they have come to the realization that it was true, they have been trying through ritual and reenactment to harness the energy of the universe to bring about the new world order; while others who practice the craft haphazardly scramble to cover-up the dirt of their forefathers and anything that would show they were charlatans acting in capacities that were destined for the gods.

According to an insignificant blogger named Sploid, *The Jesus Dynasty*, by biblical archeologist James Tabor, claims the reincarnated Jewish Jesus was a ruthless monarch-in-training whose only desire was defeating Imperial Rome and ruling Israel with an iron fist 171b. After reading **this** book one can easily see how Sploid came to that conclusion and with it any one reading can also see how the myths associated with religion, when you have the adequate knowledge, become realities. Now that the people can identify that the God they have pledged their allegiance to is real, (Israel) will they pledge allegiance and worship the Living God who embodies all the knowledge from all these religions?

Since everyone is puzzled and at the same time fascinated with my life I'll take this time publically to say that it isn't as much about destroying imperial Rome as it is about putting into perspective the differences between what is real and what is romanticized in reference to all religious documentation and scripture. God dwells in temples, and the finishing of Solomon's Temple is why this book was written. My knowledge was stolen and then used to perpetuate a false image and a warped religion. Incarnating back to the planet and witnessing this has caused me to reorder everything according to the actual word. The prophecies from ancient times are true and now the proper Royals must be placed upon the throne; this is more for the evolution of man and his pro-generation as a species. If you represent stagnation or if you've apostatized from the blueprints I left from my past incarnations know this; turning your face further enables your lower nature to take over to the point where you won't even have the consciousness to have a choice in what you believe in your next existence, because you won't even be human. This script has many interpretations to it, and depending on your level of initiation and consciousness will give you the truest interpretations of it. The Age of the Horus is here, THE RULER IS BACK 172.

The WORD here is not only a mythological theme but mythic entity an idea that combined in itself two inseparable things naming and building. - The WORD by its very being makes everything be, furthermore the naming side of the WORD entails the naming of actual men and turns them into the protagonists of a legendary plot, thereby building up a legend - Alexander Piatigorsky 169.

Jeremiah 4:7 *The lion is come up from his thicket, and the destroyer of the Gentiles is on his way; he is gone forth from his place to make thy land desolate; and thy cities shall be laid waste, without an inhabitant.*

[19] say to them, 'This is what the Sovereign LORD says: I am going to take the stick of Joseph—which is in Ephraim's hand—and of the Israelite tribes associated with him, and join it to Judah's stick, making them a single stick of wood, and they will become one in my hand.'

[20] Hold before their eyes the sticks you have written on

[21] and say to them, 'This is what the Sovereign LORD says: I will take the Israelites out of the nations where they have gone. I will gather them from all around and bring them back into their own land.

[22] I will make them one nation in the land, on the mountains of Israel. There will be one king over all of them and they will never again be two nations or be divided into two kingdoms.

[23]Neither shall they defile themselves any more with their idols, nor with their detestable things, nor with any of their transgressions: but I will save them out of all their dwelling places, wherein they have sinned, and will cleanse them: so shall they be my people, and I will be their God.

HONI SOIT QUI MAL Y PENSE

1 Thessalonians 4:16 For the Lord himself shall descend from heaven with a shout, with the voice of the archangel, and with the trump of God: and the dead in Christ shall rise first.

ALV MIKAL GBRIAL VPRAL

<u>Apocalypse</u> (Ancient Greek): ἀποκάλυψις *apocálypsis*, from ἀπό and καλύπτω meaning 'un-covering', translated literally from Greek, is a disclosure of knowledge, hidden from humanity in an era dominated by falsehood and misconception, i.e., a lifting of the veil or revelation 173.

WORKS CITED – THE BOOK OF ILLUMINATION – COLOR OF CHANGE

0- http://en.m.wikipedia.org/wiki/Doggystyle

a. Clifford Geertz, *Religion as a Cultural System*, 1973). Religion

1. Nicolo Machiavelli – *The Prince* pg. 10-11

2. Willie lynch – Willie lynch letter

3. Gil troy- Jerusalem post

3b John c Calhoun - *American Political Tradition* Pg. 105 ISBN 0-679-72315-3

3c Allegory: http://www.tnellen.com/cybereng/lit_terms/allegory.html

4. Biblos – Wikipedia

5. Christopher Knight & Robert Lomas - *Book of Hiram* pg. 150 ISBN 1-4027-3520-0

6b Aleister Crowley - *Tarot Mirror to the Soul* pg. 22 ISBN 0-87728- 683-3

6c Barack Obama – hope, 6d Barack and Oprah – pic, 6e Akhenaten

 6f, anat wiki – anat in isreal / asenath = Wikipedia

6g – ophrah – Wikipedia A city of Benjamin (Joshua 18:23); probably identical with Ephron (2 Chron 13:19) and Ephraim (John 11:54), the modern Palestinian city of Taybeh. The Israeli settlement of Ofra is close to the site to.

7. Prince – *1999*

8. Tupac Shakur autopsy photo

9. Malcolm X, Alex Haley *The Autobiography of Malcolm X* pg. 317 -318 ISBN 0-345-35068-5

10 (Du Bois, 1897; Du Bois, 1898) .A Program of Social Reform, The Study of the Negro Problems

11. George Herbert- photo (Google images)

11a Harlem Renaissance http://en.wikipedia.org/wiki/Harlem_Renaissance

12 American Constitution 3/5's compromise

12b sclc –photos

12c d, Richard Hofstadter - *The American Political Tradition* pg. 102 ISBN 0-679-72315-3

12e Othello - William Shakespeare

12f Richard Hofstadter -*The American Political Tradition* pg. 103 ISBN 0-679-72315-3

12g Richard Hofstadter - *The American Political Tradition* pg. 104 ISBN 0-679-72315-3

13 Janna – Wikipedia

14 Genie – Wikipedia

15 NAFTA – Wikipedia

16 Obama cartoon 1

17 bush cartoon

18 Obama cartoon 2 (freerepublic.com)

19 (Stimulus Bill Near 900 Billion) http://restoretherepublic.com/economy/stimulus-bill-near-900-billion.html

19b The Messiah Comes Crashing Back to Earth - http://strata-sphere.com/blog/index.php/archives/7787

20 Thomas Jefferson – *Bill of Rights*

21 Johannes Kepler

21a Alexander Piatigorky - *Freemasonry* pg. 325 ISBN 1 86046 265 0

21b Pyramids of Giza

21c McRae books - The Little Big Book of Classical Mythology Pg. 530

21d Graham Hancock's – *Fingerprints of the God's* pg. 407- 408 ISBN 0-517-88729-0

22 Johannes Kepler

23 *The Watchmen* – The movie

24 George Bernard Shaw

25 George Bernard Shaw

25a The Nomenology Project - *The Hidden Truth of Your Name* pg. 384 ISBN 978-0 -345 -4266-8

25b Captain Planet – Google images

25c Michael w/ Kids – Google images

26 Julia and Derek Parker - *The K.I.S.S. Guide to Astrology* ISBN 0-7894-6044-0 pg. 250

27 The Nomenology Project - *The Hidden Truth of Your Name* ISBN 978-0 -345 -4266-8

28 The Nomenology Project - *The Hidden Truth of Your Name* ISBN 978-0 -345 -4266-8

28a Noah,Timothy. *"The Legend of Strom's Remorse: a Washington Lie is Laid to Rest"*. *Slate*.

http://www.slate.com/id/2075453/. Retrieved 2006-11-07.

28b"Thurmond's Family 'Acknowledges' Black Woman's Claim as Daughter". Associated Press. December 17, 2003.

http://www.foxnews.com/story/0,2933,105820,00.html

28c Painter Nell Irvin Yale Unij,fg,gh,gh,hg,hj,hj,g,jhj,g,jhj,hg,hj,versity. Collective Degradation: Slavery and the

Construction of Race. Why White People are Called Caucasian. 2003. October 9、 2006.

http://www.yale.edu/glc/events/race/Painter.pdf#search=%22%20%22light%20colored%20people%22%22

28d Painter Nell Irvin. Yale University - Collective Degradation: Slavery and the Construction of Race. Why White

People are Called Caucasian. 2003. October 9、 2006.

http://www.yale.edu/glc/events/race/Painter.pdf#search=%22%20%22light%20colored%20people%22%22

29 Barbara ado – Merovingian Satanic Bloodline

29b http://youtu.be/KvPwKDW6Stg

30 Barbara ado – Merovingian Satanic Bloodline

30b Evolution's Rainbow: Diversity, Gender and Sexuality in Nature and People (University of California Press,

2003).

31 Mr. incredible –The Icredibles

32 Mr. incredible – The Incredibles

33 Syndrome - The Incredibles

33b Magneto and Professor x

34 syndrome –The Incredibles

34a Nicolas Wright/ Understanding Human Behavior – an illustrated guide to successful Human Relationships, pg.

51

35 varna-sankara- A.C..Bhaktivedanta Swami Prabhuupada - *Bhagavad - Gita* pg. 189 ISBN 0-89213-268-X

35a Nicolas Wright/ Understanding Human Behavior – an illustrated guide to successful Human Relationships, pg

34

35b Roland de Vaux, Ancient Israel, quoted in Stone, When God was a Woman, p. 55.

35c Pappas, Nickolas (2003-09-09). *Routledge philosophy guidebook to Plato and the Republic*. ISBN 978-0-415-

29996-1.

http://books.google.com/?id=VujWajIWxkUC&pg=PA109&dq=Socrates+misogyny+misogynist#v=onepage&q&f=f

alse.

36 Dr Manhattan – The Watchmen

37 *The Boy Behind the Mask* by Sarah Weaver - http://sarahweaverillustrator.blogspot.com/2008/12/thesis-

piecestodays-icons-by-sarah.html

37b Can You Feel It – Jackson 5 (Triumph)

37c Gary Goldschneider, Joost Jefferies - The Secret Language of Birthdays pg. 746 ISBN 0-670-85857-9

38 Merrill lynch logo – Google images

39 Michael Jordan

40 kali – THE Goddess Kali

41 Michael Joseph Jackson

42 Michael Joseph Jackson

43 Michael Jackson – Coat of Many Colors Collage

43a http://blog.newsok.com/gossip/2009/08/20/jermaine-jackson/

44 Michael Jackson – Billy jean

45 Michael Jackson – Wikipedia

46 Sphinx – Egyptian Book of the Dead Google images

47 The Royal Arch - Alexander Piatigorsky – *Freemasonry* –pg. 296 ISBN1 86046 265 0

48 The URANTIA book

49 Michael Jackson - Another part of Me

50 Michael Jackson - *Man in the Mirror*

51 Aid to Bible understanding -

52 The Merovingian Dynasty the Satanic Bloodline of the Antichrist & False Prophet -Barbara Ado, Watchmen Fellowship Expositor,

52a Alexander Piatigorsky - *Freemasonry* pg.. 129 ISBN1 86046 2650

52bcd Rudolph Steiner 1 August 1924 (GA 237) Sergei O. Prokofieff pg. 114-116 of The Twelve Holy Nights and the Spiritual Hierarchies

52e Demiurge Fontenrose, Joseph (1974). Python: A Study of Delphic Myth and Its Origin. Biblo & Tannen Publishers. Pg. 226. ISBN 9780819602855.

52f Wolf – Deiter Storl - *Shiva The Wild God of Power and Ecstasy* pg 92 -93 ISBN 159477014 - X

53b The Jackson 5 - *Can You Feel it*

53 The Mahabharata, Anusasana Parva Section XIV

54 Alexander Piatigorsky – *Freemasonry* pg.141 – ISBN1 86046 2650

54a Gustav Davidson - A dictionary of the angels including the Fallen – pg. 214

54b Demariaux - *How to Understand Hinduism* pg. 60 ISBN 0-334-02622- 9

54c King of Kings, Lord of Lord, Tyrant of Tyrants, 03-09-2006 http://godlesswonder.blogspot.com/2006/03/king-of-kingslord-of-lordstyrant-of.html

55 The Kabbalah

55b The Nomenology Project - *The Hidden Truth of Your Name* ISBN 978-0 -345 -4266-8

56 tarot card images

57 Aleister Crowley – *The Book of Thoth pg. 268* ISBN 0-87728-268-4

58a Alexander Piatigorsky - *Freemasonry* - pg. 279 ISBN 1 86046 265 0

58 astrology sign images – wiki -Zodiac signs, 16th century, medieval woodcuts

58b Ptah – Google images

58c Oscar – Google images

58d Barbara C. Sproul - *Primal Myths*, -http://www.touregypt.net/godsofegypt/ptah.htm

58e Alexander Piatigorsky - *Freemasonry* pg.69 ISBN 1 86046 265 0

59 Julia and Derek Parker - *The K.I.S.S. Guide to Astrology* ISBN 0-7894-6044-0 – ak-l

59a Walter Burkert, *The Orientalizing Revolution: Near Eastern Influence on Greek Culture in the Early Archaic Age* (Harvard University Press) 1992:94f, 125-27.

59B Wikipedia - Hyperion

59c Diodorus Siculus (5.67.1)

59d Wikipedia – jove

59e Jovial - Webster encyclopedia

59g Dereon: http://en.wikipedia.org/wiki/House_of_Der%C3%A9on

59f McRae books - The Little Big Book of Classic Mythology pg. 392 ISBN 978-88-6098-036-6

59h McRae books - The Little Big Book of Classic Mythology pg. 386 ISBN 978-88-6098-036-6

59j McRae books - The Little Big Book of Classic Mythology pg. 390 ISBN 978-88-6098-036-6

59i McRae books - The Little Big Book of Classic Mythology pg. 388 ISBN 978-88-6098-036-6

59j http://www.beliefnet.com/resourcelib/docs/53/Letter_from_Thomas_Jefferson_to_John_Adams_1.html

61, 61b– Aliester Crowley - *Tarot of the Egyptians, Book of Thoth* pg. 86 ISBN 0-87728-268-4

60 Wikipedia – Astrology - A. Kitson. "Astrology and English literature", Contemporary Review, October 1996 http://www.findarticles.com/p/articles/mi_m2242/is_n1569_v269/ai_18920172. Retrieved 2006-07-17,

"Essential Chaucer: Science, including astrology". M. Allen, J.H. Fisher. University of Texas, San Antonio. http://colfa.utsa.edu/chaucer/ec22.html. Retrieved 2006-07-17.

"Astronomy and Astrology in the Works of Chaucer". A.B.P. Mattar et al.. University of Singapore. http://www.math.nus.edu.sg/aslaksen/gem-projects/hm/astronomy_and_astrology_in_the_works_of_chaucer.pdf. Retrieved 2006-07-17.

"Shakespeare, Astrology, and Alchemy: A Critical and Historical Perspective". P. Brown. The Mountain Astrologer, February/March 2004. http://www.astrofuturetrends.com/id19.html.

"Shakespeare's Astrology". http://starcats.com/anima/shakespeare.html. F. Piechoski

60a McRae Books - Athena w/ centaur – *The Little Big Book of Classic Mythology* – pg. 392

60b – Beyonce and Jay – Google images

62, 86 A.E. Waite - *The Holy Kabbalah*- pg 322 – ISBN 0-486-43222 - X

63 MJ Logo

64 MJ number ones cartoon

65 Virgo- the virgin

66 H.P. Blavatsky - *Isis Unveiled*

67 Bishop Rudolph Graber, Fatima Advancing Rapidly Towards Final Fulfillment

67b Julia and Derek Parker - *The K.I.S.S. Guide to Astrology* ISBN 0-7894-6044-0 pg. 87

67f http://fc02.deviantart.net/fs51/i/2009/268/5/a/Aang__Appa__and_Momo_by_Immunox.png

67, 67 c Claas Jouco Bleeker- -"*Hathor and Thoth: Two Key Figures of the Ancient Egyptian Religion*, p22-102, BRILL, 1973, ISBN 9789004037342, "*Oxford Guide to Egyptian Mythology"*, Donald B. Redford (Editor), p157-161, Berkley Reference, 2003, ISBN 0-425-19096-X

67cc – Wikipedia – Hathor - Peter Der Manuelian *The Ancient Egyptian Pyramid Texts*, , translated by James P. Allen, p432, BRILL, 2005, ISBN 90-04-13777-7 (also commonly translated as "House of Horus")

67d horMus 937. The Mountain of Salvation: www.antiqillum.com/texts/bg/Rose_Croix/RC003.htm

67E Julia and Derek Parker - *The K.I.S.S. Guide to Astrology* ISBN 0-7894-6044 pg -146

68e precession - Google image

68a Asenath & Joseph Wikipedia, - Pirke De-Rabbi Eliezer, chap. 48.*Apocrypha Book of Joseph*

68 ichtys- Wikipedia-

69b Matsya puarana illustration

69c Bhagavad Gita

70 Age of Aquarius picture

71 All Seeing Eye

73 William Cooper - *Behold a Pale Horse* ISBN 0-929385-22-5

73 Pope Leo X – Wikipedia

74b Robert Lomas and Christopher Knight - *The Second Messiah* pg. 90 ISBN 9781862042483

75 St. Michael Statues

76 high priestess tarot mirror to the soul - Aleister Crowley

77 Dawkins, Peter *ARCADIA: THE ANCIENT EGYPTIAN MYSTERIES; ARCADIA AND THE ARCADIAN ACADEMY*, Francis Bacon Research Trust Journal Series 1, Volume 5, Publisher: Francis Bacon Research Trust, 1988

78 Saffi Crawford and Geraldine Sullivan, *The Power of Birthdays, Stars and Numbers* - pg.372 ISBN 0-965-064255

78B Volume 4 of Dawkins' series, The Great Vision: The Judaic-Christian Mysteries,

79 (James Hastings, A Dictionary of the Bible, "Astronomy and Astrology")

80 Christopher Knight and Robert Lomas –*The Hiram Key*

81, 82, 83 Volume 5 of Dawkins' series, Arcadia: The Ancient Egyptian Mysteries,

82b Dr. Raymond Faulkner , The Chapter of Making transformation into a god and giving light and darkness- The Egyptian Book of the Dead - plate 28 - 80

84 Bob Marley picture

85 The New English Dictionary

86 A.E Waite *The Holy Kabbalah* pg 317 -318, ISBN 0-486-43222 – X, *The Book of Isaiah* 13:12

86a Wikipedia : Caitanya Caritamrta Ml.20.340.

87a A.C..Bhaktivedanta Swami Prabhuupada - *Bhagavad - Gita* pg. 4 0-89213-268-X

87 cbs logo

88 nbc logo

89 King Michael pic

89b *Michael Jackson was like Krishna* - http://articles.timesofindia.indiatimes.com/2012-02-25/new-age-insight/31096132_1_maharishi-medical-students-vietnam-war

90 Janmashtami - Wikipedia

90b Major Catholic Organizations File Suit Over Contraceptive Coverage Mandate
http://www.outsidethebeltway.com/major-catholic-organizations-file-suit-over-contraceptive-coverage-mandate/

91The Mahabharata Vana Parva

92 Bhagavat Mahapurana

http://books.google.com/books?id=h56ansk4SyQC&pg=PA226. Sallis, John (1999). Chorology: On Beginning in Plato's Timaeus. Indiana University Press. p. 86. ISBN 0253213088.

http://books.google.com/books?id=gS_9aQ5mYKgC&pg=PA86.

Keightley, Thomas (1838). The mythology of ancient Greece and Italy. Oxford University. p. 44.

http://books.google.com/books?id=IWAEAAAAQAAJ&pg=PA42&lpg=PA42&dq=theogony+timaeus&source=web&ots=Ky1QUcicnt&sig=h-hUAq6p24pQmBXRsfSwV71asgI.

94 Melkart – g. Herm 1975 (1973) pp. 111-16, Tal., p. 139 c.bonnet tzavellas 1983, p. 197 Alexander Piatigorsky *Freemasonry* pg. 320 ISBN 1 86046 265 0

El – Wikipedia - Robert du Mesnil du Buisson: "Le décor asiatique du couteau de Gebel el-Arak", in BIFAO 68

(1969), pp.63-83, <u>Gebel el-Arak Knife</u>, Matthews 2004, p. 79.

94 A.E. Waite - *The Holy Kabbalah* pg. 286 ISBN 0-486-43222 - X

95a King Tut – Google images

95b A.E. Waite - *The Holy Kabbalah* pg. 287 ISBN 0-486-43222 - X

95c phalluses in Egypt Google

96 British family w/ white baby picture

97 Emanuel Swedenborg, Swedenborg Concordance, A complete work of reference to the …, volume 1 pg. 781

98 Sarah –The Book of Hiram - The Hidden Truth of Your Name – The Nomenology Project

Pg. 668 ISBN 978-0 -345 -4266-8

99 matrilineal descent xy fetus <u>http://www.stanford.edu/dept/news/pr/03/…</u>

http://answers.yahoo.com/question/index?qid=20060705220807AAlXKyn

100 Lycians Macaulay, G.C. and Lateiner, Donald. The Histories. Spark Educational Publishing, 2004, <u>ISBN</u>

<u>1593081022</u>, p. 63, Strabo. Geographica, 12.8.4. ", (Robin Hard, H.J. Rose, The Routledge Handbook of Greek

Mythology, p. 690. <u>ISBN 0-415-18636-6</u>.)

101 Paqad - *Book of Hiram* pg 132 ISBN 0-7607-0967- X

101A. Elvis Pressely and Michael Jackson – Paul Bergen Redferns, Michael Ochs archives/Getty images

101b Archangel Michael vs. Satan - <u>http://www.spiritsdelight.com/stmichael.html</u>

101 c,d <u>http://www.elvis-history-blog.com/elvis-racism_2.html</u>

101e <u>Elvis Aaron Presley: Revelations from the Memphis Mafia</u> , Wayne, Jane Ellen, The Leading Men of MGM

(2005), p.394.

102 Lebron James Giselle Bunchden

102d Gary Goldschneider, Joost Jefferies - The Secret Language of Birthdays pg. 403 ISBN 0-670-85857-9

103, 104, 126, Aleister Crowley - Tarot *Mirror to the Soul* – ISBN 0-87728-683-3

105 Homeric Hymn of Dionysus no VII recounted by Ovid

106 El elyon – *Book of Hiram* pg. 118 ISBN 0-7607-0967- X

107 sekmet – isis Barabara Ado - Merovingian Satanic Bloodline

108, 109 Alexander Piatigorsky - *Freemasonry*, on pg 141 1-86046-265-0

109a Demariaux - How to *Understand Hinduism* – pg. 41 ISBN 0-334-02622- 9

110 – Mitochondrial eve Wikipedia

111 Graham Hancock - *Fingerprints of the Gods* pg. 383 – ISBN 0-517-88729-0

112 Wikipedia – The Qur'an

112b Leick, Gwendolyn (2001), "Mesopotamia: the invention of the city" (Penguin) p.20

112c Wikipedia- Sumerian creation myth, the Eridu Genesis. 1914 by Arno Poebel

112cd Enlil - Myth Encyclopedia - mythology, god, story, names, ancient, creation, people

http://www.mythencyclopedia.com/Dr-Fi/Enlil.html#ixzz0zSxKcYbm

112 e Alexander Piatigorsky – *Freemasonry* pg. 324 ISBN 1 86046 265 0

112dd Michael Jordan – *For the Love of the Game My Story* pg. 30 - ISBN 9780609602065

113 Christopher Knight and Robert Lomas *The Book of Hiram* pg. 346 - ISBN 1-4027-3520-0

114, Alexander Piatigorsky - Freemasonry, pg. 70 - ISBN 1 86046 265 0

115, 116, 117 Wikipedia – Dr. James Anderson

118 Wikipedia – R.H. Charles - *The Book of the Prophet Enoch* – ISBN I0 -57863-259-5

119a Wikipedia - Hart, G., The Routledge Dictionary of Egyptian Gods and Goddesses, 2005, Routledge, second edition, Oxon, p 158

119b Edith R. Sanders, "The Hamitic Hypothesis: Its Origin and Functions in Time Perspective," *Journal of African History*, 10 (1969), 521-532

119c A brief history of Hamites: http://www.egyptsearch.com/forums/ultimatebb.cgi?ubb=get_topic;f=8;t=004377

119d Graham Hancock - *Fingerprints of the Gods* pg. 104- 105 – ISBN 0-517-88729-0

120 Conan – Conan the Barbarian

121 Prometheus Wikipedia –

122 A.E. Waite - *The Holy Kabbalah* pg. 223 ISBN 0-486-43222-X

123 The underworld –The Underworld the Movie Poster

124 Elijah Muhammad - Message to the Blackman - ISBN 1884855148

124b The Hidden Truth of your name – The Nomenolgy project pg. 356 ISBN 978-0-345-42266-8

124c Michael Jackson trial picture – Google images

124d Michael Jackson History album cropped – Google images

125 The age of Aquarius

126 a tarot –

126 b Genghis Kahn wiki - Genghis Khan". North Georgia College and State University.

http://www.accd.edu/sac/history/keller/mongols/empsub1.html. Retrieved 2010-01-26

126c Genghis Khan a Prolific Lover, DNA Data Implies Hillary Mayell

for National Geographic News February 14, 2003, American Journal of Human Genetics.

127,128 – min and poem

129 – Two ball cane - [Manly P. Hall, 33rd Degree, K.T., The Lost Keys of Freemasonry or The Secret of Hiram Abiff , Forward by Reynold E. Blight, 33rd Degree, K.T., Illustrations by J. Augustus Knapp, 32nd Degree, Macoy Publishing and Masonic Supply Company, Inc., Richmond, Virginia, p. 48]

129a Encyclopedia of Jewish medical ethics: a compilation of Jewish Medical Law, D. Specific Laws pg. 915 3. Laws of destroying seed in regard to a woman

129b http://prorege-forum.com/forum_entry.php?id=2163

130 W.E. Burghardt Du Bois- 1897–*THE CONSERVATION OF RACES*-

131 W.E.B. Dubois - *The Souls of Black Folks*

133, 134 Richard Nixon – wiki- Black, Conrad (2007), p. 740. Yergin, Daniel; Joseph Stanislaw (1997). "Nixon Tries Price Controls". Commanding Heights. http://www.pbs.org/wgbh/commandingheights/shared/minitextlo/ess_nixongold.html. Retrieved November 2, 2008

134d http://badsam.us/?p=41 – Badsam.org Conspiracy theories with a ring of truth to them Feb '09 Hitler and Abe agreed on one thing.

135 Burger & Fiebig *Tarot Basics* – pg. 51 ISBN 1-4027-0202-7

136 Newsweek magazine – Adam and eve black Oppenheimer, Stephen (2004), The Real Eve: Modern Man's Journey Out of Africa, New York, NY: Carroll & Graf, ISBN 0-7867-1334-8

136b Helen Thomas

137 Costco dolls

137d Obama – monkey cartoon -the New York Post

138 Planet of the apes- King Kong – Google images

139 Unbreakable – Samuel Jackson

140, George Louis Buffon - *Histoire Naturelle*

141 George Louis Buffon – Google images

142 Caucasus wiki - http://www.merriam-webster.com/dictionary/caucasia Merriam-Webster

142A De generis Humani Varietate nativa [On the Natural Varieties of Mankind] Blumenbach

143 Reggie and Kim –Google images

144 Sons of Japheth- wiki - Josephus (Antiquities of the Jews I.6):

145 Neanderthal – Wikipedia p. 302 of Karl Christoph Vogt, James Hunt, Lectures on man: his place in creation, and in the history of the earth, Publications of the Anthropological Society of London, Longman, Green, Longman, and Roberts, 1864. See also the index entry "Neanderthal skull" (only) on p. 473.

145a Alexander Piatigorsky - *Freemasonry* pg. 114 ISBN 1 86046 265 0

145b The Hidden Truth of your name – The Nomenolgy project pg. 260 ISBN 978-0-345-42266-8

146 Vishnu on bed of snakes – Google images

147,148 ot, nt canon timelines adapted from materials of Professor Paul Hahn of the University of St. Thomas,

Houston, Texas - http://www.columbia.edu/cu/augustine/a/canon.html

149 Holman - Concordance - *King James Bible Red Letter Edition* –ISBN 0-87981-463-2

149b – Lingam The Nomenology Project, *The Hidden Truth of Your Name* – Ballantine pg. 400 ISBN 978-0 -345 -

4266-8

149cde Michael Jordan and Kobe Bryant

150 Wolf- Dieter Storl - *Shiva the Wild God of Power and Ecstacy*. Pg. 58 – ISBN 1-59477-014-X

150 A.E. Waite - *The Holy Kabbalahh* pg.263 – ISBN 0-486-43222-X

151 A.E. Waite - *The Holy Kabbalah* pg. 321 - ISBN 0-486-43222-X

152 Wikipedia – Athanasius - Encyclopedia Britannica, 15th edition. Chicago: Encyclopedia Britannica, Inc. ISBN 0-

85229-633-0.

153 Wikipedia – Nicene council pg. 120 The Council of Nicaea, 325". Schaff's History of the Christian Church,

Volume III, Nicene and Post-Nicene Christianity, www.ccel.org/ccel/schaff/hcc3.iii.xii.iv.html, Ad Afros Epistola

Synodica 2

154 Nicene Creed – Wikipedia – Nicene Creed

155 Christopher Knight and Robert Lomas - *The Second Messiah* pg. 74, ISBN 9781862042483

156 The Library of Alexandria – Wikipedia - El-Abbadi, Mostafa (1990), *The life and fate of the ancient Library of*

Alexandria (2, illustrated ed.), Unesco/UNDP, pp. 159,160, ISBN 9231026321, Jean-Yves *Empereur, Alexandria -*

Jewel of Egypt, p. 41.

156a Thee library of Alexandria – theophisius The "Mithreum" Mithraeum was an underground temple for worship

of the god Mithras. Socrates; Roberts, Alexander; Donaldson (1885), Socrates: Book V: Chapter 16 , in Philip Schaff

et al., Nicene and Post-Nicene Fathers, II, U.S.

156b Wikipedia – Library of Alexandria - http://www.bede.org.uk/library.htm , Richard Stoneman, Books We Might

Have Known, Classical Association Presidential Address 2010, p 3, Classical Association, London, 2010

157 C.H. Charles *The Book of the Prophet Enoch, The Book of Noah* CVI-CVII pg. 132 ISBN 978-1-57863-259-6

158 Albino – Google images

159 Five pointed star – Google images

159b Five pointed man – Google images

159c Captain Planet Google images

160 Hilary Clinton Press Conference, Nigeria

161 Graham Hancock in Fingerprints of the Gods

161a Sacredsites.com/Africa/Egypt/sphinx.HTML

162 Solomon's Seal wiki images – no cookie.net

162a SHIN personified – Alexander Piatigorsky - Freemasonry

163 Star Wars – darth vader

164 Padma Purana –Wikipedia

165 The Masonic Testament 1813

165a The Duke – Google images

165b Cobra Commander – www.gijoe.com

166 Robert Lomas and Christopher Knight – *The Hiram Key* pg.288 ISBN 0-7607-0967- X

167 Ursa Major -The New English Dictionary

168 The Transformers Revenge of the Fallen symbol

169/112e Alexander Piatigorsky - *Freemasonry* - pg. 324 ISBN 1 86046 265 0

170 Captain America

171 Marvel comics #10 in a twelve – issue limited series SECRET WARS FEB 10 02475

171b http://godlesswonder.blogspot.com/2006/03/king-of-kingslord-of-lordstyrant-of.html

172 American Eagle – seal of America

173 Apocalypse Wikipedia

4444 Bhagavad – Gita As it is pg. 11 – Introduction ISBN 0-89213-268-X

4445 Bhagavad – Gita As it is – *xix* ISBN 0-89213-268-X

4446 Saint Seiya Wikipedia

4447 – Huffington Post – http://huffpost.com/us/entry/1628167

4448 Bhagavad – Gita As it is pg. 11 – Introduction ISBN 0-89213-268-X